THE
WHOLE WORKS

OF THE

RIGHT REV. EDWARD REYNOLDS, D.D.

LORD BISHOP OF NORWICH;

Now First Collected

WITH HIS FUNERAL SERMON, BY B. RIVELEY,

ONE OF HIS LORDSHIP'S CHAPLAINS.

TO WHICH IS PREFIXED

A MEMOIR OF THE LIFE OF THE AUTHOR

By ALEXANDER CHALMERS, F.S.A.

———————————

IN SIX VOLUMES

VOL. II.

————————

Soli Deo Gloria Publications
...for instruction in righteousness...

Soli Deo Gloria Publications
Suite 2311, The Clark Building
717 Liberty Avenue
Pittsburgh, PA 15222
(412) 232-0866/FAX (412) 232-0867

*

The Works of Edwards Reynolds
was first reprinted in 1826 in 6 volumes
in London for B. Holdsworth in
St. Paul's Church-yard.

This Soli Deo Gloria Reprint is 1993.

*

Volume 2 of
The Works of Edward Reynolds
ISBN 1-877611-62-X

CONTENTS

OF

THE SECOND VOLUME.

AN EXPOSITION OF THE HUNDRED AND TENTH PSALM.

---

viii

CONTENTS.

X CONTENTS.

AN

EXPLICATION

OF THE

HUNDRED AND TENTH PSALM,

WHEREIN

THE SEVERAL HEADS OF CHRISTIAN RELIGION THEREIN CONTAINED,
TOUCHING THE EXALTATION OF CHRIST, THE SCEPTRE OF HIS
KINGDOM, THE CHARACTER OF HIS SUBJECTS, HIS PRIEST-
HOOD, VICTORIES, SUFFERINGS, AND RESURRECTION,
ARE LARGELY EXPLAINED AND APPLIED.

THOMAS LORD COVENTRY,

BARON OF AYLESBOROUGH,

AND

LORD-KEEPER OF THE GREAT SEAL OF ENGLAND, &c.

MOST NOBLE LORD,

It was the devout profession which St. Austin [a] once made
of himself, when speaking of the great delight which he
took in Cicero's *Hortensius* (as containing a most liberal
exhortation to the love of wisdom, without any bias or
partiality towards sects,) he affirmeth, That the heat of this
his delight, was by this only reason abated, because there
was not in that book to be found the name of Christ; without which name, nothing, though otherwise never so polite
and elaborate, could wholly possess those affections, which
had been trained to a nobler study. And Gregory Nazianzen [b], that famous divine, setteth no other price upon all
his Athenian learning (wherein he greatly excelled) but only
this, 'That he had something of worth, to esteem as nothing
in comparison of Christ;' herein imitating the example of
St. Paul, who though he profited in the Jewish religion
above many others [c], yet when the Son of God was revealed
in him, laid it all aside as loss and dung, for the excellency
of the knowledge of Christ Jesus his Lord [d]. The consideration of which sacred affections in those holy men,
together with the many experiences of your Lordship's
abundant favour, hath put into me a boldness beyond my
natural disposition, to prefix so great a name before these
poor pieces of my labours in God's Church. Other argument
in this book there is none to procure either your Lordship's
view or patronage, than this one, (which that good father
could not find in all the writings of Plato or Cicero,) That it
hath that High and Holy Person for the subject thereof,—
the knowledge of whom is not only our greatest learning,
but our eternal life.

In this confidence, I have presumed to present unto your
Lordship this public testimony of my most humble duty, and
deep obligations for your many thoughts of favour and
bounty towards me, not in myself only, but in others, unto

---

a Confess. lib. 3. cap. iv.   b Orat. 1.   c Gal. i. 14, 16.   d Phil. iii. 8.

B 2

whom your Lordship's goodness hath vouchsafed under that respect to overflow.   The Lord Jesus, our eternal Melchisedec, meet your Lordship in all those honourable affairs which he hath called you unto, with the constant refreshment and benediction of his Holy Spirit, and long preserve you a faithful patron of the Church which he hath purchased with his own blood; and a worthy instrument of the justice, honour, and tranquillity of this kingdom.

Your Lordship's most humbly devoted

EDW. REYNOLDS.

TO THE READER.

CHRISTIAN READER, When I was first persuaded to communicate some of my poor labours to the public, my purpose was to have added unto those treatises which were extant before, so much of these which I now present unto thy view, as concerneth the Elogies of the Gospel of Christ, the instrument of begetting the life of Christ in us.   For little reason had I, considering mine own weakness, the frequent returns of that service wherein these pieces were delivered, and the groaning of the press of late under writings of this nature, to trouble the world a second time with any more of my slender provisions towards the work of the sanctuary, in this abundance which is on every side brought in. But finding that work grow up under mine hand into a just volume, and conceiving that it might be both more acceptable and useful to handle a whole Scripture together (especially being both of so noble a nature, and at first view of so difficult a sense, as this Psalm is) than to single out some verse and fragment by itself; I therefore resolved once more to put in my mite into the treasury of the temple, which (though for no other reason) may yet, I hope, be for this cause accepted, because it beareth the image and inscription of Christ upon it.   Some passages therein are inserted, which were delivered in another order, and on other Scriptures; and some likewise which were delivered in other places, and on other occasions; which yet being pertinent to the series of the discourse, I thought might justly seem as natural parts, and not as ἐπιβλήματα, incoherent and unsuitable pieces.   So submitting my poor labours to thy favourable censure, and commending thee to the blessing of God, I rest   EDW. REYNOLDS.

EXPOSITION

HUNDRED AND TENTH PSALM.

PSALM CX. 1.

*The Lord said unto my Lord, Sit thou at my right hand, until
I make thine enemies thy footstool.*

CHRIST JESUS the Lord, is the sum and centre of all
divine revealed truth; neither is any thing to be preached
unto men, as an object of their faith, or necessary element
of their salvation, which doth not, some way or other, either
meet in him, or refer unto him. All truths, especially divine,
are of a noble and precious nature; and, therefore, whatsoever mysteries of his counsel God hath been pleased in
his Word to reveal, the church is bound in her ministry to
declare unto men. And St. Paul professeth his faithfulness
therein, "I have not shunned to declare unto you all the
counsel of God [a]:" but yet all this counsel (which elsewhere
he calls μαρτύριον τοῦ Θεοῦ, the testimony of God) he gathers
together into one conclusion, "I determined not to know
any thing amongst you [b]," that is, in my preaching unto you
to make discovery of any other knowledge, as matter of
consequence or faith, but only of Jesus Christ and him
crucified [c]. And therefore preaching of the Word, is called
preaching of Christ,—and ministers of the Word, ministers of
Christ [d],—and learning of the Word, learning of Christ [e];
because our faith, our works, and our worship (which are
the three essential elements of a Christian, the whole duty
of man, and the whole will of God,) have all their founda-

---

[a] Acts xx. 27.   [b] 1 Cor. ii. 1, 2.   [c] 2 Cor. iv. 5.   [d] 1 Cor. iv. 1, 2.
2 Cor. iii. 6, 14.   [e] Eph. iv. 20.

tion, growth, end, and virtue, only in and from Christ crucified. There is no fruit, weight, nor value in a Christian's
title, but only in and from the death of Christ[e].

The Word, in general, is divided into the Old and New
Testament, both which are the same in substance[g], though
different in the manner of their dispensations, as Moses
veiled differed from himself unveiled. Now that Christ is
the substance of the whole New Testament, containing the
history, doctrine, and prophecies of him in the administration
of the latter ages of the church, is very manifest to all.
The Old Scriptures are again divided into the law and prophets (for the historical parts of them do contain either
typical prefigurations of the evangelical church, or induc-
tions and exemplary demonstrations of the general truth of
God's justice and promises, which are set forth by way of
doctrine and precept in the law and prophets.) Now Christ
is the sum of both these; they waited upon him in his
transfiguration, to note that in him they had their accomplishment. First, For the law, he is the substance of it;
he brought grace to fulfil the exactions, and truth to make
good the prefigurations of the whole law. The ceremonial
law, he fulfilled and abolished; the moral law, he fulfilled
and established[h]; that his obedience thereunto might be the
ground of our righteousness, and his Spirit and grace therewith might be the ground of our obedience: and therefore
it is called the law of Christ. Secondly, For the prophets,
he is the sum of them too; for to him they give all witness. He is the author of their prophecies; they spake by
his Spirit: and he is the object of their prophecies; they
spake of the grace and salvation[i], which was to come by
him: so that the whole Scriptures are nothing else but a
testimony of Christ, and faith in him, of that absolute and
universal necessity which is laid upon all the world to be-

---

[e] Totum Christiani nominis pondus et fructus mors Christi. *Tertul.* Heb. i. 1.
[g] Quid est quod dicitur Testamentum Vetus, nisi occultatio Novi? et quid aliud quod
dicitur Novum nisi Veteris revelatio? *Aug.* de Civit. Dei, l. 6. c. 26.—Hoc occul-
tabatur in Veteri Testamento pro temporum dispensatione justissima, quod re-
velatur in Novo. *Id.* de Pec. Merit. et Remiss. l. 1. c. 11, & tom. 4. de
Catech. Rud. cap. 4. Νόμος εὐαγγέλιον προκατηγγελμένον. εὐαγγέλιον νόμος πεπλη-
ρωμένος. *Justin. Mart.*   [h] Matth. v. 17, and vii. 12.   Luke xvi. 16, 31, and
ix. 28. *Hilar.* Can. 17. in Matth.   *St. Ambr.* lib. 7. in Luc.   [i] John i. 17.
Gal. vi. 2.   Acts x. 43.   1 Pet. i. 10, 11.   John v. 39.

lieve in his name [k]: it is not only 'necessitas præcepti,' because we are thereunto commanded, but 'necessitas medii' too, because he is the only ladder between earth and heaven, the alone mediator between God and man ; in him there is a final and unabolishable covenant established, and there is no name but his, under heaven, by which a man can be saved.[l]

In consideration of all which, and for that I have formerly discovered the insufficiency of any either inward or outward principle of man's happiness, save only the life of Christ,— I have chosen to speak upon this Psalm, and out of it to discover those ways, whereby the life of Christ is dispensed and administered towards his Church. For this Psalm is one of the clearest and most compendious prophecies of the person and offices of Christ in the whole Old Testament, and so full of fundamental truth, that I shall not shun to call it 'symbolum Davidicum,' the prophet David's creed. And indeed there are very few, if any, of the articles of that creed, which we all generally profess,—which are not either plainly expressed, or, by most evident implication, couched in this little model. First, The doctrine of the Trinity is in the first words; "The Lord said unto my Lord :"—There is 'Jehovah the Father,' and 'my Lord;' the 'Son,' and the 'sanctification' or consecration of him, which was by the 'Holy Ghost;' by whose fulness he was anointed unto the offices of king and priest; for so our Saviour himself expounds this word 'said,' by the sealing and sanctification of him to his office.[m] Then we have the 'incarnation' of Christ, in the words, "My Lord," together with his dignity and honour above David, as our Saviour himself expounds it.[n] *Mine*, that is, my Son by descent and genealogy after the flesh, and yet *my Lord* too, in regard of a higher sonship. We have also the sufferings of Christ, in that he was consecrated a priest, verse 4, to offer up himself once for all, and so " to drink of the brook in the way." We have his eluctation and conquest over all his enemies and sufferings, his resurrection, " He shall lift up his head :" his ascension and intercession, " Sit thou on my right hand."—And in that is comprised his descent into Hell by St. Paul's way of arguing, " That he ascended, what is it but that he descended first into the lower parts of the earth[o]?" We have a holy catholic church,

[k] 1 John iii. 23.　　[l] Acts iv. 12.　　[m] John x. 34, 35, 36.　　[n] Matth. xxii. 42, 45.　　[o] Ephes. iv. 9.

gathered together by the sceptre of his kingdom, and holding
in the parts thereof a blessed and beautiful communion of
saints ; " The Lord shall send forth the rod of thy strength out
of Sion; rule thou in the midst of thine enemies. Thy people
shall be willing in the day of thy power, in the beauties of holiness: from the womb of the morning, thou hast the dew of thy
youth." We have the last judgment ; " for all his enemies
must be put under his feet,"—which is the apostle's argument to prove the end of all things [p]: and there is the "day
of his wrath," wherein he shall accomplish that judgment
over the heathen, and that victory over the kings of the
earth, ("who take counsel, and bandy themselves against
him,") which he doth here in his Word begin. We have the
remission of sins, comprised in his priesthood; for he was to
offer "sacrifice for the remission of sins, and to put away
sin by the sacrifice of himself [q]." We have the resurrection
of the body ; because he must " subdue all his enemies under
his feet," and " the last enemy to be subdued is death," as
the apostle argues out of this Psalm [r]. And lastly, we have
life everlasting, in the everlasting merit and virtue of his
priesthood ;—" Thou art a priest for ever after the order of
Melchizedek ;" and in his " sitting at the right hand of
God," whither he is gone as our forerunner, and to prepare
a place for us [s]; and therefore the apostle from his sitting
there, and living ever, inferreth the perfection and certainty
of our salvation [t].

The sum then of the whole Psalm, without any curious or
artificial analysis, (wherein every man, according to his own
conceit and method, will vary from other) is this: The
ordination of Christ unto his kingdom, together with the
dignity and virtue thereof, ver. 1 : the sceptre or instrument
of that kingly power, ver. 2: the strength and success of
both in recovering, maugre all the malice of enemies, a kingdom of willing subjects, and those in multitudes, unto himself, ver. 2, 3: the consecration of him unto that everlasting
priesthood, by the virtue and merit whereof he purchased
this kingdom to himself, ver. 4: the conquest over all his

[p] 1 Cor. xv. 25.   [q] Ephes. i. 7. Heb. ix. 26.   [r] 1 Cor. xv. 25, 26.
[s] Heb. vi. 20. John xiv. 2.   [t] Rom. vi. 8, 11. Rom. viii. 17. Ephes. ii. 6.
Col. iii. 1, 2, 3, 4. 1 Cor. xv. 49. Phil. iii. 20, 21. 1 Thes. iv. 14. Heb. vii. 25.
1 John iii. 2.

strongest, and most numerous adversaries, ver. 5, 6: the proof of all, and the way of effecting it, in his sufferings and exaltation: He shall gather a church, and he shall confound his enemies, because, for that end, he hath finished, and broken through all the sufferings which he was to drink of, and "hath lifted up his head again."

Verse 1.—" The Lord said unto my Lord, Sit thou at my right hand, until I make thine enemies thy footstool."

Here the Holy Ghost begins with the kingdom of Christ, which he describeth and magnifieth ; 1. By his unction and obsignation thereunto : the word or decree of his Father: " The Lord said."—2. By the greatness of his person in himself, and yet nearness in blood and nature unto us, " My Lord." 3. By the glory, power, and heavenliness of this his kingdom ; for, in the administration thereof, he sitteth at the right hand of his Father : " Sit thou at my right hand." 4. By the continuance and victories thereof: " Until I make thy foes thy footstool."

" The Lord said."—Some read it, *certainly* or *assuredly said*, by reason of the affinity which the original word hath with *amen*, from which it differs only in the transposition of the same radical letters; which would afford this observation by the way ; ' That all which God says of or to his Son, is very faithful and true.'—For which cause the gospel is, by special emphasis, called, " the Word of Truth [u]," and ϖιστὸς ὁ λόγος, " A faithful saying, worthy of all acceptation [x]," or " most worthy to be believed and embraced." For so the words δέχεσθαι and λαμϐάνειν, being applied unto the Gospel, signify [y]; being opposite unto ἀποθέσθαι τὸν λόγον [z].

But the principal thing here to be noted is, the decree, appointment, sanctification, and sealing of Christ unto his regal office. For the Word of God, in the Scripture, signifies his blessing, power, pleasure, ordination. " Man liveth not by bread alone, but by every word which proceedeth out of the mouth of God [a]:" that is, by that command which the creatures have received from God to nourish by, that benediction and sanctification which maketh every creature of God good unto us [b]. God's saying, is ever doing

u Ephes. i. 13.   x 1 Tim. i. 15.   y John i. 12.   John iii. 33.   Acts xvii. 11.
z Acts xiii. 46.   a Matth. iv. 4.   b 1 Tim. iv. 5.

something; his words are operative, and carry an unction and authority along with them.

Whence we may note,—That Christ's kingdom [c] belongs to him, not by usurpation, intrusion, or violence, but legally, by order, decree, investiture from his Father.—All kings reign by God's providence, but not always by his approbation. " They have set up kings, but not by me; they have made princes, and I knew it not [d]." But Christ is a king, both by the providence, and by the good will and immediate consecration, of his Father. " He loveth him, and hath given all things into his hand [e]." " He judgeth no man, but hath committed all judgment to his Son [f]." That is, hath entrusted him with the economy and actual administration of that power in the Church, which originally belonged unto himself. " He hath made him to be Lord and Christ [g]; " " He hath ordained him to be judge of quick and dead [h];" " He hath appointed him over his own house [i]," " He hath crowned him, and put all things in subjection under his feet [k]; " " He hath highly exalted him, and given him a name above every name [l]." Therefore he calleth him " my king," set up by him upon his own holy hill, and that in the virtue of a solemn decree [m].

But we must here distinguish between ' regnum naturale,' Christ's natural kingdom which belongeth unto him as God co-essential and co-eternal with his Father; and ' regnum œconomicum,' his dispensatory kingdom, as he is Christ the mediator;—which was his, not by nature, but by donation and unction with his Father, that he might be the head of his Church, a prince of peace, and a king of righteousness unto his people. In which respect he had conferred upon him all such meet qualifications, as might fit him for the dispensation of this kingdom.—1. God " prepared him a body," or a human nature [n], and, by the grace of personal and hypostatical union, caused the Godhead to dwell bodily in him [o]. 2. He anointed him with a " fulness of his Spirit ;" not such a fulness as John Baptist and Stephen had [p], which was still κατὰ τὸ μέτρον, the fulness of a

---

[c] *Tertul.* Apolog. cap. 30. et ad Scapulam, c. 5.   Dan. vii. 14.   Matth. xi. 27.
[d] Amos viii. 4.   [e] John v. 35.   [f] John v. 22.   [g] Acts ii. 36.   [h] Acts x. 42.
[i] Heb. iii. 2, 6.   [k] Heb. ii. 7, 8.   [l] Phil. ii. 9.   [m] Psalm ii. 6. 7.   [n] Heb. x. 5.
[o] Col. ii. 9.   [p] Luke ι. 15.   Acts vii. 55.

measure or vessel, a fulness for themselves only [q] : but a
fulness without measure, like the fulness of light in the sun,
or water in the sea, which hath an unsearchable sufficiency
and redundancy for the whole church [r]. So that as he was
furnished with all spiritual endowments of wisdom, judgment, power, love, holiness, for the dispensation of his own
office [s], so from his fulness did there run over a share and
portion of all his graces unto his church [t]. 3. He did, by a
solemn and public promulgation, proclaim the kingdom of
Christ unto the church, and declare the decree in that
heavenly voice which came unto him from the excellent
glory; "This is my beloved Son, in whom I am well pleased;
hear ye him [u]." 4. He hath given him 'a sceptre of righteousness,' and hath put a sword in his mouth, and a rod of iron
in his hand, made him a preacher and an apostle, to reveal
the secrets of his bosom, and to testify the things which he
hath seen and heard [x]. 5. He hath honoured him with many
ambassadors and servants to negotiate the affairs of his kingdom, "some apostles, and some prophets, and some evangelists, and some pastors and teachers, for the perfecting of
the saints, for the work of the ministry, and for the edifying
of his body [y]." 6. He hath given him the souls and consciences of men, even to the uttermost parts of the earth
for his possession, and for the territories of his kingdom [z]. 7. He hath given him a power concerning the laws of
his church. A power to make laws, "the law of faith," (as
St. Paul calls it [a].) A power to expound laws, as "the moral
law [b]." A power to abrogate laws, as "the law of ordinances [c]." 8. He hath given him a power of judging and con-
demning enemies [d]. Lastly, He hath given him a power of
remitting sins, and sealing pardons, which is a royal prerogative [e]. And these things belong unto him as he is
Θεάνθρωπος, as well man as God [f]. For the works of Christ's
mediation were of two sorts. 'Opera ministerii, works of
service, and ministry; for he took upon himself the form of

q Ephes. iv. 7.   1 Cor. xii. 11.   Rom. xi. 3.   r John iii. 34.   Ephes. iii. 8.
Mal. iv. 2.   s Isai. xi. 2. lxi. 1.   t John i. 16.   Col. ii. 19. 3.   u Psalm ii. 7.
Mat. iii. 17. xvii. 5. 2 Pet. i. 17.   x Heb. i. 8.   Rev. i. 16. ii. 16. Psalm ii. 9.
Isai. xvi. 1.   Heb. iii. 1.   John i. 18.   John iii. 11, 12, 32, 34.   y 2 Cor. v. 20.
Eph. iv. 11, 12.   z Psalm ii. 8.   John xvii. 6.   a Rom. iii. 27.
Mark xvi. 15, 16.   b Matt. 5.   c Col. ii. 14.   d John v. 37. Luke xix. 27.
e Matth. ix. 7.   John xx. 23.   f John v. 27.

a servant, and was a minister of the circumcision [g]; and 'opera potestatis,' works of authority and government in the church. " All power is given unto me in heaven and earth [h].

The quality of this kingdom is not temporal or secular, over the natural lives or civil negotiations of men. He came not to be ministered unto, but to minister. His kingdom was not of this world ; he disclaimed any civil power in the distribution of lands and possessions ; he withdrew himself from the people, when, by force, they would have him made a king ; and himself, that in this point he might give none offence, paid tribute unto Cæsar [i]. But his kingdom is spiritual and heavenly, over the souls of men, to bind and loose the conscience, to remit and retain sins, to awe and overrule the hearts ; to captivate the affections, to bring into obedience the thoughts, to subdue and pull down strong holds, to break in pieces his enemies with an iron rod, to hew and slay them with the words of his mouth, to implant fearfulness and astonishment in the hearts of hypocrites, and to give peace, security, protection, and assurance to his people.

The way whereby he enters upon his kingdom, is ever by way of conquest. For though the souls of the elect are his, yet his enemies have the first possession ; as Canaan was Abraham's by promise, but his seed's by victory. Not but that Christ proclaims peace first, but because men will not come over nor submit to him without war. The strong man will not yield to be utterly spoiled and crucified upon terms of peace.

Hence then we may, first, learn the great authority and power of this king, who holds his crown by immediate nature from Heaven, and was, after a more excellent manner than any other kings, thereunto decreed and anointed by God himself. Much then are they to blame, who find out ways to diminish the kingdom of Christ,—and boldly affirm, that though a king he could not but be, yet he might be without a kingdom ; a king in personal right, without subjects or territories to exercise his regal power in ; a king

g Phil. ii. 8.   Rom. xv. 8.   h Matth. xxviii. 18.   i Matth. xx. 28. John xviii. 36.
Luke xii. 13, 14.   John vi. 15.   Matth. xvii. 27.

only to punish enemies, but not a king to govern or to feed
a people. But shall God give his Son the uttermost parts
of the earth for his possession, and shall men withhold it?
shall God give men unto Christ ("Thine they were, and
thou gavest them unto me[k],") and shall they detain themselves from him? what is it, that he gives unto his Son, but
the souls, the hearts, the very thoughts of men, to be made
obedient unto his sceptre[l]? and shall it then be within the
compass of human power to effect, as it is in their pride
to maintain, "fieri posse ut nulla sit ecclesia?" We know
one principal part of the kingdom and power of Christ is,
" to cast down imaginations, and every high thing that exalteth itself against the knowledge of God;" and that not only
unto conviction, but unto obedience, as the apostle shows;
to send such gifts of the Spirit unto men, as should benefit
the very rebellious, that God might dwell amongst them[m];
for inasmuch as Christ came " to destroy the works of the
Devil, that is, sin," (as the apostle shows[n],) and in their
place, to bring in the work of God, which is "faith in him"—
for so that grace is frequently styled[o]; therefore it is requisite, that none of Satan's instruments, and confederates,
such as the hearts of natural men are, should be too strong
for the grace of Christ.

But what then? doth Christ compel men against their
wills to become subject unto him? No, in no wise. He
hath ordered to bring them in by way of voluntariness and
obedience. And herein is the wisdom of his power seen[p],
that his grace shall mightily produce those effects in men,
which their hearts shall most obediently and willingly consent unto ; that he is able to use the proper and genuine
motions of second causes to the producing of his own most
holy, wise, and merciful purposes. As we see human wisdom can so order, moderate, and make use of natural motions, that by them artificial effects shall be produced; as in
a clock, the natural motion of the weight or plummet causeth

---

k John xvii. 6.   l 2 Cor. x. 5.   m Psalm lxviii. 18.   n 1 John iii. 8.
John viii. 41, 44.   o John vi. 29.   Phil. i. 29.   Col. ii. 12.   p Illud nescio
quomodo dicitur frustra Deum misereri, nisi nos velimus: si enim Deus
miseretur, etiam volumus; ad eandem quippe misericordiam pertinet ut
velimus. *Aug.* tom. 4. Ad Simplicianum lib. 1. qu. 2.—Agit Omnipotens in
cordibus hominum etiam motum voluntatis eorum, ut per eos agat, quod per eos
agere ipse voluerit. *Id.* de Grat. et Lib. Arb. c. 2.

the artificial distribution of hours and minutes: and in a mill, the natural motion of the wind or water, causeth an artificial effect in grinding the corn. How much more then shall the wisdom of Almighty God, whose weakness is stronger, and whose foolishness is wiser than men, be able so to use, incline, and order the wills of men, without destroying them or their liberty, as that thereby the kingdom of his Son shall be set up amongst them? So that though there be still an habitual, radical, fundamental, indetermination and indifferency unto several ways (unto none of which there can be a compulsion), yet by the secret, ineffable, and most sweet operation of the Spirit of grace[q], opening the eyes[r], convincing the judgment[s], persuading the affections, inclining the heart, giving an understanding, quickening and knocking the conscience[t], a man shall be swayed[u] unto the obedience of Christ, and shall come unto him so certainly, as if he were drawn,—and yet so freely, as if he were left unto himself.[x] For in the calling of men by the Word, there is a 'trahere,' and a 'venire.' The Father draweth, and the man cometh[y]. *That* notes the efficacy of grace; and *this*, the sweetness of grace. Grace worketh strongly, and therefore God is said 'to draw;' and it worketh sweetly too, and therefore man is said 'to come.'

Again, from hence we learn our duty unto this king, the honour and subjection which is due unto him. "The Father committeth all judgment unto the Son," that is, hath anointed him with the office and abilities of a king: for judgment stands for the whole duty of a king[z], and is therefore frequently attributed unto the Messias[a]. And from thence our Saviour infers, that "all men should honour the Son, even as they honour the Father[b]," with the same worship, reverence, and subjection. For "God hath highly exalted him, and given him a name above every name[c], That at the name of Jesus," that is, unto that Holy Thing, unto the power and sceptre of that divine person, which is unto us so comfortably manifested in a name of salvation, "Every knee

---

q 2 Cor. iv. 6.   r Eph. i. 17, 18. Acts xxvi. 18.   s 1 John ii. 27.
t John xvi. 8.   u Acts xvi. 14. Jer. xxxi. 18, 33. Ezek. xxxvi. 26, 27.
1 John v. 20. Psal. cxix. 34, 36.   x Nolite cogitare invitum trahi ; trahitur animus et amore. *Aug.* Tract. 26. in Johan.   y John vi. 44.   z Psalm lxxii. 1.
a Isai. xlii. 1. 4. Jer. xxiii. 5. Jer. xxxiii. 15. b John ii. 22, 23. c Acts iii. 16.

shall bow [d]," &c. This duty the Psalmist expresseth by
"kissing the Son ;" which denoteth unto us three things :—
1. Love: for a kiss is a symbol or expression of love, and therefore used by the primitive Christians [e] in their feasts of love, and
after prayer unto God, and oftentimes enjoined by St. Paul as
an expression of Christian love. Insomuch that it was a proverbial speech among the heathens; 'See, how these Christians
do love one another.'—And this is a duty which the apostle requires, under pain of the extremest curse that can light upon
a man, to "love the Lord Jesus Christ." [f] And "If any
man," saith our Saviour, "loveth father or mother, more than
me, he is not worthy of me; or son or daughter more than
me, he is not worthy of me [g] : " that is, he is utterly unqualified for the benefit of my mediation. For he that hath good
by me, cannot choose but love me. [h]—2. To kiss, in the Scripture phrase noteth worship and service. [i] " Let the men that
sacrifice, kiss the calves." [k] And thus we find the four
beasts, and the four and twenty elders, and every creature in
heaven and on earth, and under the earth, worshipping the
Lamb, and ascribing blessing, honour, glory, and power unto
him.' [l]—3. To kiss, is an expression of loyalty and obedience :
thus Samuel kissed Saul, when he had anointed him king
over Israel. [m] And therefore the Septuagint [n] and Jerome,
and, from them, our translators, render the word which sig-
nifieth to 'kiss,' by 'being obedient,' or ruled by the words
of Joseph. [o] And this likewise is a duty which we owe unto
Christ, to be obedient to him, to be ruled by his mouth, and
by the sceptre of his mouth, that is, by his word, which is
therefore called the 'law of Christ,' because it hath a binding
power in it. We are commanded from Heaven to hear him [p];
and that too, under pain of a curse : " Every soul which will
not hear that prophet, shall be destroyed from among the

[d] Phil. ii. 9, 10.   [e] Ἀλλήλους φιλήματι ἀσπαζόμεθα, παυσάμενοι τῶν εὐχῶν
Justin. Martyr. Apol. 2. Osculum pacis orationis signaculum, quæ oratio cum
divortio sancti osculi integra, &c. Tertul. de Orat.   [f] 1 Cor. xvi. 22. Ephes.
vi. 24.   [g] Matth. x. 37.   [h] Luke vii. 47.   [i] Affectatione cœlestia adorandi,
ad solis ortum labia vibratis. Tertul. Apolog. cap. 16. Cæcilius simulacro Serapidis
denotato, ut vulgus superstitiosus solet, manum ori admovens, osculum labiis
pressit. Minut. Felix in Octavio.—In adorando, dextram ad osculum referimus.
Plin. lib. 28. cap. 2. Ἰνδοὶ προσεύχονται τὸν ἥλιον, οὐχ ὥσπερ ἡμεῖς, τὴν χεῖρα
κύσαντες, &c. Lucian. de Saltatione.   [k] Hos. xiii. 2. Job xxxi. 26, 27.
[l] Rev. v. 8, 14.   [m] 1 Sam. x. 1.   [n] Ὑπακούσεται. Ad tui oris imperium
cunctus populus obediet. Hieron.   [o] Gen. xli. 40.   [p] Matth. xvii. 5.

people."q We should learn, therefore, to take his commands
as from God; for he speaketh his Father's words, and in his
name.r When Ahasuerus commanded Haman to put on the
crown upon Mordecai, he presently executed the king's pleasure, and honoured his greatest enemy, because the king required it. Now God hath made Christ our king, and "hath
crowned him with honour and majesty" (as the apostle speaks),
and requires of us to kiss this his Son, and to bow unto his
name; and therefore be we what we will, princes, or judges, or
great men of the world (who rejoice in nothing more, than in
the name of wisdom), this is our wisdom, and dutys. It is too
ordinary with great men to be regardless of God and his ways.
Yet we see the wrath of God in his creatures, fire, tempest,
pestilence, sword, sickness, make no distinction betwixt them
and others: how much less will God himself make, when all
crowns, and sceptres, and dignities shall be resigned to him,
and all men shall stand in an equal distance and condition
before the tribunal of Christ, when no titles of honour, no
eminency of station, no treasures of wealth, no strength of
dependencies, no retinue and train of servants will accompany
a man into the presence of the Lamb, or stand between him
and the judgment of that great day. We know he was a
king that feared the presence of a persecuted prophet t; and
he was a prince that trembled at the preaching of an apostle
in chains.u The Word of God cannot be bound nor limited;
it is the sceptre which his Father hath given him; and we
cannot, without open contestation against God, resist his
government therein over us. "He that despiseth you, despiseth me; and he that despiseth me, despiseth him that sent
me," saith our Saviour. It is Christ himself, whose ambassadors we are, and with whom men have to do in our ministry. And he will have it so: First, For our peace; if God
will speak again by the ministry of angels, in thunder, and
fire (as he did on Mount Sinai) we would quickly call for
Moses and ministers again.x Secondly, For his own glory,
that the excellency may be of God, and not of men y; that it
may not be "in him that planteth, nor in him that watereth,
but in God which giveth the blessing and the increase z;" that

q Acts iii. 23.   r Deut. xviii. 19.   John iii. 34.   s Psalm ii. 10, 12.
t 1 Kings xxi. 20.   u Acts xxiv. 26.   x Exod. xx. 19.   y 2 Cor. iv. 7.
z 1 Cor. iii. 7.

it may not be in him which willeth, nor in him which runneth, "but in God which showeth mercy;[a]" that the service, co-operation, and help of the church's joy might be ours, but the dominion over men's faith, and the teaching of their inner man might be Christ's.[b] Very bold therefore, and desperate is the contumacy of those men, who stand at defiance with the power of Christ, speaking in his servants. The apostle saith, there is no escape left for those, "who neglect so great salvation."[c] And yet this is the constant folly and cry of natural men, "We will not have this man to reign over us: let us break their bands asunder, and cast away their cords from us."

But, first, Every man must be subject to some king, either Christ or sin; for they two divide the world, and their kingdoms will not consist. And the subjects of sin are all slaves and servants, no liberty amongst them[d]; whereas Christ makes all his subjects kings, like himself[e]; and his is a kingdom of righteousness, peace, and joy.[f] Secondly, If men, by being the subjects of sin, could keep quite out from the judgment and sceptre of Christ, it were something: but all men must, one way or other, be subdued unto him[g], either as sons, or as captives; either under his grace, or under his wrath. "As I live, saith the Lord, every knee shall bow to me."[h] He must either be a savour of life, or of death; either for the rising, or the fall of many in Israel; either for a sanctuary, or for a stumbling-block; all must either be saved by him, or judged by him. There is no refuge nor shelter of escape in any angle of the world; for his kingdom reacheth to the uttermost corners of the earth, and will find out and fetch in all his enemies. Thirdly, The matter were not great, if a man could hold out in the opposition. But "can thine heart endure, or thine hands be strong," saith the Lord, "in the day that I shall deal with thee?"[i] What will ye do in the desolation[k] which shall come from far? when you are spoiled, what will you do? where will you leave your glory? what will become of the king whom you served before?—It may be, thy money is thine

a Rom. i. 16.　　b 2 Cor. i. 24. Ephes. iv. 20. 21.　　c Heb. ii. 3. d John viii. 34.　　e Rev. i. 6.　　f Rom. xiv. 17.　　g Eris sub pedibus, aut adoptatus aut victus; locum habebis vel gratiæ vel pœnæ. *Aug.*　　h Rom. xiv. 10, 11.　　i Ezek. xxii. 14.　　k Isai. x. 3.

idol, and thou art held in thraldom under thine own possessions. But what will remain of a man's silver and gold
to carry him through the wrath to come, but only the rust
thereof, to join in judgment against him?—It may be, thou
servest the times, and fashions of the world, rejoicest in thy
youth, in the ways of thy heart, and in the sight of thine
eyes: but thou must not rise out of thy grave in thy best
clothes[1], nor appear before Christ, like Agag, gorgeously ap-
parelled. Thou must not rise to play, but to be judged.—
It may be, thou servest thine own lust, and another's beauty.
But what pleasure will there be in the fire of lust, when it
shall be turned into the fire of Hell? or what beauty wilt thou
find on the left hand of Christ, where the characters of every
man's hellish conscience shall be written in his face?—Thou
servest thine own vain glory, and affections: but what
good will it be to be admired by thy fellow-prisoners, and
condemned by thy judge? In one word, thou servest any
of thine own evil desires:—foolish man, here they command
thee, and there they will condemn thee; they are here thy
god, and they will be there thy devils.

The second particular in the description of Christ's kingdom is the greatness, and nearness of his person unto David:
—*My Lord.* David calleth him " my Lord " upon a double
reason; by a spirit of prophecy, as foreseeing his incarnation and nativity out of the tribe of Judah, and stock of
Jesse; and so he was David's ' son; ' and by a spirit of
faith, as believing him to be his redeemer and salvation;
and so he was David's 'Lord'—" A virgin shall conceive
and bear a son;"—there we see his incarnation and descent
from David; "and shall call his name Immanuel, God with
us;" there we see his dominion over David. As man, so he
was his son; and as mediator, so he was his Lord. As
man, so he was subject unto Mary his mother; and as mediator, so he was the Lord and Saviour of his mother[m]. As
man, he was made for a little while lower than the angels, that
he might suffer death; but as mediator, God and man, in one
person, so he was made much better than the angels, all the
angels of God were his subjects to worship him, and his
ministers to wait upon him[n]. So then the pronoun *mine*

[1] Jer. iv. 30.   [m] Luke ii. 51.   Luke i. 46, 47.   [n] Heb. ii. 7, 9.   Heb. i. 4, 6, 7.

leads us to the consideration of Christ's consanguinity with David, as he was his *son;* and of his dignity above David, as he was his *Lord.*

From hence we learn, that though Christ was man, yet he was more than a bare man. For, 'jure naturæ,' no son is Lord to his father; domination doth never ascend. There must be something above nature in him to make him his father's sovereign, as our Saviour himself argueth from these words[o]. Christ then is a Lord to his people; he had dominion, and was the salvation of his own forefathers.

"A Lord." First, By right of the creation. For he is before all things, and by him all things consist[p]; which the apostle makes the argument of his sovereignty; "To us there is but one Lord Jesus Christ, by whom are all things, and we by him."[q]

Secondly, By a right of sonship and primogeniture, as the chief, the first-born, the heir of all things. He is not in the house as Moses was, a servant, but a son over his own house[r]; that is, he was not a servant, but Lord in the church;—as the apostle elsewhere gives us the same distinction; "We preach Christ Jesus the Lord, and ourselves servants[s]." For, in the Scripture-phrase, the 'first-born' notes principality, excellency, and dominion. "I will make him," saith God, "my first-born, higher than the kings of the earth[t]." So in Job, the first-born of death is the same with the king of terrors[u]: and so the apostle saith, that the heir is the Lord of all[x]. And therefore from his primogeniture[y] and designation to the inheritance of all things, he inferreth his pre-eminence and honour even above the angels[z].

Thirdly, By the right of his unction, office, and mediatorship, unto which he was designed by his Father. He was to have in all things the pre-eminence, "For it pleased the Father, that in him should all fulness dwell[a]." Where by *fulness* either we must understand fulness of the Godhead

---

[o] Mat. xxii. 42, 45.   [p] Col. i. 17.   [q] 1 Cor. viii. 6.   [r] Heb. iii. 5, 6.
[s] 2 Cor. 4, 5.   [t] Psalm lxxxix. 27.   [u] Job xviii. 13, 14.   [x] Gal. iv. 1.
[y] Christus vocatur ' Primogenitus omnis creaturæ,' hoc est, ' Dominus.' *Schindler* in voce בכר—Solet in Scripturis ' *Primogenitum*' vocari quodcunque in suo genere excellens atque summum est—' Ego primogenitum constituam eum,' hoc est, mirum in modum exaltabo et glorificabo eum. *Glass.* in Ὀνοματολογία Messiæ. Clas. 8. Appel. 7. p. 308.   [z] Col. i. 18. Heb. i. 2, 4.   [a] Col. i. 18, 19.

bodily, as the apostle speaks [b], or fulness of the Spirit of Grace, which St. John speaks of [c]. And, in both respects, he is a Lord over all : in one, by the dignity of his hypostatical union ; in the other, by the grace of his heavenly unction; and in both, as mediator, and head in the church. Therefore the apostle saith, " That God hath made him Lord and Christ [d]," and by the accomplishment of his office, in dying, rising, and reviving, he became Lord both of the dead and living [e].

And thus he is Lord in two respects : First, a Lord in power and strength; power to forgive sins [f]; power to quicken whom he will [g]; power to cleanse, justify, and sanctify [h]; power to succour in temptations [i]; power to raise from the dead [k]; power to save to the uttermost [l] all that come unto God by him; power to hold fast his sheep [n]; power to cast out the accuser of the brethren [o]; power to put down all his enemies, and to subdue all things unto himself [p]. Secondly, a Lord in authority; to judge, to anoint, to employ, to command whom and what he will. He only is Lord [q] over our persons, over our faith, over our consciences: to him only we must say, " Lord, save us, lest we perish ;" to him only we must say, " Lord, what wilt thou have me to do ?"

And such a Lord Christ was to his own forefathers. " They all did eat of the same spiritual meat, and all drank of the same spiritual drink, even of that rock which was Christ [r]." He was the substance of the ceremonies, the doctrine of the prophets, the accomplishment of the promises, the joy [s] and salvation of the patriarchs and princes, the desire and expectation of all flesh. The gospel is to us a history, and narration, and therefore delivered by the hand of witnesses [t] ; to them, a promise and prediction, and therefore delivered by the hand of prophets [u]. The apostles entered into the prophets' labours, and were servants in the same common salvation ; these as sowers, and they as

[b] Col. ii. 9.   [c] John i. 16. John iii. 34.   [d] Acts ii. 36.   [e] Rom. xiv. 9. Rev. v. 12.   [f] Matth. ix. 6.   [g] John v. 25, 26.   [h] 1 Cor. vi. 11. [i] Heb. ii. 18.   [k] John vi. 40.   Heb. vii. 25.   [n] John vi. 39, and x. 28. [o] Rev. xii. 10.   [p] Phil. iii. 21.   [q] Col. ii. 7. Luke i. 69, 70. Acts iii. 18. and xx. 24. 2 Cor. i. 20.   [r] 1 Cor. x. 3. 4.   [s] John viii. 56. Gen. xlix. 18. 2 Sam. xxiii. 5. Hag. ii. 7.   [t] Acts xxvi. 16. 1 John xii. 3.   [u] 1 Pet. i. 10, 11, 12.

reapers[x]: these as preachers of the seed hoped, and they as preachers of the same seed exhibited. The ancient Jews were not then saved by bare temporal promises, neither was their faith ultimately fixed upon ceremonies or earthly things; but as their preachers had the same spirit of Christ with ours, so the doctrine which they preached, the faith and obedience which they required, the salvation which they foretold, was the same with ours. As the same sun[y] illightens the stars above, and the earth beneath; so the same Christ was the righteousness and salvation both of his forefathers, and of his seed. They without us could not be made perfect; that is, as I conceive, their faith had nothing actually extant amongst themselves to perfect it, but received all its form and accomplishment from that better thing which was provided for, and exhibited unto us. "For the law," that is, the carnal commandment, and outward ceremonies therein prescribed, "made nothing," no grace, no person, "perfect; but the bringing in of a better hope," that is, of Christ, (who as he is unto us the hope of glory, so he was unto them the hope of deliverance, for he alone it is by whom we draw nigh unto God) "doth perfect for ever those that are sanctified[z]."

If Christ then be our Lord, we must trust in him, and depend upon him for all our present subsistence, and our future expectations. For he never faileth those, that wait upon him. "He that believeth in him, shall not be ashamed." And indeed faith is necessary to call Christ, 'Lord:' no man can call Jesus 'Lord,' but by the Spirit; because other Lords are present with us, they do with their own eye over-see, and by their own visible power order and direct us in their service: But Christ is absent from our senses; "Though I have known Christ after the flesh, yet henceforth," saith the apostle, "know I him no more."—Therefore to fear, and honour, and serve him with all fidelity,—to yield more absolute and universal obedience to his commands, though absent, though tendered unto us by the ministry of mean and despicable persons, than to

---

[x] John iv. 38.   [y] *Aug.* de Civ. Dei, l. 10. c. 25. et epist. 157. ad Optat.—Et epist. 49. ad Deograt. de Cath. Rud. c. 3. et c. 19.—de Peccat. Merit. et Remiss. lib. 2. c. 29.—de Peccat. Orig. c. 24. et 25.—de Nupt. et Concupisc. l. 2. c. 11. [z] Heb. vii. 19.   Heb. x. 14.

the threats, and sceptres of the greatest princes,—to labour that not only present, but absent we may be accepted of him,—to do his hardest works of self-denial, of overcoming and rejecting the assaults of the world, of standing out against principalities, and powers, and spiritual wickedness, of suffering and dying in his service,—needs must there be faith in the heart to see him present by his Spirit, to set our seal to the truth, authority, and majesty of all his commands, to hear the Lord speaking from Heaven, and to find, by the secret and powerful revelations of his Spirit out of the Word to the soul, evident and invincible proofs of his living by the power of God, and speaking mightily in the ministry of his Word to our consciences. Therefore when the apostle had said, " We are absent from the Lord," he presently adds, " We walk by faith ;" that is, We labour to yield all service and obedience to this our Lord though absent; because by faith (which giveth presence to things unseen, and subsistence to things that are yet but hoped) we know that he is, and that he is a rewarder of those that diligently seek him.

And indeed, though every man call him ' Lord,' yet no man doth in truth and sincerity of heart so esteem him, but those who do in this manner serve him, and by faith walk after him. " If I be a master, saith the Lord, where is my fear [a] ?" It is not every one that saith ' Lord, Lord,' but he that doth my will, that trembleth at my Word, that la boureth in my service, who declares himself to be mine indeed. For the heart of man cannot have two masters; because, which way so ever it goes, it goes whole and undivided. We cannot serve Christ, and any thing else which stands in competition with him: First, Because they are contrary masters ; one cannot be pleased, or served, without the disallowance of the other. The Spirit that dwelleth in us, lusteth to envy,—that is, grudgeth, and cannot endure that any service should be done to the Lord ; for " the friendship of the world is enmity against God [b]." And therefore saith the apostle, " If any man love the world, the love of the Father is not in him [c] ;" and the reason is, because they are contrary principles, and have contrary spirits, and lusts ; and therefore must needs overrule unto contrary services.

a Mal. i. 6.   b Jam. iv. 4, 5.   c 1 John ii. 15.

Secondly, Because both masters have employments enough to take up a whole man. Satan and the world have lusts to fill the whole head and heart of their most active and industrious servants; for the apostle saith, that " all which is in the world, is lusts."—And the heart of man is wholly, or most greedily, set in him to do that evil which it is tasked withal [d]. The all that is in man, all his faculties, all his affections, the whole compass of his created abilities, are all gone aside, or turned backward; there is no man, no part in man, that doth any good, no, not one [e]. Christ likewise is a great Lord; hath much more business than all the time, or strength of his servants can bring about. He requireth the obedience of every thought of the heart [f]; grace and edification and profit in all the words, that proceed out of our mouth [g]; a respect unto the glory of God in whatsoever works we go about [h]; the whole soul, body, and spirit should be sanctified throughout, and that even 'till the coming of our Lord Jesus Christ [i].' Christ hath service much more than enough to take up all the might, strength, studies, abilities, times, callings of all his servants: —businesses towards God and himself, worship, fear, communion, love, prayer, obedience, service, subjection : businesses towards and for ourselves, watchfulness, repentance, faith, sincerity, sobriety, growth in grace : business towards other men as instruments and fellow-members, exhortation, reproof, direction, instruction, mourning, rejoicing, restoring, relieving, helping, praying, serving in all ways of love. So much evil to be avoided,—so many slips and errors to be lamented,—so many earthly members to be crucified, — so much knowledge and mysteries to be learned,—so many vain principles to be unlearned,—so much good to be done to myself,—so much service to be done to my brother,—so much glory to be brought to my master; every Christian hath his hands full of work. And therefore Christ expostulateth it as an absurd thing, to call him " Lord, Lord," to profess and ingeminate a verbal subjection, and " yet not do the things which he requires [k]."

The third thing observed touching the kingdom of Christ, is the glory and power thereof, intimated by his ' sitting at

[d] Eccles. viii. 11.　[e] Psalm xiv. 3. and liii. 3.　[f] 2 Cor. x. 5.　[g] Ephes. iv. 29.
[h] 1 Cor. x. 31.　[i] 1 Thes. v. 23.　[k] Luke vi. 46.

the Lord's right hand.'—' God's right hand [1]' in the Scripture, is a metonymical expression of the strength, power,
majesty, and glory, that belong unto him.   " This is mine
infirmity," saith the Psalmist ; " but I will remember the
years of the right hand of the Most High [m];" where we find
God's ' power' under the metonymy of a ' right hand,' opposed to the infirmity of his servant: ' My infirmity, and
weak faith, made me apt to sink under the sense of
God's displeasure; but when I called to mind the experiences of God's former power in like distresses, I re-
collected my spirits, and was refreshed again.'   So the
right hand of the Lord is said to span, or extend the
heavens [n]; and the Psalmist expresseth the strength and salvation of the Lord by his right hand.[o]   And " his fury is the
cup of his right hand [p]."   And he strengtheneth, and helpeth,
and upholdeth his people by ' the right hand of his righteousness ;' that is, by his power and faithful promises, which in
their weakness strengthens them,—in their fear and flagging,
helps them,—in their sinking and falling, upholds them.[q]
So the Psalmist saith of wicked men, that " their right
hand, is a right hand of falsehood [r]:" that is, either confidence in their own power will deceive themselves, or they
will deceive others to whom they promise succour and assistance.   Therefore God's right hand is called " the right hand
of majesty [s] ;" and " the right hand of power [t]."   To sit then
at God's right hand [u], noteth that great honour and judiciary
office, and plenitude of power, which God the Father hath
given to his Son; after his manifestation in the flesh, in his
nativity, and justification by the Spirit, in his resurrection,
he was then, amongst other dignities, received up into
glory.[x]   This we find amongst those expressions of honour,
which Solomon showed unto his mother, that " she sate at
his right hand [y]."   And herein the apostle puts a great difference between Christ and the Levitical priests, that they

---

[1] Δεξιὰν τοῦ πατρὸς λέγομεν τὴν δόξαν καὶ τὴν τιμὴν τῆς θεότητος, ἐν ᾗ ὁ τοῦ
Θεοῦ υἱὸς πρὸ αἰώνων ὑπάρχων, ὡς Θεὸς καὶ τῷ πατρὶ ὁμοούσιος, ἐπ' ἐσχάτων
σαρκωθεὶς, καὶ σωματικῶς κάθηται συνδοξασθείσης τῆς σαρκὸς αὐτοῦ. Damasc.
lib. 4. de Orthodox. Fid. cap. 2.   [m] Psalm lxxvii. 10.   [n] Isa. xlviii. 13.
[o] Psalm cxviii. 14, 15, 16.   [p] Hab. ii. 16.   [q] Isai. xli. 10.   [r] Psalm cxliv. 11.
[s] Heb. i. 3.   [t] Luke xxii. 69.   [u] Verbum ' sedere' Regni significat potestatem. *Hieron.* in Eph. cap. 1.—' Sedere' quod dicitur Deus, non membrorum posi-
tionem, sed judiciariam significat potestatem. *Aug.* de Fide et Symbol. cap. 7.
[x] 1 Tim. iii. 16.   [y] 1 Kings ii. 19.

'stood' daily ministering, but Christ, after his offering, 'sate down' at the right hand of God.[z] Noting two things : First, that Christ was the Lord ;—and they, but servants; for standing[a] is the posture of a servant or minister [b], and not sitting.[c] Secondly, that their work was daily repeated ; whereas Christ's was consummate in one offering once for all, after which he rested or sate down again.

This sitting then of Christ at the right hand of majesty and glory, notes unto us, first, the great exaltation of the Lord Christ, whom God hath highly honoured and advanced, and given a name above every name.

First, His divine nature, though it cannot possibly receive any intrinsecal improvement or glory, (all " fulness of glory" essentially belonging thereunto,) yet so far forth as it was humbled, for the economy and administration of his office, so far it was re-advanced again. Now he emptied and humbled himself [d], not by putting off any of his divine glory ; but by suffering it to be overshadowed with the similitude of sinful flesh, and to be humbled under the form of a servant, as the light of a candle is hidden in a dark and close lanthorn : so that declaratorily, or by way of manifestation, he is, in that respect, magnified at God's right hand,—or, as the apostle speaks, "declared to be that Son of God by power in rising from the dead," and returning to his glory again.[e] Again, however in 'abstracto' we cannot say, that the deity or divine nature was exalted in any other sense, than by evident manifestation of itself in that man who was before despised, and accused as a blasphemer, for that he made himself equal with God ; yet in 'concreto,' and by reason of the communication of properties from one nature to another in the unity of one person ; it is true, that as God saved the world by his blood, and as it was the Prince of Life that was

---

[z] Heb. x. 11, 12. [a] Luke i. 19. 1 Kings xvii. 1. [b] Deut. x. i. and xvii. 12. Ezek. xliv. 24. [c] Luke xvii. 7. 2 Chro. xviii. 18. [d] Οὐ γὰρ ἡ πρὸς τὸ σὸν ἀσθενὲς συγκατάβασις ἐλάτλωσις ὀφείλει γίνεσθαι τῆς ἀξίας τοῦ δυνατοῦ· ἀλλὰ τὴν μὲν φύσιν νόει θεοπρεπῶς, τὰ δὲ ταπεινότερα τῶν ῥημάτων δέχου οἰκονομικῶς. Basil. Mag. Homil. de Fide.—Ut sol cum in nube tegitur, claritas ejus comprimitur, non cæcatur ; sic Homo ille, quem Dominus Salvatorque noster i. e. Deus, Dei Filius, induit, Deitatem in illo non intercepit, sed abscondit. Greg. Nazian. Orat. 49. de Fide.—Συνεκάθισε τὴν ἀνθρωπίνην φύσιν ἐν τῷ θρόνῳ τῷ βασιλικῷ, καὶ προσκυνεῖται νῦν ἀπὸ πάσης τῆς κτίσεως. Theophylact. in Joh. 17.—Accepit ut homo, quæ habebat ut Deus. Theodoret. in Phil. 2. [e] Rom. i. 4.

crucified, and the Lord that lay in the grave; so God
likewise was in the form of a servant humbled, and at the
right hand of majesty exalted again.

Secondly, The human nature of Christ is most highly
exalted by sitting at God's right hand: for in the right of
his hypostatical union, he hath an ample and immediate
claim to all that glory, which might, in the human nature,
be conferred upon him. So that though during the time of
his conversation amongst men, the exigence and economy of
the office which he had for us undertaken, made him a man
of sorrows, and intercepted the beams of the godhead and divine glory from the other nature; yet having finished that
dispensation, there was, in the virtue of that most intimate
association of the natures in one person, a communicating of
all glory from the Deity, which the other nature was capable
of. For as, by the Spirit of holiness, he was filled with treasures of wisdom, and knowledge, and grace, and thereby fitted
for the office of a mediator, and made the first-fruits, the
first-born, the heir of all things, the head, and captain of the
church; furnished with a residue and redundancy of the
Spirit to sanctify his brethren, and to make them joint heirs
and first-born with himself;—so, by the Spirit of glory, is he
filled with unmatchable perfections, beyond the capacity or
comprehension of all the angels of heaven; being not only
full of glory, but having in him all the fulness of glory,
which a created nature, joined to an infinite and bottomless
fountain, could receive.

From hence, therefore, we should learn to let the same
mind be in us which was in Christ; to humble ourselves first,
that we may be exalted in due time,—to finish our works of
self-denial, and service which we owe to God, that so we
may enter into our master's glory. For he himself entered
not but by a way of blood. We learn likewise to have recourse and dependence on him for all supplies of the
Spirit[f], for all strength of grace, for all influences of life, for
the measure of every joint and member; he is our treasure,
our fountain, our head; it is his free grace, his voluntary influence which habituateth and fitteth all our faculties, which
animateth us unto a heavenly being, which giveth us both
the strength and first act, whereby we are qualified to work,

<hr>

[f] Phil. i. 19. and iv. 13.   Eph. iv. 16.

and which concurreth with us in ' actu secundo' to all those works, which we set ourselves about. As an instrument, even when it hath an edge, cutteth nothing, till it be assisted and moved by the hand of the artificer ; so a Christian when he hath a will, and an habitual fitness to work, yet is able to do nothing without the constant supply, assistance, and concomitancy of the Grace of Christ, exciting, moving, and applying that habitual power unto particular actions. He it is that giveth us not only to will but to do ; that goeth through with us, and worketh all our works for us by his grace. Without him, we can do nothing ; all our sufficiency is from him. But it may be objected, If we can do nothing without a second grace, to what end is a former grace given ? Or what use is there of our exciting that grace and gift of God in us, which can do nothing without a farther concourse of Christ's Spirit ?—To this I answer, First, That as light is necessary and requisite unto seeing, and yet there is no seeing without an eye ; so without the assisting grace of Christ's Spirit concurring with us unto every holy duty, we can do nothing ; and yet that grace doth ever presuppose an implanted, seminal, and habitual grace, fore-disposing the soul unto the said duties. Secondly, As, in the course of natural effects, though God be a most voluntary agent, yet, in the ordinary concurrence of a first cause, he worketh ' ad modum naturæ,' measuring forth his assistance proportionably to the condition and preparation of the second causes : so in supernatural and holy operations (albeit not with a like certain and unaltered constancy) though Christ be a most voluntary head of his church, yet usually he proportioneth his assisting and second grace, unto the growth, progress, and radication of those spiritual habits which are in the soul before. From whence cometh the difference of holiness, and profitableness amongst the saints, that some are more active, and unwearied in all holy conversation than other ; as, in the natural body, some members are larger, and more full of life and motion than others, according to the different distribution of spirits from the heart, and influences from the head. This then affords matter enough both to *humble* us, and to *comfort* us : to *humble* us, that we can do nothing of ourselves, that we have nothing in ourselves, but sin. All the fulness of grace is in him : and therefore, whosoever hath any, must have it from him ; as in the Egyptian famine, whosoever had any corn, had it from Joseph, to whom the granaries and treasures of Egypt were, for that purpose, committed. And this lowliness of heart, and sense of our own emptiness, is that which makes us always have recourse to our fountain, and keep in favour with our head, from whom we must receive fresh supply of strength for doing any good,—for bearing any evil,—for resisting any temptation,—for overcoming any enemy; for beginning, for continuing, and for perfecting, any duty. For though it be man's heart that doth these things, yet it is by a foreign and impressed strength; as it is iron that burns, but not by its own nature, which is cold,—but by the heat which it hath received from the fire. "It was not I," saith the apostle, "but the grace of God which was with me."

To *comfort* us likewise, when we consider, that all fulness and strength is in him, as in an officer, an Adam, a treasurer, and dispenser of all needful supplies to his people, according to the place they bear in his body, and to the exigence and measure of their condition, in themselves, or service in his church. Sure we are, that what measure soever he gives unto any, he hath still a residue of spirit; nay he still retaineth his own fulness; hath still enough to carry us through any condition; and, according to the difficulties of the service he puts us upon, hath still wisdom to understand, compassion to pity, strength to supply, all our needs. And that all this he hath as a merciful and faithful depositary, as a guardian, and husband, and elder brother, to employ for the good of his church; that he is unto this office appointed by the will of him that sent him, to lose nothing of all that which is given him, but to keep and perfect it unto the resurrection at the last day; that God hath planted in him a spirit of faithfulness, and pity for the cheerful discharge of this great office, given him a propriety unto us, made us as near and dear unto him, as the members of his sacred body are to one another. And, therefore, whosoever cometh to him, with emptiness, and hunger, and faith, he will in no wise cast out: it is as possible for him to hew off, and to throw away the members of his natural body, to have any of his bones broken,—as to reject the humble and faithful desires of those, that duly wait upon him.

Again, from this exaltation of Christ in his human nature, we should learn to keep our vessels in holiness and in honour,

as those who expect to be fashioned at the last like unto
him. For how can that man truly hope to be like Christ
hereafter, that labours to be as unlike him here as he can?
" Shall I take the members of Christ, and make them the
members of a harlot?" saith the apostle. So may I say,
' Shall I take the nature of Christ, that nature which he in
his person hath so highly glorified, and make it in my person the nature of a devil?' If a prince should marry a mean
woman, would he endure to see those of her nearest kindred, her brethren and sisters, live like scullions or strum-
pets, under his own eye? Now Christ hath taken our nature
into a nearer union with himself than marriage; for man and
wife are still two persons, but God and man is but one Christ.
Death itself was not able to dissolve this union: for when
the soul was separated from the body, yet the Deity was
separated from neither. It was the Lord that lay in the
grave; and he that ascended, was the same that descended
into the lower part of the earth g. And shall we then defile
this nature by wantonness, intemperance, and vile affections,
which is taken into so indissoluble an unity with the Son of
God? Christ took it to advance it; and it is still by his
Spirit in us so much the more advanced, by how much the
nearer it comes to that holiness which it hath in him. We
should therefore labour to walk as becometh those that have
so glorious a head,—to walk worthy of such a Lord unto all
well pleasing, in fruitfulness and knowledge; to walk as
those that have received Christ, and expect his appearing
again h.

Secondly, The sitting of Christ on the right hand of God,
notes unto us the consummation of all those offices, which
he was to perform here on the earth for our redemption.
For till they were all finished, he was not to return to his
glory again : " He that hath entered into his rest, hath
ceased from his own works," saith the apostle i. First he
was to execute his office, before he was to enter into his rest :
though he were a son, and so, ' jure naturali,' the inheritance
were his own before; yet he was to learn obedience by the
things which he was to suffer, before he was made perfect
again k. " After he had offered one sacrifice for sins for

g Matth. xxviii. 6. Eph. iv. 10.   h Phil. i. 27. Colos. i. 10, and ii. 6, and
iii. 4, 5.   i Heb. iv. 10.   k Heb. v. 8, 9.

ever," that is, after he had made such a complete expiation
as should never need be repeated, but was able for ever to
perfect those that are sanctified,—he then " sate down on the
right hand of God," expecting " till his enemies be made
his footstool [k]." This is the argument our Saviour useth,
when he prayeth to be glorified again with his Father; " I
have glorified thee on earth," or revealed the glory of thy
truth and mercy to thy church ; " I have finished the work
which thou gavest me to do; and now, O Father, glorify
thou me with thine own self," [l] &c. " He humbled himself,"
saith the apostle, " and became obedient to death, even the
death of the cross ; wherefore God hath highly exalted
him," [m] &c.; noting unto us the order of the dispensation of
Christ's offices; some were works of ministry and service,
in the office of obedience and suffering for his church; others
were works of power and majesty, in the protection and
exaltation of his church; and those necessarily to precede
these. " He ought to suffer, and to enter into his glory [n]."
Necessarily I say, First, by a necessity of God's decree, who
had so fore-appointed it [o]. Secondly, by the necessity of
God's justice, which must first be satisfied by obedience,
before it could be appeased with man, or in the person of
their head and advocate, exalt them to his glory again [p].
Thirdly, by the necessity of God's word and will, signified
in the predictions of the prophets [q]. Fourthly, by the necessity of Christ's infinite person ; which, being equal with
God, could not possibly be exalted without some preceding
descent and humiliation. " That he ascended," saith the
apostle, " what is it but that he descended first into the
lower parts of the earth [r] ?" Therefore it is that our Saviour
saith, " The Spirit should convince the world of righteousness, because he was to go to the Father, and should be
seen here no more [s]." The meaning of it is, That the Spirit
shall, in the ministry of the word, reveal unto those who are
fully convinced of their sinful condition, and humbled in the
sense thereof, a treasure of full and sufficient righteousness,
by my obedience wrought for sinners. And the reason which
is given of it, stands thus : ' Our righteousness consists in

---

[k] Heb. x. 12, 13, 14.   [l] John xvii. 4, 5.   [m] Phil. ii. 8, 9.   [n] Luke xxiv. 26, 46.
[o] Acts ii. 23, 24.   [p] Rom. iii. 25, and v. 10, vi. 6, 11. Ephes. ii. 5, 6.   [q] Luke
xxiv. 46. 1 Pet. i. 10, 11.   [r] Ephes. iv. 9.   [s] John xvi. 10.

our being able to stand in God's presence.' Now Christ,
having done all as our surety here, went up unto glory as
our head and advocate, as the first-fruits, the captain, the
prince of life, the author of salvation, and the forerunner of
his people; so that his going thither, is an argument of our
justification by him :—First, because it is a sign that he hath
finished the work of our redemption on earth; a sign that
he overcame death, and was justified by the Spirit, from the
wrongs of men, and from the curse of the law. Therefore
he said to Mary after his resurrection, " Go tell my disciples, I ascend to my Father and your Father, to my God
and your God t:" That is, by my death, and victory over it,
you are made my brethren, and reconciled unto God again.
Secondly, because he hath offices in Heaven to fulfil at the
right hand of his Father in our behalf, to intercede, and to
prepare a place for us, to apply unto us the virtue of his
death and merits. If he had ascended, without fulfilling all
righteousness for the church, he should have been sent down,
and seen again : " But now," saith he, " you see me no
more ;" for by once dying, and by once appearing in the end
of the world, I have put away sin by the sacrifice of myself u.
" He was taken," saith the prophet, " from prison and judgment;" to note, that the whole debt was paid, and now
" who shall declare his generation ?" That is, he now liveth
unto numberless generations, he prolongeth his days, and
hath already fulfilled righteousness enough to justify all
those that know him, or believe in him x. Thus we see, that
Christ's deliverance out of prison, and exaltation at the right
hand of God, is an evident argument, that he is fully exone-
rated of the guilt of sin, and curse of the law, and hath
accomplished all those works, which he hath undertaken for
our righteousness.

And this likewise affords abundant matter both to *humble*,
and to *comfort* the church of Christ: to *humble* us in the
evidence of our disabilities ; for if we could have finished
the works which were given us to do, there would have been
no need of Christ. It was weakness which made way for
Christ : our weakness to fulfil obedience, and that weakness

---

t John xx. 17.   u Heb. ix. 26. vii. 27. Rom. vi. 9, 10.   x Isa. liii. 8, 10.

of the law to justify sinners [y]. All the strength we have, is
by the power of his might, and by his grace [z]. And even
this God dispenseth unto us in measure, and by degrees,
driving out our corruptions, as he did the Canaanites before
his people, " by little and little [a]." Because while we are
here, he will have us live by faith, and fetch our strength,
as we use it, from Christ, and wait in hope of a better condition, and glorify the patience and forbearance of God,
who is provoked every day.

To *comfort* us likewise : First, Against all our unavoidable
and invincible infirmities. Every good Christian desires to
serve the Lord with all his strength, desires to be enriched,
to be steadfast, unmoveable, abundant in the work of the
Lord, to do his will as the angels in Heaven do it : yet in
many things they fail, and have daily experience of their
own defects. But here is all the comfort,—Though I am
not able to do any of my duties as I should, yet Christ hath
finished all his to the full ; and therefore, though I am compassed with infirmities, so that I cannot do the things which
I would, yet I have a compassionate advocate with the
Father, who both giveth and craveth pardon for every one
that prepareth his heart to seek the Lord, though he be not
perfectly cleansed [b].

Secondly, Against the pertinacy and close adherence of
our corruptions, which cleave as fast unto us as the very
powers and faculties of our soul, as heat unto fire, or light
unto the sun. Yet sure we are, that he who forbade the fire
to burn, and put blackness upon the face of the sun at mid-
day,—is able likewise to remove our corruptions as far from
us, as he hath removed them from his own sight. And the
ground of our expectation hereof, is this ;—Christ, when he
was upon the earth, in the form of a servant, accomplished
all the offices of suffering and obedience for us : therefore,
being now exalted far above all heavens, at the right hand
of Majesty and Glory, he will much more fulfil those offices
of power which he hath there to do :—Which are, by the
supplies of his Spirit, to purge us from sin, by the sufficiency of his grace to strengthen us, by his word to sanc-

---

[y] Rom. v. 6, and viii. 3. Heb. vii. 18, 19.   [z] Ephes. vi. 10. 2 Tim. ii. 1.
     [a] Exod. xxiii. 30.   [b] 1 John ii. 2. 2 Chron. xxx. 18, 19.

tify and cleanse us, and to present us to himself a glorious church without spot or wrinkle. He that brought from the dead, the Lord Jesus, and suffered not death to hold the head, is able, by that power, and for that reason, to make us perfect in every good work to do his will, and not to suffer corruption for ever to hold the members. It is the frequent argument of the Scripture [c].

Thirdly, Against all those fiery darts of Satan, whereby he tempteth us to despair, and to forsake our mercy. If he could have held Christ under, when he was in the grave, then indeed " our faith would have been vain, we should be yet in our sins [d]." But he who himself suffered, being tempted, and overcame both the sufferings and the temptation, " is able to succour those that are tempted, and to show them mercy and grace to help in time of need [e]."

Lastly, against death itself. For the accomplishment of Christ's office of redemption in his resurrection from the dead, was both the merit, the seal, and the first-fruits of ours [f].

Thirdly, The sitting of Christ on the right hand of his Father, noteth unto us the actual administration of his kingdom: therefore that which is here said, " Sit at my right hand, until I make thine enemies thy footstool,"— the apostle thus expoundeth, " He must reign, till he hath put all enemies under his feet [g]." And " he therefore died, and rose, and revived, that he might be Lord both of dead and living," namely, by being exalted unto God's right hand [h].

Now this administration of Christ's kingdom implies several particulars: First, νομοθεσίαν, the publication of established laws. For that which in this Psalm is called " The sending forth of the rod of Christ's strength out of Sion," is thus by the prophets expounded, " Out of Sion shall go forth the law, and the Word of the Lord from Jerusalem [i]."

Secondly, The conquering and subduing of subjects to himself, by converting the hearts of men, and bringing their thoughts into the obedience of his kingdom; ministerially, by the word of reconciliation; and effectually by the power

---

[c] Heb. xiii. 20, 21. Col. ii. 12. Eph. i. 19, 20. Rom. vi. 5, 6. and viii. 11.
[d] 1 Cor. xv. 17. [e] Heb. ii. 17, 18, and iv. 15, 16. [f] 1 Cor. xv. 20, 22.
[g] 1 Cor. xv. 25. [h] Rom. xiv. 9. [i] Isai. ii. 3. Mic. iv. 2.

of his Spirit; writing his laws in their hearts, and transforming them into the image of his word from glory to glory.

Thirdly, Ruling, and leading those whom he hath thus converted, in his way, continuing unto their hearts his heavenly voice, never utterly depriving them of the exciting, assisting, co-operating grace of his Holy Spirit, but, by his divine power, giving unto them all things which pertain unto life and godliness, after he had once called them by his glorious power [k].

Fourthly, Protecting, upholding, succouring them against all temptations and discouragements. By his compassion, pitying them,—by his power and promises, helping them,—by his care and wisdom, proportioning their strength to their trials,—by his peace, recompensing their conflicts,—by patience and experience, establishing their hearts in the hope of deliverance [l].

Fifthly, Confounding all his enemies: 1. Their projects; holding up his kingdom in the midst of their malice, and making his truth like a tree, settle the faster, and like a torch, shine the brighter, for the shaking. 2. Their persons; whom he doth here gall and torment by the sceptre of his word, constraining them, by the evidence thereof, to subscribe to the justice of his wrath; and whom he reserveth for the day of his appearing, till they shall be put all under his feet. In which respect he is said to " stand at the right hand of God," as a man of war, ready armed for the defence of his church [m].

Fourthly, The sitting of Christ on the right hand of God, noteth unto us his giving of gifts, and sending down the Holy Ghost upon men. It hath been an universal custom, both in the church and elsewhere, in days of great joy and solemnity, to give gifts and send presents unto men. Thus after the wall of Jerusalem was built, and the worship of God restored, and the law read and expounded by Ezra to the people after their captivity; it is said, " That the people did eat and drink, and send portions [n]." The like form was by the people of the Jews observed in their feast of

---

[k] Isai. ii. 2. John x. 3, 4. 1 Cor. i. 4, 8. Isai. xxx. 21. 1 Pet. ii. 9. 2 Pet. i. 3.   [l] Heb. ii. 17. John xvi. 33. 1 Cor. x. 13. 2 Cor. i. 5. Phil. iv. 7, 19. Rom. xv. 4.   [m] Acts vii. 56.   [n] Neh. viii. 10, 12.

Purim [o]. And the same custom hath been observed amongst heathen princes [p] upon solemn and great occasions, to distribute donations and congiaries amongst the people. Thus Christ, in the day of his majesty and inauguration, in that great and solemn triumph, "When he ascended up on high, and led captivity captive, he did withal give gifts unto men."[q]

Christ was notably typified in the Ark of the Testament. In it, were the tables of the law,—to show that the whole law was in Christ fulfilled, and that he was the end of the law for righteousness to those that believe in him. There was the golden pot, which had manna,—to signify that heavenly and abiding nourishment, which from him the church receiveth. There was the rod of Aaron which budded; signifying either the miraculous incarnation of Christ in a virgin, or his sufferings, which are expressed by stripes [r], and our resurrection with him, noted in the budding of a dry rod ; or lastly, noting the sanctifying and fruitful virtue of his word, which is the rod of his strength. Upon it also was the mercy seat,—to note that in Christ is the foundation of all that mercy and atonement which is preached unto men. But in two things principally did it signify Christ unto our present purpose : First, It was overlaid within and without with gold, and had a crown of gold round about it [s] ; denoting the plentiful and glorious kingdom of Christ, who was crowned with glory and honour [t]. Secondly, it had rings by which it was carried up and down, till at last it rested in Solomon's temple, with glorious and triumphal solemnity [u]. So Christ, while he was here upon earth, " being anointed with the Holy Ghost, and with power, went about doing good [x]." And having ceased from his works, did at last " enter into his rest [y]," which is ' the heavenly temple [z] '

Now this carrying of the ark into his resting-place denotes

[o] Esther ix. 22.   [p] Tiberius, in triumpho Germanico, congiarium tricenos nummos viritim dedit. *Sueton.*—Divisit in populum congiarium, ut mos est imperium suscipientibus. *Herodian.* l. 5. et de Septimio Severo, Initio imperii magno congiario populum prosecutus est. Idem lib. 3. Vid. *Sueton.* Aug. cap. 41. et *Ælium Lamprid.* in Antonino.   Observatum fuit ut principes, assumpto imperio, ad conciliandum favorem, congiarium darent populo, &c. *Alex. ab Alex.* Genial. dier. lib. 5. cap. 34.   [q] Eph. iv. 10.   [r] Isai. liii. 5.   [s] Exod. xxv. 11, xxxvii. 2.   [t] Heb. ii. 7.   [u] Psalm cxxxii. 89. 2 Chron. v. 13.   [x] Acts x. 38.   [y] Heb. v. 10.   [z] Rev. xi. 19.

two things: First, a final conquest, over the enemies of God. For as the moving of the ark signified the acting and pro- curing of victory[a], so the resting of the ark noted the con- summation of victory. And therefore the temple was built, and the ark set therein in the days of Solomon, when there was not an emendicated or borrowed peace, depending upon the courtesy of the neighbour nations, but a victorious and triumphal peace, after the great victories of David, and tri- butary subjection and homage of all the Canaanites which were left in the land.[b] Secondly, it notes the conferring of gifts, as we see in that triumphal song at the removal of the ark ; being also a prediction both of that which literally happened in the reign of Solomon, and was mystically veri- fied in Christ[c]. Thus Christ, our ' prince of peace,' being now in the temple of God in Heaven, hath bound Hell, sin, and death, captive,—and hath demolished the walls of Jeri- cho, or the kingdom of Satan, thrown him down 'from Heaven like lightning,' and passed a sentence of judgment upon him ; and hath received of the Father, " the promise of the Holy Ghost, and given gifts unto men[d]." Before his entering into his rest, it was but a promise, and they were to wait at Jerusalem for it[e] ; but, after his departure and inter- cession at his Father's right hand, it was poured forth " in abundance upon them[f]."

And we are to note, that as it began with his sitting there, so it continueth as long as he shall there sit. It is true all holy Scripture which God ordained for the gathering of his people, and for the guidance of them in the militant church, is already long since by the Spirit dictated unto holy and selected instruments, for that purpose inspired with more abundance of grace, and guided by a full and infallible spirit ; but yet we must note, that, in these holy writings, there is such a depth of heavenly wisdom, such a sea of mysteries, and such an unsearchable treasure of purity and grace, that though a man should spend the longest life after the severest and most industrious manner to 'acquaint him- self with God' in the revelations of his word, yet his know- ledge would be but in part,—and his holiness, after all that,

---

[a] Josh. vi. 11, 20.   [b] 2 Chron. viii. 7, 8, ix. 26. 2 Sam. vii. 9, 12. Psalm lxviii. 29.   [c] Psalm lxviii. 18.   [d] Acts ii. 32, 35.   [e] Acts i. 4.
[f] John xiv. 16, and xvi. 7.

come short of maturity; as the enemies are not all presently under Christ's feet, but are by degrees subdued; so the Spirit is not presently conferred in fulness unto the members of Christ, but by measure and degrees, according to the voluntary influences of the head, and exigences of the members. So much of the Spirit of Grace and Truth as we have here, is but the earnest and handsel of a greater sum,[g] the seed and first-fruits of a fuller harvest.[h] Therefore the apostle mentions "a growing change from glory to glory by the Spirit of God[i]." We must not expect a fulness till 'the time of the restitution of all things,' till that day of redemption and adoption, wherein the light, which is here but sown for the righteous, shall grow up into a full harvest of holiness and of glory.

But here ariseth a question out of the seeming contradiction of holy Scripture. It is manifest, that the Spirit of Christ was in the church, long before his ascension. The prophets spake by him[k]. The ancient Jews vexed him[l], John Baptist was even 'filled' with the Spirit, to note a plentiful measure for the discharge of his office[m]; and yet St. John saith, that "the Holy Ghost was not yet given, because Christ was not yet glorified."[n] To this I answer, that the fathers were sanctified by the same Spirit of Christ with us: difference there is none in the substance, but only in the accidents and circumstances of effusion and manifestation; as light in the sun, and light in a star, is, in itself, the same original light, but very much varied in the dispensation. It was the same truth which was preached by the prophets, and by Christ; but the apostle observes in it a difference; "Sundry times, and in sundry manners, hath God spoken by the prophets, but unto us by his Son;" that is, more plentifully, and more plainly unto us, than unto the fathers.[o] Therefore though it be true, that 'Abraham saw Christ's day,' as all the fathers did (though he haply, being the father of the faithful, more than others,) in which respect Eusebius[p] saith of them, that "they were Christians really, and in effect, though not in name:" yet it is true likewise, that "many prophets and righteous men did desire

g Eph. i. 14.   h 1 John iii. 9. Rom. viii. 23.   i 2 Cor. iii. 18.   k 1 Pet. i. 11.
l Isai. lxiii. 10.   m Luke i. 15.   n John vii. 39.   o Heb. i. 1.
John xvi. 25.   p Χριστιανοὶ ἔργῳ εἰ καὶ μὴ ὀνόματι. Euseb. Hist. lib. 1. cap. 5.

to see and hear the things which the apostles saw and heard, but did not[q]," namely, in such plain and plentiful measures as the apostles did. They saw in glimpses and morning stars and prefigurations ; but these, the things themselves. They saw only the ' promises,' and those too ' but afar off[r] ;' these, the substance and gospel itself, near at hand, in their mouth, and before their eyes, and even amongst them[s]. They by prophets who " testified beforehand ;" these, by eye-witnesses, who declared " the things which they had seen and heard[t]." Therefore it is said, that " Christ was a Lamb slain from the beginning of the world," and yet " in the end of the world that he appeared to take away sin by the sacrifice of himself[u]", to note that the fathers had the benefit, but not the perfection of the promises[x]; for the apostle every where makes perfection the work of the gospel[y].

So then, after Christ's sitting on the right hand of power, the Holy Spirit was more completely sent, both in regard of manifestation and efficacy, than ever before. The difference is chiefly in three things :

First, In the manner of his mission. To the old church, in dreams and visions, in figures and latent ways : but to the evangelical churches, in power, evidence, and demonstration[z]. Therefore it is called the "Spirit of revelation and knowledge," which discovereth, and that unto principalities and powers by the church, the manifold and mysterious wisdom of God in Christ[a]. Therefore the Spirit was sent in the latter days, in winds, and fire, and tongues[b], and earthquake[c] ; all which have in them a self-discovering property, which will not be hidden. Whereas, in the time of the prophets, God did not, in any such things, save only in ' a low and still voice,' reveal himself[d].

Secondly, In the subjects, unto whom he was sent. Before, only upon the enclosed garden of the Jews did this wind blow ; but now is the Spirit poured upon all flesh[e] ; and this heavenly dew falleth not upon the fleece, but upon the whole earth. And, therefore, our Saviour opposeth Jerusalem and the Spirit[f]. Every believer[g] is of the ' Israel

[q] Matth. xiii. 17.   [r] Heb. xi. 13.   [s] Rom. x. 8.   Gal. iii. 1.   John i. 1.
1 John i. 2, 3, 4.   [t] Acts i. 8, 22. x. 41.   [u] Heb. ix. 26.   [x] Heb. xi. 40.
[y] 1 Cor. ii. 7. Ephes. iv. 13. Heb. vi. 1.   [z] 1 Cor. ii. 4. 5.   [a] Eph. i. 17.
iii. 10.   [b] Acts ii. 2, 3.   [c] Acts iv. 31.   [d] 1 Kings xix. 11, 12.
[e] Joel ii. 28.   [f] John iv. 21, 23.   [g] Rom. ii. 29. Gal. vi. 15, 16.

of God;' every Christian, a ' temple of the Holy Ghost:' no
people of the earth secluded, but "In every nation, he
that feareth God and worketh righteousness, is accepted;"
no place unclean, but every where pure hands may be
lifted up [h].

Thirdly, In the measure of his grace. At first he was
sent only in drops and dew, but after he was poured out in
showers and abundance[i]; and therefore (as I have before
observed) the grace of the gospel is frequently expressed by
the name of riches [k], to note not only the preciousness, but
the plenty thereof in the church. And it is here worth our
observation, that the Spirit, under the gospel, is compared
to things of a spreading, multiplying, and operative nature.

First, To ' *water*;' and that, not a little measure to
sprinkle or bedew, but to baptize the faithful in [l], and that
not in a font or vessel, which grows less and less, but in a
springing or living river [m]. Now water, besides its purging
property, is first of a spreading nature: it hath no bounds
nor limits to itself, as firm and solid bodies have, but receives its restraint by the vessel or continent which holds
it: so the Spirit of the Lord is not straitened in himself,
but only by the narrow hearts of men into which he comes.
"Ye are not straitened," saith the apostle, "in us," that
is, in that ministry of grace, and dispensation of the Spirit,
which is committed to us, " but in your own bowels," which
are not in any proportion enlarged unto that abundance and
fulness of heavenly grace, which in the gospel of salvation
is offered unto you. Secondly, Spring water is a growing
and a multiplying thing; which is the reason, why rivers,
which rise from narrow fountains, have yet, by reason of a
constant and regular supply, a great breadth in remote
channels, because the water lives : whereas, in pits and tor-
rents, it groweth less and less :—so the graces of the Spirit
are living and springing things; the longer they continue,
the larger they grow, like the waters of the sanctuary [n]; and
the reason is, because they " come from a fountain, which is
all life [o]." Thirdly, As water multiplies in itself, so, by in-

[h] Col. ii. 11. Phil. iii. 3. 1 Cor. vi. 19. Acts x. 35. 1 Tim. ii. 8.　　[i] Tit. iii. 6.
[k] Ephes. i. 7. ii. 7. iii. 8. Col. i. 27.　　[l] Matth. iii. 11. Acts i. 5.　　[m] John
vii. 39.　　[n] Ezek. xxxvi. 25.　　[o] John iv. 10. xiv. 6. Col. iii. 4.

sinuation and mollification, it hath a fructifying virtue in other things. Fruitful trees 'are planted by the waters' side .' so the Spirit, searching and mollifying the heart, maketh it fruitful in holy obedience P. Fourthly, Water is very strong in its own stream : we see what mighty engines it moveth, what huge vessels it rolleth like a ball, what walls and bulwarks it overthrows : so the Spirit of God is able to beat down all strong holds, which the wit of man, or the malice of Satan, can erect against the church. "The horses of Egypt are flesh, and not spirit," saith the Lord ; " not by might, nor by power, but by my Spirit;" noting that that, which might and created power could not do, the Spirit of the Lord was able to effect. And this strength of water serves to carry it as high as its own spring and level : so the Spirit will never cease to raise the hearts of his people, till it carries them up to their fountain and spring-head in Heaven.

Secondly, The Spirit is compared to the '*rushing of a mighty wind.*' The learned observe, that before Christ's time, God spake unto men in a soft still voice, which they called ' Bath Koll ;' but after, in the time of the gospel, by a mighty wind : noting thereby both the abundance of his Spirit which he would pour out in the latter days ; and the strength thereof, as of a rushing wind. Though a man have walls of brass, and bars of iron upon his conscience, though he set up fortifications of fleshly reason, and the very gates of Hell to shut out the Spirit of grace ; yet nothing is able to withstand the power of this mighty rushing wind. " Who art thou, O great mountain ? Before Zerubbabel thou shalt become a plain r," &c. No mountains, no difficulties can prevent the power of God's Spirit. He hath strength to pull down the strongest oppositions, and to enable the weakest condition unto the service which he will have done. Though there be mountains between Israel and their deliverance, yet the blind, and the lame, and the woman with child, and her that travaileth with child together, will he strengthen to climb over the precipices of the highest mountain s.

Thirdly, The Spirit is compared to ' *Fire,*' noting likewise both the multiplying or diffusive property thereof, turning

P Ezek. xi. 19, 20.   r Zech. iv. 7.   s Jer. xxxi. 8.

every thing into its own nature : and the mighty strength thereof, whereby it either cleanseth or consumeth any thing that it meets with. If thou art stubble, it will devour thee ; if stone, it will brake ; if gold, it will purge thee. The hard heart it can melt, and the foul heart it can purify. Lay down thine heart under the Word, and yield it to the Spirit, who is, as it were, the artificer which doth manage the Word ; he can frame it into ' a vessel of honour :' but if thou resist, and be stubborn against the Spirit in the Word, know that it is but a crackling of a leaf in the fire : if thou wilt not suffer it to purge thee, thou canst not hinder it to torment thee. Nothing is more comfortable, nothing more consuming than fire ; nothing more comfortable than the light, warmth, and witness of the Spirit ; nothing more terrible than the conviction, condemnation, and bondage of the Spirit.

Now this difference in the measure of the Spirit may be seen in two things. First, in a greater measure of know-ledge ; " They shall all know me, from the least of them to the greatest of them, saith the Lord[t]." And " The earth shall be full of the knowledge of the Lord, as the waters cover the sea[u]." Our Saviour told his disciples, that " All things which he had heard of his Father, he had made known unto them[x]." And yet a little after he telleth them, that " Many other things he had to say unto them, which they could not bear, till the Spirit of truth came, who should guide them into all truth[y] ;" noting that the Spirit, when he came, should enlarge their hearts to a capacity of more heavenly wisdom, than they could comprehend before. For we may observe before, how ignorant they were of many things, though they conversed with Christ in the flesh :—Philip, ig-norant of the Father[z] ; Thomas, of the way unto the Fa-ther[a] ; Peter, of the necessity of Christ's sufferings[b] ; the two disciples, of his resurrection[c] ; all of them, of the quality of his kingdom[d]. Thus before the sending of the Holy Ghost, the Lord did not require so plentiful knowledge unto salvation, as after ;—as in the valuations of money, that which was plenty two or three hundred years since, is

---

[t] Jer. xxxi. 34.   [u] Isai. xi. 9.   [x] John xv. 15.   [y] John xvi. 12, 13.
[z] John xiv. 8.   [a] John xiv. 5.   [b] Matth. xvi. 22.   [c] Luke xxiv. 45.
[d] Acts i. 6.

but penury now. Secondly, in a greater measure of strength,
for spiritual obedience. They who before fled from the company of Christ in his sufferings, did, after, " rejoice to be
counted worthy of suffering shame for his name," or as the
elegancy of the original words import, to be " dignified
with that dishonour of being Christians [e]." For suffering of
persecution for Christ, and the trial of faith by divers temptations, is, in the Scriptures, reckoned up amongst the gifts,
an hundred-fold compensations of God to his people [f]. " No
man," saith our Saviour, " putteth new wine into old bot-
tles," that is, exacteth rigid and heavy services of weak and
unqualified disciples; and therefore my disciples fast not,
while I am amongst them in the flesh : " But the days will
come, when I shall be taken from them in body," and shall
send them my Holy Spirit to strengthen and prepare them
for hard service ; and then they shall fast and perform those
parts of more difficult obedience unto me [g].

Now farther, touching this sending of the Holy Spirit
(which, together with Christ's intercession, was one of the
principal ends of his ascending up unto the right hand of
power) it may be here demanded,—Why the Holy Spirit
was not, before this exaltation of Christ, sent forth in such
abundance upon the church ? The main reason whereof, next
unto the purpose and decree of God, into which all the acts
of his will are to be resolved [h], is given by our Saviour [i];
because he was to supply the corporal absence of Christ, and
to be another ' comforter' to the church. Of which office
of the Spirit, (because it was one of the main ends of his
mission, and that one of the chief works of Christ's sitting
at God's right hand) I shall here, without any unprofitable or
impertinent digression, speak a little.

First, then, the Spirit is a ' comforter,' because ' an advocate to his people :' for so much the word signifies, and
is elsewhere rendered [k]. Now he is called " another comforter or advocate," to note the difference between Christ
and the Spirit in this particular. There is then an advocate
by office, when one person takes upon himself the cause of
another, and in his name pleads it. Thus Christ by the

[e] Acts v. 41.   [f] Mark x. 30. Phil. 1. 29. Heb. xi. 26. Jam. i. 2. 1 Pet. i.
6, 7.   [g] Matth. ix. 15, 17.   [h] Eph. i. 11.   [i] John xiv. 16, and xvi. 7.
[k] 1 John ii. 1.

office of his mediation and intercession, is an advocate for his church, and doth, in his own person in Heaven, apply his merits, and further the cause of our salvation with his Father.—There is likewise an advocate by energy and operation, by instruction and assistance; which is not when a work is done by one person in the behalf of another, but when one, by his counsel, inspiration, and assistance, enableth another to manage his own business, and to plead his own cause. And such an advocate the Spirit is, who doth not intercede, nor appear before God in person for us, as Christ doth,—but maketh interpellation for men in and by themselves, giving them an "access unto the Father," emboldening them in their fears, and helping them in their infirmities, when they know not what to pray[1].

First, then, The Spirit as our advocate, justifieth our persons, and pleadeth our causes against the accusations of our spiritual enemies. For as Christ is our advocate at the tribunal of God's justice to plead our cause against the severity of his law, and that most righteous and undeniable charge of sin which he layeth upon us; so the Holy Spirit is our advocate at the tribunal of God's mercy, enabling us there to clear ourselves against temptations, and murderous assaults of our spiritual enemies. The world accuseth us by false and slanderous calumniations, 'laying to our charge things which we never did:' the Spirit, in this case, maketh us not only plead our innocency, but to rejoice[m] in our fellowship with the prophets which were before us, to esteem 'the reproaches of Christ greater riches than the treasures of the world;' to count ourselves happy in this, that it is not such low marks as we are, which the malice of the world aimeth at, but the Spirit of glory and of God which resteth upon us, who is on their part evil spoken of[n]. "Satan, that grand accuser of the brethren," doth not only load my sins upon my conscience, but further endeavoureth to exclude me from the benefit of Christ, by charging me with impeni-

---

[1] Ephes. ii. 18. Heb. x. 15, 19. Rom. viii. 26. Ephes. iii. 16.   [m] Interpellare dicitur pro nobis, quia nobis gemendi et interpellandi imponit affectum. *August.* Quod dicitur Spiritus Sanctus ' intercedere pro nobis,' hoc non est ita intelligendum, ac si ipsa persona Spiritus immediatè intercederet. Intercedit enim per gemitus : porro non gemit Spiritus, sed nos gemimus ; itaque docendo hoc facit, efficiendo ut gemamus. *Cameron.* de Eccles. p. 98.   [n] 1 Pet. iv. 14.

tency and unbelief:—but here the Spirit enableth me to clear
myself against the father of lies. It is true indeed, I have
a naughty flesh, the seeds of all mischief in my nature; but
the first means which brought me hereunto, was the believing of thy lies, and therefore I will no longer entertain thy
hellish reasonings against mine own peace. I have a spirit
which teacheth me to bewail the frowardness of mine own
heart, to deny mine own will and works, to long and aspire
after perfection in Christ, to adhere with delight and purpose
of heart unto his law, to lay hold with all my strength upon
that plank of salvation, which, in this shipwreck of my soul,
is cast out unto me. These affections of my heart come not
from the earthly Adam; for whatsoever " is earthly, is sensual, and devilish " too. And if they be holy and heavenly,
I will not believe, that God will put any thing of Heaven
into a vessel of Hell. Sure I am, he that died for me when
I did not desire him, will in no ways cast me away when I
come unto him. He that hath given me a will to love his
service, and to lean upon his promises, will in mercy accept
the will for the deed, and in due time accomplish the work
of holiness which he hath begun. Thus the Spirit, like an
advocate, secureth his client's title, against the sophistical
exceptions of the adversary ; and when by temptations our
eye is dimmed, or by the mixture of corruptions our evidences
defaced, he by his skill helpeth our infirmities, and bringeth
those things which are blotted out and forgotten, into our
remembrance again.

Secondly, An advocate admonisheth and directeth his
client how to order and solicit his own business, what evidences to produce, what witnesses to prepare, what offices to
attend, what preparations to make against the time of his
hearing: so the Spirit doth set the heart of believers in a
right way of negotiating their spiritual affairs, 'maketh
them to hear a voice behind them,' furnishing them with
wisdom and prudence in every condition. How to grapple
with temptations,—how to serve God in all estates,—when to
reprove, direct, counsel, comfort,—when to speak, and when
to be silent,—when to let out, and when to chain up a
passion,—when to use, and when to forbear liberty,—how
to prosecute occasions, and apply occurrences unto spiritual
ends,—every where, and in all things, strengthening and

instructing us to manage our hearts unto the best advantages of peace to ourselves, and of glory to our master [o].

Thirdly, An advocate maketh up the failings of his client, and, by his wisdom and observation of the case, picks out advantages beyond the instructions, and gathereth arguments to further the suit, which his client himself observed not. So the Spirit, when we know not what to pray, when, with Jehoshaphat, " we know not what to do," when (it may be) in our own apprehension the whole business of our peace and comfort lieth a bleeding,—doth then help our infirmities, and, by dumb cries, and secret intimations, and deep and inexpressible groanings, presenteth arguments unto Him, who is ' the searcher of hearts,' and who ' knoweth the mind of the Spirit,' which we ourselves cannot express. Thus as an infant crieth and complaineth for want of sleep, and yet knoweth not that it is sleep which he wanteth;—as a sick man goeth to the physician, and complaineth that some physic he wanteth, but knoweth not the thing which he asketh for;—so the soul of a Christian, by the assistance of the Spirit, is enlarged to request things of God, which yet of themselves do pass the knowledge and understandings of those that ask them [p].

Secondly, The Spirit is a comforter by applying and representing Christ absent unto the soul again. For, First, the Spirit carrieth a Christian heart up to Christ in heavenly affections and conversation [q]. As a piece of earth, when it is out of its place, doth ever move to the whole earth; so a sparkle of Christ's Spirit will naturally move upward unto him, who hath ' the fulness' in him. A stone, though broken all to pieces in the motion, will yet, through all that peril and violence, move unto the centre : so though the nature of man abhor, and would of itself decline the passages of death [r], yet the apostle desired " to be dissolved, and to be taken asunder, that by any means he might be with Christ," who is the centre of every Christian's desire [s]. Secondly, The Spirit bringeth Christ down to a Christian, formeth him in his heart, evidenceth him, and the virtue of his passion, and resurrection, unto the conscience, in the powerful dis-

[o] Isai. xxx. 21.   Col. i. 9, 10.   Phil. iv. 12, 13.   Ephes. iv. 20, 21.   [p] Rom. viii. 26, 27. Eph. iii. 19. Phil. iv. 7. 1 Cor. 14, 15.   [q] Col. iii. 1, 3. Phil. iii. 20.   [r] 2 Cor. v. 4.   [s] Phil. i. 23.

pensation of his holy ordinances. Therefore when our
Saviour speaks of sending the Holy Spirit, he addeth, " I
will not leave you comfortless, I will come to you ;—when
the world seeth me not, yet ye see me." This noteth the
presence of Christ by his Spirit with the church : but there
is more than a presence, there is an inhabitation ; " At that
time ye shall know that I am in my Father, and ye in me,
and I in you[t]."

Thirdly, The Spirit is a comforter by a work of sweet and
fruitful illumination, not only giving the knowledge, but
the love and comfort of the truth unto a Christian ; making
him " with open face behold, as in a glass, the glory of
God," and thereby " transforming him into the same image
from glory to glory." The light of other sciences is like
the light of a candle, nothing but light : but the knowledge
of Christ by the Spirit, is like the light of the sun, which
hath influences and virtue in it. And this is that which the
apostle calls ' the Spirit of revelation, in the knowledge of
God :' for though there be no prophetical, nor extraordinary
revelations by dreams, visions, ecstasies, or enthusiasms ; yet,
according to the measure of spiritual perspicacy, and dili-
gent observation of holy Scriptures, there are still manifold
revelations or manifestations of Christ unto the soul. The
secret and intimate acquaintance of the soul with God, the
heavings, aspirings, and harmony of the heart with Christ,
the sweet illapses and flashes of heavenly light upon the
soul, the knowledge of the depths of God, and of Satan, of
the whole armour of God, and the strong man, of conflicts
of spirit, protection of angels, experiences of mercy, issues
of temptation and the like, are heavenly and constant revelations out of the Word, manifested to the souls of the faithful by the Spirit.

Lastly, and principally, The Spirit is a comforter in those
effects of ' joy and peace,' which he worketh in the heart.
For joy is ever the fruit and companion of the Spirit[u] ; and
the joy of the Spirit is like the intercession of the Spirit,
' unspeakable and glorious[x],' not like the joy of the world,
which is empty, false, and deceitful,—full of vanity, vexation, insufficiency, unsuitableness to the soul,—mingled

---

[t] John xiv. 18, 20.   [u] Gal. v. 22. Acts xiii. 52.   [x] 1 Pet. i. 8.

with fears of disappointment and miscarriage, with trem-
blings and guilt of conscience, with certainty of period and
expiration ; but clear, holy, constant, unmixed, satisfactory,
and proportionable to the compass of the soul,—more gladness than all the world can take in the 'increase of their
corn and wine.'[x]

And this joy of the Spirit is grounded upon every passage
of a Christian condition, from the entrance to the end.
First, The Spirit worketh joy in discovering, and bending
the heart to mourn for corruption. For it is ' the Spirit of
grace and supplications which maketh sinners mourn, and
loath themselves [y].' And such a sorrow as this, is the seed,
and the matter of true joy : our Joseph's heart was full of
joy, when his eyes poured out tears upon Benjamin's neck.
As in wicked laughter the heart may be sorrowful, so in holy
mourning the heart [z] may rejoice ; for all spiritual afflictions
have 'a peaceable fruit.' This was the first glimpse and
beam of the prodigal's joy, that he resolved, with tears and
repentance, to return to his father again. For there is a sweet
complacency in an humble and spiritual heart to be vile in
its own eyes, as to the hungry soul every bitter thing is
sweet. Sacrifices, we know, were to be offered up with joy [a];
and of all sacrifices 'a broken heart' is that which God
most delighteth in [b]. " There is joy in Heaven at the repentance of a sinner ;" and therefore there must needs be
joy in the heart itself which repenteth, inasmuch as it hath
heavenly affections begun in it. Therefore as the apostle
saith, " Let a man become a fool, that he may be wise ;" so
may I truly say,—Let a man become a mourner, that he may
rejoice.

If it be objected, How one contrary affection can be the
ground and inducement of another, and that he who feeleth
the weight of sin, and displeasure of God, can have little
reason to boast of much joy ; to this I answer, First, that we
do not speak of those extraordinary combats, and grapplings
with the sense of the wrath of God, breaking of bones, and
burning of bowels, which some have felt ; but of the ordinary humiliations and courses of repentance, which are

---

[x] Psalm iv. 7.   [y] Zech. xii. 10, 11. Ezek. xxxvi. 27, 31.   [z] 'Εν τοῖς πένθεσι
καὶ θρήνοις ἐγγίνεταί τις ἡδονή. Arist. Rhet.   [a] Mal. ii. 13.   [b] Psalm li. 16, 17.

common to all. Secondly, that such spiritual mourning and joy are not contrary, in regard of the Spirit, nor does one extinguish or expel the other. As black and white are contrary in the wall, but meet without any repugnancy in the eye, because, though as qualities they fight, yet, as objects, they agree ' in communi conceptu visibilis ;' so joy and mourning, though contrary, in regard of their immediate impressions upon the sense, do not only agree in the same principle, the grace of Christ,—and in the same end, the salvation of man,—but may also be subordinated to each other :—as a dark and muddy colour is a fit ground to lay gold upon ; so a tender and mourning heart is the best preparation unto spiritual joy. Therefore our Saviour compareth ' spiritual sorrow unto the pains of a woman in travail.' Other pains, growing out of sickness and distempers, have none but bitter ingredients, and anguish in them ; but that pain groweth out of the matter of joy, and leadeth unto joy : so though godly sorrow have some pain in it, yet that pain hath ever joy both for the root and fruit of it [c] : and though, for the present, it may haply intercept the exercise, yet it doth strengthen the habit and ground of joy ; as those flowers in the spring rise highest and with greatest beauty, which, in winter, shrink lowest into the earth. " I trembled," saith the prophet, " in myself, that I might rest in the day of trouble [d]."

Secondly, The Spirit doth not only discover, but heal the corruptions of the soul ; and there is no joy to the joy of a saved and cured man. The lame when he was restored by Peter, expressed the abundant exultation of his heart, "by leaping, and praising God [e]." For this cause therefore, amongst others, the Spirit is called ' the oil of gladness,' because by that healing virtue which is in him, he maketh glad the hearts of men. "The Spirit of the Lord," saith Christ, " is upon me, because the Lord anointed me to preach the glad tidings to the meek ; he hath sent me to bind the broken hearted [f] :" and again, " I will bind that which was broken, and will strengthen that which was sick [g]." Now this healing virtue of Christ is the dispensa-

<hr>

[c] John xvi. 21.   [d] Hab. iii. 16.   [e] Acts iii. 8.   [f] Isai. lxi. 6.
[g] Ezek. xxxiv. 16.

tion of his word and Spirit; and therefore the prophet saith, "The Sun of righteousness shall arise with healing in his wings [h];" where the Spirit in the word, by which he cometh and preacheth unto men [i], is called 'the wing of the Sun,' because he proceedeth from him, and was sent to supply his absence, as the beam doth the sun's: and this Spirit the apostle calleth 'the strengthener of the inner man [k].'

Thirdly, The Spirit doth not only heal, but renew, and revive again. When an eye is smitten with a sword, there is a double mischief; a wound made, and a faculty perished: and here though a surgeon can heal the wound, yet he can never restore the faculty, because total privations admit no regress or recovery;—but the Spirit doth not only heal and repair, but renew, and re-edify the spirits of men. As he healeth that which was torn, and bindeth up that which was smitten, so he reviveth and raiseth up that which was dead before[l]: and this the apostle calls 'the renovation of the Spirit [m],' whereby old things are not mended and put together again (for our fall made us all over unprofitable and little worth [n]), but are done quite away, and "all things made new" again [o]: the heart, mind, affections, judgment, conscience, members, changed from stone to flesh, from earthly to heavenly, from the image of Adam to the image of Christ [p]. Now this renovation must needs be matter of great joy; for so the Lord comforteth his afflicted people [q].

Fourthly, The Spirit doth not renew and set the frame of the heart right, and then leave it to its own care and hazards again; but being thus restored, he abideth with it to preserve and support it against all tempests and batteries. And this farther multiplieth the joy and comfort of the church, that it is 'established in righteousness,' so that no weapon which is formed against it, can prosper [r]. Victory is ever the ground of joy [s]; and the Spirit of God is a victorious Spirit. His judgment in the heart is sent forth unto victory [t]. "And before him, mountains shall be made a plain, and every high thing shall be pulled down, till he bring forth

[h] Mal. iv. 2.   [i] Eph. ii. 17. 1 Pet. iii. 19.   [k] Eph. iii. 16.   [l] Hosea vi. 1, 2.
[m] Tit. iii. 5.   [n] Rom. iii. 12. Prov. x. 20.   [o] 2 Cor. v. 17.   [p] Ezek. xi. 19.
1 Cor. xv. 49.   [q] Isa. liv. 11, 12, 13.   [r] Isa. liv. 14, 17.   [s] Isa. ix. 3.
'Ηδὺ τὸ νικᾷν. *Arist.*   [t] Mat. xii. 20.

the Head-stone with shoutings." [x]   To Stephen, he was a
Spirit of victory against the disputers of the world [y] : to the
apostles, a Spirit of liberty in the prison [z] : to all the faithful, a Spirit of joy and glory in the midst of persecutions [a].

Fifthly, The Spirit doth not only preserve the heart which
he hath renewed, but maketh it fruitful and abundant in the
works of the Lord [b]; and fruitfulness [c] is a ground of rejoicing [d]. [e] Therefore ' they which are born of God, cannot
commit sin;' that is, they are not ἐργάται τῆς ἀδικίας [f], ' workers'
or artificers, or finishers ' of iniquity,' because they have the
seed of God, that is, his Spirit in them, which fitteth them
(as seed doth the womb or the earth) to bring forth fruit
unto God : partly by teaching the heart [g], and casting [h], as
it were, in the mould of the word, fashioning such thoughts,
apprehensions, affections, judgments, in the soul, as are
answerable to the will and spirit of God in the word; so that
a man cannot but set his seal, and say ' Amen' to the written
law ;—partly, by moving, animating, applying, and most
sweetly leading the heart unto the obedience of that law,
which is thus written therein.

Lastly, Those whom he hath thus fitted, he sealeth up
unto a final and full redemption by the testimony of
their adoption, which is the handsel and earnest of their inheritance : and thereby begetteth a lively hope, an earnest
expectation, a confident attendance upon the promises, and
an unspeakable peace and security thereupon; by which
fruits of faith and hope there is a glorious joy shed abroad
into the soul, so full, and so intimately mingled with the
same, that it is as possible for man to annihilate the one, as
to take away the other.   For according to the evidence of

---

[x] Ezek. iv. 6, 7.   [y] Acts vi. 10.   [z] Acts xvi. 25, 26.   [a] 1 Pet. iv. 13, 14.
[b] Gal. v. 22. Rom. vii. 4.   [c] Ἐπεὶ δὲ φίλαυλοι πάντες, καὶ τὰ αὐτῶν ἀνάγκη ἡδέα
εἶναι πᾶσιν, οἷον ἔργα, λόγους, διὸ καὶ φιλότεκνοι· αὐτῶν γὰρ ἔργα τὰ τέκνα. Arist.
[d] Isaiah liv. 1.   [e] 1 John iii. 8, 9.   [f] Mat. vii. 23. Luke xiii. 27.   The whole
phrase, ἀμαρτίαν ποιῶν, is as much as the Latin ' operarius iniquitatis,' one that
maketh a trade of sin, or professeth iniquity, whose service is altogether incompa-
tible with the profession or hope of a Christian.   Doctor Jackson of Justif. Faith,
sect. 2. cap. 8.   [g] John xiv. 26. 1 John ii. 20. Isa. liv. 13. Jer. xxxi. 33.
2 Cor. iii. 3.   Τὸ μανθάνειν ἡδύ.   [h] Vid. Beza Annot. in Rom. vi. 17. Jer.
xxxii. 39, 40. Ezek. xxxvi. 27. Rom. viii. 14. Ephes. iv. 30. Gal. iv. 5, 6.
Ephes. i. 14. 1 Pet. i. 3. Rom. viii. 19, 23. Rom. ix. 23. 2 Cor. v. 4. Phil.
iv. 7. 1 Pet. i. 8. John xvi. 22. 24. Ἐλπίζοντες χαίρουσι. Arist.

hope, and excellency of the thing hoped, must needs the joy, therefrom resulting, receive its sweetness and stability.

By all this which hath been spoken of the mission of the Spirit in such abundance after Christ's sitting at the right hand of God, we should learn with what affections to receive the gospel of salvation,—for the teaching whereof, this holy Spirit was shed abroad abundantly on the ambassadors of Christ; and with what heavenly conversations to express the power, which our hearts have felt therein, to walk as children of the light, and as becometh the gospel of Christ, to adorn our high profession, and not to receive the grace of God in vain. Consider, first, that the word, thus quickened, will have an operation, either to convince unto righteousness, or to seal unto condemnation; as the sun, either to melt, or to harden; as the rain, either to ripen corn, or weeds; as the sceptre of a king, either to rule subjects, or to subdue enemies; as the fire of a goldsmith, either to purge gold, or to devour dross; as the waters of the sanctuary, either to heal places, or to turn them into salt-pits.[i] Secondly, According to the proportion of the Spirit of Christ, in his word revealed, shall be the proportion of their judgement who despise it. The contempt of a great salvation and glorious ministry, shall bring a sorer condemnation.[k] "If I had not come and spoken unto them," saith our Saviour, "they had not had sin."[l] Sins against the light of nature are no sins in comparison of those against the gospel. "The earth which drinketh in the rain that falls often on it, and yet beareth nothing but thorns and briers,—is rejected, and nigh unto cursing."[m] Thirdly, Even here God will not always suffer his Spirit to strive with flesh; there is a day of peace, which he calleth "our day;" a day wherein he entreateth and beseecheth us to be reconciled: but if we therein judge ourselves unworthy of eternal life, and go obstinately on till there be no remedy, he can easily draw in his Spirit, and give us over to the infatuation of our own hearts, that we may not be cleansed any more, till he have caused his fury to rest upon us.[n]

We see likewise by this doctrine whereupon the comforts of the church are founded; namely, upon Christ as the first

[i] Ezek. xlvii. 11.   [k] Heb. ii. 2, 4.   [l] John xv. 22.   [m] Heb. vi. 7, 8.
[n] Ezek. xxiv. 13.

comforter, by working our reconciliation with God; and upon the Spirit as 'another comforter,' testifying and applying the same unto our souls. And the continual supply and assistance of this Spirit is the only comfort, the church hath against the dominion and growth of sin. For though the motions of lust which are in our members, are so close, so working, so full of vigour and life, that we can see no power nor probabilities of prevailing against them; yet we know Christ hath a greater fulness of Spirit than we can have of sin: and it is the great promise of the new covenant, that "God will put his Spirit into us, and thereby save us from all our uncleannesses." [o] For though we be full of sin, and have but a seed, a sparkle of the Spirit put into us, and upheld and fed by further, though small, supplies, yet that little is stronger than legions of lust; as a little salt or leaven seasoneth a great lump, or a few drops of spirits strengthen a whole glass-ful of water. Therefore the Spirit is called a 'Spirit of judgment and of burning,' because, as one judge is able to condemn a thousand prisoners, and a little fire to consume abundance of dross; so the Spirit of God in and present with us, though received and supplied but in measure, though but a smoking and suppressed fire,—shall yet break forth in victory and judgment against all that resist it. In us indeed there is nothing that feeds, but only that which resists and quencheth it. But this is the wonderful virtue of the Spirit of Christ in his members, that it nourisheth itself. Therefore sometimes the Spirit is called *fire* [p]; and sometimes *oil* [q], to note that the Spirit is nutriment unto itself; that grace which we have received already, is preserved and excited by new supplies of the same grace. Which supplies we are sure shall be given to all that ask them, by the virtue of Christ's prayer [r], by the virtue of his and his Father's promise [s]; and by the virtue of that office which he still bears, which is to be the head, or vital principle of all holiness and grace unto the church. And all these are permanent things, and therefore the virtue of them abideth, their effects are never totally interrupted.

Fifthly and lastly, This sitting of Christ at the right hand of God, noteth his intercession in the behalf of the whole

[o] Ezek. xxxvi. 27, 29. [p] Isa. iv. 4. Mat. iii. 11. [q] Heb. i. 9. 1 John ii. 27. [r] John xiv. 16. [s] John xvi. 7. Acts i. 4.

church, and each member thereof. "Who is he that condemneth?" saith the apostle; "It is Christ that is dead, yea rather that is risen again, who is even at the right hand of God, who also maketh intercession for us."[t] But of this doctrine I shall speak more fitly in the fourth verse, it being a great part of the priesthood of Christ.

I now proceed to the last thing in this first verse, the continuance and victory of Christ's kingdom, in these words, "*until I make thy foes thy footstool*;" wherein every word is full of weight. For though ordinarily subdivisions of holy Scripture, and crumbling of the bread of life, be rather a losing than expounding of it; yet in such parts of it as were of purpose intended for models and summaries of fundamental doctrine, (of which sort, this psalm is one of the fullest and briefest in the whole Scripture,) as in little maps of large countries, there is no word whereupon some point of weighty consequence may not depend. Here then is considerable the term of duration, or measure of Christ's kingdom; *until*. The author of subduing Christ's enemies under him; I, *the Lord*. The manner thereof ' ponam,' and ' ponam scabellum ;' *put thy foes as a stool under thy feet*. Victory is a relating word, and presupposeth enemies, and they are expressed in the text. I will but touch that particular, because I have handled it more largely upon another Scripture; and their enmity is here not described, but only presupposed. It shows itself against Christ in all the offices of his mediation. There is enmity against him as a prophet:— enmity against his truth:—in opinion, by adulterating it with human mixtures and superinducements, teaching for doctrines the traditions of men :—in affection, by wishing many divine truths were razed out of the Scriptures, as being manifestly contrary to those pleasures which they love rather than God :—in conversation, by keeping down the truth in unrighteousness, and in those things which they know, as brute beasts, corrupting themselves. Enmity against his teaching, by quenching the motions, and resisting the evidence of his Spirit in the word, refusing to hear his voice, and rejecting the counsel of God against themselves. There is enmity against him as a priest, by undervaluing his per-

t Rom. viii. 34.

son, suffering, righteousness, or merits. And as a king ; enmity to his worship, by profaneness neglecting it, by idolatry communicating it, by superstition corrupting it. Enmity to his ways and service, by ungrounded prejudices, misjudging them as grievous, unprofitable, or unequal ways; and, by wilful disobedience, forsaking them to walk in the ways of our own heart.

And this is a point which men should labour to try themselves in ; for the enemies of Christ are not only out of the church, but in the midst where his kingdom is set up, verse 2.[u] And indeed by how much the more dangerous it is, by so much the more subtle will Satan and a sinful heart be to deceive itself therein ; for this is a certain truth, that men may profess and falsely believe that 'they love the Lord Jesus,' and yet be as real enemies unto his person and kingdom, as the Jews that accused, and the heathen that crucified him. " He was set up for a sign to be spoken against, for a rock of offence, and a stone of stumbling, which the very builders themselves would reject."—False brethren amongst the Philippians there were, who professed the name of Christians ; and yet, by their sensual walking and worldly-mindedness, declared themselves to be enemies to the cross of Christ.[x] To honour the bodies of the saints departed with beautiful sepulchres, is in itself a testimonial of sincere love and inward estimation of their persons and graces ; and therefore the Holy Ghost hath recorded it for the perpetual honour of Joseph of Arimathea, and Nicodemus, that " they embalmed the body of Jesus, and laid it in a new sepulchre [y]:"—yet our Saviour pronounceth " a woe against the Scribes and Pharisees, because they build the tombs of the prophets, and garnish the sepulchres of the righteous."[z] The fault was not in the fact itself; but in the hypocrisy of the heart, in the incongruity of their other practices, and in that damned protection, which, by this plausible pretext of honour to the prophets, they laboured to gain their persons, and appropriation to their attempts against Christ, in the minds of the people, who yet ordinarily esteemed Christ (whom they persecuted) a prophet sent from God. They profess, " If we had been in the days of

[u] Isa. viii. 14.   [x] Phil. iii. 18, 19.   [y] John xix. 38, 41.   [z] Matth. xxiii. 29.

our fathers, we would not have done as they did:"—but our Saviour reproves this hypocritical persuasion, by showing first, that it was no strange thing with them to persecute prophets, but a national and hereditary sin, and therefore they had no reason to boast of their descent (as their manner was[a]), or to think that God's mercies were entailed unto them, since, by their own confession, they were 'the posterity of those that had killed the prophets;' and secondly, that they did 'fulfil the measure of their fathers;'—that is, that which their fathers had been long and leisurely a-doing, they now did altogether in one blow: For it was the same Christ whom they persecuted in his person, and their fathers in his prophets; and therefore, though they seemed to honour and revive the memory of those holy martyrs, yet upon them should light the guilt of all the righteous blood which had ever been shed in the land, inasmuch as their malice was directed against that fulness, of which all the prophets had but a measure. If, by several enemies, a man be severally mangled, one cuts off a foot, another a hand, another an arm,—and after all this, there comes one who cuts off the head, and yet bestows some honourable ceremonies upon those members which the rest had abused;—he shall justly suffer, as if he had slain a whole man, insomuch as his malice did eminently contain in it the degrees of all the rest; and that pretended honour shall be so far from compensating the injury, that it shall add thereunto an aggravation of base hypocrisy. Thus, as the Jews, when they thought they did honour and admire the prophets, did yet harbour in their breasts that very root of fury, and had that self-same constitution of soul which was in their forefathers who shed their blood;—so in our days, men may say and think that they love Christ, and court him with much outside and empty service, may boast that if they had lived in the days of those unthankful Jews, they would not have partaken with them in so execrable a murder;—and yet interpretatively, and at second hand, show the very same root of bitterness, and rancorous constitution of heart against him in his spirit and ordinances, which was in those men when they cried, "Away with him, crucify him, crucify him."

[a] Luke iii. 8.   John viii. 39.

Many grounds there are of this grand mispersuasion of
the heart in its love to Christ, which I will but touch upon.
The first is the general acceptation and continuance, which
the gospel of Christ receiveth amongst the princes of this
world, who, in Christian commonwealths, do, both by their
own voluntary and professed subjection, and by the vigour of
their public laws, establish the same.   Now this is most certain, that, as in all other sciences there cannot be ' transitus
à genere in genus,' the principles of one will not serve to
beget the conclusions of another;—so here especially, if
a spiritual assent and affection be grounded upon no other
than human inducements, it is most undoubtedly spurious
and illegitimate.   That reason which the Pharisees used to
dissuade men from believing in Christ, " Have any of the
rulers or the Pharisees believed on him [d] ?" is one of the
principal arguments which many men have now why they do
believe him,—because the rulers, whose examples and laws
they observe more upon trust than trial, do lead them thereunto : and therefore we find amongst the Jews, that those
very men, who, when the government of the whole twelve
tribes was one, did all consent in a unity of religion,—upon
the distraction of the kingdom under Jeroboam, were presently likewise divided in their observance of God's worship ; and they who, before, were zealous for the Temple at
Jerusalem, were, after, as superstitious for Dan and Bethel.
The prophet giveth the reason of it, " They willingly walked after the commandment," namely of Jeroboam [c] : no
sooner did the prince interpose his authority, but the people
were willing to pin their opinions and practices upon his
word.   " If Omri make statutes, and Ahab confirm idolatrous counsels by his own practices," the prophet shows,
how forward the people are to walk in them [d].   Therefore it
is that our Saviour saith of the best sort of wicked men,
" those who with gladness " (and that is ever a symptom of
love) " received the gospel," that yet, in time of persecution,
they were offended and fell away [e].   To note unto us, that
when Christ is forsaken because of persecution, the imaginary love which was bestowed upon him before, was certainly supported by no other ground than that which is con-

[b] John vii. 48.   [c] Hos. v. 11.   [d] Micah vi. 16.   [e] Matth. xiii. 21.

trary to persecution, namely, the countenance and protection of public power.

Secondly, A great part of men profess faith and love to Christ merely upon the rules of their education. The main reason into which their religion is resolved, is not any evidence of excellency in itself, but only the customs and traditions of their forefathers ;—which is to build a divine faith upon a human authority, and to set man in the place of God. Certain it is, that contrary religions can never be originally grounded upon the same reason : that which is a true and adequate principle of faith or love to Christ, can never be suitable to the conclusions of Mahometism, or idolatry. Now then, when a professed Christian can give no other account of his love to Christ, than a Turk of his love to Mahomet; when that which moveth an idolater to hate Christ, is all that one of us hath to say why he believeth in him; certainly, that love and faith is but an empty presumption, which dishonoureth the Spirit of Christ, and deludeth our own souls. There is a natural instinct in the mind of man, to reverence and vindicate the traditions of their progenitors, and at first view to detest any novel opinions, which seem to thwart the received doctrine, wherein they had been bred : and this affection is ever so much the stronger, by how much the tradition received is about the nobler and more necessary things. And therefore it discovereth itself with most violence and impatiency in matters of religion, wherein the eternal welfare of the soul is made the issue of the contention. We find with what heat of zeal the Jews [f] contended for the Temple at Jerusalem, and with how equal and confident emulation the Samaritans ventured their lives for the precedency of their Temple on mount Gerizim ; and took an oath to produce proofs for the authority thereof; and yet all the ground of this will-worship was the tradition of their fathers. For our Saviour [g] assures us, that "they worshipped they knew not what," and only took things upon trust from their predecessors. The satirist [h] hath made

---

[f] *Joseph.* Antiq. lib. 13. cap. 6. [g] John iv. 20, 22. [h] Immortale odium, et nunquam sanabile vulnus, Ardet adhuc Coptos et Tentyra. Summus utrinque Inde-furor vulgo, quod numina vicinorum Odit uterque locus, cum solos credat habendos Esse Deos, quos ipse colit. *Juvenal.* Satir. 15, 34.

himself merry with describing the combat of two neighbour
towns amongst the Egyptians in the opposite defence of
those ridiculous idols, the several worship of which they
had been differently bred up unto : And surely if a profane
Christian and a zealous Mahometan should join in the like
contention, notwithstanding the subject itself, on the one
side defended, were a sacred and precious truth,—yet I
doubt not but the self-same reasons might be the sole motive
of the Christian, to vindicate the honour of Christ,—and of
the other, to maintain the worship of Mahomet :—I mean a
blind and pertinacious adhering to that religion, in which
they have been bred, a natural inclination to favour domes-
tical opinons, a high estimation of the persons of men, from
whom by succession they have thus been instructed, without any spiritual conviction of the truth, or experience of
the good which the true members of Christ resolve their
love unto him into.   And this (we find) was ever the reason
of the Jews' obstinacy against the prophets ;—they answered
all their arguments, with the practice and traditions they
had received from their fathers [i].

Thirdly, The heart may be mispersuaded of its love to
Christ, by judging that an affection unto him, which is indeed nothing but a self-love and a desire of advancing private ends.   The rule whereby Christ, at the last day, will
measure the love or hatred of men unto him, is their love or
hatred of his brethren and members here [k], for, in all their
afflictions, Christ himself is afflicted.   " Peter, lovest thou
me ? feed my sheep ;" make proof of thy love to me by thy
service and compassion to my people.— And how many are
there every where to be found, whose love unto themselves
hath devoured all brotherly love ! who take no pity either
upon the souls, or temporal necessities of those, with whom
they yet pretend a fellowship in Christ's own body ! who
spend more upon their own pride and luxury, upon their
backs and bellies, their pleasures and excesses, yea, bury
more of their substance in the maws of hawks and dogs, than
they can ever persuade themselves to put into the bowels
of the poor saints [l] !   Surely at the day of judgement, how-

---

[i] Jer. ix. 14, xi. 10, xliv. 17. Acts vii. 51.   [k] Mat. xxv. 40, 45.   [l] Auro
parietes, auro laquearia, auro fulgent capita columnarum, et nudus atque esuriens
, ante fores nostras Christus in paupere moritur. *Hieron.* ad Gaudentium.

ever such men here profess to love Christ, and would spit in
the face of him who with Justin Martyr [m] should say, they
were not Christians ;—it will appear that such men did as
formally and as properly deny Christ, as if with Peter they
had publicly sworn, " I know not the man." The apostle
plainly intimates thus much, when he showeth, that the experiment of the Corinthians' ministration to the necessity
of the saints was an inducement unto the churches to
praise God for their professed subjection to the gospel of
Christ [n]. Again, as Christ is present with us in his poor
members, so likewise in the power of his ordinances, and in
the light and evidence of his Spirit shining forth in the lives
of holy men. If then we are impatient of the edge of his
word, when it divides between the bone and the marrow,
when it discerneth and discovereth our secret thoughts, our
bosom-sins, our ambitious, unclean, and hypocritical intents ;
if the lives and communion of the saints be, in like manner,
an eyesore unto us in shaming and reproving our formal and
fruitless profession of the same truth, as Christ was unto the
Jews ; certainly the same affections of hatred, reproach, and
disestimation which we show unto them, we would with so
much the more bitterness have expressed unto Christ himself, if we had lived in his days, by how much that Spirit of
grace, against which the Spirit which is in us envieth, was
above measure more abundantly in him than in the holiest
of his members. " If you were of the world," saith our
Saviour, " the world would love their own ; but now I
have called you out of the world :" I have given to you
a Spirit which is contrary to the spirit of the world ;
" therefore the world hateth you." And this is evident when
men hate one another merely for that distinction, which
differenceth him from them,—they much more hate him,
from whom the difference itself originally proceedeth. We
see then, that they who openly profess Christ, may yet
inwardly hate him ; because the ground of their profession

---

[m] Οἱ δ᾽ ἂν μὴ εὑρίσκωνται βιοῦντες ὡς ἐδίδαξε, γνωριζέσθωσαν μὴ ὄντες Χριστιανοὶ,
κἂν λέγωσιν διὰ γλώτ]ης τὰ τοῦ Χριστοῦ διδάγματα.   Just. Mart. Apol. 2.—Qui
Christiano vocabulo gloriantur et perditè vivunt, non absurdè possunt videri medio
Noe filio figurari ; passionem quippe Christi, quæ illius hominis nuditate sig-
nificata est, et annunciant profitendo, et male agendo exhonorant. Aug. de Civit.
Dei, lib. 16. cap. 2.—Οὐ Χριστιανοὶ, ἀλλὰ Χριστέμποροι, &c. Ignat. Epist. ad Tral.
[n] 2 Cor. ix. 13.

is not any experimental goodness which they have tasted in
him (for, by nature, men have no relish of Christ at all,)
but only self-love and private ends, whereby Christ[o] is subordinated to their own commodities. Men are herein just
like the Samaritans[p], of whom Josephus reports, that when
Antiochus persecuted the Jews, they then utterly disavowed
any consanguinity with them,—denied their Temple on
mount Gerizim to be dedicated to the great God, and declared their lineage from the Medes and Persians. But
when before that, Alexander had showed favour unto the
Jews, and remitted the tribute of every seventh year, then
they claimed kindred with that people, and counterfeited a
descent from the tribes of Ephraim and Manasseh, that
thereby they might enjoy the privileges[q] of those people,
whom otherwise they mortally hated. And so we find that,
in the vastation of the city of Rome by the Goths and bar-
barians, when there was but one only refuge allowed the
Romans for the safety of their lives, namely, to flee unto the
Christian churches,—those very enemies of Christ and his
profession, who before had persecuted him, and after returned to their malice again,—were yet then as hasty to flee
unto his temples, and to assume the title of his servants,
as they were, after, ungratefully malicious in reproaching
Christian religion, as if that had been the provocation of
those calamities. And may we not still observe, amongst
Christians at this day, many men, who, contrary to the evidence of their judgement, and peace of their consciences, con-

---

[o] Si quis Christo temporalia præponat, non est in eo fundamentum Christus.
Aug. de Civit. Dei, lib. 21. cap. 26. Multi, amissâ caritate, propterea non ex-
eunt foras, quia secularibus emolumentis tenentur, et sua quærentes, non quæ
Jesu Christi, non à Christi unitate, sed à suis commodis nolunt recedere. *Aug.*
de Baptismo contr. Donat. lib. 4. cap. 10. [p] Ταῦτα δὲ βλέπον]ες οἱ Σαμαρεῖται
ϖάσχον]ας τοὺς Ἰουδαίους, οὐκέθ᾽ ὡμολόγουν αὐτοὺς εἶναι συΓγενεῖς αὐτῶν,οὐδε τὸν ἐν
Γαριζεὶν ναὸν τοῦ μεγίστου Θεοῦ, &c. *Joseph.* Antiq. lib. 12. cap. 7. Ἰδόν]ες ὅτι τοὺς
Ἰουδαίους᾽ Ἀλέξανδρος οὕτω λαμπρῶς τετίμηκεν, ἔγνωσαν αὐτοὺς Ἰουδαίους ὁμολογεῖν·
εἰσὶ γὰρ οἱ Σαμαρεῖς τοιοῦτοι τὴν φύσιν· ἐν μὲν ταῖς συμφοραῖς ὄντας τοὺς Ἰουδαίους
ἀρνοῦνται συΓγενεῖς ἔχειν· ὅταν δέ τι ϖερὶ αὐτοὺς λαμπρὸν ἴδωσιν ἐκ τύχης, ἐξαίφνης
ἐπιπηδῶσιν αὐτῶν τῇ κοινωνίᾳ, &c. *Joseph.* Antiq. lib. 11. cap. 8. [q] Quos vides
petulanter et procaciter insultare servis Christi, sunt in eis plurimi qui illum inte-
ritum clademque non evasissent, nisi servos Christi se esse finxissent ; et nunc,
ingratâ superbiâ atque impiissimâ insaniâ, ejus nomini resistunt corde perverso, ut
sempiternis tenebris puniantur, ad quod nomen ore vel sub dolo confugerunt, ut
temporali luce fruerentur. *Aug.* de Civ. Dei, lib. 1. cap. 1.

form themselves unto the vanities, courses, and companies of this evil world,—and, like cowards, are afraid to adventure on a rigorous and universal subjection to the truth of Christ, dare not keep themselves close to those narrow rules of St. Paul, to "abstain from jesting, which is not seemly; to avoid all appearances of evil; to reprove the unfruitful works of darkness; to speak unto edification, that their words may minister grace unto the hearers; to rejoice always in the Lord; to give place unto wrath; to recompense evil with good; to be circumspect and exact in their walking before God;"—and all this merely out of suspicion of some disrespect and disadvantages, which may hereupon meet them in the world,—of some remora's and stoppage in the order of those projects, which they have contrived for their private ends. Now if such purposes as these do startle men with a punctual and rigorous profession of the gospel of Christ and his most holy ways (notwithstanding our vow in baptism do as strictly bind us thereunto, as unto the external title of Christianity) suppose we that the same, or greater disadvantages should now (as in the primitive times) attend the naked and outward profession of Christ; would not such men as these fall into downright apostasy, and "deny the Lord that bought them?" Certainly our Saviour hath so resolved that case in the very best sort of unregenerate men, noted in the stony ground; when times of persecution happen, that they are brought to the trial who it was whom, in their profession, they loved, Christ or themselves, the excellency of the knowledge of him, or the secure enjoyment of secular contentments,—they will then certainly "fall away and be offended [r]." So profound and unsearchable is the deceitful heart of men, that by that very reason, for which men contend for the outward face and profession of religion, because they love their pleasures and profits, which without such a profession they cannot peaceably enjoy,—they are deterred from a close, spiritual, and universal obedience to the power thereof; because thereby likewise those pleasures and profits are kept within such rules of moderation, as the nature of a boundless and unsatiable lust will not admit. This is a certain rule in love, that the motions and desires thereof are strong, and therefore in any thing which the soul loves,

[r] Matth. xiii. 21.

it therein strives for excellency and perfection: and this rule holds most true in religion, because when the soul loves that, it loves it under the apprehension of the greatest good, and therefore, by consequence, sets the strongest and most industrious desires of the soul upon it. Therefore the apostle saith, that "the love of Christ," namely, that love of him which is by the Holy Ghost 'shed abroad in our hearts,' constraineth us to live unto him, and to aspire after him 'who died for us and rose again.' Love is as strong as death; it will take no denial. It is the wing and weight of the soul, which fixeth all the thoughts, and carrieth all the desires unto an intimate unity[s] with the thing it loves,—stirreth up a zeal to remove all obstacles which stand between it,—worketh a languor or failing of nature in the want of it, a liquefaction and softness of nature to receive the impressions of it, an egress of the spirits, and, as it were, a haste of the soul to meet and entertain it. Whence those expressions of the saints in holy Scripture, "Comfort me with apples, stay me with flaggons, for I am sick of love[t]: My soul breaketh for the longing which it hath unto thy judgments at all times[u].—The desire of our soul is to thy name[x], and to the remembrance of thee. My soul thirsteth for God, yea, for the living God; when shall I come and appear before God[y]?—We that have the first-fruits of the Spirit, groan within ourselves, waiting for the adoption, even the redemption of our bodies[z].—O that my ways were directed, that I might keep thy commandments; with my whole heart have I sought thee; I have stuck unto thy testimonies; I will delight myself in thy commandments; thy statutes have been my songs; my soul fainteth for thy salvation[a]," &c. By all which we see, that a true love of Christ doth excite strong desires, and an earnest aspiring and ambition of the soul to walk in all well-pleasing, and to be in all things conformable unto him. What the apostle saith of spiritual hope, we may truly say of love (which is the fundamental affection and root of all the

---

[s] Amor concupiscentiæ non requiescit in quacunque extrinsecâ aut superficiali adeptione amati, sed quærit amatum perfectè habere, quasi ad intime illius perveniens, &c. *Aquin.* 1a. 2æ. qu. 28. art. 2. vid. id. art. 4 et 5.   [t] Cant. ii. 5.
[u] Psalm cxix. 20.   [x] Isaiah xxvi. 8.   [y] Psalm xlii. 2.   [z] Rom. viii. 13.
[a] Psalm cxix. 5, 10, 31, 47, 54, 81, &c.

rest) ; he that hath it indeed in him, " purgeth himself even as Christ is pure." The love of the world, and the things and lusts of the world, may, indeed, consist with the formal profession, but no way with the truth or power of a true love to Christ or his government. For love is ever the principle and measure of all our actions ; such as it is, such likewise will they be too.

Fourthly, Something like love there may be in natural men unto Christ, grounded upon the historical assurance and persuasion of his being now in glory, attended by mighty angels, filled with all the treasures of wisdom, knowledge, grace, power, and other excellent attributes, which can attract love [b] even from an enemy ; and that he hath, and still doth procure such good things for mankind, in their deliverance from the guilt of sin, and from the wrath to come, as of which, might they but have an exemption from his spiritual government, and a dispensation to live according to their own lusts still, no man should be more greedily desirous. As Samson met the lion as an enemy, when he was alive; but after he was slain, he went unto him as to a table ; there was only terror while he lived, but honey when he was dead :—so doubtless, many men, to whom the bodily presence of Christ, and the mighty power and penetration of his heavenly preaching, whereby he smote sinners unto the ground, and spake with such authority as never man spake, would have been unsufferably irksome, and full of terror (as it was unto the Scribes and Pharisees), can yet, now that he is out of their sight, and doth, not in person [c], but only by those who are his witnesses, torment the inhabitants of the earth, pretend much admiration, and thankful remembrance of that death of his, which was so full of honey for all that come unto him. For as particular dependencies and expectations may make a man flatter and adore the greatness of some living potentate, whose very image, notwithstanding, the same man doth professedly abominate in other tyrants of the world who are dead, or upon

[b] Quodlibet agens propter amorem agit quodcunque agit. *Aquin.* 1a. 2æ. qu. 28. art. 6.   [c] Securus licet Æneam Rutulumque ferocem Committas : nulli gravis est percussus Achilles.—Quid refert dictis ignoscat Mucius, annon ? Pone Tigellinum : tædâ lucebis in illâ, Qua stantes ardent, qui fixo gutture fumant, &c. *Juvenal. Satir.* 1.

whom he hath not the same ends;—so the self-same reason
may make men, in hypocritical expressions, flatter and fawn
upon Christ himself who is absent, and yet hate with a perfect hatred the very image of his Spirit, in the power of his
word, and in the lives of his people. The very Scribes and
Pharisees, who blasphemed his Spirit, and contrived his
death, could yet be contented to be gainers thereby; for so
they confess, " It is expedient for us, that one die for the
people."

Lastly, A false love to Christ may be grounded upon a
false conceit of love to his ordinances. For as it is certain,
that he who loves the word and worship of Christ, as his,
doth love him too, who is the author of them;—so it is
certain likewise, that that love which is sometimes pretended unto them, may indeed in them fix upon nothing but accidental and by-respects. " This people," saith the Lord to
his prophet, " come and sit before thee as my people, and
they hear thy words, but they will not do them; for with
their mouth they show much love, but their heart goeth
after their covetousness." Here is love in pretence, but falsehood in the heart: What then was it in which they did
thus love the prophet? That presently follows: " Thou art
unto them as a very lovely song of one that hath a pleasant
voice, and can play well on an instrument [d] :" That is, it is
not my will which in thy ministry they at all regard, but
only those circumstantial ornaments of graceful action and
elocution, which they attend with just a like proportion of
sensual delight, as an ear doth the harmony of a well-tuned
instrument. For as a man may be much affected with the
picture of his enemy, if drawn by a skilful hand, and yet
therein love nothing of the person, but only the cunning of
the workman who drew the piece;—so a man who hates the
life and spirit of the word of God itself, as being diametrically contrary to that spirit of lust and of the world which
rules in him, may yet be so wonderfully taken with that
dexterity of wit, or delicacy of expression, or variety of
learning, or sweetness of speech, and action,—or whatsoever
other perfection of nature or industry in the dispensers
of that word, are most suitable to his natural affections,—as

[d] Ezck. xxxiii. 31, 32.

that he may from thence easily cheat his own conscience, and ground a mispersuasion of his love to God's word, which yet indeed admireth nothing but the perfections of a man. Nay, suppose he meet not with such 'lenocinia' to entice his affection, yet the very pacification of the conscience, which, by a notorious neglect of God's ordinances, would haply be disquieted,—or the credit of bearing conformity to ecclesiastical orders, and the established service of God in his church,—or some other the like sinister respect, may hold a man to such an external fair correspondence, as, by a deceitful heart, may easily be misconstrued a love of God's ordinances. Nay, further, a man may externally glory[e] in the privilege of God's oracles; he may distinctly believe, and subscribe to the truth of them; he may therein hear many things gladly, and escape many pollutions of the world;—and yet here hence conclude no clearer evidence of his love to Christ in his word, than the unbelieving Jews[f], or Herod[g], or Ahab[h], or Simon Magus[i], or the foolish virgins and apostates[k] (all which have attained to some of these degrees), could have done.

For the clearing, then, of this great case,—Touching the evidence of a man's love to Christ,—we must first know, that this is not a flower of our own garden,—for every man, by nature, is an enemy to Christ and his kingdom,—of the Jews' mind, "We will not have this man to reign over us." And the reason is, because the image of the old Adam which we bear, is extremely contrary to the heavenly image of the second Adam, unto which we are not born, but must be renewed. And this is certain, our love is according to our likeness : he who hath not the nature and spirit of Christ, can never love him or move towards him. For love is like fire ; 'congregat homogenea,' it carrieth things of a nature to one another. Our love, then, unto Christ, must be of a spiritual generation; and it is grounded upon two causes.

First, Upon the proportion which is in him unto all our desires or capacities; upon the evidence of that unsearchable and bottomless goodness which is in him, which makes him 'the fairest of ten thousand,' even altogether lovely.

---

[e] Jer. vii. 4. Rom. ii. 17, 20.   [f] Hos. ii. 2, 3.   [g] Mark vi. 20.   [h] 1 Kings xxi. 27, 29.   [i] Acts viii. 13.   [k] 2 Pet. ii. 20.

For that heart which hath a spiritual view of Christ, will be
able, by faith, to observe more dimensions[1] of love, and
sweetness in him, than the knowledge of any creature is able
to measure. In all worldly things, though of never so curious
and delicate an extraction, yet still even those hearts, which
swim in them and glut upon them, can easily discover more
dregs than spirits. Nothing was ever so exactly fitted to the
soul of man, wherein there was not some defect, or excess,
something which the heart could wish were away, or something which it could desire were tempered with it:—but in
Christ and his kingdom, there is nothing unlovely. For as
in man the *all* that is, is full of corruption, so in Christ the
all that he is, is nothing but perfection. His fulness is the
centre and treasure of the soul of man ; and therefore that
love which is thereupon grounded, must needs be in the
soul as a universal habit and principle, to facilitate every
service whereby we move unto this centre ; for love is the
weight[m] or spring of the soul, which sets every faculty on
work ; neither are any of those commandments grievous
which are obeyed in love ; and therefore it is called " the
fulfilling of the law." True love unto Christ keeps the whole
heart together, and carries it all one way ; and so makes it
universal, uniform, and constant in all its affections unto
God ; for unsteadfastness of life proceeds from a divided or
double heart[n]. As in the motions of the heavens, there is
one common circumvolution, which ' ex æquo' carrieth the
whole frame daily unto one point from east to west, though
each several sphere hath a several cross-way of its own, wherein some move with swifter, and others with a slower motion ;
so though several saints may have their several corruptions,
and those likewise in some stronger than in others, yet,
being all animated by one and the same Spirit, they all
agree in a steady and uniform motion unto Christ. If a
stone were placed under the concave of the moon, though
there be fire, and air, and water between, yet through them
all it would hasten to its own place ; so, be the obstacles
never so many, or the conditions never so various, through
which a man must pass, " through evil report and good

---

[1] Eph. iii. 18, 19.   [m] Amor meus pondus meum ; eo feror quocunque
feror. *Aug.*   [n] James i. 8.

report," through terrors and temptations, through a sea and a wilderness, through fiery serpents and sons of Anak ; yet if the heart love Christ indeed, and conclude that Heaven is its home, nothing shall be able totally to discourage it from hastening thither, whither Christ the fore-runner is gone before.

Secondly, The true love of Christ is grounded upon the evidence of that propriety which the soul hath unto him, and of that mutual inhabitation and possession which is between them : so that our love unto him, in this regard, is a kind of self-love º (and therefore very strong), because Christ and a Christian are but one P. And the more persuasion the soul hath of this unity, the more must it needs love Christ. " For we love him, because he loved us first ۹." And therefore our Saviour, from the woman's apprehension of God's more abundant love in the remission of her many and great sins, concludeth the measure and proportion of her love to him: " But," saith he, " to whom little is forgiven, the same loveth little ʳ."

Now true love of Christ and his kingdom, thus grounded, will undoubtedly manifest itself, first, in a universal extent unto any thing wherein Christ is present unto his Church.

First, The soul, in this case, will abundantly love and cherish the Spirit of Christ, entertain with dearest embraces, as worthy of all acceptation, the motions and dictates, and secret elapses of him into the soul; will be careful to hear his voice always behind him, prompting and directing him in the way he should walk ; will endeavour with all readiness and pliableness of heart, to receive the impression of his seal, and the testimony which he giveth in the inner man unto all God's promises ; will fear and suspect nothing more, than the frowardness of his own nature, which daily endeavoureth to quench, grieve, resist, rebel against this Holy Spirit, and to fling off from his conduct again.

Secondly, The soul, in this case, will abundantly love the ordinances of God (in which, by his Spirit, he is still walking in the midst of the churches) ; for the law is written in it by the finger of God ; so that there is a suitableness and

º Cant. ii. 16.   P John xiv. 23, and xvii. 21, 23.   ۹ 1 John iv. 16, 19.
ʳ Luke vii. 47.
F 2

coincidency between the law of God, and the heart of such a man. He will receive the Word in the purity thereof, and not give way to those human inventions which adulterate it,—to that spiritual treason of wit and fancy, or of heresy and contradiction, which would stamp the private image and superscription of a man upon God's own coin, and torture the Scriptures to confess that which was never in them. He will receive the Word in the power, majesty, and authority thereof,—suffering it like thunder to discover the forest, and to drive out all those secret corruptions, which sheltered themselves in the corners or deceit of his heart. He will delight to have his imaginations humbled, and his fleshly reasons nonplussed, and all his thoughts subdued unto the obedience of Christ. He will receive the Word as a wholesome potion, to that very end, that it may search his secret places, and purge out those tough and incorporated lusts, which hitherto he had not prevailed against. He will take heed of hardening his heart, that he may not hear of rejecting the counsel of God against himself,—of thrusting away the Word from him,—of setting up a resolved will of his own against the call of Christ,—as of most dangerous downfals to the soul. Lastly, he will receive the Word in the spiritualness thereof, subscribing to the closest precepts of the law, suffering it to cleanse his heart unto the bottom. He will let the consideration of God's command preponderate and over-rule all respects of fear, love, profit, pleasure, credit, compliancy, or any other charm to disobedience. He will be contented to be led in the narrowest way, to have his secretest corruption revealed and removed, to expose his conscience with patience under the saving, though severest blows of this spiritual sword. In one word, he will deny the pride of his own wit; and if it be the evident truth of God which is taught him, though it come naked, and without any dressings or contributions of human fancy, he will distinguish between the author and the instrument, between the treasure and the vessel in which it comes, and from any hand receive it with such awful submission of heart, as becometh God's own word.

Thirdly, The soul, in this case, will most dearly love every member of Christ: for these two, the love of Christ, and of his members, do infallibly accompany one another. For though there be a far higher proportion of love due unto Christ than unto men, yet our love to our brethren is, 'quoad nos' and 'à posteriori,' not only the evidence, but even the measure of our love to Christ. "He that loveth not his brother whom he hath seen, how can he love God whom he hath not seen?" saith the apostle.[s] He that hath not love enough in him for a man like himself, how can he love God, whose goodness, being above our knowledge, requireth transcendency in our love? This then is a sure rule;—he that loveth not a member of Christ, loveth not Him; and he who groweth in his love to his brethren, groweth likewise in his love to Christ. For as there is the same proportion of one to five, as there is of twenty to an hundred, though the number be far less; as the motion of the shadow upon the dial, answereth exactly to that proportion of motion and distance, which the sun hath in the firmament, though the sun goeth many millions of miles when the shadow (it may be) moveth not the breadth of a hand; so though our love to Christ ought to be a far more abundant love than to any of his members; yet certain it is, that the measure of our progress in brotherly love is punctually answerable to the growth of our love to Christ.

Thirdly, A true grounded love unto Christ, will show itself in the right manner or conditions of it. Which are principally these three :—

1. It must be an incorrupt and sincere love. "Grace be upon all those that love the Lord Jesus, ἐν ἀφθαρσίᾳ, 'in incorruption' or sincerity, saith the apostle[t]; that is, on those who love not in word or outward profession and stipulation only, but in deed and truth, or in the permanent constitution of the inner man; which moveth them to love him always and in all things, to hate every false way, to set the whole heart, the study, purpose, prayer, and all the activity of our spirits against every corruption in us, which standeth at enmity with him and his kingdom.

2. It must be a principal and superlative love, grounded upon the experience of the soul in itself, that there is ten thousand times more beauty and amiableness in him, than in all the honours, pleasures, profits, satisfactions which the world can afford; that, in comparison or competition with him,

<hr>

[s] 1 John iv. 20.   [t] Eph. vi. 24.

the dearest things of this world, the parents of our body, the children of our flesh, the wife of our bosom, the blood in our veins, the heart in our breast, must not only be laid down and lost as sacrifices, but hated as snares when they draw us away from him.

3. It must be an unshared and uncommunicable love, without any corrivals: for Christ as he is unto us all in all, so he requireth to have all our affections fixed upon him. As the rising of the sun drowneth all those innumerable stars which did shine in the firmament before ; so must the beauty of this ' sun of righteousness' blot out, or else gather together unto itself, all those scattered affections of the soul, which were, before, cast away upon meaner objects.

Lastly, True love unto Christ will show itself in the natural and genuine effects of so strong and spiritual grace. Some of the principal I before named, unto which we may add,

First, A universal, cheerful, and constant obedience to his holy commandments. " If a man," saith Christ, " love me, he will keep my commandments ; and my Father will love him, and we will come unto him, and make our abode with him."[u] There is a twofold love; a love which descends, and a love which ascends ; a love of bounty and beneficence, and a love of duty and service. So then, as a father doth then only in truth love his child, when, with all care, he provideth for his present education and future subsistence ; so a child doth then truly love his father, when, with all reverence and submission of heart, he studieth to please and to do him service. And this love, if it be free and ingenuous, by how much the more, not only pure and equal in itself, but also profitable unto him the commandment is, by so much the more carefully will it endeavour the observation thereof. And therefore since the soul of a Christian knows, that as God himself is good, and doth good[x]; so his law (which is nothing but a ray and glimpse of his own holiness) is likewise good in itself, and doth good[y] unto those which walk uprightly ; it is hereby inflamed to a more sweet and serious obedience thereunto ; in the keeping whereof, there is for the present so much sweetness ; and in the future so great a

u John xiv. 24.   x Psal. cxix. 68.   y Micah ii. 7. Isai. xlv. 19.

reward.[z] "Thy word," saith the psalmist, "is very pure;
therefore thy servant loveth it."[a]

Secondly, A free, willing, and cheerful suffering for him
and his gospel. " Unto you," saith the apostle, " it is given
in the behalf of Christ, not only to believe on him, but also
to suffer for his sake."[b] We see how far a human love,
either of their country, or of vain-glory, hath transported[c]
some heathen men, to the devoting and casting away their
own lives: how much more should a spiritual love of Christ
put courage into us to bear all things, and "to endure all
things" (as the apostle speaks[d]) "for him," who bare our
sins, and our stripes, and our burdens for us, which were
heavier than all the world could lay on! And this was the
inducement of that holy martyr Polycarp[e], to die for Christ,
notwithstanding all the persuasions of the persecutors, who,
by his apostasy, would fain have cast the more dishonour
upon Christian religion, and, as it were, by sparing him,
have the more cunningly persecuted that: "This eighty-six
years," saith he, " I have served him; and he never, in all that
time, hath done me any hurt; why should I be so ungrateful as not to trust him in death, who in so long a life hath
never forsaken me?"—" I am persuaded, saith the apostle[f],
" that neither death, nor life, nor principalities, nor powers,
nor things to come, nor height, nor depth, nor any other
creature, shall be able to separate us from the love of God
which is in Christ Jesus our Lord."[g] Nothing able to turn
away his love from us, and therefore nothing should be able
to quench our love to him. " Many waters," that is, by the
usual expression[h] of the holy scriptures, many afflictions,
persecutions, temptations, "cannot quench love, neither
can the floods drown it."[i]

Thirdly, A zeal and jealous contention for the glory, truth,
worship, and ways of Christ. Wicked men pretend much

---

[z] Psal. xix. 7, 11.   [a] Psal. cxix. 140.   [b] Phil. i. 29.   [c] Tertul.
Apolog. cap. ult.   [d] 1 Cor. xiii. 7.   [e] Ὀγδοήκοντα καὶ ἐξ ἔτη δουλεύω
αὐτῷ, καὶ οὐδέ με ἠδίκησε· καὶ πῶς δύναμαι βλασφημῆσαι τὸν βασιλέα μου τὸν
σεσωκότα με. Euseb. Hist. Eccles. lib. 4. cap. 14.   [f] Πῦρ, καὶ σταυρὸς,
θηρίων τε συστάσεις, ἀνατομαὶ, διαιρέσεις, σκορπισμοὶ ὀστέων, συγκοπαὶ μελῶν,
ἀλυσμοὶ ὅλου τοῦ σώματος, καὶ κόλασις τοῦ διαβόλου ἐπ᾽ ἐμὲ ἐρχέσθω, μόνον
ἵνα Ἰησοῦ Χριστοῦ ἐπιτύχω. Ignat. Ep. ad Rom. Ζῶν γὰρ γράφω ὑμῖν, ἐρῶν
τοῦ διὰ Χριστὸν ἀποθανεῖν. ὁ ἐμὸς ἔρως ἐσταύρωται, &c. Ibid.   [g] Rom.
viii. 38, 39.   [h] Psal. lxix. 1, 2, and cxxiv. 4, 5. Isai. viii. 7.   [i] Canticles viii. 7.

love to Christ, but they indeed only serve their own turns; as ivy, which clasps an oak very close, but only to suck out sap for its own leaves and berries. But a true love is full of care to advance the glory of Christ's kingdom, and to promote his truth and worship; fears lest Satan and his instruments should by any means corrupt his truth, or violate his church;—as the apostle to the Galatians professeth the fear which his love wrought in him towards them, " I am afraid of you, lest I have bestowed upon you labour in vain."[k] So we find what contention, and disputation, and strife of spirit, the apostles and others in their ministry used, when Christ and his holy gospel was any way either injured by false brethren, or kept out by the idolatry of the places to which they came.[l]

Lastly, A longing after his presence, a love of his appearing, a desire to be with him, which is best of all; a seeking after him, and grieving for him, when for any while he departs from the soul; a waiting for his salvation, a delight in his communion, and in his spiritual refreshments; " a communing with him in his secret chamber, in his houses of wine, and in his galleries of love." By which lovely expressions the Wise Man hath described the fellowship, which the church desireth to have with Christ, and that abiding and supping of Christ with his church, feasting the soul with the manifestations of himself, and his graces unto it.[m]

Having thus, by occasion of the enemies of Christ, spoken something of the true and false love which is in the world towards him; we now proceed to the particulars mentioned before. And the first is the term of duration or measure of time in the text, " *until.*" It hath a double relation in the words, unto Christ's kingdom, and unto his enemies. As it looks to the kingdom of Christ, it denotes both the continuance and the limitation of his kingdom. The continuance of it in his own person, for it is there fixed and intransient: he is a king without successors, as being subject to no mortality, nor defect which might be by them supplied. The kingdom of Christ (as I observed) is either na-

---

k Gal. iv. 11, 16.   l Acts xv. 2. and xvii. 16. and xviii. 25. and xix. 8. Gal. ii. 4, 5. Jude v. 2.   m Psal. xlii. 3. and cv. 4. 2 Cor. v. 2. 2 Tim. iv. 8. Phil. i. 23. Cant. iii. 1, 2. and v. 6, 8. Gen. xlix. 18. Psal. cxix. 131. Cant. i. 4. and ii. 4. and vii. 5. John xiv. 21, 23. Rev. iii. 20.

tural, as he is God ; or dispensatory and by donation from
the Father, as he is mediator : and not only of the former,
but even of this likewise, the Scripture affirms that it is
eternal. It is a kingdom set up by the God of Heaven, and
yet it shall never be destroyed, but "stand for ever."[n] "I
have set my king upon my holy hill of Sion ;"—that
notes the unction and donation.[o] And in Mount Sion where
God hath set him, "he shall reign from hence even for
ever."[p] Though he be a child born, and a son given, yet
" of the increase of his government and peace, there shall be
no end ;" upon the throne of David, and upon his kingdom,
to order it, and to establish it with judgment and justice,
" from henceforth, for ever and ever."[q] Unto the Son he
saith, "Thy throne, O God, is for ever and ever."[r]—And here
we must distinguish between the substance of Christ's kingdom, and the form or manner of administering and dispensing it. In the former respect, it is absolutely eternal ;
Christ shall be a head and rewarder of his members, an
' everlasting Father,' a ' prince of peace' unto them for ever.
In the latter respect, it shall be eternal according to some
acceptation ; that is, it shall remain until the consummation
of all things, as long as there is a church of God upon the
earth ;—there shall be no new way of spiritual and essential
government prescribed unto it, no other vicar, successor or
monarch, or usurper upon his office by God allowed, but he
only, by his Spirit in the dispensation of his ordinances,
shall order and over-rule the consciences of his people, and
subdue their enemies. Yet he shall so reign till then, as
that he shall then cease to rule in such manner as now he
doth : when the end comes, "he shall deliver up the kingdom to God the Father ; and when all things shall be subdued unto him, he also himself shall be subject unto him that
put all things under him, that God may be all in all."[s] He
shall so return it unto God, as God did confer, and, as
it were, appropriate it unto him, namely, in regard of judiciary dispensation and execution ; in which respect our
Saviour saith, that as touching the present administration of the church, "The Father judgeth no man, but
hath committed all judgement, and hath given authority

---

n Dan. ii. 44. o Psal. ii. 6. p Mic. iv. 7. q Isai. ix. 6, 7.
Heb. i. 8. s 1 Cor. xv. 24, 28.

to execute it unto his Son.[t]" Now Christ governeth his
church by the ministry of his word and sacraments, and
by the effusion of his Spirit in measure and degrees upon
his members. By his mighty, though secret power, he
fighteth with his enemies; and so shall do till the resurrection of the dead,—when Death, the last enemy, shall
be overcome, and then, in these respects, his kingdom shall
cease : for he shall no more exercise the offices of a mediator
in compassionating, defending, interceding for his church ;
but yet he shall sit and reign for ever as God, coequal with
his Father, and shall ever be the head of the church his body.
Thus we see, though Christ's kingdom, in regard of the
manner of dispensation, and present execution thereof, it be
limited by the consummation of all things ; yet in itself it is
a kingdom, which hath neither within, the seeds of mortality,
—nor without, the danger of a concussion ; but in the substance is immortal, though, in regard of the commission and
power, which Christ had as mediator, to administer it alone
by himself, and by the fulness of his Spirit,—it be at last
voluntarily resigned into the hands of the Father,—and
Christ, as a part of that great church, become subject to the
Father, that God may be all in all.

Now·the grounds of the constancy of Christ's government
over his church, and by consequence of the church itself,
which is his kingdom, are, amongst others, these :—

First, The decree and promise of God, sealed by an oath,
which made it an adamantine and unbended purpose, which
the Lord would never repent of nor reverse.   All God's counsels are immutable[u]; though he may alter his works, yet he
doth never change his will : but when he sealeth his decree
with an oath, that makes their immutability past question or
suspicion.   In that case, it is impossible for God to change,
because it is impossible for God to lie, or deny himself.[x]
Now upon such a decree is the kingdom of Heaven established : " Once have I sworn by my holiness, that I will not
lie unto David," saith the Lord.[y]   " *Once*," that notes the
constancy and fixedness of God's promise : " *By my holiness*,"

---

t John iv. 22, 27.   u James i. 17.—Non mutat voluntatem, sed vult mutatio-
nem. *Aquin.* part 1. qu. 19. art. 7.—*Aug.* Confess. lib. 2. cap. 15.—de Civit. Dei,
lib. 14. cap. 11. lib. 22. cap. 1.—de Trin. lib. 5. cap. 16.   x Heb. vi. 18.
y Psalm lxxxix. 35.

that notes the inviolableness of his promise, as if he should have said,—Let me no longer be esteemed a holy God, than I keep immutably that covenant which I have sworn unto David in my truth.

Secondly, The free gift of God unto his son Christ, whereby he committed all power and judgement unto him. And power is a strong argument to prove the stability of a kingdom, especially if it be on either side supported with wisdom and righteousness, as the power of Christ is. And therefore from his power he argues for the perpetuity of his church to the end of the world; " All power is given to me in heaven and earth ; Go ye therefore and preach the gospel to all nations; and lo, I am with you, always, to the end of the world." [z] And the argument is very strong and emphatical: for though kingdoms of great power have been and may be subdued, yet the reason is, because much power hath still remained in the adverse side ; or if they have been too vast for any smaller people to root out, yet having not either wisdom enough to actuate so huge a frame, or righteousness to prevent or purge out those vicious humours of emulation, sedition, luxury, injustice, violence, and impiety, which, like strong diseases in a body [a], are, in states, the preparations and seminaries of mortality, they have sunk under their own weight, and been inwardly corrupted by their own vices. But now, first, the power of Christ in his church is universal: there is in him all power, and no weakness ; no power without him or against him. And therefore no wonder, if from a fulness of power in him, and an emptiness in his enemies, the argument of continuance in his kingdom doth infallibly follow : for what man, if he were furnished with all sufficiency, would suffer himself to be mutilated and dismembered, as Christ should, if any thing should prevail against the church, which is his fulness.— Again, this power of Christ is supported with wisdom; it can never miscarry for any inward defect; for the wisdom is proportionable to the power; this, " all power," and that, " all the treasures of wisdom ;" power, able by weakness to confound the things which are mighty,—and wisdom, able

---

[z] Matth. xxviii. 18, 20.　　[a] Vid. *Arist.* Polit. lib. 5.—In se magna ruunt : laetis hunc numina rebus Crescendi posuere modum. *Lucan.*

by foolishness to bring to nought the understanding of the prudent: and both these are upheld by righteousness, which is indeed the very soul and sinews of a kingdom, upon which the thrones of princes are established, and which the apostle makes the ground of the perpetuity of Christ's kingdom; " Thy throne, O God, is for ever and ever; a sceptre of righteousness is the sceptre of thy kingdom." [b]

Thirdly, The quality of Christ's kingdom is to be a growing kingdom; though the original thereof be but like a grain of mustard seed, or like Elijah's cloud, to a human view despicable, and almost below the probabilities of subsistence,—the object rather of derision than of terror to the world; yet, at last, it groweth into a wideness, which maketh it as catholic as the world. And therefore that which the prophet David speaks of the sun, the apostle applies to the gospel [c], to note, that the circle of the gospel is like that of the sun, universal to the whole world. It is such a kingdom as groweth into other kingdoms, and eats them out. The little stone in Nebuchadnezzar's vision (which was the kingdom of Christ, for so Jerusalem is called ' a stone' [d]) brake in pieces the great monarchies of the earth, and grew up into a great mountain which filled the world [e]; " For the kingdoms of the earth must become the kingdoms of the Lord, and of his Christ." [f] Therefore the prophets express Christ and his kingdom, by the name of " a branch," which groweth up for a standard and ensign of the people. [g] A branch which grows, but never withers. It hath no principles of death in itself; and though it be, for a while, subject to the assaults of adversaries, and foreign violence, yet that serves only to try it, and to settle it, but not to weaken or overturn it. The gates of Hell, all the powers, policies, and laws of darkness, shall never prevail against the church of Christ. He hath bruised, and judged, and " trodden down Satan under our feet." He " hath overcome the world;" he hath subdued iniquity; he hath turned persecutions into seminaries and resurrections of the church; he hath turned afflictions into matter of glory and of rejoicing: so that in all the violence, which the church can suffer, it

b Heb. i. 8.   c Rom. x. 18.   d Zech. xii. 3.   e Dan. ii. 34, 35.   f Revel. xi. 15.
g Isai. xi. 1, 10. Zech. iii. 8.

doth more than conquer; because it conquers not by repelling, but by suffering.

And this shows the sacrilege and sauciness of the church
of Rome; which, in this point, doth with a double impiety
therefore pervert the Scriptures, that it may derogate from
the honour of Christ and his kingdom. And those things
which are spoken of the infallibility, authority, and fulness of
power, Christ hath in his body, of the stability, cons tancy,
and universality of his church upon earth,—she doth arrogate
only to the Pope and his see at Rome. As the Donatists in
Saint Austin's [h] time, from that place of the spouse in the
Canticles, " Tell me, O thou whom my soul loveth, where
thou feedest, where thou makest thy flock to rest *in meridie,*"
excluded all the world from being a church, save only a
corner of Africa, which was at that time the nest of those
hornets: so because Christ says, " his church is built upon
a rock, and the gates of Hell shall not prevail against it,"
therefore the Romanists from hence conclude all these privileges to belong to them, and exclude all the famous
churches of the world besides, from having any communion
with Christ the head. That scornful expostulation which
Harding makes with that renowned and incomparable bishop [i],
(under whose hand he was no more able to subsist, than a
whelp under the paw of a lion) ' Shall we now change the song
of Micah the prophet, " Out of Zion shall come the law,
and the word of the Lord from Jerusalem," and sing a new
song, Out of Wittenberg is come the gospel, and the word
of the Lord from Zurich and Geneva ?'—may, most truly and
pertinently, be retorted upon himself and his faction, who
boldly curse [k] and exclude all those Christian churches from
the body of Christ, and the hope of salvation, who will not
receive laws from Rome, nor esteem the cathedral determi-
nations of that bishop, (though haply in himself, an impure,
diabolical, and intolerable beast, as by their own confessions [l] many of them have been) to be notwithstanding the in-

---

[h] *Aug.* Epist. 48. & tom. 7. de Unitat. Eccles. cap. 16. [i] B. *Jewel's* Defence of the Apology, part 4. page 360. [k] Idem à Romano Pontifice dividi,
quod ab universa Ecclesia separari. *Baron.* tom. 2. A. 254. sect. 100. [l] *Crant-
zius* in Metropol. l. 5. cap. 1. in Bonifacio 6. Stephano 6. Theodoro Christophoro
Joanne 12. Sylvestro 2.—*Sigon.* de Regno Italiæ, lib. 7. Anno 964.—*Guicciard.*
de Alex. 6. l. Hist. 1 pag. 3, 4.—*Pet. Bembus* de eodem in Hist. Venet. l. 6.

fallible edicts of the Spirit of God, and as undoubtedly the word of Christ, as if St. Peter or St. Paul had spoken it;—an arrogancy, than which there is scarce any more express and characteristical note to discern Antichrist by. It is true, that Christ's regal power doth always show forth itself in upholding his catholic church, and in revealing unto it out of his sacred word such necessary truths, as are absolutely requisite unto its being and salvation: but to bind this power of Christ to one man, and to one see, (as if, like the Pope, he were infallible only in St. Peter's chair) is the mere figment of pride and ambition, without any ground at all, raised out of a heap and aggregation of monstrous presumptions, of human, and some most disputable, others most false conceits; of which though there be not the least ' vestigia ' in sacred Scriptures, yet must they be all first rested in for indubitate principles, and laid for sure foundations, before the first stone of papal authority can be raised.

As, First, that the external and visible regiment of the whole church is monarchical[m]; and that there must be a predominant mistress-church set over all the rest, to which in all points they must have recourse, and to whose decisions they must conform without any hesitancy, or suspicion at all: whereas the apostle tells us, that " the unity of the church is gathered by many pastors and teachers[n];" for as if several needles be touched by so many several loadstones (all which have the self-same specifical virtue in them) they do all as exactly bend to one and the same point of Heaven, as if they had been thereunto qualified by but one ;—so inasmuch as " apostles, prophets, evangelists, pastors, teachers," come all instructed with one and the same spiritual truth and power towards the church; therefore all the faithful, who are anywhere, by these multitudes of preachers, " taught what the truth is in Jesus," do all, by the secret sway and conduct of the same Spirit of grace (whose peculiar office it is to guide his church in all necessary and saving truth) with an admirable consent of heart, and unity of judgement, incline to the same end, and walk in the same way, acknow-

---

Platina in Christophoro 1. Joan. 13. Sylvestro 2. &c.—Vid. *Mornæum* de Ecclesia, c. 9.—*Reynold* Confer. cap. 7. divis. 1, and 5.—B. *Carlton* of Jurisdict. cap. 7.—Bishop *Usher* de Statu Ecclesiæ, c. 3, 4, 5.   [m] *Bellarm.* 1. 1. de Pontif. Rom. cap. 9.   [n] Eph. iv. 11, 12, 13.

ledging no monarch over their consciences but Christ,—nor any other ministerial application of his regal power in the catholic church, but only by several bishops and pastors,— who, in their several particular compasses, are endowed with as plenary and ample ministerial power, as the Pope and his consistory within the see of Rome.

Secondly, That Peter was prince and monarch, rock and head, in this universal church, and that he alone was 'custos clavium,' and all this in the virtue of Christ's promise and commission granted unto him, "Thou art Peter, and upon this rock will I build my church : Feed my sheep, feed my lambs, unto thee will I give the keys of the kingdom of Heaven :" in which respect Barouius[o] calleth him 'lapidem primarium'[p], the chief stone : and again, Though Christ, saith he be the author and moderator of his church, yet the prince- dom and monarchy he hath conferred upon Peter ; and therefore as[q] "no man can lay any other foundation than that which is laid," namely, Christ,—so no man can lay any other than that which Christ hath laid, namely, Peter. And it is wonderful to consider what twigs and rushes they catch at, to hold up this their monarchy. Because Peter[r] did preach first, therefore he is monarch of the church. By which reason, his monarchy is long since expired : for his pretended successors scarce preach at all. And yet if that may be drawn to any argument, it proves only that he was ' lapis primus,' the first in order and forwardness to preach Christ (as it became him who had three times denied him) but not 'lapis primarius,' the chief in dignity and jurisdic- tion over the rest : and why should it not be as good an argument to say, that James had the dignity of precedence before Peter, because Paul first names James and then Ce- phas, and that in a place where he particularly singles them out as pillars and principal men in the church ; as to say that Peter hath jurisdiction over James and the rest, because

o *Baron.* An. 33, sect. 17. *Bellar.* de Pont. Rom. lib. 1. cap. 10.   p Quod non audet *Bozius* :—Præter Christum (inquit) non potest aliud fundamentum poni, quod sit item primarium. De Sign. Ecclesiæ, l. 18. cap. 1. ob. 5.   q Sicut (quod certum est) nemo potest aliud ponere fundamentum præter id quod positum est, quod est Christus ; ita etiam nec aliud quispiam ponet, quàm quod posuit Christus, neque convellet quod ipse firmavit, dicens, ' Tu es Petrus,' &c. *Baron.* An. 33. sect. 20.   r *Baron.* A. 34. sect. 247. *Bozius* de Signis Ecclesiæ, lib. 18. cap. 1, 2. *Bellarm.* de Roman. Pontifice, lib. 1. c. 17, 25.

in their synods and assemblies he was the chief speaker?
Because [s] Peter cured the lame man that sat at the gate of
the Temple, therefore he is universal monarch.   By which
reason likewise Paul, who in the self-same manner cured a
cripple at Lystra, should fall into competition with Peter for
his share in the monarchy.   But the people there were not
so acute disputants as these of Rome: for though they saw
what Paul had done, yet they concluded the dignity and
precedence for Barnabas ; they called him Jupiter,—and Paul,
Mercury.   Again, because Peter [t] pronounced sentence upon
Ananias, therefore he is monarch of the universal church :
and why Paul should not here likewise come in for his share,
I know not; for he also passed judgment upon Elymas the
sorcerer ; (and we nowhere find that he derived his authority,
or had any commission, from Peter to do so.   And surely,
if by the same apostolical and infallible Spirit of Christ,
(which they both immediately received from Christ himself)
St. Paul did adjudge Elymas to blindness, by the which St.
Peter adjudged Ananias to death ; I see not how any logic
from a parity of actions can conclude a disparity of persons,
except they will say that it is more monarchical to adjudge
one to death, than another to blindness.   Again, because
Peter [u] healed the sick by his shadow, therefore Peter is
monarch of the universal church : and even in this point
Paul likewise may hold on his competition: for why is not
the argument as good, that Paul is monarch of the church,
because the handkerchiefs and aprons which came from his
body, did cure diseases, and cast out devils, as that Peter is
therefore monarch, because, by the overshadowing of his
body, the sick were healed ?   But the truth is, there is no
more substance in this argument for Peter's principality,
than there is for their supposed miraculous virtue of images
and relics of saints, because the shadow (which was the
image of Peter) did heal the sick ; for that also is the cardi-
nal's great argument.   Again, because Peter [w] was sent to
Samaria to confirm them in the faith, and to lay hands on
them that they might receive the Holy Ghost, and to confound Simon Magus the sorcerer, therefore he is primate of

---

[s] *Baron.* A. 34. sect. 264.   [t] *Baron.* Ibid. sect. 269.   [u] *Baron.* Ibid.
        sect. 274.   [w] *Ibid.* sect. 275. An. 35, sect. 9. 25.

the catholic church, and hath monarchical jurisdiction. And
yet the Pope is, by this time, something more monarchical
than Peter; for he would think scorn to be sent as an ambassador of the churches, from Rome to the Indians,
amongst whom his gospel hath been in these latter ages
preached; and, doubtless, they would be something more
confirmed than they are, by the sovereign virtue of his
prayers and presence. But, alas! what argument is it of
monarchy, to be sent by others in a message, and that too
not without an associate, who joined with him in the confirmation of that church? and if the confuting or cursing of
Simon Magus were an argument of primacy, why should
not St. Paul's cursing of Elymas, and Hymeneus, and Alexander, and St. John's of Cerinthus, be arguments of their
primacy likewise?—Again, because Paul [x] went up to Jerusalem to see Peter, therefore Peter was monarch of the
catholic church. And why should not, by this argument,
Elizabeth be concluded a greater woman than the Virgin
Mary, and indeed the lady of all women,—because the
blessed Virgin went up into the hill country of Judea, and
entered into the house of Zacharias, and saluted Elizabeth?
But we find no argument but of equality in the text; for he
went to see him as a brother, but not to do homage to him,
or receive authority from him as a monarch: else why went
he not up immediately to Jerusalem, but stayed three
years, and preached the gospel by the commission he had
received from Christ alone? and how came St. Paul to be
so free, or St. Peter to be so much more humble than any of
his pretended successors, as the one to give with boldness,
the other with silence and meekness to receive, so sore a
reproof, in the face of all the brethren, as, many years after
that, did pass between them? Certainly St. Paul, in so long
time, could not but learn to know his distance, and in what
manner to speak to his monarch and primate. By these
particulars we see, upon what sandy foundation this vast and
formidable Babel of papal usurpation and power over the
catholic church is erected;—which yet, upon the matter, is
the sole principle of Romish religion, upon which all their
faith, worship, and obedience dependeth. But we say, that

[x] *Baron.* An. 39. sect. 6.

as Peter was a foundation, so were all the other apostles likewise [y], and that upon the same reason: for the apostles were not foundations of the church by any dignity of their persons, as Christ the chief corner-stone was, but by the virtue of their apostolical office, which was universal jurisdiction in governing the people of Christ, universal commission in instructing them, and a spirit of infallibility in revealing God's will unto them throughout the whole world; and therefore as Peter had the "keys of the kingdom of Heaven, to remit or retain the sins of men," so likewise had the other apostles [z]. That Christ's charge to Peter, "Feed my sheep, feed my lambs," is no other in substance, than his commission to them all, "Go teach all nations, baptizing them in the name of the Father, the Son, and the Holy Ghost;" and that the particular directing of it unto Peter, and praying for him,—was, with respect unto his particular, only by way of comfort and confirmation, as being then a weak member,—not by way of dignity, or deputation of Christ's own regal power to him in the visible church. For all the offices of Christ are intransient and incommunicable to any other; inasmuch as the administration and execution of them dependeth upon the dignity of his person, and upon the fulness of his Spirit, which no mortal man or immortal angel is capable of. But all this is not enough to be granted them for the raising their authority. But then, Thirdly, We must grant them too, that Peter, thus qualified, was bishop of Rome: for proof whereof, they have no testimony of holy scriptures, but only human tradition, "Cui impossibile non est subesse falsum." So that in this, which is one of the main principles they build upon, their faith cannot be resolved into the word of God, and therefore is no divine faith. Fourthly, That he did appoint that church to be the monarchical and fundamental see to all other churches: for he was bishop as well of Antioch as of Rome, by their own confession. And I wonder why some of his personal virtue should not cleave to his chair at Antioch, but all pass over with him to another place. Fifthly [a], That he did transmit all his prerogatives to his successors in that chair. By which assertion they may as well prove, that they all

[y] Eph. ii. 20. Rev. xxi. 14.   [z] John xx. 23.   [a] *Bellarm*. de Rom. Pontif.
lib. 2. cap. 12.—*Baron*. An. 39. sect. 16, 26.

(though some of them have been sorcerers, others murderers, others blasphemous atheists) were inheritors of St. Peter's love to Christ: for from thence our Saviour infers, "Feed my sheep," to note, that none feed his sheep, but those that love his person. Lastly, that that long succession from St. Peter until now, hath ever since been legal and uninterrupted:—or else the church must sometimes have been a monster without a head. We grant that some of the ancients [b] argue from succession in the church: but it was while it was yet pure,—and while they could, by reason of the little space of time between them and the apostles, with evidence resolve their doctrine through every medium into the preaching of the apostles themselves. But, even in their personal succession, who knoweth not what simonies and sorceries have raised divers of them unto that degree? and who is able to resolve, that every episcopal ordination of every bishop there hath been valid, since thereunto is requisite, both the intention and orders of that bishop that ordained him? These, and a world the like uncertainties, must the faith of these men depend upon, who dare arrogate to themselves the prerogatives of Christ, and of his catholic kingdom. But I have been too long upon this argument.

Again, This point of the stability of Christ's kingdom is a ground of strong confidence and comfort to the whole church of Christ, against all the violence of any outward enemies, wherewith sometimes they may seem to be swallowed up. Though they associate themselves, and gird to the battle; though they take counsel, and make decrees against the Lord's anointed and against his spouse; yet it shall all come to nought, and be broken [c] in pieces: all the smoke of Hell shall not be able to extinguish, nor all the power of Hell to overturn, the church of God; and the reason is, "Emmanuel, God is with us." That anointing which the church hath received, shall deliver it at last from the yoke of the enemy.[d] Though it seem, for the time, in as desperate a condition as a dry stick in the fire, or a dead body in the grave, yet this is not indeed a sepulture, but a semination. Though it seem

[b] *Tertul.* de Præscript. cap. 19, 22.—*Aug.* Epist. 165. de Dissidio Donatist.
[c] Isai. viii. 9, 10.　　[d] Isai. x. 27.

to be cast away for a season, yet in due time it will come up and flourish again.[e] And this is the assurance that the church may have, that the Lord can save and deliver a second time [f]; that he is the " same God yesterday, and to-day, and for ever." And therefore such a God as the church hath found him heretofore, such a God it shall find him to-day, and for ever, in the returns and manifestations of his mercy. Which discovers the folly, and foretells the confusion of the enemies of Christ's kingdom; they conceive mischief, but they bring forth nothing but vanity.[g] They conceive chaff, and bring forth stubble.[h] " They imagine nothing but a vain thing;" their malice is but like the fighting of briars and thorns with the fire [i]; like the dashing of waves against a rock ; like a madman's shooting arrows against the sun, which at last return upon his own head ; like the puffing of the fan against the corn, which driveth away nothing but the chaff; like the beating of the wind against the sail, or the foaming ·and raging of the water against a mill ; which by the wisdom of the artificers are all ordered unto useful and excellent ends. " And surely when the Lord shall have accomplished his work on Mount Sion, when he shall by the adversary, as by a fan, have purged away the iniquity of Jacob, and taken away his sin, he will then return in peace and beauty unto his people again." Look on the preparation of some large building ; in one place, you shall see heaps of lime and mortar,—in another, piles of timber,—every where, rude and indigested materials, and a tumultuary noise of axes and hammers ; but at length the artificer sets every thing in order, and raiseth up a beautiful structure : such is the proceeding of the Lord in the afflictions and vastations of his church; though the enemy intend to ruin it, yet God intends only to repair it. Thus far as ' *Donec*' respects Christ's kingdom in itself.

Now, as it respecteth the enemies of Christ, it notes ; First, The present inconsummateness of the victories, and, by consequence, the intranquillity of Christ's kingdom here upon the earth ; all his enemies are not yet under his feet; Satan is not yet shut up ; the rage of Hell, the persecutions

e Zech. iii. 2. Ezek. xxxvii. 11.   f Isai. xi. 11.   g Job xv. 35.   h Isai. xxxiii. 11.   i Isai. xxvii. 4. Nahum i. 10.

and policies of wicked men, the present immunity of desperate sinners, are evidences, that Christ hath much work to
do in his church. But doth not the apostle say, that " all
things are put under his feet [k] ? It is true, ' quoad judiciariam
potestatem,' but not ' quoad exercitium potestatis.' He shall
not receive any new power to subdue his enemies, which he
hath not already; but yet he can execute that power, when
and how he will. And he is pleased to suffer his enemies, in
this respite of their reprisal, to rage, and revile, and persecute him in his members. Every wicked man is " condemned
already, and hath the wrath of God abiding upon him[1];" only
Christ doth suspend the execution of them for many weighty
reasons. As first, To show his patience and long-suffering
towards the vessels of wrath; for he ever comes first with
an offer of peace, before he draws the sword [m]. Secondly, To
magnify the power of his protection and providence over the
church in the midst of their enemies: for if the Lord were
not on the church's side, when man riseth up against it,—if
he did not rebuke the proud waves, and set them their
bounds how far they should go,—there could be no more
power in the church to withstand them, than in a level [n] of
sand, to resist an inundation of the sea [o]. Thirdly, To reserve " wicked men unto the great day of his appearing," and
of the declaration of his power and righteousness, wherein
all the world shall be the spectators and witnesses of his just
and victorious proceedings against them [p]. Fourthly, To
show forth his mighty power in destroying the wicked altogether. They who here carried themselves with that inso-
lence, as if every particular man meant to have plucked
Christ out of his throne, shall there altogether be brought
forth before him. That as the righteous are reserved to have
their full salvation together [q]; so the wicked may be bound
up in bundles, and destroyed together.[r] Fifthly, To fill up
the measure, and to ripen the sins of wicked men: for the
Lord puts the wickedness of men into an ephah; and when
they have filled up their measure, he then sealeth them up

---

[k] Eph. i. 22. 　　[l] John iii. 18, 36. 　　[m] Rom. ii. 4, and ix. 22. Deut.
xx. 10. 13. Luke x. 5, 11. 　　[n] Jer. v. 22. Ægyptus maris concavitate depressior;
et tamen præcepto Creatoris, tanquam compedibus, coercetur mare Rubrum, ne in
Ægyptum irrumpat. *Basil. Mag.* Hexamer. Homil. 4. 　　[o] Psalm cxxiv. 1, 5,
[p] Acts xvii. 31. 　　[q] 1 Thes. iv. 17. 　　[r] Psalm xxxvii. 38. Isai. i. 28.

unto the execution of his righteous judgments. And hence it is that the Scripture calleth wicked men " Vessels, fitted for destruction ;" for they first fill themselves with sin, and then God filleth them up with wrath and shame. Sixthly, To fill up ' the number of his elect ;' for he hath many sheep, which are not within his fold, and they many of them the posterity of wicked men.[s] Seventhly, To fill up the measure of his own sufferings in his members, that they may follow him unto his kingdom, through the same way of afflictions as he went before them.[t] Eighthly, To exercise the faith of his church, to drive the faithful with the prophet Habakkuk into their watch-tower, and with David, into the sanctuary of the Lord,—there to wait upon him in the way of his judgements, to consider that the end of the righteous man is peace, and that the pride and prosperity of the wicked is but as the fat of lambs, and as the beauty of grass ; that God hath set them in slippery places, and will cast them down at the last.[u] Lastly, To wean the faithful from earthly affections, and to kindle in them the desires of the saints under the altar,—"How long, O Lord, holy and true, dost thou not judge and avenge our blood on them that dwell on the earth [x] ?"

Secondly, As ' Donec' notes the patience of Christ towards his enemies, so it notes likewise that there are fixed bounds and limits unto that patience, beyond which he will no longer forbear them. There is " an appointed day, wherein he will judge the world with righteousness [y]." There is ' a year of vengeance,' and of recompenses for the controversies of Sion.[z] The wild ass that sucketh up the wind at her pleasure, may be found in her month.[a] The Lord seeth, that the day of the wicked is coming : it is an appointed time : though it tarry, yet if we wait for it, it will " surely come, it will not tarry [b]." Well then, let men go on with all the fierceness and excess of riot they will, let them walk in the way of their heart, and in the sight of their eyes,—yet all this while they are in a chain; they have but a compass to go, and God will bring them to judgement at the last. When the day of a drunkard and riotous person is come,—

<hr />

[s] John x. 16.   [t] Col. i. 24. Rev. vi. 11.   [u] Hab. ii. 1, 3. Psalm xxxvii. 2, 10, 20, and lxxiii. 18.   [x] Rev. vi. 10.   [y] Acts xvii. 31.   [z] Isai. xxxiv. 8.   [a] Jer. ii. 24.   [b] Psalm xxxvii. 13. Hab. ii. 3.

when he hath taken so many hellish swallows, and hath filled up the measure of his lusts,—his marrow must then lie down in the dust : though the cup were at his mouth, yet from thence it shall be snatched away ; and for everlasting he shall never taste a drop of sweetness, nor have the least desire of his wicked heart satisfied any more. A wicked man's sins will not follow him to Hell to please him, but only the memory of them to be an everlasting scourge and flame upon his conscience. O then take heed of ripening sin by custom, by security, by insensibility, by impudence and stoutness of heart, by making it a mock, a matter of glory and of boasting, by stopping the ear against the voice of the charmer, and turning the back upon the invitations unto mercy, by resisting the evidence of the Spirit in the word, and commiting sin in the light of the sun : for as the heat of the sun doth wither the fruit which falls off, and ripen that which hangs on the tree ; so the word doth weaken those lusts, which a man is desirous to shake off, and doth ripen those which the heart holds fast and will not part with. When was Israel overthrown, but when they mocked the messengers of God, and despised his Word, and misused his prophets, and rejected the remedy of their sin ? And when was Judah destroyed, but when they hardened themselves against the Word, and would not take notice of the day of their peace ? Alas, what haste do men make to promote their own damnation, and go quickly to Hell, when they will break through the very law of God, and through all his holy ordinances, that they may come thither the sooner, as if the gate would be shut against them, or as if it were a place of some great preferment ; as if they had to do with a blind God which could not see, or with an impotent God which could not revenge their impieties ! Well, for all this the wise man's speech will prove true at the last, " Know, that God will bring thee into judgement."

Thirdly, ' *Donec* ' notes the infallible accomplishment of Christ's victories and triumph over his enemies at the last, when the day is come wherein he will be patient towards them no longer. The prophet giveth three excellent reasons hereof in one verse. " The Lord is our judge [c], the Lord is our law-

---

[c] Isai. xxxiii. 22.

giver, the Lord is our king, he will save us." He is " our
judge ;" and therefore certainly, when the day of trial is
come, he will plead our cause against our adversaries, and
will condemn them.[d] But a judge cannot do what pleaseth
himself; but he is bound to his rule, and proceedeth according to established laws. Therefore he is " our lawgiver"
likewise ; and therefore he may appoint himself laws according to his own will : but when the will of the judge, and the
rule of the law do both consent in the punishing of offenders,
yet then still the king hath a liberty of mercy, and he may
pardon those whom the law and the judge have condemned.
But Christ, who shall judge the enemies of his church
according to the law which himself hath made, is himself
" the king;" and therefore when he revengeth, there is none
besides nor above him to pardon. So at that day there shall
be a full manifestation of the kingdom of Christ: none of
his enemies [e] shall move the wing, or open the mouth, or
peep against him.

The second thing, formerly proposed in this latter part of
the verse, was the author of subduing Christ's enemies under his feet ; I, the Lord. Wicked men will never submit
themselves to Christ's kingdom, but stand out in opposition
against him in his word and ways. When God's hand is
lifted up in the dispensation of his word and threatenings
against sin, men will not see [f]; and therefore he saith, " My
Spirit shall not always strive with men,"—to note, that men
would of themselves always strive with the Spirit, and never
yield nor submit to Christ. Though " the patience and
goodness of God should lead them to repentance, and fore-
warn them to fly from the wrath to come, yet they, after
their hardness and impenitent heart, do hereby treasure
up against themselves the more wrath [g]; and " because judgement is not speedily executed, their heart is wholly set in
them to do mischief."[h]—" Let favour," saith the prophet [i],
" be showed unto a wicked man, yet will he not learn righteousness ; in the land of uprightness will he deal un-
justly, and will not behold the majesty of the Lord." Certainly, if a wicked man could be rescued out of Hell itself,

d Micah vii. 9.   e Oportet eum ad tantam evidentiam regnum suum per-
ducere, donec inimici ejus nullo modo audeant negare quod regnat. *August.*
f Isai. xxvi. 11.   g Rom. ii. 4, 5.   h Eccles. viii. 11.   i Isai. xxvi. 10.

and brought back into the possibilities of mercy again, yet
would he, in a second life, fly out against God, and while
he had time, take his fill of lusts again. We see clay will
but grow harder by the fire; and that metal which melted in
the furnace, being taken thence, will return to its wonted
solidity. When Pharaoh [k] saw "the rain, and the hail, and
the thunders were ceased,"—though, in the time of them, he
was like melted metal, and did acknowledge the righteousness of God, and his own sin, und make strong promises
that Israel should go,—"yet then he sinned more, and hardened his heart, he and his servants, and would not let the
children of Israel go."—Do we not see men sometimes cast
on a bed of sickness, brought to the very brink of Hell, and
to the smell of that sulphury lake,—when, by God's wonderful patience, they are snatched like a brand out of the fire,
and have recovered a little strength, to provoke the Lord
again; when they should now set themselves to make good
those hypocritical resolutions of amendment of life, wherewith in their extremity they flattered God, and deceived
themselves,—suddenly break forth into more filthiness than
before, as if they meant now to be revenged of God, and to
fetch back that time which sickness took from them, by an
extremity of sinning; as if they had made a covenant with
Hell, to do it more service, if they might then be spared?
All the favours and methods which God useth, are not
enough to bring wicked men home unto him of their own
wills. "Though I redeemed them," saith the Lord, "yet
have they spoken lies against me [l]; they have not cried unto
me with their heart, when they howled upon their beds.—The
people turned not unto him that smiteth them, neither do
they seek the Lord of Hosts." [m] So many judgements did
the Lord send upon Israel in the neck of one another, and
yet still the burden of the prophet is, "yet have you not
returned unto me [n]," saith the Lord. Dam up the passage
of a river, and use all the art that may be, to over-rule it;
yet you can never carry it backward in its own channel: you
may cut it out into other courses and diverticles, but no art
can drive it into a contrary motion, and make it retire into

---

[k] Exod. ix. 27, 28, 34, 35.   [l] Hos. vii. 13, 14.   [m] Isai. ix. 13.
[n] Amos iv. 6, 8, 9, 10, 11.

its own fountain : so though wicked men may, haply, by divers reasons which their lusts will admit, be so far wrought upon, as to change their courses,—yet it is impossible to change themselves, or to turn them quite out of their own way into the way of Christ. There is but a bivium in the world, a way of life, and a way of death ; and the Lord, in the ministry of the Word, gives us our option, " I have set before you this day, life and death, blessing and cursing ;" and " he that believeth shall be saved, and he that believeth not, shall be damned." To the former, he inviteth, beseecheth, enticeth us with promises, with oaths, with engagements, with prevention of any just objection which might be made ; " We beseech you," saith the apostle, "in Christ's stead, that ye be reconciled unto God." From the other, he deters us by forewarning us of the wrath to come, and of the period which death will put to our lusts with our lives.—And as Tertullian once spake of the oath of God, so may I of his entreatings and threatenings ; " O blessed men whom the Lord himself is pleased to solicit and entice unto happiness ! but, O miserable men that will not believe nor accept of God's own entreaties !"—And yet thus miserable are we all by nature. There is in men so much atheism, infidelity, and distrust of God's word,—so close an adherency of lust unto the soul,—that it rather chooseth to run the hazard, and to go to Hell entire, than to go halt and maimed unto Heaven ;—yea, to make God a liar, to bless themselves in their sins, when he curseth,—and to judge of him by themselves, as if he took no notice of their ways. It is not therefore without just cause, that God so often threateneth to remember all the sins of wicked men, and to do against them whatsoever he hath spoken.—We see then, that men will never submit themselves unto the sceptre of Christ, nor prevent the wrath to come by a voluntary subjection. It remains therefore, that God take the work into his own hands, and put them perforce under Christ's feet. They will not submit to his kingdom of grace and mercy, they will not believe his kingdom of glory and salvation ; but they shall be made subject to the sword of his wrath,

o Deut. xxix. 16, Psal. l. 21. Hosea v. 2, 3. and vii. 2. 12. Amos viii. 7. Deut. xxxii. 34, 35. Psal. l. 21. Jer. xvii. 1.

and that without any hope of escape, or power of opposition; for God himself doth it immediately by his own mighty power. He will interpose his own hand, and magnify the glory of his own strength in the just confusion of wicked men. So the apostle saith, that "The Lord will show his wrath, and make power known in the vessels fitted for destruction."[p] Two means, the apostle showeth, shall be used in the destruction of the wicked, to effect it,—the presence or countenance, and the glorious power, of the Lord.[q] The very terror of his face, and the dreadful majesty of his presence, shall slay the wicked. The kings of the earth, and the great men and the rich men, and the chief captains, and the mighty men, those who all their lifetime were themselves terrible, and had been acquainted with terrors,—shall then beg of the mountains and rocks to fall upon them, and hide them "from the face of him that sitteth upon the throne, and from the wrath of the Lamb."[r] Whence that usual expression of God's resolution to destroy a people, "I will set my face against them." O then, how sore shall the condemnation of the wicked men be, when therein the Lord purposeth to declare τὴν δόξαν τῆς ἰσχύος αὐτοῦ, the glorious strength of his own almighty arm. Here, when the Lord punisheth a people, he only showeth how much strength and edge he can put into the creatures to execute his displeasure. But the extreme terror of the last day shall be this, that men shall fall immediately into the hands of God himself, who hath said, "Vengeance belongeth unto me, and I will recompense."[s] And therefore the apostle useth this expostulation against idolaters; "Do we provoke the Lord to jealousy? Are we stronger than he?"[t] Dare we meet the Lord in his fury, do we provoke him to put out all his wrath?[u] He will at last stir up all his wrath against the vessels that are fitted for it. And for that cause he will punish them himself. For there is no creature able to bring all God's wrath unto another; there is no vessel able to hold all God's displeasure. The apostle telleth us that we have to do with God in his word[w]; but herein he useth the ministry of weak men; so that his majesty is covered, and wicked men have a veil upon

[p] Rom. ix. 22. [q] 2 Thes. i. 9. [r] Rev. vi. 15, 16. Isa. ii. 10.
[s] Heb. x. 30, 31. [t] 1 Cor. x. 22. [u] Psal. lxxviii. 38. [w] Heb. iv. 13.

their hearts, that they cannot see God in his word. "When thy hand is lifted up," namely, in the threatenings and predictions of wrath out of the word, "they will not see :" for it is a work of faith to receive the word as God's word, and therein before-hand to see his power, and to hear his rod.[x] Other men belie the Lord, and say it is not he. But though they will not acknowledge that they have to do with God in his word, though they will not see when his hand is lifted up in the preparations of his wrath, yet they shall see and know that they have to do with him in his judgements, when his hand falleth down again in the execution of his wrath. So the Lord expostulateth with them :[y] " Can thine heart endure, or thine hands be strong, in the days that I shall deal with thee ?" The prophet Isaiah resolves that question, " The sinners in Sion are afraid, fearfulness hath surprised the hypocrites," (namely, ' a fearful looking for of judgement and fiery indignation,' as the apostle speaks [z]). " Who amongst us shall dwell with devouring fire ? who amongst us shall dwell with everlasting burnings [a] ?" That is, in the words of the prophet, " Who can stand before his indignation? and who can abide in the fierceness of his anger ? His fury is poured out like fire, and the rocks are thrown down by him.[b] Confirmations of this point we may take from these considerations : First, the quarrel with sinners is God's own, the controversy his own, the injuries and indignities have been done to himself and his own Son, the challenges have been sent unto himself and his own Spirit : and therefore no marvel, if he take the matter into his own hands ; and the quarrel so immediately reflecting upon him, if he be provoked to revenge it by his own immediate power.[c]

Secondly, Revenge is his royalty and peculiar prerogative [d] ; from whence the apostle infers, that " it is a fearful thing to fall into the hands of the living God." [e] And there are these arguments of fearfulness in it; First, It shall be " in judgement without mercy [f]:" there shall be no mixture of any sweetness in the cup of God's displeasure, but all poison and bitterness : there shall not be afforded a drop of water to a lake of fire, a minute of ease to an

---

x Micah vi. 9.   y Ezek. xxii. 14.   z Heb. x. 27.   a Isa. xxxiii. 14.
b Nahum i. 6.   c Levit. xxvi. 25. Hosea xii. 2. Psalm ii. 2. Isa. lxv. 3.   d Deut.
xxxii. 35, 41.   e Heb. x. 30, 31.   f James ii. 13.

eternity of torment. Secondly, It shall be in fury without compassion : in human judgements where the law of the state will not suffer a judge to acquit or show mercy, yet the law of nature will force him to compassionate and grieve for the malefactor whom he must condemn. There is no judge so senseless of another's misery, nor so destitute of human affections, as to pronounce a sentence of condemnation with laughter. But the Lord will condemn his enemies in vengeance without any pity. " I will laugh," saith the Lord, " at your calamity ; I will mock when your fear cometh."ᵍ Thirdly, It shall be in revenge and recompense, in reward and proportion; that is, in a full and everlasting detestation of wicked men ; the weight whereof shall, peradventure, lie heavier upon them, than all the other torments which they are to suffer, when they shall look on themselves as scorned, and abhorred exiles from the favour and presence of him that made them. For as the wicked did here hate God, and set their hearts and their courses against him ' in suo æterno,' in all that time which God permitted them to sin in ; so God will hate wicked men, and set his face and fury against them ' in suo æterno' too, as long as he shall be judge of the world.

Thirdly, This may be seen in the inchoations of Hell in wicked men upon the earth. When the door of the conscience is opened, and that sin which lay there asleep before, riseth up like an enraged lion to fly upon the soul,—when the Lord suffers some flashes of his glittering sword to break in like lightning upon the spirit, and to amaze a sinner with the pledges and first-fruits of Hell,—when he melteth the stout hearts of men, and grindeth them unto powder ; what is all this but the secret touch of God's own finger upon the conscience? For there is no creature in the world, whose ministry the heart doth discern in the estuations and invisible workings of a guilty and unquiet spirit.

Fourthly, The torments of wicked angels, whence can they come ? There is no creature strong enough to lay upon them a sufficient recompense of pain for their sin against the majesty of God. And for the disputes of schoolmen touching corporal fire in Hell, and the manner of elevating and

ᵍ Prov. i. 26.

applying corporal agents to work upon spiritual substances, they are but the intemperate niceties of men, ignorant of the Scriptures, and of the terror of the Lord, who is himself a consuming fire. The devils acknowledge Christ their tormentor,—and that, when he did nothing but rebuke them : there was no fire, nor any other creature by him supplied, but only the majesty of his own word, power, and person, which wrung from them that hideous cry, " Art thou come to torment us before the time ?" [h]

Lastly, Consider the heaviness of Christ's own soul, his agony and sense of the curse due unto our sin, when he was in the garden [i]; the trouble, astonishment, and extreme anguish of his soul, which wrought out of his sacred body that woful and wonderful sweat. Whence came it all? We read never of any devils let loose to torment him; they were ever tormented at his presence. We read of no other angels, that had commission to afflict him : we read of an angel, which was sent to strengthen him. [k] There is no reason to think that the fear of a bodily death, which was the only thing that men could inflict upon him,—was that which squeezed out those drops of blood and extorted those bitter and strong cries from him. There were not in his innocent soul, in his most pure and sacred body, any seeds or principles of such tormenting distempers. His compassion towards the misery of sinners, his knowledge of the guilt and cursedness of sin, was as great at other times as now. What then could it else be, but the weight of his Father's justice, the conflict with his Father's wrath against the sins of men, which wrought much extremity of heaviness in his soul? And he was our surety, he stood in our stead : that which was done to the green tree, should much more have been done to the dry. If God laid upon him the strokes which were due unto our sin,—how much more heavy shall his hand be upon those, whom he thoroughly hateth ?

But shall not the angels, then, be executioners of the sentence of God's wrath upon wicked men ?—I answer, the angels shall have their service in the coming of the Lord. First, as attendants, to show forth the majesty and glory of

h Matth. viii. 29.   i Matth. xxvi. 37. Luke xxii. 44. John xii. 27. Mark xiv. 33, 34.   k Luke xxii. 43.   l 2 Thes. i. 7. Matth, xxiv. 31.

Christ to the world.[l] Secondly, as executioners of his will,
which is to gather together the elect and the reprobate, to bind
up the wicked as sheaves or faggots for the fire.[m] But yet
still the Lord interposeth his own power. As a schoolmaster
setteth one scholar to bring forth another unto punishment;
but then he layeth on the stripes himself.

But why is it said, that the Father shall put Christ's enemies under his feet? Doth not Christ himself do it as well
as the Father?—Yes, doubtless. " God hath given the Son
authority to execute judgement also," and put into his hands
a rod of iron, to dash his enemies to pieces like a potter's
vessel; for " whatsoever things the Father doth, those also
doth the Son likewise."[n] But we are to note, that the subjecting of Christ's enemies under his feet is a work of divine
power. And therefore though it be attributed to Christ as an
officer, yet it belongeth to the Father as the fountain of all
divine operations. So God is said to set forth his Son as a
propitiation[o]; and yet the Son came down and manifested
himself.[p] The Father is said to have raised him from the
dead[q]; and yet the Son raised himself by his own power.[r]
The Father is said to have set Christ at his own right hand
in heavenly places[s]; and Christ is said to have sat down
himself on the right hand of the majesty on high.[t] The
Father is said to give the Holy Ghost[u]: and yet the Son
promiseth to send him himself[x]; so here, though the Son
have received power sufficient to subdue all his enemies
under his feet (for he is able to subdue all things unto himself[y];) yet the Father, to show his hatred against the enemies
of Christ, and his consent to the victories of his Son, will
likewise subdue all things unto him.[z]

O then, that men would be, by the terror of the Lord, persuaded to flee from the wrath to come,—to consider the
weight of God's heavy hand,—and, when they see such a
storm coming, to hide themselves in the holes of that rock
of mercy. It is nothing but atheism and infidelity, which
bewitcheth men with desperate senselessness against the

[l] 2 Thes. i. 7. Matth. xxiv. 31.   [m] Matth. xiii. 30, xxiv. 31.   [n] John
v. 19, 27. Psalm ii. 9.   [o] Rom. iii. 25.   [p] Phil. ii. 7, 8. Heb. ix. 26.
[q] Acts ii. 32. Rom. vi. 4.   [r] John x. 18.   [s] Ephes. i. 20.   [t] Heb.
i. 3. 10, 12.   [u] John xiv. 16.   [x] John xvi. 7.   [y] Phil. iii. 21.   [z] 1 Cor.
xv. 27, 28.

vengeance of God. And, therefore, as the Lord hath seconded his word of promise with an oath, that they might have strong consolation, who flee for refuge to lay hold on the hope which is set before them [a]; so hath he confirmed the word of his threatenings with an oath too; " If I lift up my hand to heaven, and say I live for ever——I will render vengeance to mine enemies, I will reward them that hate me [b]:" and again, " The Lord hath sworn by the excellency of Jacob, Surely I will never forget any of their works [c]:" and again, " I have sworn by myself, that unto me every knee shall bow [d]." And this he doth, that secure and obdurate sinners might have the stronger reasons to flee from the wrath which is set before them. " O nos miseros, qui nec juranti Deo credimus !" How wonderful is the stupidity of men, that will neither believe the words, nor tremble at the oath of God ! He hath warned us to flee from the wrath to come, and we make haste to meet it rather : we fill up our measure and commit sin with both hands greedily, with unclean and intemperate courses : we bring immature deaths upon ourselves, that so we may hasten to Hell the sooner, and make trial whether God be a liar or no. For this indeed is the very direct issue of every profane exorbitancy which men rush into. Every man hath much atheism in his heart by nature; but such desperate stupidity doth wonderfully improve it, and bring men by degrees to the hellish presumption of those in the prophets,—" The Lord will not do good, neither will he do evil ; it is not the Lord, neither shall evil come upon us; the prophets shall become wind, and the word is not in them [e]. The days are prolonged, and the vision shall fail ; this man prophesies of things afar off [f];"—of doomsday, of things which shall be long after our time. Unto these men, I say, in the words of the apostle, though they sleep, and see nothing, and mock at the promise of Christ's coming, yet their " damnation sleepeth not [g]," but shall come upon them soon enough, even like an armed man. " Be ye not mockers," saith the prophet [h], " lest your bands be made strong." Atheism and scorn of God's judgement will make him bind them the faster upon us ; he will get the better of

[a] Hebr. vi. 17, 18.   [b] Deut. xxxii. 40, 41.   [c] Amos viii. 7.   [d] Isai. xlv. 23.   [e] Jer. v. 11, 12.   [f] Ezek. xii. 22.   [g] 2 Pet. ii. 3.   [h] Isai. xxviii. 22.

the proudest of his enemies. We may mock, but "God will
not be mocked [i]." He that shooteth arrows against the sun,
shall never reach high enough to violate it: but the arrows
shall return upon his own head. Contempt of God and his
threatenings doth but tie our damnation the faster upon us,
and make our condition the more remediless.[k] The rage and
wrestling of a beast, with the rope that binds him, doth make
the knot the faster. Nay, there is no atheist in the world,
but, some time or other, feeleth by the horrors of his own
bosom, and by the records of his own conscience, that there
is a consumption decreed, and a day of slaughter coming for
the bulls of Bashan.

Again, others I have known acknowledge indeed, the
terror of the Lord, but yet go desperately on in their presumptions, and that upon two other dangerous downfals.
First, they thus argue,—Peradventure I belong to God's
election of grace; and then he will fetch me in, in his time;
and, in the mean time, his mercy is above my sins, and it is
not for me to hasten his work till he will himself.—O what a
perverseness is this, for the wickedness of man to perturb
the order of God! His rule is, that we should argue from a
holy conversation to our election, and, by our diligence in
adding one grace unto another, to make it sure unto ourselves; not to argue from our election to our calling, nor to
neglect all diligence, till our election appear. It is true, the
mercy of Christ is infinitely wider than the very rebellious
men, and, it may be, he will snatch such a wicked disputer as
this like a brand out of the fire. But then know withal,
that every desperate sin thou dost now wilfully run into, will,
at last, cost thee such bitter throes, such bloody tears, as
thou wouldst not be willing, with the least of them, to purchase the most sweet and constant pleasure, which thy heart
can now delight in. And in the mean time, it is a bloody
adventure upon the patience of God, for any man upon expectation of God's favour to steal [l] time from his service,
and to turn the probability of the mercy of God into an
occasion of sinning. The Ninevites [m] gathered another conclusion from these premises; "Let man and beast be covered with sackcloth and cry mightily unto God: yea, let

---

[i] Gal. vi. 7. 8.   [k] 2 Chro. xxxvi. 16.   [l] Medium interim furantur tempus,
et commeatum faciunt delinquendis. *Tertul.*   [m] Jonah iii. 8, 9.

them turn every one from their evil way, and from the violence which is in their hands:" and the ground of this resolution is this, " Who can tell if God will turn and repent,
and turn away from his fierce anger that we perish not ?"—
And the prophets teach us to make another use of the
possibility of God's mercy : " Rend your hearts and not your
garments, and turn unto the Lord your God; for he is
gracious and merciful, slow to anger, and of great kindness,
and repenteth him of the evil. Who knoweth if he will return and repent, and leave a blessing behind him [n] ?" &c.
And again : " Seek ye the Lord, all ye meek of the earth ;
seek righteousness, seek meekness; it may be, ye shall be hid
in the day of the Lord's anger [o]."

But then, secondly, there are not wanting desperate
wretches, who will thus hellishly argue against the service
of God :—It may be, the decree is gone forth, and I am rejected by God : and why should I labour in vain, and go
about to repeal his will, and not rather, since I have no
Heaven hereafter, take the fill of mine own ways and
lusts here ?—Thus we find the wicked epicures conclude,
" We shall die to-morrow; therefore, let us eat and drink to-
day [p]."—Nay, but who art thou, O man, who disputest
against God? who rather choosest to abuse the secrets of
God, that thou mayest dishonour him, than to be ruled by
his revealed will, that thou mayest obey him ? Let the potsherds strive with the potsherds of the earth; but let not
the clay dash itself against him that made it. Remember
and tremble at the difference, which our Saviour makes even
amongst the wicked in Hell. " It shall be easier for Sodom
and Gomorrah, and for Tyre and Sidon, in the day of judgment," than for those cities which have heard and despised
him. Wicked men are treasuring up of wrath, and hoarding
up of destruction against their own souls. Every new oath
or blasphemy heaps a new mountain upon their conscience ;
every renewed act of any uncleanness plungeth a man deeper
into Hell, giveth the Devil more holdfast of him, adds more
fuel unto his Tophet, squeezeth in more dregs and woful ingredients into the cup of astonishment which he must swallow. Doubtless, a sinner in Hell would account himself a

blessed creature, if he did not feel there the weight and worm of such and such particular sins, which with much easiness he might have forborne, nay, which without pain and labour he could not commit. We see Dives in Hell begged for but a drop of water to cool his tongue in that mighty flame. Now suppose a man in a burning furnace: what great comfort could he receive from but a drop of water against a furnace of fire? Certainly, the abatement of so much pain as the abiding of one drop would remove, could, in no proportion, amount to the taking away the punishment of the smallest sin, of the least idle word, or unprofitable thought: and yet, in that extremity, there shall not be allowed a drop of refreshment against a lake of fire. O that men would, therefore, in time consider, what a woful thing it is to fall into the hands, and to rouse up the jealousy of the living God! that because he will do thus and thus unto obdurate sinners, they would therefore in time humble themselves under his mighty hand, and prepare to meet him in the way of his judgements. For, certainly, no sooner doth the heart of a sinner yield to God, but he meeteth him in his return, and preventeth him with goodness; his heart likewise is turned within him, and his repentings are kindled together. With much more delight will he put a man into the arms of Christ, than force him under his feet. " He doth not afflict willingly, nor grieve the children of men; he taketh no pleasure in the death of a sinner, but he delighteth in mercy."

The last thing observed, was the manner of this victory, expressed in those words, *ponam*, and *ponam scabellum:* To *put*, and to *put as a stool* under Christ's feet. Now this expression, that the conquest of Christ's enemies shall be but as the removing of a stool into his place, noteth unto us two things :—

First, The easiness of God's victory over the enemies of Christ. They are before him as nothing, less than nothing, the drop of a bucket q, the dust of a balance, a very little thing. What thing is heavier than a mountain? what thing easier than a touch? what lighter than chaff? or softer than wax? and yet they, who, in the eyes of men, are as strong and immovable as mountains, — if God but touch them, they

q Isa. xli. 15.

shall be turned into chaff, and flow [r] at his presence. If a
man had a deadly pestilence, and of infallible infection ; how
easily might that man be avenged on his enemy, but with
breathing in his face ! Now the breath of the Lord is like
a stream [s] of brimstone to devour the wicked. As easily as
fire [t] consumeth flax or stubble, as easily as poison invadeth
the spirits of the body,—as easily as a rod of iron breaketh
in pieces a potter's vessel [u],—as easily as a burthensome stone [x]
bruiseth that which it falls upon ; so, and much more irresisti-
bly, doth the wrath of the Lord consume his enemies.

Not to insist long on so certain and obvious a truth : far
easier, we know, it is to destroy than to build up : there is no
such art required in demolishing, as there is in erecting of an
edifice ; those things which are long and difficult in growing
up, are suddenly extinguished.[y] Since, therefore, God hath
power and wisdom to make the creature,—no wonder if he
can, most easily, destroy him.

Again ; God's power is, as it were, set on by his jealousy
and fury against sinners. Anger, we know, is the whetstone
of strength : in an equality of other terms, it will make a
man prevail. Nothing is able to stand before a fire, which is
once enraged. Now God's displeasure is kindled, and
breaketh forth into a flame against the sins of men [z] ; like a
devouring lion [a], or a bereaved bear,—like the implacable
rage [b] of a jealous man ;—so doth the fire of the Lord's revenge break forth upon the enemies of his son.

Add hereunto our disposition and preparedness for the
wrath of God. Strength itself may be tired out in vain upon
a subject, which is incapable of any injury therefrom. But
if the paw of a bear meet with so thin a substance as the
caul of a man's heart, how easily is it torn to pieces ! Every
action is then most speedily finished, when the subject on
which it works, is thereunto prepared. Far easier is it to
make a print in wax than in an adamant ; to kindle a fire in dry
stubble, than in green wood. Now wicked men have fitted
themselves for wrath [c], and are the procurers [d] and artificers

---

[r] Isa. lxiv. 3.   [s] Isa. xxx. 33.   [t] Isa. xxvii. 4. Isa. xlvii. 14.   [u] Psalm
ii. 9.   [x] Zech. xii. 3, 6.   [y] Corpora tarde augescunt, cito exstinguuntur. *Tac.*
[z] Deut. xxix. 20.   [a] Hosea xiii. 7, 8.   [b] Prov. vi. 34. Cant. viii. 6. Ezek.
xxxvi. 5.   [c] Rom. ix. 22. Isa. iii. 9. Jer. ii. 17.   [d] Jer. iv. 18.

of their own destruction.[e] They are vessels; and God is never without treasures of wrath : so that the confusion of a wicked man is but like the drawing of water out of a fountain, or the filling of a bag out of a heap of treasure.

Lastly, Add hereunto our destituteness of all help and succour. Even fire amongst pitch might be quenched, if a man could pour down water in abundance upon it. But the wicked shall have no strength, either in or about them, to prevent or remove the wrath to come. Here, indeed, they have some helps (such as they are) to stand out against God in his word. Wealth and greatness to be the provisions of their lusts ; the countenance of the wicked world, to encourage them in their ways ; Satan and the wisdom of the flesh, to furnish them with arguments, and cast a garnish upon uncleanness : but when a lion comes, the shepherd can do the sheep no good ; when the fire comes, the rotten post shall perish with the varnish which covered it. He that was here strong enough to provoke God, shall at last be bound hand and foot; and so have no faculty left, either to resist him, or to run from him.

There is a foolish disposition in the hearts of men, to think that they shall ever continue in that estate, which they are once in. The proud and wicked man hath said in his heart, " I shall never be moved, I shall never be in adversity : God hath forgotten, he hideth his face, he will never see it[f]." And the prophet David was overtaken with this gross error, " I said in my prosperity, I shall never be moved." This was the vain conceit of the fool in the Gospel ; "thou hast much laid up for many years, take thine ease, eat, drink, and be merry[g]." This ever hath been the language of secure and wicked men : " No evil shall come upon us[h] ; I shall have peace[i], though I walk in the imagination of mine heart. To-morrow[k] shall be as this day, and much more abundant." And so also in afflictions : " Hath the Lord forgotten to be gracious, and shut up his lovingkindness in displeasure ?—from day even to night wilt thou make an end of me[l]? I said, My hope is lost, and I am cut off from my part[m]:" I shall never overcome such an afflic-

---

[e] Hosea xiii. 9.   [f] Psalm x. 6, 11.   [g] Luke xii. 19.   [h] Micah iii. 11.
[i] Deut. xxix. 19.   [k] Isai. lvi. 12.   [l] Isai. xxxviii. 12.   [m] Ezek. xxxvii. 11.

tion, I shall never break through such a pressure.—And both
these come from want of faith, touching the power of God
to subdue all enemies under Christ's feet. If men would
but consider how easily God can break down all their cob-
webs, and sweep away their refuge of lies,—how easily he
can spoil them of all the provisions of their lusts, and leave
them like a lamb in a large place; they would be more fearful of him, and less dote upon things which will not profit;
they would take heed how they abuse their youth, strength,
time, abilities, as if they had a spring of them all within
themselves, and consider that their good is not in their own
hand; that the scythe can get as well through the green
grass as the dry stubble; that consuming fire can as well
melt the hardest metal as the softest wax. What is the
reason, why men, in sore extremities, make strong resolutions, and vow much repentance and amendment of life,—
and yet, as soon as they are off from the rack, return again
to their vomit, and wallow in their wonted lusts,—but because their sense made them feel that then, which, if they
had faith, they might still perceive, and so still continue in
the same good resolutions,—namely, that God's hand was
near unto them? But what? " is not God a God afar off,
as well as near at hand?" doth not he say of wicked men,
that in " the fulness of their sufficiency, they shall be in
straits [n] ?" cannot he blast the corn in the blade [o], in the
harvest [p], in the barn [q], in the very mouth of the wicked [r]?
Did he not cut off Belshazzar in his cups, and Herod in his
robes, and Babylon and Tyrus in their pride, and Haman in
his favour, and Jezebel in her paint? Have but faith enough
to say,—I am a man, and therefore no human events should
be strange unto me;—and even that one consideration may
keep a man from outrage of sinning. It may be, I have
abundance of earthly things, yet am I still but a gilded potsherd: it may be, I have excellent endowments, but I have
them all in an earthen vessel. And shall the potsherd strive
with the potter, and provoke him that made it? This would
teach us to fear and tremble at God's power. Though we
look upon death and judgement as afar off, yet God can
make them near when he will: for he hath said, that the

---

[n] Job xx. 22.   [o] Amos iv. 7.   [p] Hosea ii. 9.   [q] Hag. i. 9. Hos. ix. 2.
[r] Psalm lxxviii. 30, 31.

damnation of wicked men is swift[s], and that they are near
unto cursing[t]. His judgements are like lightning, and have
wings[u] suddenly to overtake a sinner. He requires but a
month[x], nay, but a morning[y], nay, but a moment[z] to consume his enemies, and bring desolation upon those who said
they should sit as a lady for ever, and did never remember
the latter end. "Though a sinner do evil a hundred times,
and his days be prolonged," namely, by the patience and
permission of God, in whose hands his days are,—" yet it
shall go well at last only with those that fear God."[a] The
wicked are not able to prolong their own days.

Again, For afflictions and temptations, it is a great fruit
of the infidelity of men's hearts, and a foolish charging and
chiding of our Maker, to account ourselves swallowed up of
any present pressure. If we did but consider that it is as
easy with God to subdue our enemies, and to rebuke our
afflictions, as it is with us to put a stool under our feet,
—we would then learn to wait on him in all our distresses ;
and when we cannot answer difficulties, nor extricate ourselves out of our own doubts or fears,—to conclude, that his
thoughts[b] are above our thoughts, and his ways above our
ways, and so to cast ourselves wholly upon his power. It is
an argument which the Lord everywhere useth to establish
his church withal : "Fear not the fear of men[c], nor be afraid,
but sanctify the Lord of hosts himself, and let him be your
fear.—Who art thou, that thou shouldest be afraid of a man
that shall die[d], and of the son of man which shall be made
as grass; and forgettest the Lord thy maker, and hast feared
every day because of the fury of the oppressor? And where
is the fury of the oppressor? If it be marvellous in the eyes
of the remnant of this people, should it be marvellous in mine
eyes, saith the Lord of hosts?[e] Behold, I am the Lord, the
God of all flesh; is there any thing too hard for me?[f]
Blessed is the man[g] that trusteth in the Lord, and whose
hope the Lord is. He shall be as a tree planted by the
waters, which shall not be careful in the year of drought.
When the poor and needy seek water, and there is none, and

[s] 2 Pet. ii. 1.   [t] Heb. vi. 8.   [u] Hosea viii. 1. Zech. v. 1.
[x] Hos. v. 7.   [y] Hos. x. 15.   [z] Isai. xlvii. 9.   [a] Eccles. viii. 12, 13.
[d] Isai. lv. 8, 9.   [c] Isai. viii. 12, 13.   [d] Isai. li. 12, 13.   [e] Zech.
viii. 6, 7.   [f] Jer. xxxii. 27. Gen. xviii. 14.   [g] Jer. xvii. 7, 8.

their tongue faileth for thirst, I the Lord will hear them, I
the God of Israel will not forsake them.[h] Though the fig-
tree shall not blossom [i], neither shall fruit be in the vines, the
labour of the olive shall fail, and the field shall yield no
meat, the flock shall be cut off from the fold, and there shall
be no herd in the stalls: yet I will rejoice in the Lord, I
will joy in the God of my salvation." He is able to do
above all that we can ask or think. God would never so
frequently carry man to the dependence upon his power, if
they were not apt, in extremities, to judge of God by themselves, and to suspect his power.

Secondly, As this putting of Christ's enemies like a stool
under his feet, noteth easiness, so also it noteth order or
beauty too. When Christ's enemies shall be under his foot,
then there shall be a right order in things; then it shall indeed appear, that God is a God of order: and therefore the
day wherein that shall be done, is called " the time of the
restitution of all things."[k] The putting of Christ's enemies
under his feet, is an act of justice ; and of all other, justice[l]
is the most orderly virtue, that which keepeth beauty upon
the face of a people, as consisting itself in a symmetry and
proportion. Again ; Every thing out of its own place, is
out of order; but when things are all in their proper places
and due proportions, then there results a beauty and comeliness from them. In a great house, there are many vessels,
—some, of wood and brass,—others, of gold and silver ;
some, for honourable,—others, for base and sordid uses.
Now if all these were confusedly together in one room, a
man would conclude that things were out of order ; but when
the plate is in one place, the brass and wood in another, we
acknowledge a decency and cleanliness in such a house.
Let a body be of never so exact temperature and delicate
complexion, yet if any member therein be misplaced, the
eye in the room of the ear, or the cheek of the forehead,
there can be no beauty in such a body : so in the church,
till God set every one in his right place, the order thereof
is but imperfect. Therefore when Judas was put under
Christ's feet, he is said to have gone εἰς ἴδιον τόπον, " unto
his own place."[m]

h Isai. xli. 17, 18.   i Heb. iii. 17, 19.   k Acts iii. 21.   l Ethic.
lib. 5. cap. 1. Τὸ δίκαιον νόμιμον καὶ ἴσον· τὸ δὲ ἄδικον παράνομον καὶ ἄνισον.
Arist.   m Acts i. 25.

Why then should any man murmur at the prosperity of wicked men, or conceive of God's proceedings, as if they were irregular and unequal [n]?—as if there were no profit[o] for those who walk mournfully, but the proud, and wicked workers were set up. This is to revile the workman, while he is yet in the fitting of his work. The pieces are not yet put together in their proper joints ; and therefore no marvel, if the evenness and beauty of God's works be not so plainly discovered. For every thing is ' beautiful in its time.' What though the corn in the field hang down the head, and the weeds seem to flourish and overtop it ; stay but till the harvest ; and it will then appear which was for the garner, and which for the fire. Go into the sanctuary of the Lord, and by faith look unto the day of the revelation of God's righteous judgements ; and it will appear " that the ways of the Lord are right, though the transgressors stumble in them[p]," or be offended at them.

Secondly, From hence every man may learn how to bring beauty and order into himself, namely, by subduing those enemies of Christ, those lusts and evil affections which dwell within him. Laws, we know, are the ligaments and sinews of a state ; the strings, as it were, which, being touched and animated by skilful governors, do yield that excellent harmony, which is to be seen in well-constituted commonwealths : the more they prevail, so much the more unity is preserved, and faction abated, and community cherished in the minds of men. Even so, where the sceptre of Christ, the law of the mind, the royal law of liberty and grace, do more prevail over the lusts of the heart,—by so much the more excellent is the harmony and complexion of such a soul.

Now the last thing in this verse is, "Scabellum pedibus tuis," *a stool under thy feet.* Things are under Christ's feet two manner of ways : either by way of subjection, as servants unto him ; and so he hath dominion [q] over all the works of God's hands, and hath all things put under his feet. So the apostle saith[r], that God hath set him at his own right hand in heavenly places, far above all principality, and power, and might, and dominion, and every name that is named, not only in this world, but also in that which is to come ; " and hath put all things under his feet," and gave

n Ezek. xviii. 25.   o Mal. iii. 14. 15.   p Hosea xiv. 9.   q Psal. viii. 6.   r Eph. i. 21, 22.

him to be the head over all things to the church.—Which St.
Peter [s] expresseth in a like manner: he is gone into Heaven,
and is on the right hand of God, "angels and authorities
and powers being made subject to him." Or, secondly, by
way of victory and insultation; and so all Christ's enemies
are put under his feet, which is the most proper way. For
the members of Christ are indeed under the head; so we
find, that the sheep of Christ are in his hands; "no man shall
pluck them out of my hand."[t] And the lambs of Christ are
in his arms and bosom:[u] He shall gather the lambs with
his arms, and carry them in his bosom.[x] But the enemies
of Christ are under his feet to be trampled upon, till their
blood be squeezed out, and his garments stained with it.
All the multiplied multitudes of the wicked in the world
shall be but as so many clusters of ripe grapes [y] to be
cast into the great wine-press of the wrath of God, and
to be trodden by him who went forth on a white horse
conquering [z], and to conquer, till the blood come out of
the wine-press even unto the horse-bridles. And this is
a usual expression of a total victory in holy Scripture, the
laying of an adversary even with the ground [a], that he may
be crushed and trampled upon. This was the curse of the
serpent [b], that he should crawl with his belly upon the dust
of the earth, and that the seed of the woman should bruise
his head. And it is the curse of God's enemies, that
they should lick the dust, and that the feet of the church,
and the tongue of her dogs, should be dipped in the blood
of her enemies.[c] Thus David [d] put the people of Rabbah
under harrows; and Jehu [e] trod Jezebel under his horses'
feet. And therefore the church [f] chooseth that phrase to
express the greatness of her calamity by, "The Lord hath
trodden under feet all my mighty men in the midst of me;
he hath called an assembly against me to crush my young
men. The Lord hath trodden the virgin, the daughter of
Judah, as in a wine-press."

Now this putting of Christ's enemies as a stool under his
feet, notes unto us, in regard of Christ, two things: first,
his rest, and secondly, his triumph. To *stand* in the Scrip-

[s] 1 Pet. iii. 22.   [t] John x. 28.   [u] Isai. xl. 11.   [x] Isai. lxiii. 1, 3.
[y] Joel iii. 13, 14.   [z] Rev. xiv. 20.   [a] Luke x. 19. Rom. xvi. 20.
[b] Gen. iii. 14.   [c] Psal. lxviii. 23.   [d] 2 Sam. xii. 31.   [e] 2 Kings ix. 33.
[f] Lam. i. 15.

ture-phrase (as I have before observed) denoteth *ministry;*
and to *sit, rest;* and there is no posture more easy, than to
sit with a stool under one's feet : till Christ's enemies then
be all under his feet, he is not fully in his rest. It is true,
in his own person he is in rest ; he hath finished the work
which was given him to do, and therefore is entered into his
rest. He hath already ascended up on high, and led captivity captive ; yet in his members he still suffers, though
not by way of pain or passion, yet by way of sympathy or
compassion ; he " is touched with a feeling of our infirmities."[g] As by the things which he suffered, he learned obedience[h] towards God, so by the same sufferings he learned
compassion[i], and thereupon mercy and fidelity towards his
members ; for no man can be more tenderly faithful in the
business of another, than he who by his own experience knoweth the consequence and necessity of it. And therefore he
is said to be afflicted[k], in all the afflictions of his people :
and the apostle[l] tells us, that the afflictions of the saints
" fill up the remainders," or " that which is behind of the
sufferings of Christ." For as the church is called ' the fulness of Christ,' who yet of himself is so full, as that he " filleth all in all " (neither doth the church serve to supply his
defects, but to magnify his mercy); so the church's sufferings are esteemed the fulness of the sufferings of Christ,
although his were of themselves so full before, as that they
had a ' consummatum est,' to seal up both their measure
and their merit. And therefore our sufferings are called *his*,
not by way of addition, or improvement unto those, but by
way of honour and dignity unto us : they show Christ's compassion towards us, and our union and conformity to him, but
no way either any defect of virtue in his, or any value of
merit in ours ; or any ecclesiastical treasure, or redundancy
out of a mixture of both. Very profitable they are for the
edification of the church, but very base and unworthy for
the expiation of sin; very profitable for the comfort of men,
but very unprofitable to the justice of God. So then, though
Christ rest from suffering in himself, yet not in his saints ;
though the serpent cannot come to the head, yet it is still
bruising of his heel. Here then the apostle's inference is
good, " There remaineth therefore a rest unto the people of

g Heb. iv. 15.   h Heb. v. 8.   i Heb. ii. 17, 18.   k Isai. lxiii. 9.
l Col. i. 24.

God," and that such a glorious rest as must arise out of the ruin of their enemies; when the wicked perish, they shall see it, and rejoice, and shall wash their feet in the blood of their adversaries. The revenge of God against his enemies is such as shall bring an ease with it: "Ah," saith the Lord, "I will ease me of mine adversaries, I will avenge me of mine enemies."[m] This is the comfort which the Lord giveth his people,—That they shall be full, when their enemies shall be hungry [n]; and that he will appear to their joy, when their enemies shall be ashamed.[o]

This must teach wicked men, to take heed of persecuting the members of Christ, for they therein are professed enemies to him, whom yet they would seem to worship. This is certain, that all the counsels and resolutions which are made against the subjects or laws of Christ's kingdom, are but 'vain imaginations,' which shall never be executed. He will at last avenge the quarrel of his people, and, in spite of all the power or malice of Hell, make them to sit actually in heavenly places with him, whom he hath virtually and representatively carried thither already. And it should comfort the faithful in all their sufferings for Christ's sake: because hereby they are, First, Conformable unto him: Secondly, They are associates with him: Thirdly, They are assured that they are in a way to rest: "for," saith the apostle, "it is just with God to recompense tribulation to them that trouble you, and to you who are troubled, *rest*, when the Lord Jesus shall be revealed from Heaven."[p] And "inasmuch," saith St. Peter[q], "as you are partakers of Christ's sufferings, —when his glory shall be revealed, ye shall be glad also with exceeding joy." And this joy shall be so much the greater, because it shall grow out of the everlasting subjection of the enemies under Christ's feet; and those whom here they persecuted and despised, shall there with Christ be their judges.[r]

Secondly, As it noteth the rest, so likewise the triumph of Christ, when he shall set his feet on the neck of his enemies. The apostle saith, that he "triumphed over them in his cross."[s] And there are two words [t] which have an allusion unto the forms of triumph, *exspoliation*, and *publication*, or

m Isai. i. 24.   n Isai. lxv. 13.   o Isai. lxvi. 5.   p 2 Thes. i. 6, 7.
q 1 Pet. iv. 13.   r 1 Cor. vi. 2, 3.   s Col. ii. 15.   t *Alex. ab Alex.*
Gen. Dier. lib. 6. cap. 6. *Rosin.* Antiq. Rom. 1. 10. cap. 29.

representation of the pomp, unto the world of the faithful.
"He spoiled principalities and powers," that is, he took
from them all their armour, wherein they trusted, and "divided the spoils."[u] The armour of Satan was, principally,
"the hand-writing of the law which was against us," or contrary unto us. So long as we were under the full force and
rigour of that, so long we were under the possession and
tyranny of Satan: but when Christ nailed that unto the
cross, and took it out of the way, then all the other panoply
of Satan was easily taken from him. He was then spoiled
of all his weapons and provisions of lust: for the world, and
therewithal the things which are in the world, were unto us
crucified in the cross of Christ[x]; so that now by faith in
him, we are able to overcome the world[y], to value it aright,
to esteem the promises thereof thin and empty, and the
threatenings thereof vain and false; the treasures thereof
baser than the very reproaches of Christ[z]; and the afflictions
thereof not worthy to be compared with the glory which shall
be revealed in us[a], as being in their measure but light, and
but momentary in their duration.[b] The power and wisdom
of Satan was likewise in the cross of Christ most notably
befooled and disappointed: for when he thought that he had
now swallowed up Christ, he found a hook under that bait;
he found that which neither himself, nor any of his instruments could have suspected, that Christ, crucified, was indeed the wisdom of God, and the power of God ; and that,
through death, he chose to destroy him who had the power
of death.[c]

Again, He made "a show," or public representation of this
his victory, and of these his spoils, openly unto the world.
As the cross was his triumphal chariot, so was it likewise
'ferculum pompæ,' the pageant, as it were, and table of his
spoils. For though to a carnal eye there was nothing but
ignominy and dishonour in it, yet to those that are called,
there is an eye of faith given to see, in the cross of Christ,
Hell disappointed, Satan confounded, his kingdom demolished, the earthly members of the old man crucified, affections and lusts abated, and captivity already led captive.
And indeed what triumph of any the most glorious con-

[u] Luke xi. 22.   [x] Gal. vi. 14.   [y] 1 John v. 4, 5.   [z] Heb. xi. 26.
[a] Rom. viii. 18.   [b] 2 Cor. iv. 17.   [c] 1 Cor. i. 24. Heb. ii. 14.

queror was ever honoured with the opening of graves,
the resurrection of the dead, the conversion of enemies,
the acclamation of mute and inanimate creatures, the
darkness of the sun, the trembling of the earth, the compassion of the rocks, the amazement of the world, the
admiration of the angels of Heaven, but only this triumph of Christ upon the cross? And if he did so triumph
there, how much more at the right hand of the Majesty on
high, where he is crowned with glory and honour,—and at
that great day, which is therefore called "the day of the
Lord Jesus," because he will therein consummate his triumph over all his enemies, when he shall come with the attendance of angels, in a chariot of fire, with all the unbelievers of the world bound before his throne, and with the
clamour, applause, and admiration of all the saints.

And this is a plentiful ground of comfort to the faithful in
all their conflicts with Satan, sin, temptations, or corruptions;
—they fight under his protection, and with his Spirit, who
hath himself already triumphed, who accounteth our temptations his, and his victories ours; who turned the sorest
perplexities which the world shall ever see, into a doctrine
of comfort unto his disciples.[d] Whenever, then, we are assaulted with any heavy temptation to discomforts, fears,
faintings, weariness, despair, sinful conformities, or the like;
let us not toss over our own store, nor depend upon any
strength or principles of our own,—but look only by faith
unto the victories of Christ, and to this great promise which is
here made unto him, as head and captain of the church, by
whom we shall be able to do all things, and, though we were
surrounded with enemies, to escape, as he did, through the
midst of them all. We know the cat's 'unum magnum,' in
the fable, was more worth than the fox's thousand shifts,
notwithstanding all the which he was caught at the last.
Our enemies come against us in armies, with infinite methods and stratagems to circumvent us; this only is our
comfort, that we have "unum magnum," one refuge which
is above all the wisdom of the enemy,—to climb up unto
the cross of Christ, and to commit the keeping of our souls
unto him, out of whose hands no man can take them. When
David went forth against Goliah, he did not grapple with

d Luke xxi. 25, 28.

him by his own strength, but with his sling and his stone at a distance overthrew him. It is not good to let Satan come too close unto the soul, to let in his temptations, or to enter into any private and intimate combat with him : this was for our captain only to do, who, we know, entered into the field with him, as being certain of his own strength :—but our only way to prevail against him, is to take faith as a sling, and Christ as a stone; he will undoubtedly find out a place to enter in and to sink the proudest enemy. We are beset with enemies, yea, we are enemies unto ourselves ; the burden of the flesh,—the assaults of the world,—the fiery darts of Satan,—treason within, and wars without,—swarms of Midianites,—troops of Amalekites,—the sea before us, the Egyptian behind us ;—sin before, Satan and the world behind :—either I must run on and be drowned in sin ; or I must stand still and be hewed in pieces with the persecutions of wicked men ; or I must revolt and turn back to Egypt, and so be devoured in her plagues. In these extremities the apostle hath given us our " unum magnum,"—" Look unto Jesus [d] ;" he that is the author, will be the finisher of our faith : it is yet but a little while, he will come, and will not tarry [e] : he is in the view of our faith, he is within the cry of our prayers, he sitteth at the right hand of power ; nay, he there standeth, and he is risen up already in the quarrel of his saints.[f] The nearer the Egyptian is to Israel, the nearer he is to ruin, and the nearer Israel is to deliverance. Though Moses have not chariots, nor multitudes of weapons, yet he hath a rod[g], a branch[h], an Angel of God's presence [i], which can open the sea, and give an issue to the greatest dangers, which can turn the enemy's rage into his own ruin. There is no enemy so close, so dangerous, so unavoidable as our own lusts. Now the Lord promiseth to deal with the sins of his people, as he did with the Egyptians. We know their tyranny he subdued with plagues ; their first-born, the strength and flower of the land, he slew before ; and those who afterwards joined themselves against his people, he drowned in the bottom of the sea. So saith the prophet, " He will subdue our iniquities," he will purge [k] them away; the power and strength of them

[d] Heb. xii. 1, 2.   [e] Heb. x. 36, 37.   [f] Acts vii. 56.   [g] Isa, xi. 1.
[h] Zech. iii. 8.   [i] Exod. xxxiii. 14. 16.   [k] Psalm lxv. 3.

he will abate by his Spirit; and as for those remainders thereof, by which we are yet behind, and rebel against his grace, he
" will cast all of them into the depth of the sea [1] ;" that is,
He will remove them utterly away from us [m], he will drown [n]
them in everlasting forgetfulness; he will not only blot them
out [o], that they may not be, but he will not remember them
neither, which is in some sort to make them even not to have
been. And which yet makes the assurance of all this the
stronger, the ground of it all is only in God himself, his
covenant and mercy. Now though our condition alters, yet
his mercy is still the same [p]: if the root of the covenant were
in us, then as we change, that also would vary too; but the
root is in God's own grace, whose mercy is therefore without repentance in himself, because it is without reason or
merit in us.

Now lastly, This footstool under Christ's feet, in regard of
his enemies, noteth unto us four things : First, The extreme
shame and confusion which they shall everlastingly suffer,
the utter abasing [q] and bringing down of all that exalteth
itself against Christ. In victories amongst men, the part
conquered goes many times off upon some honourable
terms; at the very worst, when they are led captives, yet
they go like men still: but to be made a stool for the conqueror to insult over, to lick the dust [r] like a serpent, and
move out of holes like the worms of the earth, to be so low
as not to have any farther degree of calamity, or dishonour
left unto which a man may be debased; this is the extremity
of shame. It is to be noted for the greatest indignity which
Bajazet the Grand Seignior ever suffered, when Tamerlane [s]
his adversary trampled upon his neck;—and of Valerian [t],
that cruel persecutor of the church, that he was trod under
foot by Sapores the Persian king, and after flayed like a
beast. It notes the extremest degree of revenge, which
hath no mixture of mercy or compassion in it: so that by
this we see the enemies of Christ and his kingdom shall be
put to utter and everlasting shame: that as the faithful, in

---

[1] Mic. vii. 19, 20.   [m] Psalm ciii. 12.   [n] Quod in profundum maris abjici-
tur, penitus non exstat. *Theodoret.*   [o] Isa. xliii. 25, xliv. 22.   [p] Mal. iii. 6.
[q] Isa. ii. 11. Psalm lxxii. 9.   [r] Micah vii. 17. Isa. xlix. 23.   [s] Qui Con-
stantini toties perterruit urbem, Sub Tamberlano sella canisque fuit.   [t] Aurel.
Victor et Eutropius.

that great day of their redemption, shall lift up their heads, and
have boldness in the presence of the Lamb ; so the wicked [u]
shall fall flat upon their faces, and cleave unto the dust, when
the books shall be unsealed, and the consciences of men
opened, and the witnesses produced, and the secrets of uncleanness revealed on the house-top, and the mouths of the
wicked, who here for a little while dispute against the ways of
Christ, and cavil at his commands, shall be everlastingly
stopped ; when men shall be like a deprehended thief, (as the
prophet [x] speaks) then shall their faces be as a flame, full of
trembling, confusion, and astonishment. The very best that
are, find shame enough in sin: how much more they who give
themselves over unto vile and dishonourable affections ?

Secondly, Hereby is noted the burden which wicked men
must bear.   The footstool beareth the weight of the body ;
so must the enemies of Christ bear the weight of his heavy
and everlasting wrath upon their souls. Sin in the committing seems very light, no bigger than the cloud which the
prophet showed his servant; but at last it gathers into such
a tempest, as, if the soul make not haste, it will be swept
away, and overwhelmed by it. Weighty bodies do, with
much difference, affect the sense according to the difference
of places wherein they are. That vessel or piece of timber,
which when it is on the water, may be easily drawn with the
hand of a man, on the land cannot be stirred with much
greater strength : So it is with sin upon the conscience : in
the time of committing it, nothing more easy,—but, in the
time of judging it, nothing more unsupportable. A wild ass [y]
in the time of her lusting traverseth her ways, with much
petulancy, and snuffeth up the wind at her pleasure ; no man
can turn her: but " in her month," that is, when she is bur-
dened with her foal, she then feeleth the event of her former
lustfulness, and will easily be overtaken. So the wicked in
sin, however for the time they may bear it out with much
mirth, and cheer up their hearts in the days of their pleasure ;
yet when sin is come to the birth, and so fully finished, that
it is now ready to bring forth death unto the soul,— they shall
then find, that it is but like the roll which the prophet
swallowed, sweet to the palate, but bitter in the belly ; like

[u] Ezra ix. 6. Dan. ix. 7, 8. Rom. vi. 21.   [x] Jer. ii. 26.   [y] Jer. ii. 24.

a cup of deadly poison, pleasant in the mouth, but torment in the bowels. On whomsoever the Son of Man shall fall with the weight of his heavy displeasure, he will grind him to powder.[z] That must needs be a heavy burden, which men would most joyfully exchange for the weight of rocks and mountains to lie everlastingly upon their backs. And yet the wicked at that great day shall all in vain beg of the mountains and rocks to fall upon them, and to hide them from the wrath of the Lamb; shall choose rather to live eternally under the weight of the heaviest creature in the world, than under the fury of him that sitteth upon the throne[a].

Thirdly, Herein likewise is noted the relation of a just and equal recompense unto ungodly men. The Lord useth often to fit punishments to the quality and measure of the sins committed[b]. He that on the earth denied a crumb of bread, in Hell was denied a drop of water. Man who, being in honour, would needs affect to be as God, was thereby debased to become like the beasts that perish. Nadab and Abihu offered strange fire, and perished by strange fire from the Lord. Sodom and Gomorrah burnt in unnatural lusts, and they were drowned in an unnatural tempest of fire. That apostate in St. Cyprian[c], who opened his mouth against Christ in blasphemy, was immediately smitten with dumbness, that he could not open it unto Christ for mercy. Eutropius[d] the eunuch, when he persuaded the emperor to take from malefactors the benefit of refuge at the altars, did therein prevent his own mercy, and beg away the advantage of an escape from himself, the privilege whereof he did afterwards in vain lay hold on. And thus will Christ deal with his enemies at the last day. Here they trample upon Christ, in his word, in his ways, in his members. They make the saints[e] bow down for them to go over, and make them as the pavements on the ground. They tread under foot the blood[f] of the covenant, and the sanctuary[g] of the Lord, and put Christ[h] to shame here: and there their own measure shall be returned into their own bosom: they shall

---

[z] Matth. xxi. 44. [a] Revel. vi. 16. [b] Ὁ τῆς κολάσεως τρόπος τῆς ἁμαρτίας μεμίμηται. *Chrys.* Hom. 20 ad Pop. Antioch. [c] Inde pœna cœpit unde cœpit et crimen. *Cyprian.* de Lapsis. [d] *Socrat.* Hist. lib. 6. cap. 5. et *Sozom.* lib. 8, cap. 7. [e] Isa. li. 23. [f] Heb. x. 29. [g] Isa. lxiii. 18. Revel. xi. 2. [h] Heb. vi. 6.

be constrained to confess as Adonibezek [i], " I have done, so
God hath requited me." Yea, this they shall suffer from the
meanest of Christ's members, whom they here insulted over.
They shall then as witnesses, and, as it were, co-assessors [k]
with Christ, judge the very wicked angels, and tread them
under their feet.[l] " They shall take them captives whose
captives they were, and shall rule over their oppressors.[m]
All they that despised them, shall bow themselves at the
soles of their feet.—They who gathered themselves against
Sion, and said, " Let her be defiled [n], and let our eye see it,
shall themselves be gathered as sheaves into the floor, and
the daughter of Sion shall arise and thresh them with horns
of iron, and with hoofs of brass. Then [o] (saith the church)
she that is mine enemy, shall see it ; and shame shall cover her
which said unto me, Where is the Lord thy God ? Mine eyes
shall behold her ; now shall she be trodden down as the mire
of the streets." Even so let all thine enemies perish, O Lord ;
but let them which love thee, be as the sun when he goeth
forth in his might.

Lastly, Herein we may note the great power and wisdom
of Christ, in turning the malice and mischief of his enemies
unto his own use and advantage ; and in so ordering wicked
men [p], that though they intend nothing but extirpation and
ruin to his kingdom, yet they shall be useful unto him, and,
against their own wills, serviceable to those glorious ends, in
the accomplishing whereof he shall be admired by all those
that believe. As, in a great house, there is necessary use of
vessels of dishonour, destinated unto sordid and mean, but
yet daily services ; so, in the great house of God [q], wicked
men are his utensils and household instruments, as footstools
and staves, and vessels wherein there is no pleasure, though
of them there may be good use. The Assyrian [r] was the rod
of his anger,—his axe wherewith he pruned, and his saw

[i] Judg. i. 7.   [k] 1 Cor. vi. 2, 3.   [l] Rom. xvi. 20.   [m] Isai. xiv. 2.
[n] Mic. iv. 11, 12, 13.   [o] Mic. vii. 10.   [p] Voluntas humana, perverse utendo
bonis, fit mala; ille ordinatè etiam malis utendo, permanet bonus. *Aug.* Epist.
120.—Sicut ergo ipsi benignitate, et patientia, id est, bonis Dei malè utuntur, dum
non corriguntur ; sic contra, Deus etiam malis eorum bene utitur, non solum ad
justitiam suam, quà eis digna in fine retribuet, sed etiam ad exercitationem et pro-
fectum Sanctorum suorum, ut ex ipsa etiam malorum perversitate, boni proficiant,
et probentur, et manifestentur. *Idem*, Epist. 141.   [q] 2 Tim. ii. 20.   [r] Isai.
x. 5, 6, 7.

wherewith he threatened, his people. Pharaoh [s] was a vessel fitted to show the glory and power of his name. It is necessary, saith our Saviour [t], that offences come ; and there must be heresies [u], saith the apostle. Because, as a skilful physician ordereth poisonful and destructive ingredients unto useful services ; so the Lord, by his wisdom, doth make use of wicked men's persons and purposes to his own most righteous and wonderful ends, secretly [x] and mightily directing their wicked designs, to the magnifying of his own power and providence, and to the furthering of his people in faith and godliness.

[s] Rom. ix. 17.   [t] Matth. xviii. 7.   [u] 1 Cor. xi. 19.   [x] Isa. xxxvii. 28, 29.

VERSE II.

*The Lord shall send the Rod of thy strength out of Sion :
Rule thou in the midst of thine enemies.*

THIS verse is a continuation of the former, touching the
kingdom of Christ; and it contains the form of its spiritual
administration. Wherein is secretly couched another of the
offices of Christ, namely, his prophetical office. For that is,
as it were, the dispensation and execution of his regal office
in the militant church. The sum of this administration consists in two principal things: First, In matters military, for
the subduing of enemies, and for the defence and protection
of his people. Secondly, In matters civil and judicial, for
the government, preservation, and honour of his kingdom.
And both these are in this psalm; the former, in the latter
part of this verse, " Rule thou in the midst of thine enemies."
The other, in the third verse, "Thy people shall be willing,"
&c.; and the way of compassing and effecting, in the former
words of this verse, "The Lord shall send forth the rod of
thy strength out of Sion."

Every king [a] hath his 'jura regalia,' certain royal prerogatives and peculiar honours proper to his own person, which
no man can use but with subordination unto him. And if
we observe them, we shall find many of them as exactly
belong unto Christ in his kingdom, as to any secular prince
in his. First, Unto kings do belong 'armamentaria publica,'
the magazines for military provision, and the power and disposition of public arms. Therefore he is said by the
apostle [b] to " bear the sword," because arms properly belong
unto him, and unto others under his allowance and protection. So to Christ alone doth belong,—and in him only is
to be found, the public armoury of a Christian man The
weapons of our warfare are mighty only through him. Nay,
he is himself the armour and panoply of a Christian, and
therefore we are commanded " to put on the Lord Jesus."

[a] *Greg. Tholos.* de Repub. lib. 9. cap. 1.   [b] Rom. xiii. 4. 1 Sam. x. 16, 17

Again, 'via publica' is 'via regia;' the high way is the king's
way, wherein every man walketh freely under the protection of his sovereign. So that law of faith and obedience
under which we are to walk, which St. Paul[e] calleth the law
of Christ, is by St. James[d] called 'lex regia,' a royal law,
and ' a law of liberty;' in which while any man continueth,
he is under the protection of the promises and of the angels
of Christ[e]. Again, ' bona adespota seu incerti domini,'
lands that are concealed and under the evident claim of no
other person or lord, do belong unto the prince, as he that
hath the supreme and universal dominion in his countries.
And this is most certainly true of Christ, in his kingdom : if
any man can once truly say, ' Lord, I am not the servant of
any other master; no other king hath the rightful dominion,
or peaceable possession of my heart,' he may most truly from
thence infer;—Therefore, Lord, am I thy servant, and therefore, Lord, my heart is thine. True it is, Lord our God, that
"other lords besides thee have had dominion over us ; but
now by thee only will we make mention of thy name[f]."
Again ; ' vectigalia,' and ' census,' tributes, and customs, and
testifications of homage and fidelity are personal prerogatives
belonging unto princes, and, as the apostle[g] saith, "due
unto them," for that ministry and office, which, under God,
they attend upon. So in Christ's kingdom, there is a worship which the psalmist saith is " due unto his name[h]."
They which came unto the Temple, which was a type of
Christ, were not to come empty-handed, but to bring testimonies of their reverence, and willing subjection unto that
worship. When Abraham met Melchisedec, a figure of
Christ,—as from him he received a blessing, so unto him he
gave an expression of a loyal heart, the tenth of the spoils.
When the people of Israel entered into the land of Canaan,
(which was a type of Christ's church, which he should conquer unto himself,) if any people accepted of the peace which
they were first to proclaim, they were to become tributaries
and servants unto Israel[i]. So it is said of Solomon[k] (whose
peaceable kingdom was a type of Christ's after his many
victories) that "he levied a tribute of bond-service upon all

---

[e] Gal. vi. 2.   [d] James ii. 8, and i. 25.   [e] Psalm xci. 11. Prov. x.29.
[f] Isai. xxvi. 13.   [g] Rom. xiii. 6, 7.   [h] Psalm xcvi. 8.   [i] Deut. xx. 11.
[k] 1 Kings iv. 21. 1 Kings ix. 21, x. 10.

the nations about Israel;" and that those princes with whom he held correspondency, brought unto him presents, as testimonies of his greatness and wisdom. So when the wise men (the first-fruits [1] of the Gentiles, after Christ exhibited) came to submit unto his kingdom, they opened their treasure, and presented him with gifts, gold, frankincense, and myrrh." Again; ' Monetarum leges et valores,' the authorizing and valuations of public coins belong unto the prince only; it is his image and inscription alone, which maketh them current. Even so unto Christ only, doth belong the power of stamping and creating, as it were, new ordinances in his church : nothing is with God, nor should be current with us, which hath not his image or express authority upon it. Neither can any man falsify or corrupt any constitution of his, without notable contempt against his royal prerogative. —Again ; ' Judicium,' or ' potestas judiciaria,' a power of judging the persons and causes of men, is a peculiar royalty, the administration whereof is from the prince, as the fountain of all human equity (under God) deposited in the hands of inferior officers, who are, as it were, the mouth of the prince, to publish the laws, and to execute those acts of justice and peace, which principally belong to his own sacred breast. And so Christ saith of himself, " The Father hath committed all judgement unto the Son, and hath given him authority to execute judgement.[m]" Again ; ' Jus vitæ et necis ;' a power to pardon condemned persons, and deliver them from the terror of the law's sentence, is a transcendent mercy, a gem which can shine only from the diadems of princes. Now unto Christ likewise belongeth, in his church, a power to forgive sins : it is the most sacred royalty of this ' prince of peace,' not only to suspend, but for ever to revoke, and, as it were, annihilate, the sentence of malediction under which every man is born. There are likewise ' ornamenta regia,' regal ornaments [n], a crown, a throne, a sceptre, and the like. Thus we find the Romans [o] were wont to send to those foreign kings with whom they were in league, as testimonies and

[1] Matt. ii. 11.—Primitiæ Gentium Sacramentalia munera proferunt de thesauris, &c. *Cyprian.* Serm. de Stell. & Magis.—*Brisson.* De Reg. Persarum 1. i. 26.   [m] John v. 22. 27   [n] 2 Kings xi. 12. 1 Kings x. 18.   *Liv.* lib. 30.—*Tacit.* An. l. 4. *Dionys. Halicar.* lib. 3.

confirmations of their dignity, scipionem eburneum, togam pictam, sellam curulem, an ivory sceptre, a royal robe, and a chair of state. And the like honours we find, in the Scriptures, belonging unto Christ, that he was ' crowned with glory and honour [p],' and that he had ' a throne and righteous sceptre [q],' belonging to his kingdom. Thus we have seen in several particulars, how Christ hath his royalties belonging to his kingdom. Some principal of them we find in this place; a throne, a sceptre, ambassadors, armies, for the right dispensing of his sacred power. We will first consider the words, and then raise such observations as shall offer themselves.

First, What is meant by the *rod of Christ's strength*, or his strong rod? It notes a thing which a man may lean upon, or lay the whole weight of his body on in his weariness. But being spoken of Christ's kingdom, we take it for a sceptre or rod of majesty [r]. I will not hold you with the variety of acceptions in expositors. Some take it for the branch, that groweth out of that root of Jesse:—some, for the wood of the cross:—some for the body of Christ born of a Virgin:—some, for the kingdom of Christ's power, taking the sign for the thing signified:—some, for the power of his mighty works and preaching. That of the body and of the cross of Christ, except by them we understand the virtue of Christ crucified, I conceive to be not so pertinent to the purpose of the prophet; the rest agree in one. But for the more distinct understanding of the words, we may consider, out of the holy scriptures, what things were ' sent out of Sion.' And we find there two things: First, the word of the Lord, or his holy gospel: "The law shall proceed out of Sion, and the word of the Lord from Jerusalem." [s] Secondly, The Spirit of the Lord, which was first sent unto Sion; for at Jerusalem, the apostles were to wait for the promises of the Father [t], and from thence " was shed abroad into the world upon all flesh [u];" and both these are the power or strength of Christ. His Word, " a gospel of power unto salvation [x]," and his Spirit, " a spirit of power [y]," which

---

[p] Heb. ii. 9.   [q] Psal. xlv. 6. 8.   [r] Insigne majestatis regiæ. *Hieron.*
Theodoret. Arnobius. Aug. et Prosp. Euthymius.   [s] Mic. iv. 2.   [t] Acts i. 4.
[u] Acts ii. 17.   [x] Rom. i. 16. 2 Cor. iv. 7, x. 4.   [y] 1 Cor. ii. 4. 2 Tim. i. 7.

is therefore called the finger and the arm of the Lord.[z] So by the *rod* is meant the gospel and the Spirit of Christ.

Secondly, What is meant by " God's *sending* this rod of Christ's strength?" It notes the manifestation of the gospel: we knew it not, before it was sent:—the donation of the gospel; we had it not before it was sent: the invitations of the gospel; we were without God in the world, and strangers from the covenant of promise, before it was sent. The commission of the dispensers of the gospel; they have their patent from Heaven; they are not to speak until they be sent.

Thirdly, What is meant by " sending it *out of Sion?*" It is put in opposition to Mount Sinai, from whence the law was sometimes sent with thunders and fire, and much terror unto the people of Israel. " Ye are not come," saith the apostle, " unto the mount that burned with fire, nor unto blackness and darkness, and tempest, &c., but ye are come unto Mount Sion, and unto the city of the living God, the heavenly Jerusalem, and to an innumerable company of angels, and to Jesus the mediator of the new covenant[a]," &c. and the apostle elsewhere showeth us the meaning of this allegorical opposition between Sinai and Sion, between Sarah and Hagar; namely, the two covenants of the law and of grace, or of bondage and liberty.[b] Sion was the place, whither the tribes resorted to worship the Lord; the place, towards which that people prayed; the place of God's merciful residence amongst them; the beauty of holiness; the place, upon which first the gift of the Holy Ghost was poured forth, and in which the gospel was first of all preached after Christ's ascension. We may take it by a synecdoche, for the whole church of the Jews, unto whom the Lord first revealed his covenant of grace in Christ.[c]

" *Rule thou:*"—that is, *Thou shalt rule;*—which is a usual form to put the imperative for the future indicative. It is not a command, which hath relation unto any service; but it is a promise, a commission, a dignity conferred upon Christ.

[z] Luke xi. 20. Matth. xii. 28. Isai. liii. 1. [a] Heb. xii. 18, 24. [b] Gal. iv. 24, 25. [c] Acts iii. 26. xiii. 46. Rom. ii. xx.

" *In the midst of thine enemies:*"—Some understand it of
changing the hearts of his enemies, and converting them,
as captives, unto his obedience. Others understand the
wonderful effect of the power of Christ's kingdom, that he
can, by his word and spirit, hold up his church in despite
of all the enemies thereof round about.[d] The church ever
was, and will be, pestered with divers kinds of adversaries,
heretics, and hypocrites, and false brethren, with profaneness, temptations, persecutions, spiritual wickednesses; and,
in the midst of all these, the church of Christ groweth as
' a lily amongst the thorns.' Now this ' in medio' noteth
two things; ' dominium plenum,' and ' dominium securum,'
a perfect and full government, without mutilation, without
impediment; the church being amongst the wicked as a rock
in the midst of the sea, or as a garrison in an enemy's town.
' Media dominantur in urbe,' is an expression of such a rule,
as can no way be hindered or removed. The church of God
is a burdensome stone : they who go about to remove it
out of that place where Christ will plant it, shall be cut in
pieces, though all the people of the earth should gather together against it.[e] A secure and confident government: so
in the scripture-phrase, *in the midst,* notes confidence and
security. When the prophet asked the Shunammite, "Wouldst
thou be spoken for to the King, or to the captain of the
host ?" she answered, " I dwell amongst mine own people;"
that is, I am safe and have enough already[f]. When they of
the synagogue would have cast Christ down headlong from
the brow of a hill, it is said, that " he passed through the
midst of them, and went his way ;" that is, with much confidence, safety, and assurance, he withdrew himself.[g] As
the prophet was full of security and quietness, in the midst
of the Syrian siege.[h]

The words being thus unfolded, we may observe in them
three of Christ's principal regalities, ' sceptrum, solium, and
imperium ;' the sceptre, the throne, and the power or government of his kingdom. His sceptre is the word of his
gospel, animated by the power of his Holy Spirit, and

---

d Qui alieni erant, tui esse incipient.   Dignare esse Dominus inimicorum
tuorum. *Hieron.*   e Zech. xii. 3.   f 2 Kings iv. 13.   g Luke iv. 29. 30.
h 2 Kings vi. 14, 16.

accompanied with the blessing and authority of God the Father, who sendeth it abroad into the world :—His throne, from whence this his sceptre is extended, Sion, the church of the Jews :—His victorious, plenary, and secure government, " *Rule thou in the midst of thine enemies.*"

First, the sceptre; Here is the gospel and the spirit of Christ. Christ is a shepherd towards his flock the church [i]: a *great* shepherd [k]; that notes his power and majesty over them :—and a *good* shepherd [l]; that notes his care and tenderness towards his sheep. Kings, in the Scripture, are called shepherds to lead, and to feed, and to govern the people. So David is said to have been taken from the sheepfolds, to feed Jacob and Israel [m] ; and thus Christ is a shepherd and a king. " I will set up one shepherd over them, and he shall feed them, even my servant David—I the Lord will be their God, and my servant David a prince among them." [n] Prophets and teachers are, in the Scripture, likewise called shepherds [o]: and so Christ is a shepherd and a bishop ; " Ye were as sheep going astray, but now ye are returned unto the shepherd and bishop of your souls." [p] And therefore we find in the Scripture, that Christ hath two pastoral staves, to note his great care and double office in his church. " The Lord is my shepherd, I shall not want—I will fear no evil, for thou art with me ; thy rod and thy staff they comfort me." [q]—" I took unto me two staves ; the one I called Beauty, and the other I called Bands; and I fed the flock." [r] So then, the rod of Christ's strength, or his strong staff, doth in these several relations note unto us three things : as it is a staff of strength, so it notes the power of Christ :—as it is the sceptre of a king, so it notes the majesty of Christ :—as it is the staff of a bishop or prophet, so it notes the care and superintendency of Christ over his church. So then this first particular of the rod of Christ's kingdom, affords unto us three observations : First, That Christ, in his gospel and spirit, is full of power and strength towards the church. Secondly, That Christ, in his gospel and spirit, is full of glory and majesty towards his church.

---

[i] Isai. xl. 11.   [k] Heb. xiii. 20.   [l] John x. 14.   [m] Psal. lxxviii. 71.
2 Sam. v. 2.   [n] Ezek. xxxiv. 23, 24.   [o] Jer. xxiii. 1, 4.   [p] 1 Pet. ii. 25.
[q] Psal. xxiii. 4.   [r] Zech. xi. 7.

Thirdly, That Christ in his gospel and spirit, is full of care, and of tenderness towards his church.

First, The word of the gospel with the Spirit is full of power and strength. No man will deny, that Christ, in his own person, is full of power. And as the power of a prince is principally seen in his laws, edicts, pardons, and gracious patents; so is the power of Christ wonderfully magnified towards the church in his gospel, which unto us is both a covenant of mercy, and a law of obedience. We may observe how Christ is frequently pleased to honour his gospel with his own titles and attributes. And therefore the apostle [s] speaks of him and his word, as of one and the same thing : " The word of God is quick and powerful, a discerner of the thoughts and intents of the heart; neither is there any creature which is not manifest in his sight; but all things are naked and open unto the eyes of him, with whom we have to do." That which is the ' Word' in one verse, is ' Christ himself' in another; which hath given occasion to some learned men to take the ' Word' there for the ' essential Word of God,' or ' the person' of Christ himself. We know, that Christ was crucified at Jerusalem ; and yet the apostle [t] saith, that he was crucified amongst the Galatians. Certainly, " in that he died, he died but once, unto sin." St. Paul could not do that himself, which he curseth others for doing, " Crucify again the Lord of glory." So then at Jerusalem he was crucified in his person, and, at Galatia, in the ministry of his word. One and the same crucifying, was as lively set forth in St. Paul's preaching, as it was really acted upon Christ's person : for Christ is as really present to his church now in the spiritual dispensation of his ordinances, as he was corporally present with the Jews in the days of his flesh. And therefore I say it is, that we find the same attributes given to both : " Christ the power of God, and the wisdom of God [u];" and the gospel elsewhere " the power of God [x]," and " the wisdom of God in a mystery [y]" to them that are perfect. Again, " Christ the Lord of glory [z]," and the gospel " the gospel of glory [a]," or the glorious gospel. " Christ the prince of life [b]," yea, " the word of life [c],"

s Heb. iv. 12, 13.   t Gal. ii. 1.   u 1 Cor. i. 24.   x Rom. i. 16.
y 1 Cor. ii. 6, 7.   z 1 Cor. ii. 8.   a 1 Tim. i. 11.   b Acts iii. 15.
c 1 John i. 1.

and the gospel " the word of life [d] " too. " Christ a judge [e]," and " the word of Christ a judge [f] " too ; " the word which I have spoken, the same shall judge you at the last day :"— Christ [g] a Saviour and salvation unto men ; " mine eyes have seen thy salvation :" and the gospel of Christ [h], ' a salvation' too ; " We know," saith Christ to the woman of Samaria, " what we worship, for salvation is of the Jews." The force of the reason leads us to understand by ' salvation,' the ' oracles of God,' which were committed unto that people ; for out of them only it is, that we know what and how to worship, and this is not unusual in holy Scriptures. " If the word [i]," saith the apostle, " spoken by angels, was steadfast, and every transgression and disobedience received a just recompense of reward ; how shall we escape, if we neg- lect so great salvation, which, at the first, began to be spoken by the Lord," &c. Where we find salvation set in opposition to the word spoken by angels, which was the law of God, or the ministry of condemnation,—and therefore it must needs signify the gospel of Christ. " Be it known unto you," saith the apostle [k] to the unbelieving Jews, " that the salvation of God," that is, the gospel of God (as appeareth plainly by the like parallel speech in another place [l]) " is sent unto the Gentiles, and that they will hear it." So the apostle [m] saith, that " the engraffed word is able to save the souls of men." All which, and many other the like particulars note unto us, that as Christ is the power and image of his Father, so the gospel is in some sort of Christ. For which reason the apostle, as I conceive, calleth the gos- pel, ' the face of Jesus Christ:'—" God who commanded the light to shine out of darkness, hath shined in our hearts, to give the light of the knowledge of the glory of God in the face of Jesus Christ." [n] Where is it that we behold " the glory of God but in a glass [o]?" and what is that glass, but " the word of God," as St. James calls it [p] ? Christ is not pleased any other ways ordinarily to exercise his power, or to reveal his glory, but in these ordinances of his which we dispense. Therefore he walketh in his church with ' a sword

[d] Phil. ii. 16.　　[e] John v. 27.　　[f] John xii. 48.　　[g] Luke i. 69, 77, and ii. 30. Isai. lxii. 11. Gen. xlix. 18.　　[h] John iv. 22.　　[i] Heb. ii. 2, 3. 2 Cor. iii. 9.　　[k] Acts xxviii. 28.　　[l] Acts xiii. 46.　　[m] James i. 21.　　[n] 2 Cor. iv. 6.　　[o] 2 Cor. iii. 18.　　[p] James i. 23.

in his mouth [q],' and with ' a rod in his mouth [r],'—to note
that he giveth no greater testification of his strength, than in
the ministry of his gospel;—which is therefore sometimes
called ' a sword [s],' ' a hammer [t],' ' a fire,' sometimes only ' a
savour of life and death [u],'—to note the mighty working
thereof, that can kill as well by a scent as by a wound, as
well by a breath as by a blow.

To consider this point a little more distinctly. This power
of the gospel of Christ appears in both these regards, as it is
a savour of life unto life, and as it is a savour of death unto
death,—towards his church who shall be saved, and towards
his enemies who shall perish. Many ways, is the gospel of
Christ, and his Spirit, a *rod of strength* unto his church.

First, In their calling and conversion from the power of
Satan unto God. Satan is a strong man [x]; and he is armed,
hath a whole panoply and full provision of military instruments, and (which is a great advantage) hath both the first
possession, and the full love of the hearts of men before
Christ attempts any thing upon them. And therefore that
which pulleth [y] a man from under the paw of such a lion, and
forceth him away from his own palace, must needs be much
stronger than he. And therefore the apostle [z] commendeth
the power of the Word by this argument, that it is a sword
fit to overcome " principalities, and powers, and rulers of
the darkness of this world, and spiritual wickedness in heavenly places."—Again, the old man in our nature is a strong
man too [a]; a reigning king, which setteth himself mightily
against the word and will of Christ, and cherisheth the disease against the remedy. And by that likewise the apostle
commendeth the power of the gospel, that it is " mighty,
through God, to the pulling down of strong holds, and imaginations or fleshly reasonings." When Christ stilled the
winds and the sea with but two words, " peace, be still,"
they were exceedingly amazed at his power, and said one to
another, " What manner of man is this, that even the winds
and the sea obey him [b]?" The conversion of a man is a far
greater work than the stilling of the sea; that will be some-

---

[q] Revel. i. 16.　　[r] Isai. xi. 4.　　[s] Eph. vi. 17.　　[t] Jer. xxiii. 29. Jer. v. 16.
[u] 2 Cor. ii. 16.　　[x] Luke xi. 20, 21. Eph. ii. 2.　　[y] 2 Tim. ii. 26.　　[z] Eph.
vi. 12, 17.　　[a] Ἀνδρεῖοί ἐσμεν καθ᾽ ἑαυτῶν, καὶ κατὰ τῆς ὑγείας ἡμῶν ἐπιστήμονες.
Greg. Naz. Orat. 1.　　[b] Mar. iv. 39. 41.

times calm of itself, when the fury of the wind ceaseth. The wicked indeed are like the sea, but not at any time ; but, " like a troubled sea, when it cannot rest."[c] The sea, we know, is subject unto several motions. An inward boiling and unquietness from itself, its ordinary fluxes and refluxes from the influence of the moon,—many casual agitations from the violence of the winds, and from its own waves, one wave precipitating, impelling, and repelling another : so are the hearts of wicked men, by the foaming, estuations, and excesses of natural concupiscence,—by the provisions and materials of sinful pleasures,—by the courses of the world, by the solicitations and impulsions of Satan,—by a world of hourly casualties and provocations so tempestuous, that they always cast out, upon the words and actions of men, mire and dirt. Now, in the dispensation of the word by the ministry of a weak man, Christ stilleth the raging of this sea, quells the lusts, correcteth the distempers, scattereth the temptations, worketh a smoothness and tranquillity of spirit in the soul of a man. Surely, when this is done, the soul cannot but stand amazed at its own recovery, and admire that wonderful and invisible power which could so suddenly rebuke such raging affections, and reduce them unto calmness and beauty again. " What ailed thee, O thou sea, that thou fleddest, and thou Jordan, that thou wert driven back ? ye mountains, that ye skipped like rams,—and ye little hills, like lambs [d]?" It is an expression of God's power towards his people in their triumphal entrance into the land of Canaan. We may apply it to the conquest and possession, which the Word takes of the souls of men. What ailed a man that he was driven back from his own channel, and made suddenly to forget his wonted course? what ailed those strong and mountainous lusts, which were as immovably settled upon the soul, as a hill upon his base, to fly away at the voice of a man like a frighted sheep? what ailed those smaller corruptions and intemperances, which haply had before lost their names, and were rather customs and infirmities, than sins, to fly away, like lambs, from the word of Christ? A man went into the church with a full tide and stream of lusts ; every thicket in his heart, every reasoning and imagination of his

---

c Isai. lvii. 20.   d Psalm cxiv. 5, 6.

soul, did before shelter whole flocks of evil affections : when
he came out, the tide was driven back, the stream turned, the
centre of his heart altered, his forest discovered, his lusts
scattered and subdued. What ails this man ? He hath but
heard an hour's discourse, the same which others hear, and
their tide riseth [e] the higher by it. Certainly these devils
were not cast out, these streams were not turned back, but by
the finger of God himself. When the minister of Christ
shall whisper in the ears of a dead man, whom no thunder
could have awakened, and he shall immediately rise up and
give glory to God ; when Christ shall call men to ' deny themselves,' — to get above themselves, — to ' hate father, and
mother, and wife, and children, and their own life,'—to ' sell
all that they have,'—to ' crucify, and be cruel to their own
members,'—to ' pull out their right eyes, to cut off their right
hands,' to part from those sins which before they esteemed
their choicest ornaments, and from those too, which, before,
they made their chiefest support and subsistence ; to stand
at defiance with the allurements or discouragements of the
world ; to be set up for signs and wonders, for very proverbs
of scorn, and objects of hatred to those of their own house ;
to receive persecutions as rewards, and entertain them not
with patience only, but with thankfulness and with rejoicing ;
to be all their life long in the midst of enemies, put to tedious
conflicts with the powers of the world and of darkness ; to
believe the things which they have not seen, and to hope for
things which they do not know ; and yet, maugre all this,
to refuse to consult with flesh and blood, to stand still more
in awe of God's word, than of any other thing ;—certainly
that which, with the voice of a weak man, bringeth such
great things to pass, must needs be ' virga virtutis,' a rod of
strength.   A rod like the rod of Moses, which can lead us
through such seas as these, to one whom we have never seen
nor known before [f].

Secondly, The gospel of Christ is a *rod of strength* in the
justification of men, as it is ' sceptrum justitiæ,' a sceptre of
righteousness [g]; a word of reconciliation [h]; a gospel of salvation [i]; a law of the Spirit of life [k]; a ministration of the
Spirit of life, and of righteousness [l]; an opening of prisons,

---

[e] Acts xvii. 32, 34.   [f] Isai. lv. 5.   [g] Heb. i. 8.   [h] 2 Cor. v. 19.
[i] Eph. i. 13.   [k] Rom. viii. 2, 3.   [l] 2 Cor. iii. 6, 8, 9.

and a proclaiming of liberty unto captives [m]; in these respects likewise it is full of power. There was a mighty power in the law of God, typified in those thunderings and terrors, with which it was administered upon Mount Sinai. The apostle calleth it 'a schoolmaster [n]' to scourge and drive us unto Christ,—and the psalmist 'an iron rod [o],' able to break in pieces all the potsherds of the earth. And we know boys in a school do not apprehend so much terror in the king, as in their master. Yet in comparison of the power of the gospel, the law itself was very "weak and unprofitable [p]," able to make nothing perfect. The power of the law was only to destruction; the power of the gospel, for edification. The law could only hold under him that was down before; it could never raise him up again. Now the power is far greater to raise than to kill,—to forgive sins than to bind them. Herein is the mighty "strength of God's mercy seen, that it can pass by iniquities, transgressions, and sins." [q] To preach the gospel of Christ in his name and authority [r], is an evident argument of that plenary power which is given unto him, both in heaven and earth. And the very dispensing of this word of reconciliation, which is committed unto the ministers of the gospel (how basely soever the ungrateful world may esteem of them), hath honoured them with a title of as great a power as a man is capable of, to be called 'Saviours [s],'—to have the custody of the keys of Heaven, ministerially and instrumentally under Christ and his Spirit, to save the souls, and to cover the sins of men. [t] Now then that word, which from the mouth of a weak man, is able to reconcile a child of wrath unto God, and, by the words of one hour, to cover and wipe out the sins of many years, which were scattered as thick in the souls of men as the stars in the firmament, must needs be 'virga virtutis,' *a rod of strength.*

Thirdly, The gospel of Christ is a *rod of strength* in the sanctification of men [u], as it is 'sceptrum cum unctione,' a sceptre which hath ever an unction accompanying it; as it is a sanctifying truth, a heavenly teaching [x], a forming of

---

m Isai. lxi. 1.   n Gal. iii. 24.   o Psal. ii. 9.   p Rom. viii. 3.
Heb. vii. 18, 19.   q Exod. xxxiv. 5, 6, 7. Mic. vii. 18, 19.   r Mat.
ix. 6. xxviii. 18, 19.   s Obad. v. 21.   t John xx. 23. 1 Tim. iv. 16.
James v. 20.   u John xvii. 17.   x Isai. liv. 13.

Christ in the soul[y]; a making of the heart[z], as it were, his epistle, by writing the law therein, and manifesting the power and image of Christ in the conscience. If a man should touch a marble or adamant stone with a seal, and taking it off, should see the print of it left behind, he could not but conceive some wonderful and secret virtue to have wrought so strange an effect. Now our hearts are, of themselves, as hard as the nether millstone: when then a holy word, so meekly and gently laid on upon them, shall leave there an impression of its own purity; when so small a thing as a grain of mustard-seed shall transform an earthy soul into its own nature; when the eyes, and hands, and mouth of Christ, being in the ministry of his word, spread upon the eyes, and hands, and mouth of a child, shall revive the same from death; when, by looking into a glass, we shall not only have a view of our own faces, but shall see them changed into the image of another face, which from thence shineth upon us,—how can we but conclude, that certainly that word, by which such wonders as these are effected, is indeed ' virga virtútis,' a *rod of strength.*

Fourthly, The gospel of Christ is a *rod of strength* in the preservation and perseverance of the saints, as it is 'virga germinans,' a rod like Aarons rod, which blossomed; and the blossoms perished not, but remained in the ark for a testimony of God's power. For as those buds, or the manna, in the ark did not perish, so neither doth the word of the gospel in the hearts of the faithful. The apostle[a] saith, that we are " kept by the power of God unto salvation;" and St. Jude[b], that " God's power keepeth the saints from falling, and presenteth them faultless before the presence of his glory." And what is this power of God whereby he doth it, but the gospel of Christ? which St. Peter calleth ' semen incorruptibile[c],' uncorruptible seed; and the Spirit of Christ, which St. John[d] calleth 'semen manens,' an abiding seed. If I should see a tree with perpetual fruit, without any variation from the difference of seasons,—a tree like that in St. John's paradise, which every month did bring forth fruit of twelve several kinds; I should conclude that it had an extraordi-

[y] Gal. iv. 19.　　[z] 2 Cor. iii. 2.　　[a] 1 Pet. i. 5.　　[b] Jude v. 24.
[c] 1 Pet. i. 24.　　[d] 1 John iii. 9.

nary vital power in it:—so when I find Christ in his word promising, and, by the planting and watering of his labourers in the vineyard, making good that promise unto his church, 'that every branch, bringing forth fruit' in him, shall not only be as Aaron's rod, have his fruit preserved upon him, but 'shall bring forth more fruit[e],' and shall have 'life more abundantly;' how can I but conclude, that the word which is the instrument of so unperishable a condition, is indeed ' virga virtutis,' a *rod of strength*, a rod cut out of the tree of life itself?

Fifthly, The gospel of Christ is a *rod of strength* in comforting and supporting of the faithful, as it is ' virga pulchritudinis et colligationis,' a rod of beauty and of binding ; as it is a word which doth bind that which was broken, and give unto them which mourn in Sion [f], beauty for ashes, and the garment of praise for the Spirit of heaviness: as it quencheth all the fiery darts, and answereth all the bloody reasonings of Satan against the soul, as it is a staff which giveth comfort and subsistence in the very valley of the shadow of death.[g] The 'shadow of death' is a usual expression in the Scripture for all fears, terrors, affrightments, or any dreadful calamities, either of soul or body. The whole misery of our natural condition is thereby signified.[h] Many ways doth the prophet David set forth the extremities he had been drawn unto: " My bones are vexed, and dried like a potsherd, and turned into the drought of summer ; my couch swimmeth with tears, mine eye is consumed and waxen old with grief. I am poured out like water; all my bones are out of joint ; my heart is like melted wax in the midst of my bowels. Thine arrows stick fast in me ; thine hand presseth me sore. There is no soundness in my flesh ; my wounds stink and are corrupt. I am feeble and sore broken; I have roared by reason of the disquietness of my heart. Innumerable evils compass me about, I am not able to look up. Fearfulness and trembling are come upon me, and horror hath overwhelmed me. My soul is amongst lions ; I lie amongst them that are set on fire. The waters are come in unto my soul, I sink in the deep mire ; the floods overflow me, &c." These all, and the like, are com-

e John xv. 2.   f Isai. lxi. 1, 3.   g Psal. xxiii. 4.   h Luke i. 79.

prehended in that one word, ' the shadow of death.' And
in that it was only the word, and the Spirit of God which
did support him: "This is my comfort in my affliction,"
saith he [i], "for thy word hath quickened me. When my
afflictions had brought me to the very brink and darkness of
the grave, thy word revived me again, and made me flourish.
Unless thy law had been my delight, I should have perished
in mine affliction."—Now then when I see a man, upon whom
so many heavy pressures do meet, the weight of sin, the
weight of God's heavy displeasure, the weight of a wounded
spirit, the weight of a decayed body, the weight of scorn
and temptations from Satan and the world,—in the midst of
all this, not to turn unto lying vanities, not to consult with
flesh and blood, nor to rely on the wisdom or help of man,
but to lean only on this word, to trust in it at all times [k], and
to cast all his expectations upon it, to make it his only rod
and staff, to comfort him in such sore extremities; how can I
but confess, that this word is indeed ' virga virtutis,' a *rod
of strength?*

Lastly, The gospel of Christ is a *rod of strength* in sanctifying and blessing of our temporal things ; as it is ' baculus
panis,' a staff of bread. "Man liveth not by bread alone,
but by the word which proceedeth out of God's mouth [l]; "
not by the creature, but by the blessing which prepareth
the creature for our use. Now it is the Word of God,
namely, his promises in Christ, of things concerning this
life, as well as that which is to come, that doth sanctify the
creatures of God [m], to those who with thankfulness receive
them. The fall of man brought a pollution upon the creatures, a curse upon the stone and timber of a man's house, a
snare upon his table, a poison and bitterness upon his meat,
distractions and terrors upon his bed, emptiness and vexation
upon all his estate ; which cleaves as fast thereunto, as
blackness to the skin of an Ethiopian, or sin to the soul of
man. For all the creatures of God are by sin mischievously
converted into the instruments and provisions of lust." :—the
sun and all the glorious lights of nature, but instruments to
serve the pride, covetousness, adultery, vanity of a lustful

---

[i] Psal. cxix. 50, 52.   [k] 2 Chron. xxxii. 8.   [l] Mat. iv. 4.   [m] 1 Tim.
iv. 5.   [n] Rom. xiii. 14. 1 John ii. 16.

eye: all the delicacies which the earth, air, or sea can
afford, but materials to feed the luxury and intemperance of
a lustful body:—all the honours and promotions of the
world, but fuel to satisfy the haughtiness and ambition of a
lustful heart. That Word then which can fetch out this leprosy from the creatures, and put life, strength, and comfort
into them again, must needs be 'virga virtutis,' a *rod of
strength.*

Secondly, The gospel and spirit of Christ, is a *rod of
strength,* in regard of his, and his church's enemies; able
both to repel, and to revenge all their injuries; to disappoint
the ends and machinations of Satan; to triumph and get
above the persecutions of men; to get a treasure which no
malice nor fury of the enemy can take away,—a nobleness of
mind, which no insultation of the adversary can abate,—a
security of condition, and calmness of spirit, which no
worldly tempests can any more extinguish than the darkness
of a cloud, or the boisterousness of a wind can blot out the
lustre, or perturb the order of celestial bodies; a heavenly
wisdom able to prevail against the gates of Hell, and to stop
the mouths of every gainsayer. The Word hath ever 'a
readiness to revenge disobedience [o],' as the apostle speaks;
it hardens the faces of men [p], and arms them, that they may
break [q] all those who fall upon them.

This power of the Word towards wicked men showeth
itself in many particulars : First, In a mighty work of conviction. The Spirit was therefore sent into the world, to
convince it by the ministry of the gospel; which one word
containeth the ground of the whole strength here spoken of;
for all, which the Word bringeth to pass, it doth it by the
conviction of the Spirit. This conviction is twofold: A conviction unto conversion, whereby the hearts of men are wonderfully over-ruled, by that invincible evidence of the Spirit
of truth, to feel and acknowledge their woful condition by
reason of sin, so long as they continue in unbelief,—to take
unto themselves the just shame and confusion of face which
belongs unto them,—to give unto God the glory of his
righteous and just severity, if he should destroy them,—and
hereupon to be, secondly, by the terror of the Lord per-

o 2 Cor. x. 6.   p Jer. i. 8, 9. vi. 27. Ezek. iii. 8, 9.   q Mat. xxi. 44.

suaded to count worthy of all acceptation any deliverance
out of that estate, which shall be tendered unto them ;—to
admire, adore, and greedily embrace, any terms of peace
and reconciliation which shall be offered them ;—to submit
unto the righteousness, and, with all willing and meek affection, to bend the heart to the sceptre of Christ, and to whatsoever form of judicature and spiritual government he shall
please to erect therein.　And this magnifies the strength of
this rod of Christ's kingdom, that it maketh men yield upon
any terms: When we see the little stone grow into a mighty
mountain, and eat into all the kingdoms of the world ; when
we see emperors and princes submit their necks and sceptres
to a doctrine, at first everywhere spoken against, and that
upon the words of a few despicable persons,—and that such
a doctrine too as is diametrically contrary to the natural constitution of the hearts of men, and teacheth nothing but self-
denial,—and this for hope of reward from one, whom they
never saw, and whom if they had seen, they should have
found, by a natural eye, no beauty in him, for which he
should be desired ; and this reward too, whatever it be, de-
ferred for a long time, and in the interim no ground of assurance to expect it, but only faith in himself that promiseth it,
and, in the mean time, a world of afflictions for his name
sake ;—How can we think that a world of wise and of great
men, should give ear most willingly unto such terms as these,
if there were not a demonstrative and constraining evidence
of truth and goodness therein, able to stop the mouths, and
to answer the objections of all gainsayers ?　Of this point,
I have spoken more copiously upon another Scripture.—Secondly, there is a conviction unto condemnation of those,
who stand out against this saving power of the gospel and
Spirit of grace, driving them from all their strong holds, and
constraining them perforce to acknowledge the truth which
they do not love.　Thus we find our Saviour[r] disputing with
the Jews, till no man was able to answer him a word : and
as he did so himself, so he promiseth that his messengers
should do so too ; " I will give you a mouth and wisdom,
which all your adversaries shall not be able to gainsay, nor
resist[s]."　And this promise we find made good : the ene-

mies of Stephen [t] were not able to resist the Spirit by which
he spake: and Apollos [u] mightily convinced the Jews, showing by the Scriptures that Jesus was Christ. And this the
apostle [x] numbereth amongst the qualifications of a bishop,
that he should be able, by sound doctrine, to convince the
gainsayers, and to stop the mouths of those unruly deceiv-
ers, whose business it is to subvert men: for this is the
excellent virtue of God's word, that " it concludeth [y]" or
shutteth men in, and leaveth not any gap or evasion of corrupted reason unanswered, or unprevented. Thus we find
how the prophets [z] in their ministry did still drive the Jews
from their shifts, and press them with dilemmas, the incon-
veniences whereof they could on no side escape:—either
there must be a fault in you, or else in God who rebuketh
you; but now, "What iniquity," saith the Lord, "have
your fathers found in me, that they are gone far from me?
Have I been a wilderness unto Israel, or a land of darkness?
Wherefore say my people, We are Lords, we will come no
more unto thee? O my people, what have I done unto
thee, and wherein have I wearied thee? testify against me [a].
I raised up of your sons for prophets, and of your young
men for Nazarites: Is it not even thus, O ye children of
Israel [b]?" Here the Scripture useth that figure which is
called by the rhetoricians ' communicatio,' a debating and
deliberating with the adverse party; an evidencing of a
cause so clearly, as that at last a man can challenge the
adversary himself to make such a determination, as himself
shall, in reason, judge the merit of the cause to require:
" How shall I pardon thee for this [c]?" and " How shall I do
for the daughter of my people [d]?" Set me in a way, determine the controversy yourselves; and I will stand to the
issue, which your own consciences shall make. " O inhabitants of Jerusalem, and men of Judah, judge, I pray you,
between me and my vineyard [e];" that is, do you yourselves
undertake the deciding of your own cause. When a band
of armed men came against Christ to attack him, and at
the pronouncing but of two words, *I am he* [f], fell all down
backward to the earth; we must needs confess, that there

[t] Acts vi. 10.   [u] Acts xviii. 28.   [x] Tit. i. 9, 11.   [y] Gal. iii. 22.
[z] Jer. xxv. 31.   [a] Micah vi. 3, 4.   [b] Amos ii. 11.   [c] Jer. v. 7.
[d] Jer. ix. 7.   [e] Isai. v. 3.   [f] John xviii. 6.

was some mighty power and evidence of majesty in him that uttered them. What, think we, can he do, when he reigneth and judgeth the world [g], who did let out so much power when he was to die and be judged by the world? Now Christ reigneth and judgeth the world by his word, and that more mightily after his ascending up on high; and therefore he promiseth his apostles, that they should do greater works [h] than he himself had done. When I shall see a man, —armed with scorn against Christ in his word, standing proudly upon the defence of his own ways, by his own wisdom, and wrapping up himself in the mud of his own carnal reasonings,—by a few postulata, and deductions from God's word, to be enforced to stop his own mouth [i], to be condemned [k] by his own witness, to betray his own succours, and to be shut up in a prison [l] without bars; when I shall force such a man, by the mighty penetration and invincible evidence of God's word, to see his own conscience a hand subscribing to the truth which condemns him, and belying all those delusions which he had framed to deceive himself withal; who can deny but that the rod of God's mouth is indeed ' virga virtutis,' *a rod of strength;* a rod of iron, able to deal with all human reasonings, as a hammer with a potsherd [m]? which though to the hand of a man it may feel as hard as a rock, yet it is too brittle to endure the blow of an iron rod. Strange it is to observe how boldly men venture on sins, under the names of custom, or fashions, or some other pretences of corrupted reason, contrary to the clear and literal evidence of holy Scripture: the most immediate and grammatical sense whereof is ever soundest, where there doth not some apparent and unavoidable error in doctrine, or mischief in manners, follow thereupon [n]. Men will justify the cause of the wicked for reward [o], and by dexterity of wit put a better colour upon a worse business, as hath been observed of Protagoras and Carneades [p]: and yet the Lord saith expressly, " Thou shalt not speak in a cause to

---

[g] Quid judicaturus faciat, qui judicandus hoc fecit? quid regnaturus poterit, qui moriturus hoc potuit? *Aug.* [h] John xiv. 12. [i] Luke xix. 22. [k] Tit. iii. 11. [l] Wis. xvii. 11, 16. [m] Jer. xix. 11. [n] *Aquin.* par. 1. qu. 1. art. 10. ad primum.—*Alphons. à Castro* contra Hæres. lib. 1. cap. 3.—*Glass.* Philog. Sacra, lib. 2, page 338.—*Hooker* lib. 5. sect. 59. [o] Isai. v. 23. Exod. xxiii. 2, 7. [p] Τὸν ἥττω λόγον κρείττω ποιῶν. *A. Gell.*

wrest judgement, thou shalt keep thee far from a false matter:" for God (whom thou oughtest to imitate) will not justify the wicked. Men will follow the sinful fashions of the world, in strange apparel, in prodigious hair, in lustful and unprofitable expense of that precious moment of time, upon the abuse or right improvement whereof dependeth the several issues of their eternal condition; though the Lord say expressly, "Be not conformed to this world [q]: they that walk according to the course of the world, walk according to the prince of the power of the air [r]." "The Lord will punish all such as are clothed with strange apparel," who take up the fashions of idolaters, or any other nation, or other sexes (as that place is differently expounded [s]). Nature [t] itself teacheth, that it is a shame for a man to wear long hair. Nay, nature itself taught that honest heathen to stand at defiance with the sins of his age, and not comply with the course of the world, upon that slight apology, as if the commonness [u] had taken away the illness; and that which, committed by one [x], would have been a sin,—being imitated after a multitude, were but a fashion. To conclude this particular: the apostle is peremptory, "Neither fornicators, nor idolaters, nor effeminate, nor covetous, nor thieves, nor drunkards, nor revilers, nor extortioners shall inherit the kingdom of God [y]:" and the consciences of many men, who yet will never yield to the conclusion, cannot choose but subsume, as the apostle goes on, "such are some of us;" nay, and such we will be too. But now if we should bespeak these men in the word of the prophet [z], "Produce your cause, saith the Lord, bring forth your strong reasons, saith the King of Jacob,"—they should find at the last their reasons to be like themselves, vanity, and lighter than nothing; that the Word of the Lord will at last prevail, and sweep away all their refuge of lies [a].

Secondly, The power of the Word towards wicked men is seen in affrighting of them: there is a spirit of bondage, and a savour of death [b], as well as a spirit of life and liberty,

q Rom. xii. 2.   r Ephes. ii. 2,   s Zeph. i. 8. *Hieron. Theodoret. Ribera.*
t 1 Cor. xi. 14.   u Nec virtutem aut vitium seculum vocavit. *Tacit.* in Agric.
x Homicidium cum admittunt singuli, crimen est; virtus vocatur, cum publice geritur. *Cypr.* 1. 2. Ep. 2.   y 1 Cor. vi. 9.   z Isal. xli. 21.   a Isai. xxviii. 17.   b 2 Cor. ii. 16.

which goeth along with the Word. Guilt is an inseparable
consequent of sin,—and fear, of the manifestation of guilt.
If the heart be once convinced of this, it will presently faint
and tremble, even at the shaking of a leaf[c], at the wagging
of a man's own conscience: how much more at the voice
of the Lord, which shaketh mountains, and maketh the
strong foundations of the earth to tremble ! If I should see
a prisoner at the bar pass sentence upon his judge ; and the
judge thereupon surprised with trembling, and forced to
subscribe and acknowledge the doom, I could not but stand
amazed at so inverted a proceeding: yet in the Scripture
we find precedents for it; Micaiah [d], a prisoner, pronouncing
death unto Ahab, a king: Jeremiah, a prisoner [e], pronouncing
captivity unto Zedekiah, a king : Paul, in his chains [f], preaching of judgement unto Felix in his robes, and making his
own judge to tremble. It is not for want of strength in the
Word,—or because there is stoutness in the hearts of men to
stand out against it,—that all the wicked of the world do not
tremble at it ; but merely their ignorance of the power and
evidence thereof. The devils are stronger and more stubborn creatures than any man can be; yet because of their
full illumination, and that invincible conviction of their
consciences from the power of the Word, they believe and
tremble at it [g]. Though men were as hard as rocks, the
Word is a hammer [h] which can break them: though as sharp
as thorns and briers [i], the Word is a fire [k] which can devour
and torment them: though as strong as kingdoms and nations, the Word is able to root them up [l], and to pull them
down: though as fierce as dragons and lions [m], the Word is
able to trample upon them, and chain them up.

Thirdly, The power of the Word is seen towards wicked
men, in that it doth judge them. " Son of man, wilt thou
judge, wilt thou judge the bloody city ?" saith the Lord: [n]
" Yea, thou shalt show them their abominations :"—to note,
that when wicked men are made to see their filthiness in the
Word, they have thereby the wrath of God, as it were, sealed
upon them. " He that rejecteth me, the Word which I have

c Levit. xxvi. 36.   d 1 Kings xxii. 27, 28.   e Jer. xxxvii. 16, 17.
f Acts xxiv. 25.   g Jam. ii. 19.   h Jer. xxiii. 29.   i Ezek. ii. 6.
k Jer. v. 14. Deut. xxxiii. 2.   l Jer. i. 10.   m Psalm xci. 13.   n Ezek.
xxii. 2.

spoken, the same shall judge him at the last day," saith our Saviour.[o] And " if all prophesy," saith the apostle [p], " and there come in one that believeth not, or one unlearned, he is *convinced* of all, he is *judged* of all, and the secrets of his heart are made manifest." Nay, the Word doth, in some sort, execute death and judgement upon wicked men: therefore it is said, that " The Lord would smite the earth with the rod of his mouth, and with the breath of his lips would slay the wicked [q] :" and again, " I have hewed them by the prophets, I have slain them by the words of my mouth [r]." And therefore the word of the Lord is called " *fury*" by the prophet [s], to note, that when wrath and fury is poured out upon a land, they are the effects of God's word. If a pestilence devour a city, and a sword come and glean after it, it is the Word only which slays; they are but the instruments, which are, as it were, actuated and applied by the word of God to their several services. Therefore it is that the prophet [t] saith, that wise men " see the voice of God, and hear his rod." A rod is properly to be seen, and a voice to be heard; but here is a transposition, and, as it were, a communication of properties between the word of God and his punishments; to note, that towards wicked men there is a judging, and tormenting virtue in the Word; " For judgement," saith our Saviour [u], " am I come into the world, that they which see not, might see, and that they which see, might be made blind." If it be here objected that Christ saith of himself [x], " The Son of Man is not come to destroy men's lives, but to save them ; and that he came not to condemn the world, but that the world through him might be saved;" I answer, that there are two events of Christ's coming, and by consequence, of his gospel :—the one principal, and by him intended ; the other accidental and occasional, growing out of the ill disposition of the subject unto whom he was sent. The main and essential business of the gospel, is to declare salvation, and to set open unto men a door of escape from the wrath to come : but when men willingly stand out, and neglect so great salvation, then, secondarily, doth Christ prove unto those men a stone of offence, and

---

o John xii. 48.   p 1 Cor. xiv. 24.   q Isai. xi. 8.   r Hosea vi. 5.
s Jer. vi. 11.   t Micah vi. 9.   u John ix. 30.   x Luke vi. 5

the gospel a savour of death unto death; as that potion which was intended for a cure by the physician, may, upon occasion of the indisposedness of the body, and stubborn radication of the disease, hasten a man's end sooner than the disease itself would have done: so that, to the wicked, the Word of God is a two-edged sword indeed, an edge in the law, and an edge in the gospel. They are on every side beset with condemnation; if they go to the law, that cannot save them; because they have broken it: if they go to the gospel, that will not save them, because they have contemned it.

Fourthly, The power of the Word towards wicked men is seen in this, that it doth ripen their sins, and make them so much the more sinful, and so much the sooner fill up their measure. " If I had not come," saith Christ ʸ, " and spoken unto them, they had had no sin; but now they have no cloak for their sin." A tree which is fastened unto a wall, in which the heat of the sun is more permanent and united, will bring forth ripe fruit before the ordinary season: so a people upon whom the light of the gospel hath constantly shined, and which doth often drink in the rain which falleth upon it, must needs bring forth summer-fruit ᶻ, sins speedily ripe, and therefore be so much nearer unto cursing. There is but a year between such a tree and the fire ᵃ. We shall never find, that the sins of Israel and of Judah (for which they were at any time plagued with captivity) were so long in ripeness as the sins of the Canaanites, upon whom there did no light shine. The land had rest sometimes forty years: but we never find, that they were suffered to provoke the Lord to his face four hundred years together. We find, when to Nineveh he sent a prophet to reveal unto them the guilt and merit of their sins, he then set them a very short time, in which they should either forsake or ripen them, " Yet forty days and Nineveh shall be destroyed."

Fifthly, The power of the engraffed Word towards wicked men is seen even in the rage and madness, which it excites in them. It is a sign that a man hath to do with a strong enemy, when he buckleth on all his harness, and calleth together all his strength for opposition. When I see a river without any sensible noise or motion, I am ready to esteem it a

standing pool; but when I look further, and there observe
what huge engines it carries about, and what weighty bodies
it rolleth before it,—I then believe a strength in it which I
did not see: So when I see the word of Christ rouse up the
rage and lusts of men, and force them to set up against it
strong holds and high imagination, even the wisdom and
strength of the gates of hell to keep it out; I must needs
then conclude that it is indeed ' virga virtutis,' *a rod of
strength.* The most calm and devout hypocrites in the
world have, by the power of this word, been put out of
their demure temper, and mightily transported with outrage
and bitterness against the majesty thereof. One time, filled
with wrath b; another time, filled with madness c; another
time, filled with envy and indignation d; another time, filled
with contradiction and blasphemy; another time, cut to the
heart, and, like reprobates in hell, gnashing with their
teeth e;—such a searching power, and such an extreme con-
trariety there is in the gospel to the lusts of men, that if it
do not subdue, it will wonderfully swell them up f,—till it
distemper even the grave, prudent men of the world with
those brutish and uncomely affections of rage and fury,
and drive disputers from their arguments unto stones.g Sin
cannot endure to be disquieted, much less to be shut in and
encompassed with the curses of God's word. Therefore as a
hunted beast, in an extremity of distress, will turn back, and
put to its utmost strength to be revenged on the pursuers,
and to save its life; so wicked men to save their lusts will
let out all their rage, and open all their sluices of pride and
malice, to withstand that holy truth which doth so closely
pursue them. Thus as beggarly masters deal with their servants, or bankrupts with their creditors,—when they should
pay them their money (which they are unable to do), they
then pick quarrels, and create pretences to withhold it; or
as froward men, in suits of law, when their cause fails, endeavour to piece it out with rage and passion;—so do wicked
men deal with God in his word, when they should pay him
that service which he therein requireth of them, and which
they have neither will nor power to do, when he produceth

b Luke iv. 28. e Luke vi. 11. d Acts v. 17. xiii. 45. e Acts vii. 54.
f Acts vi. 10, 11. vii. 57, 58. g John viii. 59.

his cause, and entereth into controversy with them, convincing them in the court of their own consciences, so that they are not able to stand out,—they have then no other refuge left, but either to submit (which they will in no wise endure) or to fly into the face of the Word, and withstand it with malice, when they cannot with reason. Till men can be persuaded to lay apart all filthiness and superfluity of naughtiness, they will never receive the engraffed word[h] with meekness. For till then it is a binding word[i], which sealeth their guilt and condemnation upon them.

Lastly, The mighty power of the Word towards wicked men is seen in altering them : in their semipersuasions and semiconversions unto goodness, in restraining them from those lusts which they dearly love, and in forcing them to those external conformities, which have no inward principles to support them. The humiliation of Ahab[k], the observation of Herod[l], the incomplete persuasion of Agrippa[m], the forced obedience and flatteries of the dissembling Jews, the essays and offers of hypocrites towards religion, the velleities and hankerings of unresolved[n] wills after Christ, are notable evidences of the power and majesty which is in the gospel. If I should see a millstone in the air, not falling constantly and swiftly down, but swag and waver, and float about in a kind of unresolved motion, as if it were in a deliberation which way to go, one while yielding to its own weight, another while lingering, and by fits attempting to ascend,—how could I sufficiently wonder at that secret virtue, and those strange impressions which did retardate the natural descent of so weighty a body ? So when I see men, who still retain the principles of their own corrupt nature, which carry them with as strong an impulsion to sin and Hell, as a millstone is moved unto its centre, hanker notwithstanding after goodness,—and, when they yield unto their lusts, do it not without much hesitancy and conflict of a natural conscience; I must needs acknowledge a mighty strength in that Word, which setteth bounds to the raging of so proud a sea.

From hence then the messengers of Christ, who are entrusted with the dispensation of this *rod of strength*, may be instructed how to behave themselves in that ministry. Few

---

[h] James i. 21.   [i] Mat. xviii. 18. Mark xvi. 16.   [k] 1 Kings xxi. 27.
[l] Mark vi. 20.   [m] Acts xxvi. 28.   [n] Psalm lxxviii. 34, 36.   Luke ix. 57, 61.

men will lose any thing of that power which is given them; for every thing, in its kind, doth affect power. Now Christ, hath committed unto us the custody of his own power; and therefore we ought to manage it as "a word of power," able alone by itself, without the contemperations of human fancies, or the superstruction of human opinions, to work mightily to the salvation of those that believe, and to the conviction of gainsayers. Our commission is to charge even the great men of the world.[o] It is true, the ministers of the gospel are "servants[p]" to the church: in compassion, to pity the diseases, the infirmities, the temptations, of God's people; in ministry, to assist them with all needful supplies of comfort, or instruction, or exhortation in rightcousness; in humility, to wait upon men of lowest degree, and to condescend unto men of weakest capacity. And thus the very angels in Heaven are servants to the church of Christ. But yet we are servants only for the church's good,—to serve their souls, not to serve their humours. And therefore we are such servants as may command too. "These things *command*[q] and *teach;* let no man despise thy youth."

And again, "These things speak and rebuke with all authority, let no man despise thee[r]." No ministers are more despicable than those who, by ignorance, or flattery, or any base and ambitious affections, betray the power and majestical simplicity of the gospel of Christ. When we deliver God's message, we must not then be the servants of men.[s] "If I yet please men, I were not then the servant of Christ," saith the apostle. To captivate the truth of God unto the humours of men, and to make the Spirit of Christ in his gospel to bend, comply, and compliment with human lusts,—is, with Jonah, to play the runagates from our office, and to prostrate the sceptre of Christ unto the insultation of men. There is a wonderful majesty and authority in the Word, when it is set on with Christ's spirit. He taught men ὡς ἐξουσίαν ἔχων, as one who had power[t] and authority, or privilege to speak; as one that cared not for the persons[u] of men. And, therefore, wherever his Spirit is, there will this power[x] and liberty[y] of Christ appear: for he hath given it to his minis-

[o] 1 Tim. vi. 17. [p] 2 Cor. iv. 5. [q] 1 Tim. iv. 11, 12. [r] Tit. ii. 15.
[s] 1 Cor. vii. 23. [t] Matth. vii. 29. [u] Matth. xxii. 16. [x] 1 Cor. ii. 4.
[y] 2 Cor. iii. 17.

ters [z], that they may commend themselves in the consciences [a] of those that hear them,—that they may harden their faces [b] against the pride and scorn of men,—that they may go out in armies against the enemies [c] of his kingdom,—that they may speak boldly [d] as they ought to speak,—that they may not suffer his Word to be bound, or his Spirit to be straitened, by the humours of men.

Again; We should all labour to receive the Word in the power thereof, and to expose our tender parts unto it. A cock is in comparison but a weak creature: and yet the crowing of a cock will cause the trembling of a lion. What is a bee to a bear, or a mouse to an elephant? and yet if a bee fasten his sting in the nose of a bear, or a mouse creep up and gnaw the trunk of an elephant; how easily do so little creatures, upon such an advantage, torment the greatest! Certainly the proudest of men have some tender part, into which a sting may enter. The conscience is as sensible of God's displeasure, as obnoxious to his wrath, as subject to his word in a prince, as in a beggar. If the Word, like David's stone, find that open, and get into it,—it is able to sink the greatest Goliah. Therefore, we should open our consciences unto that word, and expect his Spirit to come along with it, and receive it, as Josiah did, ' with humility and trembling.' We should learn to fear the Lord in his word, and, when his voice crieth in the city, to see his name and his power therein. " Will ye not fear me? saith the Lord ; [e] will ye not tremble at my presence, who make the sand a bound to the sea ?" No creature so swelling, and of itself so strong and encroaching as the sea; nothing so small, weak, smooth, and passable as the sand ; and yet the sand, a creature so easily removed and swept away, decreed to hold in so raging an element. What, in appearance, weaker than words spoken by a despised man ? and what, in the experience of all the world, stronger than the raging of an army of lusts ? and yet that hath the Lord appointed to tame and subdue these, that men might learn to fear his power.

Again; It should teach us to rest upon God in all things, as being unto us all-sufficient, a sun, a shield, an exceeding great reward in the truth and promises of his gospel. The

[z] 2 Cor. xiii. 10.   [a] 2 Cor. iv. 2.   [b] Jer. i. 6, 7, 8. Ezek. iii. 8, 9.
[c] Psalm cx. 3.   [d] Ephes. vi. 20.   [e] Jer. v. 22.

word of God is a sure thing [f], that which a man may cast [g] his whole weight upon, and lean confidently on in any extremity.[h] All the creatures in the world are full of vanity, uncertainties, and disappointments ; and then usually do deceive a man most, when he most of all relies upon them. And, therefore, the apostle chargeth us ' not to trust' in them.[i] But the word of the Lord is ' an abiding word,' as being founded upon the immutability of God's own truth. He that maketh it his refuge, relieth on God's omnipotency, and hath all the strength of the Almighty engaged to help him. Asa [k] was safe while he depended on the Lord, in his promises, against the hugest host of men that was ever read of: but when he turned aside to collateral aids, he purchased to himself nothing but perpetual wars. And this was that which established the throne of Jehoshaphat, and caused " the fear of the Lord to fall upon the kingdoms of the lands which were round about him [l] ;" because he honoured the word of God, and caused it to be taught unto his people. Whensoever Israel and Judah did forget to lean upon God's word, and betook themselves to human confederacies, to correspondence with idolatrous people, to facility in superstitious compliances, and the like fleshly counsels ; they found them always to be but very lies, like waxen and wooden feasts, made specious, of purpose to delude ignorant comers; things of so thin and unsolid a consistence, as were ever broken with the weight of those who did lean upon them. Let us not, therefore, rest upon our own wisdom, nor build our hopes or securities upon human foundations ; but let us, in all conditions, " take hold of God's covenant [m]," of this staff of his strength, which is able to stay us up in any extremities.

Again ; Since the gospel is a word of such sovereign power, as to strengthen us against all enemies and temptations, to uphold us in all our ways and callings, to make us strong in the grace of Christ (for ever a Christian man's knowledge of the Word, is the measure of his strength and comfort) ; we should therefore labour to acquaint ourselves with God in his word, to hide it in our hearts, and grow rich in the knowledge of it. In Heaven, our blessedness shall consist in

f Psalm xix. 7.   g 2 Pet. i. 19.   h Acts xiii. 34.   i 1 Tim. vi. 17.
k 2 Chron. xvi. 8, 9.   l 2 Chron. xvii. 9, 10.   m Isai. lvi. 2, 4, 6.

the knowledge and communion with the Father, and with his Son Jesus Christ. So that the gospel and the Spirit, are, to us upon earth, the preludes and supplies of Heaven; for by them only, is this knowledge and communion begun. And that man doth but delude himself, and lie to the world, who professeth his desire to go to Heaven, and doth not here desire to know so much of God, as he is pleased to afford to men on the earth. The gospel is the patent and charter of a Christian; all that he hath to show for his salvation; the treasure of his wealth and privileges; all that he hath to boast in, either for this life or another; the armoury of a Christian, all that he hath to hold up against the temptations and conflicts of his sorest enemies; the only tool and instrument of a Christian, all that he hath to do any action of piety, charity, loyalty, or sobriety withal; the only glass of a Christian wherein he may see his own face, and so learn to deny himself, and wherein he may see the face of God in Christ, and so learn to desire and to follow him. So that upon the matter, for any man to be ignorant of the gospel, is to unchristian himself again, and to degenerate into a heathen. " Pour out thine indignation upon the heathen, that *know thee not* [n]." Ignorance makes a man a very heathen. " This I say and testify," saith the apostle [o], " that ye henceforth walk not as other Gentiles walk in the vanity of their mind:—for you have not so learned Christ." It is not the title, nor the profession which maketh a man a real Christian, and distinguisheth him from other heathen men; but the learning of Christ in his Spirit and gospel. For as he [p] who was only outwardly, and in the flesh a Jew, might be uncircumcised in his heart; so he who is only in title and name a Christian, may be a heathen in his heart: and that more fearfully than Sodom and Gomorrah, or Tyre and Sidon, because he hath put from himself the salvation of the Lord, and judged himself unworthy of eternal life.

Lastly; If there be indeed such power in the gospel, we should labour to bear witness unto the testimony which God giveth of his Word, in a holy conversation. It is a reproach cast upon the ordinances of God, when men do, in their lives, deny that virtue, which God testifieth to be in them.

n Jer. x. 25.   o Ephes. iv. 17, 20.   p Rom. ii. 28, 29. Col. ii. 11.
Philip. iii. 3.

Wicked men are said to ' crucify Christ again,' to ' put him
to shame,' to ' make him a liar :' not that these things can
so really be, but because men, in their evil lives, carry
themselves, as if indeed they were so. And, in this sense,
the gospel may be said to be weak too; because the
pride of men holds out against the saving power thereof.
But these men must know, that the Word returneth not
empty unto God, but accomplisheth some work or other;
either it ripeneth weeds or corn. There is thunder and
lightning both in the Word : if the one break not a heart,
the other will blast it; if it be not humbled by the Word,
it will certainly be withered, and made fruitless. Shall the
clay boast itself against the fire, because, though it have
power to melt wax, yet it hath not power to melt clay ? Is
it not one and the same power which hardeneth the one, and
which softeneth the other ? Is not the Word a sweet savour
unto God, as well in those that perish, as in those that are
saved ? Certainly there is as wonderful a power in adding
another death to him who was dead before (which, upon the
matter, is to kill a dead man), as in multiplying and enlarging life. And the gospel is to those that perish, ' a savour
of death unto death ;' such a word as doth accumulate the
damnation of wicked men, and treasure up wrath upon wrath.
If it do not convert, it will certainly harden ; if it do not
save, it will undoubtedly judge and condemn. The Lord
doth never cast away his Gospel. He that gave charge to
gather up the broken meat of loaves and fishes, that nothing
might be lost, will not suffer any crumb of his spiritual manna
to come to nothing. Yet we find the Lord giveth a charge
to his prophets [q] to preach even there where he foretold them,
that their words would not be heard: " Thou shalt speak all
these words unto them, but they will not hearken to thee ;
thou shalt also call unto them, but they will not answer thee.
Son of man, I send thee to the children of Israel, to a rebellious nation; they are impudent children, and stiff-hearted.
Yet thou shalt speak my words unto them, whether they will
hear, or whether they will forbear, for they are rebellion itself.
They will not hearken unto thee, for they will not hearken
unto me ; for all the house of Israel are impudent and hard-

[q] Jer. vii. 27. Ezek. ii. 3, 4, 7, and iii. 7.

hearted."—Certainly, when the Lord taketh pains by his prophets, to call those who will not hear, he doth it not in vain; they shall know at length, that a prophet hath been amongst them.   Therefore as the apostle saith, that "The gospel is a sweet savour even in those that perish;" so we find those messages which have contained nothing but curses against an obstinate people, have yet been as honey for sweetness in the mouth of those that preached them.   I did eat the roll, saith the prophet [r] "and it was in my mouth as honey for sweetness;"—and yet there was nothing in it written but lamentations, and mourning, and woe.   Jeremy [s] did not desire the woful day, but did heartily say Amen to the false prophets, in their predictions of safety; yet in regard of his ready service unto God, and of that glory which God would work out unto himself into the punishment of that sinful people, the word of prophecy which was committed unto him, was the joy and rejoicing of his heart:—so that in all respects, the gospel of Christ is a word of power, and therein we do and must rejoice.

We observed before, that this *rod of strength* is both ' sceptrum majestatis,' and 'pedum pastorale;' both the sceptre of Christ as he is a king, and his pastoral staff as he is a bishop. It denoteth the administration of Christ's kingdom, which consisteth in the dispensing of his gospel, as it is a word of majesty, and of care.   So then here are (as I before observed) two observations, yet remaining to be noted out of these words, ' virga virtutis,' the *rod of thy strength.*

The first, That the gospel of Christ, accompanied with his Spirit, is a word of great glory and majesty.   For we must ever make these concomitants, "We preach the gospel," saith St. Peter, " with the Holy Ghost sent down from Heaven[t]."   And indeed the Spirit is peculiar to the gospel, and not belonging to the law at all, if we consider it alone by itself, under the relation of a distinct covenant.   For though as it proceedeth out of Sion [u], that is, as it is an appendix and additament unto the gospel, it tends unto liberty, and so cometh not without the Spirit; yet, by itself, it gendereth nothing but bondage [x].   And therefore when the apostle [y] showeth the excellency of the gospel above the law, he

---

[r] Ezek. iii. 2, 10.   [s] Jer. xvii. 16, xxviii. 6, and xv. 16.   [t] 1 Pet. i. 12.
[u] Micah. iv. 2.   [x] Rom. viii. 3. Jam. i. 25. Gal. iv. 24.   [y] 2 Cor. iii. 6, 7.

calleth the one ' a ministration of death, and of the letter,'
the other ' a ministration of the Spirit and life ;'—to show
that, properly, the Spirit belongeth unto the gospel of
grace.   Now then this spiritual gospel of Christ is the sceptre of his kingdom ; and therefore as it is ' insigne regium,'
an ensign of royalty, it importeth glory and majesty.   It is
a gospel full of glory : we may observe that the very typical
prefigurations of that mercy, which is the sole business of
the gospel of Christ, are in the Scriptures honoured with the
name of ' glory.'   The garments of the priests [z], being types
of the evangelical righteousness of the saints, were made for
glory and beauty.   The tabernacle which was ordained for an
evidence and seal of God's evangelical presence with that
people, is called, by the prophet David [a], a tabernacle of *honour ;* the place which God did use to fill with his own glory.
The ark of God, which was nothing else but ' evangelium
sub velo,' the gospel under veils and shadows, is called, by
excellency, the *glory* [b] of Israel ;—which is the attribute of
Christ " All kings shall see thy *glory* [c]."   The temple at
Jerusalem was the place of God's *rest* [d] ; " This is my rest
for ever, here will I dwell.—Arise, O Lord God, into thy resting place, thou and the ark of thy strength."   It was so
called, to note, first, the stability of God's evangelical covenant in Christ : it was not to be changed [e], nor to be repented of, but to be sure and fixed [f] in Christ for ever : his
kingdom, a kingdom which was not to be shaken [g] ; his priesthood, a priesthood [h] which was not to pass away ; his teaching, a teaching which was to continue to the world's end [i].
And secondly, to note the delight of God in Christ [k], and
in the mercy which through him was unto the world revealed ; therein the Lord resteth and reposeth himself, as in
the crown and accomplishment of all his works.   And this
temple is called a glorious rest [l], a glorious high throne, [m] a
house of glory [n], of beauty [o], and of holiness [p].   It is said at
the first dedication thereof, that " The glory of the Lord filled
it."   It was not the gold or silver (wherewith, before that de-

[z] Rev. vi. 11. vii. 14, xix. 8. Exod. xxviii. 2, 40.   [a] Psalm xxvi. 8. Exod.
xl. 34.   [b] 1 Sam. iv. 22.   [c] Isai. lxii. 2.   [d] Psalm cxxxii. 8, 14. 2 Chron. vi. 41.
[e] Isai. liv. 9, 10.   [f] Heb. viii. 13.   [g] Heb. xii. 28.   [h] Heb. vii. 24.   [i] Matth.
xxviii. 20, and iii. 17.   [k] Jer. ix. 24. Mic. vii. 18.   [l] Isai. xi. 10.   [m] Jer.
xvii. 12.   [n] Isai. lx. 7.   [o] Isai. lxiv. 11.   [p] 1 Kings viii. 11.

dication, it was beautified) wherein the glory thereof did consist, but in the evidence of God's presence; which, at that time, was but a cloud, whereas the true glory thereof, himself, was a sun, as the prophet q calls him.   And with this did the Lord fill the second temple, which, for this cause, is said to have been " more glorious than the former r," though, in the magnificence of the structure, far inferior.   Now then, as the apostle s, in a case of just alike proportion, useth a πόσω μᾶλλον, a term of excess, when he speaketh of the substance in comparison of the type; " If the blood of bulls and goats did sanctify to the purifying of the flesh, *how much more* shall the blood of Christ?" so may we in this case,—If the types of evangelical things were thus glorious, *how much more* glorious must the gospel itself needs be? And therefore, as I before observed in other things, so in this is it true likewise,—that Christ and his gospel have the same attributes of glory frequently given unto them.   Christ is called ' the glory of the Lord t, and of his people Israel u :' and the gospel ' a glorious mystery x,' a ' royal law y,' ' a ministration of glory z :' nay ' glory itself a ;' for so I understand that place of the apostle, that " ye would walk worthy of God, who hath called you unto his kingdom and glory," that is, unto the knowledge of his gospel ; for of that in all the antecedent parts, and in the verse immediately following, doth the apostle speak :—a glory, which draweth the study and amazement of the most glorious b creatures of God unto it.

To consider this point more particularly : The glory and majesty of the gospel of Christ appeareth principally in four things : in the author of it : in the promulgation and publishing of it : In the matter which it contains ; and in the ends, purposes, or uses, for which it serves.

First, In the author of it ; Many things of small worth, have yet grown famous by the authors of them, and, like the unprofitable children of renowned progenitors, hold their estimation and nobility from the parents which begat them. And yet from men who are unclean, there will ever descend some uncleanness upon the works which they do.   But the

---

q Mal. iv. 2.   r Hag. ii. 7, 9.   s Heb. ix. 13, 14.   t Isai. xl. 5, and lxvi. 18.   u Luke ii. 32.   x Col. i. 27.   y James ii. 8.   z 2 Cor. iii. 8, 9.   a 1 Thes. ii. 12.   b 1 Pet. i. 12.

gospel is therefore indeed a glorious gospel, because it is ' the gospel of the blessed God.' There is glory in all the works of God, because they are his; for it is impossible that so great a workman should ever put his hand to an ignoble work. And, therefore, the prophet David useth his ' glory ' and his ' handy-work,' promiscuously for the same thing; " The heavens declare the glory of God, and the firmament showeth his handy-work ;"—to note, that there is an evidence of glory in any thing which he puts his hand unto. And yet the prophet there showeth, that there is more glory in the law of his mouth, than in the works of his hands : " The Lord is better known by Sion, and his name greater in Israel," than in all the world besides : the more God doth communicate himself unto any of his works, the more glorious it is. Now there is nothing wherein God hath so much put himself, wherein he may be so fully known, communicated with, de-pended upon, and praised,—as in his gospel. This is a glass, in which the blessed angels do see and admire the unsearch-able riches of his mercy to the church, which they had not, by their own observation, found out from the immediate view of his glorious presence. In the creatures, we have him a God of power and wisdom,—working all things in number, weight and measure, by the secret vigour of his providence,—upholding that being which he gave them, and ordering them to those glorious ends for which he gave it. In the law, we have him a God of vengeance and of recompense,—in the publication thereof threatening, and in the execution thereof inflicting, wrath upon those that transgress it. But, in the gospel, we have him a God of bounty and endless com-passion ; humbling himself, that he might be merciful to his enemies,—that he might himself bear the punishments of those injuries which had been done unto himself,—that he might not offer only but beseech his own prisoners to be par-doned and reconciled again. In the creature, he is a God above us; in the law, he is a God against us ; only in the gospel he is ' Emmanuel, a God with us,' a God like us, a God for us.

There is nothing doth declare God so much to be God, as his mercy in the gospel. He is invisible in himself; we can-not see him but in his Son. He is unapproachable in him-self; we cannot come unto him but by the Son. Therefore

when he maketh himself known in his glory to Moses, he
sendeth him not to the creation, nor to Mount Sinai, but
putteth him ' into a rock' (being a resemblance of Christ)
and then maketh a proclamation of the gospel unto him.
Moses' prayer was, " I beseech thee, show me thy glory."
How doth the Lord grant this prayer? " I will make all my
goodness to pass before thee ;"—and then revealeth himself
unto him almost all by mercy :—" The Lord, the Lord God,
merciful and gracious, long-suffering, and abundant in goodness and truth, keeping mercy for thousands, forgiving iniquity, transgression, and sin [c];" to note unto us, that the
glory of God is in nothing so much revealed, as in his goodness. " Who is a God like unto thee, that pardoneth iniquity, and passeth by the transgression of the remnant of
his people [d]?"

Besides ; Though the law be indeed from God, as from the
author of it, so that, in that respect, there may seem to be
no difference of excellency between that and the gospel ; yet
we must observe that, by the remainders of creation, though
God should not have revealed his law again unto Moses in
the Mount,—much of the law, and by consequence of God
himself, might have been discovered by human industry, as
we see by notable examples of the philosophers and grave
heathens. But the gospel is such a mystery [e], as was for
ever hidden from the reach and very suspicion of nature, and
wholly of divine revelation. " Eye hath not seen, nor ear
heard, neither have entered into the hearts of men, the things
which God hath prepared for them that love him :"—the
apostle [f] speaketh it of the mystery of the gospel ; noting,
that it is above the observation, or learning, or comprehension, of nature, so much as to suspect it. Nay, the natural
enquiry of the angels themselves could never have discovered
it ; even unto them it is ' made known by the church [g];'
that is, If it had not been for the church's sake, that God
would reveal so glorious a mystery, the angels in Heaven
must have been for ever ignorant of it. So extremely
desperate was the fall of man, that it wanted the infinite
and unsearchable wisdom of God himself to find out a

  [c] Exod. xxxiii. 18, 19, and xxxiv. 6, 7.   [d] Mic. vii. 18.   [e] Rom. xvi. 25.
  [f] 1 Cor. ii. 7, 9.   [g] Ephes. iii. 9, 10.

remedy against it. If the Lord should have proceeded thus far in mercy towards man, and no farther,—Thou art a wretched creature, and I am a righteous God; yea, so heavy is my wrath, and so woful is thy condition, that I cannot choose but take compassion upon thee; and therefore I will put the matter into thine own hands; requisite it is, that my pity towards thee should not swallow up the respects to mine own justice and honour, that my mercy should be a righteous and a wise mercy. Consult therefore together, all ye children of men, and invent a way to reconcile my justice and mercy to one another; set me in a course to show you mercy, without parting from mine own right, and denying the righteous demands of mine offended justice,—and I will promise you to observe it;—I say, if the mercy of the Lord should have confined itself within these bounds, and referred the method of our redemption unto human discovery, we should for ever have continued in a desperate estate, everlastingly unable to conceive, or so much as in fancy to frame unto ourselves, a way of escape. As the creatures, before their being, could have no thought or notion of their being educed out of that nothing which they were before; so man, fallen, could not have the smallest conjecture or suspicion of any feasible way to deliver himself out of that misery into which he fell. If all the learning in the world were gathered into one man, and that man should employ all his time and study to frame unto himself the notions of a sixth or seventh sense, which yet are as expressly fashioned amongst those infinite ideas of God's power and omniscience, as these five which are already created,—he would be as totally ignorant of the conclusion he sought at last, as he was at first. For all human knowledge of natural things is wrought by a reflection upon those phantasms or ideas, which are impressions made from those senses we already use; and are indeed nothing else but a kind of notional existence of things in the memory of man, wrought by an external and sensible perception of that real existence, which they have in themselves. And yet, in this case, a sixth or a seventh sense would agree 'in genere proximo,' and so have some kind of cognation with those we already enjoy. But a new covenant, a new life, a new faith, a new salvation, are things, 'toto genere,' beyond the strain and sphere of nature. That two should become one, and yet remain two still, as God and man do in one Christ; that he who maketh, should be one with the thing which himself hath made; that he who is above all, should humble himself; that he who filleth all, should empty himself; that he who blesseth all, should be himself a curse; that he who ruleth all, should be himself a servant; that he who was the 'Prince of life,' and 'by whom all things in the world do consist,' should himself be dissolved and die; that mercy and justice should meet together, and kiss each other; that the debt should be paid, and yet pardoned; that the fault should be punished, and yet remitted; that death, like Sampson's lion, should have life and sweetness in it, and be used as an instrument to destroy itself;—these and the like evangelical truths are mysteries which surpass the reach of all the princes of learning in the world. It is to be believed by a spiritual light [h], which was not so much as possible to a human reason. We may observe, that every person in the Trinity, setteth himself to teach the mystery of the gospel. The Father revealeth it unto men : " Flesh and blood hath not revealed it unto thee, but my *Father* which is in Heaven.[i]—It is written in the prophets, They shall be all taught of God. Every man therefore that hath heard and learned of the *Father*, cometh unto me.[k]"—The Son likewise teacheth it unto men : therefore he is called the " angel of God's covenant and counsel [l]," that is, the revealer thereof, because unto the world he made known that deep project of his Father's counsel, touching the restoring of mankind. " No man hath seen God at any time; the only begotten Son which is in the bosom of the Father, he hath declared him [m]." He only it is who openeth the bosom of his Father, that is, who revealeth the secret and mysterious counsels, and the tender and compassionate affections (for the bosom is the seat of secrets of love) of his Father unto the world. And there he is said to be a " teacher sent from God [n]," and to be " the Lord which speaketh from Heaven [o]" in the ministry of his gospel; and

---

[h] Non humana ratione possibile, sed spiritus efficacia credibile. *Ambros.* Ideo certum, quia impossibile. *Tertul.*   [i] Matth. xvi. 17.   [k] John vi. 45.
[l] Officii non naturæ vocabula, quia magnum cogitatum patris super hominis restitutione annunciavit seculo. *Tertul.* [m] John i. 18. [n] John iii. 2. [o] Heb. xii. 25.

the doctrine which he teacheth, is called " a heavenly doctrine P," and " a heavenly calling q," and " a high calling r,"
and oft by the apostle to the Hebrews, τὰ ἐπουράνια, " heavenly things s;"—to note, that they are not of a natural or earthly condition, and therefore not within the comprehension of
an earthly understanding. It is " a wisdom which is from
above t."—The Holy Ghost likewise is a revealer of the gospel unto the faithful. He was sent that he might " convince
the world, not only of sin, but of righteousness and judgement too u," which are evangelical things. " The Spirit
searcheth all things, even the deep things of God x," that is,
his unsearchable love, wisdom, and counsel, in the gospel.
Therefore the gospel is called " the law of the Spirit of life y,"
and " The ministration of the Spirit z," and " The revelation
of the Spirit a;" and " No man can call Jesus Lord, but
by the Holy Spirit b;" that is, though men may, out of external conformity to the discipline and profession under
which they live, with their mouths acknowledge him to be
the Lord ; yet their hearts will never tremble, nor willingly
submit themselves to his obedience ; their conscience will
never set to its seal to the spiritual power of Christ over
the thoughts, desires, and secrets of the soul, but by the
overruling direction of the Holy Ghost. Nature taught the
Pharisees to call him Beelzebub and Samaritan c; but it is
the Spirit only, which teacheth men to acknowledge him a
Lord. Christ is not " the power nor the wisdom of God to
any, but to those who are called d;" that is, to those unto
whose consciences the Spirit witnesseth the righteousness,
which is to be found in him. So then the publication of the
gospel belongeth unto men ; but the effectual teaching and
revelation thereof unto the soul e, is the joint work of the
Holy Trinity, opening the heart to attend, and persuading
the heart to believe the gospel, as a thing worthy of all
acceptation. Thus the gospel is a glorious thing, in regard
of the original and author of it.

p John iii. 12.   q Heb. iii. 1.   r Phil. iii. 14.   s Heb. viii. 5. ix. 23.
t James iii. 17.   u John xvi. 8. 11.   x 1 Cor. ii. 10, 11, 12.   y Rom.
viii. 2.   z 2 Cor. iii. 8.   a Ephes. i. 17. and iii. 16, 19. 1 Pet. i. 11, 12.
b 1 Cor. xii. 3.   c Matth. xii. 24. John viii. 44.   d 1 Cor. i. 24.   e 2 Thes.
ii. 13, 14. Acts xvi. 14.—Deus nos adjuvat et ut sciamus, et ut amemus. Aug.
Epist. 143.

From whence we may infer,—That whatever men think of
the ministry and dispensation of the Word, yet undoubtedly
the neglect and scorn which is showed it, is done unto
Christ himself, and that in his glory.—He that receiveth not
his word, rejecteth his person [f]; and the sin of a man against
the Word, which we speak in the name and authority of
Christ, and in the dispensation of that office wherewith he
hath entrusted us, is the same with the sins of those men,
who despised him in his own person. You will say,—Christ
is in Heaven ; how can any injuries of ours reach unto him ?
—Surely though he be in Heaven, (which is now the court
of his royal residence) yet he hath to do upon earth, as one
of the chief territories of his dominion ; and, in the ministry
of his Word, he speaketh from Heaven still [g]. He it was,
who, by his ambassador St. Paul, " came and preached
peace [h] to the Ephesians, who were afar off." His Spirit it
was, which " in the prophets did testify of his sufferings and
glory [i]." He it was, who gave manifest proof of his own
power [k], speaking in his apostles. He then who refuseth
to obey the words of a minister in the execution of his office,
when he forewarneth him of the wrath to come, and doth not
discern the Lord's voice therein,—but in despite of this ministerial citation unto the tribunal of Christ, will still persist in
the way of his own heart, and as he hath been, so resolveth
to continue, a swearing, blasphemous, luxurious, proud, re-
vengeful, and riotous person, thinking it baseness to mourn
for sin, and unnecessary strictness to humble himself to walk
with God ; and yet because all men else do so, will profess
his faith in the Lord Jesus ;—that man is a notorious liar ;
yea (as the apostle speaketh) " he maketh God a liar" too, in
not believing [l] the record which he giveth of his Son, which
is that he should " wash away the filth, and purge out the
blood of his people with a spirit of judgement, and a spirit
of burning [m] :" that " he should sit as a refiner and purifier
of silver [n], purging his priests that they might offer unto the
Lord an offering in righteousness." He walketh contrary
to that covenant of mercy which he professeth to lay hold on ;
for this is one of the great promises of the covenant,—" I
will sprinkle clean water upon you [o], and ye shall be clean

f John xii. 48.   g Heb. xii. 25.   h Eph. ii. 17.   i 1 Pet. i. 11.   k 2 Cor.
xii. 3.   l John v. 10.   m Isai. iv. 4.   n Mal. iii. 3.   o Ezek. xxxvi. 25, 27.

from all your filthiness; and from all your idols will I cleanse
you. I will put my Spirit within you, and cause you to walk
in my statutes."—He walketh contrary to the quality of that
fear of God, which yet he professeth to feel as well as others:
For the fear of the Lord is a clean thing [p]. He walketh contrary to the virtue of that blood, with which, notwithstanding, he professeth to be sprinkled : for the blood of Christ
cleanseth not only the lives, but the very consciences of
men from dead works [q] : that is, makes them so inwardly
labour for purity of heart, as that they may not be conscious
to themselves of any, though the most secret allowed sin.—
He walketh contrary to the fruitfulness of that grace, which
alone he professeth to boast in : for the Spirit of grace which
is poured from on high [r], maketh the very wilderness a
fruitful field.—He walketh contrary to the properties of that
faith, by which alone he hopeth to be saved : for true faith
purifieth the heart [s]; and therefore a pure heart and a good
conscience are the inseparable companions of an unfeigned
faith [t]. And therefore whatever verbal and ceremonious
homage he may tender unto Christ, yet, in good earnest, he
is ashamed of him, and dares not prefer the yoke of Christ
before the lust of the world, or the reproaches of Christ
before the treasures of the world.

Why should it be treason to kill a judge in his ministry
on the bench ; or esteemed an injury to the state, to do any
indignity to the ambassador of a great prince ; but because,
in such relations, they are persons public and representative,
" ut eorum bona malaque ad rempublicam pertineant ?" why
should the supreme officer of the kingdom write ' Teste
meipso,' in the name and power of his prince, but because
he hath a more immediate representation of his sacred person, and commission thereunto? Surely, the case is the
same between Christ and his ministers in their holy function. And therefore we find the expressions promiscuous :
sometimes εὐαͿγέλιον τοῦ Χριστοῦ, 'The gospel of Christ [u];'
and sometimes εὐαͿγέλιόν μου, ' My gospel [x];' sometimes τὸ
κήρυγμα 'Ιησοῦ Χριστοῦ, ' The preaching of Jesus Christ [y];' and
sometimes τὸ κήρυγμά μου, ' My preaching.' [z] In the virtue

---

p Psal. xix. 9.   q Heb. ix. 14.   r Isai. xxxii. 15.   s Acts xv. 9.   t 1 Tim. i. 5.
u Rom. xv. 19.   x Rom. ii. 16.   y Rom. xvi. 25.   z 1 Cor. ii. 4.

of which synergy [a] and copartnership with Christ and with
God, as he saveth, so we save [b]; as he forgiveth sins, so we
forgive them [c]; as he judgeth wicked men, so we judge
them [d]; as he beseecheth, so " we also beseech [e]," saith the
apostle, " that ye be reconciled, and receive not the grace
of God in vain;" we by his grace and he by our ministry[f].—
He therefore that despiseth any conviction out of the book
of God (and he that obeyeth not, doth despise, for the Lord
calleth disobedience rebellion, stubbornness, and a rejecting
of his Word [g]); he that persisteth in any known sin, or in the
constant omission of any evident duty,—fighteth against
Christ himself, throweth away his own mercy, stoppeth his
ears at the entreaties of the Lord, and committeth a sin
directly against Heaven. And if he so persist, God will
make him know, that there is flaming fire prepared for those
that obey not the gospel of our Lord Jesus Christ. [h]

Therefore, whensoever we come unto the Word read or
preached, we should come with an expectation to hear
Christ himself speaking from Heaven unto us, and bring
such affections of submission and obedience as becometh
his presence. " Let him that hath an ear, hear what the
Spirit saith unto the churches. [i]—I will hear what God the
Lord will speak ; for he will speak peace unto his people. [k]—"
Christ's sheep [l] discern his voice in the dispensation of the
gospel, and will not know the voice of strangers. And this
was the honour of the Thessalonians [m], and the men of
Berea [n], that, in the preaching of the Word, they set themselves as in God's presence, expecting it in his authority,
and receiving it in his name. Dareth any man to rush with
a naked weapon into the presence of his prince, and, with
scorn, to throw back his own personal command into his
face again? and shall we dare to come armed with high
thoughts, and proud reasonings [o], and stubborn resolutions
against the majesty of the Lord himself, who speaketh from
Heaven unto us ? " Receive with meekness," saith the apostle, " the engraffed word, which is able to save your souls [p]."

---

a 1 Cor. iii. 9. 2 Cor. vi 1.   b James v. 20.   c John xx. 23.   d Ezek. xx. 4.
e 2 Cor. v. 20.   f δι' ἡμῶν τῶν τὸ ἐκείνου ἀναδεξαμένων ἔργον. Chrys.   g 1 Sam.
xv. 22, 23.   h 2 Thes. i. 8.   i Revel. ii. 7.   k Psal. lxxxv. 8.   l John
x. 4, 5.   m 1 Thes. ii. 13.   n Acts xvii. 11.   o Jer. xiii. 15, 17.
p James i. 21.

—The Word doth not mingle nor incorporate, and, by consequence, doth not change nor save the soul, but when it is received with meekness; that is, when a man cometh with a resolution to lay down his weapons, to fall down on his face, and give glory to God; he that is " swift to wrath," that is, to set up stout [q] and fretful affections against the purity and power of the Word, to snuff [r] against it, and to fall backward [s] like pettish children which will not be led, will be very slow to hear, to obey it; for " the wrath of man doth not work the righteousness of God [t]." A proud hearer will be an unprofitable liver. Ever therefore come unto the Word with this conclusion,—It may be, this day will God strike me in my master-vein : I am an unusual profaner of his glorious name; a name which I should fear for the greatness, and love for the goodness, and adore for the holiness of it; he will peradventure lay close to my conscience that guilt, which himself hath declared to be in this great sin, that whatsoever is more than yea and nay, is sin unto me,— and whatsoever is sin, is Hell to my soul. I am a vain person, a companion of loose and riotous men : it may be, the Lord will urge upon my conscience the charge of his own Word, not to company with fornicators, to have no fellowship with the unfruitful works of darkness, not to follow a multitude to do evil, and that though hand join in hand, yet sin shall not go unpunished. I am unprofitable, loose, and rotten in my discourse; and he will ply me with his own authority, that for every idle word I must render an account. I am full of oppression and unjust gain; and the Lord will now urge the instructions of Nehemiah [u], and the restitution of Zaccheus [x] upon me. In these or any other the like cases, if a man can come with St. Paul's temper of heart, 'not to consult with flesh and blood [y],' but 'Lord, what wilt thou have me to do [z]?' or with the answer of Samuel, 'Speak, Lord, for thy servant heareth [a];' or with the resolution of Cornelius, 'I am here present before God, to hear all things that shall be commanded of God [b];' I am come with a purpose of heart to cleave unto thy holy will in all things ; here

q Mal. iii. 13.   r Mal i. 13.   s Πνεύμαλι τῷ ἁγίῳ ἀντιπίπλετε. Acts vii. 51.
t Jam. i. 19, 20.   u Nehe. v. 11, 12.   x Luke xix. 8.   y Gal. i. 16.
z Acts ix. 6.   a 1 Sam. iii. 10.   b Acts x. 33.

I am in my sins, strike where thou wilt, cut off which
of mine earthly members thou wilt,—I will not arm it,
I will not extenuate it, I will not dispute with thee, I
will not rebel against thee, I will second thee in it; I
will praise thee for it:—this is to give God the glory of
his own gospel.—It is not to part from a little money
towards the maintenance of the Word, or to vouchsafe a
little countenance to the dispensers of it (and yet, alas,
how few are there, who repay unto the ministers of the gospel that double honour, which God, and not they, hath given
unto them!); but to part from our lusts, and to suffer our old
man to be crucified, which giveth honour to the Word. If a
man had a thousand of rams, and ten thousand rivers of oil,
and would be content to part from them all for God's worship; if a man had children enough, and, in a famine of the
Word, would buy every sermon which he heareth, with the
sacrifice of a son;—yet all this would not give glory enough
to the ordinance of God. Men naturally love their lusts,
the issue of their evil hearts, better than their lands, or the
children of their body. If Herod's son stand in the way of
his ambitious security, it were better to be his hog than his
child. The loss of cattle, and fruits, and water, and light,
and the first-born of all the land, was not enough to make
Pharaoh let go his sin; he will once more rush into the
midst of a wonderful deliverance of Israel, and venture his
own and his people's lives, for but the bondage of his enemies,
and the satisfaction of his lust. To do justly then, to love
mercy, and to walk humbly before God, to acknowledge his
name in the voice of the minister, and to put away the treasures of wickedness out of our hands,—this only is to give
God the glory which is due unto his Word.[c]

Secondly, The gospel is glorious in the promulgation and
publishing of it unto the world. And this may appear
whether we consider the initial promulgation in Christ's own
personal preaching; or the plenary revelation thereof, in the
sending of the Holy Ghost to those selected vessels, who
were to carry abroad this treasure unto all the world. For
the former we may note, that there was a resemblance of
state and glory observed in the preaching of Christ. A fore-

c Micah vi. 6, 10.

runner sent to prepare his way [d], and to bear his sword before him, as a herald to proclaim his approach, and then at last is revealed the glory of the Lord. And thus we may observe, how he sent his harbingers " before his face into every city and place, whither he himself would come [e]:" that so men might prepare themselves, and lift up their everlasting gates, against this prince of glory should enter in. When one poor ordinary man intendeth to visit another, there is no state nor distance, no ceremonies, nor solemnities observed; but when a prince will communicate himself unto any place, there is a publication, and officers sent abroad to give notice thereof, that meet entertainments may be provided. So doth Christ deal with men; he knoweth how unprepared we are to give him a welcome, how foul our hearts, how barren our consciences: and, therefore, he sendeth his officers before his face with his own provision, his graces of humiliation, repentance, desire, love, hope, joy, hungering and thirsting, after his appearance; and then, when he is esteemed worthy of all acceptation, he cometh himself.

Look upon the more consummate publication of the gospel (for Christ in his own personal preaching is said but to have *begun* to teach [f]) and we shall see, that as princes, in the time of their solemn inauguration, do some special acts of magnificence and honour, open prisons, proclaim pardons, create nobles, stamp coin, fill conduits with wine, distribute donatives, and congiaries to the people; so Christ, to testify the glory of his gospel, did reserve the full publication thereof unto the day of his instalment, and solemn re-admission into his Father's glory again. " When he ascended up on high, he then led captivity captive, and gave gifts unto men [g]," namely, the Holy Ghost, who is called ' the gift of God [h],' and, in the plural number, 'gifts;' as elsewhere he is called ' seven spirits [i],' to note the plenty and variety of graces, which are by him shed abroad upon the church,— wisdom, and faith, and knowledge, and healings, and prophecy, and discerning, and miracles, and tongues: " All these works one and the self-same spirit, dividing to every

---

[d] Isa. xl. 3, 4, 5. Mal. iii. 1, 4, 5.   [e] Luke x. 1.   [f] Acts i. 1. Heb. ii. 3.   [g] 1 Cor. xii. 8, 11.   [h] Acts ii. 38. Acts viii. 20. Joh. iv. 10.   [i] Rev. i. 4.

man severally as he will." And these gifts were all shed abroad for evangelical purposes, for the perfecting of the saints, for the work of the ministry, and for the edifying [k] of the body of Christ. And this spirit, St. Peter [l] tells us, is 'a spirit of glory:' and therefore, that gospel, for the more plentiful promulgation whereof he was shed abroad, must needs be a gospel of glory too.

And this farther appears, because, in this more solemn publication of the gospel, there was much more abundance of glorious light and grace shed abroad into the world. The Sun of Righteousness, in his estate of humiliation, was much eclipsed with the similitude of sinful flesh, the communion of our common infirmities, the poverty of a low condition, the grief and vexation of the sins of men, the overshadowing of his divine virtue, the form and entertainment of a servant, the burden of the guilt of sin, the burden of the law of God, the ignominy of a base death, the agony of a cursed death. But when he ascended up on high, like the sun in his glory, he then dispelled all these mists; and now sendeth forth those glorious beams of his gospel and Spirit, which are the two wings, by which he cometh unto the churches, and under which the healing and salvation of the world is treasured.[m] John Baptist[n] was the last and greatest of all the prophets, who foretold of Christ; a greater had not been born of women: and yet he was 'less than the least in the kingdom of heaven,' that is, than the least of those upon whom the promise of the Spirit was shed abroad, for the more glorious manifestation of the kingdom of his gospel. All the prophets and the law prophesied until John; but, at the coming of Christ, they seemed to be taken away, not by way of abrogation and extinguishment, as the ceremonies,— but by way of excess and excellency, " ut stellæ exiliores ad exortum solis," as the orator speaks. So saith the apostle [o], —"Even that which was made glorious, had no glory in this respect, by reason of the glory that excelleth." Therefore the full revelation of the gospel is called ' an effusion of the Spirit,' not in dew but in showers of rain [p], which multiply into ' rivers of living water,' (for the rain of the Spirit

k Eph. iv. 12, 13.   l 1 Pet. iv. 14.   m Mal. iv. 2. Ezek. xlvii. 8, 9.
Isai. xxxv. 5, 6, 7.   n Mat. xi. 11, 13.   o 2 Cor. iii. 10.   p Heb.
vi. 7. John vii. 38. iv. 14. Isa. xi. 9. xliv. 3.

floweth from heaven as from a spring) and into ' wells of salvation,' and into 'a sea of knowledge.' Which attributes note unto us two things. First, The abundance of spiritual grace [q] and knowledge by the gospel ; it should be a river : —Secondly, The growth and increase thereof ; it should be ' living water [r],' multiplying and swelling up like the waters of the sanctuary [s], till it came to a bottomless and unmeasurable sea of eternal life. And to touch that which was before spoken of, very glorious are the virtues of the Spirit in the gospel, intimated in this similitude of ' living water.' To quench the wrath of God, that otherwise consuming and unextinguishable fury, which devoured the adversaries with everlasting burnings :—To satisfy those desires of the thirsty soul which itself begetteth : for the Spirit is both for medicine and for meat ; for medicine, to cure the dull and averse appetites of the soul ; and for meat, to satisfy them. The Spirit is both 'a Spirit of supplication [t],' and ' a Spirit of grace or satisfaction ;'—a Spirit of supplication, directing us to pray ; and a Spirit of grace, supplying those requests, and satisfying those desires which himself did dictate :—to cleanse [u], to purify, to mollify, to take away the barrenness of our natural hearts [x]:—to overflow and communicate itself to others [y]:—to withstand and subdue every obstacle [z] that is set up against it :—to continue and to multiply to the end.

By this then we learn the way how to abound in grace and glory, and how to be transformed into the image of Christ. The beam and light of the sun is the ' vehiculum' of the heat and influence of the sun ; so the light of the gospel of Christ is that which conveyeth the virtue and gracious working of the Spirit upon the soul. And therefore we are to seek those varieties of grace, which are for meat to satisfy the desires, and for medicine to cure the bruises, of the soul, only upon the banks of the waters of the sanctuary [a]; that is, in the knowledge of the word of truth, which is the gospel of salvation. The more of this glorious light a man hath, the more proportion of all other graces will he have too. And, therefore, the apostle [b] puts the growth of these two together, as contributing a mutual succour unto one another,

[q] Tit. iii. 6.　　[r] John iv. 10.　　[s] Ezek. xlvii. 12.　　[t] Zech. xii. 10.
[u] Ezek. xxxvi. 25.　　[x] Isa. xxxv. 6, 7. Ezek. xi. 19.　　[y] Mal. iii. 16.
Gal. vi. 1, 2.　　[z] Gal. v. 17. Phil. i. 27.　　[a] Ezek. xlvii. 12.　　[b] 2 Pet. iii. 18.

" Grow in grace, and in the knowledge of our Lord Jesus
Christ:" your grace will enlarge your desires of knowledge;
and your knowledge will multiply your degrees of grace.—
And St. Paul[c] makes the knowledge of the will of God in
wisdom, and after a spiritual manner, to be the ground of
fruitfulness in every good work; and that again an inducement to increase in knowledge: as, in the twisting together
of two cords into one rope, they are by art so ordered, that
either shall bind and hold in the other. As, in the heavens,
the inferior orbs have the measure and proportion of their
general motions from the supreme; so, in the motions of
grace in the soul, the proportion of all the rest ariseth from
the measure of our spiritual and saving light. The more
distinctly and thoroughly the spirit of a man's mind is convinced of the necessity, beauty, and gloriousness of heavenly things, the more strong impressions thereof will be
made upon all subordinate faculties; for we move towards
nothing without preceding apprehensions of its goodness;—
which apprehensions as they more seriously penetrate into
the true and intimate worth of that thing, so are the motions
of the soul thereunto proportionably strengthened. As the
hinder wheels in a coach ever move as fast as the former
which lead them; so the subordinate powers of the soul
are overruled in their manner and measure of working towards grace, by those spiritual representations of the truth
and excellency thereof, which are made in the understanding
by the light of the gospel. Thus the apostle [d] telleth us,
that "the excellency of the knowledge of Christ" was that
which made him so earnest to win him; "the knowledge of
the power of his resurrection, and fellowship of his sufferings," was that which made him reach forth, and press forward unto the mark and price of that high calling which was
before him.

Thirdly, The glory of the gospel of Christ with his Spirit
may be considered in regard of the matters which are therein contained, namely, the glory, the excellency, the treasure,
of God himself. "We all," saith the apostle [e], "with open
face behold, as in a glass" (that is, in the spiritual ministration of the gospel, having the veil of carnal stupidity taken

c Col. i. 9, 10.   d Phil. iii. 8, 14.   e 2 Cor. iii. 18.

away by the Spirit) " the glory of the Lord." What glory
do we here behold, but that which a glass is able to represent? Now ' in speculo nisi imago non cernitur,' nothing
can be seen in a glass but the image of that thing which
sheddeth forth its species thereupon: and therefore he
immediately addeth, " We are changed into the same image
from glory to glory." And elsewhere [f] he putteth these two
together, " Man is the image and glory of God :" for nothing
can have any thing of God in it, any resemblance or form of
him, but so far it must needs be glorious. But how do we
in the gospel see the image of God who is invisible? The
apostle expresseth that elsewhere [g]; " God who commanded
the light to shine out of darkness, hath shined in our hearts,
to give the light of the knowledge of the glory of God in the
face of Jesus Christ. Christ is the image and express character of his Father's glory, as the impression in the wax is
of the form and fashion of the seal. There is no excellency
in God, which is not completely, adequately, and distinctly,
in Christ: so that in that glass, wherein we may see him,
we may likewise see the glory of the Father. Now the gospel is ' the face of Jesus Christ,'—that which as lively setteth
forth his grace and Spirit to the soul, as if he were present
in the flesh amongst us. Suppose we that a glass could
retain a permanent and unvanishing species of a man's face
within it; though he himself were absent, might we not
truly say, This glass is the face of that man, whose image it
so constantly retaineth? So, inasmuch as Christ is most
exactly represented in his gospel (so that when we come
into his personal and real presence, to know even as we are
known, we shall be able truly to say, This is indeed the very
person who was so long since, in his gospel, exhibited to my
faith, ' sic ille manus, sic ora gerebat') it is therefore justly
by the apostle called ' the face of Jesus Christ;' and the
' glass wherein we see the image and glory of God.' As it
is the same light which shineth from the sun upon a glass,
and from a glass upon a wall ; so it is the same glory which
shineth from the Father upon the Son, and from the Son
upon the gospel : so that in the gospel we see the unsearchable treasures of God, because his treasures are in his Son.

f 1 Cor. xi. 7.   g 2 Cor. iv. 4, 5, 6.

Therefore, that which is usually called 'preaching the gospel [h],' is, in other places, called 'preaching the kingdom [i], and the riches of Christ [k],' to note the glory of those things which are in the gospel revealed unto the church.

It containeth the glory of God's wisdom, and that wisdom is Πολυποίκιλος σοφία, 'a manifold, and various wisdom [l]' as the apostle speaketh [m]; who therefore calleth Christ and his gospel by the name of 'wisdom:' "We preach Christ crucified, to those that are called, the power of God, and the wisdom of God;" and "we speak wisdom amongst them that are perfect :" wisdom to reconcile his own attributes of mercy and truth, righteousness and peace,—which, by the fall of man, seemed to be at variance among themselves; wisdom in reconciling the world of obstinate and rebellious enemies unto himself; wisdom in sanctifying the whole [n] creation by the blood of the cross, and repairing those ruins which the sin of man had caused; wisdom in concorporating Christ and his church, things, in their own distinct natures, as unapt for mixture, as fire and water in their remotest degrees; wisdom in uniting the Jews and Gentiles, and reducing their former jealousies and disaffections unto an intimate fellowship in the same common mysteries: in one word, wisdom above the admiration of the blessed angels, in finding out a way to give greater satisfaction to his offended justice, by showing mercy and saving sinners, than he could ever have received by either the confusion or annihilation of them. It containeth the glory of God's goodness and mercy, of that εὐδοκία 'good will' towards men, which brought glory to God, and to the earth peace: for the gospel is, as it were, a love-token or commendatory epistle of the Lord unto his church. God left not himself without witnesses [o] of his care, and evidences of some love, even to those whom he suffered to walk in their own ways, without any knowledge of his gospel: he did them good, he gave them rain from heaven, and fruitful seasons: so even they had experience of some of his goodness, the goodness of his providence; for he is the Saviour of all men. But the gospel containeth all God's goodness, as a heap and miscellany of universal

h Rom. xv. 19. 1 Cor. xv. 1.   i Acts xx. 25.   k Ephes. iii. 8.
l Ephes. iii. 10.   m 1 Cor. i. 24. ii. 6, 7.   n Rom. viii. 22.   o Acts xiv. 16, 17.

mercy : "I will make all my goodness pass before thee, and I will proclaim the name of the Lord before thee, and will be gracious to whom I will be gracious, and I will show mercy to whom I will show mercy." God's special and gracious mercy, the mercy of his promises in Christ, doth convey unto the soul an interest in all his goodness : nay, it maketh all things good unto us; so that we may call them ours, as gifts and legacies from Christ. He hath given to us all things that pertain to life and godliness[p], the world, and life, and death, and things present, and things to come; "all are yours," saith the apostle.[q] Death itself and persecutions are amongst the legacies of Christ unto the church, and a portion of all that goodness, with which, in the gospel, she is endowed. It contains the glory of God's power and strength ; for it is "the power of God unto salvation," as hath been declared. It containeth the glory of God's grace: The grace of his favour towards us, and the grace of his Spirit in us. "The law was given by Moses, but grace came by Christ[r];" that is, favour instead of God's fury, and strength instead of man's infirmity. For because man was unable to fulfil the law, therefore the law came with wrath and curses against man ; but in the gospel of Christ there is abundance, even a whole kingdom of grace : the apostle saith, that by Jesus Christ "grace reigned."[s] There is grace to remove the curse of the law by God's favour towards us : so that on all sides the law is weak ; unable, by reason of man's sin, to save ; and unable, by reason of God's favour, to condemn. And there is grace to remove the weakness of man by God's Spirit in us : for though our own spirit lust unto envy[t], or set itself proudly against the law of God ; yet he giveth more grace, that is, strength enough to overcome the counterlustings of the flesh against his will, and to enable us in sincerity and evangelical perfection, to fulfil the commands of the law. Lastly, It containeth, in some sort, the glory of God's heavenly kingdom, in that therein are let in the glimpses and first-fruits, the seals and assurances thereof unto the soul by the promises, testimonies and comforts of the Spirit. And therefore it is frequently called

p 2 Pet. i. 3, 4.   q 1 Cor. iii. 21.   r John i. 17.   s Rom. v. 21.
t James iv. 5, 6.

'the gospel of the kingdom [u],' and 'the mysteries of the kingdom of God;' namely, that kingdom which beginneth here, but shall never end. As if a man, born in Ireland, be afterward transplanted into England, though he change his country, he doth not change his king, or his law, but is still under the same government:—so when a Christian is translated from earth to heaven, he is still in the same kingdom: in heaven it is the kingdom of glory, mended much by the different excellency of the place, and preferment of the person: in earth, it is the same kingdom, though in a less amene and comfortable climate, the kingdom of the gospel. These and many other the like things, are the glorious matters which the gospel containeth.

Here then we see, how, and wherein, we are to look upon God, so as that we may abide his glory, and be comforted by it. We must not look upon him in his own immediate brightness and essence,—nor, by our saucy curiosities, pry into the secrets [x] of his unrevealed glory, for he is a consuming fire, an invisible, an unapproachable light [y]; we may see "his back-parts [z]," in the proclaiming of his mercy; and we may see "the horns [a]" or bright beams "of his hands," in the publishing of his law: but yet all this was under a cloud, or under the hiding of his power; "His face no man can see, and live." We must not look upon him only in ourselves. Though we might, at first, have seen him in our own nature,—for we were created after his image in righteousness and true holiness, yet now that image is utterly obliterated, and we have by nature the image only of Satan and the old Adam in us. We must not look upon him only in Mount Sinai, in his law, lest the fire devour us, and the dart strike us through: we can find nothing of him there but rigour, inexorableness, wrath and vengeance; but we must acquaint ourselves with him in his Son, we must know him, and whom he hath sent together [b]; there is no fellowship [c] with the Father, except it be with the Son too. We may have the knowledge of his hand, that is, of his works and of his punishments, without Christ: but we cannot have the knowledge of his bosom [d], that is, of his counsels, and of his com-

---

[u] Mat. xiii. 19. Mark i. 14. Luke viii. 10.   [x] Deut. xxix. 29.   [y] Exod. xix. 21.   [z] Exod. xxxiii. 23.   [a] Habak. iii. 4.   [b] John xvii. 3.   [c] 1 John i. 3.   [d] John i. 18.

passions; nor the knowledge of his image [e], that is, of his holiness, grace, and righteousness; nor the knowledge of his presence, that is, of his comforts here, and his glory hereafter, but only in and by Christ.[f] We may know God in the world, for in the creation is manifest τὸ γνωστὸν τοῦ Θεοῦ "that which may be known of him;" namely, his eternal power and godhead. But this is a barren and fruitless knowledge, which will not keep down unrighteousness; for "the wise men of the world when they knew God, they glorified him not as God, but became vain in their imaginations," and held that truth of him which was in the creation revealed, in unrighteousness. We may know him in his law too; and that in exceeding great glory; "When God [g] came from Teman, and the holy one from Mount Paran" (whereabout the law was the second time repeated by Moses) "his glory covered the heavens, and the earth was full of his praise, his brightness was as the light," &c. But this is a killing knowledge, a knowledge which makes us fly from God, and hide ourselves out of his presence, and fight against him as our sorest enemy, and come short of his glory: therefore the law is called 'a fiery law [h],' or 'a fire of law,' to show not only the original thereof, for it was spoken out of the midst of the fire [i]; but the nature and operation of it too, which of itself is to heap fire and curses upon the soul [k]; and therefore it is called 'the ministration of death.'[l] But now to know the glory of God in the face of Jesus Christ, is both a fruitful and a comfortable knowledge. We know the pattern we must walk by; we know the life we must live by; we know the treasure we must be supplied by; we know whom we have believed; we know whom we may be bold with in all straits and distresses; we know God in Christ full of love, full of compassion, full of ears to hear us, full of eyes to watch over us, full of hands to fight for us, full of tongues to commune with us, full of power to preserve us, full of grace to transform us, full of fidelity to keep covenant with us, full of wisdom to conduct us, full of redemption to save us, full of glory to reward us. Let us, therefore, put ourselves into this rock, that God's goodness may pass be-

e Col. i. 15.   f John xiv. 6. Ephes. ii. 18. iii. 12. Heb. x. 19, 22.   g Habak. iii. 3, 4. Deut. i. 1.   h Deut. xxxiii. 2.   i Deut. v. 22.   k Gal. iii. 10. Rom. xii. 20.   l 2 Cor. iii. 7.

fore us; that he may communicate the mysteries of his
kingdom, and of his glory unto us ; that by him our persons
may be accepted, our prayers admitted, our services regarded, our acquaintance and fellowship with the Lord increased by that blessed Spirit, which is from them both shed
abroad in his gospel upon us.

Now lastly, The gospel of Christ is glorious in those ends,
effects, or purposes for which it serveth. And in this respect principally, doth the apostle so often magnify the
glory of the gospel above the law. The law was a glorious
ministry, as appears by the thunderings and lightnings [m],
the shining of Moses' face, and trembling at God's presence, the service of the angels, and sound of the trumpet,
the ascending of the smoke, and the quaking of the mountain: but yet still the glory of the gospel was far more excellent, a better covenant [n], a more excellent ministry. The
law had 'weakness and unprofitableness' in it,—both terms
of diminution from the glory thereof ;—and therefore it could
make nothing perfect [o]: but that which the law could not
do, inasmuch as it was weak through the flesh, the 'law of
the Spirit of life in Christ Jesus' (which is a periphrasis of the
gospel, as appeareth 2 Cor. iii. 6.) did do for us, namely, make
us free from the law of sin and death. So then the law was
glorious; but the gospel, in many respects, did excel in glory [q].

To take a more particular view of the spiritual glory of
the gospel of Christ in those excellent ends and purposes
for which it serveth : First, it is full of light, to inform, to
comfort, to guide those who sit in darkness and the shadow
of death, into the way of peace. Light was the first of all
the creatures which were made ; and the apostle magnifieth
it for a glorious thing in those other luminaries which were
after created.[r] How much more glorious was the light of
the gospel ! The apostle calleth it φῶς θαυμαστὸν, 'a marvellous
light [s]:' and therefore the kingdom of the gospel is expressed
by 'light and glory' together, as terms of a promiscuous
signification [t]. Of all other learning [u], the knowledge of the
gospel doth infinitely excel in worth, both in regard of the
object thereof, which is God manifested in the flesh, and in

[m] Exod. xix. 16, 21.　[n] Heb. viii. 6.　[o] Heb. vii. 18, 19.　[q] 2 Cor. iii. 10.
[r] 1 Cor. xv. 41.　[s] 1 Pet. ii. 9.　[t] Isai. lx. 1, 2, 3.　[u] Ἄσοφος σοφία
πᾶσα ἡ τοῦ αἰῶνος τούτου δύναμίς τε καὶ παίδευσις. Greg. Naz. Orat. 3.

regard of the end thereof, which is flesh reconciled and
brought unto God. ' A knowledge which passeth knowledge ˣ ;' a knowledge which bringeth fulness with it, even
all the fulness of God ; a knowledge so excellent, that all
other human excellences are but dung ʸ in comparison of it.
What angel in Heaven would trouble himself to busy his
noble thoughts (which have the glorious presence of God,
and the joys of Heaven to fill them) with metaphysical, or
mathematical, or philological contemplations, which yet are
the highest delicacies which human reason doth fasten on to
delight in? And yet we find the angels in Heaven, with much
greediness of speculation ᶻ stoop down, and, as it were, turn
away their eyes from that expressless glory which is before
them in Heaven, to gaze upon the wonderful light, and
bottomless mysteries of the gospel of Christ ᵃ. In all other
learning, a devil in Hell (the most cursed of all creatures) doth
wonderfully surpass the greatest proficients amongst men :
but, in the learning of the gospel, and in the spiritual revelations and evidences of the benefits of Christ, to the soul
from thence, there is a knowledge which surpasseth the comprehension of any angel of darkness ; for it is the Spirit of
God only, which knoweth the things of God. It was the
devilish flout of Julian the apostate ᵇ against Christian religion,
that it was an illiterate rusticity, and a naked belief ; and that
true, polite learning, did belong to him and his ethnic faction : and, for that reason, he interdicted Christians the use
of schools and human learning, as things improper to their
believing religion ;—a persecution esteemed by the ancients
as cruel as the other bloody massacres of his predecessors.
To which slander, though the most learned father might
have justly returned the lie, and given proofs, both in the
canonical books of holy Scripture, and in the professors of
that religion, of as profound learning, as invincible argumen-
tation, and as forcible eloquence, as in any heathen author,
(for I dare challenge all the Pagan learning in the world,
to parallel the writings of Clemens of Alexandria, Origen,
Justin, Tertullian, Cyprian, Minutius, Augustin, Theodoret,

ˣ Ephes. iii. 18.   ʸ Phil. iii. 8.   ᶻ 1 Pet. i. 12.   ᵃ ῝Ον τοῦτο ἀπήλαυσα
μόνον, τὸ περιϊδεῖν καὶ ἐσχηκέναι ὧν Χριστὸν προετίμησα. Greg. Naz. Orat. 1.
ᵇ Ἡμέτεροι, φησὶν, οἱ λόγοι, καὶ τὸ Ἑλληνίζειν, ὧν καὶ τὸ σέβειν θεούς· ὑμῶν δὲ ἡ
ἀλογία καὶ ἀγροικία· καὶ οὐδὲν ὑπὲρ τὸ, πίστευσον, τῆς ὑμετέρας ἐστὶ σοφίας. Greg.
Naz. Orat. 3.

Nazianzen, and the other champions of Christian religion against gentilism) yet he rather chooseth thus to answer,— That that authority, which the faith he so much derided, was built upon, came to the soul with more self-evidence, and invincible demonstration, than all the disputes of reason or learning of philosophy could create [c]. Though therefore it were to the Jews an offence, as contrary to the honour of their law,—and to the Greeks foolishness, as contrary to the pride of their reason; yet to those that were perfect, it was a hidden and mysterious wisdom, able to convince the gainsayers, to convert sinners, to comfort mourners, to give wisdom to the simple, and to guide a man in all his ways with spiritual prudence. For, whatever the prejudice of the world may be, there is no man a wiser man, nor more able to bring about those ends which his heart is justly set upon, than he who, being acquainted with God in Christ by the gospel, hath the Father of Wisdom, the treasurer of wisdom, the spirit of wisdom, and the law of wisdom, to furnish him therewithal. It is not for want of sufficiency in the gospel, but for want of more intimate acquaintance and knowledge thereof in us, that the children of this world are more wise in their generation, than the children of light.

Secondly, Another glorious end and effect of the gospel, is to be a ministration of righteousness, a publication of a pardon to the world,—and that so general, that there is not one exception therein of any other sin, than only of the contempt of the pardon itself. And in this respect likewise, the gospel exceeds in glory. " If the ministration of condemnation" (saith the apostle) " be glory, much more doth the administration of righteousness exceed in glory [d]." It is the glory of a man to pass by an offence; and the Lord proclaimeth his glory to Moses, in " that he would forgive iniquity, transgression and sin," that is, multitudes of sins, and sins of all degrees [e]. And thus the Lord magnifies his mercy and thoughts towards sinners, above all the ways and thoughts of men, even as the heavens are higher than the earth, because " he can abundantly pardon," or multiply forgivenesses

c Βούλεται γὰρ ἡμῖν ὁ λόγος μὴ ἐξεῖναι διαστατεῖν τοῖς ὑπὸ τῶν θεοφόρων ἀνδρῶν εἰρημένοις· ἀλλ᾽ ἀπόδειξιν εἶναι τοῖ λόγου, τὸ ἐκείνων ἀξιόπιστον, πάσης δυνάμεως λογικῆς καὶ ἀντιλογικῆς ἰσχυρότερον. Greg. Naz. 16.   d 2 Cor. iii. 9.   e Exod. xxxiv. 7.

upon those who forsake their ways, and turn to him [f]. And therefore justifying faith, whereby we rely upon the power of God to forgive and subdue our sins, is said to " give glory to God :" Abraham staggered not at the promise through unbelief, but being strong in faith, he gave " glory to God," namely, the glory of his power and fidelity [g]. " Ye shall not bring this congregation into the land which I have given them," saith the Lord to Moses and Aaron [h], " because ye believed me not, to sanctify me in the eyes of the children of Israel :" that is, to give me the glory of my power and truth (for to ' sanctify the Lord of Hosts,' signifies to ' glorify his power, by fearing him more than men, and by relying on him against the power and confederacies of men [i].' And therefore in the same argument touching the happiness of the saints, if they suffer for righteousness' sake, or be reproached for the name of Christ, St. Peter [k] useth in one place ' sanctifying of the Lord ' in our hearts, and in another, ' glorifying of him,' as terms equivalent; and therefore unbelief is said ' to make God a liar [l];' that is, to dishonour him, and to rob him of the glory of his truth ; and despair [m], to rob God of his mercy, and to make the guilt of sin greater than the power of God. And therefore murmurers and unbelievers are said " to speak against God, and to grieve him, to tempt, to limit him [n]," that is, to call in question the glory of his power and truth. Herein then consisteth another glorious effect of the gospel of Christ,—that, being a ministration of righteousness, it is a glass of that power, truth, mercy, and fidelity of God, which by faith we rest upon, for the forgiveness and sub-duing of sin.

Thirdly, Another glorious end of the gospel is to be a ministration and a law of life. " If the ministration of death" (saith the apostle) " were glorious, how shall not the ministration of the Spirit be rather glorious [o]? The law alone by itself is towards sinners but a dead letter ; only the rule, according unto which a man ought to walk, not any principle enabling him to walk. If Moses alone should speak unto men, he could only tell them what they ought to do; he could in no wise enable them to do it. Nay, farther, the law hath occasionally, from the sin of man, a malignant

---

[f] Isai. lv. 7, 8, 9.   [g] Rom iv. 20, 21.   [h] Numb. xx. 12.   [i] Isai. viii. 12, 13.   [k] 1 Pet. iii. 14, 15. 1 Pet. iv. 14.   [l] 1 John v. 10.   [m] Gen. iv. 13.   [n] Psalm lxxviii. 18. xix. 40, 41.   [o] 2 Cor. iii. 6, 7, 8.

property in it, to irritate and exasperate lust the more,
to beget an occasional rage and fierceness in our nature :
as the sun, shining on a dunghill, exhaleth noisome vapours,
and maketh it stink the more. But now the gospel of
the Spirit doth not only teach, but help too [p]; sheweth us
what we should do, and giveth us strength to do it. We do
not only therein see the glory of God, but are withal changed
into the same image, even " from glory to glory [q];—that is,
(as I conceive from that allusion to a glass) the glory of the
Lord, shining upon the gospel, and from the gospel shining
upon our hearts, doth change them into the image of the
same glory; even as the glory of the sun, shining upon a
glass, and from that glass reflecting on a wall, doth therein
produce a more extraordinary image of its own light : so
that the apostles ἀπὸ δόξης εἰς δόξαν, is the same with the
poets ' è speculo in speculum:' from the glory of the gospel,
which is one glass of God's image, there is shaped the same
glory in the heart, which is another glass of his image.
This is that which the apostle calleth, the ' forming of Christ
in the soul,' and ' the planting of it into the likeness of his
death and resurrection.'

Fourthly, It is a glorious gospel in the judicature thereof.
The Spirit in the gospel doth convince, not of righteousness
only, but of ' judgement' too [r]; that is, the Spirit shall erect
a throne in the hearts of men, shall pull down the prince of
this world, and dispossess him ; shall enable men's own hearts
to proceed like upright judges, with truth and with victory [s]
(which are two of the principal honours of judgement) against
their own lusts, to censure, to condemn, to crucify them,
though before they were as dear as their own members ; to
throw all their idols away as menstruous rags, and to judge [t]
and revenge [u] themselves. " Ephraim shall say, What have
I to do any more with idols [x]?—In that day, saith the Lord,
every man shall cast away his idols of silver, and his idols of
gold, which your own hands have made unto you for a sin [y].
I have surely heard Ephraim bemoaning himself : after that

---

[p] Quod operum lex minando imperat, hoc fidei lex credendo imperat.—Lege
operum dicit Deus, ' Fac quod jubeo;' lege fidei dicitur Deo, ' Da quod jubes.
Aug. tom. 3, lib. de Spiritu et Litera, cap. 13. 19.   [q] 2 Cor. iii. 3, 18.   [r] John
xvi. 11. Isai. xlii. 3.   [s] Matth. xii. 20.   [t] 1 Cor. xi. 31.   [u] 2 Cor. vii. 11.
[x] Hosea xiv. 8.   [y] Isai. xxxi. 7.

I was turned, I repented; and after that I was instructed, I smote upon my thigh [z]."—Thus the government of the gospel in the heart, makes a man severe to sentence every sin, to hang up his Haman, his favourite lusts, to give up himself to the obedience of Christ, and to have his conversation [a], his trading, his treasure, his privileges, his freedom, his fellowship in heaven, as being now constituted under the gracious and peaceable government of a heavenly prince.

Fifthly, It is a glorious gospel, in that it was to be a continuing ministration, and an immortal seed. "If that which was done away," saith the apostle, "was glorious, much more that which remaineth, is glorious [b]." Now the gospel is able to preserve a man blameless unto the coming of our Lord Jesus: it will not suffer a man to be shaken, nor overturned by all the powers of darkness: there is strength enough in it to repel, and wisdom to answer, all the temptations and assaults of the enemies of our salvation. If the world set upon us with any temptations on the right hand or on the left, with disgraces, persecutions, discomforts, exprobrations, ' Lo, this was the man who made God his help, and would needs be more excellent than his neighbours ;'—the gospel furnisheth us with sure promises and sure mercies. This is answer sufficient against all the discouragements of the world, " I know whom I have believed ; I know that he hath overcome the world ; I know that he is able to keep that which I have committed unto him, until the last day ; and, in the mean time, the world is crucified unto me, and I unto the world ;" that is, " we are at an equal point of distance and defiance, the world contemns me, and I am as careless of the world." If with pleasures, honours, and gilded baits to' draw us away from God, faith in the gospel easily overcometh the world: for it giveth both the promises and first-fruits of such treasures, as are infinitely more precious and massy, than all the world can afford : the very reproaches of Christ (how much more his promises, how infinitely more his performances at the last?) are far greater riches than the treasures of Egypt. The daily sacrifice of a godly life, and the daily feast of a quiet conscience, put more sweetness into the afflictions of Christ, than is in

z Jer. xxxi. 19.   a Phil. iii. 20.   b 2 Cor. iii. 11.

all the profits, pleasures, or preferments of the world, being
made bitter with the guilt of sin.   If Satan, or our own
reasonings stand up against the kingdom of Christ in us,
the gospel is a storehouse, which can furnish us with ar-
mory of all sorts to repel them.   Faith can quench fiery
darts ; the weapons of the Spirit can captivate the very
thoughts of the heart unto the obedience of Christ; no
weapon which is formed against it, can prosper; and every
tongue which riseth up against it in judgement, it shall condemn; it is a staff which can carry a man over any Jordan,
and can support and comfort him in any shadow of death.
This is the honour of the Word, that it doth not only
' sanctify' men, but ' preserve' their holiness in them.   If
it were not for the treasure of the Word in the heart, every
little thing would easily turn a man out of his way, and
make him revolt from Christ again.   How easily would
afflictions make us mistrust God's affection to us, and so
change our's unto him, (for this is certain, his love to us is
the original of our love to him) make us murmur, repine,
struggle, fret under his hand,—if, in the gospel, we did
not look upon them as the gentle corrections of a Father,
who loves us, as the pruning and harrowing of our souls,
that they may bring forth more fruit?   " Except thy law
had been my delight, I should have perished in mine affliction [c] :"   My affliction would have destroyed me, and made
me perish from the right way, if it had not been tempered
and sanctified by thy Word.—It wrought so with that wicked
king of Israel [d] ; " Behold, this evil is of the Lord ; what
should I wait upon the Lord any longer? what profit is
there to walk humbly before him [e]," or to afflict our souls
before him, who will not see nor take knowledge of it, but
continue to be our enemy still ?—But the gospel teacheth a
man's heart to rest in God ; assureth it that there is hope in
Israel, and balm in Gilead ; that they which believe, should
not make haste to limit, or to misconstrue God, but wait for
his salvation, which will ever come in that due time, wherein
it shall be both most acceptable and most beautiful.   Again ;
how easily would temptations overturn the faith of men, if
it were not daily supported by the Word !   What is the

c Psalm cxix. 92.   d 2 Kings vi. 33.   e Mal. iii. 14.   Isai. lviii. 3.

reason that the sheep of Christ will not follow strangers, nor know their voice, that is, will not acknowledge any force, nor subscribe in their hearts to the conviction or evidence of any temptation which would draw them from God,—but only because they hear and know [f] the voice of Christ in his gospel, and feel a spirit in their own hearts setting to its seal, and bearing witness to that truth, from whence those solicitations would seduce them? The apostle [g] foretold the elders of Ephesus at his solemn departure from them, that "grievous wolves would enter in among them, and that some of themselves would arise, speaking perverse things, to draw away disciples after them." And the main remedy which the apostle gives them against this danger, was, "I commend you to God, and to the Word of his grace, which is able to build you up," &c. ;—noting, that it is the word of God which keepeth men from being drawn away with perverse disputes. And the same intimation he gives them in his epistles [h] unto them, "He gave some apostles, and some prophets, and some evangelists, and some pastors and teachers.—That we henceforth be no more children tossed to and fro, and carried about with every wind of doctrine by the slight of men, and cunning craftiness, whereby they lie in wait to deceive." The more richly the word of God, in the love and evidence thereof, doth dwell in any man, and enable him to prove all things, —the more steadfastly will he hold that which is good, and stand immovable against the slights and solicitations of men.—Again; How easily would our own evil hearts gather a rust and unaptness for service over themselves, if they were not daily whet and brightened upon the word of God. That only it is, which scrapeth away that leprosy and mossiness, which our souls are apt to contract out of themselves. A man may lose all that he hath wrought, all the benefit of what he hath done already, and all the strength to do any more, only by not abiding in the doctrine of Christ [i]. He is no doer of the Word, who only looketh [k] in it, as a man on a glass, and presently forgetteth the image and state of his conscience again : it is only he that continueth therein, who is a doer of the work, and blessed in his deed.

[f] John x. 4, 5.   [g] Acts xx. 29, 32.   [h] Eph. iv. 11, 14. 1 Thess. v. 21.
[i] 2 John viii. 9.   [k] Jam. i. 23, 25.

He that treasureth up the gospel in his heart, and laboureth
to grow rich in the knowledge thereof, can never be turned
quite out of his way, or become an apostate from the grace
of Christ.

Lastly, It is a glorious gospel in regard of those noble
and majestical endowments, with which it qualifieth the soul
of a Christian: for there is no nobility to that of the gospel.
It giveth men the highest privilege in the world; to be called
the 'sons of God [1],' to be 'kings and priests [m]' before him, to
be 'a royal priesthood [n],' a 'holy nation,' a 'peculiar people,'
a 'nation of priests.' Nothing doth so honour a land, as to
be the seat of the gospel. It was the honour of the Jews,
that unto them were committed the oracles of God [o]. Therefore the ark [p] is called 'the glory of Israel,' and Christ 'the
glory of Israel [q],' and 'the excellency of Jacob [r]:' neither is
there any thing else allowed a man to glory in, save only
this [s] that he understandeth and knoweth the Lord in his
Word. It putteth magnanimity into the breasts of men, high
thoughts, regal affections, public desires and attempts, a
kind of heavenly ambition [t]—to do, and to gain the greatest
good. The main ends of a Christian are all high and noble:
the favour of God, the fellowship of the Father and the Son,
the grace of Christ, the peace of the church; his traffic and
negotiation is for Heaven, his language the dialect of Heaven, his order a heavenly order, innumerable companies of
angels, and the spirits of just men made perfect. A holy
man, who hath the spirit of his mind raised and ennobled
by the gospel, is an agent in the same affairs, and doth, in
his thoughts, desires, prayers, emulations, pursue the same
high and heavenly ends, for the advancement of the glory of
Christ, and demolishing the kingdom of Satan, with the
blessed angels of God. His desires look no lower than a
kingdom, a weight of massy, and most superlative exceeding
glory. That which other men make the utmost point, even
of their impudent and immodest hopes, the secular favours
and dignities of the world, they put lowest under their feet;
but their wings, the higher and more aspiring affections of
their soul, are directed only unto Heaven and heavenly

---

[1] John i. 12. 1 John iii. 1.   [m] Revel. i. 6.   [n] 1 Pet. ii. 9.   [o] Rom.
iii. 1, 2.   [p] 1 Sam. iv. 22.   [q] Luke ii. 32.   [r] Amos. viii. 7.   [s] Jer.
ix. 24.   [t] Οὕτω φιλοτιμούμενον εὐαγγελίζεσθαι. Rom. xv. 20.

things. They no sooner are placed in the body of Christ, but they have public services, some to preach, some to defend, all to pray, to practise, to adorn the profession they have undertaken. For indeed every Christian hath his talent given him, his service enjoined him. The gospel is a ' depositum,' a public treasure, committed to the keeping of every Christian; each man having, as it were, a several key of the church, a several trust for the honour of this kingdom delivered unto him. As, in the solemn coronation of the prince, every peer of the realm hath his station about the throne, and with the touch of his hand upon the royal crown, declareth the personal duty of that honour which he is called unto, namely, to hold on the crown on the head of his sovereign; to make it the main end of his greatness, to study, and by all means endeavour the establishment of his prince's throne;—so every Christian, as soon as he hath the honour to be called unto the kingdom, and presence of Christ, hath immediately no meaner a ' depositum' committed to his care, than the very throne and crown of his Saviour, than the public honour, peace, victory, and stability of his master's kingdom. The gospel is committed to the custody of the bishops [u], and pastors of the church, to preach it. They are, as it were, the heralds, and forerunners of Christ, to prepare his way in the souls of men. To the custody of the princes and judges of the earth to defend it, to be a guard about the person and truth of Christ, to command the obedience, and to encourage the teaching of it. The gospel is the law of Christ's throne, and the princes of the world are the lions about his throne, set there to watch and guard it against the malice of enemies. And therefore it is recorded for the honour of David [x], that he set in order the courses of the priests, and appointed them their forms and vicissitudes of service:—of Solomon, that he built, adorned, and dedicated a temple for God's solemn worship:—of Josiah [y] that he made the people to serve the Lord their God;—of Hezekiah [z], that he restored the service, and repaired the temple of God; that he spake comfortably to the Levites, who taught the good knowledge of the Lord;

[u] 2 Tim. i. 14. ii. 2.   [x] 1 Chron. xxiii. 24.   [y] 2 Chron. xxxiv. 33.
[z] 2 Chron. xxix. 3. xxx. 1. 22. xxxi. 2, 3, 4.

that he proclaimed a solemn passover; that he ordered the
courses of the priests and Levites; that he gave commandment concerning the portion of their due maintenance, that
they might be encouraged in the law of the Lord (a pattern
worthy the admiration and imitation of all Christian princes,
in spite of the sacrilegious doctrine of those men, who would
rob them of that power and office, which God hath given
them for the establishment of his gospel, and it was imitated
by the first Christian prince [a] that ever the world had): Lastly,
The gospel is committed to the keeping of every Christian
to practise it, to adorn it, to pray for it, to be valiant and
courageous [b] in his place and station for the truth of it.
And for a man to neglect these duties, is to betray and
dishonour the kingdom of Christ, and to degenerate from
that high and public condition in which God hath placed
him.

Again: It putteth a spirit of fortitude and boldness into
the hearts of men. Boldness to withstand the corruptions
of the times; to walk contrary to the courses of the world;
to outface the sins and the scorns of men; to be valiant for
a despised truth, or power of religion ; not to be ashamed
of a persecuted profession; to spread out ' contra torrentem
brachia;' to stand alone against the power and credit of a
prevailing faction, as Paul [c] against the contradictions of the
Jews, and Peter [d] and John against a Synod of Pharisees;
and those invincible champions of Christ,—Athanasius against
the power of Constantius, the frequent synodical conventions
of countenanced heretics, and the general deluge of Arianism
in the world; Ambrose against the wrath and terror of the
emperor of the world, to whom, having imbrued his hands
in much innocent blood, that holy Father durst not deliver
the blood of Christ ;—Chrysostom against the pride and persecution of the Empress Eudoxa ;—Luther against the mistress of fornications, the princess of the earth, and, as himself professed, if it had been possible, against a whole city
full of devils;—the Christians of all ages against the fire,
fury, and arts of torment, executed by the bloody persecutors
of the church. Nay farther, the gospel giveth boldness

---

[a] *Euseb.* de vit. Constant. lib. 2. cap. 37, 38, 39.   [b] Acts xiii. 26. Jude ver. 3.
2 Thes. ii. 15.   [c] Acts xiii. 46. xxviii. 28. 1 Thes. ii. 2.   [d] Acts ii. 14.
xxiii. 36. iv. 8, 12. iii. 19. v. 29, 32.

against that universal fire, which shall melt the elements, and shrivel up the heavens like a roll of parchment. "Herein," saith the apostle [e], "is our love made perfect, that we may have boldness in the day of judgement, because, as he is, so we are in this world;" that is, we have his image in us, and his love shed abroad in our hearts; and therefore we are able to assure our hearts before him, and to have confidence towards him. Now he who hath boldness to stand before God, to dwell with consuming fire, and with everlasting burnings; who can get the Lord on his right hand, and put on the Lord Jesus, though he be not out of the reach, or beyond the blow, yet is he above the injury of the malice of men: they may kill, but they can never overcome him. "I am he that comforteth you; who art thou" (saith the Lord [f]) "that thou shouldest be afraid of a man that shall die, and forgettest the Lord thy maker?" &c. What an invincible courage was that of Elijah [g], which retorted the slander of Ahab upon his own face: "I have not troubled Israel, but thou and thy father's house." And that of Micaiah [h] against the base request of a flattering courtier, who thought God to be such a one as himself, that would magnify and cry up the ends of a wicked king: "As the Lord liveth, what the Lord saith unto me, that will I speak." And that of Amos [i] against the unworthy instructions of Amaziah, the priest of Bethel: "Thou sayest, Prophesy not against Israel, and drop not thy words against the house of Isaac;—therefore thus saith the Lord, Thy wife shall be a harlot in the city, and thy sons and thy daughters shall fall by the sword, and thy land shall be divided by line, and thou shalt die in a polluted land, and Israel shall surely go into captivity forth of his land."—And that of Jeremiah [k], who boldly gave the lie to Irijah, the captain of the ward; "It is false; I fall not away to the Chaldeans."—The time would fail if I should speak of the unbended constancy [l] (or as the gentiles styled it, obstinacy) of Ignatius, Polycarp, Justin, Cyprian, Pionius, Sabina, Maximus, as those infinite armies of holy martyrs, who posed the inventions, tired out the cruelties, withstood the flatteries, and with one word, "Christiani sumus [m]," over-

---

[e] 1 John iv. 17. [f] Isai. li. 12, 13. [g] 1 Kings xviii. 18. [h] 1 Kings xxii. 14. [i] Amos vii. 16, 17. [k] Jer. xxxvii. 13, 14. [l] *Tertul. Apolog.* cap. ult. *Baron.* A. 179. num. 27. *Euseb.* Hist. lib. 5. cap. 1. [m] Christiani

came all the tyrannies, quenched the fire, and stopped the
mouths of their proudest persecutors.

Again; The gospel putteth a kind of lustre and terror on
the faces of those in whom it reigneth,—and maketh them,
as the law did Moses, to shine as lights in the world, and to
be more excellent than their neighbours; worketh in others
towards them a dread and awfulness. Though Jeremiah[n]
were a prisoner, cast into the dungeon, and in such extremity
as he was there likely to perish; yet such a majesty and
honour did God even then put upon him, and that in the
thoughts of the king himself, that he could not be in quiet,
till he consulted with him about the will of the Lord, and,
by his many conferences with him, made it plainly appear,
that he stood in awe of his person and prophecies. So it is
said, that " Herod feared John, knowing that he was a just
and a holy man, and observed him[o];" to note, that holiness
maketh men's persons and presence dreadful to the wicked,
by reason of that grace and majesty which God hath put
into them The whole counsel of scribes and pharisees,
they who afterward gnashed on Stephen with their teeth,
were forced to acknowledge the majesty of holiness shining
upon him; " They steadfastly looked on him, and saw his
face as it had been the face of an angel[p]." The mighty
power of the gospel of Christ maketh unbelievers fall[q] on
their faces, and confess of a truth that God is in those who
preach it. This we find verified in the poor astonished
keeper of the prison, into which Paul and Silas had been
cast; he sprang in, and came in trembling, and fell down
before them, and brought them forth, and said, Κύριοι,
" Sirs," (which is an honourable appellation, fit rather for
princes than for prisoners,) " what must I do to be saved?"
It is true, that naturally men hate Christ and his servants;
but this is not as a man hateth a toad (which he can easily
crush) with a simple hatred: but as a man hateth a lion,
or as a malefactor hateth his judge, or as a thief hateth the
light,—with a compounded hatred, mixed with a fear and
dread of that majesty within them. Which majesty hath
sometimes shined so brightly even under torments and per-

---

sumus, Christiani; et Deos tuos, imperator, non colemus. *Baron.* A. 301. num.
46. A. 195. n. 4.   [n] Jer. xxxvii. 16, 17. xxxviii. 15, 16.   [o] Mark vi. 20.
[p] Acts vi. 15.   [q] 1 Cor. xiv. 24, 25. Acts xvi. 29, 30.

secutions, that it hath forced from heathen emperors a desire
of the Christians' prayers; sometimes not astonished only,
but converted the adversaries [r].

Lastly, The gospel bringeth liberty and joy into the hearts
of men with it. The liberty 'a glorious liberty [s],' and the
joy 'a glorious joy [t].' Therefore the gospel is called 'a
gospel of great joy [u].' Liberty is so sacred a thing, that
indeed it belongs, in the whole compass of it, only to the
prince: for though other men be free from servitude, yet
they are not free from subjection. Now the gospel giveth a
plenary freedom to the consciences of men; they may be
commanded by their own consciences, but their consciences
cannot be commanded by any but by Christ. The Son hath
made them free from all others, that he might only be the
Lord over them. These are those noble effects of the majesty of the gospel in the hearts of men, and all so many
several evidences of that glory which belongs unto it.

Now then to draw some inferences from the most useful
and excellent doctrine of the glory of the gospel, we learn
from thence, first, what liberty, and what sincerity the ministers of Christ ought to use in the administration of this his
kingdom in the Word. First, What liberty. The officers of
a prince who go before him to prepare his way, make bold to
strike, and to scatter those unruly throngs of men, who press
too near upon his sacred person. We are the messengers
of Christ, sent beforehand with his royal proclamation of
peace, to make room in the hearts of men for him, and to open
their everlasting doors, that this King of glory may enter in.
We may therefore boldly smite [x] with the rod of his mouth;
we may cry aloud, and not spare [y]; pull down mountainous
lusts; subdue strong holds; take unto us iron pillars, and
brazen walls, and faces of flint to root up, to pull down, to
batter and destroy; not to teach only, but to command [z]
with all authority, and to commend ourselves to every man's
conscience [a] in the sight of God. This use the apostle [b]
maketh of the glory of the gospel, "Seeing we have such
hope;" that is, seeing in this glorious gospel we have the

[r] Adjectos ideo vocabant, quia cum in eo essent ut torquerent martyres, ipsi
martyres fuerunt, verbo Dei et constantiâ martyrum permoti. *Cameron.* De Ecclesia, pag. 83.   [s] Rom. viii. 21.   [t] 1 Pet. i. 8.   [u] Luke ii. 10.   [x] Jer. i.
17, 18.   [y] Ezek. iii. 8, 9.   [z] 1 Tim. iv. 11.   [a] 2 Cor. iv. 1, 2.   [b] 2 Cor. iii. 12.

dispensation of a blessed hope unto men ; or the revelation of Christ, who is unto us the hope of glory ; or the assured confidence of doing excellent works by the virtue of this so glorious a word ; πολλῇ παῤῥησίᾳ χρώμεθα, " we use great boldness or liberty of speech." For why should he who bringeth unto men glad tidings of glorious things, which offered unto them the blessed hope of eternal life, be afraid or ashamed of his office ?[c] Though Rome were the seat, and that emperor the first dedicator of the persecutions of the church, yet even unto that place the apostle was not ashamed to preach the gospel of Christ, because it was " the power of God unto Salvation."[d] There is no shame in being a saviour : and therefore it is both the honour and duty of the dispensers of the gospel, " to speak boldly as they ought to speak [e] ;" and of the people to pray that that excellent Spirit might ever accompany so glorious a message. This was the prayer of the primitive saints for the apostles of Christ, " Grant unto thy servants, that, with all boldness they may speak thy word."[f] And this duty lies upon us with a heavy necessity.

For first, We are dispensers of all God's counsels [g]: there must not be a word [h] which God hath commanded, that we should refuse to make known unto the people ; for the things revealed are for them and their children.[i] Thus we find when the angel of the Lord brought forth the apostles out of prison, he gave them this command—"Go, stand and speak in the temple to the people, all the words of this life [k]:" and certainly some of these words will require boldness. When we lay the axe to the root of the tree,—when we hew off men's very members,—when we snatch them, like brands out of the fire,—when we make them to see their own faces in the law of liberty, the face of a guilty, and therefore cursed conscience,—there will be need of much boldness. A surgeon who is to search an inveterate wound, and to cut off a putrified member, had not need to be faint-hearted, or bring a trembling hand to so great a work.

Secondly, The severest message we are sent withal, and which men are most unwilling to hear, is for them expe-

[c] *Tertul.* Apol. cap. 5.   [d] Rom. i. 16.   [e] Ephes. vi. 20.   [f] Acts iv. 29.   [g] Acts xx. 27.   [h] Josh. viii. 35.   [i] Deut. xxix. 29.
[k] Acts v. 20.

dient. No news could be so unwelcome to the apostles, as to hear of Christ's departure; " Because I have said these things, sorrow hath filled your heart: nevertheless, I tell you the truth, it is expedient for you that I go away.[1]" The first news which we bring unto men, is of Christ's absence,— of their false conceits and presumptions of their being in him,—of the distance and unacquaintance which is between them,—of our fears of them, and of their condition; and, in all this, we are not their enemies, because we tell them the truth[m]. As it is our office to speak, so it is the people's duty and profit to hear all things which shall be told them of God; for ' all Scripture[n],' as well that which reproveth and correcteth, as that which teacheth and instructeth in righteousness, ' is profitable,' and tends to the perfection of the saints. All his precepts concerning all things are right.[o] The contempt of one is, virtually and interpretatively, in the constitution and preparation of heart, the violation of all;[p] because they are all grounded upon the same divine authority, and directed unto the same saving ends: and, therefore, we ought not to pick and choose, either in the preaching or practising thereof.

Thirdly, We are to answer for the blood of people, if we prevaricate. If we let their sins alone, they will have a double edge, to kill them and us both, like the mutual embracements of two in a river, which is the means to drown them both. " Speak unto them all that I command thee; be not dismayed at their faces," saith the Lord to his prophet[q], " lest I confound thee before them.—If thou warn not the wicked from his wicked way, that he may live, he shall die in his wickedness," (thy bashfulness shall do him no good,) " but his blood will I require at thy hands[r]." Is it at all congruous, that men should have boldness enough to declare their sins, to speak them, to proclaim them, to wear them, to glory in them; and that those officers who are sent for no other business, but in the name and authority of Almighty God to fight against the corruptions of the world, should, in the mean time, hang down the head and be tongue-tied? That men should have more boldness to destroy

---

[1] John xvi. 6, 7.   [m] Gal. iv. 16.   [n] 2 Tim. iii. 16, 17. Deut. xii. 28.
[o] Psal. cxix. 128.   [p] Jam. ii. 10, 11.   [q] Jer. i. 17.   [r] Ezek. iii. 18.

themselves, and to do Satan's works, than we to save them, or to serve God?

Fourthly, We are to speak in the person of Christ, and in the virtue of his Spirit. We must speak as the ' oracles of God [s],' and ' with his words [v], as if ' he himself did by us speak unto the people.' [u] We must give manifestation of Christ's speaking by us, [x] that men may be convinced that God is in us of a truth [y], and that we are full of power by his Spirit [z]; that his Spirit setteth to his seal to authorize our commission, and, so to countenance our ministry. And therefore we must use ' judgement, and might,' that is, spiritual discretion, and inflexible constancy against the sins of men, (for these two are contrary to the two grand props of Satan's kingdom, which are παvουργία, and πανοπλία, his craftiness, and his weapons of power :) for " where the Spirit of the Lord is, there is liberty [a]:" " his Spirit will not be straitened, [b] neither will the Lord keep silence." He that speaketh by the Spirit of Christ, must speak, though not in equality (which is impossible) yet in some similitude and proportion as he spake, that is, as those that have " authority and power [c]," committed to them for the edification of the church.

Lastly, A partial, unsearching, and unreproving minister is one of God's curses and scourges against a place, the forerunner of a final and fearful visitation. " The days of visitation and recompense come," saith the Lord [d]. The prophet is a fool, the spiritual man is mad, for the multitude of thine iniquity, and the great hatred.—" If a man be walking in the spirit and falsehood," that is, professing the work of a spiritual man, and yet betraying his office,—or in a false and lying spirit, ' prophesying of wine and strong drink,' that is, cherishing and encouraging sensual livers in their pernicious courses, ' he shall even be the prophet of this people.' [e]—And, therefore, when the Lord will punish with an extreme revenge the rebellion of a people against his gospel who judge themselves unworthy of so great salvation, he either removeth their candlestick [f], and taketh it away from

---

[s] 1 Pet. iv. 11.   [t] Ezek. iii. 4.   [u] 2 Cor. v. 20.   [x] 2 Cor. xiii. 3.
[y] Cor. xiv. 25.   [z] Micah iii. 8.   [a] 2 Cor. iii. 17.   [b] Micah ii. 7.
[c] Mat. vii. 29.   [d] Hos. ix. 7.   [e] Mich. ii. 11.   [f] Rev. ii. 5.

them; [g] or else sealeth up the mouth of his prophets [h], that they may be dumb, and reprove them no longer, and that " they may not be purged any more from their filthiness [i]; or else infatuates their prophets, and suffereth Satan to seduce them, and to be a lying spirit [k] in their mouths, that he may destroy them; as we see in the ruin of Ahab, and in the captivity of Judah. [l]

Again; As the ministers of the gospel must use liberty, so must they likewise use sincerity [m] in the dispensation thereof, because it is a ' glorious gospel.' This likewise is the apostle's inference: for having spent a whole chapter in this one argument of the glory of the gospel, he presently concludeth, " Therefore, seeing we have this ministry," that is, the dispensation of such a gospel committed unto us, " we faint not, but have renounced the hidden things of dishonesty;" that is, as I conceive, the arts of daubing, and palliating, and covering over unclean courses with plausible reasonings, and fleshly apologies, which is the use of false prophets; " not walking in craftiness," that is, not using human slights, or cogging, to carry men about with every wind of doctrine, [n] (as sinners are very willing to be deceived, [o] and love to have it as false prophets [p] say it is) " nor handling the word of God deceitfully [q]," that is, falsifying and adulterating it with corrupt glosses, and so tempering it to the palate of sinners, that the working and searching virtue thereof, whereby of itself it is apt to purge out and wrestle with the lusts of men, may be deaded;—and so it may well consist with the power of lusts still; as physicians so use to qualify and allay poison by other correctives and cross ingredients, that it shall serve as an instrument to strengthen us, not extinguish life: or as immodest poets may so tamper with the chaste expressions of Virgil or Homer, as by them both to notify, and in corrupt minds, to kindle unclean lustings; " but by manifestation of the

---

[g] Mat. xxi. 41. xxxiii. 23, 37, 38.   [h] 1 Thes. ii. 16.   [i] Ezek. xxiv. 13. [k] 2 Kings xxii. 20, 23.   [l] Jer. iv. 10. xiv. 13. xxiii. 13. xxxiii. 40. Lam. ii. 14.   [m] 2 Cor. iv. 1, 2. 2 Cor. ii. 17.   [n] Ephes. iv. 14. Col. ii. 4. 8. [o] Ezek. xiii. 10.   [p] Jer. xiv. 13. v. 31.   [q] Ὡς οἱ καπηλεύοντες τὸν λόγον. τ. ε. ἀναμἴγνύντες τὸν οἶνον ὕδατι—τὰς ἑαυτῶν ἡδονὰς θεραπεύοντας λόγοις ἐκ γῆς φωνουμένοις καὶ δυομένοις εἰς γῆν, &c. Greg. Naz. Orat. 1. & Isid. Pelus. lib. 1. ep. 169.

truth [r]," that is, by such spiritual and perspicuous demonstrations, as under which there cannot ' subesse falsum,' there can no falsity or deceit lurk, " commending ourselves to every man's conscience in the sight of God;" that is, working not the fancies, or humours, or fleshly conceits of men, (which always take the part of sin,) but their very consciences (which always is on God's side) to bear witness unto the truth which we speak,—to receive it not as the wit or learning of a man, but as the Word and wisdom of God,—to acknowledge the conviction, the judicature, the penetration thereof, and so to fall down upon their faces, and to glorify God and report that he is in us of a truth;—and all this " in the sight of God;" that is, so handling the Word as that we may please and approve ourselves to his eye, whose servants we are, and whose work we do. This is that which the apostle [s] calleth ἀ᾽διαφθορίαν, σεμνότητα, ἀφθαρσίαν, λόγον ὑγιῆ, ὑγιαίνουσαν διδασκαλίαν, " Uncorruptedness, gravity, sincerity, soundness of doctrine," such as the very adversaries themselves shall not be able to pick quarrels withal, or to speak against. We must not, then, make account to adorn the gospel with our own inventions, or with superstructions of human wit and fancy. Though these things may, to fleshly reason, seem full of beauty, yet indeed they are but like the mingling of glass beads with a chain of diamonds, or of lime with pure and generous wine : they are indeed but ' latebræ dedecoris,' lurking places for unclean lusts to hide themselves under, or to escape away, while the corrupt fancies of men stand gazing at that which pleaseth them ; as Agag when he was gloriously arrayed, thought nothing of the bitterness of death; or Sisera, of the nail and the hammer, while he saw nothing but the milk and the butter. Some there are not unlike Praxiteles [t], the painter, who made the silly people worship the image of his strumpet, under the title and pretence of Venus; who, by slight and cunning craftiness, impose upon weak and incautious hearers, the visions of their own fancy, the crude and unnourishing vapours of empty wit (things infi-

---

[r] Ἐν ἀποδείξει πνεύματος καὶ δυνάμεως. 1 Cor. ii. 4.—Demonstratio autem nihil relinquit aut inevidentiæ in re, aut formidinis in intellectu.   [s] Titus ii. 1, 7, 8.   [t] *Clem. Alex.* in Protrept.

nitely unsuitable to the majesty and seriousness of the foundation in the gospel) for the indubitate truth of God in his Word; which (with reverence may it be spoken) is nothing else but to put the holy prophets and apostles into a fool's coat. But however these men may please and puff up themselves in the admiration of their own wind, yet certain it is that the gospel of Christ doth as much scorn human contemperations, as a wall of marble doth a roof of straw, or the sun at noon doth the light of a candle. And, therefore, the palate of those who cannot away with the naked simplicity of the gospel, without the blandishments of human wit,—who must needs have quails to their manna,—is hereby discovered to be manifestly distempered with an itch [u] of lust, and their eyes blinded by the god of this world. [x]

Secondly, This glory of the gospel, may teach us what admiration and acceptation it should find amongst men, even as it doth with the blessed angels themselves. This is " a faithful saying, and worthy of all acceptation [y];" worthy to be received with all readiness of mind [z]; worthy to be gazed upon, like the star of the wise men [a], ' with exceeding great joy ;' worthy to be enamelled in the crowns of princes, and to be written in the soul of every Christian with a beam of the sun,—" That Jesus Christ came into the world to save sinners." And indeed the faithful have ever found " beauty in the feet of those, that bring them glad tidings of this their king ;" that is, in the coming of this Word of grace and salvation unto them, which is the usual phrase of the scripture setting forth more abundantly the mercy of the Lord [b], who did not choose one fixed place for his gospel to reside in, and unto which all nations, who would have benefit by it, should take the pains to resort, as he did for the Jews at Jerusalem; but hath made it an itinerary salvation, and hath sent it abroad to the very doors of men, who else would never have gone out of doors to seek it. What man in a sad and disconsolate estate would not spread wide open his heart, and let out his spirits, to run upon the embraces of that man who was coming unto him with a message of

---

[u] 2 Tim. iv. 3.   [x] 2 Cor. iv. 3.   [y] 1 Tim. i. 15. iv. 9, 10.   [z] Acts xvii. 11.   [a] Matt. ii. 10.   [b] Rom. x. 5. i. 10. Eph. ii. 17. Col. ii. 6. 1 Thes. i. 5. ii. 1. Rom. x. 6, 7, 8. Jer. xxvi. 4. Isai. lxv. 1.

more lovely and acceptable news, than the very wishes of
his heart could have framed to himself? When Joseph was
sent for out of prison unto Pharaoh's court, when Jacob saw
the chariots which were brought to carry him unto Joseph
his son, how were they revived and comforted after their
distresses! When Caligula the emperor sent for Agrippa
(the same which was afterwards smitten by the angel) whom
Tiberius had bound in chains, and cast into prison, caused
him to change his garments, and cut his hair (it seems that
long and ugly hair was then the fashion of discontented prisoners) and placed a diadem on his head, made him Tetrarch
of Iturea and Trachonitis, and governor of Judea, and for
his chain of iron, gave him another of gold, of equal weight,
as the historian relateth [c], he saith that men were ἐν ἀπιστίᾳ
ϖερι τῶν γεγονότων, they could not believe so wonderful a
change ; for things of extraordinary goodness are very diffi-
cultly believed. " When the Lord turned away the captivity of Sion, we were like them that dream [d] :" the thing was
so incredibly suitable to their desires, that it seemed rather
the imaginary wish of a dream, than a deliverance really
acted: as Peter [e] when he was delivered out of prison,
thought he had seen a vision ; Jacob [f] could not at first believe the news of the life and honour of Joseph his son ;
and the disciples [g] for very joy were not able to believe the
resurrection of Christ.—Now what are all the good tidings
to the gospel, which is a word of salvation, which opens
prisons and lets out captives, which brings our king unto us,
and makes us kings too, which gives us such a joy, as the
whole world cannot rob us of? " Your joy shall no man
take from you." The joy which Caligula gave unto Agrippa,
Claudius might have taken from him, as he did after from
Agrippa his son ; and though he did not, yet we see the
angel did. But the joy of the gospel is invariable. The
angels themselves (to whom, one might think, the joys of
men should seem but small) call it χαρὰν μεγάλην, ' a great
joy.[h] ' It is the ' joy of a treasure [i],' infinitely more worth
than all which a man hath besides. ' A joy of a triumphal

[c] *Joseph.* Antiq. lib. 18. cap. 8.   [d] Psal. cxxvi. 1.   [e] Acts. xii. 9.
[f] Gen. xlv. 26.   [g] Luke xxiv. 41.   [h] Luke ii. 10.   [i] Matth. xiii. 44.

harvest [k],' and of ' victorious spoils,' wherein there is not
only an escape from dangerous hazard, but a large reward of
peace and plenty. It is ' a full joy [l];' there is no sorrow mingled with it ; nay, it is ' all joy [m],' and therefore there is nothing but sorrow without it. All joy in itself, and all joy
in the midst of opposition too. A joy in the heart like gold
in the mine, which turneth every thing about it into joy.
Divers temptations take not away one scruple of it, no more
than fire doth of gold; it is all joy still. " My brethren,"
saith the apostle [n], " count it all joy, when ye fall into divers
temptations." It turneth the reproaches of men into riches,[o]
nay, in the midst of all other tribulations, it is our peace [p]
and our glory [q]. Therefore being so full of joy, when once
aright apprehended, needs must it likewise be worthy of all
acceptation too. And therefore the prophet [r] calleth the time
of the gospel ' tempus acceptabile,' the acceptable time or
year of the Lord ;—which Baronius [s] falsely understands of
the first year of Christ's preaching only, since the apostle
useth the same phrase for the whole time of evangelical dispensation.[t]

And indeed, if we look into the church, we shall see what
worthy acceptation this gospel hath found. Zaccheus [u] made
haste, and received Christ in his house ' gladly ;' so did the
brethren at Jerusalem [x] receive the apostles ; so did the men
of Berea [y] receive the Word, μετὰ πάσης προθυμίας, " with all
readiness of mind," or forward affection : so did the Galatians [z] receive St. Paul with " the honour of an angel, yea,
even as Christ Jesus himself;" for indeed Christ and his gospel
go still together : the man in the gospel sold all he had for
it :[a] the saints did earnestly contend for it, and take ' the
kingdom of heaven by violence.' Though they suffered the
loss of all for Christ, yet they counted godliness great gain
still. In a shipwreck I throw my goods overboard, and get
my life for a prey : in this case I come no loser to Heaven ;
' vita sibi merces ;' a man's life is sufficient treasure in such
an adventure. We are all, by nature, ' in maligno positi,'

---

[k] Isai ix. 3, 4.   [l] John xv. 11.   [m] Rom. xv. 3.   [n] James i. 2.
[o] Heb. xi. 26.   [p] Mic. v. 5.   [q] Rom. v. 3.   [r] Isai. lxi. 2.   [s] Baron.
An. 31. numb. 78.   [t] 2 Cor. vi. 2.   [u] Luke xix. 26.   [x] Acts xxi. 17.
[y] Acts xvii. 11.   [z] Gal. iv. 14.   [a] Mar. x, 29.

every man is a sea and a tempest to himself; as impossible
to escape ruin, as to put off himself. Now, in the gospel,
Christ showeth a man a way to get out of himself, and so to
escape the tempest; showeth a way, how with him he shall
walk upon the sea and not sink; how he shall be in the
world, and not of it, nor swallowed by it. O how willingly
will the man who is convinced of his danger, cast off every
thing which would press him down,—and account it a plentiful deliverance to have his soul saved from such a tempest
of wrath as was falling upon him! We see what hazards men
run to get temporary riches, to the bottom of rocks for diamonds, to the bowels of the earth for gold and silver;—such
affections have the saints had towards the gospel. If they
must dig in mines for Christ (as it was an usual condemnation, ' Christiani ad metalla') they were most willing so to
do: they had a treasure there which the emperor knew not
of; they had infinite more precious wealth from thence than
he. If they must fetch Christ in the fire, or wrestle for him,
as for a precious price, with the wild beasts of the earth; if
they be not suffered to wear Christ, except they put off themselves, how willing, how thankful are they for so rich a
bargain! " Look to your life," said the governor to St.
Cyprian, that blessed martyr; " be not obstinate against
your own safety, but advise well with yourself;"—" Fac quod
tibi præceptum est," saith the holy man, " in re tam justa
nulla est consultatio ; Sir, you are my judge, you are none
of my counsellor; do the office which is committed to you;
in so righteous a cause there is no farther need of consultation [b]."—" Take pity upon yourself; and sacrifice, and save
your life," said the officers [c] to Polycarp ;—" No," saith the
martyr, " these eighty-six years I have served Christ, and
he hath done me no harm, I will not do what you persuade
me."—That rich and blessed virgin in Basil [d], who was, for
Christianity, condemned to the fire, and was offered, if she
would worship idols, to have her life and estate safe restored
unto her, was obstinate in her resolution ; " Valeat vita, pe-
reat pecunia ;" I shall have more life in Christ, than in myself; all the emperors, all the physicians in the world, can-

---

[b] *Baron.* An. 261. num. 30.   [c] *Euseb.* lib. iv. hist. cap. 14.   [d] *Schulten.*
Exercitat. Evangel lib. 2. cap. 5.

not make my life, which I have in myself, so long to-morrow as it is to-day; but in Christ, my life is not only an
abiding, but an abounding life: I shall have more of that
by losing mine own; my life in him is an hidden life, free
from all injuries and persecutions of men: I shall have more
riches in him than in myself, even unsearchable riches, which
can never be stolen away, because they can never be exhausted. It is as possible for thieves to draw out the mines
of India, or to steal away the sun out of his orb, as for any
human violence to take away Christ from a man." Alike
honourable was the answer of Frederic, the elector of
Saxony, who, being prisoner to Charles V. was promised
enlargement and restitution of dignity, if he would come
to mass. "Summum in terris dominum agnosco Cæsarem,
in cælis Deum," in all civil accommodations I am ready to
yield unto Cæsar, but for heavenly things, I have but one
master, and therefore I dare not serve two; Christ is more
welcome to me in bonds, than the honours of Cæsar without
Christ.—Such acceptation hath the gospel found amongst the
renowned worthies heretofore: and the like entertainment
should we all give unto it, even prefer it above our greatest
glory; and as the Thessalonians ᵉ did, receive it with joy in
the midst of afflictions,—abide with Christ in his temptations ᶠ; esteem his gospel glorious, as the stars are in the
darkness of the night,—or as a torch, which blazeth most
when it is most shaken.

This alone it is, which proves our love to Christ to be ἐν
ἀφθαρσίᾳ, "sincere and incorrupt," when we embrace his
gospel for itself, and can therein, in any condition, see
Christ full of glory, grace, and truth: when a man can with
St. Paul ᵍ, not rejoice only in the name and profession of the
cross of Christ, but in conformity and obedience thereunto,
in that virtue of the gospel which crucifies him unto the
world, and the world unto him. In days of peace and religion, men may easily afford to magnify the gospel, because
they get by it. The Persians, who, had the bloody decree
held, would have been the slaughterers of the Jews; yet
when leave was given to that people, to deliver themselves
from the malice of Haman, "even many of them turned

ᵉ 1 Thes. i. 6.   ᶠ Luke xxii. 28, 29.   ᵍ Gal. vi. 14.

Jews themselves, because the fear of that people fell upon them."—We may observe this affection in the woman of Samaria : the first reason why she gave some heed to Christ, speaking of his water of life unto her, was, because " she should thirst no more, nor come thither to draw[h]." So long as Ephraim might have her work and her wages together, she was contented to do God some service, " like an heifer that loveth to tread out the corn[i];" that is, while she hath no yoke on her neck, no muzzle on her mouth, while she is not put to plough, but to easy and pleasant service, she is willing to yield unto it :—to note, that it is but base and hypocritical obedience, which is supported by no other than present rewards. " They seek me daily," saith the Lord of the hypocrites, among his people, " and delight to know my ways, as a nation that did righteousness[k]." But the end was, that they might have their own wills, and, as it were, oblige God to reward them : and therefore as soon as God seemeth to neglect them and their services, they proudly expostulate with him, and even twit him with their works; " Wherefore have we fasted, and thou seest not?" &c. This then is the proof of our sincere love unto Christ, which is not raised upon mercenary respects, when we can receive the gospel with persecution. Persecution[l] is amongst Christ's legacies, a part of the church's portion, and of God's gifts unto her[m]; no man that will live godly[n], can be without them. Even in Abraham's house, which was, at that time, if not the sole, yet the most glorious church on the earth, there was a persecutor, and " as it was then, so is it now," saith the apostle.[o] The saints of God ever have been, and ever will be, to the world's end esteemed for 'wonders[p],' and 'marks,' and 'mad men[q],' and ' proverbs of reproach.'[r] And hereby the Lord did provide to make his gospel more glorious, because he giveth men's hearts to suffer scorn and reproach for it. " To receive the word in affliction, and yet with joy," is an exemplary thing, which maketh the sound and glory of the gospel to spread abroad. Now then, if persecution be thus an appendant to the gospel,—every man must resolve to

h John iv. 14.   i Hos. x. 11.   k Isai. lviii. 2, 3.   l Mark x. 30.
m Phil. i. 29.   n 2 Tim. iii. 12.   ● Gal. xciv. 29.   p Zech. iii. 8.
Isai. viii. 18.   q 2 Kings ix. 11. Jer. xxix. 26.   r Wisd. v. 6.

receive it in some affliction, when he must be put to discard his wicked companies, to shake off his flattering and sharking lusts, to forsake his own will and ways, to run a hazard of undeserved scorn, disreputation, and misconstructions in the world,—and yet, for all this, to set a high price upon the precious truths of the gospel still, is not this to receive 'the Word in much affliction?' And surely till a man can resolve upon this conclusion, "I am ready to be bound, and to die for the name of Jesus, I count not my life, much less my liberty, peace, credit, secular accommodations dear, so I may finish my course with joy ; Lord, my will is no more mine, but it shall be in all things subject unto thee ;"—he can never give such entertainment to the Word, as becometh so glorious a gospel. All his seeming profession and acceptation, is but like the Gadarenes' courtesy in meeting of Christ, which was only to be rid of him.[s]

Lastly, We should from hence learn a farther Christian duty, which is, to adorn this glorious gospel in a holy conversation. This use the apostle everywhere makes of the gospel of Christ; that " we should walk as becometh the gospel[t]; " that " we should in all things adorn the doctrine of God our Saviour[u];" that " we should walk worthy of him, who hath called us unto his kingdom and glory[x]; " that " we show forth the virtues of him who hath called us out of darkness into his marvellous light[y];" that we should not receive so great a grace as the ministry of reconciliation in vain[z], but that we should walk fittingly[a] to the holiness and efficacy of so excellent a rule, as becometh 'a royal nation,' a people of glory, 'a peculiar[b] and selected inheritance,' even 'zealous of good works.'—It was once the expostulation of Nehemiah[c] with his enemies, " Should such a man as I flee" from such men as you?—Such should be our expostulation with Satan, and our own lusts: 'Should such men as we are, who have the gospel of Christ for our rule, conform ourselves unto another law?'—Is not this the end why the gospel is preached[d], that we should live unto God? Doth it become the son of a king to go in rags, or to converse

s Mat. viii. 34.   t Phil. i. 27.   u Tit. ii. 10.   x 1 Thes. ii. 12.
y 1 Pet. ii. 9.   z 2 Cor. vi. 1, 3.   a Gal. vi. 16.   b Tit. ii. 14.
c Nehem. vi. 11.   d 1 Pet. iv. 3, 6.

with mean and ignoble persons? Now, by the gospel, we
have that great honour and privilege given us, to be called
' the sons of God:' and shall we then walk as servants of
Satan? Would any prince endure to see the heir of his
crown, live in bondage to his own vassals and most hated
enemy? Herein is the greatest glory of the gospel above
the law, that it is a law of life and liberty; a word which
transformeth men into the image of Christ, and maketh
them such as it requireth them to be. So that to walk still
according to the course of the world, as we did before, is,
as much as in us lies, to make the gospel as weak and unprofitable as the law. " How do you say we are wise," saith
the prophet[e], "and the law of the Lord is with us? ´Cer-
tainly in vain made he it, the pen of the scribe is in vain:"
that is, the privilege of having the oracles and ordinances
of God committed unto us, will do us no more good, if we
walk unworthy of so great a grace,—than if those ordinances
had never been written or revealed to men.

Here then it is needful to enquire, in what manner we are
to adorn and set forth the glory of the gospel. To this I
answer, That the first and greatest honour we can do unto
the gospel, is to set it up in our hearts, as our only rule by
which we are to walk; that we prefer it above all our own
counsels, and venture not to mingle it with the wisdom and
reasonings of the flesh; that we raise up our conversation
unto it, and never bend it unto the crookedness of our own
ends or rules. " As ye have received Christ Jesus the Lord,
so walk ye in him[f]," saith the apostle; that is, fashion
your conversation to the doctrine of Christ; let that have
the highest room, and the overruling suffrage in your
hearts. There is ' all wisdom[g],' in the gospel: it is able
to make men ' wise unto salvation[h];' that is, there is
wisdom enough in it to compass the uttermost and most
difficult end. And what can the reasonings of the flesh
contribute to that which was all wisdom before, and
which can thoroughly " furnish a man unto every good
work?" This glory St. Paul (though a man of great learning, of strong intellectuals, of a working and stirring

---

[e] Jer. viii. 8.   [f] Col. ii. 6.   [g] Col. i. 28.   [h] 2 Tim. iii. 15, 16, 17.
Psal. cxix. 98, 99. Jer. viii. 9.

spirit, qualities very unapt to yield and be silent) did, at the very first revelation thereof, give unto the gospel; "Immediately," saith he, "I conferred not with flesh and blood [i];" I did not compare the gospel of Christ with the principles of my carnal wisdom; I did not resolve to dispute against God's grace, or to conform unto this mystery no farther than the precepts of mine own reason, or the co-existence of mine own secular ends and preferments would allow: but I captivated all my thoughts, and laid down all the weapons of the flesh, at Christ's feet,—resting only on this Word as a treasury of wisdom,—and yielding up my whole heart, to be in all things ordered by this rule. It is a horrible boldness in many men to rest, and torture, and distinguish the gospel into all shapes, for their own lusts' sake. As we see what shifts men will use, to make the way of life broader than it is, by looking upon it through their own multiplying glasses; what evasions and subterfuges, sin will find out to escape by, when the letter of the Word presseth sore upon them. O how many sins might men escape, how wonderfully might they improve the image of Christ in their hearts, if they did, with David [k], make the law their counsellor and weigh every action which they go about:—those especially which they have any motions of reluctancy in the spirit of their mind unto, "Non in statera dolosa consuetudinum, sed in recta statera scripturarum [l]," not in the deceitful balance of human custom, but in the balance of the sanctuary, the holy scriptures: if they would seriously remember, that they must always "walk in Christ [m]," make him the rule, the way, the end, the judge, the companion, the assistant in all their works;—that as the members of the body do nothing at all but in the fellowship of the body, and as they are thereunto applied by the same common soul which animates them all; so Christian men should do nothing but as parts of Christ, and as actuated by the same gracious Spirit, which is in him. This is the meaning of our being Christians, and of that consent which, in our baptism, we yield unto that covenant of Christ,—that we will not follow, nor be led by Satan, the world, or the flesh;—that is, by that wisdom which

i Gal. i. 16.   k Psal. cxix. 24.   l *Aug.* contr. Ep. Parmen. lib. 3. c. 2.
m Col. ii. 6.

is earthly, sensual, devilish ;—but that we will be ordered by that Spirit of regeneration, the seal of whose baptism we receive in our sacramental washing. O then what is become of the Christianity of many men, who forget that they have been purged! who live as if they had never been 'baptized into Christ,' who live as if they never 'learned Christ!' What a prodigy and contradiction is it, that that tongue which even now professed itself to be a Christian, and said *Amen* to a most clean and holy prayer, should like those beasts which Seneca speaketh of, which by but turning aside their head to some other spectacle, do immediately forget the meat which they most greedily ate before, break forth presently into blasphemies, oaths, lies, revilings, clamours, obscenities, which are the very fumes and evidences of Hell in the heart! That those hands which even now were reached forth to receive the sacred pledges and most dreadful mysteries of salvation, which were even now employed in distributing alms to the members of Christ, or in helping to heave and lift up a prayer unto Heaven, which seemed, like the hands of Ezekiel's living creature, to have wings of devotion over them,— should suddenly have their wings melted off, and fall down to covetous and cruel practices again ! that those feet which, in the morning, carried men into the Lord's sanctuary, and into the presence of Christ,—should, the same day, turn the backs of the same men upon the temple of the Lord, and carry them to stews and stages, the nurseries of uncleanness! that those eyes which even now seemed to have been nailed unto Heaven, and to have contended with the tongue and the hand, which should more earnestly have presented the prayers of the soul to God,—should, almost in the space of their own twinkling, be filled with sparks of uncleanness, gazing and glutting themselves upon vain or adulterous objects! What is this but for men to renounce their baptism, to tear off their seal, and dash out their subscription from the covenant of grace, 'to deny the Lord that bought them,' to repent their bargain, which they had made for salvation, and really to dishonour that gospel which they hypocritically profess? This then is the first honour which we can do unto the gospel of Christ, when we set it up in our hearts as a most adequate rule of all wisdom, and the alone principle of every action.

Secondly, We continue to honour the gospel of Christ, by walking in obedience of faith, receiving it, and leaning upon it, laying hold on the covenant which is therein revealed, as on the only hope which is set before us : for this is a great acknowledgment of the glory and praise of God, when we trust in him for salvation. Therefore the apostle, having showed the glory of Christ above Moses, maketh this use of it, that therefore " they should hear his voice, and take heed of an unbelieving heart, in departing from him[n]." " We," saith he, " are to the praise of God's glory, who trust in Christ [o]."

Secondly, In obedience of life and holiness. When, for the honour of the gospel, we can deny ourselves, and dishonour our lusts, and part from all that we had before, as from dung and dross, and express the image of Christ in our conversations. This is indeed the true learning of Christ[p], when we show forth his life in ours ; when we walk as he also walked[q] ; when as he was, so we are in this world[r]; when the same mind[s], judgement, affections are in us which were in Christ. Thus the faithful are said to honour God[t], when they sanctify his sabbath, and to glorify him[u] when they bring forth much fruit.

Thirdly, We honour the gospel of Christ by constancy and continuance in our faith and obedience thereunto : for ' standing fast,' or persisting immovably in our course without sorrow or repentance, is an argument of the excellency of the gospel. " Walk," saith the apostle[x], " as becometh the gospel"———" that I may hear of your affairs, that you stand fast in one spirit."—Lusts ever bring inconstancy[y] with them, and make the soul like weary and distempered bodies, never well in any posture or condition. Wicked men flee like bees from one flower to another, from one vanity to another, can never find enough in any to satiate the endless intemperancy of unnatural desires : only the gospel being spiritually apprehended, hath treasures enough for the soul to rest in, and to seek no farther. And therefore falling away from the truth, power, or purity of the gospel, is said to ex-

[n] Heb. iii. 3, 12.   [o] Ephes. i. 12.   [p] Ephes. iv. 20, 22.   [q] 1 John ii. 6.
[r] 1 John iv. 17.   [s] Phil. ii. 5.   [t] Isai. lviii. 13.   [u] John xv. 8.   [x] Phil.
i. 27.   [y] Non stant uno loco vitia, sed mobilia, et inter se diffidentia tumultu-
antur, pellunt invicem, et fugantur. *Sen.* de Beuef. l. i. c. 16.

pose Christ to shame, and to crucify him again.   For as, in
baptism, when we renounce sin, and betake ourselves to
Christ, we do, as it were, expose sin [z] unto public infamy,
and nail it on the cross of Christ; so when we revolt from
Christ unto sin again, and in our hearts turn back unto Egypt,
and thrust him from us,—we do then put him to shame again,
as if he were either in his power deficient, or unfaithful in
those promises which before we pretended to rely upon.   If
Israel, as they consulted, should likewise actually have rebelled against Moses, and returned in body as well as in heart
unto Egypt again, what a scorn would it have wrought in
that proud nation, that their vassals should voluntarily re-
sume their thraldom, after so many boasts and appearances of
deliverance! If a man should relinquish the service of some
noble person, and apply himself unto some sordid master for
subsistence,—would not the mouths of men be quickly open,
or their minds jealous to suspect that however such a man
carries a high name, and there be great expectations from attending on him, yet, in truth, he is but a dry master, whom
his own servants do so publicly dishonour [a] ?   So when any
men turn apostates from the power and profession of the gospel of Christ, presently wicked men are apt to blaspheme,
and to conceive desperate prejudices against our high and
holy calling.   If any man make a boast of the law, and yet
break it, he dishonoureth God the more : for, (saith the
apostle) " The name of God is blasphemed among the gentiles through you, as it is written."   So then constancy in
Christ's service, giveth him the glory of an honourable master,—and his law, of a royal law; putteth to silence the ignorance of those foolish men [b], who lie in wait to take advantages, that they may blaspheme [c] the name of God, and
his doctrine.

Fourthly, The gospel of Christ is honoured by the unity
of the Spirit, and concurrent judgements and affections of
men towards it.   When all the sincere professors thereof, do
unanimously strive together [d], and " earnestly contend for it [e];"
when all that ever have been, or are acquainted therewith, do

---

[z] Δείξῃς ὅτι τὴν ἁμαρτίαν ὄντως μεμίσηκας, παραδειγματίσας αὐτήν· καὶ θριαμ-
βεύσας, ὡς ἀξίαν ὕβρεως. *Greg. Naz.* Orat. 40. de Baptismo.   [a] Rom. ii. 23, 24.
[b] 1 Pet. ii. 15, 16.   [c] 2 Cor. vi. 3. 1 Tim. vi. 1.   [d] Phil. i. 27.   [e] Jude
verse 3.

glorify it with their suffrages and subscription. " Nemo
omnes, neminem omnes fefellere ;" it must needs be a glorious
gospel, if all that ever looked on it, do so conclude.—Nothing
was ever able to deceive all men, neither did so many ever
combine to deceive others.—When the philosophers severally
strove for the precedence of their several sects, and every
man, after his own order, gave the next place unto Plato, it
was undoubtedly concluded, that his was the most excellent,
because, after their own prejudice and personal respects, it
was honoured by the equal suffrages of all the rest. How
much more must the gospel needs be glorious, which hath
the joint attestation of angels[f], and all holy men, since the
world began to honour it withal ! Therefore when the apostle
proveth the greatness of this heavenly mystery, he useth a
word which importeth the consent of men, καὶ ὁμολογουμένως
" without any doubt," or by a universal confession, " Great
is the mystery of godliness." Doth it not much set forth
the glory of a law, that there should be so much wisdom,
power, equity, majesty, beauty in the face of it, that every
true subject in a realm should concur in a constant and uniform love and obedience to it? Let us, therefore, express the
glory of the gospel, not only in our joint confessions, but in
our united obedience thereunto, and in our unanimous zeal
and contention for it, in our brotherly affections and compassions to one another thereby : for the schisms and disaffections of Christians, bring much dishonour upon their holy
profession, which, in all their miscarriages, doth ever, by occasion of the unreasonableness of wicked men, suffer together
with them. Therefore the apostle, from the unity of Christ
in himself, concludeth that such he should be in his members too. " Is Christ divided ?" hath he divers opinions ? or
hath he the truth of God in respect of persons ? such as he
is, such should you be likewise ; lest, by your contentions,
you seem to make another Christ, or another gospel, than
that which you have received.

Fifthly, The gospel of Christ is honoured in our studying
of it, and digging after it in our serious and painful enquiries
into the mysteries of it. St. Paul despised all other knowledge, and shook off every weight, that he might press for-

[f] 1 Tim. iii. 16.

ward with the more unwearied affections towards so excellent
a treasure. Surely, if men had the spirit of the apostle, or
of those blessed angels which desire to pry into the gospel of
Christ, they would not mispend so much precious time in
frothy and fruitless studies, nor waste away that lamp of reason in their bosoms, in empty and unnourishing blazes ; but
would set more hours apart to look into the patent of their
salvation (which is the book of God), and to acquaint themselves with Christ beforehand, that when they come into his
presence, they may have the entertainment of friends, and
not of strangers. Men that intend to travel into foreign
kingdoms with any advantage to their parts, or improvement
of their experience, do, beforehand, season and prepare
themselves with the language, with some topographical observations of the country, with some general notions of the
ingeny, manners, forms, civilities, entertainments of the
natives there ; do delight to converse with those men, who
are best learned in these, or the like particulars. Surely, we
all profess a journey to Heaven, a pilgrimage in this present
world, to have our conversation now, where we look to have
our everlasting abode with the Lord hereafter. Now in the
gospel of Christ we have, as it were, a map, a topographical
delineation of those glorious mansions, which are there prepared for the church ; we have a taste and description of the
manners of that people; we have some rudiments of the
heavenly language ; in one word, we have abundantly enough,
not only to prepare us for it, but to inflame all the desires of
our soul unto it, even as exiles and captives desire to return
to their native country. Now then, if we no way regard to
study it, or acquaint ourselves with it ; if we seem to desire
the sight of Christ in Heaven,—and when we may, every day,
have a blessed view of his face in the glass of his gospel, we
turn away our eyes, and regard it not ; we do as good as proclaim to all the world, that either our hopes of Heaven are
very slender, or our care thereof little or none at all. And
this I take for a most undoubted truth, that there is so much of
the knowledge, grace, and Spirit of Christ, and, through him,
of the Father, in the holy Scriptures (and those only are the
things, which make Heaven to be the home and the hope of
men), as that whosoever neglecteth the study of them, and
suffereth the Scriptures to lie by him as a sealed book, would

be every whit as unwilling, if Heaven' gates were wide open
unto him, to relinquish his portion in the earth, and to spend
his time in the fruition or contemplation of that glorious
country.

Lastly, We honour the gospel, when, in our greatest distresses, we make it our altar of refuge, our door of escape,
the ground of all our hope and comfort, the only anchor to
stay our souls in any spiritual tempest, the only staff to lean
upon in our greatest darkness. Whatever other carnal comforts men may, for a time, rejoice in, they will all prove but
as a fire of sparks, or as a blaze of thorns, which can yield
no solid or abiding light unto the soul. When sinners in
Sion begin once to be afraid, and to be surprised with the
fearfulness of a guilty soul; when the affrighted conscience
shall put that dreadful question, in the prophet [g], to itself,
' How can I dwell with devouring fire? how can I dwell with
everlasting burning?'—there will no other answer allay the
scorching terror thereof, but that in the end of the same chapter, " The people that dwell therein, shall be forgiven their
iniquity." A man may as soon drink up the water of the sea
with sponges, or remove mountains with one of his fingers, as
be able to drain out these close and incorporated sorrows,
which together with sin, do soak through the whole substance of the soul, with vain company, worldly employments,
or youthful pleasures. All these do but respite them for a
time, that they may return the stronger. But if thou wilt
indeed be comforted, sue out thy pardon, flee to the court of
mercy which is erected in the gospel. This was our Saviour's
argument [h] to the man that was sick of the palsy,—" Son, be
of good cheer; thy sins be forgiven thee." There is no
worldly affliction goeth closer to the life of a man than sickness: and yet, as in the midst of laughter, the heart of a
wicked man is sorrowful, because it is still under the guilt of
sin,—so, in the midst of pain and sorrow, the heart of a godly man may be cheerful, because his sins are forgiven.

To conclude this point, we may, for our better encouragement in so necessary a duty, lay together these considerations: First, In point of honour, we should learn to walk, as
becometh the gospel; for the gospel is a Christian's glory,

[g] Isai. xxxiii. 14, 24.　　[h] Matth. ix. 2.

and therefore ought to be preserved in his heart, as his
chiefest privilege. The Spirit of God will not endure to have
holy things profaned, as if they were common or unclean.
Belshazzar converted the consecrated vessels of the temple
into instruments of luxury and intemperance ; but the Lord
tempered his wine with dregs, and made them prove unto
him as cups of trembling and astonishment. Herod [i] polluted the sepulchres of the saints with a sacrilegious search
of treasures, presumed to have been there hidden, and God
made fire rise there out of the earth, to devour the overbusy
searchers. Antiochus [k] ransacked the temple of the Lord ;
Heliodorus emptied the treasuries of their consecrated monies ;
Pompey [l] defiled the sabbath and the sanctuary ; Crassus [m]
robbed the house of God of ten thousand talents. But enquire into the event of these insolences ; and we shall find
that true then, of which later ages have given many examples, and are still likely to give more, that stolen bread hath
gravel in it to choke those that devour it,—that ruin is ever
the child of sacrilege,—that mischief setteth a period to the
lives and designs of profane men. Now then, if the Lord
were thus jealous for the types of his gospel, how think we,
can he endure to see the gospel itself dishonoured by an unsuitable profession, or the blood of the covenant trampled under
foot, as if it were a common or unclean thing ? In the contempt of the gospel, there is more dishonour done unto every
person of the blessed Trinity, than can be by any other sin.
An undervaluing of the Father's wisdom, that great mystery
and counsel of redemption, which was hidden from former
ages : and what an indignity is it unto him, for a man to
shut out the light of the sun, that so he may enjoy that
pitiful benefit of darkness, to gaze upon the false glistering
of rotten wood, or of earthly slime, the deceit whereof would
be by the true light discovered ? An undervaluing of his
wonderful love, as if he had put himself unto a needless compassion, and might have kept it still in his own bosom ;—a
scorn unto the Son of God, when we suffer him to stand at
our doors, with his locks wet with the dew of Heaven, to
put his finger into the hole of the lock, as if he desired to
steal an entrance upon the soul ; to empty, to humble, to

i *Joseph.* Antiq. lib. 6. cap. 11.   k 2 Mac. iii. 5.   l *Tacit.* Hist. l. 5.
m *Joseph.* Antiq. lib. 12. cap. 13.

deny himself, to suffer the wrongs of men, and the wrath of God ; and after all this, to have that precious blood, which was squeezed out with such woful agonies, counted no other than the blood of a common malefactor,—nor that sacred body which was thus broken, discerned from the bodies of the thieves which were crucified with him. An indignity beyond all apprehension to the Spirit of grace, when we suffer him to wait daily at our Bethesda, our houses of mercy, and all in vain ; to spend his sacred breath in the ministry of reconciliation, in doubling and redoubling his requests unto our souls, that we should be contented to be saved; and we shall harden our hearts, and stop our ears, and set up the pride and stoutness of our own reasonings, till we do even weary him, and chide him away from us. Now this is a certain rule, God will not lose any honour by men's sins: if they refuse to give him the glory of his mercy, he will show the glory of his power and justice, in treading down the proud enemies of Christ under his feet. As they that honour him, shall be honoured; so they who cast any disgrace upon his truth and covenant, shall be sure to meet with shame and dishonour at the last.

Secondly, To avoid scandal. The gospel is the light of a nation: and sins in the light, as they are committed with more impudence, so likewise with more offence :—an offence or scandal tending unto sin in misguiding the weak, in heartening and confirming the obdurate, in opening the mouths of adversaries to revile our holy profession; and a scandal tending unto sorrow, in wounding the hearts of the godly, and vexing their righteous spirits with a filthy con-versation.

Thirdly, We should learn to walk as becometh the gospel, even in respect to the state ; for the gospel is the foundation of true peace and tranquillity in a common weal : and those who show forth the power thereof, are, as it were, lions about the throne of their king. " By righteousness the throne is established, but sin is a reproach unto any people[n]." One Joseph in Egypt, is a storehouse to all the kingdom : One Elisha, an army of chariots and of horsemen unto Israel : One Moses, a fence to keep out an inundation of

[n] Prov. xvi. 12. xx. 28. xxv. 5.

wrath which was breaking in upon the people: One Paul, a haven, an anchor, a deliverance to all that were in the ship with him.   And now, " si stellæ cadunt, venti sequentur[o];" If the stars fall, we must needs look for tempests to ensue: if the salt be infatuated, we cannot look that any thing should be long preserved.   If Christians live as if they had no gospel, or as if they had another gospel; what can we expect, but that God should either plague us, or forsake us, either send his judgements, or curse his blessings?

Lastly, The gospel makes sin more filthy, if it do not purge it; as a taper in the hand of a ghost makes him seem more ghastly than he was before.   Sweet ointment causeth rank and strong bodies to smell worse than they did before[p]. So the sweet savour of the gospel maketh the sins of men more noisome and odious in the nostrils of the Almighty. And therefore we see what a fearful doom the apostle[q] pronounceth against those, who having " tasted of the good Spirit of God, and been illightened," and in some sort affected with his grace, do yet afterwards " fall away;"—even an impossibility of repentance or renovation.   From which place, perversely wrested, though the Novatians[r] of old, did gather a desperate and uncomfortable conclusion, that " sin, committed after regeneration, was absolutely unpardonable," (to avoid the danger of which damnable and damning doctrine, some have boldly questioned both the author and authenticalness of that epistle,) yet, all these inferences being denied, we learn from thence this plain observation, that " precedent illumination from the gospel of Christ, doth tend much to the aggravation of those sins which are committed against it."   And therefore in all these considerations, we should labour to walk worthy of so glorious a gospel, and of so great a salvation.

Thus have we at large spoken of the rod of Christ's strength, as it is ' insigne regium,' or ' sceptrum majestatis,' an ensign and rod of majesty :—we are now to speak a little of it as it is ' pedum pastorale,' an episcopal rod, which denoteth much heedfulness and tender care.   This is the pre-

---

[o] *Arist.* Prob. sect. 26. q. 27.   [p] Qui hircos redolent, fœdiùs olent cum se unguentaverint.   *Arist.* Prob.   [q] Heb. vi. 4, 7. x. 26.   [r] Vid. *Sixt. Senens.* Bibliot. 1. 7.—*Melch. Can. loc.* Theolog. 1. 2. cap. 10.—*Greg. Tholos.* de Rep. lib. 12. cap. 7.

cept which the apostle giveth unto the pastors of the church, that they would προσέχειν τῷ ποιμνίῳ, " take special heed to all the flock, over which the Holy Ghost had made them overseers [s]." And the apostle again reckoneth ' vigilancy' or care over the flock [t], amongst the principal characters of a bishop : and he professeth of himself, that there did daily lie upon him μέριμνα πασῶν τῶν ἐκκλησιῶν, " the care of all the churches [u]." And this consideration affordeth us another note out of the words, namely, That Christ, in the ministry of his gospel, and dispensation of his Spirit, is full of care and tenderness towards his church. This Christ maketh one main point of opposition between himself and hirelings, that these ' care not for the flock [x],' but suffer the wolf to come and to scatter them while they flee away ; whereas he keepeth them, that none may be lost, and prayeth unto the Father [y] to keep them through his own name. The Lord committed the church unto Christ as their head ; gave them into his hands, not as an ordinary gift, wherein he did relinquish his own interest in them, or care of them (for he careth [z] for them still) but as a blessed ' depositum ;' intrusted them with him, as the choicest of his jewels [a], as the most precious casket amongst all the treasures of the creation, that he should polish, preserve, present them faultless, and " without spot, before the presence of his glory at the last day [b]." And for this purpose he gave him a commandment of the greatest care and tenderness that ever the world knew,—that he should ' lay down his life [c]' for his sheep, and should ' lose nothing [d]' of all that was given him, but should ' raise it up at the last day.' So that now, want of care, or compassion of Christ towards his church, would be an argument of unfaithfulness; if he had not been a ' merciful high-priest [e],' neither could he have been ' faithful' to him that appointed him : for he was appointed to be merciful,—and was, by the Spirit of God, filled with most tender affections, and qualified with a heart fuller of compassion, than the sea is of waters, that he might commiserate the distresses of his people, and take care of their salvation.

Notably doth this care of Christ show itself: First, In the

[s] Acts x. 28.   [t] 1 Tim. iii. 2.   [u] 2 Cor. xi. 28.   [x] John x. 12, 13.
[y] John xvii. 11, 12.   [z] 1 Peter v. 7.   [a] Mal. iii. 17.   [b] Jude v. 24. Eph. v. 26. 27.
[c] John x. 18.   [d] John vi. 39.   [e] Heb. ii. 17. iii. 2.

apportioning and measuring forth to every one his due ' de-
mensum,' and in the midst of those infinite occasions and exigences of his several members, in providing such particular
passages of his Word, as may be thereunto most exactly suitable; for this showeth, that his care reacheth unto particular
men.   It is the duty of a faithful bishop [f], ὀρθοτομεῖν, to make
such a difference [g] between men, and so ' to divide or distribute the Word aright,' as that every one may have the portion which is due unto him.   Some are but lambs in Christ's
flock, young, tender, weak [h], easily offended or affrighted;
others, sheep grown up to more strength and maturity : some
in his garner are but cummin seed; others, fitches [i],—and
some, harder corn : some can but bear a little rod, others
a greater staff or flail, and some the pressure of a cart
wheel : that which doth but cleanse some, would batter
and break others into pieces : some are ' great with young [k],
in the pangs of a loaden conscience, in the travail under
some sore affliction, or in the throws of a bitter repentance, as it were in fits of breeding, or new forming of
Christ in their soul : and these he leadeth with a gentle hand :
others are, as it were, ' new-born,' past their pains, but yet
very tender, weak, and fearful; and these he gathers with
his arm, and carries in his bosom ; shows them that his care
doth not only reach unto the least of his kingdom, but that
his compassions are most enlarged to those that are too weak
to help themselves ; but he hath ' breasts of consolation [l],'
to satisfy and delight with abundance, the smallest infant
of his kingdom.   Some are ' broken-hearted,' and those he
bindeth [m] : some are ' captives,' to those he proclaimeth liberty : some are ' mourners' in Sion, and for them he hath
beauty, and oil of joy, and garments of praise : some are
' bruised reeds,' whom every curse or commination is able to
crush : and some are ' smoking flax,' whom every temptation is able to discourage : and yet even these doth he so
carefully tend and furnish with such proportionable supplies
of his Spirit of Grace, as makes that seed and sparkle of
holiness, which he began in them, get up above all their own
fears, or their enemy's machinations, and grow from a judge-

---

[f] 2 Tim. ii. 15.   [g] Jude v. 22, 23.   [h] John xx. 15, 16.   [i] Isai.
xxviii. 27, 28.   [k] Isai. xl. 11.   [l] Isai. lxvi. 11.   [m] Isai. lxi. 1, 2, 3.

ment ' of truth' and sincerity, as it is called by the prophet [n];
unto a ' judgement of victory' and perfection, as it is termed
by the evangelist [o]. In one word, some are strong, and others
are weak; the strong he feedeth, the weak he cureth; the
strong he confirmeth, the weak he restoreth ; he hath trials
for the strong to exercise their graces, and he hath cordials
for the weak to strengthen theirs. According unto the
several estates, and unto the secret demands of each member's condition, so doth the care of Christ severally show itself towards the same in his Word : there is provision for any
want, medicine for any disease, comforts for any distress,
promises for any faith, answers to any doubt, directions in
any difficulty, weapons against any temptation, preservatives
against any sin, restoratives against any lapse ; garments to
cover my nakedness, meat to satisfy my hunger, physic to
cure my diseases, armour to protect my person, a treasure to
provide for my posterity. If I am rich, I have there the
wisdom of God to instruct me ; and if I am poor, I have
there the obligations of God to enrich me. If I am honourable, I have there the sight of my sins to make me vile, and
rules of moderation, to make me humble : if I am low of
degree, I have there the communion and consanguinity of
Christ, the participation of the divine nature, the adoption of
God the Father, to make me noble. If I am learned, I have
there a law of charity to order it unto edification ; and if I
am unlearned, I have there a spirit which searcheth the deep
things of God, which can give wisdom unto the simple,
which can reveal secrets unto babes, which can command
light to shine out of darkness, which can give the light of
the knowledge of the glory, fulness, and love of God in the
face of Jesus Christ ; which can make me, though ignorant
of all other things, to learn Christ in whom there is more
wisdom, more various and admirable curiosity, more filling
and plentiful satisfaction, more proportion to the boundless
desires of a soul once rectified, more fruit and salvation
(which should be the end of every Christian man's learning)
than in all other knowledge, which either past or present
ages can afford. In one word, every where, and in all things,
I am there " taught how to want, and how to abound, and

[n] Isai. xlii. 3.   [o] Matth. xii. 20.

how to do all things through Christ that strengthens me." A
Christian can be set in no estate, wherein the abundant care
of Christ over him is not, in the gospel, wonderfully magnified. And commonly, in the greatest straits, he showeth the
greatest care, as waters run strongest in the narrowest
passages: when we walk in darkness and have no light,—
when we seek water, and there is none, and our tongue faileth
for thirst, then is his fittest time to help us, and then is our
fittest time to stay upon him. Israel were delivered by
miracles of mercy from their Egyptian bondage, and in the
wilderness conducted by a miraculous presence, and fed with
angels' food. Isaac was upon the altar, and then in the mount
was the Lord seen, and his mercy stepped between the knife
and the sacrifice. Jacob in great fear of his brother Esau,
and then comforted by prevailing with an angel which was
stronger than Esau. Peter [p] in sorest distress for denying
Christ, and he the first man to whom Christ sent news of his
resurrection. Paul in the ship visited by an angel. Peter in
prison delivered by an angel. The distressed women at
Christ's sepulchre comforted by an angel. Such as the extremities of the saints are, such is Christ's care for their deliverances.

And care is thus farther commended, that it proceedeth
solely from the grace and compassion of Christ: there is no
affection naturally in us to desire it, there is no virtue in us
to deserve it. When we were in our blood [q], well pleased
with our own pollution, he doubled his goodness, and used a
kind of violence and importunity of mercy to make us live.
When we did not seek after him,—when we did not so much
as ask whether he were fit to be sought,—when we were
aliens from his covenant, and strangers to his name, he even
then multiplied his invitation unto us ; " I said, Behold me,
behold me, unto a people, that were not called by my name [r]."
When we were weak [s], full of impotency; when we were
sinners, full of antipathy; when we were enemies, full of
obstinacy and rebellion; when we cared not for him,
but turned our backs and stopped our ears, and suffered
him to throw away in vain so many sermons, so many sacraments, so many mercies, so many afflictions upon us; when

p Mark xvi. 7.   Vocatur ex nomine, ne desperaret ex negatione. *Gregor. Mag.*
q Ezek. xvi. 6.   r Isai. lxv. 1.   s Rom. v. 6, 8. 10.

we cared not for ourselves, no man repented, or said, What have I done? even then did he magnify his compassion towards us; he cared for us, when we neglected ourselves, despised him; he bestowed his mercy not only upon the unthankful, but upon the injurious.

But then a little compassion is enough for those that had deserved none, for those that had provoked scorn and displeasure against themselves: but herein is the care and tenderness of Christ abundantly magnified, that it hath in it all the ingredients of a most sovereign mercy, that nothing more could have been done[t], than he hath done for us. First, For the foundation and original of all mercy, there is in him an overflowing of love, without stint or measure, — a turning of heart[u],—a rolling and sounding of bowels[x],—a love which surpasseth all knowledge[y], which is as much beyond the thoughts or comprehensions[z], as it is above the merits of men.

Secondly, There is a study and inquisitiveness how to do good,—a debating within himself, a consulting and projecting how to show mercy,—an arguing, as it were, of his grace with man's sin, and his own severity: " How shall I give thee up, Ephraim? How shall I deliver thee, Israel? How shall I make thee as Admah? How shall I set thee as Zeboim? Mine heart is turned within me, my repentings are kindled together[a]." True it is, thou hast been unto me as the rulers of Sodom, and as the people of Gomorrah[b]: but I shall be unto thee, as I have been unto them. Am I not God, and not man? shall I change my covenant, because thou hast multiplied thy backslidings?—The Lord useth such humane expressions of his proceedings with men, as if their sins had put him to a stand, and brought him to difficulties in showing mercy. " I said, How shall I put thee amongst the children, and give thee a pleasant land[c]?" &c. Thy case is very desperate, and thou hast stopped up the courses of my mercy towards thyself: how then shall I make good my resolutions of compassion towards those that reject and nullify it to themselves? Surely, there is no way but one, to overrule the hearts of obstinate sinners, that they may not

t Isai. v. 4.   u Hosea xi. 8.   x Jer. xxxi. 20.   y Ephes. iii. 19.   z Isai. lv. 9. Jer. xxix. 11.   a Hosea xi. 8.   b Isai. i. 10.   c Jer. iii. 19.

turn away any more. 'Thou shalt call me My father;' that
is, I will put filial affections, awful thoughts, constant resolutions into thy heart, and thou shalt not turn away from
me. I will melt them and try them, saith the Lord; for how
shall I do for the daughter of my people [d]? The Lord setteth
himself to study and contrive mercy for his people, that as
they set up their sins, as it were, in pride to pose his covenant; so he gathereth together his thoughts of mercy, as it
were, to conquer their sins.

Thirdly, There is constancy and continuance in this his
care: " His mercy endureth, his compassions fail not, but
are renewed every morning [e]."—And therefore ' the mercies of
David,' that is, of Christ, for so he is called, or the mercies
of the covenant made with David, are called ' Sure mercies [f];' they have a foundation, the everlasting love and
counsel of God, upon which they are built; they have many
seals [g] by which they are confirmed, the faithfulness [h], the
immutability, and the oath of God. If there were not continuance in his mercies [i]; if he were not the same yesterday,
and to-day, and for ever [k], in his truth and fidelity to his
church: if he should change and turn from us, as oft as we
forsake him; if he should leave us in the hand of our own
counsel, and not afford us such daily supplies of his Spirit, as
might support us against the ruinous disposition of our own
nature; we should be children of wrath every day anew.
But herein doth the abundant care of Christ in the gospel
declare itself unto us, that, though we are worms in ourselves, full of weakness, and of earthly affections, yet God
hath ' a right-hand of righteousness [l],' which can uphold us;
that, though we are bent to back-sliding, yet ' he is God and
not man;' unchangeable in his covenant with the persons;
almighty in his power and mercy towards the sins of men,
both to cover them with his righteousness, and to cure them
by his Spirit,—both to forgive for the time past, and to heal
and prevent backslidings [m] for the time to come.

Fourthly, That he might be fit for so mean and humble a
service, there was " a lessening and emptying of himself:"
he was contented to be subject to his own,—to be the child
of his own creature,—to take upon himself not the similitude

d Jer. ix. 7.   e Lam. iii. 22. 23.   f Acts xiii. 34.   g 2 Tim. ii. 19.
h Psalm lxxxix. 2.   i Mal. iii. 6. Isai. lxiv. 5.   k Hebr. xiii. 8.   Isai.
i. 10, 14.   m Hosea xi. 7, 11.

only, but the infirmities of sinful flesh[n],—to descend from his throne, and to put on rags,—in one word, " to become poor for us, that we, through his poverty, might be made rich [o]."—Amongst men, many will be willing to show so much mercy as will consist with their state and greatness, and may tend to beget a farther distance, and to magnify their height and honour in the minds of men ; but when it comes to this exigent, that a man must debase himself to do good unto another,—that his compassion will be to a miserable man no benefit, except he suffer ignominy, and undergo a servile condition for him, and do, as it were, change habits with the man whom he pities ; what region of the earth will afford a man, who will freely make his own honour to be the price of his brother's redemption ? Yet this is the manner of Christ's care for us, who, though he were the Lord of glory, the brightness of his Father's majesty, and the express image of his person, did yet humble himself to ' endure shame, and the contradiction of sinners,' that he might be the ' author and finisher of our faith.'

Fifthly, There was not only an humbling or metaphorical emptying of himself, in that he ' made himself of no repu- tation ;' but there was likewise a real and proper emptying of himself : he therein testified his wonderful care of the businesses of men, that for them he put himself to the great- est expense, and to the exhausting of a richer treasure than any either heaven or earth could afford besides. " Ye were not redeemed," saith the apostle, " with corruptible things, as silver and gold, from your vain conversation, but with the precious blood of Christ, as of a lamb without blemish, and without spot." That which no man will bestow upon himself, and that which was in nature, and might justly in love have been nearest to Christ himself, even the soul in his body and the blood in his veins,—he was contented to make a sacrifice for them, who poured it out as the blood of a malefactor.

Sixthly, Besides this great price which he paid to his Father for us, he hath opened another treasure of his grace and spirit, out of which he affordeth us daily supplies, and putteth into our hands, as it were, a heavenly stock, for the better negotiating and improvement of our salvation. He setteth up his Spirit in our hearts, thereby conversing

---

[n] Phil. ii. 7. 8. Gal. iv. 5. Rom. viii. 3. [o] 2 Cor. viii. 9.

and communing with us, teaching us the trade of the citizens of Heaven, and of laying up treasures there, where our final abode must be,— of having our conversation and commerce with innumerable companies of angels, and with the spirits of just men made perfect, and with all that general assembly or church of the first-born, which is enrolled in Heaven.

Lastly, To all this he addeth preparations and provisions, for the future for us: he doth not only give, but he *prepareth* things for those that love him[o], and whatever is wanting now, he will make it up unto us in the riches of his glory.[p] It was for our expediency that he left the church on earth (in regard of his carnal presence) and went unto his Father again. He was not beholding to change of place for his own glory, for his heaven was within him as a fountain. And indeed it is his presence, which maketh Heaven to be the place of glory: therefore St. Paul desired to depart[q], and to be with Christ; noting that it is not heaven, but Christ's presence which is the glory of the saints. Therefore I say, it was for us, that he went to Heaven again ; " for their sakes," saith he, " I sanctify myself[r] ;—it is expedient for you that I go away[s]." *Expedient,* to sell and secure our full and final redemption unto us: for as the Levitical priest entered not into the holiest of all without blood, so neither did Christ into Heaven, without making satisfaction. He first obtained ' eternal redemption' for us, and then he entered into the holy place.[t] And *expedient* to prepare[u] a place for us; that the glory which is given to him, he may give unto us[x]; that being raised up together, we may likewise sit together with him in heavenly places.[y] For when the head is crowned, the whole body is invested with royal honour. He, by the virtue of his ascension, opened the kingdom of Heaven for all believers. Even the fathers before Christ entered not in, without respect unto that consummate redemption, which he was, in the fulness of time, to accomplish for his church :—As a man may be admitted into an actual possession of land, only in the virtue of covenants, and under the intuition of a payment to be afterwards per-

---

o 1 Cor. ii. 9.   p Phil. iv. 19.   q Phil. i. 23.   r John xvii. 19.
s John xvi. 7.   t Heb. ix. 12.   u John xiv. 2, 3.   x John xvii. 22.
y Eph. ii. 6.

formed. Thus we see in how many things the abundant care of Christ doth show itself towards the church.

And as there are therein all the particulars of a tender care, so, by the gospel likewise, do all the fruits and benefits thereof redound unto the faithful. First, In the gospel he feedeth [z] and strengtheneth them ; even in the presence of their enemies he prepareth them a table, and feedeth them with his rod [a]; and, according to their coming out of Egypt, he showeth unto them marvellous things. And therefore our Saviour calleth his gospel, " The children's bread [b]." It is that which quickeneth, which strengtheneth them [c], which maketh them fruitful in spiritual works.[d]

Secondly, He upholdeth them from fainting : if their strength at any time fail, he leadeth them gently, and teacheth them to go. As Jacob [e] led on his cattle and his children softly, according as they were able to endure; so Christ doth lead out his flock [f], and hold his children by the hand, and teach them to go [g], and draweth them ' with the cords of a man [h],' that is, with meek and gentle institution, such as men use towards their children [i], and not to their beasts, and ' with bands of love.' As an eagle fluttereth over her young,[k] and spreadeth abroad her wings, and taketh them and beareth them on her wings; so doth the Lord, in his gospel, sweetly lead on and institute the faithful unto strength and salvation : he dealeth with them as a compassionate nurse with a tender infant, condescendeth to their strength and capacity; when we stumble, he keepeth us ; when we fall, he raiseth us ; when we faint, he beareth us in his arms [l] ; when we grow weary of well-doing, the gospel is full of encouragements to hearten us, full of spirit to revive us, full of promises to establish us, full of beauty to entice us. When we seem to be in a wilderness, a maze, where there is no issue, nor view of deliverance,—even there he openeth a door of hope, and allureth and speaketh comfortably unto us.[m]

Thirdly, He healeth our diseases, our corruptions, our

[z] Psal. xxiii. 5.   [a] Mic. vii. 13, 15. Ezek. xxxiv. 14, 23.   [b] Matt. xv. 26. [c] Phil. iv. 13. Heb. vi. 12.   [d] John xv. 4.   [e] Gen. xxxiii. 14.   [f] John x. 3.   [g] Hos. xi. 3, 4.   [h] Psal. lxxviii. 52. Isai. lxiii. 13.   [i] Deut. i. 31. [k] Deut. xxxii. 11, 12.   [l] Isai. xl. 11. xli. 13.   [m] Hos. ii. 14. 15.

backslidings.[n] Easily are the best of us misled out of the
right way, drawn and enticed away by our own lusts, driven
away by the temptations of Satan, the frowns or follies of
the world; possessed with carnal prejudices against the
ways of God, as if they were ' grievous [o],' ' unprofitable,[p]'
and ' unequal ' ways [q]; apt to take every pretence to flinch
away, and steal from the eye of God; apt to turn aside into
every diverticle, which a carnal reason, and a crooked heart
can frame unto itself; for a corrupt heart is like a wild
beast [r], that loveth ' confusa vestigia,' to have intricacies
and windings in his holes; it cannot away with straight
paths, but loveth to wry and pervert the rule of life.[s] In
these cases it is the care and office of Christ to gather that
which was scattered [t], to seek that which was lost, to bring
again that which was driven away, to bind up that which
was broken, to strengthen that which was sick, and to restore by his spirit of meekness, those which are overtaken
with a fault: his gospel is like the trees of the sanctuary,
not for meat only, but for medicine too.

Fourthly, As he healeth our diseases, and giveth us
strength, so, in the midst of enemies and dangers, he removeth our fears, and giveth us comfort and refreshment.
" I will make them," saith he, " a covenant of peace, and
I will cause evil beasts to cease out of the land, and they
shall dwell safely in the wilderness, and sleep in the woods.
—When the Assyrian shall be in our land, and shall tread
in our palaces, then shall he raise up seven shepherds, and
eight principal men ;" namely, the ministers of his gospel in
abundance, to establish the heart of his people against all
dangers. This is that Shiloh who should bring tranquillity
and peace into the church, even when the sceptre should
depart from Judah. When the heart is full of doubts and
distresses, disquieted with the fear of God's displeasure, accused by the law, pursued by the adversary, and condemned
by itself; then doth he still the raging of the sea, and com-

---

[n] Hos xiv. 4.　　[o] John vi. 60. Matth. xxv. 24. Job. xxi. 14, 15. Mal.
iii. 14, 15.　　[p] Ezek. xviii. 25.　　[q] Jer. xi. 10. Acts vii. 39. Psal. xiv. 3.
[r] Animalia quædam, ne inveniri possint vestigia sua, circa cubile ipsum confun-
dunt. *Senec.* ep. 68. χεῦδος μυρίας ἐκτροπὰς ἔχει. *Clem. Alex.*　　[s] Gal. i. 7.
2 Peter iii. 16.　　[t] Ezek. xxxiv. 16. Gal. vi. 1 Ezek. xlvii. 12. xxxiv. 25.
Micah v. 5. *Scultet.* Exercit. Evang. l. 1. cap. 4.

mand the evil spirit to be dumb ; then doth he wipe away
tears from the conscience, and refresh it with living waters[u],
even with the sweet communion of his Spirit, and with the
abundance of his graces.

Lastly, He keepeth a continual watch over us by his spiritual presence and protection.   As Jacob testified his great
care for the good of Laban [x], that " the drought consumed
him by day, and the frost by night, and that sleep departed
from his eyes;" so doth the Lord commend his care towards
the church, in that he is the keeper or watchman of Israel,
which doth neither slumber nor sleep.[y] His presence is with
his people [z] to guide them in their pilgrimage, and unto
which they have daily recourse for comfort and establishment.   In that great tempest when Christ was asleep in the
ship, his disciples awaked him and expostulated with him,
" Master, carest thou not that we perish ?[a]"   But when he
had rebuked the wind and the sea, he then rebuked them
likewise : he had another storm of fear and unbelief to calm
in their hearts, who could not see him in his providence
watching over them, when his body slept.

The grounds of this great care, which Christ in his gospel testifieth towards his church, are these : First, He is our
kinsman, there is affinity in blood, and therefore a natural
care and tenderness in affection.   We know, amongst the
Jews [b], when a woman had buried a husband without fruit
of his body, the next of the kindred was to take care of her,
and to raise up the name of the dead upon his inheritance.
And if any man had waxen poor,[c] and sold any of his possession, the nearest kinsman was to have the first option
in the recovery and redemption of it.   And from hence the
apostle argueth to prove the mercifulness and fidelity of
Christ, in ' sanctifying' or ' bringing many sons unto glory'
(for I take those phrases to be, in that place,[d] equivalent), because he was not " ashamed to call us brethren, but was made
in all things like unto us."   And we may observe that, in the
Scripture, he hath almost all the relations of consanguinity,
to note that his care is universal, and of all sorts.—He is a

[u] Rev. vii. 17.   [x] Gen. xxxi. 40.   [y] Psal. xi. 42.   [z] Exod. xxxiii. 14.
[a] Mark iv. 38, 40.   [b] Deut. xxv. 5. Ruth iii. 9. iv. 5.   [c] Levit. xxv. 25.
[d] Heb. ii. 11, 17.

father;—" Behold, I and the children which thou hast given me [e];"—and the care of a father is to govern, to nourish, to instruct, to lay up for his children.   He is as a mother; [f] he carries his young ones in his bosom [g] he gathereth them as a hen her chickens[h], he milketh unto them out of the breasts of consolation.[i] And thus he hath a care of indulgence and compassion.—He is a brother; " Go to my brethren, and say unto them,—I ascend unto my Father, and your Father, and unto my God, and your God [k]."   And the care of a bro- ther is to counsel, advise, and comfort.   " A brother is born for adversity [l]."—Lastly, He is a husband : Ye are married to him who is raised from the dead [m], and that word com- priseth all care, to love, [n] to cherish, to instruct, to main- tain, to protect, to compassionate, to adorn, to communi- cate both his secrets and himself.   A father may maintain his child, but he cannot suckle it ; a mother may give it a breast, but she cannot ordinarily provide it a portion ; a brother can give counsel, but he cannot give himself unto his brother: a husband may comfort his wife, but it becomes him not to correct her.   There is no degree of nearness that hath power enough to answer all the offices of love, but, in one point or other, it will be defective.   Therefore Christ is set forth unto us under all relations of blood and unity ; to note, that there can be no case or condition of the church be supposed, wherein the care of Christ shall be impotent or deficient towards it, wherein he is not able to correct, to nourish, to instruct, to counsel, to comfort, to provide for it.

Secondly, He is our companion in sufferings.   He himself suffered, and was tempted ; and this the apostle [o] maketh a main ground of his care towards us, and of our confidence in him: ' We have not a high Priest which cannot be touched with a feeling of our infirmities, but was, in all points, tempted as we are, only without sin ; and therefore he is able to suc- cour those that are tempted, and to take compassion on those that are out of the way, because he was compassed with such infirmities, as were much less grievous than the weight of sin.'

e Isai. viii. 18.   f Isai. xlix. 15.   g Isai. xl. 11.   h Matt. xxiii. 37.
i Isai. lxvi. 11.   k John xx. 17.   l Prov. xvii. 17.   m Rom. vii. 4.
n Eph v. 25, 32.   o Heb. iv. 15. ii. 17. v. 2.

Thirdly, He is our head, and so is one with us in a nearer relation than that of affinity, in a relation of unity: for he and his members make but one Christ. And being head, he is the seat of care, and the fountain of influences into the rest of the body. All the wisdom, spirit, senses, which are in the head, are there placed as in a watch tower, or council-chamber, to consult and provide for the good of the whole: the eye seeth, the ear heareth, the tongue speaketh, the fancy worketh, the memory retaineth for the welfare of the other members, and they have all 'the same care one for another[p].'

Fourthly, He is our advocate[q], and mediator; he is the only practiser in the court of Heaven, and therefore he must needs be full of the businesses of his church. It is his office to despatch the affairs of those that come unto him, and crave his favour and intercession to debate their causes; and he is both faithful[r] and merciful in his place, and, besides, furnished with such unmeasurable unction of spirit, and vast abilities to transact all the businesses of his church, that whosoever cometh unto him for his counsel and intercession, "he will in nowise cast them out[s]," or refuse their cause. And this is one great assurance we may take comfort in,—that be our matters never so foul and inexcusable in themselves, yet the very entertaining of him of our counsel, and the leaning upon his wisdom, power, fidelity, and mercy, to expedite our businesses, to compassionate our estate, and to rescue us from our own demerits, doth, as it were, alter the property of the cause, and produce a clean contrary issue to that, which the evidence of the thing in trial, would, of itself, have created. And as we may observe, that men of extraordinary abilities in the law, delight to wrestle with some difficult business, and to show their learning in clearing matters of greatest intricacy and perplexity before; so doth Christ esteem himself most honoured, and the virtue and wisdom of his cross magnified, when, in cases of sorest extremity, of most hideous guilt, of most black and uncomfortable darkness of soul, which pose not only the presumptions, but the hope, faith, conjectures, thoughts, contrivances which the hearts of men can, even in wishes, make to themselves for mercy, they do yet trust him "whose

[p] 1 Cor. xii. 25. [q] 1 John ii. 2. [r] Heb. iii. 3. [s] John vi. 37.

thoughts are infinitely above their thoughts, and whose ways above their ways [t]."—" Who is there among you that feareth the Lord, that obeyeth the voice of his servant, that walketh in darkness, and hath no light? Let him trust in the name of the Lord, and stay upon his God [u]." When the soul can go unto Christ with such complaints and acknowledgments as these; " Lord, when I examine my cause by mine own conscience, and judgement of it, I cannot but give it over as utterly desperate, and beyond cure: my bones are dried, my hope is cut off, I am utterly lost; my sins, and my sorrows are so heavy, that they have broken my spirit all to pieces, and there is no sound part in me: but, Lord, I believe thou knowest a way to make dead bones live [w]; that thy thoughts and ways are above mine; that thou knowest thine own thoughts of peace and mercy [x], though I cannot comprehend them; that thy riches are unsearchable; that thy love is above human knowledge; that thy peace passeth all created understanding [y]; that though I am the greatest of all sinners, and feel enough in myself to sink me as low as Judas into Hell, yet thou hast not left me without patterns [z] of all-suffering, of thy royal power in enduring, and in forgiving sins. And now, Lord, though thou afford me no light, though thou beset me with terrors, though thou make me to possess the sins of my youth,—yet I still desire to fear thy name, to walk in thy way, to wait upon thy counsel. I know there is not, in men or angels, so much wisdom, compassion, or fidelity as in thee; and therefore if I must perish, I will perish at thy feet; I will starve under thy table; I will be turned away and rejected by thee, who has promised to cast away none that come unto thee. I have tried all ways, and I here resolve to rest, and to look no farther. Thou that hast kept such a sinner as I am, out of Hell thus long, canst, by the same power, keep me out for ever; upon thy wisdom and compassion (who canst make dried bones to flourish like a herb [a], and broken bones to rejoice and sing,) I cast [b] the whole weight of my guilty spirit; into thy bosom I empty all the fears, cares, and requests of my distracted and sinking soul:"—I

[t] Isai. lv. 8.   [u] Isai. l. 10.   [w] Ezek. xxxvii. 3.   [x] Jer. xxix. 11.
[y] Eph. iii. 8, 19.   [z] 1 Tim. i. 16.   [a] Isai. lxvi. 14.   [b] Psalm li. 8.
1 Pet. v. 7.

say, when a man can thus pour out himself unto Christ, he esteemeth the price and power of his blood most highly honoured when men believe in him against reason and above hope, and beyond the experience or apprehensions they have of mercy: for Christ loveth to show the greatness of his skill in the salvation of a Manasseh, a Mary Magdalen, a crucified thief, a persecutor, and injurious blasphemer, in giving life unto them that nailed him to his cross :—the more desperate the disease, the more honourable the cure.

Fifthly, He is our purchaser, our proprietary. We belong unto him by grant from the Father, " Thine they were, and thou gavest them unto me [c] :"—and by payment from him unto the Father, " Ye are bought with a price [d]." There is no good that concerns the church, that he hath not fully paid for with his own precious blood : and Christ will not die in vain, he will take order for the accomplishing of that redemption, which himself hath merited. And this is the greatest argument of his care and fidelity, that he is not as a servant, but a lord, and his care is over his own house [e]. An ordinary advocate is faithful only ' ratione officii,' because the duty of his office requireth it ; but the businesses which he manageth, come not close unto his heart, because he hath no personal interest in them : but Christ is faithful, not as Moses, or a servant only, but ' ratione dominii,' as Lord in his own house: so that the affairs of the church concern him in as near a right, as they concern the church herself. So that, in his office of intercession, he pleadeth his own causes with his Father; and, in the miscarriages of them, himself should lose that which was infinitely more precious, than any thing in the world besides,—even the price and merit of his own blood. These are the grounds of the great care of Christ towards his people.

And from hence we should learn faith and dependence on Christ in all our necessities, because we are under the protection and provision of him who careth for us, and is able to help us. A right judgement of God in Christ, and in his gospel of salvation, will wonderfully strengthen the faith of men. Paul was not ashamed of persecutions [f], because he knew whom he had believed ; he doubted neither of his

---

c John xvii. 6.   d 1 Cor. vi. 20.   e Heb. iii. 6.   f 2 Tim. i. 12.

care or power, and therefore he committed the keeping of his soul unto him, against the last day; and therefore when all forsook him, he stood to the truth, "because the Lord forsook him not [g]." The reason why men trust in themselves or their friends, is, because they are assured of their care and good-will to help them: but if men did compare the affections of Christ to other succours, they would rather choose to build their hopes and assurances on him. This consideration of the care and power of God, made the three children,[h] at a point, *rebel* against the edict of an idolatrous king, " Our God is able to deliver us, and he will deliver us." And this made Abraham, at a point, to offer his son [i] without staggering, because he rested upon the promise [k] and the power of God, who was able to raise him from the dead, from whence, in a sort, he had received him before, namely, from a dead body, and from a barren womb. And this is the ground of all diffidence, that men consider not the power [l], and the care of God towards them, but conceive of him, as if he had forgotten to be gracious, as if he had cast them out of his sight, as if he had given over his thoughts of them; and that maketh them fear second causes, and seek unto things which cannot profit. And therefore the Lord suffereth second causes to go cross, to fail and disappoint a man, because he loveth to be glorified by our dependence on his all-sufficiency and protection. He suffereth friends to fail, to be off and on,—promises to be uncertain,— assurances to vanish,—projections and frames of businesses to be shattered; that men may know how to trust him: for man, being impotent in himself, must needs have something without himself to subsist upon. Now when a man findeth the creatures to be deceitful, and second causes vain, and considereth that God is *I Am*, a most certain rewarder of those that diligently seek him [m], then the soul findeth it good to draw near to God [n], to live under his fidelity, and to cast all its care on him [o], because he careth for it.

And indeed a right judgement of God will help us to employ our faith in any condition. In wealth, men are apt to trust in their abundance, to stand upon their mountain, and

---

[g] 2 Tim. iv. 16, 17, 18. [h] Dan. iii. 16, 17. [i] Heb. xi. 17, 19. [k] Rom. iv. 20, 21. [l] Jer. xvii. 5, 8. [m] Heb. xi. 6. [n] Psalm lxxiii. 28. [o] 1 Pet. v. 7.

to say, 'I shall never be moved.'—But now, in this estate, if
a man conceive aright of God, that it is he who giveth
strength to be rich, and who giveth riches strength to do us
good; that he can blast the greatest estate with an impercep-
tible consumption, and, in the midst of a man's sufficiency,
make him be in straits; that he can imbitter all with his
sore displeasure, and not suffer the floor nor the wine-press
to feed him :—in great wisdom and deep counsels, if a man
consider that the counsel of the Lord shall stand, and that
he can turn the wisdom of the oracles into foolishness, and
catch the wise in their own craftiness :—in great provisions
of worldly strength, and human combinations, if he consider
that God can take off the wheels, and amaze the phantasies,
and dissipate the affections, and melt the spirits, and way-
lay the enterprises of the hugest hosts of men, that he can
arm flies, and lice, and dust, and wind, and stars, and every
small unexpected contingency against the strongest opposition ;—it must needs make him set his rest, and hang his
confidences and assurances upon a higher principle.

Again, In poverty and the extremest straits which a man
can be in, if he consider that God is a God as well of the
valleys as of the hills ; that he will be seen in the mount,
when his people are under the sword, and upon the altar ;
that the Lord knoweth the days of the upright, and will
satisfy them in the time of famine ; that when the
young lions famish for hunger, (they which live not by the
fruits on the earth, but by their prey ; they which can feed
of the dead bodies of those other creatures, whom a famine
had devoured,) yet even then he can provide abundantly for
his ; that when things are marvellous unto us [p], then they
are easy unto him ; that when they are impossible unto us [q],
then they are possible with him ; that he can lead in a wilderness [r], and feed with an unknown and unsuspected bread ;
that when the light of the sun and the moon shall fail, he
can be an everlasting light and glory to his people [s] ; that as
a Father, so he pittieth ; and as a heavenly Father [t], so he
knoweth and can supply all our needs ; that when we are
without any wisdom to disappoint, or strength to withstand,

[p] Zech. viii. 6.   [q] Mark x. 27. Psal. cxxxvi. 16. Jer. ii. 6.   [r] Amos
ii. 10. Deut. viii. 15, 16.   [s] Isai. lx. 19.   [t] Mat. vi. 32.

the confederacies of men, when they come with chariots of
iron, and walls of brass, even then the eyes of the Lord run
to and fro [u], to show himself valiant in the behalf of those
that walk uprightly, that he can then order some accident,
produce some engine, discover some way, to extricate and to
clear all ;—then will a man learn to be careful, and distracted
in nothing, but in every thing by prayer and supplication,
with thanksgiving, make his request [x] known unto him who
is at hand, and who careth for him.

The like may be said of men's spiritual condition. When
men despair, as Cain, that their sin is greater than can be forgiven ; the only ground is, because they judge not aright of
God in Christ: they look not on him in his gospel, as a God
that careth for them ; they do not lean upon the staff of his
strength. Despair is an affection growing out of the sense
of sin and wrath, as it is ' malum arduum, instans, et ine-
luctabile,' an evil too heavy to be borne, and yet impossible
to be removed. All victory ariseth either out of an inward
power of our own, or by the assistance of foreign power,
which is more than our own. Now then, when we despair
because of sin, this cometh, First, From the consideration of
our own disability to break through sin by our own strength;
and this is a good despair, which helpeth to drive men unto
Christ.

Secondly, It cometh from a mis-conceiving, either of the
power or care of those which might assist us. Sometimes
from the mis-judging of God's power ; for the forgiveness of
sins is an act of omnipotency : and therefore when the Lord
proclaimeth himself a forgiver of iniquity, transgression, and
sin, he introduceth it with his titles of power, " The Lord,
the Lord God, gracious and merciful," [y] &c. To pardon malefactors, is a power and royalty which belongeth only unto
princes. There is much strength required in bearing burdens ; and therefore patience, especially towards sinners, is
an act of power ; and impatiency, ever a sign of impotency.
And therefore [z] the weakest affections are ever most revenge-
ful : children, old men, sick, or indigent persons, are ever
most subject to anger, and least able to concoct an injury:

---

[u] 2 Chron. xvi. 9.   [x] Phil. iv. 6.   [y] Exod. xxxiv. 6.   [z] Προοδο-
ποιεῖται γὰρ ἕκαστος πρὸς τὴν ἑκάστου ὀργὴν ὑπὸ τοῦ ὑπάρχοντος πάθους. *Arist.*
Rhet. l. 2. c. 2.

so that to conceive sin greater than can be forgiven, is to misjudge the omnipotency of God. But, ordinarily, despair proceedeth from the misjudging of God's affection and good will towards men ; the soul conceives of him, as of one that hath cast off all care or respect towards it. This is an error touching God's benevolence, and the latitude of his mercy, and height of his thoughts towards sinners. He hath declared himself "willing that all men should be saved [a];" he had set forth examples [b] of the compass of his long-suffering; his invitations run in general terms, that no man may dare to pre-occupate damnation, but look unto God as one that careth for his soul. Let a man's sins be never so crimson, and his continuance therein never so obdurate (I speak this for the prevention of despair, not for the encouragement of security or hardness), yet as soon as he is willing to turn, God is willing to save ; as soon he hath a heart to attend, God hath a tongue to speak salvation unto him. We see, then, the way to trust in Christ, is to look upon him as ' the bishop of our souls ;' as the officer of our peace ; as one that careth and provideth for us; as one that hath promised to save to the uttermost [c], to give supplies of his Spirit and grace in time of need [d], to give us daily bread and life in abundance [e], to be with us all always to the end of the world, never to fail us nor forsake us.[f]

And we may hereby learn our duty one to another, to put on the affections of members [g], and the mind of Christ, in compassionating, considering, and seeking the good of one another, in bearing one another's burdens, in pleasing not ourselves, but our neighbour for his edification ; for even Christ pleased not himself ;—that man cannot live in honour, nor die in comfort, who liveth only to himself, and doth not, by his prayers, compassions, and supplies imitate Christ, and interest himself in the good of his brethren.

Now the ground of all this power, majesty, and mercy of the gospel is here set forth unto us in two words : First, It is the strength of Christ; Secondly, It is sent by God himself : *The Lord shall send the rod of thy strength out of Sion.*

Here then we may first note, That the gospel is Christ's

[a] 2 Pet. iii. 9. John v. 34.   [b] 1 Tim. i. 16.   [c] Heb. vii. 25.   [d] Heb. iv. 16.   [e] John x. 10.   [f] Heb. xiii. 5.   [g] Col. iii. 12, 13. Ephes. v. 2. Phil. ii. 4, 5. Rom. xiv. 7, 15. xv. 2, 3.

own power and strength, and the power of God his Father,
by whom it is sent abroad. So the apostle calls it, The
power of God unto salvation [h], and the demonstration of the
Spirit, and of power ; that our faith should not stand in the
wisdom of men, but in the power of God. Therefore, in one
place, we are said to be taught of God [i], and, in another,
to be taught of Christ [k]; in one place it is called the
gospel of the blessed God [l],—and, in another, the gospel
of Christ [m];—to note, that whatsoever things the Father
doth in his church, the same the Son doth also [n], and
that the Father doth not make known his will of mercy but
by his Son: that as, in the Son, he did reconcile the
world unto himself [o], so, in the Son, he did reveal himself unto the world. [p] " No man hath seen the Father at any
time, but the Son, and he to whom the Son shall reveal
him." Christ is both the matter and the author of the gospel. As, in the work of our redemption, he was both the
sacrifice, and the priest to offer, and the altar to sanctify it ;
so, in the dispensation of the gospel, Christ is both the sermon and the preacher, and the power which giveth blessing
unto all. He is the sermon ; " We preach Christ crucified [q]," saith the apostle ; " we preach not ourselves, but
Christ Jesus the Lord." And he is the preacher ; " See that
ye refuse not him that speaketh. [r]——He came and preached
peace to those afar off, and to those that were nigh." And
lastly, He is the power, which enliveneth his own Word ;
" The dead shall hear the voice of the Son of man, and they
that hear, shall live [s];" for " as the Father hath life in himself, so hath he given to the Son to have life in himself."—
" My sheep hear my voice, and I know them, and they follow
me, and I give unto them eternal life," &c. He is the " Lord
of your faith [t];—we are but the helpers of your joy." He
is the master in the church [u], we are but your servants for
Jesus' sake. [x] He is the chief shepherd [y], the Lord of the
sheep ; the sheep are his own [z]; we are but his depositaries [a],
entrusted with the ministry of reconciliation ; unto us is

[h] Rom. i. 16. 2 Cor. ii. 4, 5. [i] John vi. 45. [k] Eph. iv. 20, 21.
[l] 1 Tim. i. 11. [m] Rom. xv. 19. [n] John v. 19. [o] 2 Cor. v. 19.
[p] John i. 18. John xiv. 17. [q] 1 Cor. i. 23. 2 Cor. iv. 5. Col. i. 28.
Heb. xii. 25. Eph. ii. 17. 1 Pet. iii. 19. [s] Joh. v. 25, 26. x. 27, 28.
2 Cor. i. 24. [u] Joh. xiii. 13, 14. [x] 2 Cor. iv. 5. [y] 1 Pet.
v. 3, 4. [z] Joh. xxi. 15. [a] 2 Cor. v. 19. Eph. iii. 2. 2 Tim. i. 14.
1 Pet. iv. 11. 1 Cor. iv. 1. 2 Cor. v. 19, 20.

committed the dispensation of the grace of God. So then the Word is his, but the service ours.

From whence, both the ministers of the Word, and they which hear it, may learn their several duties. First, We should learn to speak as the oracles of God, as the servants and stewards of a higher master, whose Word it is which we preach, and whose church it is which we serve. We should therefore do his work, as men that are set in his stead; preach him and not ourselves. There can be no greater sacrilege in the world, than to put our own image upon the ordinances of Christ, than to make another gospel than we have received. St. Paul durst not please men [b], because he was the servant of Christ; neither durst he preach himself, because he was the servant of the church. For hereby men do even justle Christ out of his own throne, and, as it were, snatch the sceptre of his kingdom out of his hand, boldly intruding upon that sacred and uncommunicable dignity which the Father hath given to his Son only, which is to be the author of his gospel, and the total and adequate object of all evangelical preaching. This sacrilege of self-preaching is committed three manner of ways: First, When men make themselves the authors of their own preaching, when they preach their own inventions, and make their own brains the seminaries and forges of a new faith; when they so gloss the pure word of God, as that withal they poison and pervert it. This is that which the prophet [c] calleth "lying visions and dreams of men's own hearts;" which St. Peter [d] calls "perverting," or making crooked the rule of faith; and St. Paul [e], the huckstering, adulterating, and "using the word of God deceitfully." Which putteth me in mind of a speech in the prophet [f], "The prophet is the snare of a fowler in all his ways." Birds, we know, use to be caught with the same corn wherewith they are usually fed; but then it is either adulterated with some venomous mixture, which may intoxicate the bird, or else put into a gin which shall imprison it: and such were the carnal preachers in the prophet's, and in St. Paul's time, who turned the truth of God into a snare, that by that means they might "bring the

b Gal. i. 10.　c Ezek. xiii. 3, 9, 17. Jer. xiv. 14. xxiii. 16.　d 2 Pet. iii. 16.　e 2 Cor. ii. 17. 2 Cor. iv. 2.　f Hosea ix. 8.

church into bondage."[g] The occasions and originals of
this perverse humour are, First, Without men, the seduce-
ments of Satan, unto which, by the just severity of God[h],
they are sometimes given over, for the punishment of
their own and others' sins. Secondly, Within them (upon
which the other is grounded) as pride of wit[i], joined
with ambition and impatiency of repulse in vast desires,
which hath anciently been the ground of many heresies and
schisms: nothing hath ever been more dangerous to the
church of God, than greatness of parts unsanctified and
unallayed with the love of truth, and the grace of Christ.
Secondly, Envy against the pains and estimation of those
that are fearful.[k] This was one of the originals of Arius's
cursed heresy, — his envy against Alexander the good
bishop of Alexandria, as Theodoret reports. Thirdly, Impatiency of the spiritualness and simplicity of the holy
Scriptures, which is ever joined with the predominancy of
some carnal lust, whereby the conscience is notoriously
wasted or defiled. He that hath once put away a good conscience, and doth not desire truth in order and respect to
that, that thereby his conscience may be illightened, purified, and kept even towards God,—will, without much ado,
make shipwreck of his faith, and change the truth for any
thriving error. And this impatiency of the Spirit of truth in
the Scriptures, is that which caused heretics[l] of old to reject
some parts, and to add more to the canon of sacred Scriptures,—and, in these days, to superadd traditions and apo-
cryphal accessions thereunto ; and in those which are pure,
and on all sides confessed, to use such licentious and carnal
glosses, as may hale the Scripture to the countenancing of
their lusts and prejudices, rather than to the rectifying of
their own hearts by the rule of Christ

Secondly, Men preach themselves when they make
themselves the object of their preaching, when they
preach self-dependency, and self-concurrency, making
themselves, as it were, joint-saviours with Christ. Such
was the preaching of Simon Magus, who gave out that

---

g Gal. ii. 4. Mic. iii. 5, 6.   h 1 Kings xxii. 23. 2 Thes. ii. 10, 12,
i Mater omnium Hæreticorum, superbia. *Aug.* de Gen. contr. Manic. lib. 2. c. 8.
et Conf. l. 12. c. 24.   k *Theod.* Eccl. Hist. l. i. c. 2.—Vid. *Petr. Ærod.* Decret.
lib. 1. Tit. 6. sect. 12.   l *Tertul.* cont. Merc. l. 4. c. 6. et 43. et lib. 5. cap. 4.

himself was some great one, even the great power of
God. Of Montanus and his scholars, who preached him
for the comforter that was promised. Of Pelagius and his
associates, who though they did acknowledge the name of
grace [m], to decline envy, and avoid the curse of the great
council of Carthage, yet still they did but shelter their proud
heresies under equivocations and ambiguities. Of the
Massilienses in the time of Prosper and Hilary, and of some
ancient schoolmen, touching pre-existent congruities for the
preparations of grace, and co-existent concurrences with the
Spirit, for the production of grace. Of the Papists, in their
doctrines of indulgences, authoritative absolution, merits of
good works, justification, and other like,—which do, all in
effect, out-face, and give the lie unto the apostle, when he
calleth Christ an 'able or sufficient Saviour.' [n]

Thirdly, Men preach themselves [o], when they make themselves the end of their preaching, when they preach their
own parts, passions, and designs, and seek not the Lord ;
when out of envy, or covetousness, or ambition, or any other
servile or indirect affection, men shall prevaricate in the
Lord's message, and make the truth of God serve their own
turns ; when men shall stand upon God's holy mount, as
on a theatre, to act their own parts, and as on a step to their
own advancement [p]; when the truth of God, and the death
of Christ, and the kingdom of Heaven, and the fire of Hell,
and the souls of men, and the salvation of the world shall be
made basely serviceable and contributary to the boundless
pride of an atheistical Diotrephes. [q] Such as these were they,
who, in the times of Constantius the emperor [r], poisoned the
world with Arianism, and, in the times of St. Cyprian, provoked persecutions against the church ; and, in the times of
Israel [s], ensnared the ten tribes, till they were utterly destroyed,—and blinded the two tribes, till they were led away
captive by the Babylonians :—so horrid are the consequences
of taking away the gospel of Christ from him, and making
it *the rod*, not *of his strength*, but of our own pride or passion.

---

m Gratiæ vocabulo frangens invidiam, offensionemque declinans, *Aug.* de Grat.
Christ. l. 1. c. 37. et epist. 105.　　n Heb. vii. 25.　　o Jer. x. 21. Phil.
i. 16. Ezek. xxxiv. 25.　　p Isai. lvi. 11. Mich. iii. 5. 2 Pet. ii. 14, 15. Jude
v. 11.　　q 3 John ver. 9. Amos vii. 12, 13.　　r *Sulpit. Sever.* lib. 2.
—*Cyprian.* de Lapsis.　　s Hos. v. 1. ix. 7, 8. Jer. xxiii. 28, 29.

We must, therefore, always remember, that the gospel is Christ's own, and that will encourage us to speak it as we ought to speak :

First, With authority and boldness, without silence or connivance at the sins of men. Though, in our private and personal relations, we are to show all modesty, humility, and lowliness of carriage towards all men ; yet, in our master's business, we must not respect the persons, nor be daunted at the faces of men. Paul a prisoner was not afraid to preach of righteousness, and temperance, and judgement to come, before a corrupt and lascivious prince, though it made him tremble.

Secondly, With wisdom, as a scribe[t], instructed to the kingdom of Heaven. This was St. Paul's[u] care to work as a wise master-builder. When Christ's enemies watched him to pick something out of his mouth, whereby they might accuse him, we find so much depth of wisdom in the answers and behaviours of Christ, as utterly disappointed them of their expectations, and struck them with such amazement, that they never durst ask him questions more.[x] So should we endeavour to behave ourselves in such manner, as that our ministry may not be blamed[y], nor the truth of God exposed to censure or disadvantages : for sacred truths may be sometimes either so unseasonably, or so indigestedly, and incoherently delivered, as may rather open than stop the mouths of gainsayers, and sooner discredit the truth, than convert the adversary. The apostle[z] saith, that we are to "make a difference, to save some with compassion, others with fear." This is to speak ' a word in due season,' and, as our Saviour did, ' to speak as men are able to hear;' to press the Word upon the conscience with such seasonable and suitable enforcements as may be most likely to convince those judgements, and to allure those affections, which we have to do withal. It is not knowledge in the general, but the right use thereof, and wise application unto particulars, which winneth souls. " The tongue of the wise useth knowledge aright."[a] This is that heavenly craft wherewith the apostle[b] caught the Corinthians, as it were, by guile : such art he useth towards the philosophers of Athens [c], not exasperating men who are heady and confident of their own rules, but seeming rather to make up the defects, which themselves in the inscription of their altar confessed, and to reveal that very God unto them, whom they worshipped, but did not know. Therefore we find him there honouring their own learning, and, out of that, disputing for a resurrection, and against idolatry, to show that Christian religion was no way against that learning, or rectified reason, which they seemed to profess. The like art he used towards king Agrippa [d], first presuming of his knowledge and credit which he gave to the prophets, and then meeting, and setting on his inclinable disposition to embrace the gospel; like the wisdom of the servants of Benhadad unto Ahab, " They did diligently observe, whether any thing would come from him, and did hastily catch it; and they said, Thy brother Benhadad [e]." And the like wisdom he used everywhere, he denied himself his own liberty, and made himself a servant [f] unto all; to the Jew, as a Jew ; to the Greek, as a Greek ; to the weak, as weak ; and all things to all, that by all means he might save some, and so further the gospel. One while, he used circumcision, that he might thereby gain the weak Jews : another while, he forbad circumcision, that he might not misguide the converted Gentiles, nor give place by subjection unto false brethren. " Who is weak," saith he [g], " and I am not weak ? who is offended, and I burn not ?" His care of men's souls made him take upon him every man's affection, and accommodate himself unto every man's temper ; that he might not offend the weak, nor exasperate the mighty, nor dishearten the beginner, nor affright those which were without, from coming in,—but be all unto all for their salvation. The same love is due unto all ; but the same method of cure is not requisite for all [h]. With some, love travelleth in pain ; with others, it rejoiceth in hope : some, it laboureth to edify ; and others, it feareth to offend : unto the weak, it stoopeth; unto the strong, it raiseth itself: to some, it is compassionate ; to others, severe ; to none, an enemy ; to

[c] Acts xvii. 23, 28.   [d] Acts xxvi. 2, 3, 27, 29.   [e] 1 Kings xx. 33.
[f] 1 Cor. ix. 19, 23.   [g] 2 Cor. xi. 29.   [h] Eadem omnibus debetur charitas, non eadem medicina, &c. *Aug.* de Catech. Rud. cap. 15.

all, a mother. But all this it doth, ' non mentiendo, sed
compatiendo,' not by belying the truth, but by pitying the
sinner. It is not the wisdom of the flesh, nor to be learned
of men. The scripture alone is able to make ' the man of
God, wise unto the work of salvation.'

Thirdly, With meekness ; for that is the child of wisdom.
" Who is a wise man ?" saith St. James [i]; " let him show out
of a good conversation his works, ἐν πραΰτητι σοφίας, with meekness of wisdom ;" and again, " The wisdom which is from
above, is pure, peaceable, gentle, easy to be entreated, full
of mercy." The gospel is Christ's gospel, and it must be
preached with Christ's Spirit, which was very meek and
lowly [k]. When the disciples would have called for fire from
Heaven upon the Samaritans, for their indignity done unto
Christ, he rebuketh them in a mild and compassionate manner, " Ye know not, what spirit ye are of [l]." A right evangelical spirit is ever a meek and a merciful spirit. " If a
man" (saith the apostle [m]) " be overtaken in a fault, ye which
are spiritual, restore such an one in the spirit of meekness ;"
and again, " In meekness," saith the apostle [n], " instruct
those that oppose themselves," if God, peradventure, will
give them repentance to the acknowledging of the truth.

Lastly, With faithfulness [o]; inasmuch as the gospel is none
of ours, but Christ's, whose servants and stewards we are [p].
Christ was faithful, though he were a son over his own
house ; and therefore, might, in reason, have assumed the
more liberty to do his own will : Much more doth it become
us, who are but his officers, to be faithful too, not to dissemble any thing, which the estate and exigence of those
souls committed to our charge, shall require us to speak :
not to add, diminish, or deviate from our commission [q],
preaching one gospel in one place, and another in another [r];
but to deliver only the counsel of God [s], and to watch over
the souls of men, as they that must give an account [t].

Again, Since the gospel is Christ's own power, we must
all learn from thence two duties : First, to receive it as from
him, with the affections of subjects which have been bought
by him, that is, first in hearing of the Word, to expect prin-

i James iii. 13, 17.　k Matth. xi. 29, xxi. 5.　l Luke ix. 55.　m Gal. vi. 1.
n 2 Tim. ii. 25.　o Heb. iii. 2.　p 1 Cor. iv. 2. 2 Tim. ii. 2.　q Deut. iv. 2.
r Gal. i. 6.　s Acts xx. 27.　t Heb. xiii. 17.

cipally his voice, and to seek him speaking from Heaven. This is the nature of Christ's sheep [u], to turn away their ears from the voice of strangers, and ' to hear him.' Two things principally there are, which discover the voice of Christ in the ministry of the Word : First, It is a spiritual and heavenly doctrine [x], full of purity, righteousness, and peace [y], touching the soul with a kind of secret and magnetical virtue,—whereby the thoughts, affections, conscience, and conversation are turned from their earthly centre, and drawn up unto him, as eagles to a carcase. Secondly, It is a powerful, an edged [z], a ' piercing' doctrine. If the Word thou hearest, speak unto thy conscience ; if it search thy heart ; if it discover thy lusts ; if it make thy spirit burn within thee ; if it cast thee upon thy face, and convince and judge thee for thy transgressions ; if it bind up thy sores, and cleanse away thy corruptions ; then it is certainly Christ's Word,— and then it must be received with such affections, as becometh the Word of Christ.

First, With faith : If we confer with flesh and blood, we shall be apt to cavil against the truth : for he that rejecteth Christ [a], doth never receive his Word. A fleshly heart [b] cannot submit unto a heavenly doctrine. Christ [c] and his apostles [d] did every where endure the contradiction of sinners. But yet he claimeth this honour over the consciences of men, to overrule their assents against all the mists and sophistical reasonings of the flesh. The apostles [e] themselves preached nothing, but either by immediate commission from him, or out of the law and the prophets. But his usual form was, " Verily, I say unto you [f];"—noting, that he only was, unto the church, the author and fountain of all heavenly doctrine ; that unto him only belongeth that authoritative and infallible Spirit, which can command the subscription and assent of the conscience ; that he only can say with boldness to the soul, as he did to the Samaritan woman, " believe me [g]." And that therefore no authority, either of men, or churches, either episcopal, papal, or synodical, can, without open sacrilege, usurp power to overrule the faith of men, or impose any immediate and doctrinal necessity upon the conscience

---

[u] John x. 4, 5, 27.   [x] John iii. 12.   [y] James iii. 17.   [z] Heb. iv. 12.
[a] John xii. 48.   [b] Rom. viii. 7.   [c] Heb. xii. 3.   [d] Acts xiii. 45. xxviii. 23.
[e] 1 John i. 1, 2. Gal. i. 12.   [f] Matth. v. 22.   [g] John iv. 21.

in any points, which are not, ultimately and distinctly, resolved into the evident authority of Christ in his Word. St.
Paul [h] himself durst not assume dominion over the faith of
men ; nor St. Peter [i] neither suffer any elders (amongst whom
he reckoneth himself as an elder) also καλακυριεύειν, ' to over-
rule,' or prescribe unto the heritage of God. It is only
Christ's Word which the hearts of men must stoop and attend
unto, and which they must 'mingle with faith [k],' that it may
be profitable unto them ; that is, they must let it into their
hearts with this assurance, that it is not the breath of a man,
but the message of Christ [l], who is true in all his threatenings,
and faithful in all his promises, and pure in all his precepts ;
that he sendeth this ministry abroad for the perfection of the
saints [m], and the edification of his church,—and therefore if
they be not hereby cleansed, and built up in his body, they
do, as much as in them lieth, make void the holy ordinance
of God, which yet must never return in vain [n]. The word
of God doth ' effectually work' only in those that believe.
It worketh in hypocrites, and wicked hearers,—according to
the measure of that imperfect faith which they have ; it
worketh not effectually; that is, it doth not consummate
nor accomplish any perfect work, but only in those that believe ; in the rest, it proves but an abortion, and withers in
the blade.

Secondly, With love and readiness of mind [o], without despising or rejecting it. No man can be saved, who doth not
receive the truth in love; who doth not receive it (as the
primitive saints did) with gladness and readiness of mind ;
as Eli [p], though from the hand of Samuel, a child ; as David [q],
though from the hand of Abigail, a woman; as the Galatians [r],
though from the hand of Paul, an infirm and persecuted
apostle. For herein is our homage to Christ the more apparent, when we suffer a little child to lead us [s].

Thirdly, With meekness and submission of heart [t], reverencing and yielding unto it in all things. Wresting, shift-
ing, evading, perverting the Word, is as great an indignity
unto Christ, as altering, interlining, or rasing a patent which

h 2 Cor. i. 24.   i 1 Peter v. 3.   k Heb. iv. 2.   l 1 Thes. ii. 13.
m Ephes. iv. 12.   n Isa. lv. 11.   o 2 Thes. ii. 10. Acts ii. 41. xvii. 11. xxi. 17.
p 1 Sam. iii. 18.   q 1 Sam. xxv. 32.   r Gal. iv. 14.   s Isa. xi. 6.
t James i. 21. Levit. xxvi. 2. Acts x. 33.

the king hath drawn with his own royal hand, is an offence against him. Patience and effectual obedience even in affliction, is an argument that a man esteems the Word to be indeed God's own Word [u], and so receives it. He only who putteth off the old man [x], the corrupt, deceitful lusts of his former conversation, and is renewed in the spirit of his mind, is the man that hath heard, and been taught by Christ, that hath received the truth in him.

Again, Inasmuch as the gospel is the rod of Christ's own strength, or the instrument of his arm, ('Who hath believed our report, and to whom is the arm of the Lord revealed [y] ?') and the instrument is no farther operative or effectual, than according to the measure of that impressed virtue which it receiveth from the superior cause ; therefore we should learn always to repair unto Christ for the success of his Word. For he only is the teacher of men's hearts, and the author of their faith. To him only it belongeth to call men out of their graves, and to quicken whom he will. We have nothing but the ministry : he keepeth the power in his own hands, that men might learn to wait upon him, and to have to do with him, who only can send a blessing with his Word, and teach his people to profit thereby.

Another ground of the power of the Word is, that it is sent from God. "The *Lord* shall send forth the rod of thy strength :" From which particular likewise, we may note some useful observations ; as,

First, That God's appointment and ordination is that which gives being, life, majesty, and success to his own Word; authority, boldness, and protection to his servants. When he sendeth his word, he will make it prosper [z]. When Moses [a] disputed against his going down into Egypt to deliver his brethren, sometime alleging his own unfitness and infirmity, sometimes the unbelief of the people ; this was still the warrant with which God encouraged him ; "I will be with thee, I have sent thee ; do not I make man's mouth? I will be with thy mouth, and teach thee what thou shalt say."—"I was no prophet, neither was I a prophet's son," (saith Amos [b]) "but I was a herdsman, and a gatherer of sycamore fruit: and the Lord took me as I followed the

[u] 1 Thes. ii. 13, 14.   [x] Ephes. iv. 20, 22.   [y] Isai. liii. 1.   [z] Isai. lv. 11.
[a] Exod. iii. 4.   [b] Amos vii. 14, 15.

flock, and said unto me, Go, prophesy unto my people Israel." And this made him peremptory in his office to prophesy against the idolatry of the king's court, and against
the flattery of the priest of Bethel. And this made the
apostles [c] bold, though otherwise unlearned and ignorant
men, to stand against the learned council of priests and
doctors of the law, " We ought to obey God rather than
men." Upon which, grave was the advice of Gamaliel : " If
this counsel or work be of men, it will come to nought ; but
if it be of God, ye cannot overthrow it, lest, haply, ye be
found even to fight against God." For to withstand the
power or progress of the gospel, is to set a man's face against
God himself.

Secondly, Inasmuch as the gospel is sent forth by God,
that is, revealed and published out of Sion,—we may observe, that evangelical learning came not into the world by
human discovery or observation, but it is utterly above the
compass of all reason or natural disquisition ; neither men
nor angels ever knew it but by divine revelation. And therefore the apostle everywhere calleth it a ' mystery [d],' a ' great
and hidden mystery,' which was ' kept secret since the
world began.' There is a natural theology, without the
Word, gathered out of the works of God [e], out of the resolution of causes and effects into their first originals, and out
of the law of nature written in the heart. But there is no
natural Christianity. Nature is so far from finding it out by
her own enquiries, that she cannot yield unto it, when it is
revealed, without a spirit of faith to assist it. The Jews
stumbled at it, as dishonourable to their law ; and the Gentiles derided it, as absurd in their philosophy. It was a hidden and secret wisdom, the execution and publication whereof was committed only to Christ. In God, it was an eternal
gospel [f] ; for Christ was a lamb slain from before the foundations of the world [g], namely, in the predeterminate counsel
and decree of his Father : but revealed it was not till the
dispensation of the fulness of time ; wherein he gathered together, in one, all things in Christ. The purpose and ordination of it was eternal ; but the preaching and manifesta-

c Acts iv. 13, v. 29, 35, 36   d Rom. xvi. 25. 1 Cor. ii. 7, 9.   e Rom. i. 20.
ii. 14, 15.   f Revel. xiv. 6.   g 1 Peter i. 20. 1 Cor. ii. 7. 10. Ephes. i. 9, 10.
iii. 9, 11.

tion of it reserved until the time of Christ's solemn inauguration into his kingdom, and of the obstinacy of the Jews,
upon whose defection the Gentiles were called in.

Which might teach us to adore the unsearchableness of
God's judgements unto former ages of the world, whom he
suffered to walk in their own ways[h], and to live in times
of utter ignorance, destitute of any knowledge of the gospel,
or of any natural parts or abilities to find it out. For if
these things be true ; First, That, without the knowledge of
Christ, there is no salvation; "This is eternal life to know
thee, and him whom thou hast sent, Jesus Christ[i];"—" By
his knowledge shall my righteous servant justify many[k]."
Secondly, That Christ cannot be known by natural, but evangelical and revealed, light: "The natural man cannot know
the things of the Spirit of God," because they are spiritually
discerned[l]. The light shined in darkness[m], and the darkness was so thick and fixed that it did not let in the light,
nor apprehend it. Thirdly, That this light was, at the first,
sent only unto the Jews[n], as to the first-born people, excepting only some particular extraordinary dispensations and
privileges to some few first-fruits and preludes of the Gentiles, " He showeth his word unto Jacob, his statutes and his
judgements unto Israel.—He hath not dealt so with any nation[o]." He hath not afforded the means of salvation ordinarily unto any other people ; the world, by wisdom, knew
him not. Fourthly[p], That this several dispensation towards
one and other, the giving of saving-knowledge to one people,
and withholding it from others, was not grounded upon any
preceding differences and dispositions thereunto in the people, but only in the love of God : " The Lord thy God hath
chosen thee to be a special people unto himself, above all
people that are upon the face of the earth; The Lord did
not set his love upon you, nor choose you because ye were
more in number than any people, (for ye were the fewest of
all people)but because the Lord loved you[q]," &c. " The Lord
thy God giveth thee not this good land to possess it, for thy
righteousness ; for thou art a stiff-necked people[r].—Your fathers dwelt on the other side of the flood in old time, and

[h] Acts xiv. 16, 17, 30.   [i] John xvii. 3.   [k] Isai. liii. 11.   [l] 1 Cor. ii. 14.
[m] John i. 5.   [n] Exod. iv. 22.   [o] Psalm cxlvii 20.   [p] Vide *Cameron*. de
Eccl. pag. 81.   [q] Deut. vii. 6, 7.   [r] Deut. ix. 6.

they served other gods [s];" there was no difference between them and the Gentiles from which I gathered them. Fifthly, That the gospel was hidden for others in God [t]; his own will and counsel was the cause of it. He forbad men to go into the cities of the Gentiles [u] ; neither were they to go unto them without a special gift [x], and commission [y]. The same 'Beneplacitum' was the reason of revealing it to some, and of hiding it from others [z]; " Even so, O Father, for so it seemed good in thy sight :"—If all these particulars be true, needs must we both admire the inscrutableness of God's judgements [a] towards the Gentiles of old (for no human presumptions are a fit measure of the ways and severities of of God towards sinners) ; and also everlastingly adore his compassions towards us, whom he hath reserved for these times of light, and, out of the alone unsearchable riches of his grace, hath, together with principalities and powers in heavenly places, made us to see what is the fellowship of that great mystery, which, from the beginning of the world, was hidden in himself.

Thirdly, In that the Lord doth send forth the gospel of Christ out of Sion into the world, we may farther observe, that the gospel is a message and an invitation from Heaven unto men [b]. For that end was it sent, that thereby men might be invited and persuaded to salvation. The Lord sendeth his Son up and down, carrieth him from place to place ; he is set forth before men's eyes, he comes, and stands, and calls, and knocks at their doors, and beseecheth them to be reconciled. He setteth his word before us at our doors, and in our mouths and ears. He hath not erected any standing sanctuary or city of refuge for men to fly for their salvations unto, but hath appointed ambassadors to carry this treasure unto men's houses where he inviteth them, and intreateth them, and requireth them, and commandeth them, and compelleth [c] them to come unto his feast of mercy. And this must needs be πλοῦτος ἀνεξιχνίαστος, an unsearchable riches of grace, for mercy, pardon, preferment, life, salvation to go a-begging, and sue for 'acceptance ; and very un-

---

[s] Josh. xxiv. 2, 3.   [t] Ephes. iii. 9.   [u] Matth. x. 5.   [x] Ephes. iii. 7, 8.
[y] Matth. xi. 25. 26.   [z] Ephes. iii. 9, 11.   [a] Rom. xi. 33.   [b] Gal. iii. 1.
Col. i. 6.   Revel. iii. 20.   Jer. xxvi. 4.   Deut. xxx. 19.   Rom. x. 8.   2 Cor. v. 20.
Matth. xi. 28.   Mic. vi. 8.   1 John iii. 23.   [c] Luke xiv. 23.

searchable likewise must needs be the love of sin, and madness of folly in wicked men, to trample upon such pearls, and to neglect so great salvation when it is tendered unto them. O what a heavy charge will it be for men, at the last day, to have the mercy of God, the humility of Christ, the entreaties of his Spirit, the proclamations of pardon, the approaches of salvation, the days, the years, the ages of peace, the ministers of the Word, the book of God, the great mystery of godliness, to rise up in judgement, and testify against their souls !

Lastly, In that the gospel is sent from God, the dispensers thereof must look upon their mission, and not intrude upon so sacred a business before they are thereunto called by God[d]. Now this call is twofold : extraordinary, by immediate instinct and revelation from God[e], which is ever accompanied with immediate and infused gifts (of this we do not now speak); and ordinary, by imposition of hands, and ecclesiastical designation. Whereunto there are to concur three things. First, An act of God's providence, casting a man upon such a course of studies, and fashioning his mind unto such affections towards learning, and disposing of him in such schools and colleges of the prophets, as are congruous preparations, and were appointed for nurseries and seminaries of God's church. It is true, many things fall under God's providence, which are not within his allowance ; and therefore it is no sufficient argument to conclude God's consent or commission in this office, because his wisdom hath cast me upon a collegiate education. But when therewithal, he in whose hands the hearts of all men are as clay or wax, to be moulded into such shapes as the counsel of his will shall order,—hath bended the desires of my heart to serve him in his church, and hath set the strongest delight of my mind upon those kinds of learning, which are unto that service most proper and conducent ; when measuring either the good will of my heart, or the appliableness of my parts, by this, and other professions of learning, I can clearly conclude that that measure and proportion which the Lord hath given me, is more suitable unto this, than other learned callings ;—I suppose, other qualifications herewith concurring, a

[d] Heb. v. 4.   [e] Gal. i. 12.

man may safely from thence conclude, that God, who will have every man live in some profitable calling, doth not only by his providence permit, but by his secret direction lead him unto that service whereunto the measure of gifts which he hath conferred upon him, are most suitable and proper. And therefore, Secondly, There is to be respected in this ordinary mission, the meet qualification of the person, who shall be ordained unto this ministry. For if no prince will send a mechanic from his loom, or his shears, in an honourable embassage to some other foreign prince; shall we think that the Lord will send forth stupid and unprepared instruments about so great a work as the perfecting of the saints, and edification of the church? It is registered for the perpetual dishonour of that wicked king Jeroboam (who made no other use of any religion, but as a secondary bye thing, to be the supplement of policy) that " he made of the lowest of the people [f]," those who were really such as the apostles were falsely esteemed to be, the scum and off-scouring of men, "to be priests unto the Lord." Now the qualities more directly and essentially belonging unto this office, are these two; fidelity and ability. "The things," saith the apostle[g], " which thou hast heard of amongst many witnesses, the same commit thou to faithful men, who shall be able to teach others also."

We are stewards of no meaner a gift than the ' Grace of God,' and the ' Wisdom of God;' that Grace which by St. Peter [h] is called ποικίλη Χάρις, a manifold grace ; and that wisdom which, by St. Paul [i], is called πολυποίκιλος σοφία, ' the manifold wisdom of God.' We are the depositaries and dispensers of the most precious treasures which were ever opened unto the sons of men,—the incorruptible and precious blood of Christ, the exceeding great and precious promises of the gospel, the word of the grace of God, and of the unsearchable riches of Christ. Now it is required of stewards, that a man be found faithful [k]; that he defraud not Christ of his purchase, which is the souls of men, nor men of their price and privilege, which is the blood of Christ; that he never favour the sins of men, nor dissemble the truth of God; that he watch, because he is a

[f] 1 Kings xii. 31.   [g] 2 Tim. ii. 2.   [h] 1 Pet. iv. 10.   [i] Eph. iii. 10.
[k] 1 Cor. iv. 2.

seer ; that he speak, because he is an oracle ; that he feed, because he is a shepherd; that he labour, because he is a husbandman ; that he be tender, because he is a mother ; that he be careful, because he is a father; that he be faithful, because he is a servant to God and his church : in one word, that he be instant in season and out of season, to exhort, rebuke, instruct, to do the work of an evangelist, to accomplish and make full proof of his ministry, because he hath an account to make, because he hath the presence of Christ to assist him, the promises of Christ to reward him, the example of Christ, his apostles, prophets, evangelists, bishops, and martyrs of the purest time, who have now their palms in their hands, to encourage him. It was Christ's custom to enter into their synagogues on the Sabbath days [1], and to read and expound the Scriptures to the people. It was St. Paul's [m] manner to reason in the synagogues, and to open the Scriptures on the Sabbath days. Upon Sunday, saith Justin Martyr [n], all the Christians that are in the cities or countries about, meet together, and, after some commentaries of the apostles and writings of the prophets have been read, the senator or president doth, by a sermon, exhort the people, and admonish them to the imitation and practice of those divine truths, which they had heard read unto them. And St. Austin [o] telleth us of Ambrose, that he heard him rightly handling the word of God unto the people, every Lord's day. Yea it should seem by the homilies of St. Chrysostom, that he did often preach, daily, unto the people ; and therefore we frequently meet with his χθὲς 'yesterday,' this and this I taught you.—And Origen [p] intimateth this frequency of expounding the Scriptures in his time : " If," saith he, " you come frequently unto the church of God, and there attend unto the sacred Scriptures, and to the explication of those heavenly commandments, thy soul

---

[1] Luke iv. 16, 31. [m] Acts xvii. 2. xviii. 4. [n] Τῇ τοῦ ἡλίου λεγομένῃ ἡμέρᾳ, πάντων κατὰ πόλεις ἢ ἀγροὺς μενόντων ἐπὶ τὸ αὐτὸ συνέλευσις γίνεται· εἶτα παυσαμένου τοῦ ἀναγινώσκοντος, ὁ προεστὼς διὰ λόγου τὴν νουθεσίαν καὶ πρόκλησιν τῆς τῶν καλῶν τούτων μιμήσεως ποιεῖται. *Just. Martyr.* Apol. 2.— Tertul. Apol. cap. iii. 9. [o] Eum in populo verbum veritatis recte tractantem, omni die Dominico, audiebam. *Aug.* Confes. 1. vi. c. 3. [p] Si ad Ecclesiam frequenter venias, aurem divinis literis admoveas, explanationem mandatorum cœlestium capias, sicut cibis caro, ita spiritus verbis divinis convalescet. *Orig.* Hom. 9. in Levit.

will be strengthened, as thy body with food."—And ^q our
church, in her ecclesiastical constitutions, hath provided for
the continuance of so faithful and pious a custom, enjoining
every allowed preacher to have a sermon every Sunday in
the year, and in the afternoon besides to spend half an hour
in catechising the younger and ruder sort in the principles
of Christian religion. The neglect of which most necessary
duty no man can more bewail, nor more urge the necessity
thereof, than those who, looking abroad into the world, have
experience of more thick and palpable darkness in the minds
of men, concerning those absolute necessary doctrines of
the passion, merits, and redemption of Christ, and of faith
in them, than men who have not, with their own eyes, observed it, can almost believe; and that too in such places
where sermons have been very frequently preached. I will
close this point with the assertion and profession of holy
Austin: "Nothing ^r," saith he, "is in this life more pleasant and easy, than the life of a bishop or minister, if it
be perfunctorily and flatteringly executed; but then in
God's sight 'nihil turpius, miserius, damnabilius;'" and it
was his profession, ^s that he was never absent from his
episcopal service and attendance, upon any licentious and
assumed liberty, but only upon some other necessary service of the church.

Touching the ability required in the discharge of this
great office, there are (as I conceive) two special branches
thereunto belonging. First, Learning, for the right infor-
mation of the consciences of men, that men may not pervert
the Scripture: Secondly, Wisdom, or spiritual prudence,
for seasonable application of the truth to particular circumstances; which is that which maketh 'a wise builder.' For
this latter, it being so various, ^t according to those infinite
varieties of particular cases and conditions, which are
hardly reducible unto general rules, I cannot here speak,
but refer the reader to the grave and pious counsels of

q Canon. 45. 59.   r Nihil in hac vita lætius aut hominibus accepta-
bilius Episcopi aut Presbyteri Diaconi officio, si perfunctorie atque adulatorie
res agatur, &c. Aug. Epist. 148.   s Illud noverit dilectio vestra, nunquam me absentem fuisse licentiosâ libertate, sed necessaria servitute. Aug.
Epist. 138.   t τῶν καθ' ἕκαστά ἐστιν ἡ φρόνησις, ἃ γίνεται γνώριμα ἐξ
ἐμπειρίας. Arist. Ethic. lib. 6. cap. 8. Bell i. 274.

those holy men [u], who have given some directions herein. For the other two great works which belong to this high calling, there are,—instruction of the scholar, and conviction of the adversary. Unto the perfection of which two services, when we duly consider how many different parts of learning are requisite, as knowledge of the tongues [x], for the better understanding of the holy Scriptures by their original idiom and emphasis; of the arts, to observe the connexion, and augmentation, and method of them; of ancient customs, histories, and antiquities of the Babylonians, Persians, Greeks, and Romans, without insight whereinto the full meaning of many passages of holy Scripture cannot be clearly apprehended; of school learning, for discovering and repelling the subtilty of the adversaries, a thing required in a rhetorician by Aristotle and Quintilian, insomuch, [y] that Julian the apostate complained of the Christians, that they used the weapons of the Gentiles against them, and therefore interdicted them the use of schools of learning; lastly [z], of histories and antiquities of the church, that we may observe the succession of the professors and doctrines hereof, the originals and sproutings of heresy therein, the better to answer the reproaches of our insolent adversaries, who lay innovation to our charge;—I say, when we duly consider these particulars, we cannot sufficiently admire nor detest the sauciness of those bold intruders, who, when they have themselves need to be taught what are the first principles of the oracles of God, become teachers of the ignorant, before themselves have been disciples of the learned; and before either maturity of years or any severe progress of studies have prepared them, boldly leap, some from their manual trades, many from their grammar and logic rudiments, into this sacred and dreadful office, unto which heretofore the most learned and pious men have trembled to approach. To these men I can give no better advice than that which

---

[u] *Aug.* in lib. de Doct. Christ. et de Catechiz. Rud.—*Gregor. Mag.* de Officio Pastoral. par. 3. cap. 1. &c.   [x] *Hieron.* Apol. adver. Ruffin.—*Aug.* de Doctr. Christ. lib. 2. cap. 16, 17, 39.   [y] *Theodoret*, Hist. 3. cap. 7.   [z] *Aug.* de Doct. Christ. l. 2. c. 28.   Vid. *Greg. Nazianz.* Orat. 1.—Docent Scripturas quas non intelligunt; prius imperitorum magistri, quam doctorum discipuli, &c. *Hieron.* Ep. 8. ad Demetr. ad Apol. et To. 3. Epistol. Ep. ad Paulinum.

Tully once gave unto Aristoxenus, a musician, who would needs venture upon philosophical difficulties, and, out of the principles of his art, determine the nature of a human soul, "Hæc magistro relinquat Aristoteli, canere ipse doceat:" let them spend their time in the work which best befits them, and leave great matters unto abler men.

Thirdly and lastly, Unto this call is requisite the imposition of hands[a], and the authoritative act of the church, ordaining and setting apart, and deriving actual power upon such men, of whose fidelity and ability they have sufficient evidence (for "hands are not to be laid suddenly on any man") to preach the Word, and to administer the sacraments, and to do all those ministerial acts, upon which the edification of the people of Christ doth depend. I have now done with the first of Christ's regalities in the text, which was the sceptre of his kingdom.

Now to speak a word of the second, which is 'solium,' the throne of his kingdom, "The Lord shall send the Rod of thy strength *out of Sion*." Which notes unto us: First, That the church of the Jews was the chief original, metropolitan church of all others. Therefore our Saviour chargeth his disciples to "tarry in the city of Jerusalem, till they should be endued with power from on high[b]." The apostle saith, that they had the advantage or precedence and excellency above other people, because "unto them were committed the oracles of God[c].—To them did pertain the adoption, and the glory, and the covenants, and the giving of the law, and the service of God, and the promises[d]. Of them was Christ after the flesh." All the fathers, patriarchs, prophets, apostles, and writers of the holy Scriptures were of them. There is no church can show such privileges, nor produce such authentic records for her precedency as the church of the Jews. Therefore they are called by an excellency 'God's first-born[e],' and 'the first-fruits of the creatures[f];' they are called 'the children of the kingdom[g],' whereas others were at first 'dogs[h],' and

---

[a] Hi sunt qui se ultro apud temerarios convenas sine divinâ dispositione præficiunt; qui se præpositos sine ulla ordinationis lege constituunt; qui, nemine Episcopatum dante, Episcopi sibi nomen assumunt. *Cyprian.* de unitat. Ecclesiæ.   [b] Luke xxiv. 49.   [c] Rom. iii. 1, 2.   [d] Rom. ix. 4.   [e] Jer. xxxi. 9.   [f] Jam. i. 18.   [g] Matt. viii. 12.   [h] Eph. ii. 12.

' strangers '.' Their titles, ' Sion, Jerusalem, Israel [k],' are
used as proper names to express the whole church of God
by, though amongst the Gentiles. Christ Jesus, though he
came as 'a Saviour unto all,' yet he was sent to be ' a
prophet and a preacher' only unto them: therefore the
apostle calleth him ' the ministry of the circumcision [l],' that
is, of the Jews; and He saith, " I am not sent but unto
the lost sheep of the house of Israel [m]." And when he gave
his apostles their first commission [n], he sent them only ' into
the cities of the Jews.' The Gentiles [o] were incorporated
into them, were brought in upon their rejection and refusal
of the gospel, took the Christians of Judea for their pattern in their profession [p]; and from that church were rules
and constitutions sent abroad into other churches, as binding and necessary things [q]. To that church [r] the churches of
the Gentiles were debtors, as having been made partakers of
their spiritual things; and though they be now a rejected
people, yet when the fulness of the Gentiles is come in,
Israel shall be gathered again, and made a glorious church.
And, in the mean time, their dispersion tendeth unto the
conversion of the Gentiles. For though they were enemies
to the faith of Christians, yet they did bear witness unto
those Scriptures [s], out of which the Christians did prove
their faith. And there is no greater evidence in a cause,
than the affirmative testimony of that man who is an enemy
to the cause. If the church of Rome had such evidences
as these out of the book of God, to prove their usurped
primacy by, how proud and intolerable would they be in
boasting thereof, and obtruding it unto others—who are
now so confident upon far slenderer grounds!

And from hence we may learn to take heed of the sins of
that people, which were principally the rejecting of the
corner-stone, and the putting off the gospel of Christ away
from them, as every obstinate and unbelieving sinner doth

---

[i] Matt. xv. 26.   [k] Gal. iv. 26. vi. 16. Rom. ii. 29. Heb. xii. 22.   [l] Rom.
xv. 8.   [m] Matt. xv. 24.   [n] Matt. x. 5, 6.   [o] Rom. xi. 11, 12, 15, 30.
[p] 1 Thes. ii. 14.   [q] Act. xv. 2, 22.   [r] Rom. xv. 27. xi. 25, 26.   [s] Magnum est quod Deus præstitit Ecclesiæ suæ ubique diffusæ, ut gens Judæa, merito
debellata et dispersa per terras, ne à nobis hæc composita putarentur, codices
Prophetarum nostrorum ubique portaret, et, inimica fidei nostræ, testis fieret
veritatis nostræ. *Aug.* To. 4. de Cons. Evang. lib. 1. cap. 26. et Epist. 3. ad
Volusianum.

from himself. This is that, which hath made them, of all nations, the most hated and the most forsaken, and hath brought wrath to the uttermost upon them, because when Christ came unto his own, they received him not. " Because of unbelief they were broken off," saith the apostle; " and thou standest by faith; be not high-minded, but fear: for if God spared not the natural branches, take heed lest he also spare not thee." And we should likewise learn to pray for the fulness of the Gentiles, and for the restoring of this people unto their honour and original privileges again; for we are their debtors: we entered upon the promises which were made to them; and therefore good reason we have to do for them now, as they did for us before: " We have a little sister," or rather an elder sister, " and she hath no breasts;" the oracles and ordinances of God are taken from her; " What shall we do for our sister, in the day when she shall be spoken for.[s] "

Secondly, This notes unto us the calling of the Gentiles into the fellowship of the same mystery, which was first preached unto the Jews, that they might be the daughters [t] of this mother-church, that they " may take hold of the skirt [u] of the Jew, and say, We will go with you, for we have heard that God is with you." The church of Jerusalem was set up as a beacon, or an ensign, or a public sanctuary [x], to which the nations shall flee, as doves to their windows. Of this merciful purpose, some evidences and declarations the Lord gave before in Rahab, Job, Nineveh, the Wise men, and others, who were the preludes and first-fruits of the Gentiles unto God: and did after fully manifest the same in his unlimited commission to his apostles, " Go preach the gospel unto every creature."

And now alas, what were we that God should bring us hitherto? St. Paul saith, that we were ' filled with all unrighteousness; that we did neither understand God, nor seek after him.' All our faculties were full of sin, and the fulness of all sin was in us. We were ruled by no laws but the course of the world, the Prince of the air, and the lusts of the flesh, without God in this world, and without any hope for the world to come. Here,

---

[s] Cant. viii. 8.　　[t] Ezek. xvi. 61.　　[u] Zech. viii. 23.　　[x] Isai. ii. 2, 3.

vessels of lust and poison; and fitted to be, hereafter, vessels of destruction and misery. We were no nation; a foolish people, a people that sought not, nor enquired after God, and yet his own people hath he set by, and called us to the knowledge of his love and mercy in Christ. And that, not as many other Gentiles are called, who hear of him indeed, and worship him, but have his doctrine corrupted and overturned with heresy, and his worship defiled with superstition and idolatry ; but he hath for us purged his floor, and given unto us the wheat without the chaff; he hath let the light of his glory to shine purely upon us only in the face of Jesus Christ, without any human supplements or contributions. How should we praise him for it, and as we have received Christ purely, so labour to work worthily in him! How should we run to him that called us, when we knew him not! How should we set forward, and call upon one another, that we may flee, like doves, in companies unto the windows of the church! How earnestly should we contend for this truth, the custody whereof he hath honoured us withal! How should we renew our repentance, and remember our first works, lest so excellent a privilege be removed from us! There is no wrath that is wrath to the uttermost, but that which depriveth a people of the gospel, and taketh away their candlestick from them.

Thirdly, It notes unto us the difference of the two covenants, the one out of Sinai, the other out of Sion; at first the law proceeded out of Sinai, wherein, though the end were merciful, yet the manner was terrible[y], and, therefore, the effect nothing but bondage:[z] but, after, it was sent out of Sion with the Spirit of grace and adoption, observed with cheerfulness and liberty, as by those that know God will spare them, as a man spareth his child that serveth him: for in my bondslave, I look to the perfection of the work; but in my son, to the affection and disposition of the heart.

Lastly, It notes unto us, that the seat of saving truth, the custody of the promises, and gospel of salvation, doth still belong unto Sion, to the church of God. Out of the church[a]

---

[y] Heb. xii. 18, 22.   [z] Gal. iv. 25, 26.   [a] Quomodo potest esse cum Christo, qui cum sponsa Christi, atque in ejus Ecclesia non est ? *Cypr.* lib. 2. Epist. 8. et lib. 4. Epist. 2. ad Anton. et lib. de unitat. Eccl.—*Aug.* To. 1. de Vera Relig. cap. 5.

there is no gospel; and, therefore, out of the church there
is no salvation. The apostle [b] saith of children which are
born out of the church, that " they are unclean :" unto the
church (above all congregations of men) belongeth this excellent privilege, to be the treasurer of the riches of Christ,
and " to hold forth the Word of Life unto men. [c] " In which
sense the apostle saith, that it is " the pillar and the ground
of truth [d] ;" not that which giveth being to the truth, for the
law must not fail nor perish; nor that which giveth authority, imposeth a sense, canonizeth and maketh authentical,
is a judge or absolute determiner of the truth ; for in that
sense, the church is held up by the Word, and not that by
it [e] ; for " the church is built upon the foundation of the
prophets and apostles [f] ," namely, upon that fundamental
doctrine which they have laid. But the church is the depo-
sitory of the truth [g] ; that orb out of which this glorious
light shines forth ; unto it appertain the covenants and the
giving of the law, and the service of God, and the promises.
Her office and her honour, it is to be ' the candlestick [h],'
which holdeth up the Word of truth; to set-to her seal
unto the evidence and excellency thereof by her ministry [i],
authority, consent, and countenance ; to conciliate respect
thereunto, in the minds of aliens, and to confirm it in the
minds of unbelievers; to fasten the nails and points thereof,[k]
like masters of the assemblies, under one principal Shepherd, which is Christ, in the hearts of men; not to dishonour it by their usurped authority above it (for by that
means all controversies of religion are turned, not into
means to discover doctrine, that that may be rested in,
which doth appear to have in it most intrinsecal majesty,
spiritualness, and evidence; but into factions and emulations of men, that that sect may be rested in, who can, with
most impudence and ostentation, arrogate a usurped authority to themselves,) but, by their willing submission thereunto, to credit it in the affections of men, and to establish
others in the love and obedience thereunto; for the autho-

---

[b] 1 Cor. vii. 14.   [c] Phil. ii. 16.   [d] 1 Tim. iii. 16.   [e] Ἡ γὰρ ἀλήθειά
ἐστι τῆς ἐκκλησίας καὶ στύλος καὶ ἑδραίωμα. *Chrysost.* Hom. 11. in Tim.
[f] Ephes. ii. 20.   [g] Rom. iii. 1. Rom. ix. 4.   [h] Rev. i. 12.   [i] *Reynolds'*
Confer. with Hart. cap. 8. divis. 6.   [k] Eccl. xiii. 11.

rity of the church is not ' auctoritas jurisdictionis [1],' an authority of jurisdiction above the Scriptures: but only ' auctoritas
muneris,' an authority of dispensation and of trust, to proclaim, exhibit, present the truth of God unto the people, to
point to the star,[m] which is directed unto by the finger, but
is seen by the evidence of its own light; to hold forth [n], as
a pillar [o], that law and proclamation of Christ, the contents
whereof we discover out of itself. In one word, that place
showeth the duty of the church to preserve knowledge, and
to show forth the truth of sacred Scriptures out of themselves; but not any infallibility in itself, or authority over
others to bind their consciences to assent unto such expositions of Scripture, as derive not their evidence from the
harmony and analogy of the Scriptures themselves, but only
from ' Ipse dixit,' because the church hath spoken it.

To conclude this point, we are to note, for the clear understanding of the office of the church, concerning the holy
Scriptures,—First, That some things therein are " Hard to be
understood,[p]" as St. Peter speaks, either by reason of their
allegorical and figurative expressions, as the visions of Ezekiel, Daniel, Zechariah, &c.; or by reason of the obscure
and strange connexion of one part with another; or of the
dependence thereof, upon foreign learning, or the like. But
then we must note, that the knowledge of such things as
these, is not of absolute necessity unto salvation; for though
the perverting of hard places be damnable (as St. Peter telleth us,) yet that ignorance of them which groweth out of
their own obscurity, and not out of our neglect, is not
damnable. Secondly, Some things have evidence enough
in the terms that express them, but yet are " Hard to be believed," by reason of the supernatural quality of them. As
when we say that Christ was the son of a virgin, or that he
died and rose again,—there is no difficulty in the sense of
these things, it is easily understood what he that affirmeth
them, doth mean by them: all the difficulty is to bring the
mind to give assent unto them. Thirdly, Some things,

---

[1] *Cameron.* de Eccles. p. 44.   [m] *August.* in Prœm. lib. de Doctrin. Christ.
[n] Dr. *White* in his Way to the Church, nu. 15.   [o] Figi enim solebant leges,
aut quandoque in æs incidi, et in locis celeberrimis, ut à quolibet legerentur,
proponi. vid. *Brisson.* de formul. l. 2. p. 137. et. lib. 3. pag. 323.   [p] 2 Peter
iii. 16.

though easy in their sense to be understood, and, it may be, easy likewise in their nature to be believed, are yet ' Hard to be obeyed and practised,' as repentance, and forsaking of sin, &c. Now, according unto these differences, we may conceive of the office and power, which the church hath in matters of holy Scripture.

First, For hard places, in regard of the sense and meaning of the place, it is the duty of the church to open them to God's people with modesty and moderation. And therein God alloweth the learned a Christian liberty,[q] with submission of their opinions always to the spirits of the prophets, so long as they do therein nothing contrary to the analogy of faith,—to the general peace and unity of the church,—to the rules of charity, piety, loyalty, and sobriety ; to abound in their own sense, and to declare, for the further edifying of the church, what they conceive to be, in such difficult places, principally intended. And further than this no church nor person can go : for if, unto man or chair, there were annexed an infallible spirit, enabling him to give such a clear and indubitate exposition of all holy Scriptures, as should leave no inevidence in the text, nor hesitancy in the minds of men ; how comes it to pass that hitherto so many difficulties remain, wherein even our adversaries amongst themselves do give several conjectures and explications ? and how can that man, to whom so excellent a gift of infallibility is bestowed, clear himself of envy, and abuse of the grace of God, who maketh not use thereof to expound the Scriptures, and to compose those differences thereabouts, which do so much perplex the world ?

Secondly, For those places which in their meaning, are easy to be understood, but in their excellent and high nature hard to be believed (as all articles of faith, and things of absolute necessity are, in their terms, perspicuous, but, in their heavenly nature, inevident unto human reason) the office of the church [r] is not to bind men's consciences to be-

---

[q] Necesse est eos qui Scripturas edisserendo pertractant, etiamsi rectæ atque unius fidei fuerint, varias parere in multorum locorum obscuritate sententias : quamvis nequaquam ipsa varietas ab ejusdem fidei unitate discordet ; sicut etiam unus tractator secundum eandem fidem aliter atque aliter eundem locum potest exponere, quia hoc ejus obscuritas patitur. *Aug.* Ep. 19. [r] *Theodoret*, de curand. Græc. affect. lib. 8—*Cypr.* Serm. de Baptis. Christi.—*Aug.* Epist. 3 ad Volus. et To. 3. de Doct. Christ. lib. 2. cap. 9.

lieve these truths upon her authority : for we have not dominion over the faith of men; neither are we Lords in
Christ's flock ; and how shall any scrupulous mind, which is
desirous to bolt things to the bran, be secure of the power
which the church in this case arrogates, or have any certainty that this society of men must be believed in their religion, who will allow the same honour to no society of men
but themselves ? But in this case, the office of the church
is, both to labour by all good means, to evidence the credi-
bility of the things which are to be believed ; to discover unto
men those essential and intimate beauties of the gospel,
which to spiritual minds and hearts, raised to such a proportionable pitch of capacity, as are suitable to the excellency
of their natures, are apt to evidence and notify themselves ;
and also to labour to take men off from dependence on their
own reason or corrupted judgement ; to work in their heart
an experience of the Spirit of grace, and an obedience to
those holy truths which they already assent to ; with which
preparations and persuasions, the heart, being possessed,
will, in due time, come to observe more clearly, by that
spiritual eye, the evidence of those things which were at first
so difficult. So then the act of the church is, in matter
of faith, an act of introduction and guidance[s]; but that
which begetteth the infallible and unquestionable assent
of faith, is that spiritual taste, relish, and experience of the
heavenly sweetness of divine doctrine, which, by the ministry of the church, accompanied with the special concurrence
of Almighty God therewithal, is wrought in the heart; for it
is only the Spirit of God which writeth the law in men's
hearts, which searcheth the things of God, and which maketh
us to know them.

Thirdly, For those places which are difficult, rather to be
obeyed than to be understood, the work of the church is to
enforce upon the conscience the necessity of them, to persuade, rebuke, exhort, encourage with all authority.

Which should teach us all to love the church of Christ,
and to pray for the peace and prosperity of the walls of Sion,
for the purity, spiritualness, power and countenance of the

[s] Dr. *Field* of the Church, lib. 4. cap. 8. Singulis credentibus suus gustus est
judicii à spiritu, ut hominibus à natura suus. *Jun.* contr. Bellar. controv. 1.
lib. 3. cap. 3. num. 13.

Word therein, which is able to hold up its own honour in the minds of men, if it be but faithfully published. We should, therefore, study to maintain, to credit, to promote the gospel, to encourage truth, discountenance error, to stand in the gap against all the stratagems and advantages of the enemies thereof, and to hold the candlestick fast amongst us, to buy the truth, and sell it not, betray it not, forsake it not, temper it not, misguise it not. This is to be a pillar, and to put the shoulder under the gospel of Christ. And surely, though the Papists boast of the word and name of the church, (as none more apt to justify and brag of their sobriety, than those whom the wine hath overtaken,) yet the plain truth is, they have far less of the nature thereof, than any other churches, because far less of the pure service and ministration thereof. For instead of sending forth the Word of Life, they pull it down, denying unto the people of Christ the use of his gospel ; dimidiating the use of his sacrament, breeding them up in an ignorant worship, to beg they know not what ; in all points disgracing the Word of truth, and robbing it of its certainty, sufficiency, perspicuity, authority, purity, energy, in the minds of men. And this is certain,—the more they set themselves against the light and general knowledge of the Word of truth, the less of the nature of the church they have in them, whatever ostentation they may make of the name thereof.

The last thing observed in this second verse, amongst the regalities of Christ, was ' imperium,' his rule and government in his church by his holy word, maugre all the attempts and machinations of the enemies thereof against it : *Rule thou in the midst of thine enemies ;* that is, Thou shalt rule safely, securely, undisturbedly, without danger, fear, or hazard from the enemies round about ; their counsels shall be infatuated, their purposes shall vanish ; their decrees shall not stand ; their persecutors [t] shall but sow the blood of Christ and the ashes of Christians the thicker ; they shall see it, and gnash with their teeth, and gnaw their tongues, and be horribly amazed, at the emulation and triumph of a Christian's sufferings, over the malice and wrath of men.

[t] Ne quicquam proficit exquisitior quæque crudelitas vestra ; illecebra est magis sectæ ; plures efficimur, quoties metimur à vobis. Semen est sanguis Christianorum.—Inde est quod sententiis vestris gratias agimus, ut est æmulatio divinæ rei et humanæ. *Tertul. Apolog.* cap. ult.

The kingdom of Christ is twofold : his kingdom of glory, of which there shall be no end, when he shall rule *over* his enemies, and tread them under his feet; and his kingdom of grace, whereby he ruleth *amongst* his enemies, by the sceptre of his Word.   And this is the kingdom here spoken of; noting unto us, that Christ will have a church and people gathered unto him by the preaching of his gospel on the earth, maugre all the malice, power, or policy of all his enemies.   Never was Satan so loose; never heresy and darkness so thick; never persecution so prevalent; never the tail of the dragon so long, as to sweep away all the stars of Heaven, or to devour the remnant of the woman's seed. The gates of Hell, all the policy, power, and machinations of the kingdom of darkness, shall never root out the vine which the Father hath planted, nor prevail against the body of Christ.   His gospel must be preached to the world's end, and, till then, he will be with it to give it success.   Though the kings of the earth stand up, and the rulers gather together against the Lord and his Christ, yet they imagine but a vain thing ; and he that sitteth in Heaven, shall laugh them to scorn.

The grounds of the certainty and perpetuity of Christ's evangelical kingdom, is not the nature of the church in itself considered, either in the whole or parts; for Adam and Eva were a church at first, a people that were under the law of obedience and worship of God, and yet they fell away from that excellent condition.   And the prophet tells us, that except the Lord had left a very small remnant, the Church had been all as Sodom, and like to Gomorrah.   But the grounds hereof are ; First, The decree, ordination, and appointment of God [u]; and we know whatever men project, the counsel of the Lord must stand.   Secondly, God's gift unto Christ ; " Ask of me, and I will give thee the Heathen for thine inheritance [x]," &c.   " Thine they were, and thou gavest them me [y]."   " My Father which gave them me, is greater than all, and none is able to pluck them out of my Father's hand [z]." Thirdly, God's oath, which is the seal of his irreversible decree and covenant with Christ;—" Once have I sworn by my holiness, that I will not lie unto David ; his seed shall

[u] Psal. ii. 7. Acts x. 42. Heb. iii. 2.   [x] Psal. ii. 8.   [y] John xvii. 6
[z] John x. 29.

endure for ever, and his throne as the sun before me [a]."
Fourthly, Christ's own purchase and price which he paid
for it. The apostle saith, " Christ died not in vain," and the
virtue of his blood lasteth to the end of the world : for as
his blood was shed from the beginning of the world, in regard
of God's decree ; so doth it continue to the end, in regard of
its own merit and efficacy : so long as he sitteth at the right
hand of God, which must be till the time of the restitution
of all things [b], the merit of his blood shall work amongst men.
Fifthly, Christ's own power, to keep inviolably the propriety
he hath gotten ; " My sheep hear my voice; and I give unto
them eternal life, and they shall never perish, neither shall any
man pluck them out of my hand [c]." Sixthly, The Father's
command unto his Son; " This is the Father's will, that of
all which he hath given me, I should lose nothing [d]," &c.
Seventhly, Christ's love and care. The church is his spouse,
under his coverture and protection ; and therefore as he hath
power and office, so he hath delight to preserve it still. His
love is better able to help, than the malice of the enemy is to
hurt. Eighthly, Christ's intercession, which is not for the
world, but for those whom God hath given him out of the
world, and those he demandeth of his Father (who heareth
him always) in the virtue of that covenant which between
them was ratified, on God's part, by a promise and oath,—
and on Christ's part, by a merit and purchase. Now Christ's
intercession shall last till his returning to judge the world ;
and therefore still he must have a church, for whom to intercede. Lastly, Christ's own promise, to be with the
preaching of his gospel ; that is, to give it assistance and
success, for the gathering together and perfecting of the
saints unto the end of the world [e].

Here then may be answered two great questions : First,
Whether the church may ' deficere,' fail upon the earth or
no ? To which I answer, That the church may be taken either
mystically, spiritually, and universally : and in that sense it
can never fail ; but there must be upon the earth, a true
church of Christ, not only ' certitúdine eventus,' by the certainty of the event, which is on all sides agreed ; but ' cer-

[a] Psal. lxxxix. 35, 36.   [b] Acts iii. 21.   [c] John x. 27, 28.   [d] John vi. 39.
[e] Matt. xxviii. 20.

titudine causæ' too, by a certainty growing out of those irresistible causes, upon which the being of the mystical body of Christ on the earth dependeth. Or it may be considered particularly in the several parts and places of the world, where the gospel is planted; and hierarchically and politically, denoting a company of men, professing the faith of Christ, and reduced into a quiet, peaceable, composed, and conspicuous government;—and so we affirm, that there is no church in the world so safe, but that it may ' deficere,' fail, and be extinguished out of its place. The church of the Jews did, and, after them, any may. Else the apostle's [f] argument, even to the Roman church itself (which was then a famous church throughout the world, and of that passage in the apostle, Baronius makes a long boast,) were very weak, when ' à majore ad minus,' he thus argueth, " Be not highminded, but fear God ; for if he spared not the natural branches, take heed lest he also spare not thee [g]." Thus we find the ten tribes in their apostasy, till they became ' loammi [h],' to be no more a people ; and their brethren after fall into their condition. " Wrath," saith the apostle [i], " is come to the uttermost upon them." And he telleth us [k], that ' the man of sin, the son of perdition, should be revealed by apostasy,' to note unto us, that antichrist was to be generated out of the corruption, or falling away of some eminent church, and that by a mysterious and insensible declination.

A second question which may be made, is this ;—That since the church doth not totally fail from off the earth, whether that which remaineth thereof, be always visible? To which we answer, That if we take the church for the spiritual and mystical body of Christ, which is indeed the house of God [l], so it is in a sort still invisible ; because the qualities and principles which constitute a man in the body of Christ, as faith and the spirit of grace, are invisible things. Seen indeed they may be, by an eye of charity, in their fruits,—but not by an eye of certainty in their own

---

[f] Rom. i. 8. *Baron.* An. 58. sect. 47, 48, 49, 50.　　[g] Rom. xi. 21, 22. [h] Hos. i. 9.　　[i] 1 Thess. ii. 16.　　[k] 1 Tim. iv. 1. 2 Thess. ii. 3, 7. *Cameron.* de Eccles. p. 265, 268.　　[l] Ex illis omnibus, qui intrinsecè et in occultò intus sunt, constat ille Hortus conclusus, Fons signatus, &c. *Aug.* de Bapt. cont. Donat. lib. 5. cap. 27. Alii ita sunt in domo Dei, ut ipsi etiam fint eadem domus Dei : alii ita, ut non pertineant ad compagem domus, &c. De Bapt. lib. 7. cap. 51.

infallible being. Secondly, If we take the church for a
company of men, professing the true doctrine of Christ,
we answer, That take the men in themselves so truly professing,—and impossible it is but their faith should show
itself in the fruits thereof: for the kingdom of Christ is in
the heart like leaven, which will manifest itself in the whole
lump; and so we can, in all, even in the worst ages of the
church, show some who have witnessed the truth against
that deluge of ignorance, error, and idolatry, which had
invaded the world, like gray hairs here and there mingled
on a black head; as if you single out fire from the ashes, it
will be seen by its own evidence, though it may be so raked
up that it is not observed. But then if we speak of these men
' in aggregato,' as concurring to make up a distinct external
body, or church,—so we say, that the professors of the
truth may be so few, and they persecuted, traduced, suppressed, cried down, driven into the wilderness, without
any apparent separated conspicuousness, and government
of its own, (as in the time of Constantius the emperor, the
public professors of the divinity of Christ's person, against
the damnable heresy of the Arians, were used,) as that, in
this sense, we may justly deny the church to have been
always visible; that is, the few true professors of Christ in
power and purity, to have had a free, open, uncontrolled,
distinct ecclesiastical body of their own, notoriously and ' in
conspectu hominum' different from that tyrannical and pom-
pous hierarchy under which they suffered: for though Christ
rule, yet it is *in the midst of his enemies;* and the enemies may
be so many, and Christ's subjects in whom he rules, so few,
—that the corn may be invisible, for the abundance of weeds
amongst which it grows, though in itself very apt to be
seen.

And this giveth a full answer to that question, Where our
church was before the late reformation began by Luther?—
for that reformation did not new make the church, but purge
it. And that it stood in need of purging, the papists themselves were fain to confess, and declare to the world, in their
council of Trent. Only herein is the difference; the council
pretended a reformation in points of discipline and manners;
and we made a reformation in points of doctrine too. When
Christ purged the temple of buyers and sellers, it was the

same temple after, which before. When a man separateth the wheat from the chaff, it is the same corn which before. In these corrupter ages, then the pure professors of Christ, who denied not his faith, did dwell where Satan had his seat. The members of Christ were amongst the rulers of antichrist[m]. We are not another church newly started up, but the same which before, from the apostles' times, held the common and necessary grounds of faith and salvation; which grounds being, in latter ages, perverted and overturned by antichristianism, have been, by valiant champions for the faith of Christ, therefrom vindicated, who have only pruned the Lord's vine, and picked out the stones, and driven the boars out of his vineyard, but have not made either one or other new.

Now this point, That "Christ ruleth in the midst of his enemies," is ground of great confidence in his church, inasmuch as she subsisteth not upon any corruptible strength of her own, but upon the promise, decree, oath, power, and love of God, things invincible by all the powers of darkness. Let the enemies rage never so much, they cannot dethrone Christ, nor extinguish his gospel, for it is an everlasting gospel[n]. It is but as the coming forth of a shepherd against a lion, as the prophet[o] compareth it. For either Christ is unable to protect his people; and that is against St. Jude[p], "He is able to keep you from falling, and to present you faultless," &c. Or else he is unwilling; and that is against St. Paul[q], "This is the will of God, even your sanctification:"—or else both his power and his will are suspended, upon expectation of human concurrence, or nullified and disappointed by us, and that is against the influence of his grace, which giveth us both 'the will and the deed[r];'—against the mercy of his gracious promise; "I will be merciful to their unrighteousness, and their sins and their iniquities will I remember no more[s];—I will heal their backslidings, I will love them freely[t];"—against the immutability of his covenant and holy nature, "I am God and not man, I change not[u]; therefore the sons of Jacob are not destroyed[x]."

[m] Ut sub Antichristi sacerdotibus Christi populus non excideret. *Hilar.* [n] Rev. xiv. 6.   [o] Isai. xxxi. 2.   [p] Jude v. 24.   [q] 1 Thes. iv. 3.   [r] Phil. ii. 13.   [s] Heb. viii. 12.   [t] Hos. xiv. 4.   [u] Hos. xi. 9.   [x] Mal. iii. 6. Isai. liv. 9, 10.

Now besides this general observation, the words afford some particular notes, which I will but briefly touch. As First, That Christ's kingdom in this world is 'regnum crucis,' a kingdom beset with enemies; of all other, the most hated and opposed. They that submit unto it, must resolve to be herein conformable to their head: a cross was his throne, and thorns were his crown; and " every one which will live godly, must suffer persecution," and " through many afflictions enter into his Master's kingdom."—' Quod erat Christus, erimus Christiani.' No marvel, if the world hate the church of Christ, for it hated him first. In his Word, he is resisted, disobeyed, belied, and, if it were possible, silenced and corrupted; in his officers, mocked and misused; in his subjects, persecuted and reviled; in his spirit, thrust away and grieved; in his worship, neglected and polluted; in all his ways, slandered and blasphemed.

The reasons of which strange entertainment of the kingdom of Christ, are, First, Because it is a ' new kingdom,' which enters into the world by way of challenge and dispossession of former lords, and therefore no wonder if it find opposition. Secondly, It is an invisible, unconspicuous, unattended, desolate, and, in appearance, ignoble kingdom. It began in the form of a servant, in the ignominy of a cross; none of the princes of this world [y], none of the learned of this world to countenance or help to set it up; but amongst them all, esteemed as an offensive and foolish thing [z]. Thirdly, It is a universal kingdom; ' Nec parem patitur nec superiorem,' Christ will admit of no consorts [a] or corrivals in his government. Body, and soul, and spirit, he will have wholly and throughout unto himself. And this amongst others is given for the reason, why when Tiberius [b] proposed Christ unto the Roman senate with the privilege of his own suffrage, to be worshipped, they rejected him, because he would be a God alone. If he would exempt some of the earthly members from his subjection, let lust have the eye, or folly the ear, or, violence the hand, or covetousness the heart, or any other evil affection share with him, —he would be the easier tolerated :- but when he will be

[y] John vii. 48.   [z] 1 Cor. i. 21, 22.   [a] 1 Cor. vi. 20. 1 Thes. v. 23.
[b] *Laurent. de Lau. Bar.* in Tertul. Apol. cap. 5.

absolute, and nothing must remain in our hearts but as his vassal, to be spoiled, subdued, condemned, and crucified by him, if the whole state of sin must be ruined, and the body destroyed, no wonder if the world cannot away with him. Fourthly, which is the sum of all, It is a heavenly kingdom, a spiritual kingdom, " My kingdom is not of this world;" and therefore no marvel if the devils of hell, and the lusts of the flesh, do set themselves against him.

Note, Secondly, Even there where Christ's throne and kingdom is set up, he hath enemies. Satan hath his seat[c], even where Christ dwelleth. Men may say they are Jews, and are not, but of the synagogue of Satan[d]; and men may say they are Christians, and are not, but of the kingdom of Satan too. A wen in the body seemeth to belong unto the integrity of the whole, when indeed it is an enemy and thief therein. Ivy about a tree seemeth to embrace it with much affection, when indeed it doth but kill and choke it. Men may take upon them the profession of Christians, and, like a wen, be skinned over with the same outside which the true members have, may pretend much submission, worship, and ceremony unto him ; and yet (such is the hellish hy- pocrisy of the heart) the same men may haply inwardly swell and rankle against the power of his truth and Spirit. "This people[e]," saith the Lord, "draw near me with their mouth, and honour me with their lips, but have removed their heart far from me, and their fear toward me is taught by the precepts of men."—In the apostles'[f] times there were false brethren, and false teachers, who crept in to spy out and betray the liberty of the church, and privily to bring in damnable heresies, and to speak lies in hypocrisy ; that is, under the pretext of devotion and carnal humility, to cor- rupt the doctrine of Christ, and, under a form of godliness, to deny the power thereof. Therefore antichrist is called

---

[c] Rev. ii. 13.   [d] Rev. ii. 9.   [e] Isai. xxix. 13.   [f] Gal. ii. 4. 2 Pet. ii. 1. 1 Tim. iv. 1, 2. Col. ii. 23. 2 Tim. iii. 5, 6. Occultæ obreptiones, *Aug.* Tom. 4. de fid. et op. cap. 5. Τῇ χρηστολογίᾳ τὰς ἑαυτῶν κακονοίας καλύπτοντες, ἀγκι- στρεύουσι τοὺς ἁπλουστέρους πρὸς θάνατον.   *Isid. Pelus.* l. 1. Ep. 102. Sub ipso Christiani nominis titulo fallit [inimicus] incautos, &c.   *Cypr.* de unit. Eccl.——Usitatissima hæc Hæreticorum fraus de personarum reverentiâ et prætextu pietatis sibi fidem præstruere, vid. *Aug.* Tom. 1. De morib. Eccl. lib. 1. c. 1. et Epist. 120. c. 37.   De peccat. merit. et remis. lib. 2. c. 16. et lib. 3. cap. 1. et 3.

'a whore [g],' because he should seduce the Christian world with much expression of love, and creep, peaceably and by flatteries, into the kingdom of Christ. Of these several enemies of Christ, under the profession of his name and worship, some are Christians, but not in purity, as heretics; some, not in unity, as schismatics; some, not in sincerity, as hypocrites; some, not so much as in external conformity, as evil workers: the heretic corrupteth Christ; the schismatic divideth him; the hypocrite mocketh him; the profane person dishonoureth him; and all deny him.

Let us then learn to look unto our hearts, for we may flatter Christ [h], when we do not love him; we may enquire and seek early after him [i], and yet have no desire to find him; we may come unto his school as untoward children, not for love of his doctrine, but for fear of his rod; we may call him husband, and yet be wedded to our own lusts; we may be baptized in his name, so was Simon Magus [k]; we may preach him, so did the false brethren [l]; we may flock after him, so did the multitude [m] who followed him not for his words or miracles, but for the loaves; we may bow unto him, so did his crucifiers [n]; we may call upon his name, so did the hypocrites that said, " Lord, Lord [o]," and yet did not enter into the kingdom of Heaven; we may confess and believe him, so do the very devils in Hell [p]; we may give him our lips, our eyes, our tongues, our knees, our hands, and yet still our kingdom, our throne, our hearts may be Satan's. And all this is to make him but a mock-king, as the Jews did, when indeed we crucify him.

Note, Thirdly, Christ's word and spirit are stronger than all adverse opposition. This is his glory, that his kingdom cometh in unto him by way of conquest, as Canaan unto Israel. Therefore, at the very first erecting of his kingdom, when, in all presumption, it might most easily have been crushed, he suffered his enemies to vent their utmost malice, and to glut themselves with the blood of his people, that so it might appear, that though théy did fight against him, they could not prevail against him [q]; but that his counsel should

g Rev. xvii. 1, 4.   h Psalm lxxviii. 36, 37.   i Nihil laborant nisi non invenire quod quærunt. *Aug.* de Gen. con. Manic. l. 2. c. 2.   k Acts viii. 13. l Matth. vii. 22. Phil. i. 16.   m John vi. 26.   n Matth. xxvii. 29.   o Matth. vii. 21.   p Luke viii. 28. James ii. 19.   q Isai. viii. 7, 10. Dan. ii. 44. vii. 25, 26. Zech. xii. 3, 4. Isai. xxxi. 8.

still stand and flourish, and should consume and break in pieces all the kingdoms which set themselves against it: that they all should be afraid of the ensign of the gospel, and should fly from it.

This jealousy of God for his church may be seen, in frustrating the attempts, and pulling off the wheels, on which the projects which are cast against his church, do move, as he dealt with Pharaoh. He can dissolve the confederacies, shatter the counsels, cast a spirit of treachery, unfaithfulness, and mutinous affections into the hearts of his enemies; as he did into the Midianites [r], and into the children of Ammon [s], Moab, and Edom, when they gathered together against his people. He can infatuate their counsels [t], and make them the contrivers and artificers of their own ruin, as we see in the consultation of Rehoboam with his young men, and of Jeroboam with his idolatrous policy, and of Haman in his gallows. He can defeat their expectations, and disannul their decrees, and make his own counsel alone to stand [u].

But when all this is done, this is only to rule in spite of his enemies. But besides this, his kingdom fetcheth his enemies under, and in some sort ruleth over their consciences, and striketh them to the ground ; maketh the devils in Hell, the stoutest of all sinners, to tremble; breaketh the rocks asunder [x]; affrighteth, judgeth, sealeth, hardeneth, thresheth, revengeth the pride of men [y] ; maketh them, before-hand, to taste the bitterness of that damnation, which waketh over them, and cometh swiftly against them.

Let us take heed, then, of being Christ's enemies, in opposing the power and progress of his Word, the evidence and purity of his Spirit in the lives of men. It is but to make a combination to pull the sun out of Heaven ; or for a wave to contend with a rock. For as the ruins of a house are broken on the things upon which they fall; so are the enemies of Christ, which gather together against his church, and fall upon the rock [z], at length ruined by their own malice. Sampson's foxes were themselves burnt amongst the corn which they fired : the land brought forth corn the next year again (and, it may be, more plentifully, by reason of

r Judg. vii. 22.   s 2 Chron. xx. 22, 23.   t Isai. xix. 6, xxix. 14. Mic. iv. 11, 12. Isai. xxxvii. 33, 34.   u Psalm xxxiii. 10, 11.   xJer. xxiii. 29.
y 2 Cor. x. 6.   z Luke x. 18.

that fire); but the foxes never came up any more.   Even so
can the Lord deal with those enemies, which waste and depo-
pulate his church ; make them the authors of their own utter
confusion, and bring forth his church with shouting, and
with doubled graces.

Who then is the man that desireth tranquillity of life and
security against all evil ?   Let him become a subject in this
conquering kingdom, and cast himself under the banner and
protection of Christ, and he cannot miscarry.   " He that
walketh uprightly, walketh surely.—The name of the Lord is
a strong tower ; the righteous flieth unto it and is safe.—The
Lord is a sun and a shield, a fountain of all good.—Grace and
glory will he give ; and no good thing will he withhold from
them, that walk uprightly."—And a protection against all evil ;
" I will not be afraid of ten thousands of men," saith the
prophet David, " that compass me about."   When there is
no light, nor issue; nor, in nature, possibility of escape, he can
open a door of deliverance, to relieve his church.   As a man
in the king's highway is under the king's protection ; so in
Christ's way, we are under his protection.   Let us, then,
never repine at the miscarriages of the world, nor murmur
against the wise proceedings of God in the several dispensations towards his church on earth.   When he punisheth, he
doth it in measure, less than our sins deserved ; and when we
search and try our ways, and return unto him, he knoweth
how to work his own glory in our deliverance.   Those
stones which are appointed for a glorious building, are first
under the saw and the hammer, to be hewn and squared; and
those Christians in whom the Lord will take most delight, he
usually thereunto fitteth by trials and extremities.   He that is
brought to tremble in himself [a], may, with most confidence,
expect to rejoice in God.

Note, Fourthly, This is the honour of Christ's kingdom to
be a peaceable, quiet, and secure kingdom, not only after the
victory, but in the midst of enemies.   "This man," saith the
prophet of Christ [b], " shall be the peace, when the Assyrian,
the enemy, is in the land."   We have peace in him, when we
have tribulation in the world [c].   Christ saith of himself, " I
came not to send peace, but a sword [d];" and yet the apostle

[a] Hab iii. 16.   [b] Micah v. 5.   [c] John xvi. 3.   [d] Matth. x. 34.

saith, that "he came and preached peace to those which were afar off, and to those which were near[e]." How shall these things be reconciled? Surely as a man may say of a rock, ' Nothing more quiet, because it is never stirred; and yet nothing more unquiet, because it is ever assaulted ;' so we may say of the church. ' Nothing more peaceable, because it is established upon a rock ; and yet nothing more unpeaceable, because that rock is in the midst of seas, winds, enemies, persecutions.' But yet still the prophet's conclusion is certain, " The work of righteousness is peace, and the effect of righteousness, quietness, and assurance for ever[f]."

[e] Eph. ii. 17.　　[f] Isai. xxxii. 17.

VERSE III.

Thy people shall be willing in the day of thy power, in the beauties of holiness from the womb of the morning : thou hast the dew of thy youth.

THE prophet, before, showed the reign of Christ over his enemies; he now speaketh of his reign over his people, and describeth what manner of subjects or soldiers Christ should have. I will not trouble you with a variety of expositions (occasioned by the many metaphors, and different translations), but give, in a few words, those which I conceive to be most literal and pertinent to the place.

" *Thy people;*"—that is, those whom thou dost receive from thy Father, and by setting up the standard and ensign of thy gospel, gather to thyself. " *Shall be willing ;*"—the word is *willingnesses,* that is, a people of great willingness and devotion, or (as the original word is elsewhere used [a]) shall be *freewill offerings* unto thee. The abstract [b] being put for the concrete, and the plural for the singular, notes how exceeding forward and free they should be ; as the Lord, to signify that his people were most rebellious, saith that they were " Rebellion itself." [c] So then the meaning is, " Thy people shall, with most ready and forward cheerfulness, devote, consecrate, and render up themselves to thy government as a reasonable sacrifice ; shall be of a most liberal, free, noble, and unconstrained spirit in thy service, they shall be *voluntaries* in the wars of thy kingdom."—" In the day of thy power," or " of thine armies ;" by these words we may understand two things, both of them aiming at the same general sense: First, So as that " *armies* "—shall be the same with " *thy people* " before ;—" In the day when thou shalt assemble thy soldiers together, when thou shalt set up thine ensigns for them to seek unto; that is, When thou shalt cause the preaching of thy gospel to sound like a trumpet, that men may prepare themselves in armies to fight

---

a Psal. cxix. 108.　　b Eph. iv. 8. v. 8.　　c Ezek. ii. 8.

thy battles, then shall all thy people, with great devotion
and willingness, gather themselves together under thy colours, and freely devote themselves to thy military service."
Secondly, So as that by *power* or *armies* may be meant the
means whereby this free and willing devotion in Christ's
people is wrought: that is, "When thou shalt send forth
the rod of thy strength, when thou shalt command thy
apostles and ministers to go forth and fight against the kingdoms of sin and Satan; when thou shalt, in the dispensation of thine ordinances, reveal thy power and spiritual
strength unto their consciences,—then shall they most willingly relinquish their former service, and wholly devote
themselves unto thee, to fight under thy banners, and to take
thy part against all thine enemies."

"*In the beauties of holiness.*" This likewise we may severally understand; Either, "In thy holy church;" which
may well so be called with an allusion to the temple at Jerusalem, which is called the 'beauty of holiness [d],' and a
'holy and a beautiful house [e],' and a 'glorious high throne.' [f]
And hither did the tribes [g] resort in troops, as it were, in
'armies,' to present their free-will offerings, and celebrate the
other services of the Lord. Or else we may understand it
casually, thus: "*In the day of thy power,*" that is, "When
thou shalt reveal thy strength and Spirit in '*the beauties of
holiness,*'" that is, "When thou shalt reveal how exceeding
beautiful, and full of loveliness thy holy ways and services
are, then shall thy people be persuaded, with all free and
willing devotion of heart, to undertake them." Or lastly,
thus, As the priests who offered sacrifices to the Lord, were
clothed with 'holy and beautiful garments [h];' or as those
who, in admiration of some noble prince, voluntarily follow
the service of his wars, do set themselves forth in the most
complete furniture and richest attire, as is fit to give notice
of the nobleness of their minds (for beautiful armour [i] was
wont to be esteemed the honour of an army); so they who
willingly devote themselves unto Christ, to be soldiers and
sacrifices unto him, are not only armed with strength, but

d Psal. xxix. 2.   e Isai. lxiv. 11.   f Jer. xvii. 12.   g Psal. lxxxiv. 7.
h Exod. xxviii. 2, 40.   i Judg. v. 30.   *Curtius* lib. 3. et 5.—Vid. *Brisson.*
de Reg. Persarum, l. 3. p. 323.—Et *Tho. Demsteri.* ad Rosin. Antiq. Paralipom.
lib. 10. cap. 1.

adorned with such inward graces, as make them "beautiful as Tirza, comely as Jerusalem, fair as the moon, clear as the sun, and terrible as an army with banners."[k]   All which three explications meet in one general, which is principally intended, that holiness hath all beauties in it, and is that only which maketh a man lovely in the eyes of Christ.

"*From the womb of the morning: thou hast the dew of thy youth.*" There is a middle point after those words, "*the womb of the morning*," which may seem to disjoin the clauses, and make those words refer wholly to the preceding. In which relation, there might be a double sense conceived in them. Either thus, "*In the beauties of holiness*, or in holiness very beautiful, more than the aurora or *womb of the morning*, when she is ready to bring forth the sun:"—and then it is a notable metaphor to express the glorious beauty of God's ways.—Or thus, "*Thy people shall be a willing* people from the very *womb of the morning*;" that is, "from the very first forming of Christ in them, and shining forth upon them, they shall rise out of their former nakedness and security, and shall adorn themselves with the beautiful graces of Christ's Spirit, as with 'clothing of wrought gold, and raiment of needlework; and shall, with gladness and rejoicing, with much devotion and willingness of heart, be brought unto the king[l],' and present themselves before him as voluntaries in his service."—But because the learned conceive, that the middle point is only a distinction for convenient reading, not a disjunction of the sense,—I shall therefore rest in a more received exposition: "Thy children shall be born in great abundance unto thee, by the seed of thy Word, in the womb of the church, as soon as the morning, or sun of righteousness shall shine forth upon it. As the dew is born out of the cool morning air, as out of a womb, distilling down in innumerable drops upon the earth; so thine elect shall be born unto thee, by the preaching of thy Word, and first approach of thy heavenly light, in innumerable armies."—And this explication is very suitable to the harmony of holy Scripture, which useth the same metaphors to the same purpose in other places. "The remnant of Jacob," saith the prophet[m], "shall be in the midst of

---

k Cant. vi. 4. 10.   l Psal. xlv. 13, 14, 15.   m Mich. v. 7.

many people as a dew from the Lord." And Christ is called
" the bright morning-star[n]," and " the day-spring[o]," and
" the sun of righteousness[p];" and the time of the gospel is
called "the time of day[q]," or the approach of day. So
that *"from the womb of the morning"* is, From the heavenly
light of gospel, which is the wing or beam, whereby the sun
of righteousness revealeth himself, and breaketh out upon
the world; as the rising sun, which rejoiceth like a giant
to run his race, shall the succession increase, and armies of
the church of God be continually supplied.

The words, thus unfolded, do contain in them a lively
character of the subjects in Christ's spiritual kingdom; described, First, by their relation to him, and his propriety to
them, *thy people.* Secondly, by their present condition, intimated in the Word, *willing* or voluntaries, and (if we take
thy people and *armies* for synonymous terms, the one notify-
ing the order and quality of the other) expressed in the text,
and that is, to be military men. Thirdly, by their thorough
and universal resignation, subjection and devotedness unto
him. For when he conquereth by his Word, his conquest is
wrought upon the wills and affections of men. " Victorque
volentes per populos dat jura:" *thy people shall be willing.*
The ground of which willingness is farther added, (for so
chiefly I understand those words) *the day of thy power.* So
that the willingness of Christ's subjects is effected by the
power of his grace and Spirit in the revelation of the gospel.
Fourthly, by their honourable attire, and military robes, in
which they appear before him, and attend upon him, *in
beauties of holiness,* or in the various and manifold graces of
Christ, as in a garment of divers colours. Fifthly and
lastly, by their age, multitudes, and manner of their birth;
they are the *dew of the morning,* as many as the small drops
of dew; and they are born to him out of the *womb of the
morning,* as dew is generated, not on the earth, but in the
air, by a heavenly calling, and by the shining of the morning-
star, and day-spring upon their consciences. " Ye are all
the children of light," saith the apostle, " and the children
of the day; we are not of the night, nor of darkness."[r]

[n] Rev. xxii. 16.   [o] Luke ii. 78.   [p] Mal. iv. 2.   [q] Rom. xiii. 12.
1 John ii. 8.   [r] 1 Thes. v. 5.

I said before, that I approve not the mincing and crumbling of holy Scriptures. Yet in these parts of them, which are written for models and summaries of Christian doctrine, I suppose there may be weight in every word, as, in a rich jewel, there is worth in every sparkle. Here then, first, we may take notice of Christ's propriety to his people; *thy people;* all the elect and believers do belong unto Christ. They are his people. They are his " own sheep [s]." There is a mutual and reciprocal propriety between him and them. " I am my beloved's, and my beloved is mine [t]. His desire is towards me." " His," I say, not as he is God only, by a right of inseparable dominion, as we are his creatures; for all things were created [u] by him and for him; and he is over all, God blessed for ever [x].—Nor his only, as he is the first-born and heir of all things [y]. In which respect he is Lord of the angels, and God hath set him " over all the works of his hands."—But as he is the mediator and head in his church. In which respect the faithful are his by a more peculiar propriety. " We are thine; thou never barest rule over them, they were not called by thy name [z]." The devils are his vassals: the wicked of this world his prisoners. The faithful only are his subjects and followers; his jewels, his friends, his brethren, his sons, his members, his spouse. His, by all the relations of intimateness that can be named.

Now this propriety Christ hath unto us upon several grounds. First, By constitution and donation from his father. God hath made him Lord and Christ. He hath put all things under his feet, and hath given him to be head over all things to the church. " Ask of me, and I will give thee the heathen for thine inheritance, and the uttermost parts of the earth for thy possession [a]." " Behold, I and the children whom thou hast given me [b]." " Thine they were, and thou gavest them to me [c]."—For as, in regard of God's justice, we were bought by Christ in our redemption; so in regard of his love, we were given unto Christ in our election, that he might redeem us.

Secondly, By a right of purchase, treaty, and covenant between Christ and his Father. For we, having sold away

[s] John x. 3.　　[t] Can. ii. 16. vii. 10.　　[u] Col. i. 16, 17.　　[x] Rom. ix. 5.
[y] Heb. i. 2, 3. ii. 7, 8.　　[z] Isai. lxiii. 19.　　[a] Psalm ii. 8.　　[b] Isai. viii. 18.
[c] John xvii. 6.

ourselves, and being now in the enemies' possessions, could not be restored unto our primitive estate without some intervening price to redeem us. Therefore, saith the apostle, he was made under the law, ἵνα ἐξαγοράσῃ " that he might *buy out*, those that were under the law [d]." And again, "Ye are bought with a price [e]." He was our surety [f], and stood in our stead, and was set forth to declare the righteousness of God [g]. God dealt in grace with us, but in justice with him.

Thirdly, By a right of conquest and deliverance. He hath plucked us out of our enemies' hand; he hath dispossessed and spoiled those that ruled over us before; he hath delivered us from the power of Satan, and translated us into his own kingdom. We are his freemen: he only hath made us free from the law of sin and death, and hath rescued us as spoils out of the hands of our enemies [h], and therefore we are become his servants [i], and owe obedience unto him as our patron [k] and deliverer. As the Gibeonites [l], when they were delivered from the sword of the children of Israel, were thereupon made hewers of wood, and drawers of water for the congregation; so we, being rescued out of the hands of those tyrannous lords which ruled over us, do now owe service and subjection unto him, that hath so mercifully delivered us. "Being made free from sin," saith the apostle [m], "ye become the servants of righteousness."—And "we are delivered from the law," that being dead wherein we were held, "that we should serve in newness of spirit."—And again, "He died for all, that they which live, should not henceforth live unto themselves, but unto him which died for them and rose again [n]."

Fourthly, By covenant and stipulation. "I entered into covenant with thee, and thou becamest mine [o]." Therefore, in our baptism, we are said to be ' Baptized into Christ [p],' and to ' put on Christ [q],' and to be ' Baptized into his name [r];' that is, wholly to consecrate and devote ourselves to him as the servants of his family. Therefore they which were bap-

---

[d] Gal. iv. 5.   [e] 1 Cor. vi. 20. Tit. ii. 14.   [f] Heb. vii. 22.   [g] Rom. iii. 25.
[h] Luke xi. 22.   [i] Isai. xxvi. 13, 14, 15.   [k] Ingratus Libertus, qui Patrono non præstat obsequium.   [l] Josh. ix. 26, 27.   [m] Rom. vi. 18. vii. 6.
[n] 2 Cor. v. 15.   [o] Ezek. xvi. 8.   [p] Rom. vi. 3. iii. v.   [q] Gal. iii. 27.
[r] Acts xix. 5.

tized in the ancient church [s], were wont to put on white raiment, as it were the livery and badge of Christ, a testimony
of that purity and service which therein they vowed unto
him. And therefore it is, that we still retain the ancient
form of vow, promise, or profession in baptism, which was
' to renounce the Devil and all works [t], the world, with the
pomp, luxury, and pleasures thereof.' And this is done in a
most solemn and deliberate manner by way of answer to the
question and demand of Christ. For which purpose St.
Peter[u] calleth baptism, συνειδήσεως ἀγαθῆς ἐπερώτημα ' The answer,' or ' the interrogatory trial of a good conscience' towards God. He that conformeth himself to the fashions,
and setteth his heart upon the favours, preferment, empty
applause, and admiration of the world ; that liveth κατ' αἰῶνα
according to the rules and courses and sinful maxims of
worldly men,—in such indifferency, compliancy, and connivance as may flatter others and delude himself; he that is
freely and customarily overruled by the temptations of
Satan ; that yieldeth to looseness of heart, to vanity of
thoughts, lusts of the eye, pride of life, luxury, intemperance,
impurity of mind or body, or any other earthly and inordinate affection,—is little better in the sight of God than a
perjured and a runagate person, flinging off from that service unto which he had bound himself by a solemn vow, and
robbing Christ of that interest in him which, by a mutual
stipulation, was agreed upon.

Lastly, By the virtue of our communion with him, and
participation of his grace and fulness. All that we are in
regard of Spirit and life, is from him. We are nothing of
ourselves[y]. And " we can do nothing of ourselves[z]." All
that we are, is from the grace of Christ. " By the grace of
God I am what I am[a]."—And all that we do, is from the
grace of Christ; " I am able to do all things through Christ
that strengtheneth me[b]." As when we do evil, it is not we
ourselves, but sin that dwelleth in us[c] ; so when we do

---

[s] *Socrat.* Hist. lib. 7. cap. 17.—*Laurent. de la Bar.* in Tertul. lib. de Coron.
milit. cap. 1. — *Ambros.* Tom. 4. lib. de iis qui mysteriis initiantur. c. 7.
[t] *Tertul.* de Corona milit. c. 3. et de Spectaculis, cap. 4.—*Ambros.* To. 4. de Sacram.
lib. 1. c. 2.—*Basil. Mag.* To. 2. de Spir. Sancto, cap. 11.—*Vid. Brisson.* Comment.
in lib. Dominico, &c. page 137.   [u] 1 Pet. iii. 21.   [x] Ephes. ii. 2.   [y] 2 Cor.
xii. 11.   [z] John xv. 5.   [a] 1 Cor. xv. 10.   [b] Phil. iv. 13.   [c] Rom
vii. 20.

good, it is not we, but Christ that liveth in us [d].   So that in
all respects we are not our own, but his that died for us.

Now this being a point of so great consequence, needful it
is that we labour therein to try and secure ourselves, that we
belong unto Christ.   For which purpose we must note, that
a man may belong unto Christ two manner of ways : First,
By a mere external profession [e].   So all in the visible church
that call themselves Christians, are his, and his Word and
oracles theirs : in which respect they have many privileges,
as the apostle showeth of the Jews.   Yet notwithstanding
such men, continuing unreformed in their inward man, are
nearer unto cursing than others, and subject unto a sorer condemnation, for despising Christ in his Word and Spirit, with
whom, in their baptism, they made so solemn a covenant.
For God will not suffer his gospel to be cast away, but will
cause it to prosper [f] unto some end or other, either to save
those that believe ; or to cumulate the damnation of those
that disobey it.   He will be more careful to cleanse his garner [g], and to purge his floor, than of other empty and barren
places.   A weed in the garden is in more danger of rooting
out, than in the field.   Such belong unto Christ no otherwise
than ivy unto the tree, unto which it externally adheres.
Secondly, A man may belong unto Christ by implantation
into his body, which is done by faith.   But here we are to
note, that as some branches in a tree have a more faint and
unprofitable fellowship with the root than others, as having
no farther strength than to furnish themselves with leaves,
but not with fruit ; so, according unto the several virtues or
kinds of faith, may the degrees of men's ingrafture into
Christ be judged of.   There is a dead [h], unoperative faith,
which, like Adam after his fall, hath the nakedness thereof
only covered with leaves, with mere formal and hypocritical
conformities.   And there is an unfeigned, lively, and effectual
faith ; which is available to those purposes for which faith
was appointed, namely, to justify the person, to purify the
heart [i], to quench temptations, to carry a man with wisdom
and an unblamable conversation through this present world, to
work by love, to grow and make a man abound in the service
of the Lord.   And this distinction our Saviour giveth us,

[d] Gal. ii. 20.   [e] Isai. xxix. 13.   [f] Isai. lv. 10, 11.   [g] Luke iii. 17.
[h] James ii. 26.   [i] 1 Tim. i. 5.

that " there are some branches in him which bear not fruit,
and those he taketh away ; and others which bear fruit, and
those he purgeth that they may bring forth more [k]." Those
only are the branches, which he desires to own.

And thus to belong unto Christ is that only which maketh
us λαὸς περιούσιος, and εἰς περιποίησιν, 'A purchased, a peculiar people unto him.' And there are several ways of evidencing it. I will only name two or three, and most in the
text. First, We must know that Christ is a morning star, a
sun of righteousness ; and so ever comes to the soul with
self-evidencing properties. Unto him belongeth that royal
prerogative, to write ' Teste Meipso' in the hearts of men, to
be himself the witness to his own acts, purchases, and covenants. Therefore his Spirit came in tongues of fire, and in a
mighty wind, all which have several ways of manifesting themselves, and stand not in need of any borrowing or foreign
confirmations. If Christ then be in the heart, he will discover himself. His Spirit is the original of grace and
strength, as concupiscence is of sin. It is a seed in the
heart, which will spring up and show itself. And, therefore,
as lust doth take the first advantage of the faint and imperfect stirrings of the reasonable soul in little infants, to evidence itself in pride, folly, stubbornness, and other childish
sins ; so the Spirit of grace in the heart cannot lie dead, but
will work, and move, and, as a Spirit of burning, by the
light, heat,—purging, comforting, inflaming, combating.virtue
which is in it, make the soul which was barren, and settled
on the lees, and unacquainted with any such motions before,
stand amazed at its own alteration, and say with Rebekah,
" If it be so, why am I thus ?" Externals may be imitated
by art; but no man can paint the soul or the life, or the
sense and motion of the creature. Now Christ and his
Spirit are the internal forms, and active principles in a
Christian man ; " Christ liveth in us ;—When Christ who is
our life, shall appear," &c. Therefore impossible it is, that
any hypocrite should counterfeit, and by consequence obscure those intimate and vital workings of his grace in t
soul, whereby he evidenceth himself thereunto. It is true, a
man that feareth the Lord, may walk in darkness, and be in
such discomforts, as he shall see no light ; and yet even in
that condition, Christ doth not want properties to evidence

[k] John xv. 2.

himself, in tenderness of conscience, fear of sin, striving of
spirit with God, closeness of heart, and constant recourse
to him in his Word, and the like ; only the soul is shut up
and overclouded that it cannot discern him. The Spirit of
Christ is a ' seal,' a ' witness,' an earnest [1], an handsel, a
first-fruit of that fulness which is promised hereafter. It is
Christ's own Spirit ; and therefore fashioneth the hearts of
those in whom it is, unto his heavenly image, to long for
more comprehension of him, for more conformity unto him,
for more intimacy and communion with him, for more grace,
wisdom, and strength from him ; it turneth the bent and
course of the soul from that earthly and sensual end unto
which it wrought it before ; as a good branch, having been
ingrafted into a wild stock, converteth the sap of a crab
into pleasant fruit.

Again ; If a man be one of Christ's people, then there
hath a *day of power* passed over him, the sword of the Spirit
hath entered into him ; he hath been conquered by the rod of
Christ's strength ; he hath felt John's axe laid to the root
of his conscience, and hath been persuaded by the terror
of the Lord ; for the coming of Christ is with shaking : the
conscience hath felt a mighty operation in the Word, though
to other men it hath passed over like empty breath ; for the
Word " worketh effectually in those that believe," and
bringeth about the purposes for which it was sent. To
those that are called, it is the power of God. [m]

Again ; Where Christ comes, he comes with ' beauty and
holiness :' those who lay in their blood [n] and pollutions,
before, bare and naked, are made exceedingly beautiful,
and renowned for their beauty, " perfect through the comeliness which he puts upon them [o]." He comes unto the soul
with beauty and precious oil, and garments of praise,—that
is, with comfort, joy, peace, healing, to present the church
a holy church, without spot or wrinkle to his Father.

Lastly, Where Christ cometh, he cometh with the *womb
of the morning*, with much light to acquaint the soul with his
truth and promises ; and with much fruitfulness, making the
heart, which was barren before, to flow with rivers of living

[1] Ephes. i. 14. 1 John iv. 13.   [m] 1 Cor. i. 22.   [n] Ezek. xvi. 9, 14.
[o] Isai. lxi. 3.

water P, to bring forth fruit q more and more, and to abound in the works of the Lord. These are the particular evidences of our belonging to Christ in the text, and by these we must examine ourselves:—Do I find in my soul the new name of the Lord Jesus written, that I am not only in title, but in truth, a Christian? Do I find the secret nature and figure of Christ fashioned in me, swaying my heart to the love and obedience of his holy ways? Do I hear the voice, and feel the hand and judicature of his blessed Spirit within me, leading me in a new course, ordering mine inner man, sentencing and crucifying mine earthly members? Am I a serious and earnest enemy to my original lusts and closest corruptions? Do I feel the workings and kindlings of them in mine heart with much pain and mourning, with much humiliation for them, and deprecation against them? Is Christ my centre? Do I find in mine heart a willingness to be with him, as well here in his word, ways, promises, directions, comforts ; yea, in his reproaches and persecutions, as hereafter in his glory? Is it the greatest business of my life, to make myself more like him, to walk as he also walketh, to be as he was in this world, to purify myself even as he is pure? Hath the terror of his wrath persuaded me, and shaken my conscience out of its carnal security, and made me look about for a refuge from the wrath to come,—and esteem more beautiful than the morning brightness, the feet of those who bring glad tidings of deliverance and peace? Hath his gospel an effectual seminal virtue within me, to new form my nature and life daily unto his heavenly image? Is it an ingrafted word which mingleth with my conscience, and hideth itself in my heart, actuating, determining, moderating, and overruling it to its own way? Am I cleansed from my filthiness, careful to keep myself chaste, comely, beautiful, a fit spouse for the fairest of ten thousand? Do I rejoice in his light, walking as a child of light, living as an heir of light, going on, like the sun, unto the perfect day, labouring to abound always in the work of the Lord? Then I may have good assurance that I belong unto Christ. And if so, that will be a seminary of much comfort to my soul.

P John vii. 38. xv. 2.　Cant. iv. 2.　q Isai. xxxii. 15.　Rom. vii. 4.

For first, If we are Christ's, then he ' careth for us ;' for
propriety is the ground of care. " He that is a hireling,"
saith.our Saviour,[r] " and not the shepherd, whose own the
sheep are not, seeth the wolf coming, and leaveth the
sheep," &c. " Because he is a hireling, he careth not for
the sheep. But I am the good Shepherd, and know my
sheep, and am known of mine ;" therefore I am careful of
them. He watcheth over us, he searcheth and seeketh us
out in our stragglings, and feedeth us. This is the principal argument we have to believe, that God will look upon
us for good, notwithstanding our manifold provocations, because he is pleased to own us, and to take us as his own
peculiar people. Though the church be full of ruins, yet
because it is his own house [s], he will repair it ; though it be
black as well as comely, yet because it is his own spouse,
he will pity and cherish it [t]; though it bring forth wild
grapes, and be indeed meet for no work, yet because it is
his own vine [u], planted by his own right hand, and made
strong for himself, he will be therefore careful to fence and
prune it.[x] This is the only argument we have to prevail
with God in prayer, that in Christ we call him ' Father ;'
we present ourselves before him as his ' own ;' we make
mention of no other Lord or name over us ;[y] and therefore he cannot deny us the things which are good for us.

Secondly, If we are Christ's, then he will certainly ' purge
us,' and make the members suitable to the head. " I swear
unto thee, and entered into covenant with thee, saith the
Lord, and thou becamest mine ;" and immediately it follows, " Then washed I thee with water, yea, I thoroughly
washed away thy blood from thee [x]."—" Every branch in me
that beareth fruit, he purgeth it, that it may bring forth
more fruit [a]."—" He purifieth to himself a peculiar people.[b] "
If we be his ' peculiar people,' and set apart for himself (as
the prophet David [c] speaks), he will undoubtedly purify us,
that we may be honourable vessels, sanctified and meet for
the Master's use, and prepared unto every good work.[d] He
will furnish us with all such supplies of the Spirit of grace,

[r] Joh. x. 12, 13, 14. Eze. xxxiv. 11, 15.   [s] Heb. iii. 5, 6.   [t] Ezek. xvi. 8. 9.
xv. 5.   [u] Psal. lxxx. 15.   [x] Isai. lxiii. 8, 19.   [y] Isai. xxvi. 13.   [z] Ezek.
xvi. 8, 9.   [a] John xv. 2.   [b] Tit. xxi. 14.   [c] Psal. iv. 3.   [d] 2 Tim. ii. 21.

as the condition of that place in his body requires, in the
which he hath set us.   Grace and glory will he give, and no
good thing will he withhold from those who walk uprightly.
Our propriety to Christ giveth us right unto all good things:
" All is yours, and you are Christ's."

Thirdly, If we are Christ's, then he will spare us.   This
was the argument which the priest was to use between the
porch and the altar[e] ; " Spare thy people, O Lord, and give
not thine heritage to reproach.—Then will the Lord be jealous for his land, and pity his people.[f]—They shall be mine,
saith the Lord, in the day that I make up my jewels; and
I will spare them, as a man spareth his own son that serveth
him.[g]"—Of my servant, to whom I give wages for the merit
of his work, not out of love or grace, I expect a service
proportionable to the pay he receives : but, in my child, I
reward not the dignity of the work, but only the willingness,
the loving and obedient disposition of the heart : and therefore I pass over those failings and weaknesses which discover themselves for want of skill or strength, and not of
love, praising the endeavours, and pardoning the miscarriages.   Thus doth the Lord deal with his children.

Fourthly, If we be Christ's, he will pray for us[h] ; " I
pray not for the world, but for them which thou hast given
me, for they are thine ; and all mine are thine, and thine
are mine," &c. so that we shall be sure to have help in all
times of need, because we know that the Father heareth his
Son always[i]; and those things which, in much fear, weakness, and ignorance, we ask for ourselves, if it be according
to God's will, and by the dictate and mouth of the Spirit in
our heart, Christ himself in his intercession demandeth for
us the same things.   And this is the ground of that confidence which we have in him, that if we ask any thing according to his will, he heareth us, and we have the petitions
that we desire of him.   For as the world hateth us, because
it hateth him first[k], so the Father loveth and heareth us,
because he loveth and heareth him first.

Fifthly, If we be Christ's, then he will teach us, and
commune with us, and reveal himself unto us, and lead us

---

e Joel ii. 17, 18. Exod. xxxii. 12. Num. xiv. 13.   f Isai. lxiv. 9.   g Mal.
iii. 17.   h John xvii. 9, 10.   i John xi. 42.   k 1 John v. 14.

with his voice. " He calleth his own sheep by name, and leadeth them, and putteth them forth, and goeth before them.[l]" Because Israel was his own people, therefore he showed them his words.[m] The law was theirs, and the oracles theirs. When he entereth into covenant with a people, that they become his; then he writeth his law in their hearts, and teacheth them. This is the prophet David's argument; " I am thy servant, give me understanding[n] :" Because I am thine in a special relation, therefore acquaint me with thee in an especial manner. " The earth is full of thy mercy[o]," there is much of thy goodness revealed to all the nations of the world, even to those that are not called by thy name : but as for me, whom thou hast made thine own by a nearer relation, let me have experience of a greater mercy,—" Teach me thy statutes."

Sixthly, If we be his, he will chastise us in mercy, and not in fury ; though he leave us not altogether unpunished, yet he will punish us less [p] than our iniquities deserve ; he will not deal with us as with others; " Though I make a full end of all nations whither I have driven thee, yet I will not make a full end of thee, but I will correct thee in measure [q] :" I will correct thee to cure, [r] but not to ruin thee.

The second thing, considered in the words, was the present condition of the people of Christ, which was to be ' military men,' to join with the armies of Christ against all his enemies. As he was, so must we be, in this world. No sooner was Christ consecrated by his solemn baptism unto the work of a mediator, but presently he was assaulted by the tempter : and no sooner doth any man give up his name to Christ, and break loose from that hellish power under which he was held, but presently Pharaoh and his hosts, Satan and his confederates, pursue him with deadly fury, and pour out floods of malice and rage against him. Hell and death are at truce with wicked men, there is a covenant and agreement betwixt them. Satan holdeth his possession in peace : but when a stronger than he cometh upon and overcometh him, there is, from that time, implacable venom

l John x. 3, 4. m Psal. cxlvii. 19. n Psal. cxix. 125. o Psal. cxix. 64. p Ezra ix. 13. q Jer. xxx. 10, 11. r Qui trucidat, non considerat quemadmodum laniat; qui curat, considerat quemadmodum secat. *Aug.*

and hostility against such a soul; the malice, power, policy, stratagems, and machinations of Satan; the lusts and vanities, the pleasures, honours, profits, persecutions, frowns, flatteries, snares of the wicked world; the affections, desires, inclinations, deceits of our own fleshly hearts, will ever ply the soul of a Christian, and force it to perpetual combats.

There is in Satan an everlasting enmity against the glory, mercy, and truth of God, against the power and mystery of the gospel of Christ. This malice of his exerciseth itself against all those that have given themselves to Christ, whose kingdom he mightily laboureth to demolish: by his power, persecuting it,—by his craftiness and wily insinuations, undermining it; by his vast knowledge and experience in palliating, altering, mixing, proportioning, and measuring his temptations and spiritual wickedness in such a manner, as that he may subvert the church of Christ, either in the purity thereof, by corrupting the doctrine of Christ with heresy, and his worship with idolatry and superstition; or in the unity thereof, by pestering it with schism and distraction; or in the liberty thereof, by bondage of conscience; or in the progress and enlargement thereof, endeavouring to blast and make fruitless the ministry of the gospel. And this malice of Satan is wonderfully set on and encouraged, both by the corruption of our nature, those armies of lusts and affections which swarm within us, entertaining, joining force, and co-operating with all his suggestions; disheartening, reclaiming, and pulling back the soul, when it offers to make any opposition; and also by the men, and materials of this evil world;— by the examples, the threats, the interests, the power, the intimacy, the wit, the tongues, the hands, the exprobrations, the persecutions, the insinuations and seductions of wicked men; by the profits, the pleasures, the preferments, the acceptation, credit and applause of the world.

By all which means, Satan most importunately pursueth one of these two ends, either to subvert the godly, by drawing them away from Christ to apostasy, formality, hypocrisy, spiritual pride, and the like; or else to discomfort them with diffidence, doubts, sight of sin, opposition of the times, vexation of spirit, and the like affections. And these oppositions of Satan meet with a Christian in every respect or consider-

ation, under which he may be conceived: consider him in
his spiritual estate, in his several parts, in his temporal relations, in his actions or employments; and in all these, Satan
is busy to overturn the kingdom of Christ in him. In his
spiritual estate, if he be a weak Christian, he assaulteth him
with perpetual doubts and fears touching his election, conversion, adoption, perseverance, Christian liberty, strength
against corruptions, companies, temptations, persecutions,
&c.: if he be a strong Christian, he labourcth to draw him
unto self-confidence, spiritual pride, contempt of the weak,
neglect of further proficiency, and the like. There is no natural part or faculty which is not aimed at likewise by the
malice of Satan: for Christ when he comes, takes possession
of the whole man, and therefore Satan sets himself against
the whole man. Corporeal and sensitive faculties, tempted
either to sinful representations, letting in and transmitting
the provisions of lust unto the heart, by gazing and glutting
themselves on the objects of the world: or to sinful execu-
tions; finishing and letting out those lusts, which have been
conceived in the heart: the phantasy tempted by satanical
injections and immutations, to be the forge of loose, vain,
unprofitable, and unclean thoughts: the understanding to
earthly wisdom, vanity, infidelity, prejudices, mispersuasions,
fleshly reasonings, vain speculations, and curiosities, &c.:
the will to stiffness, resistance, dislike of holy things, and
pursuit of the world: the conscience to deadness, immobility,
and a stupid benumbedness, to slavish terrors and evidences
of Hell, to superstitious bondage, to carnal security, to desperate conclusions: the affections to independence, distraction, excess, precipitancy, &c.—In temporal conditions, there
is no estate of health, wealth, honour, estimation, or the con-
traries unto these;—no relation of husband, father, magis-
trate, subject, &c.,—unto which Satan hath not such suitable
suggestions, as, by the advantage of fleshly corruptions,
may take from them occasion to draw a man from God.
Lastly, In regard of our actions and employments, whether
they be divine, such as respect God, as acts of piety, in
reading, hearing, meditating, and studying his Word, in
calling upon his name, and the like; or such as respect ourselves, as acts of temperance and sobriety, personal examina-
tions, and more particular acquaintance with our own hearts;

or such as respect others, as acts of righteousness, charity, and edification; or whether they be actions natural, such as are requisite to the preservation of our being, as sleep and diet: or actions civil; in our callings or recreations;—in all these Satan laboureth, either to pervert us in the performance of them, or to divert us from it.   There is then no condition, faculty, relation, or action of a Christian man, the which is not always under the eye and envy of a most raging, wise, and industrious enemy.   And therefore, great reason there is, that Christians should be ' military men,' well instructed in the whole armour of God, that they may be able to stand against the wiles of the devil, and to quench all his fiery darts.   It is our calling to wrestle against principalities and powers, and spiritual wickedness in high places, to resist the devil, to strive against sin, to mortify earthly members, to destroy the body of sin, to deny ourselves, to contradict the reasonings of the flesh, to check and control the stirrings of concupiscence, to resist and subdue the desires of our evil hearts, to withstand and answer the assaults of Satan, to out-face the scorns, and despise the flatteries of the present world, in all things to endure hardness as the soldiers of Jesus Christ[s].   Our cause is righteous, our captain is wise and puissant, our service honourable, our victory certain, our reward massy and eternal; so that, in all respects, great encouragements we have to be volunteers in such war, the issue whereof is our enemy's perdition, our Master's honour, and our own salvation.

The third thing observed was, The thorough and universal resignation and devotedness of Christ's people unto him. " Thy people shall be *willing*," or a people of a great devotion, " in the day of thy power."   From whence I shall gather two observations: First, They that belong unto Christ as his people, are most thoroughly and willingly subject unto his government, do consecrate, resign, and yield up their whole souls and bodies to serve in his wars against all his enemies.   For the distinct understanding of which point we are to observe first, That by nature we are utterly unwilling to be subject unto Christ.   The carnal mind is enmity against God[t], it is not subject to the law of God, neither in-

---

[s] 2 Tim. ii. 3.   [t] Rom. viii. 7, 8, 10.

deed can be. For if Christ be over us, the body of sin must die; it once crucified him, and he will be revenged upon it. By nature we are willingly subject unto no law, but the law of our members ; to no will, but the will of the flesh ; full of contumacy, rebellion [u], and stoutness of spirit against the truth and beauty of the Word or ways of God. The love of corrupted nature is wholly set upon our own ways [x], as an untamed heifer [y], or a wild ass. Men wander [z], and go about [a], and weary themselves in their full compass and swing of lust [b], and will not be turned. And therefore it is, that they bid God depart from them [c], and desire not the knowledge of his ways ; that they leave the paths of uprightness ; that having crooked hearts [d] of their own, they labour likewise to pervert and make crooked the gospel of Christ [e], that they may from thence steal countenance to their sins, contrary to the holy affection of David [f], "make my way straight before me ;" that they snuff and rage [g], and pull away the shoulder [h], and fall backward [i], and thrust away God from them [k]. And hence it is, that men are so apt to cavil, and foolishly to charge the ways of God; First, As grievous ways, too full of austerity, narrowness, and restraint. " I knew that thou wert an austere man [l] ;"—and " this is an hard saying, who can bear it [m] ?"—" The land is not able to bear all his words [n]."—" There is a lion in the way [o] ;" a certain damage and unavoidable mischief will follow me, if I keep in it. Thus as Israel [p], when they heard of giants and sons of Anak, had no heart to Canaan, but cried, and whined, and rebelled, and mutinied, and in their heart turned back into Egypt,—that is, had more will to their own bondage than to God's promise ; so when a natural man hears of walking in a narrow way with much exactness and circumspection, that come what bait of preferment, pleasure, profit, or advantage will, yet he must not turn to the right hand nor to the left, nor commit the least evil for the greatest good ; that as the people in the wilderness were to go only where

[u] Mal. ii. 17. 1 Sam. xv. 23.   [x] Eccles. viii. 11. Prov. xiv. 14.   [y] Jer. ii. 24. viii. 6. Hos. iv. 16.   [z] Jer. ii. 20.   [a] Jer. xxxi. 22.   [b] Isai. lvii. 10.   [c] Job xxi. 14.   [d] Deut. xxxii. 5.   [e] Gal. i. 7. 2 Pet. iii. 16.   [f] Psal. v. 8.   [g] Mal. i. 13.   [h] Neh. ix 29.   [i] Acts vii. 51.   [k] Acts vii. 39.   [l] Matt. xxv. 24.   [m] John vi. 60.   [n] Amos vii. 10.   [o] Prov. xxii. 13.   [p] Num. xiii. 31. xiv. 1, 4.   Neh. ix. 16, 17.

the cloud and pillar of God's presence led them, though he
carried them through giants, terrors, and temptations; so a
Christian must resolve to follow the Lamb whithersoever he
goeth;—he then turneth back to his iniquities [q], and refuseth
to hear the words of the Lord. Secondly, As unprofitable
ways: for "who will show us any good [r]?" is the only language of carnal men. "What can the Almighty do for us [s]?"
say the wicked in Job; "It is in vain to serve God; what
profit have we that we have kept his ordinances [t]?" &c. If
we must take our conscience along in all the businesses of our
life, there will be no living in the world : notwithstanding
the Lord saith, that his words "do good to those that walk
uprightly [u];" that godliness hath the promises even of this
life [x];" that "God will honour those that honour him [y]."—
Thirdly, As unequal and unreasonable ways [z], as a strange [a],
a mad, and a foolish strictness, rather the meteor of a specu-
lative brain, than a thing of any real existence ; rather ' vo-
tum' than ' veritas :' a wish or figment, than a solid truth.
And from such prejudices as these, men grow to wrestle with
the Spirit of Christ, to withstand his motions, to quench his
suggestions, and to dispute against him. "This people are
as they that strive with the priest [b];" such a bitter and unre-
concilable enmity there is between the two seeds !

Secondly, We may observe, that notwithstanding this natural averseness, yet many, by the power of the Word, are
wrought violently, and compulsorily, to tender some unwilling services to Christ, by the spirit of bondage, by the fear
of wrath, by the evidences of the curse due to sin, and by the
wakefulness of the conscience. "They have turned their
back unto me and not their face [c]," saith the Lord :—that
notes the disposition of their will. "But, in the time of
their trouble, they will say, Arise and save us :"—that notes
their compulsory and unnatural devotion. "They shall go
with their flocks and their herds," that is, with their pretended sacrifices, and external ceremonies, "to seek the
Lord; but they shall not find him, he hath withdrawn himself." As when the Lord sent lions amongst the Samaritans,

q Jer. xi. 10.   r Psal. iv. 6.   s Job xxii. 7.   t Mal. iii. 14, 15.   u Mic.
ii. 7.   x 1 Tim. iv. 8.   y 1 Sam. ii. 30.   z Ezek. xviii. 25.   a 1 Pet.
iv. 4. Isai. viii. 18. Zech. iii. 8. 1 Cor. i. 21.   b Hos. iv. 4.   c Jer. ii. 27.
Hos. v. 5, 6.   2 Kings xvii. 25, 26.

then they sent to enquire after the manner of his worship,
fearing him, but yet still serving their own gods. But this
compulsory obedience doth not proceed from fear of sin [d]
but a fear of Hell. And that plainly appears in the readiness
of such men [e], to apprehend all advantages for enlarging
themselves, and in making pretences to flinch away and steal
from the Word of grace, in consulting with carnal reason, to
silence the doubts, to untie the knots, and to break the
bonds of the conscience asunder, and to turn into every diverticle which a corrupted heart can shape, in taking every
occasion and pretext to put God off, and delay the payment
of their service unto him. Thus Felix [f] when he was fright-
ened with the discourse of St. Paul, put it off with pretence
of some further convenient season; and the unwilling Jews [g],
in the time of re-edifying the temple at Jerusalem, " This
people say the time is not come, the time that the Lord's
house should be built ;"—in slighting the warnings, and dis-
tinguishing the words of the Scripture out of their spiritual
and genuine purity, and so " belying the Lord, and saying,
It is not he [h]."—" The word of the Lord," saith the prophet,
" is to them a reproach, they have no delight in it ;" that is,
They esteem me when I preach thy words unto them, rather
as a slanderer than as a prophet.—Wouldst thou then know
the nature of thy devotion? Abstract all conceits of danger,
all workings of the spirit of bondage, the fear of wrath, the
pre-occupations of Hell, the estuations and sweatings of a
troubled conscience ; and if, all these being secluded, thou
canst still afford to dedicate thyself to Christ [i], and be
greedily ambitious of his image, that is an evident assurance
of an upright heart.

Thirdly, We may observe that, by the power of the Word,
there may yet be further wrought in natural men a certain

[d] Qui gchennas metuit, non peccare metuit, sed ardere : ille autem peccare
metuit, qui peccatum ipsum, sicut gehennas, odit. *Aug.* Ep. 144.—In ipsa intus
voluntate peccat, qui non voluntate sed timore non peccat. *Idem* con. 2. Ep. Pelag.
l. 1. cap. 9. et lib. 2. cap. 9.—Non, sicut feram et timeo et odi, ita etiam patrem
vereor quem timeo et amo. *Clem. Alex.* Strom. l. 2.   [e] *Aug.* de Nat. et Grat.
c. 57. cont. 2. ep. Pelag. lib. 3. c. 4. et Tom. 4. l. de Sp. et lit. c. ult.   [f] Acts
xxiv. 25.   [g] Hag. i. 2.   [h] Jcr. v. 12, 13. vi. 10.   [i] Nec si, per hypothesin,
à Deo potestatem acceperit faciendi ea, quæ sunt prohibita citra ullam pœnam :—
sed nec si persuasum habuerit, fore ut Deum lateant quæ gerit, in animum unquam
inducet, ut aliquid agat præter rectam rationem. *Clem. Alex.* Strom. lib. 4.

velleity, a languid and incomplete will, bounded with secret reservations [k], exceptions, and conditions of its own, which maketh it, upon every new occasion, mutable and inconstant. When the hypocritical Jews came with such a solemn protestation unto the prophet Jeremiah, " The Lord be a true and faithful witness between us, if we do not according to all things for the which the Lord thy God shall send thee unto us [l]," &c. I suppose they then meant as they spake; and yet this appears in the end, to have been but a velleity and incomplete resolution, a zealous pang of that secret hypocrisy which, in the end, discovered itself, and brake forth into manifest contradiction. When Hazael answered the prophet, " Is thy servant a dog, that he should do thus and thus [m]?" he then meant no otherwise than he spake; upon the first representation of those bloody facts, he abhorred them as belluine and prodigious villanies : and yet this was but a velleity and fit of good-nature for the time, which did easily wear out with the alteration of occasions. When Judas asked Christ, " Master, is it I that shall betray thee?" (though a man can conceive no hypocrisy too black to come out of the Hell of Judas' heart,) yet possible, and, peradventure, probable it may be, that hearing at that time, and believing that woful judgement pronounced by Christ against his betrayer, " It had been good for that man if he had never been born [n],"—he might then, upon the pang and surprisal of so fearful a doom, secretly and suddenly relent, and resolve to forsake his purpose of treason : which yet, when that storm was over, and his covetous heart was tempted with a bribe, did fearfully return and gather strength again. When the people returned and enquired early, and remembered God their maker, they were in good earnest for the time; and yet that was a velleity, and ungrounded devotion ; their heart was not right towards him, neither were they steadfast in his covenant. When Saul [o], out of the force of natural ingenuity, did, upon the evidence of David's integrity, who slew him not when the Lord had delivered him into his hands,—relent for the time and weep, and acknowledge his righteousness above his own, he spake all this in earnest, as he thought, and yet we find, that he afterwards returned to pursue him again, and was

---

[k] Vid. *Aqu.* p. 3. q. 21. Art. 4. c. Semisauciam hac atque hac versare et jactare voluntatem, &c. *Aug.* Conf. 1. 8. cap. 8.　　[l] Jer. xlii. 3, 5, 6, 20. xliii. 2.
[m] 2 Kings viii. 13.　　[n] Matt. xxvi. 5.　　[o] 1 Sam. xxiv. 16, 19.

once more, by the experience of David's innocency, reduced
unto the same acknowledgment.   The people, in one place,
would have made Christ a king, so much did they seem to
honour him; and yet, at another time, when their over-pliable
and unresolved affections were wrought upon by the subtile
Pharisees, they criedagainst him, as against a slave, " Crucify him, crucify him." So may it be in the general services
of God ; men may have wishings and wouldings, and good
liking of the truth, and some faint and floating resolutions to
pursue it,—which yet having no firm root, nor proceeding
from the whole bent of the heart, from a thorough mortification of sin and evidence of grace, but from such weak and
wavering principles, as may be perturbed by every new temptation,—like letters written in sand, they vanish away like
a morning dew, and leave the heart as hard and scorched as it
was before.   The young man (whom, for his ingenuity and
forwardness, Christ loved) came in a sad and serious manner
to learn of Christ the way to Heaven : and yet we find there
were secret reservations, which he had not discerned in himself ; upon discovery whereof by Christ he was discouraged
and made repent of his resolution [p].   The apostle speaketh
of " a repentance not to be repented of [q]," which hath firm,
solid, and permanent reasons to support it : therein secretly
intimating that there is likewise a repentance, which, rising
out of an incomplete will, and admitting certain secret and
undiscerned reservations, doth, upon the appearance of them,
flag and fall away, and leave the unfaithful heart to repent
of its repentance.   St. James tells us, that " a double-minded man is unstable in all his ways [r]," never uniform nor constant to any rules.   Now this division of the mind stands
thus :—The heart, on the one side, is taken up with the
pleasures of sin for the present ; and, on the other, with the
desires of salvation for the future : and now according as the
workings and representations of the one or other, are at the
time more fresh and predominant, in like manner is sin, for
that time, either cherished or suppressed.   Many men at a
good sermon, when the matter is fresh and newly presented,
while they are looking on their face in the glass ; or in any
extremity of sickness, when the provisions of lust do not

p Mark x. 21, 22.   q 2 Cor. vii. 10.   r James i. 8.

relish for the present, when they have none but thoughts of salvation to depend upon, are very resolute to make promises, vows, and professions of better living: but when the pleasures of sin grow strong to present themselves again, they return, like a man recovered of an ague, with more stomach and greediness to their lusts again :—as water which hath been stopped for awhile, rusheth with the more violence, when its passages are opened.   A double heart is like the bowls of a scale ; according as more weight is put into one or other, so are they indifferently overruled unto either motion, up or down.   When I see a vapour ascend out of the earth into the air, why should I not think that it will never leave rising, till it get up to Heaven ? and yet because the motion is not natural, but caused either by expulsion from a heat within, or by attraction from a heat without, when the cause of that ascent is abated, and the matter gathers together into a thicker consistence, it grows heavy and falls down again.   Even such is the affection of those faint and unresolved desires of men, who, like Agrippa, are but ' half-persuaded' to believe in Christ.

But now lastly, We must observe, that in the day of Christ's power, when he, by his Word and Spirit, worketh effectually in the hearts of men, they are then made " free-will offerings," totally willing to obey and serve him in all conditions.   The heart of every one stirreth him up, and his Spirit maketh him willing for the work and service of the Lord[s].   They ' yield themselves' unto the Lord, and their members as weapons of righteousness unto him[t].   They ' offer and present themselves' to God as a living sacrifice ; and therefore they are called προσφορὰ, ' an oblation,' sanctified by the Holy Ghost[u].   Therefore they are said to ' come unto Christ,' by the virtue of his Father's teaching[x]. To ' run' unto him[y] ; to ' gather themselves' under him as a common head, and to ' flow or flock together' with much mutual encouragement unto the mountain of the Lord[z] ; to ' wait upon him' in his law[a]; to ' enter into a sure covenant,' and to write and seal it[b]; in one word, ' To serve him with a perfect heart, and with a willing mind[c]:'—when

---

[s] Exod. xxxv. 21.   [t] 2 Chron. xxx. 8. Rom. vi. 19.   [u] Rom. xii. 1. xv. 16.
[x] John vi. 45.   [y] Isai. lv. 5.   [z] Hos. i. 11. Isai. ii. 2, 3.   [a] Isai. xlii. 4.
[b] Neh. ix. 38.   [c] 1 Chron. xxviii. 9.

the heart is perfect, undivided, and goeth all together, the mind will be willing to serve the Lord.

This willingness of Christ's people showeth itself in two things: First, In begetting most cordial and constant enmity against all the enemies of Christ, never holding any league or intelligence with them, but being always ready to answer the Lord as David did Saul, " Thy servant will go and fight with this Philistine."—He that is a voluntary in Christ's armies, is not disheartened with the potency, policy, malice, subtilty, or prevailing faction of any of his adversaries. He is contented to deny himself; to renounce the friendship of the world; to bid defiance to the allurements of Satan; to smile upon the face of danger; to hate father and mother, and land and life; to be cruel to himself, and regardless of others, for his Master's service. Through honour and dishonour, through evil report and good report, through a sea and a wilderness, through the hottest services, and strongest oppositions, will he follow the Lamb, whithersoever he goeth: though he receive the Word ' in much affliction,' yet he will receive it ' with joy' too. Secondly, In begetting most loving, constant, and dear affections to the mercy, grace, glory, and ways of God, an universal conformity unto Christ our head, who was contented to take upon him the form of a servant, to have his ear bored, and his will subjected unto the will of his Father. " I delight to do thy will, O my God; yea, thy law is within my heart.[d]" And as he was, so are all his, in this world,—of the same mind, judgement, spirit, conversation, and therefore of the same will too.

Now this dear and melting affection of the heart toward Christ and his ways, whereby the soul longeth after him, and hasteth unto him, is wrought by several principles: First, By the conviction of our natural estate, and a thorough humiliation for the same. Pride is ever the principle of disobedience. They were the ' proud ' men, who said unto Jeremiah, " Thou speakest falsely ; the Lord hath not sent thee[e]." And they were the proud men, who hardened their necks, and withdrew the shoulder, and would not hear, and refused to obey, (Nehem. ix. 16, 17, 29.) A man must be

<hr />

d Psal. xl. 8.   e Jer. xliii. 2.

first brought to deny himself, before he will be willing to follow Christ, and to lug a cross after him. A man must first humble himself, before he will walk with God.[f] The poor only receive the gospel. The hungry only find sweetness in bitter things. Extremities will make any man not only willing, but thankful, to take any course wherein he may recover himself and subsist again; when the soul finds itself in darkness, and hath no light, and begins to consider whither darkness leads it; that it is even now in the mouth of Hell, under the paw of the roaring lion, under the guilt of sin, the curse of the law, and the hatred and wrath of God;—it cannot choose, but most willingly pursue any probability, and, with most enlarged affections, meet any tender of deliverance. Suppose we that a prince should cause some bloody malefactor to be brought forth, should set before his eyes all the racks and tortures which the wit of man can invent to punish prodigious offenders withal, and should cause him to taste some of those extremities; and then, in the midst of his howling and anguish, should not only reach out a hand of mercy to deliver him, but should further promise him, upon his submission, to advance him like Joseph from the iron which enters into his soul, unto public honour and service in the state;—would not the heart of such a man be melted into thankfulness, and with all submission resign itself unto the mercy and service of so gracious a prince? Now the Lord doth not only deal thus with sinners; doth not only cause them, by the report of his Word, and by the experience of their own guilty hearts, to feel the weight, fruitlessness, and shame of sin, and the firstfruits of that eternal vengeance which is thereunto due;—nor only set forth Christ before them as a rock of redemption, reaching out a hand to save, and offering great and precious promises of an exceeding, eternal, abundant weight of glory;—but besides all this, doth inwardly touch the heart by the finger of his Spirit, framing it to a spiritual and divine conformity unto Christ. How can the soul of such a man in these present extremities of horror, which yet are but the pledges of infinite more which must ensue; and in the evidence of so wonderful and sweet promises, the seals of

[f] Micah vi. 8.

the eternal favour and fellowship of God, choose but, with much importunity of affection, to lay hold on so great a hope which is set before it, and, with all readiness and ambition of so high a service, yield up itself into the hands of so gracious a Lord, to be by him ordered and overruled unto any obedience?

Secondly, This willingness of Christ's people is wrought by a spiritual illumination of the mind. And therefore the conversion of sinners is called a ' conviction,' because it is ever wrought in us ' secundum modum judicii,' as we are reasonable and intelligent creatures. I take it (under favour and submission to better judgements) for a firm truth, that if the mind of man were once, thoroughly and in a spiritual manner (as it becometh such objects, as are altogether spiritual), possessed of the adequate goodness and truth which is in grace and glory,—the heart could not utterly reject them ; for human liberty is not a brutish, but a reasonable thing: it consisteth not in contumacy or headstrongness, but in such a manner of working, as is apt to be regulated, varied, or suspended by the dictates of right reason. The only cause why men are not willing to submit unto Christ, is, because they are not, thoroughly and in a manner suitable to the spiritual excellency of the things, enlightened in their mind. The apostle often maketh mention of ' fulfilling ᵍ' and ' making full proof of our ministry ʰ,' and of ' preaching the gospel fully ⁱ,' namely, with ' the evidence of the Spirit and of power,' and with such ' a manifestation of the truth, as doth commend itself unto the conscience of a man.'— " The word of God," saith the apostle ᵏ, " is not yea and nay," that is, a thing which may be admitted or denied at pleasure, but such a word as hath no inevidence in itself, nor leaveth any uncertainty or hesitancy in a mind fitted to receive it. And as we may thus distinguish of preaching, that there is an imperfect and a full preaching ; so may we distinguish of understanding the things preached : in some, it is full,—and in others, superficial. For there is a twofold illumination ˡ of the mind, the one theoretical and merely notional, consisting in knowledge ; the other practical, ex-

---

ᵍ Col. iv. 17. Acts xiv. 26.   ʰ 2 Tim. iv. 5.   ⁱ Rom. xv. 19 .
ᵏ 2 Cor. i. 18.   ˡ Luke xxiv. 32.

perimental, and spiritual, consisting in the irradiation of the
soul by the light of God's countenance, in such an apprehension of the truth, as maketh the heart to burn thereby,
" when we know things as we ought to know them [m];" that
is, when the manner and life of our knowledge is answerable
to the nature and excellency of the things known, when the
eye is spiritually opened to believe and seriously conclude,
that the things spoken are of most precious and everlasting
consequence to the soul, as things that concern our peace
with God.   This is the learning of Christ,—the teaching of
the Father,—the knowing of the things which pass knowledge,—the setting to the seal of our own hearts that God is
true,—the evidence of spiritual things not to the brain but to
the conscience.   In one word, this is that which the apostle
calleth a ' spiritual demonstration.'   And surely, in this
case, the heart is never overruled contrary to the full, spiritual, and infallible evidence of divine truths unto a practical judgement.   Therefore the apostle saith, that " Eve,
being deceived, was in the transgression [n];" and there is frequent mention made of the ' deceitfulness of sin,' to note,
that sin got into the world by error and seduction.   For certainly the will is ὄρεξις μετὰ λόγου, a ' rational appetite,' and
therefore (as I conceive) doth not stir from such a good as is
fully and spiritually represented thereunto, as the most universal, adequate, and unquestionable object of the desires
and capacities of a human soul.   For the freedom and willing consent of the heart is not lawless, or without rules to
moderate it; but it is therefore said to be free, because
whether, out of a true judgement, it move one way,—or out
of a false, another,—yet in both it moves naturally, ' secundum modum sibi competentem,' in a manner suitable to its
own condition.

If it be objected, that the heart, being unregenerate, is
utterly averse unto any good, and therefore it is not likely
to be made willing by the illumination of the mind ;—To
this I answer, That it is true, the will must not only be
moved, but also renewed and changed [o], before it can yield
to Christ.   But withal, that God doth never so fully and

---

[m] 1 Cor. viii. 2.   [n] 1 Tim. 2. 14.   [o] Oportet non tantum moveri,
sed etiam novam fieri.   *Prosper.*

spiritually convince the judgement, in that manner of which I have spoken, without a special work of grace thereupon, opening the eye, and removing all natural ignorance, prejudice, hesitancy, inadvertency, mispersuasion, or any other distemper of the mind, which might hinder the evidence of spiritual truth. By which means he also frameth and fashioneth the will to accept, embrace, and love those good things, of which the mind is thus prepossessed.

Thirdly, This willingness of Christ's people is wrought by the communion and aspiration of the Spirit of grace, which is a free spirit, ᵖ a spirit of love ᑫ, and a spirit of liberty ʳ; a spirit which is in every faculty of man as the soul and principle of its Christianity, or heavenly being and working. And therefore it makes every faculty, ' secundum modum sibi proprium,' to work unto spiritual ends and objects. As the soul in the eye causeth that to see,—and in the ear, to hear,—and in the tongue, to speak; so the Spirit of grace in the mind causeth it rightly to understand, and in the will causeth it freely to desire heavenly things; and in every faculty causeth it to move towards Christ, in such a way and manner of working, as is suitable to its nature.

Fourthly, This willingness of Christ's people ariseth from the apprehensions of God's dear love, bowels of mercy, and riches of most unsearchable grace revealed, in the face of Jesus Christ, to every broken and penitent spirit. Love is naturally, when it is once apprehended, an attractive of love. And therefore it is that the apostle saith, " Faith worketh by love ;" that is, by faith, first, the heart is persuaded and affected with God's love unto us in Christ. " I live by the faith of the Son of God, who loved me, and gave himself for me ˢ." Being thus persuaded of his love to us, the heart is framed to love him again : for who can be persuaded of so great a benefit as the remission of sins, and not be most deeply inflamed with the love of him, by whom they are remitted ᵗ? And lastly, by this reciprocal love of the heart to Christ, " faith becometh effectual" to work obedience and conformity to his will. " Love is the fulfilling of the law ;" he that loves God, would, with all joyfulness,

ᵖ Psal. li. 12.　　ᑫ 2 Tim. i. 7.　　ʳ 2 Cor. iii. 17.　　ˢ Gal. ii. 20.
Eph. iii. 17, 18.　　ᵗ 1 John iv. 19. Luke vii. 47.

fulfil every jot of God's law, if it were possible: "This is the love of God," saith the apostle, "that we keep his commandments; and his commandments are not grievous." True love overcomes all difficulties; is not apt to pretend occasions for neglecting any service of God, nor to conceive any prejudices against it, but puts an edge and alacrity upon the spirit of a man.   He can no more be said to love Christ, who doth not willingly undergo his yoke, than that woman to love her husband, who is ever grieved at his presence, and delighteth more in the society of strangers.

Fifthly, This willingness of Christ's people ariseth from the beauty and preciousness of those ample promises, which, by the love of Christ, are made unto us.   It is said of Moses, that he did " choose" (and that is the greatest act of will-ingness) "rather to suffer affliction with the people of God, than to enjoy the pleasures of sin for a season;" and the ground of this willingness was, "he had a respect unto the recompense of the reward ᵘ."   So Christ endured the cross, and despised the shame; that is, the shame (which would much have staggered and disheartened an unresolved man) was no prejudice or discouragement unto him, to abate any of his most willing obedience; and the motive was, " for the joy that was set before him ˣ."   And St. Paul professeth of himself, that he " pressed forward;" he was not only willing, but importunate and contentious, to put forth all his spirits, and, like riders in a race, to rouse up himself in a holy fervour and emulation; and all this was " for the price of the high calling of God in Christ Jesus," which was, as it were, before his face in the promises thereof ʸ.   So the apostle assureth us, that a Christian's hope to be like unto Christ hereafter, will cause him "to purify himself even as he is pure ᶻ."   When a man shall sit down and re-count with David, what God hath done for him already; "Who am I, O Lord God, and what is my house, that thou hast brought me hitherto ?"   And what God hath farther promised to do for him more,—" Thou hast also spoken of thy servant's house for a great while to come :" of a child of wrath, thou hast called me to an inheritance of the saints in light, and into the fellowship of more glory than can be

ᵘ Heb. xi. 25, 26.   ˣ Heb. xii. 2.   ʸ Phil. iii. 14.   ᶻ John iii. 3.

shadowed forth by all the lights of Heaven, though every star were turned into a sun ;—I say, when the soul shall thus recount the goodness of God, how can it be but wonderfully enlarged with thoughts of thankfulness, and grieved at the slow and narrow abilities of the other parts to answer the urgent and wide desires of a willing soul ?

Sixthly, This willingness of Christ's people ariseth from the experience of that peace, comfort, liberty, triumph, and security, which accompanieth the Spirit and the service of Christ. Nothing makes a man more fearful of wars, than the dangers and hazards which are incident thereunto. But if a man can serve under such a prince, whose employments are not only honourable but safe; if he, who is able and faithful to make good his words, promise us, that none either of the stratagems or forces of the enemy shall do us hurt, but that they shall fly before us, whilst we resist them ; who would not be a voluntary in such services, as are not liable to the casualties and vicissitudes, which usually attend other wars, wherein he might fight with safety, and come off with honour ?—David had experience of God's power in delivering him from the lion and the bear; and was well assured, that God, who was careful of sheep, would be more pitiful to his people Israel ; and that made him with much willingness ready to encounter Goliah, whose assurance was only in himself, and not in God. When a man shall consider what God *might have done* with him,—he might have sent him from the womb to Hell ; deprived him of the means of grace; left him to the rebellion and hardness of his evil heart, and to the rage of Satan ; burnt his bones, and dried up his bowels with the view of that wrath which is due to sin :—And what he *hath done* with him ;—he hath called him to the knowledge of his will, refreshed him with the light of his countenance, heard his prayers, given an issue to his temptations, and a reviving out of bondage, fastened him as a nail in his holy place, given him his favour which is better than life, and spoken of his servant for a long time to come ; —O how readily will the spirit of such a man conclude, " Lord, according to thine own heart, hast thou done all this unto me, and I have found so much sweetness in thy service above all mine own thoughts or expectations, that

now, O Lord, my heart is prepared, my heart is prepared,
I will sing and rejoice in thy service."

Lastly, This willingness of Christ's people ariseth from
that excellent beauty and attractive virtue, which is in holiness. " Thy law is pure; therefore thy servant loveth it."—
And therefore we find Christ and his church do kindle the
coals of love, and stir up those flames of mutual dearness
towards one another ; do cherish those longing, languishing,
and ravishing affections, and suspirings of hearts, by the frequent contemplations of each other's beauty. " Behold,
thou art fair, my love; behold, thou art fair; thou hast
dove's eyes. Behold, thou art fair, my beloved, yea pleasant," &c. [a]. These are the principles of that great devotion
and willingness, which is in the people of Christ unto his
service.

And hereby we may make trial of the truth of that profession, subjection, and obedience, which we all pretend to
the gospel of Christ. It is then only sound, when it proceeds from a willing and devoted heart, from purpose, fervour, and earnestness of spirit [b]. For as God, in mercy,
accounts the will for the deed; because where there is a
willing mind, there will certainly be all answerable endeavours to execute that will, and reduce it into an act; so he
esteems the deed nothing without the will [c]. Cain and Abel
did both sacrifice; it was the heart, which made the difference between them. Let the outward conversation be what
it will, yet ' if a man regard iniquity in his heart,' God will
not hear him. " Gravius est diligere peccatum quam fa-
cere:" It is a worse token (saith Gregory) of an evil man
to love sin, than to commit; for it may be committed out
of temptation and infirmity, and so may be either in part the

---

[a] Cant. i. 15, 16.   [b] Acts xi. 23. Rom. xii. 11. Gal. iv. 18.   [c] Qui per-
spicit apud te paratam fuisse virtutem, reddet pro virtute mercedem. Nunquid
Cain cum Deo munus offerret, jam peremerat fratrem ? Et tamen parricidium
mente conceptum Deus providus ante damnavit; ut illic cogitatio prava, et
perniciosa conceptio Deo providente prospecta est: ita et in Dei servis, apud
quos confessio cogitatur et martyrium mente concipitur, animus ad bonum
deditus, Deo judice coronatur. Aliud est martyrio animum deesse, aliud animo
defuisse martyrium—nec enim sanguinem vestrum quærit Deus, sed fidem.
Cypr. de mortal.—Neque enim in sacrificiis quæ Abel et Cain primi obtulerunt,
munera eorum Deus, sed corda intuebatur, ut ille placeret in munere qui place-
bat in corde. Idem de Orat. Domini.

sin of another that tempteth us, or at least not the sin of
our whole selves, but of those remainders of corruption
which dwell within us. But our love is all our own;—Satan
can but offer a temptation, the heart itself must love it : and
love is strong as death, it worketh by the strength of the
whole man ; and therefore ever such as the will is, which is
the seat of love, such is the service too. And the reason is :

First, Because the will is the first mover, and the master-
wheel in spiritual work, that which regulateth all the rest,
and keepeth them right and constant; that which holdeth
together all the faculties of the soul and body in the execution of God's will. In which sense, among others I understand that of the apostle, that "love is the bond of perfection ;" because when love resideth in the heart, it will put
together every faculty to do that work of God perfectly,
which it goes about. And therefore by a like expression it
is called, " The fulfilling of the law ;" because love aims
still at the highest and at the best, in that thing which it
loves ;—it is ever an enemy to defects. He that loves learning, will never stop, and say, " I have enough ;"—in this
likewise, love is as death. And he that loves grace, will be
still ambitious to abound in the work of the Lord, and to
press forward unto perfection ; to make up that which is
wanting to his faith ; to be sanctified throughout; to bring
forth more fruit; to walk in all pleasing ; to be holy, and
unblamable, and unreprovable, without spot or wrinkle.
It is an absurd thing in religion to dote upon mediocrities of
grace : " in eo non potest esse nimium, quod esse maximum
debet ;"—He that, with all the exactness and rigour of his
heart, can never gather together all grace, can surely never
have too much. In false religions, no man is so much magnified as he that is strictest : that Papist which is most cruel
to his flesh, most assiduous at his beads, most canonical in
his hours, macerated with superstitious penance, most frequently prostrated before his idols, is, of all other, most
admired for the greatest saint. O why should not a holy
strictness be as much honoured as a superstitious ? Why
should not exactness, purity, and a contending unto perfection, be as much pursued in a true as in a false religion ?
Why should not every man strive to be filled with grace,
since he can never have enough till he have it all, till he is

brimful? He that truly loves wealth, would be the richest; and he that loves honour, would be the highest of any other: certainly grace is in itself more lovely than any of these things. Why then should not every man strive to be most unlike the evil world, and to be more excellent than his neighbour; to be holy as God is holy, to be as Christ himself was in this world, to grow up in unity of faith, and in the knowledge of him, unto a perfect man? Certainly if a man once set his will and his heart upon grace, he will never rest in mediocrities; he will labour to abound more and more; he will never think himself to have apprehended; but forgetting the things which are behind, he will reach forth to those things which are before him;—for all the desires of the heart are strong, and will overrule any other natural desire. The grief of David's heart made him forget to eat his bread. The desire of Christ's heart to convert the Samaritan woman, made him careless of his own hunger: "It is my meat to do the will of him that sent me, and to finish his work."—A true heart will go on to finish the work which it hath begun. "The wicked sleep not," saith Solomon, "except they have done mischief;" and the enemies of St. Paul, provided to stop the clamours and demands of an empty stomach, with a solemn vow that they would neither eat nor drink, till they had slain Paul. Lust never gives over, till it finish sin; and therefore the love of Christ should never give over, till it finish grace.

Secondly, Because God is more honoured in the obedience of the will, than of the outward man. Human restraints may rule this, but nothing but grace can rule the other; for herein we acknowledge God to be the searcher of hearts, the discerner of secret thoughts, the judge and Lord over our consciences. "Whatsoever ye do," saith the apostle, "do it heartily, as to the Lord, and not to men:"—noting unto us that a man doth never respect the Lord in any service which cometh not willingly, and from the inner man. Now he worketh in vain, and loseth all that he hath wrought, who doth not work for him who is the master of the business he goes about, and who only doth reward it. Therefore saith the apostle, "Do it heartily as to the Lord, knowing that of the Lord you shall receive the reward of the inheritance; for ye serve the Lord Christ." He only is the pay-

master of such kind of work ; and therefore do it only as to
him, so that he may approve and reward it.

Before I leave this point touching the willingness of
Christ's people, here is a great case, and of frequent occur-
rence, to be resolved,—Whether those who are truly of Christ's
people, may not have fears, torments, uncomfortableness,
weariness, unwillingness in the ways of God. St. John, in
general, states the case ; " There is no fear in love ; but
perfect love casteth out fear, because fear hath torment [d] ; "
so that it seems where there is torment and weariness, there
is no love. For the clearing of this case, I shall set down
some few positions :—

First, In general, where there is true obedience, there is
ever a willing and a free spirit, in this degree at the least, a
most deep desire of the heart, and serious endeavour of the
spirit of a man to walk in all well-pleasing towards God : a
longing for such fulness of grace, and enlargement of soul, as
may make a man fit to run the way of God's commandments.

Secondly, Where there is this will, yet there may, upon
other reasons, be such a fear as hath pain and torment in it,
and that in two respects : First, There may be a fear of God's
wrath ; the soul of a righteous man may be surprised with
some glimpses and apprehensions of his most heavy displeasure ; he may conceive himself set up as " God's mark to
shoot at [e]," that " the poisoned arrows and terrors of the
wrath of God do stick fast upon him [f]," that " his transgressions are sealed up and reserved against him [g]." The hot
displeasure of the Lord may even " vex his bones and make
his soul sore within him [h]." He may conceive himself " forgotten and cast out by God," surprised with fearfulness,
trembling, and the horror of death.[i] Christ may withdraw
himself and be gone, in regard of any comfortable and sensible fruition of his fellowship ; and, in that case the soul
may fail, and seek him, but not find him ; and call upon him,
but receive no answer [k]. A man may fear the Lord, and yet
be in darkness and have no light.[l]

Secondly, There may be a great fear, even of performing
spiritual duties. A broken and dejected man may tremble
in God's service, and upon a deep apprehension of his own

<hr/>

[d] 1 John iv. 18.   [e] Job vii. 20.   [f] Job. vi. 4.   [g] Job. xiv. 17.
[h] Psal. vi. 1, 2, 3.   [i] Psal. xiii. 1. lv. 4, 5.   [k] Cant. v. 6.   [l] Isai. l. 10.

unworthiness, and erroneous applying of that sad expostulation of God with wicked men, "What hast thou to do to take
my covenant in thy mouth [m]?" And, "What hath my beloved
to do in mine house, seeing she hath wrought lewdness
with many?"[n] He may be startled, and not dare adventure
upon such holy and sacred things, without much reluctancy
and shame of spirit. "O my God," saith Ezra, "I am
ashamed and blush to lift up my face to thee my God: for
our iniquities are increased over our heads."[o] Thus it is
said of the poor woman who, upon the touch of Christ's
garment, had been healed of her bloody issue, that "she
came fearing and trembling, and fell down" before Christ,
and told him the truth [p]; but yet great difference there is between this fear of the saints and of the wicked. The fear of
the wicked ariseth out of the evidences of the guilt of sin;
but the fear of the saints, from a tender apprehension of the
majesty of God, and his most pure eyes, which cannot endure to behold uncleanness (which made Moses himself to
tremble [q]), and out of a deep sense of their own unworthiness
to meddle with holy things. And such a fear as this may
bring much uncomfortableness and distraction of spirit; but
never at all any dislike or hatred of God, or any stomachful
disobedience against him. For as the fear of the soul deters, so the necessity of the precept drives him to an endeavour of obedience and well-pleasing. Slavish fear forceth a
man to do the duty some way or other, without any eye or
respect unto the manner of doing it: but this other, which
is indeed a filial, but yet withal, an uncomfortable fear,
rather dissuades from the duty itself,—the heart being so
vile, and unfit to perform so precious a duty, in so holy a
manner as becomes it.

Thirdly, As the saints may have fear and uncomfortableness (which are contrary to a free spirit), so they may have a
weariness and some kind of unwillingness in God's service.
Their spirits, like the hands of Moses in the mount, may
faint and hang down, may be damped with carnal affections,
or tired with the difficulty of the work, or plucked back by
the importunity of temptations; so that though they begin
in the Spirit, yet they may be bewitched and transported

m Psal. l. 16.   n Jer. xi. 15.   o Ezra ix. 6.   p Mark v. 33.
q Acts vii. 32.

from a thorough obedience to the truth.[r] A deadness, heaviness, insensibility, inactiveness, confusedness of heart, unpreparedness of affections, insinuation of worldly lusts and earthly cares, may distract the hearts, and abate the cheerfulness of the best of us. And hence come those frequent exhortations to stir up ourselves, to prepare our hearts to seek the Lord, to whet the law upon our children, to exhort one another, lest the deceitfulness of sin harden us,—to be strong in the grace of Christ, not to faint or be weary of well doing,—and the like. All which, and sundry like, intimate a sluggishness of disposition, and natural bearing-back of the will from God's service.

Fourthly, The proportion of this discomfort and weariness ariseth from these grounds : First, From the strength of those corruptions, which remain within us : for ever so much fleshliness as the heart retains, so much bias a man hath to turn him from God and his ways, so much clog and incumbrance in holy duties. And this remainder of flesh is in the will as well as in any other faculty, to indispose it unto spiritual actions. As it is in our members, that we cannot do the things which we would[s]; so, in proportion, it is in our wills, that we cannot with all our strength desire the things which we should. And therefore David praiseth God for this especial grace, " Who am I, and what is my people, that we should be able ' to offer so willingly after this sort ?' for all things come of thee, and of thine own have we given thee[t]."

Secondly, From the dulness or sleepiness of grace in the heart, which, without daily reviving, husbanding, and handling, will be apt to contract a rust, and to be overgrown with that bitter root of corruption within. As a bowl will not move without many rubs and stops in a place overgrown with grass, so the will cannot move with readiness towards God, when the graces which should actuate it, are grown dull and heavy. A rusty key will not easily open the lock unto which it was first fitted ; nor a negligent grace easily open or enlarge the heart.

Thirdly, From the violent importunity and immodesty of some strong temptations, and unexpellible suggestions, which, frequently presenting themselves to the spirit, do

<hr>

[r] Gal. iii. 1, 3.   [s] Gal. v. 17.   [t] 1 Chro. xxix. 14.

there beget jealousies to disquiet the peace of the heart. For Satan's first end is to rob us of grace; for which purpose he hearteneth our lusts against us :—but his second is to rob us of comfort, and to toss us up and down between our own fears and suspicions : for unwearied and violent contradictions are apt to beget weariness in the best. " Consider him that endured such contradiction of sinners against himself," saith the apostle, " lest ye be wearied and faint in your minds.[u]

Fourthly, From the present weight of some heavy fresh sin, which will utterly indispose the heart unto good. As we see how long security did surprise David, after his murder and adultery. Thus, as Jonah, after his flight from God, fell asleep in the ship ; so stupidity, and unaptness to work is ever the child of any notable and revolting sin. When the conscience lieth bleeding under any fresh sin, it hath first a hard task to go through, in a more bitter renewing the tears of repentance. And hard works have, for the most part, some fears and reluctances in the performing of them. Secondly, It hath not such boldness and assurance to be welcome to God. It comes with shame, horror, blushing, and want of peace, and so cannot but find the greater conflict in itself. Thirdly, Sin diswonts a man from God, carries him to thickets and bushes. The soul loves not to be deprehended by God in the company of Satan or any sinful lust. That child cannot but feel some strugglings of shame and unwillingness to come unto his father, who is sure when he comes, to be upbraided with the companions which he more delights in.

Fifthly, From the proportion of the desertions of the Spirit : for the Spirit of God bloweth where and how he listeth ; and it is he that worketh our wills unto obedience. If he be grieved and made retire, (for he is of a delicate and jealous disposition,) if he turn his wind from our sails, alas, how slow and sluggish will our motion be ! How poor our progress ! Upon these and several other the like grounds, may the best of us be possessed with fears, discomforts, and unwillingness in God's service. But yet,

Sixthly, None of all this takes off the will ' à toto,' though

u Heb. xii. 3.

it do ' à tanto,' but that the faithful, in their great heaviness and unfitness of spirit, have yet a stronger bias towards God, than any wicked man when he is at best : for it is true of them in their lowest condition, that they desire to fear God's name [x] ; that the desire of their soul is towards the remembrance of him [y] ; that they are seriously displeased with the distempers and uncomfortableness of their spirit [z] ; that they long to be enlarged, that they may run the ways of God's commandments [a] ; that they set their affection unto God and his service [b] ; that they prepare their heart to seek the Lord God [b] ; that they strive, groan, wrestle, and are unquiet in their dumps and dulness, earnestly contending for joy and freedom of spirit [d] : in one word, that they dare not omit those duties, which yet they have no readiness and disposedness of heart to perform ; but when they cannot do them in alacrity, yet they do them in obedience, and serve the Lord when he hideth his face from them. " I said, I am cast out of thy sight, yet I will look again towards thy holy temple [e]." " He that feareth the Lord, will obey his voice, though he walk in darkness, and have no light [f]." So then the faithful have still thus much ground of comfort, that God hath their wills always devoted and resigned unto him ; though thus much likewise they have to humble them too, the daily experience of a backsliding and tired spirit in his service ; and should therefore be exhorted to stir up the Spirit of grace in themselves, to keep fresh and frequent their communion with Christ. The more acquaintance and experience the heart hath of him, the more abundantly it will delight in him, and make haste unto him, that it may, with St. Paul, apprehend him in fruition, by whom it is already apprehended, and carried up unto heavenly places in assurance and representation. As long as we are here, there will be something lacking to our faith, some mixture of unbelief and distrust with it [g]. Corruptions, temptations, afflictions, trials, will be apt to beget some fears, discomforts, weariness, and indisposedness towards God's service. The sense whereof should make us long after our home, and, with the apostle, groan, and wait for the adoption, even the redemption of our bodies, for the manifestation of the sons of God (for "though we are now

---

[x] Neh. i. 11.   [y] Isai. xxvi. 8.   [z] Psalm xlii. 5.   [a] Psalm cxix. 32.
[b] 1 Chron xxix. 3.   [c] 2 Chron. xxx. 19.   [d] Psalm li. 8, 11, 12.   [e] Jonah
ii. 4.   [f] Isai. l. 10.   [g] 1 Thes. iii. 10. Mark ix. 24.

sons, yet it doth not appear what we shall be [h]);" should make us pray for the accomplishment of his promises, for the hastening of his kingdom, where we shall be changed into a universal spiritualness, or purity of nature;—where those relics of corruption, those strugglings of the law of the members against the law of the mind shall be ended ; those languishings, decays, ebbs and blemishes of grace shall be removed ; where all deficiencies of grace shall be made up, and that measure and first-fruits of the Spirit which we here receive, shall be crowned with fulness, and everlasting perfection.   Here we are like the stones and other materials of Solomon's temple, but in the act of fitting and preparation : no marvel if we be here crooked, knotty, uneven, and therefore subject to the hammer, under blows and buffets.   But when we shall be carried to the heavenly building which is above, and there laid in, there shall be nothing but smoothness and glory upon us, no noise of hammers, or axes, no dispensation of word or sacraments, no application of censures and severity ; but every man shall be filled with the fulness of God, Faith turned into sight, Hope turned into fruition, and Love everlastingly ravished with the presence of God, with the face of Jesus Christ, with the fulness of the holy Spirit, and with the communion and society of all the saints.—And so much for the first observation out of the third particular concerning the *willingness* of Christ's people.

There was farther therein observed the principle of this willingness, " *In the day of thy power*, or of thine armies ;" that is, When thou shalt send abroad apostles, and prophets, and evangelists, and doctors, and teachers, for evidencing the Word and Spirit unto the consciences of men.   Whence we may secondly observe, That the " heart of Christ's people is made willing to obey him by an act of power," or by the strength of the Word and Spirit.   It is not barely enticed, but it is conquered by the gospel of Christ [i]; and yet this is not a compulsory conquest (which is utterly contrary to the nature of a reasonable will, which would cease to be itself, if it could be compelled), but it is an effectual conquest.   The will (as all other faculties) is dead naturally in trespasses and sins : and a dead man is not raised to life again by any

h 1 John. iii. 2.   i 2 Cor. x. 4, 5.

enticements, nor yet compelled unto a condition of such exact complacency and suitableness to nature by any act of violence. So then a man is made willingly subject unto Christ, neither by mere moral persuasions, nor by any violent impulsions ; but by a power in itself, supernatural, spiritual, or divine, and, in its manner of working, sweetly tempered to the disposition of the will, which is never, by grace, destroyed, but perfected. Therefore the apostle saith, that " It is God who worketh in us to will and to do [k]." First, he frameth our will according to his own (as David was said to be ' a man after God's own heart') ; and secondly, by that will, and the imperate acts thereof, thus sanctified and still assisted by the Spirit of grace, he setteth the other powers of nature on work in farther obedience unto his will. And therefore the prophet David praiseth God, that had enabled him and his people to 'offer willingly' unto the service of God's house, and prayeth him that he would ever keep that willing disposition in the imaginations and thoughts of the hearts of his people [l]. Therefore, the apostle saith, that " Our faith standeth not in the wisdom of men, but in the power of God [m]." Therefore likewise it is called " The faith of the operation of God who raised Christ from the dead [n]."

For the more distinct opening and evidencing this point, how Christ's people are made willing by his power, I will only lay together some brief positions, which I conceive to be thereunto pertinent,—and proceed to that which is more plain and profitable. First, Let us consider the nature of the will, which is to be a free agent or mover, to have, ' ex se' and within itself, an indifferency and undeterminateness unto several things ; so that when it moves or not moves, when it moves one way or other, in none of these it suffers violence, but works according to the condition of its own nature.

Secondly, We may note that this indifferency is twofold, either habitual, belonging to the constitution of the will, which is nothing else but an original aptitude, or intrinsecal non-repugnancy in the will, to move unto contrary extremes, to work ; or to suspend its own working; or else actual, which is in the exercise of the former, as objects present themselves ;—and this is twofold ; either a freedom to good or evil, or a freedom to will or not to will.

[k] Phil. ii. 13.　　[l] 1 Chron. xxxi. 14, 18.　　[m] 1 Cor. iv. 5.　　[n] Col. ii. 12.

Thirdly, Notwithstanding the will be in this manner free, yet it may have its freedom in both regards so determined, as that, in such or such a condition, it cannot do what it should, or forbear what it should, or cannot do what it should not, nor forbear what it should not. Man fallen, without the grace of God, is free only unto evil ; and Christ, in the time of his obedience, was free wholly unto good. Man free to evil,—but yet so, as that he only doth it voluntarily ; he cannot voluntarily leave it undone. Christ free only to good,— yet so, as that he doth it most freely, but could not freely omit the doing of it.

Fourthly, The will worketh not in this condition of things unto moral objects without some other concurrent principles, which sway and determine it several ways : so that the will is ' principium quod,' the faculty which moves ; and the other, ' principium quo,' the quality or virtue by which it moves. And these qualities are, in natural men, the flesh or the original concupiscence of our nature, which maketh the motions of the will to be θελήματα σαρκὸς, the will of the flesh ; and, in the regenerate, the grace and Spirit of Christ, so far forth as they are regenerate.

Fifthly, As the will is ever carried either by the flesh or the spirit to its objects, so neither to the one nor the other, without the preceding conduct and direction of the practical judgement, whether by grace illightened to judge aright, or by corrupt affections bribed and blinded to misguide the will ; for the will, being a rational appetite, never moveth but ' per modum judicii,' upon apprehension of some goodness and convenience in the thing, whereunto it moves.

Sixthly, The judgement is never thoroughly illightened to understand spiritual things in that immediate and ample beauty and goodness which is in them, but only by the Spirit of Christ,—which makes a man to have the self-same mind, judgement, opinion, and apprehension of heavenly things which he had :—so that Christ and a Christian do τοῦτο φρονεῖν " think the same thing," as the apostle speaks [o]. By which the Spirit of grace, working first upon the judgement to rectify that, and to convince it of the evidence and necessity of that most universal and adequate good which it presenteth,

o Phil. ii. 5.

the whole nature is proportionably renewed, and Christ formed as well in the will and affections, as in the understanding: as the body in the womb is not shaped by piecemeal, one part after another, but altogether by proportionable degrees and progresses of perfection. So that at the same time when the Spirit of grace, by an act of heavenly illumination, is present with the judgement of reason to evidence, not the truth only, but the excellency of the knowledge of Christ thereunto,—it is likewise present by an act of heavenly persuasion, and most intimate allurement unto the will and affections, sweetly accommodating its working unto the exigence and condition of the faculties, that they likewise may, with such liberty and complacency, as becomes both their own nature, and the quality of the obedience required, apply themselves to the desire and prosecution of those excellent things, which are with so spiritual an evidence set forth unto them in the ministry of the Word. As by the same soul the eye seeth, and the ear heareth, and the hand worketh; so when Christ by his Spirit is formed in us (for the Spirit of Christ is the ' actus primus,' or soul of a Christian man, that which animateth him unto a heavenly being and working),[p] every power of the soul and body is, in some proportionable measure, enabled to work ' suo modo,' in such a manner, as is convenient and proper to the quality of its nature, to the right apprehension and voluntary prosecution of spiritual things. The same Spirit which, by the word of grace, doth fully convince the judgement, and let the light of the knowledge of the glory of God shine upon the mind, doth, by the same word of grace, proportionably excite, and assist the will to affect it; that as the understanding is elevated to the spiritual perception, so the will likewise is enabled to the spiritual love of heavenly things.

By all which we may observe, that this working of the Spirit of grace, whereby we become voluntaries in Christ's service, and whereby he worketh in us, both to will and to do those things which, of ourselves, we were not obedient unto, neither indeed could be,—is both a sweet and powerful work; as in the raising of a man from the dead (to which, in the Scriptures, the renewing of a sinner is fre-

[p] Rom. viii. 9, 10, 11. 1 Cor. vi. 17.

quently compared) there is a work of great power,—which yet, being admirably suitable to the integrity of the creature, must needs bring an exact complacency and delight with it. We may frequently in holy Scripture observe, that of the same effect several things may be affirmed, by reason of its connexion unto several causes, and of the several casualties of manners or concurrence, with which those several causes have contributed any influence unto it. As the obedience of Christ was, of all other, the most free and voluntary service of his Father, if we consider it with respect unto his most holy, and therefore most undistracted and unhindered will (for if it were not voluntary, it were no obedience): and yet notwithstanding, it was most certain and infallible, if we consider it with respect to the sanctity of his nature, to the unmeasurableness of his unction, to the plenitude of his unseducible and unerring Spirit, to the mystery of his hypostatical union, and the communication of properties between his natures, whereby whatever action was done by him, might justly be called the action of God, in which regard it was impossible for him to sin;—in like manner, the passive obedience of Christ was most free and voluntary, as it respected his own will: for he troubled himself, he humbled and emptied himself, he laid down his own life, he became obedient unto death, even the death of the cross; and yet, thus it was written, and thus it behoved, or was necessary for Christ to suffer, if we respect the predeterminate counsel and purpose of God, who had so ordained [q]. God would not suffer a bone of Christ to be broken, and yet he did not disable the soldiers from doing it; for they had still as much strength and liberty to have broken his, as the others who were crucified with him: but that which, in regard of the truth and prediction of holy Scriptures, was most certainly to be fulfilled, in regard of the second causes by whom it was fulfilled, was most free and voluntary. We find what a chain of mere casualties and contingencies (if we look only upon second causes) did concur, in the offence of Vashti, in the promotion of Esther, in the treason of the two chamberlains, in the wakefulness of the king, in the opening of the chronicles, in the accept-

q Acts iv. 28.

ance of Esther's request, and in the favour of the king unto her, and all this ordered by the immutable and efficacious providence of God (which moderates and guides causes and effects of all sorts to his own fore-appointed ends) for the deliverance of his people from that intended slaughter determined against them, the execution whereof would evidently have avoided that great promise of their returning out of captivity after seventy years: with relation unto which promise their deliverance at this time was, in regard of God's truth and purpose, necessary, though in regard of second causes, brought about by a cumulation of contingencies. In like manner, when the hearts of men do voluntarily dedicate and submit themselves to the kingdom of Christ, if we look upon it with relation unto the Spirit of grace, which is the ' principium quo,' the formal virtue, whereby it is wrought,—so it is an effect of power, and, as it were, an act of conquest; and yet look upon it with relation to the heart itself, which is ' principium quod,' the material efficient cause thereof; and so it is a most free, sweet, connatural action, exactly tempered to the exigency of the second cause, and proceeding therefrom with most exact delight, answerable to the measure of the grace of illumination, or spiritual evidence in the mind; whereby our natural blindness, prejudices, and mispersuasions may be removed;—and to the measure of the grace of excitation, assistance, and co-operation in the heart, whereby the natural frowardness and reluctancy thereof may be subdued.

In one word, there are but three things, requisite to make up a free and voluntary action. First, It must be ' cum judicio rationis,' with a preceding judgement. Secondly, It must be ' cum indifferentia ;' there must be an internal indeterminateness and equal disposition of itself unto several extremes. Thirdly, It must be ' cum dominio actus;' the will must have the power of her own work. And all these three do sweetly consist with the point of the text, That the heart is made willing to obey Christ by an act of power.

For, First, this power we speak of, is only the power of the Word and Spirit, both which do always work in the ordinary course of God's proceeding by them with men, ' secundum judicium,' by way of judgement and conviction, by a way of teaching and demonstration, which is suitable to a rational faculty.

Secondly, Which way soever the will is, by the Spirit of grace, directed and persuaded to move, it still retains an habitual or internal habitude unto the extremes; so that if it should have moved towards them, that motion would have been as natural and suitable to its condition, as this which it followeth: for the determination of the act, is no extinguishment of the liberty thereunto.

Thirdly, When the Spirit, by power of the word of grace, doth work the will in us, yet still the will hath the dominion of its own act; that is, it is not servilely or compulsorily thereunto overswayed, but worketh ' ex motu proprio,' by a self-motion, unto which it is quickened and actuated by the sweetness of divine grace, as the seed of that action; according to that excellent known speech of St. Austin, " Certum est nos velle cum volumus, sed Deus facit ut velimus." Thus we see how the subjection of Christ's people unto his kingdom, is a voluntary act in regard of man's will, and an act of power in regard of God's spirit, inwardly illightening the mind with the spiritual evidence, not only of the truth, but the excellency and superlative goodness of the gospel of Christ; and inwardly touching the heart, and framing it to a lovely conformity and obedience thereunto.

The ground of this point, why there is an act of power required to conquer the wills of sinners unto Christ, is that notable enmity, stoutness, reluctancy, rebellion, weariness, averseness; in one word, fleshliness which possesseth the wills of men by nature: such forwardness unto evil, so much frowardness against good, such a spring and bias from private ends and worldly objects, such fears without, such fightings within, such allurements on the right hand, such frowns and affrightments on the left; such depths of Satan, such hellish and unsearchable plots of principalities and powers, to keep fast and faithful to themselves, this chief mistress of the soul of man; such sly and soaking, such furious and fiery temptations, to flatter or to fright it away from Christ; such strong prejudices, such deep reasonings, such high imaginations, such scornful and mean conceits of the purity and power of the ways of Christ, such deceitfulness of heart, such mispersuasions and presumptions of our

present peace, or, at least, of the easiness of our future
reformation, such strong surmises of carnal hopes which
will be prevented, or worldly dangers incurred, or private
ends disappointed; such lusts to be denied, such members
to be hewed off, such friends to be forsaken, such passions
to be subdued; such certain persecutions from the world,
such endless solicitations of Satan, such irreconcilable contentions with the flesh ; in the midst of all these pull-backs,
how can we think the will should escape and break through,
if God did not send his Spirit, as once the angel unto Lot[r],
to lay hands upon it, while it lingers and hankers after its
wonted course, to use a merciful conquest over it, and, as
the Scriptures express it, to lead[s] it, to draw[t] it, to take it
by the arm[u], to carry it in his bosom[x], to bear it as an eagle
her young ones[y] on her wings ; nay, by the terrors of the
Lord, and the power of his Word and wrath, to pull and
snatch it as a brand out of the fire[z] ?   Certainly, there is so
much extreme perverseness, so much hellishness, and devilish
antipathy to God and his service, in the heart, by nature,
that if it were left to its own stubbornness to kick and rebel,
and fall back and harden itself, and were not set upon by
the grace of Christ, no man living would turn unto him, or
make use of his blood.   By the same reason that any one
man perisheth, every man would too,—because in all, there
is as fundamental and original enmity to the ways of grace,
as there is in any.

The consideration whereof may justly humble us, in our
reflection upon ourselves, whom neither the promises of
Heaven can allure, nor the blood and passion of Christ persuade, nor the flames of Hell affright from our sins, till the
Lord, by the sweet and gracious power of his holy Spirit,
subdue and conquer the soul unto himself.   If a man should
rise from the dead, and truly relate unto the conscience, the
woful and everlasting horrors of Hell ; if a man's natural capacity were made as wide to apprehend the wrath, fury, and
vengeance of a provoked God, the foulness, guilt, and venom
of a soul, fuller of sins than the Heaven of stars, as the most
intelligent devils of Hell do conceive them ; if an archangel
or seraphim should be sent from Heaven to reveal unto the

[r] Gen. xix. 16.   [s] Rom. viii. 14.   [t] John vi. 44.   [u] Hosea xi. 3.
[x] Isai. xl. 11.   [y] Deut. i. 31. xxxii. 11.   [z] Jude ver. 23.

soul of a natural man, the infinite glory of God's presence,
the full pleasures of his right hand, the admirable beauty of
his ways, the intimate conformity and resemblance between
his divine nature in himself, and the image of his holiness
in the creature, the unsearchable and bottomless love of
Christ in his incarnation and sufferings, the endless incom-
prehensible virtue and preciousness of his blood and prayers ;—yet so desperately evil is the heart of man, that if, after
all this, God should not afford the blessed operation and
concurrence of his own gracious Spirit, the revelation of his
own arm and power upon the soul, to set on those instru-
mental causes,—it would be invincible by any evidence,
which all the cries and flames of Hell, which all the armies
and hosts of Heaven, were able to beget. There is no might
or power, able to snatch a man out of the hands of his sin,
but only God's spirit. Notable are the expressions which
the Holy Ghost everywhere useth to set forth this wretched
condition of the heart by nature : Wilfulness and self-willed-
ness ; " We will not hearken, we will not have this man to
reign over us [a] ;"—Θελήματα, many *wills* in one : Rebellion and
stubbornness [b], stoutness of heart [c], contestation with God [d],
and gainsaying his Word ; impudence, stiffness, and hard
heartedness [e], mischievous profoundness, and deep reasonings against the law of God [f] ; pertinacy, resolvedness, and
abiding in mischief [g] ; they hold fast deceit, obstinacy, and
self-obduration, " They have hardened their necks, that they
might not hear [h] :" Impotency, immovableness, and undocile-
ness,—" their heart is uncircumcised, they cannot hear,
there is none that understandeth or seeketh after God [i] :"
scorn and slighting of the messages of the Lord ; " Where is
his Word ? Where is the promise of his coming [k] ?"—Incre-
dulity and belying the Lord in his Word, saying, it is not
he : "Who hath believed our report, and to whom is the arm
of the Lord revealed [l] ?"—Wrestling, resisting, and fighting
with the Word, rejecting the counsel of God, vexing and
striving with his holy Spirit ; " Ye have always resisted the

a Gen. xlix. 6. Jer. vi. 17. xliv. 16. Luke xix. 27. Ephes. ii. 3.   b 1 Sam.
xv. 13.   c Mal. iii. 13.   d Rom. ix. 19. x. 21.   e Ezek. ii. 3, 4.   f Hos. v. 2.
2 Cor. x. 5.   g Jer. vii. 27, viii. 5, 6. xviii. 18.   h Jer. xix. 15. Zech. vii. 11.
i Jer. vi. 10. Rom. iii. 11. 2 Thes. iii. 2. Isai. i. 3.   k Jer. xvii. 15. 2 Chr.
xxx. 10. 2 Pet. iii. 4.   l Isai. liii. 1. Jer. v. 12.

Holy Ghost [m] :"—Rage and fierceness of disordered affections, despising of goodness, traitorous, heady, and high-
minded thoughts [n] : Brutishness of immoderate lust [o], the
untamed madness of an enraged beast, without restraint of
reason or moderation : In one word, a Hell and gulf of unsearchable mischief [p], which is never satisfied. It is impossible that any reasonable man, duly considering all these
difficulties, should conceive such a heart as this, to be
overcome with mere moral persuasions, or by any thing less
than the mighty power of God's own grace. To him, therefore, we should willingly acknowledge all our conversion
and salvation. So extremely impotent are we, O Lord, unto
any good, so utterly unprofitable, and unmeet for our
master's use, and yet so strongly hurried by the impulsion of
our own lust towards Hell, that no precipice, nor danger,
no hope, nor reward, no man or angel is able to stop us,
without thine own immediate power ; and therefore " Not
unto us, O Lord, not unto us, but unto thy name" only be
attributed the glory of our conversion.

Again, By this consideration we should be provoked to
stir up and call together all our strength in the Lord's service,
to recover our mispent time, to use the more contention and
violence for the kingdom of Heaven, when we consider how
abundant we have been in the works of sin, in the pursuing
of vast desires which had neither end nor hope in them. O
how happy a thing would it be, if men could serve God with
the same proportion, and vigour, and willingness of mind,
as they served Satan and themselves before ! I was never
tired in that way ; I went on indefatigably towards Hell,
like a swift dromedary, or an untamed heifer; I pursued those
evil desires, which had vanity for their object, and misery
for their end, no fruit but shame, and no wages but death.
But, in the service of Christ, I have a price before me, an
abiding city, an enduring substance, an immarcescible crown
to fix the highest of my thoughts upon. I have the promises
of Christ to strengthen me, his angels to guard, his Spirit to
lead, his Word to illighten, me. In one word, I have a
soul to save, and a God to honour. And why should

m Gen. vi. 3. Luke vii. 30. Isai. lxiii. 10. Acts vii. 51.   n 2 Tim. iii. 2, 3, 4.
Rom. i. 29, 31.   o Jer. ii. 24. viii. 6. Hos. viii. 9.   p Jer. xvii. 9. Habak.
ii. 5.

not I apply my power, to serve him who did reach forth his
own power to convert me ? A long way I have to go, and I
must do it in a span of time; so many temptations to overcome, so many corruptions to shake off, so many promises
to believe, so many precepts to obey, so many mysteries to
study, so many works to finish, and so little time for all :
my weaknesses on one side, my businesses on another, mine
enemies and my sins round about me take away so much,
that I have scarce any left to give to God. And yet, alas !
if I could serve God on earth, as he is served in Heaven;
if I had the strength of angels and glorified saints, to do his
will ; it would come infinitely short of that good will of God
in my redemption, or of his power in my conversion. If
God should have said to all the angels in Heaven, " There is
such a poor wretch posting with full strength towards Hell,
go stand in his way and drive him back again,"—all those
glorious armies would have been too few to block up the
passage between sin and Hell, without the concurrence of
God's own spirit and power ; they could have returned none
other answer but this, " We have done all we can to persuade and turn him, but he will not be turned." If then the
Lord did put to his own power to save me, great reason
there is that I should set my weak and impotent faculties to
honour him ; especially since he hath been pleased both to
mingle with his service great joy, liberty, and tranquillity here,
and also to set before it a full, a sure, and a great reward,
for my further animation and encouragement thereunto.

The fourth thing, observed in this verse, was the attire,
wherein Christ's people should attend upon his service, " *in
the beauties of holiness.*" These words refer to those before ;
and that either to the word "*people*" or to the word " *willing.*"
If to "*people*," then they are a further description of Christ's
subjects or soldiers ; they shall be all like servants in princes'
courts, beautifully arrayed, like the priests of the law that
had garments of beauty and glory ;—and so Schindler expounds it, ' in societate sacerdotum.' If to the word "*willing*,"
then it notes the ground and inducement of their great devotion and subjection unto Christ's kingdom, that, as the
people came up in troops to the Lord's house, which was the
beauty of his holiness, or, as men do flock together to the
sight of some honourable and stately solemnity ; so Christ's

people should, by the beauty of his banners, be allured to gather unto him, and fly in multitudes as doves unto their windows. Which way soever we understand the words, we may from them observe,—First, That holiness is a glorious and a beautiful thing. The holy oil [q] with which all the vessels of the sanctuary were to be consecrated, was a type of that Spirit which sanctifieth us, and maketh us kings and priests unto God ; and it was to be compounded of the purest and most delicate ingredients, which the art of the apothecary could put together. Therefore our Saviour still calleth his spouse " the fairest of women [r],"—to note, that no other beauty in the world is to be compared with holiness. Therefore our faith and holiness is called " a wedding garment [s]," at which solemnity men use, above all other, to adorn themselves with their costliest and most beautiful attire. Therefore we are said to " put on the Lord Jesus [t]," and to " put on bowels of mercy, and humbleness of mind, and meekness [u]," &c.; and therefore likewise the church is compared to a bride [x], decked in her choicest ornaments and jewels [y], broidered work, silk, fine linen, bracelets, chains, jewels, crowns, gold, silver, perfect comeliness, garments of salvation, and of praise, robes of righteousness [z], &c. And Christ the husband of this spouse [a], " the chiefest and most amiable of ten thousand," even " altogether lovely [b];" the " desire of all nations [c]," and the allurement of all hearts that can look upon him. And Jerusalem [d], the palace of this glorious couple, described by the most precious stones, and desirable things which can be thought on : jasper the wall, gold the pavement, pearl the gates, precious stones the foundation, and the Lord the light thereof. Of ourselves, by reason of sin, we are full of filthiness and deformity in flesh and spirit [e], clothed with filthy garments [f], and overspread, from the head to the foot, with blains and putrefaction [g]. It is only the holy Word of God, which maketh us clean from our filthiness, and from our pollutions. " By the washing of water through the Word, Christ sanctifieth us,

q Exod. xxx. 23.   r Cant. iv. 12.   s Matt. xxii. 12.   t Rom. xiii. 14.
u Col. iii. 12.   x Psal. xlv. 13, 14.   y Jer. ii. 32.   z Isai. lxi. 10.
a Ezek. xvi. 8. 14.   b Cant. v. 10. 16.   c Hag. ii. 7.   d Psal. lxxxiv. 1.
lxxxvii. 3. Rev. xxi. 18, 23.   e 2 Cor. vii. 1.   f Zech. iii. 3, 4.   g Isai.
i. 5, 6. John xv. 3. xvii. 17.

that he may present unto himself ἔνδοξον ἐκκλησίαν, a glorious church without spot or wrinkle, that it might be holy and without blemish[h]." And therefore the apostle St. Peter exhorteth Christian women to adorn the inner man of the heart with the ornament of a meek and quiet spirit, which is in the sight of God (whose pure eye they ought rather to please, than the wanton eye of man) of great price[i]. And the truth hereof may be proved, even from the practice of hypocrites themselves : for no man will counterfeit villanies, and make a show of the vices, which indeed he hath not, except he be desperately thereunto swayed by a humour of pleasing his wicked companions. And therefore St. Austin complaineth of it as a prodigious corruption of his nature, that he did sometimes belie himself to his wicked associates, and boasted of the wickedness which he durst not practise. No woman will paint herself with dung ; or spread ink upon her face. It must be beautiful in itself, which any man will ordinarily counterfeit : so that holiness hath the prerogative of an enemy's suffrage, which is one of the strongest evidences, to testify the beauty and excellency thereof.

This point will more distinctly appear, if we consider either the author, nature, properties, or operations of this holiness. First, The author is God himself by his Spirit. " The very God of peace sanctify you wholly," saith the apostle[k], and " the God of peace make you perfect to do his will[l]." Therefore the Spirit is called ' a Spirit of holiness ;' by the power whereof Christ, rising from the dead, was " declared to be the Son of God[m]," — to note, the answerableness between raising from the dead, or giving life where there was none before, and the sanctification of a sinner. Therefore the apostle calleth it, the ' renewing of the Holy Ghost[n], and the forming of Christ in us[o], the quickening[p], and creating us to good works.' By all which we may note, that what beauty the creation brought upon that empty and unshaped chaos, when it was distributed into this orderly frame, which we now admire ; or what beauty the reunion of a living soul unto a dead and ghastly body doth restore unto it ; the same beauty doth holiness bring unto the soul of a man,

[h] Ephes. v. 27. [i] 1 Pet. iii. 3, 4. [k] 1 Thes. v. 23. [l] Heb. xiii. 20, 21.
[m] Rom. i. 4. [n] Tit iii. 5. [o] Gal. iv. 19. [p] Ephes. ii. 5, 10.

which was filthy before.   But yet further we must note, that
God did not make man, as other ordinary creatures, for some
low and inferior use, (and yet Solomon saith, that " they were
made all beautiful in their time") but there was a pause, a
consultation, a more than common wisdom, power, and mercy
revealed in the workmanship of man.   For God made man
for his own more peculiar delight, company, and communion ;
one whom he would enter into a more intimate league and
covenant withal ; " The Lord hath set apart the man, that is
godly, for himself[q] ;—This people have I formed for myself,
they shall show forth my praise[r] :" I will magnify the beauty
of my glorious virtues in those, whom I have sanctified for
myself.—Thus we find what perfect comeliness the Lord hath
bestowed upon his people, when he entered into covenant
with them, and made them his own; one of which was always
to lean on his bosom, and to stand in his own presence[s].
The church is the Lord's own house[t], a temple[u] in the which
he will dwell and walk : it is his throne in which he sitteth
as our ' prince and law-giver.'   And, in this regard, it must
needs be extraordinary beautiful ; " for the Lord will beautify
the place of his sanctuary, and will make the place of his
feet glorious[x]."   Now then, if " by holiness we are made
God's building[z]," and that not as the rest of the world is for
his creatures to inhabit, but as ' a temple' for himself to dwell
in, as a gallery[a] for himself to walk and refresh himself in ;
certainly, holiness, which is the ornament and engraving of
this temple, must needs be a glorious thing ; for there is
much glory and wisdom in all God's works.

Secondly, If we consider the nature of holiness, it must
needs be very beautiful.   In general, it consists in a relation
of conformity, as all goodness, save that of God doth ; for
no creature is so absolute, as to have its being from itself,
and therefore its goodness cannot consist in any thing which
hath its original in itself.   It is the rule and end which deno-
minateth the goodness of any created thing : that therefore
which ought not to work for its own end, ought not to work
by its own rule ; for he who is lord of an end, must needs be
lord of the means and directions which lead unto that end.

q Psalm iv. 3.   r Isai. xliii. 21.   s Ezek. xvi. 8, 14.   t 1 Tim. iii. 15.
u 2 Cor. vi. 16.   x Jer. iii. 13.   y Isai. lx. 13.   z 1 Cor. iii. 9.   a Cant.
vii. 5.

And this is indeed the ground of all sin, when men make themselves, their own will, wit, reason, or resolutions, to be the spring and fountain of all their actions. Therefore sin is called our ' own ways,' and the lusts of our own hearts, and our own counsels; because it is absolutely from ourselves, and hath no constituted rule to moderate and direct it. Impossible it is for any creature, as it comes out of God's hands, to be without a law, or to be an original law unto itself: for as he who hath none over him, cannot possibly be subject unto any law, inasmuch as the law is but the declaration of a superior's will, what he requires to be done, and what he threateneth on default thereof to inflict; so he that is under the wisdom and ends of another, must needs likewise be subject to the laws which his will prescribes for advancing and compassing his own ends; who if he be, in his own nature and ends, most holy, must needs be holy in the laws which he enacts. By all which we may observe, that holiness consisteth in conformity; so that according to the excellency of the pattern, whereunto it refers, so is the measure of its beauty to be conjectured. And the pattern of our holiness is God himself; "Be ye holy, as your Father which is in Heaven, is holy." Other creatures have some prints and paths of God in them, and so are all beautiful in their time; but man had the image of God created in him: his will was set up in our heart as a law of nature, most pure, right, holy, good, wise and perfect, and that law did bear the same relation to man's life, as his soul doth unto his members, to animate, form, and organize every motion of the heart, every word of the mouth, every action of the soul and body, according unto the will of God. When, after this, man threw away his image, and God was pleased in mercy again to renew holiness in him, he did it again by another pattern, or rather the same, exhibited in another manner. He made him then conformable to the image of his Son [b], the heavenly Adam [c],—who is himself the image of the invisible God, the express character of his Father's brightness, a sun of righteousness, a morning star, the light of the world, the fairest of ten thousand. So that compare holiness with the first original draught thereof in Paradise, the nature of Adam, as it came

---

[b] Rom. viii. 29.   [c] 1 Cor. xv. 49.

new out of God's fashioning, or that with the law of God written in his heart, or that with the holiness of God, of which it was a ray shining into the soul, or that image of God with itself in Christ the second Adam; and, every way, holiness in its nature consists in a conformity and commensuration to the most beautiful things.

Thirdly, If we consider some of the chief properties of holiness, we shall find it, in that regard likewise, very beautiful. First, Rectitude and uprightness, sincerity and simplicity of heart: " God made man upright, but they have found out many inventions [d];" that is, have sought up and down, through many turnings and by-ways, to satisfy crooked affections. It was David's prayer, " Make thy way straight before my face [e];" and it is the apostle's instruction, " Make straight paths for your feet, lest that which is lame, be turned out of the way [f]." True holiness is a plain and an even thing, without falsehood, guile, perverseness of spirit, deceitfulness of heart, or starting aside. It hath one end, one rule, one way, one heart ; whereas hypocrites are, in the Scripture, called " double-minded men [g]," because they pretend to God, and follow the world :—And " crooked men [h]," like the swelling of a wall [i], whose parts are not perpendicular, nor level to their foundation. Now rectitude, sincerity, and singleness of heart, is ever, both in the eyes of God and man, a beautiful thing.

Secondly, Harmony and uniformity within itself. The philosopher saith of a just man, that " he is like a die,"—which is every way even and like itself; turn it how you will, it falls upon an equal bottom. And so holiness keeps the heart like itself in all conditions. As a watch, though altogether it may be tossed up and down with the agitation of him that carrieth it about him ; yet that motion doth no way perturb the frame, or disorder the workings of the spring and wheels within : so though the man may be many ways tempted and disquieted, yet the frame of his heart, the order of his affections, the government of the spirit within him, is not thereby stopped, but holdeth on in the same tenor. We know, in the body, if any part do exceed the due pro-

---

[d] Eccles. vii. 29. Jer. xxxi. 22. Isai. lvii. 10.   [e] Psal. v. 8.   [f] Heb. xii. 13.   [g] Jam. i. 8.   [h] Deut. xxxii. 5.   [i] Isai. xxx. 12, 13.

portion, it destroys the beauty and acceptableness of the
rest. Symmetry and fitness of the parts unto one another,
is that which commends a body. Now holiness consisteth
in this proportion; there is in it an ἀκρίβεια, ' an exactness' of
obedience, an equal respect unto all God's commandments, a
hatred of every false way, a universal work upon the whole
spirit, soul and body,—a supply made unto every joint,—a
measure dispensed unto every part; not a grace due unto
Christian integrity, which is not, in some proportion, fashioned in a man. Christ hath no monsters begotten by his spiritual seed : for monsters are ever caused, either by an
excess, or by a defect of seed: in one case, nature, being
over-charged, is forced to labour that which remains, and
will not be laid aside, into some superfluous members ; and,
in the other, for want of materials to leave her work unfi-
nished, and destitute of some necessary parts. But now
first, we are to note, that a man can have no superfluity of
grace ; we can never have too much of that, the fulness
whereof we should labour to get: and for the other danger,
we know Christ hath a residue of spirit to supply any defect,
and to make up whatsoever is away for the fashioning of
Christ in us: so then holiness fashioneth the whole man.
He that leaves any one faculty of his soul neglected, or any
one part of the service or law of God disobeyed (I speak of
a total and constant neglect), is undoubtedly a hypocrite,
and disobeys all.[k] As David with a little stone slew Goliah,
because his forehead was open; so can our enemy easily deal
with us, if he observe any faculty naked and neglected.
The actual and *total* breach of any one commandment, (*total*
I mean, when the whole heart doth it, though haply it execute not all the obliquity which the compass of the sin ad-
mits) is an implicit, habitual, interpretative, and conditional breach of all ; his soul stands alike disaffected to the
holiness of every commandment; and he would undoubtedly
adventure on the breach of this, if such exigencies and conditions as misguided him in the other, should thereunto as
strongly induce him. He that hath done any one of these
abominations, hath done all these abominations in God's
account.[l] There being then in a Christian man a suitable

k James ii. 10, 11.   l Ezek. xviii. 10, 13.

life and vigour of holiness in every part, and a mutual con-
spiring of them all in the same ways and ends, there must
needs likewise be therein an excellent beauty.

Thirdly, Growth and farther progress in these proportions : for it is not only uprightness and symmetry of parts,
which causeth perfect beauty and comeliness, but stature
likewise. Now holiness is a thriving and growing thing.
The Spirit is seed, and the Word is rain, and the Father
is a husbandman, and therefore the life of Christ is an
abounding life.[m] The rivers of the Spirit of grace spring up
into eternity.[n] As Christ hath no monsters, so neither
hath he any dwarfs in his mystical body ; but all his grow
up unto the pitch of perfection, which it becometh them to
have in him, even " unto the measure of the stature of the
fulness of Christ.[o]" The meaning of the apostle is, that
Christ is not always an infant in us as when he is first formed ; but that he doth ' grandescere in sanctis,' as Musculus
well expresseth it, that he groweth up still unto the stature
of a man : for wheresoever there is faith and holiness, there
is ever ingenerated an appetite for augmentation ; faith is of
a growing, and charity of an abounding nature [p]. By the
Word of truth [q], as by incorruptible seed [r] we were begotten ;
and, by the same Word, as by the sap and milk, are we
nourished, and grow up thereby [s]. This affection holiness
ever works, as it did in the disciples ; " Lord, increase our
faith [t] ; " and in David, " Strengthen, O God, that which
thou hast wrought for us [u]."

Fourthly, Besides the rectitude, harmony, and maturity,
which is in holiness, there is another property ; which
maketh the beauty thereof surpass all other beauty, and that
is, indeficiency. The measure of Christ must be the rule of
our growth ; but Christ never was overtaken by old age or
times of declining, he never saw corruption : so we must
proceed from strength to strength, like the sun to the perfect
day ; but there is no sinking or setting of holiness in the
heart. They that are planted in God's house, do still
bring forth fruit in their old age [x], and are even then fat and

---

m Joh. x. 10.   n Joh. iv. 14.   • Eph. iv. 12, 13.   p 2 Thes. i. 3.
q Jam. i. 18, 21.   r 1 Peter i. 23.   s 1 Peter ii. 2.   t Luke xvii. 5.
u Psal. lxviii. 28.   x Psal. xcii. 14.

flourishing. " As our outward man decayeth, so our inward man groweth day by day." Our holiness is a branch of the life of Christ in us, which doth never of itself run into death, and therefore is not ' apta nata' of itself to decay: for that is nothing but an earnest, inchoation, and assurance of death. "That which waxeth old," saith the apostle, " is ready to vanish away.ʸ"

Fifthly and lastly, If we consider the operations of holiness, that likewise will evidence the beauty thereof ; for it hath none but gracious and honourable effects. It filleth the soul with joy, comfort, and peace. All joy ᶻ, unspeakable, and glorious joy, peaceᵃ, quietness, assurance, songs, and everlasting joy. It maketh the blind see ᵇ, the deaf hear, the lame leap, the dumb sing, the wilderness and parched ground to become springs of water. It entertaineth the soul with feasts of fatted things, and of refined wines ᶜ, and carrieth it into the banqueting house ᵈ unto apples and flagons. It giveth the soul a dear communion with God in Christ, a sight of him, an access unto him, a boldness in his presence, an admission into most holy delights and intimate conferences with him in his bed-chamber ᵉ, and in his galleries of love.ᶠ In one word, it gathers the admiration of men, it secures the protection of angels, and (which is argument of more beauty than all the creatures in the world have besides), it attracteth the eye and heart ᵍ, the longings and ravishments, the tender compassions and everlasting delights, of the Lord Jesus.

I have insisted on these properties of holiness, which denote inward beauty, because all the graces of the Spirit do beautify inherently. But the word properly signifying ' decus ' or ' ornatum,' ' outward adorning,'—by a metaphor of rich apparel, expressing the internal excellency of the soul,— notes unto us two things more :—

First, That the people of Christ are not only sanctified within, but have interest in that unspotted holiness of Christ, wherewith they are clothed as with an ornament. So the priests of God are said to be ' clothed with righte-

ʸ Heb. viii. 13.   ᶻ Rom. xv. 13. 1 Peter i. 8.   ᵃ Isai. xxxii. 17.
ᵇ Isai. xxxv. 5, 10.   ᶜ Isai. xxv. 6.   ᵈ Cant. ii. 4, 5.   ᵉ Psal. xlv. 16.
Cant. i. 4.   ᶠ Cant. vii. 5.   ᵍ Psal. xlv. 11. Cant. iv. 9.

ousness[h],' and we are said to ' put on Christ:[i]' and the
righteousness of Christ is frequently compared to ' long
white robes[k],' fit to cover our sins, to hide our nakedness,
and to protect our persons from the wrath of God; so that
to the eye of his justice we appear, as it were, parts of
Christ; as when Jacob wore Esau's garment, he was as
Esau to his Father, and, in that relation, obtained the blessing. God carrieth himself towards us in Christ, as if we
ourselves had fulfilled all righteousness, as if there were no
ground of contestation with us, or exception against us [l].
And this is indeed ' the beauty of holiness :' the model,
prototype, and original of all beauty.

Secondly, From the metaphorical allusion (as it is usually understood) it notes unto us likewise, that all the people of Christ are ' Priests unto God,' to offer up sacrifices [m]
acceptable unto him by Jesus Christ: they have all the
privileges, and the duties of priests [n]. To approach unto
God: we have liberty ' to enter into the holiest[o]' by the
blood of Jesus, to consult and have communion with him, to
be his remembrancers ; for as his Spirit is his remembrancer
unto us, " he shall bring all things to your remembrance,
whatsoever I have said unto you [p];" so is he our remembrancer unto God, to put him in mind of his mercy and promises [q], to make mention of him, and to give him no rest.
To know, and propagate his truth : this was the office of the
priest, to be the keeper of the knowledge [s], and to teach it
unto others: and this knowledge in the gospel doth overflow the earth [t], and make every man, in a spiritual sense, a
priest, an instructor and edifier of his brother.[u] To offer to
him such sacrifices as he now delighteth in ;—the sacrifices
of thanksgiving [x], the sacrifices of a broken and a contrite
spirit[y], the sacrifices of praise [z], confession, good works,
and mutual communicating unto one another [a] ; in one word,
the sacrificing of a man's whole self,[b] to be consecrated as
a kind of first-fruits unto God[c], being sanctified by the

---

h Psal. cxxxii. 9.   i Gal. iii. 27.   k Rev. iii. 18. iv. 4. vi. 11. vii. 9.
l Psal. xxxii. 1.   m 1 Pet. ii. 5. Isai. lvi. 7.   n Rev. i. 6.   o Heb. x. 19.
p John xiv. 26.   q Isai. xliii. 26.   r Isai. lxii. 6, 7.   s Mal. ii. 7.
t Isai. xi. 9.   u Col. iii. 16. Heb. iii. 13. Jude ver. 20.   x Psal. cvii. 22.
y Psal. li. 17.   z Heb. xiii. 15, 16.   a Phil. iv. 18.   b Rom. xii. 1.
Isai. lxvi. 20.   c James i. 18.

Holy Ghost.[d] There is no man actually belonging unto the
kingdom of Christ, who hath not all these holy affections
wrought in him, and maketh conscience of them, as of his
calling, and the duties of his life.

We see then that holiness is the badge of Christ's subjects; they are called ' The people of his holiness[e] :' Israel
was ' holiness unto the Lord[f],' and the ' first-fruits' of his
increase consecrated unto him and his service as a kind of
first-fruits.[g] The livery of Christ's servants is a parcel of the
same holy Spirit, with which his own human nature was
clothed. All the vessels and ministerial instruments of the
tabernacle were anointed with the holy oil[h]; and the house
of the Lord was a house of holiness[i], to signify that every
Christian should be, by the Spirit of God, sanctified, because he is a temple[k]; and every member, because it is a
vessel and instrument for the master's use.[l] The Spirit of
holiness is that which distinguisheth, and, as it were, mark-
eth the sheep of Christ from the wicked of the world : " Ye
are sealed with the holy Spirit of promise[m]: ye have not
received the spirit of the world, but the Spirit which is of
God[n]." Holiness setteth us apart for God's service[o], for his
presence, and fruition[p]; protecteth and privilegeth us from
the wrath to come, in the day when he shall separate between
the precious and the vile, and make up his jewels;—without
this, no man can either serve, or see, or escape God ; either
do his will, enjoy his favour, or decline his fury. All our
services without this are but dung[q]: and who would thank
that man for his service, who, with wonderful officiousness,
should bring nothing but heaps of dung into his house ? If
a man could pour out of his veins rivers of blood, and offer
up every day as many prayers as thoughts unto God ; if his
eyes were melted into tears, and his knees hardened into
horn with devotion ;—yet all this, if it be not the fruit of
holiness, but of will-worship, or superstition, or opinion of
merit and righteousness, it is but as dung in God's sight.
" Wherefore liest thou upon thy face? There is an accursed

d Rom. xv. 16.   • Isai. lxiii. 18.   f Jer. ii. 3.   g James i. 18.
h Exod. xl. 9.   i Psal. xciii. 5.   k 2 Cor. vi. 16.   l Rom. vi. 13.
m Ephes. i. 13.   n 1 Cor. ii. 12.   o Tit. ii. 14.   p Heb. xii. 14. Ezek.
ix. 4.   q Malach. ii. 3.

thing in the camp." Whatever sin thy conscience telleth thee lieth next thy heart, and warms it, so that thou art unwilling to part from it, take heed of bringing it into God's presence, or provoking him with thy services; for he will throw them back like dung into thy face. " What hath my beloved to do in mine house, seeing she hath wrought lewdness with many [r]? What hast thou to do to take my covenant in thy mouth, seeing thou hatest instruction [s]? Who hath required this at your hands, to tread in my courts? Bring no more vain oblations, incense is an abomination unto me [t]," &c. Till a man put away the evil of his doings, and cleanse himself, all his worship of God is but mocking of him, and profaning his ordinances. In vain did the mariners pray, while Jonah was in the ship; in vain did Joshua intercede, while the accursed thing was in the camp. A man shall lose all which he hath wrought in God's worship, and have neither thanks nor reward for it, so long as he harboureth any unclean affection in his heart, and will not yield to part from it. Any sin which wasteth the conscience (as every great presumptuous sin doth in whomsoever it is) unqualifieth that person for the kingdom of Heaven. Grace maketh a believer sure of salvation, but it doth not make him wretchless, or secure in living. Though there be not an extinguishment, yet there is a suspension of his right upon any black and notorious fall, that a man must not dare to lay claim to Heaven, that hath dared, in a presumptuous manner, to provoke the Lord. Our holiness is not the cause of our salvation, but yet it is the way thereunto. He which, by any wasting and presumptuous sin, putteth himself out of that way, must by repentance turn into it again, before he can hope to find out Heaven; for " without holiness no man shall see the Lord." He that is a hundred miles from his own house, notwithstanding his propriety thereunto, shall yet never actually enter therein, till he have travelled over the right way which leads unto it. There is an order, ' a primo ad ultimum,' in the salvation of men; many indeterminate passages between their vocation and their glory: justification, repentance, sanctification, as a scale or ladder betwixt earth and Heaven. He that falls from his holiness

[r] Jer. xi. 15.   [s] Psal. l. 16, 17.   [t] Isai. i. 11, 14.

and purity of conscience, though he be not quite down the ladder, and hath the whole work to begin again as much as ever, yet doubtless he shall never get to the top, till he recover the step from which he fell.

And if, in this case, it be true that the righteous shall scarcely be saved ; O then where shall that man appear whom God, at the last, shall find without this garment and seal upon him? When there was a tempest, he who slept, and least thought of it, was thrown into the sea ; and when the day of wrath shall come, those that have neglected their estate most, shall doubtless be in the greatest danger. And, therefore, we should labour to go to God's throne with our garments and our mark upon us ; for all other endowments, our learning, our honours, our parts, our preferments, our earthly hopes and dependences, will none follow us ; but we shall live to see them, or the comforts of them depart. Ahitophel had wisdom like an oracle of God ; but he lived to see it bid him quite farewell : for he died like a very fool or child,—who, when he may not have his own will, will be revenged upon himself. Haman had more honour than the ambition of a subject usually aspires unto ; and yet he lived to see it bid him farewell, and died the basest death which himself could devise for his most hated and despised enemy. Jehoiakim, a king, lived to see his crown take its leave, and was buried with the burial of an ass, and dragged like carrion out of the gates of the city. There will be nothing at last left for any man to cast his trust upon, but God, or angels, or our fellows ; and if then God be against us, though all which remains were on our side, alas what is a handful of stubble to a world full of fire ? But yet there will not be that advantage, but the combat must be single between God and a sinner. The good angels rejoice to do good God's will, and the wicked will rejoice to do man any mischief : these will be only ready to accuse, and those to gather the wicked together unto the wrath of him that sitteth on the throne. O what would a man give then for that holiness, which he now despiseth ! what covenants would such a man be content to subscribe unto, if God would then show him mercy, when the court of mercy is shut up ! Wouldst thou return to the earth, and live there a thousand years under contempt and persecution for my service ?   O yes, not under thy service only, but under the rocks and mountains of the earth, so I may be hid from the face of the Lamb.—Wilt thou be content to go to Hell, and serve me there a thousand years in the midst of hellish torments, and the reviling of damned creatures ?   O yes, even in Hell infinitely better would it be to be thy servant than thine enemy.—Wilt thou revenge every oath with a year of prayers, every bribe or corruption with a treasury of alms, every vanity with an age of preciseness ?   Yes, Lord, the severest of thy commands to escape but the smallest of thy judgements.—O let us be wise for ourselves: there shall be no such easy conditions then proposed, when it will be impossible to observe them; and there are now far easier proposed, when we are invited to observe them.

Lastly, From hence we learn, that none will be willing to come unto Christ, till they see beauty in his service, which, with a carnal eye, they cannot do : for naturally the heart is possessed with much prejudice against it,—that the way of religion, in that exactness which the Word requires, is but the phantasm of more sublimated speculation, a mere notional and airy thing, which hath no being at all, but in the wishes of a few men, who fancy unto themselves the shape of a church, as Xenophon did of a prince, or Plato of a commonwealth.   And therefore though with their tongues they do not, yet in their hearts, men are apt to lay aside that rigour and exactness, which the Scripture requires ;—namely, to pull out our right eyes, to cut off our right hands, to hate father, and mother, and wife, and lands, and our own life ; to deny ourselves, to cross our own desires, to mortify our earthly members ; to follow the Lamb through evil report and good report, through afflictions and persecutions and manifold temptations, whithersoever he goeth ; to war with principalities and powers, and spiritual wickednesses ; to acquaint ourselves with the whole counsel of God, and the like ; and instead thereof to resolve upon certain more tolerable maxims of their own to go to Heaven by, certain mediocrities between piety and profaneness, wherein men hope to hold God fast enough, and yet not to lose either the world, or their sinful lusts.   This is a certain and confessed truth, that the spirit which is in us by nature, is contrary to the

Spirit of purity and power which is in the Word : and therefore the universal and willing submission of the heart unto
this, must needs find both many antipathies within, and
many discouragements and contempts without. Christ was
set up for "a sign of contradiction to be spoken against [u],"
and that "in the houses of Israel and Judah ;" and as it was
then, so is it now, even in Abraham's family, in the household and visible church of Christ, "They that are of the flesh,
persecute those that are after the Spirit;" Christ had never
greater enemies than those which professed his name. This
is one of the sorest engines Satan hath against his kingdom,
to make it appear in the eyes of men as a despicable [x], con-
temptuous, and unbeautiful thing. And therefore no man
comes under Christ's government, till that prejudice by manifest evidence of the Spirit be removed. And for this reason, the ways of Christ are set forth as beautiful, even under
crosses and afflictions. "I am black" with persecution,
with the beating of the sun upon me ; "but yet I am comely,
O ye daughters of Jerusalem." [y] When the watchmen smote
the church, and wounded her, and took away her veil, yet
still she acknowledged Christ, for whose sake she suffered
these persecutions, to be "white and ruddy, the fairest of
ten thousand [z]:" and the same opinion hath Christ of his
church, though she be afflicted and tossed with tempest [a],
yet he esteemeth of her as of a beautiful structure : "How
fair and pleasant art thou, O love, for delights [b]." And this
is that we should all endeavour to show forth in a shining
and unblamable conversation, the beauty of the gospel, that
the enemy may have no occasion,—from any indiscretions,
affectations, unnecessary reservedness, and deformities, ungrounded scrupulosities, over worldly affections, or any other
miscarriages of those who profess not the name only, but the
power of religion,—to blaspheme or fling off from a way,
against which they have such prejudices offered them : for
all that which the faithful have common with the world,
shall yet be sure to be charged upon their profession
by wicked men, who have not either reason or charity

---

[u] Isa. viii. 14, 18. Zech. iii. 8. Luke ii. 34.   [x] Quantus in Christiano
populo honor Christi, ubi religio ignobilem facit ?—per hoc omnes quodammodo
mali esse coguntur, ne viles habeantur. *Salv.*   [y] Cant. i. 5, 8.   [z] Cant.
v. 7, 10.   [a] Isai. liv. 11, 12.   [b] Cant. iv. 1, 7.

enough to distinguish between God's rule and man's error. "Submit yourselves," saith the apostle, "to every ordinance of man for the Lord's sake," &c. "for so is the will of God, that, with well-doing, ye may put to silence the ignorance of foolish men:" for this is certain, the ignorance of foolish men will not so much lay the blows upon your persons, as upon that truth and religion which you profess, when you needlessly withstand any such ordinances, as you might without sin obey.

The last thing observed in this verse was the multitudes of Christ's subjects, and the manner of their birth; " *From the womb of the morning, thou hast the dew of thy youth:*" thy children are born in as great abundance unto thee, as the dew which falleth from the morning womb.

From whence we may note; First, That Christ, in the day of his power, in the morning of his church, had multitudes of children born unto him. This promise the Lord made to Abraham [c],—and it is not to be limited to his children after the flesh, but to his children of promise, that his seed should be as the 'stars,' and as the 'dust [d]' for multitude. And the prophet applies that promise to Israel by promise, when those after the flesh should be dissipated and become no people, yet saith the prophet, "The number of the children of Israel, shall be as the sand of the sea which cannot be measured nor numbered, [e]" &c. meaning the Israel of God amongst the Gentiles. [f] Thus the faithful are said to flock like doves unto their windows, and to swell into a sea of great waters, 'a hundred and four and forty thousand,' with an innumerable company more, all sealed and standing before the Lamb. [g]

Now this was 'in die copiarum,' in the time when Christ first sent abroad his armies and the rod of his strength into the world. Before this God suffered men to walk in their own ways [h]; yea, in his own lifetime, he forbid his disciples to enter into the cities of the Samaritans, or to the Gentiles. And he promised them that they should do greater works than he himself had done, "because he went unto his Father [i]:" for when he ascended up on high, he then led cap-

c Gen. xxii. 17. xxviii. 14.   d Numb. xxiii. 10.   e Hos. i. 10.
f Isai. xi. 9.   g Rev. vii. 4, 9.   h Acts xiv. 16. xvii. 30.   i John xiv. 12.

tivity captive ; that ignorance and thraldom under which the
world was held, he triumphed over, and gave gifts of his
Spirit unto men of all sorts in abundance; visions to the
young, dreams to the aged, and his gracious Spirit unto all.
We never read of so many converted by Christ's personal
preaching (which was indeed but the beginning of his preaching ; for it is the Lord which speaketh from Heaven still) as
by the ministry of his apostles; he thereby providing to
magnify the excellency of his spiritual presence, against all
the carnal superstitions of those men, who seek for an invisible corporal presence of Christ on the earth, charmed
down out of Heaven, under the lying shapes of separated accidents ; and who cannot be content with that all-sufficient
remembrancer, which himself hath promised to his church [j],
except they may have others, and those such as the holy
Scriptures everywhere disgrace as teachers of lies and
vanity, the crucifixes and images of their own erecting :
therein infinitely derogating from that all-sufficient provision
which the Lord, in his Word and sacraments (the only living
and full images of Christ crucified [k]) hath proposed unto
men as alone able to make them wise unto salvation ; being
opened and represented unto the consciences of men, not by
human inventions, but by those holy ordinances and offices
which himself hath appointed in his church, the preaching
of his Word, and administration of his sacraments. And
surely they who, by Moses and the prophets, by that ministry which Christ after his ascension did establish in his
church, do not repent,—would be no whit the nearer, no
more than Judas or the Pharisees were, if they should see or
hear Christ in the flesh. Therefore it is observed, after
Christ's ascension, that the Word of God "grew mightily,
and prevailed [l];" and that there were " men daily added
unto the church [m];" that " the saviour of the gospel was
made manifest in every place [n];" that "the children of the
desolate were more than of the married wife [o]." Therefore
the believers, after Christ's ascension, are called πλῆθος τῶν
πιστευσάντων, " the multitude of them that believed [p]," and

j John xiv. 26.   k Gal. iii. 1.   l Acts xix. 20.   m Acts iii. 47.
n 2 Cor. ii. 14.   o Isa. liv. 1.   p Acts iv. 32.

"multitudes of men and women were added to the Lord ᵍ."
Ten to one of that there was before ; "Ten men shall take
hold, out of all languages of the nations, of the skirt of him
that is a Jew, saying, We will go with you ʳ ;" that is, shall
take the kingdom of Heaven by violence ˢ, as Saul laid hold
of the skirt of Samuel's mantle, that he might not go from
him.ᵗ

The reason hereof is to magnify the exaltation and spiritual
presence and power of Christ in the church. While he was
upon the earth, he confined his ordinary residence and personal preaching unto one people, because his bodily presence was narrow, and could not be communicated to the
whole world. For he took our nature with those conditions
and limitations, which belong thereunto. But his Spirit
and power is over the whole church ; by them he walketh in
the midst of the candlesticks. Christ's bodily presence and
preaching the Jews withstood, and "crucified the Lord of
glory." But now, to show the greatness of his power by
the gospel, he goes himself away, and leaves but a few poor
and persecuted men behind him, assisted with the virtue of
his Spirit, and by them wrought works, which all the world
could not withstand. He could have published the gospel,
as he did the law, by the ministry of angels ; he could have
anointed his apostles with regal oil, and made them not
preachers only, but princes, and defenders of his faith in
the world :—but he rather chose to have them to the end of
the world, poor and despised men, whom the world (without
any show of just reason, which can be by them alleged)
should overlook, and account of as low and mean-condi-
tioned men, that his Spirit might in their ministry be the
more glorified. "God hath chosen the foolish things of
the world to confound the wise, and weak things of the
world to confound things that are mighty, and base things
of the world and things which are despised, hath God
chosen, yea, and things that are not, to bring to nought
things that are, that no flesh should glory in his presence ᵘ ;"
but that his own Spirit might have all the honour. "Therefore I was with you in weakness," saith the apostle, "and in

ᵍ Acts v. 14.　　ʳ Zech. viii. 20, 23.　　ˢ Matt. xi. 12.　　ᵗ 1 Sam. xv. 27.
ᵘ 1 Cor. i. 27, 28.

fear, and in much trembling," &c. "that your faith should
not stand in the wisdom of men, but in the power of God [x]."
—And again; "We have this treasure in earthen vessels,
that the excellency of the power may be of God and not of
us [y]; not by might, nor by power, but by my Spirit, saith
the Lord [z]." Thus we find, that when the church was most
persecuted, it did then most grow ; and in the worst times it
brought forth the greatest fruit ; to note, the power of Christ's
kingdom, above all the attempts of men. "A great door
and effectual is opened unto me," saith the apostle, "and
there are many adversaries [a];" intimating, that the gospel of
Christ had great success, when it was most resisted. All
persecutors (as St. Cyprian [b] observes) are like Herod ; they
take their times, and seek to slay Christ, and overthrow his
kingdom in its infancy ; and therefore, at that time, doth he
most of all magnify the power and protection of his Spirit
over the same. Never were there so many men converted,
as in those infant times of the church, when the dragon
stood before the woman ready to devour her child, as soon
as it should be born. The great potentates of the world
which did persecute the name of Christ, were themselves at
last thereunto subjected, "Non à repugnantibus, sed à mo-
rientibus Christianis [c]," not by fighting but by dying Christians. As a tree shaken sheds the more fruit, and a perfume burnt diffuseth the sweeter savour ; so persecuted Christianity doth the more flourish by the power of that holy
Spirit, whose foolishness is wiser, and whose weakness is
stronger than all the oppositions and contradictions of men.—
But if there be such multitudes belonging unto Christ's kingdom, is not universality [d], and a visible pomp a true note to
discern the church of Christ by ?—To this I answer, that a
true characteristical note or difference, ought to be conver-
tible with that of which it is made a note, and only suitable
thereunto ; for that which is common unto many, can be no
evident note of this or that particular. Now universality is
common to antichristian, idolatrous, and malignant churches.

---

[x] 1 Cor. ii. 3, 4, 5.   [y] 2 Cor. iv. 7.   [z] Zech. iv. 6.   [a] 1 Cor. xvi. 9.
[b] Infantiam Christi studiosè persequuntur, et antequàm formetur Christus in nobis, in ipso piæ conversationis initio ut extinguatur Spiritus, et suffocetur vita
justitiæ, penitus elaborant. *Cypr.* Serm. de stella et Magis.   [c] *Aug.* ep. 42.
[d] ποῦ εἰσιν οἱ πλήθει τὴν ἐκκλησίαν ὁρίζοντες ; *Nazian.* Orat. 25.

The Arian heresy invaded the world, and by the imperial countenance spread itself into all churches. The whore [e] was to sit upon many waters, which were peoples, and multitudes, and nations, and tongues; the kings of the earth were to be made drunk with the wine of her fornications, and all nations to drink thereof. Therefore, touching these multitudes in the church, we are thus to state the point :— Consider the church in itself, and so it is a very vast body; but yet consider it comparatively, with the other more prevailing and malignant part of the world, and so it is but a little flock; as many grains and measures of corn may lie hid under a greater heap of chaff. Secondly, The church now is many, comparatively with the old church of the Jews; " More are the children of the desolate, than of the married wife [f]," but not comparatively with the adversaries of the church in general. We see of thirty parts of the world, nineteen are either idolatrous or Mahomedan [g]; and the other eleven serving Christ in so different a manner, as if there were many Christs or many gospels, or many ways to the same end. Thirdly, Though Christ always have a numerous offspring, yet, in several ages, there is observable a different purity and conspicuousness, according to the different administrations and breathings of the Spirit upon his garden. In some ages, the doctrine is more uncorrupt, the profession and acceptation more universal than in others. In the apostles' time, there were many born unto Christ, by reason of the more abundant measure of Spirit which was shed abroad upon them [h]. In the times of the primitive persecutions, there were many likewise born, because God would glorify the foundations of his church, and the power of his Spirit, above the pride of men [i]. In the first countenancing of it by imperial laws and favours, it was very general and conspicuous, because professed by the obedience and introduced by the power of those great emperors, whom the world followed. But after that long peace and great dignities had corrupted the minds of the chief in the church, and made them look more after the pomp, than the purity thereof,—

[e] Rev. xvii. 15. xviii. 3.　　[f] Isai. liv. 1.　　[g] *Brierwood*, of Religion.
[h] Tit. iii. 6.　　[i] Manifesta se tum Dei virtus contra odia humana porrexit, cum tanto magis Christus prædicaretur, quanto magis prædicari inhiberetur. *Hilar.* contra Auxent.

the mystery of iniquity, like a weed, grew apace, and over-spread the corn,—first abusing, and after that subjecting the power of princes, and bewitching the kings of the earth with its fornications.

Hence, likewise, we may learn to acknowledge God's mercy in the worst times. In those ages, wherein the church was most oppressed, yet many have yielded them-selves unto Christ. "The woman was with child, and was delivered, even when the dragon did persecute her [k];" and even then God found out in the wilderness a place of refuge, defence, and feeding for his church. As in those cruel times of Arianism when heresy had invaded the world, and in those blind and miserable ages wherein Satan was loosed, God still stirred up some notable instruments by whom he did defend his truth, and amongst 'whom he did preserve his church, though they were driven into solitary places, and forced to avoid the assemblies of heretical and antichristian teachers [l].

We learn, likewise, not to censure persons, places, or times. God had seven thousand in Israel, when Elias thought none but himself had been left. All are not alike venturous or confident of their strength. Nicodemus came to Christ by night; and yet even then Christ did not reject him. Therefore we must not presently censure our neigh-bours as cold or dead, if they discover not immediately the same measure of courage and public stoutness in the profes-sion of Christ with ourselves. Some men are, by nature, more retired, silent, unsociable, unactive men; some by the engagement of their places, persons, and callings wherein they are of more public and necessary use in the church, are put upon more abundant caution and circumspection in the moderate carriage of themselves than other men. Paul was of himself very zealous and earnest in that great confu-sion, when Gaius and Aristarchus were haled into the theatre, to have gone in unto the people, in that their out-rage and distemper: but the wisdom of the disciples and some of his chief friends is herein commended, that they sent unto him, desiring him that he would not adventure

---

[k] Rev. xii. 1, 4.   [l] *Hieronymus*, Contr. Luciferianos.—*Vincentius Lyrinensis* in Commonitorio.

into the theatre, and that they suffered him not[1]. It is a grave observation which Gregory Nazianzen [m] makes of that great champion, and universal agent for composing the differences and distractions of the church, St. Basil, that, "pro temporis ratione et hæreticorum principatu," by reason of the prevalency of adversaries and condition of the times, he did, in the controversies concerning the Deity of the Holy Ghost, abstain from some words, which others of an inferior rank did with liberty and boldness use: and that this he did in much wisdom, and upon necessary reasons ; because it was not fit for so eminent a person, and one who had such general influence by the quality of his place and greatness of his parts in the welfare of the church, by the envy of words or phrases, to exasperate a countenanced enemy, and to draw upon himself, and, in him, upon the church of God, any inevitable and unnecessary danger. And surely, if the wisdom and moderation of that holy man were, with the same pious affection, generally observed,— that men, when they do earnestly contend for the truth once delivered (which is the duty of every Christian) did not, in heat of argument, load the truth they maintain, with such hard and severe, though (it may be) true expressions,— as beget more obstinacy in the adversary, and (it may be) suspicion in the weak or unresolved looker on ; differences amongst men might be more soberly composed, and the truth with more assurance entertained.

Again, We have from hence an encouragement to go on in the ways of Christ, because we go in great and in good company : many we have to suffer with us, many we have to comfort and encourage us. As the people of Israel when they went solemnly up to meet the Lord in Sion, went on from troop to troop [n],—the further they went, the more company they were mixed withal, going to the same purpose ; so when the saints go towards Heaven to meet the Lord there, they do not only go unto "an innumerable company of angels, and just men [o]," but they meet with troops in their way, to encourage one another. All the discouragement that Elias [p] had, was, that he was alone: but we have no

[1] Acts xix. 30, 31.   [m] *Gregor. Nazian*. Orat. 20.   [n] Psalm lxxxiv. 7.
[o] Heb. xii. 22, 23.   [p] 1 Kings xix. 14.

such plea for our unwillingness to profess the truth and power of religion now. We are not like a lamb in a wide place, without comfort or company; but we are sure to have an excellent guard or convoy unto Christ's kingdom. And this use the apostle makes of the multitudes of believers, that we should, by so great "a cloud of witnesses," be the more encouraged in our patient running of that race, which is set before us [q].

Lastly, It should teach us, to love the multitudes, the assemblies, and the communion of the saints; to speak often to one another, to encourage and strengthen one another, nor to forsake the assembling of ourselves together, as the manner of some is; to concur in mutual desires, to conspire in the same holy thoughts and affections; to be of one heart, of one soul, of one judgement; to walk by one and the same rule, to besiege Heaven with armies of united prayers; to be mutually serviceable to the city of God, and to one another as fellow-members. Therefore hath the Lord given unto men several gifts, and to no one man all; that thereby we might be enabled to, and induced to work together unto one end, and by love to unite our several graces, for the edification of the body of Christ [r].

Now, for the manner of producing or procuring these multitudes, it is set forth unto us in two metaphors. *A womb*, and *dew of the morning*. Now the birth or dew is, first, 'generatio cœlestis.' That which is exhaled, is an earthly vapour, but the heavenly operation changeth it into dew: no art of man is able to do it. It is also undiscerned and secret: when it is fallen, you may see it, but how it is made, you cannot see. Lastly, it is a sudden birth; in a night or morning, it is both begotten, conceived, and brought forth. Here then we have four notes;—

First, That all Christ's subjects are withal his children. They are ' born unto him.' Christianity is a birth;—" Except a man be *born* again, he cannot see the kingdom of God [s]." There is a father: Christ our father by generation; " Behold, I and the children whom thou hast given me [t]:" as we are his brethren by adoption; " He is not ashamed to call us brethren [u]."—There is a mother; " Jerusalem, which

---

[q] Heb. xii. 1.   [r] Eph. iv. 11, 13.   [s] John iii. 3.   [t] Isai. viii. 18.
[u] Heb. ii. 12, 13.

is the mother of us all [x]." And there are subordinate instruments, both of one and other, the holy apostles, evangelists, doctors, and pastors, who therefore are sometimes
called " fathers begetting us [z];"—" In Christ Jesus I have
begotten you through the gospel :"—and sometimes mothers
bearing, and bringing forth ; " Of whom 1 travel in birth
again, until Christ be formed in you [a]." There is a ' holy
seed,' out of which these children of Christ are formed ;
namely, the ' word of God [b],' which liveth and abideth for
ever. For the heart of a man, new born unto Christ, cometh
from the Word, as a paper from the press, or as a garment
from a perfume, transformed into that quality of spiritualness and holiness which is in the Word. There is a vis
πλαστικὴ, or ' formative virtue,' which is the energy and concurrence of the Spirit of grace with the Word. For the
truth is not obeyed but by the Spirit [c]; " Except a man be
born of water and the Spirit,"—water as the seed, and the
Spirit as the formative virtue, quickening and actuating that
seed,—" he cannot enter into the kingdom of God [d]." There
are throes and pains, both in the mother and in the child;
much trouble and care, in the ministry of the Word, οὓς
πάλιν ὠδίνω ; " with whom I travel in pain again [e] :—I ceased
not to warn every one, night and day, with tears [f]." As a
woman with child, by reason of the fear and danger of miscarriages, doth abridge herself of many liberties, in meats,
physic, violent exercise, and the like ; so those who travel
in birth with the children of Christ, are put to deny themselves many things, and to suffer many things, for the success of their service. " I will eat no flesh while the world
standeth, rather than make my brother to offend [g].—I am
appointed a preacher and an apostle, a teacher of the Gentiles ; for the which cause I also suffer these things [h].—I
endure all things for the elect's sakes, that they may obtain
the salvation which is in Christ Jesus [i]." And there is pain
in the child too : a sinner doth not leave the warmth and
pleasure of his former condition without pain ; Christ comes
not, without shaking, unto the soul. There is a new being

[x] Gal. iv. 26. [y] Isai. li. 18. [z] 1 Cor. iv. 15. Philem. v. 10. [a] Gal.
iv. 19. [b] 1 Pet. i. 1, 22. [c] 1 Pet. i. 22. [d] John iii. 5. [e] Gal. iv. 19.
[f] Acts xx, 31. [g] 1 Cor. viii. 13. [h] 2 Tim. i. 11, 12. [i] 2 Tim. ii. 10.

or nature [k] ; a corruption of our old man, and a formation of
the new. " Old things are done away, behold all things are
become new [l]:" the same holy nature, the same mind, judgement, will, affection, motions, desires, dispositions, spirit
wrought in us which was in him. " He that hath this hope,
purifieth himself, even as he is pure [m] ; as he is, so are we in
this world [n];" patient, as he is patient [o]; holy, as he is
holy [p]; humble, as he is humble [q]; compassionate, as he
is compassionate [r]; loving, as he is loving [s]; in all things,
labouring to show Christ fashioned in our nature, and in
our affections. There is a new conversation answerable to
our new nature ; that as God is good in himself, and doth
good in his works [t],—so we both are as Christ was [u], and
walk as he walketh [x]. There is new food and appetites
thereunto suitable : a desire of the sincere, immediate, un-
tempered, uncorrupted milk [y] of the word, as it comes with
all the spirits and life in it, that we may grow thereby. New
privileges and relations ;—the Son of God, the brethren of
Christ, the citizens of Heaven, the household of the saints.—
New communion and society ; the fellowship of the Father
and the Son by the Spirit; fellowship with the holy angels,
we have their love, their ministry, their protection ; fellowship with the spirits of just men made perfect, by the seeds
and beginnings of the same perfection, by the participation
of the same spirit of holiness, by expectance of the same
glory, and final redemption.

In the mean time, then, we should walk as children of the
light [z]—as it is here, as " children of the morning." The
day is given us to work in ; and therefore in the morning, as
soon as we have our day before us, we should endeavour ' to
walk honestly [a].' Night-works are commonly works of uncleanness, violence, dishonour ; and therefore want a cover
of darkness to hide them. Thieves use to come in the
night.[b] The eye of the adulterer waiteth for the twilight,
saying, No eye shall see me,—and disguiseth himself.[c] In
the twilight, in the evening, in the black and dark night, he

    k Tit. iii. 5.   l 2 Cor. v. 17. Eph. iv. 22, 23. Rom. xii. 2.   m 1 John iii. 3.
n 1 John iv. 17.   o Heb. xii. 2.   p 1 Pet. i. 15. -   q John xiii. 14.   r Col.
iii. 13.   s Ephes. v. 2.   t Psalm cxix. 68.   u 1 John iv. 17.   x 1 John
ii. 6.   y 1 Pet. ii. 2.   z Eph. v. 8.   a Rom. xiii. 12.   b 1 Thess. v. 2.
c Job xxiv. 15.

goeth to the house of the strange woman.[d] The oppressor diggeth through houses in the dark. For "the morning is to them as the shadow of death [e]."—"They that are drunken, are drunken in the night [f]." Sins are of the nature of some sullen weeds, which will grow no where but in the side of wells, and of dark places. But works of Christianity are neither unclean, nor dishonourable ; they are beautiful and royal works, they are exemplary, and therefore public works; they are themselves light ("let your light shine before men"); and therefore they ought to be done in the light.

If we be children, we should express the affections of children [g]. The innocency, humility, and dove-like simplicity of little children; as the sons of God, blameless [h], pure, and without rebuke : "Children in malice [i], though men in understanding."—The appetite of little children ; "As new born babes, desire the sincere milk of the Word, that ye may grow thereby [k]." In all impatiency, the breast will pacify a little infant ; in all other delights, the breast will entice it and draw it away: even so should the Word and worship of God work upon us in all our distempers, and in all our deviations. Christ was hungry and faint with fasting ; it was about the sixth hour, and he had sent his disciple to buy meat ; and yet having an occasion to do his Father service, he forgat his food, and refused to eat [l].—The love of children ; " He that is begotten, loveth him that did beget him [m],"—with a love of thankfulness ; "We love him because he loved us [n];" "I love the Lord, because he hath heard my voice, and my supplication [o],"—with a love of obedience ; " Faith worketh by love [p];" " Love is the fulfilling of the law [q];" "If a man love me, he will keep my words [r]." With a love of reverence and awful fear, " A son honoureth his father [s];" "If ye call on the Father," &c. " Pass the time of your sojourning here in fear [t]."—The faith of children : For whom should the child rely on for maintenance and supportance, but the Father ? " Take no thought, saying, What shall we eat, or what shall we drink, θ wherewith shall we be clothed ? For your heavenly

d Prov. vii. 9.   e Job. xxiv. 16, 17.   f 1 Thes. v. 7.   g Mark x. 15.
h Phil. ii. 15.   i 1 Cor. xiv. 20.   k 1 Pet. ii. 2, 3.   l John iv. 6, 8, 34.
m 1 John v. 1.   n 1 John iv. 19.   o Psal. cxvi. 1.   p Gal. v. 6.
q Rom. xiii. 10.   r John xiv. 23.   s Mal. i. 6.   t 1 Pet. i. 17.

Father knoweth, that ye have need of all these things ᵘ?"
—The hope, assurance, and expectation of children: For as
children depend on their parents for present supply, so for
portions and provisions for the future ; fathers lay up for
their children, and God doth for his.   There is " an inheritance reserved for us ˣ."—Lastly, The prayers and requests of
children : " Because ye are sons, God hath sent forth the
Spirit of his Son into your hearts, crying, Abba, Father ʸ."

Note, Secondly, The birth of a Christian is a divine and
heavenly work.   God is both father and mother of the dew :
by his power and wisdom, a father ; by his providence and
indulgence, a mother ; ' Progenitor, genitrixque :' therefore
he is called in Clemens Alex. " Metripater,"—to note that
those casualties, which are in the second agents divided, are
eminently and perfectly in him united, as all things are to be
resolved into a first unity.   " Hath the rain a father, or who
hath begotten the drops of dew ?" saith Job.   " Out of
whose womb came the ice ? and the hoary frost of Heaven,
who hath gendered it ?"   None but God is the parent of the
dew ; ' it doth not stay for ' nor expect any human concurrence, or causality ᶻ: such is the call and conversion of a man
to Christ ; " A heavenly calling ᵃ," " the operation of God
in us ᵇ," a birth " not of blood, nor of the will of the flesh,
nor of the will of man, but of God ᶜ."   " Paul may plant, and
Apollos may water, but it is God " that must bless both ; nay,
it is God who, by them, as his instruments, doth both ; " of
his own will begat he us ᵈ."   The ministers are ' a savour of
Christ ᵉ.' It is not the garment, but the perfume in it, which
diffuseth a sweet scent ; it is not the labour of the minister,
but Christ whom he preacheth, that worketh upon the soul :
—" I laboured more abundantly than they all ; yet not I, but
the grace of God which was with me ᶠ."

It is not good, therefore, to have the faith of God in respect of persons : the seed of this spiritual generation cannot otherwise be given us, than in earthen vessels, by men
of like passions and infirmities with others.   Therefore, when
pure and good seed is here and there sowed,—to attribute

ᵗ ᵘ Matt. vi. 31, 32.   ˣ 1 Pet. i. 4.   ʸ Gal. iv. 6.   ᶻ Mic. v. 7.
Isa. lv. 10.   ᵃ Heb. iii. 1.   ᵇ Col. ii. 12.   ᶜ John i. 13. iii. 9.
ᵈ Jam. i. 18.   ᵉ 2 Cor. ii. 15.   ᶠ 1 Cor. xv. 10.

any thing to persons, is to derogate from God: where gifts are fewer, parts meaner, probabilities less,—God may, and often doth, give an increase above hope as to Daniel's pulse, that the excellency of the power may be of him, and not of man. Though it be a lame or a leprous hand which soweth the seed, yet the success is no way altered: good seed depends not, in its growth, on the hand that sows it,—but on the earth that covers, and on the heavens that cherish it: so the Word borroweth not its efficacy from any human virtue, but from the heart which ponders, and the Spirit which sanctifies it.

When, then, thou comest unto the Word, come with affections suitable unto it. All earth will not bear all seed; some, wheat; and some, but pulse: there is first required a fitness, before there will be a fruitfulness. Christ had many things to teach, which his disciples at the time could not carry away, because the Comforter [g] was not then sent, who was to lead them into all truth: they who by use have their senses exercised, are fit for strong meat [h]. The truth of the gospel is a heavenly truth: and therefore, it requires a heavenly disposition of heart to prosper it. It is wisdom to those that are perfect; though, to others, foolishness and offence [i]. The only reason why the Word of truth doth not thrive, is, because the heart is not fitted nor prepared unto it. The seed of itself is equal unto all grounds, but it prospers only in the honest and good heart: the rain in itself alike unto all, but of no virtue to the rocks, as to other ground, by reason of their inward hardness and incapacity. The Pharisees had covetous hearts, and they mocked Christ: the philosophers had proud hearts, and they scorned Paul: the Jews had carnal hearts, and they were offended at the gospel: the people in the wilderness had unbelieving hearts, and the Word preached did not profit them. But now a heavenly heart comes with the affections of a scholar, to be taught by God; with the affections of a servant, to be commanded by God; with the affections of a son, to be educated by God; with the affections of a sinner, to be cured by God. It considers, that it is the Lord from Heaven, who speaks in the ministry of the Word to him that is but dust and ashes;

g John xvi. 12, 13.   h Heb. v. 14.   i 1 Cor. ii. 6.

z 2

and therefore he puts his hand on his mouth, dares not reply
against God, nor wrestle with the evidence of his holy Spirit,
but falleth upon his face, and giveth glory unto God ; be-
lieves when God promiseth, trembles when God threateneth,
obeys when God commandeth, learns when God teacheth,
bringeth always meekness and humility of Spirit, ready to
open unto the Word, that it may incorporate.

Lastly, From hence we must learn to look unto God in all
his ordinances, to expect his arm and Spirit to be therein
revealed, to call on, and depend on him for the blessing of
it. If a man could, when he enters into God's house, but
pour out his heart in these two things ; A promise and a
prayer ;—" Lord, I am now entering into thy presence, to
hear thee speak from Heaven unto me, to receive thy rain
and spiritual dew [k], which never returneth in vain [l], but ripeneth a harvest either of corn or weeds, of grace or judgement. My heart is prepared, O Lord, my heart is prepared,
to learn and to love any of thy words. Thy law is my counsellor, I will be ruled by it; it is my physician, I will be
patient under it; it is my schoolmaster, I will be obedient
unto it. But who am I that I should promise any service
unto thee? and who is thy minister that he should do any
good unto me, without thy grace and heavenly call? Be thou
therefore pleased to reveal thine own Spirit unto me, and to
work in me that which thou requirest of me;"—I say, if a
man could come with such sweet preparations of heart unto
the Word, and could thus open his soul when this spiritual
manna falls down from Heaven, he should find the truth of
that which the apostle speaketh, " Ye are not straitened in
us," or in our ministry ; we come unto you with abundance of
grace ; but ye are straitened only in your own bowels, in the
hardness, unbelief, incapacity, and negligence of your own
hearts, which receiveth that in drops, which falleth down in
showers.

Note, Thirdly, As it is a divine, so it is a secret and undiscerned birth. " As the wind blows where it listeth, and
thou hearest the sound thereof, but canst not tell whence
it cometh, nor whither it goeth ; So," saith our Saviour, " is
every one that is born of God [m]." The voluntary breathings

---

[k] Deut. xxxii. 2. Amos vii. 16.   [l] Isa. lv. 10.   [m] John iii. 8.

and accesses of the Spirit of God unto the soul, whereby he cometh mightily, and, as it were, clotheth a man with power[n] and courage, are of a very secret nature; and notwithstanding the power thereof be so great, yet there is nothing in appearance but a voice[o],—of all other, one of the most empty and vanishing things. As dew falls in small and insensible drops, and as a child is born by slow and undiscerned progresses (as the prophet David saith, " Fearfully and wonderfully am I made[p] "), such is the birth of a Christian unto Christ, by a secret, hidden, and inward call; " Vocatione Altâ," as St. Austin calleth it; by a deep and intimate energy of the Spirit of grace is Christ formed, and the soul organized unto a spiritual being. A man hears a voice, but it is behind him[q], he seeth no man; he feels a blow in that voice[r] which others take no notice of, though externally they hear it too. Therefore it is observable, that the men which were with Paul at his miraculous conversion, are in one place said to " hear a voice[s]," and in another place, " not to have heard the voice" of him that spake unto Paul[t]. They heard only a voice, and so were but astonished; but Paul heard it distinctly as the voice of Christ, and so was converted[u].

Note, Fourthly, As it is a divine and secret, so is it likewise a sudden birth. In natural generations, the more vast the creature, the more slow the production;—an elephant ten years in the womb. In human actions, " magnarum rerum tarda molimina," great works move like great engines, slowly and by leisure to their maturity. But in spiritual generations, children are born unto Christ like dew, which is exhaled, conceived, formed, produced, and all in one night. Paul to-day a wolf, to-morrow a sheep; to-day a persecutor, to-morrow a disciple, and not long after, an apostle of Christ. The nobleman of Samaria[x] could see no possibility of turning a famine into a plenty within one night: neither can the heart of a man, who rightly understands the closeness and intimate radication of sin and guilt

---

n Judg. xiv. 6. vi. 34.   o Matth. x. 20. 2 Pet. i. 21.   p Psal. cxxxix. 14.
q Isa. xxx. 21.   r Acts ix. 8.   s Acts ix. 7.   t Acts xxii. 9.
u Glass. Philolog. Sacr. page 232.   x 2 Kings vii. 1, 2. Tarnov.
Exerc. Biblic. Edit. 2. page 84, 85.

in the soul, conceive it possible to remove either in a sudden change; yet such is the birth of men unto Christ, "Before she travailed, she brought forth: before her pain came, she was delivered of a man-child:" the earth bringeth forth in one day, and a nation is born at once: it is spoken of Jerusalem, the mother of us all.[y]

y Isai. lxvi. 7, 8.

VERSE IV.

*The Lord hath sworn, and will not repent; Thou art a Priest
for ever, after the order of Melchizedek.*

FROM the regal office of Christ, and the administration
thereof, by the sceptre of his Word and Spirit, to the conquering of willing people unto himself,—the prophet now
passeth to his sacerdotal office ; the vigour and merit whereof is, by the two former, applied unto the church. Therefore [a] we may observe, that though the tribes were interdicted
confusion with one another in their marriages [b], yet the regal
and Levitical tribes might interchange and mingle bloods ; to
intimate (as I conceive) that the Messiah, with relation unto
whose lineage that confusion was avoided, was to be both a
king and a priest. Thus we find Jehoiada the priest married
Jehoshabeath, the daughter of king Jehoram [c]. And Aaron,
of the tribe of Levi, took Elisheba, the daughter of Ammi-
nadab, who was of the tribe of Judah [d]. In which respect
I suppose Mary, and Elizabeth the wife of Zachary the priest,
are called cousins [e]. In the law, indeed, these two offices
were distinct. " Our Lord," saith the apostle, " sprang out
of the tribe of Judah, of which tribe Moses spake nothing
concerning priesthood [f];" and therefore when king Uzziah en-
croached on the priest's office, he was smitten with a le-

[a] Poterant Levitæ ex Regia familia ducere, quippe quæ etiam peculiari privilegio
hinc est exempta, &c. *Tarnov.* Exercit. Biblic. page 21, edit. 2.—Communicabant
inter se regia tribus ac sacerdotalis, propterea quod Christus Dominus secundum
humanitatem Rex futurus erat et Sacerdos. *Theodoret.* in Num. qu. 52.   Αἱ
δύο φυλαὶ συνῆπτοντο μόναι πρὸς ἀλλήλας, ἥτε βασιλικὴ τῇ ἱερατικῇ, καὶ ἡ ἱερατικὴ
τῇ βασιλικῇ. *Epiphan.* contra Antidiconarionitas Hæres. 78.   Νόμος δὲ ἦν μη
μνηστεύεσθαι φυλὴν ἐξ ἑτέρης φυλῆς. *Damascen.* de Orthodoxa fide, lib. 4. c. 15.
But notwithstanding these authorities, upon more deliberate consideration of this
matter, I conceive myself to have been herein mistaken ; and am rather persuaded
that marriages were lawful between several tribes, save only in the case when
daughters did inherit, to avoid confusion of possessions amongst the tribes. Judg.
xxi. 1. *Aug.* quæst. 47. in Judic. Joseph. Antiq. lib. 4. cap. 7.—*Philo Judæus* de
Monarchia. lib. 2.—*Luc. Brugens.* in Matth. i. 16.   [b] Numb. xxxvi. 7.
[c] 2 Chron. xxii. 11.   [d] Exod. vi. 23. Numb. i. 7.   [e] Luke i. 36.   [f] Heb. vii. 14.

prosy [g]. But amongst the Gentiles (amongst whom Melchizedek is thought to have been a priest [h]) it was usual for the same person to have been both king and priest [i].

The words contain the doctrine of Christ's priesthood, the quality of it, eternal: the order, not of Aaron, but of Melchizedek : the foundation of both, God's immutable decree and counsel: he cannot repent of it, because he hath confirmed it by an oath. I shall handle the words in the order as they lie.

" *The Lord hath sworn :*" Here are two things to be enquired : First, How God is, said to swear? Secondly, Why he swears in this particular case of Christ's priesthood? The former of these the apostle resolves in one word ἐμεσίτευσεν ὅρκῳ [k], ' He interposed in or by an oath,' namely, himself: for that is to be supplied out of the thirteenth verse, where it is said, that " he sware by himself." So elsewhere it is said, that " he sware by the excellency of Jacob," that is, by himself [l]. " By myself have I sworn, saith the Lord, that in blessing I will bless thee [m]." The meaning is, that God should deny himself (which he cannot do [n]), and should cease to be God, if the word which he hath sworn, should not come to pass. So that usual form, "as I live," is to be understood,— Let me not be esteemed a living God, if my word come not to pass. So elsewhere the Lord interposeth his holiness, " I have sworn by my holiness, that I will not lie unto David [o];" as impossible for him to break his word as to be unholy.

For the second question, Why God swears in this particular? I answer: First, and principally, to show, τῆς βουλῆς αὐτοῦ ἀμετάθετον [p], The immutable and irreversible certainty of what he speaks [q]. " I have sworn by myself;" the Word is gone out of my mouth, " and it shall not return [r]," &c. Thus we find God confirming the unmovableness of his covenant by ' an oath [s].' When the Lord doth only say a thing (though

[g] 2 Chron. xxvi. 18, 21.   [h] Sacerdos Ecclesiæ habentis præputium. *Hieron.* To. 3. lib. Quæst. Heb. in Genes.—Verisimile est illum esse ex illis gentibus, quæ Palestinam incolebant. *Theodoret.* Quest. 63. in Genes.   [i] Vid. *Casaub.* in Sueton. August. cap. 31.—Rex Anius, Rex idem hominum Phœbique Sacerdos. *Virgil.* Æneid. lib. 3.   [k] Heb. vi. 17.   [l] Amos viii. 7. vi. 8.   [m] Gen. xxii. 16.   [n] 2 Tim. ii. 13.   [o] Psalm lxxxix. 35.   [p] Τὸν ὅρκον δὲ πολλαχοῦ καὶ τὴν ἀμετάθετον περὶ ἑκάστου πράγματος ἀναβεβαίωσιν ὀνομάζει, ὥστε ὤμοσε Κύριος καὶ οὐ μεταμεληθήσεται, ὅτι ἀτρέπτοις καὶ ἀκινήτοις δόγμασι τὴν τῆς ἐπαγγελίας χάριν τῷ Δαβὶδ ἐβεβαίωσεν.   [q] Heb. vi. 17.   [r] Isai. xlv. 23.   [s] Isai. liv. 9, 10. Psalm lxxxix, 34, 35.

his word be as certain in itself as his oath, for it is as impossible for him to lie as to forswear himself), yet there is an implicit kind of reservation for the altering, revoking, or reversing that word by some subsequent declarations. As, in the covenant and priesthood of Aaron, though God made it for a perpetual ordinance, yet there was, after, a change of it, for the weakness and unprofitableness thereof. So when the Lord sent Jonah to preach destruction unto Nineveh within forty days, though the denunciation came not to pass, yet was it not any false message, because it was made reversible upon an implicit condition ; which condition the Lord is pleased sometimes in mercy to conceal, that men may be the sooner frighted out of their security, upon the apprehension of so approaching a danger. " At what time, saith the Lord, I shall speak concerning a nation, and concerning a kingdom, to pluck up, and pull down, and destroy : if that nation against whom I have pronounced, turn from their evil, I will repent of the evil that I thought to do unto them[t]." But when the Lord swears any absolute act, or promise of his own (for the revocation whereof there can no other ground ' de novo' arise, than was extant at the time of making it, and yet was no bar or hindrance unto it, namely, the sin of man), he then, by that oath, seals and assures the immutability thereof to those that rely upon it.

Secondly, It is to commend the excellency and pre-eminence of that above other things, which hath this great seal of Heaven, the oath of God, to confirm and establish it. " Inasmuch," saith the apostle, " as not without an oath he was made priest, by so much was he made a surety of a better testament[u] ;" and this is a consequent of the former : for by how much the more abiding, by so much the more glorious is the ministry of the gospel. " If that which is done away, were glorious, much more that which remaineth, is glorious[x]." The more solemn and sacred the institution was, the more excellent is the priesthood. Now this oath was that seal of God, by which he designed and set apart his Son for that great office, in a more solemn manner of ordination, than was to others usual. " Him hath God the Father

sealed [y]." It was but " He hath said," unto others, " Ye are
Gods ;" but it is, " He hath sanctified," to his Son [z].

Thirdly, It is to commend God's great compassion and good-
will [a], for the establishing of the hearts of men in comforts
and assurance. He therefore confirmed his promise by an
oath, "That by two immutable things, wherein it is impossible
for God to lie, we might have strong consolation, who have
fled for refuge to lay hold on the hope, which is set before
us [b]." An oath, even amongst men, is ' the end of all controversy,' the determination and composing of all differences :
how much more, when he sets his seal upon his mercy and
covenant, should the hearts of men be secure, and lay fast
hold thereon without doubt or scruple ! Therefore we find
the saints, in the Scripture, make mention of the oath of
God, for establishing their hearts against fears or dangers:
" Thou wilt perform the truth to Jacob, and the mercy to
Abraham, which thou hast sworn to our fathers from the days
of old [c]." " Thy bow was made quite naked, according to the
oaths of the tribes, even thy word [d] :"—that is, Thou didst
make it appear to thine enemies that thou didst fight for thy
people, and remember thy Word or covenant of mercy which
thou didst swear unto Abraham the father of the faithful,
and so oftentimes new ratify unto his seed, the tribes which
proceeded from him.—And this is the ground of all the
church's comfort and stability: for alas ! we, every day, deserve to have God abrogate his covenant of mercy with us,
but he is mindful of the oath which he hath sworn [e]. There
was wickedness enough in the world, to have drawn down
another flood after that of Noah ; the same reason that caused
it, did remain after it was removed [f]. But God's oath bound
him to his mercy [g]. The meaning then of this first clause is
this :—The Lord, to show the immutability of his counsel, the
unchangeableness of Christ's priesthood, the excellency of it
above the priesthood of Aaron, the strong consolation which

---

[y] John vi. 27.   [z] John x. 34, 36.   [a] Quod Deus tantopere commendat,
quod etiam humano more sub dejeratione testatur, summâ utique gravitate et
aggredi et custodire debemus, ut in asseveratione Divinæ gratiæ permanentes, in
fructu quoque ejus et emolumento proinde perseverare possimus. *Tertul.* de
pœnitent. cap. 4.—Quid est Dei veri veracisque juratio, nisi promissi confirmatio,
et infidelium quædam increpatio ? *Aug.* de Civit. Dei, lib. 16. cap. 13.   [b] Heb.
vi. 17, 18.   [e] Micah vii. 20.   [d] Hab. iii. 9.   [e] Deut. vii. 7, 8. ix. 5.
[f] Gen. vi. 12. 13. viii. 21.   [g] Isai. liv. 9.

the saints may there-hence receive, hath sealed it by an oath : so that he is a priest by a decree, which cannot be removed. It notes unto us, the solemn call of Christ unto the office of *priesthood*, as before of King, verse 1. He did not usurp this honour to himself, as Nadab and Abihu did, when, of their own heads, they offered strange fire unto the Lord ; nor encroach upon it, as Uzziah ; but he was ordained and begotten, and called of God thereunto, after the order of Melchizedek [h]. " He was sanctified and sent, and had a commandment, and a work set him to do [i]." In which respect, he was called ' a servant' or a chosen officer, formed for a special employment [k]. Here then is the consent of the whole Trinity unto Christ's priesthood : First, The Father's consent in his act of ordination ; for " him hath God the Father sealed [l]." " Thou art my Son, this day have I begotten thee [m]." Secondly, The Son's, by voluntary susception and vadimony for mankind : for he was the ' surety of the covenant [n].' The apostle joineth these two together [o]. " Lo, I come to do thy will, O God :" there was God's will, and Christ's submission thereunto, in which regard he is said to ' sanctify' himself [p]. There was a covenant between God and Christ; Christ was to undertake an office of service and obedience for men, to suffer himself a sacrifice for sin [q], to be made of a woman under the law, &c. And for this God was to prolong his days, to give him a seed, and a generation that could not be numbered,—a kingdom which cannot be bounded,—a portion with the great, and a spoil with the strong,—a name above every name,—to set a joy and a glory before him, after he should have finished his work [r], &c.— Thirdly, Here is the consent of the Holy Ghost, which did hereunto anoint him, which came along with him, which formed him in the womb of the virgin, and descended upon him in his solemn susception of this office in John's baptism ; by which Spirit he was consecrated, warranted, and enabled unto this great function [s].

---

[h] Heb. v. 5, 10.   [i] John x. 18, 36, 37.   [k] Isai. xlii. 1, xlix. 5. liii. 11. Phil. ii. 7.   [l] John vi. 27.   [m] Heb. v. 5, 6.   [n] Heb. viii. 22.   [o] Heb. x. 9, 10.   [p] John xvii. 19.   [q] Isai. liii. 1, 10, 11, 12.   [r] Psalm ii. 7, 8. Phil. ii. 7, 9. John xvii. 2, 4. 5. Heb. ii. 8, 9. xii. 2.   [s] Isai. lxi. 1. xlii. 1. Matth. iii. 16, 17. Heb. i. 9.

If, then, God call Christ unto his priesthood by a solemn oath, and make him surety of a better covenant, we ought to take the more especial notice thereof: for when God swears, he must be heard. The more excellent any thing is, the more earnest heed should be given unto it: for "how shall we escape," saith the apostle, "if we neglect τηλικαύτης σωτηρίας, so great salvation," so sure a covenant[t].

This is the only rock, on which we may cast anchor in any trouble, doubt, or fear of spirit. It is not our own will or strength, that holds us up from ruin, but only God's oath, by which Christ is made a priest, "able to save, to the uttermost, all, that come unto God by him." St. Paul and his company were in a great tempest; all hope that they should be saved, was taken away[u]: yet he exhorts them to be of good cheer, because there should not be the loss of any man's life amongst them: and the ground hereof was God's promise, which he believed[x]. The case is the same with us; we are encompassed about with infirmities, with enemies too hard, and with sins too heavy for us; with fears and doubtings, that we shall lose all again: how can we, in such tempests of spirit, be cheered, but only by casting anchor upon God's covenant which is established by an oath? by learning to hope above hope[y]; to be strong in him, when we are weak in ourselves; to be faithful in him, when we are fearful in ourselves; to be steadfast in him, when we stagger in ourselves? In the midst of Satan's buffets and our own corruptions, to find a sufficiency in his grace, able to answer and to ward off all[z];—to catch hold of his covenant and to fly to the hope that is set before us, as the only refuge and sanctuary of a pursued soul, when we are not able to stand by ourselves[a]. It is a very hard thing, when a man hath a distinct view of his filthiness and guilt, by reason of sin, not to give over himself and his salvation as desperate things. It is nothing but ignorance and insensibility, which make men presume of the pardon of sin. In this case, then, we must consider God's oath and covenant with his people. First, Not to reject them for their sins;—" Israel hath not been forsaken, nor Judah of his God, though their land was filled with sin against the Holy One of Israel[b]." " My peo-

---

[t] Heb. ii. 1, 3. [u] Acts xxvii. 20. [x] Acts xxiv. 15. [y] Rom. iv. 18.
[z] 2 Cor. xii. 10. [a] Isai. lvi. 6. Heb. vi. 18. [b] Jer. li. 5.

ple are bent unto backsliding," &c. "and yet I will not execute the fierceness of mine anger ;"—" I will not return to destroy Ephraim, for I am God, and not man [c]," &c.

Secondly, Not always to suffer them to lie under sin, but in due time 'to heal their backslidings [d].' He will not only remove our transgressions from himself, but he will remove them from us too, and that so far, as that it shall be as possible for the East and West to meet together, as for a man and his sin [e]. Though we made him to serve with our sins, and wearied him with our iniquities, yet " He will not remember against us our sins past [f];" " neither will he see against us the sins which remain [g]." Those, he will forgive,— and these, he will subdue ; and all this, because of his " truth unto Jacob, and his mercy unto Abraham, which he sware unto our fathers from the days of old [h]." He hath given us ground for both our feet to stand upon, and holdfast for both our hands to cleave unto : a promise, and an oath ; that, by two immutable things, we might have strong consolation [i]. So the apostle saith, that " All the promises of God in Christ are Yea and Amen :" *yea,* to note their truth,—and *amen,* to note their certainty and stability,— being confirmed by the oath of Christ. For so that word may be conceived, either as an oath [k], or at least as a very strong and confident affirmation [l], which is equivalent unto an oath [m]; except haply we will understand ναὶ and Ἀμὴν to be the same thing expressed in several tongues ; as " Abba Pater" in other places ; thereby noting not only the stability, but the universality, of God's promises.

Many things there are in this call of Christ unto his office, to confirm this consolation, and upon which the troubled soul may cast anchor.

First, From the Father he hath received a command and call unto this service, and so as a servant he hath fidelity : for God chooseth none but faithful servants. He was an

[c] Hosea xi. 7, 9. [d] Hosea xiv. 4. [e] Psal. ciii. 12. [f] Isai. xliii. 25. [g] Numb. xxiii. 11. [h] Micah vii. 18, 19, 20. [i] Heb. vi. 18. [k] Quodammodo, si dici fas est, juratio ejus est ' Amen, Amen, dico vobis.' *Aug.* Tract. 41. in Johan. [l] Confirmationis verbum. *Ambros.* in Psal. xl. Εἰσί τινες λόγοι σχήματα μὲν ὅρκων ἔχοντες, οὐχ ὅρκοι δὲ αὐτοί, ἀλλὰ θεραπεία πρὸς τοὺς ἀκούοντας. *Basil Mag.* in Psal. xiv.—Vid. *Nicol. Fulleri* Miscellan. lib. `. cap. 2. [m] 2 Cor. i. 20.

apostle and high priest sent to preach the will, and to pacify the wrath of God, and he was "faithful to him that appointed him, as Moses was[n]." And if he be faithful, we may trust him, for he will do the work which is given him to do. " Faithful is he that calleth you, who also will do it[o]."

Secondly, From himself there is a voluntary submission, whereby he gives himself for his church, and lays down his own life[p]. For being of himself equal with the Father, he could not be by him commanded, ordained, or overruled, to any service, without a voluntary concurring to the same decree ; emptying himself and taking on him the form of a servant; making himself less than his Father[q], and, in some sort, for a while, lower than the angels, that so he might be commanded. So that besides his fidelity to rest on as a servant, here is his especial mercy as a concurring agent in the decree, whereby he was ordained unto this office : he is not only a ' faithful,' but a ' merciful High-priest,' to make reconciliation for the sins of men[r]. But a man may, both by his fidelity as a servant, and by his mercy as having the same tender compassion with him that sent him,—be willing to help another out of mercy ; and yet may not be able to effect his own desires, for want of power. And therefore,

Thirdly, By the unction of the holy Spirit, who proceedeth from the Father and himself, he is said to be ' sanctified by the Father[s],' and to ' sanctify himself[t];' to have received power and authority from his Father[u], and to have power likewise within himself[x]. That Spirit, which, for the discharge of this office, he brought with him in fulness, and unto all purposes of that service, into the world, is a "spirit of power[y]," whereby he is enabled perfectly to save all comers[z]; so that unto his fidelity and mercy, here is added ability likewise.

Fourthly, As he received an office and a service, so he received a promise from his Father likewise, which did much encourage him in this service. And this promise is twofold : First, The promise of a great seed, which, by the execution of his office, he should gather unto himself, and of a great

n Heb. iii. 11, 2.   o 1 Thes. v. 24.   p Ephes. v. 25. Tit. ii. 14. John x. 11.   q John xiv. 28.—*August.* de Trinit. lib. 1. cap. 7. et 9.   r Heb. ii. 17.   s John x. 36.   t John xvii. 19.   u Matt. xxviii. 18. John v. 27. xvii. 2.   x John x. 18.   y 2 Tim. i. 7.   z Heb. vii. 25.

conquest over all his enemies. God conferred this honour upon him, to be the king of a mighty people, whom he should save and sanctify to himself.—They " were given unto him ª ;" so that unto his fidelity, mercy, and power, here is farther added a propriety to the thing which he saves : and who would not use all fidelity in his own business, all mercy towards his own seed, all the power he hath to deliver his own house from the fire? And Christ was faithful, " as a son over his own house, whose house are we ᵇ." Secondly, There was the promise of 'a great glory and crown,' which the nature he had assumed, should, in his person, receive after the fulfilling of his service. After he had been a little while lower than the angels, he was to be " crowned with glory and honour ᶜ;" and therefore we may be sure, that he hath fulfilled all righteousness, and done for his church all which he was to do upon the earth, " because he is gone, and we see him no more :" for his sufferings were to go before, and his glory to follow ᵈ. This is the apostle's argument, why we are not in our sins, but delivered from them, Because Christ is risen ᵉ : "Who is he that condemneth? It is Christ that died, yea rather that is risen again ; who is even at the right hand of God, who also maketh intercession for us ᶠ." And it is his argument again, why we ought to hold fast our profession, and to come boldly to the throne of grace for help in time of need,—because we have a great High-priest, that is passed into the Heavens ᵍ.

Fifthly, As he had a promise from the Father to encourage him, so he had a nature from us, to incline him unto the execution of his office. He was made of a woman ; made like unto us in all things, sin only excepted ; tempted and afflicted as we are : and so there are two things, which the heart of a believer may rest upon in him, in any discomforts. First, His sympathy ; for besides his essential mercy, as he is God, there was in him a mercy, which he learned by being like unto us. " In all things it behoved him to be made like unto his brethren, that he might be a merciful and a faithful High-priest ʰ." Such was his compassion towards the hunger of the multitude ⁱ, because he himself knew what

ª Psal. ii. 8. John xvii. 6.   ᵇ Heb. iii. 6.   ᶜ Heb. ii. 7.   ᵈ 1 Pet. i. 11.
ᵉ 1 Cor. xv. 17.   ᶠ Rom. viii. 34.   ᵍ Heb. iv. 14, 15, 16.   ʰ Heb. ii. 17.
ⁱ Matt. xv. 32.

hunger was [k]; and such was his compassion towards the
sorrows of Mary and Martha [l], because he himself was acquainted with grief [m]; and such was his compassion towards
Peter in that state of desertion wherein he lay [n], because he
himself knew what it was to be forsaken [o]. And this is
the apostle's assurance, that we shall obtain mercy and grace
to help in time of need; " Because he had a feeling of our
infirmities, and was tempted as we are [p]."—Secondly, His
consanguinity;—" He is not ashamed to call us brethren:"
he is our goel or kinsman, and therefore our redeemer [q].

" And will not repent." Many things God hath said,
which he hath revoked, as the destruction of Nineveh, the
death of Hezekiah, and the like; which implying a tacit
condition, fit in the particular cases to be concealed, upon
the varieties of that, God might be said either to persevere,
or to repent.[r] God is ever most unchangeable in all his
ways, counsels, and purposes; they stand for ever. Nothing
can fall out to make God more wise, more merciful, more
provident, more powerful than he was before; and, therefore, nothing can make him truly to change his will, or to
repent of his former actions or resolutions. There is with
him " no variableness nor shadow of changing:—He is not
a man that he should repent:—I the Lord change not [s]."
Only in mercy unto our weakness [t], God condescends unto
the manner of human expressions, retaining still the steadfastness of his own working, which receiveth no variation
nor difference from the contingencies of second causes.
He speaketh according to our capacity, but he worketh according to his own counsel; so that God is then said to repent, when that which is once willed to be, he, after, by the
counsel of the same will, causeth not to be; therein not
changing his own counsel [u], but only willing the change of
the things, that the same thing, for this period of this time,

---

k Matt. iv. 2.   l John xi. 33, 35.   m Isai. liii. 3.   n Luke xxii 61.
o Matt. xxvii. 46.   p Heb. iv. 15, 16.   q Heb. xi. Ruth. iii. 9. iv. 4.
r Jer. xviii. 7, 8. xxvi. 13, 19.   s Jam. i. 17. 1 Sam. xv. 29. Mal. iii. 6.
t Humanæ capacitati aptiora quam Divinæ sublimitati, &c. Vid. Aug. To. 4. ad
Simplicia, lib. 2. qu. 2. vid. de Civ. Dei, lib. 14. cap. 11. lib. 15. cap. 25.—Tertul.
cont. Marc. lib. 2. cap. 16.   u Ubi legitur quod ' pœnituit eum,' mutatio rerum
significatur, immutabili manente præsentia divina. Aug. de Civ. Dei. lib. 17.
cap. 7. et lib. 22. cap. 1, 2.—Just. Martyr. Quæst. et Resp. ad Orthodox. qu. 60.

shall be,—and then shall cease. As when a rope is fixed to either side of a river, by the same, without any manner of change or alteration in it, I draw the boat wherein I am, backward or forward : so the same will and counsel of God stands constant and unmoved in the several mutations of those things, which are wrought or removed by it.

Now then, when not only the counsel of God is immutable in itself, but also he hath ordained some law, covenant, or office, which he will have for ever to endure, without either natural expiration, or external abolishment, then is God said ' not to repent.' To apply this to the present business: The apostle, speaking of a new covenant which is established upon this new priesthood of Christ (for the priesthoods and the laws go both together; the one being changed, there is made, of necessity, a change of the other [m]), maketh the introducing of this new covenant, which is founded upon the oath of God, to make the preceding covenant old and transitory : " In that he saith a new covenant, he hath made the first old. Now that which decayeth and waxeth old, is ready to vanish away [n]." And he saith peremptorily, that it was therefore disannulled, because of " the weakness and unprofitableness thereof [o]," and this he affirmeth even of the moral law ;— that law, the righteousness whereof was to be fulfilled in us by the Spirit of Christ, namely, in sincerity and in love, which is the bond of perfection, and the fulfilling of the law [p]. For the full understanding, then, and applying the words to the priesthood of Christ, and the law of grace, or the second covenant thereupon grounded, it will be needful to resolve these two questions :—First, whether God hath repented him of the law, which was the rule and measure of the covenant of works ? Secondly, upon what reasons or grounds the immutability of the second covenant or law of grace standeth ?

For the first of these, the Psalmist telleth us, that " The commandments of God are sure, and that they stand fast for ever, and ever [q]. And we may note, that the same form of speech, which the Lord useth to show the stability of the new covenant,—" The mountains shall depart, and the hills

[m] Heb. vii. 12.   [n] Heb. viii. 13.   [o] Heb. vii. 18.   [p] Rom. viii. 3, 4.   [q] Psal. cxi. 7, 8.

be removed, but my kindness shall not depart from thee, neither shall the covenant of my peace be removed, saith the Lord that hath mercy on thee [r],"—the same kind of form doth our Saviour use to express the stability of the law;— " It is easier for Heaven and earth to pass, than for one tittle of the law to fail [s]." Now the law hath a twofold obligation; the one principal, which is to obedience, whereunto is annexed a promise of righteousness or justification: the other, secondary and conditional, which is unto malediction, upon supposal of disobedience. For " cursed is every one, which continueth not in all things which are written in the book of the law, to do them [t]." Now if no tittle of the law must fail, then neither of these two must fail, but be both fulfilled; and then it should seem, that the first covenant is not removed notwithstanding the weakness thereof.

For resolving hereof [u], we must note, that, in point of validity or invalidity, there can but five things be said of the law: for, first, either it must be obeyed; and that it is not, " For all have sinned, and come short of the glory of God [x]." Or, secondly, it must be executed upon men, and the curse or penalty thereof inflicted; and that it is not neither, " For there is no condemnation to them that are in Christ [y]." Or, thirdly, it must be abrogated, or extinguished; and that it is not neither, for " Heaven and earth must sooner pass away." If there were no law, there would be no sin; for sin is the transgression of the law: and if there were no law, there would be no judgement; for the world must be judged by the law. Or, fourthly, it must be moderated and favourably interpreted by rules of equity, to abate the rigour and severity thereof; and that cannot be neither, for it is inflexible, no jot nor tittle of it must be abated. Or, lastly, the law itself remaining, the obligation thereof notwithstanding, must, towards such or such persons, be so far forth dispensed withal, as that a surety shall be admitted (upon a concurrence of all their wills, who are therein interested; God willing to allow, Christ willing to perform, and man willing to enjoy:) both to do all the duties, and to suf-

---

[r] Isai. liv. 10. [s] Luke xvi. 17. [t] Gal. iii. 10. [u] Vid. *Grotii* defens. fidei Cathol. de satisfactione Christi, cáp. 3. [x] Rom. iii. 23. [y] Rom. viii. 1.

fer all the curses of the law in the behalf of that person, who, in rigour, should himself have done and suffered all. So then neither the law, nor any jot or tittle thereof is abrogated, in regard of the obligations therein contained ; but they are all reconciled in Christ with the second covenant. Yet notwithstanding to the purpose of a covenant, or rule of righteousness between us and God, so he hath repented of it, and removed that office or relation from it, that righteousness should come to us thereby, by reason of the weakness and unprofitableness which is in it to that purpose by the sin of man; yet thus much the law hath to do with justification, that the fulfilling of the whole law is thereunto ever some way or other pre-supposed. Only in the first covenant, we were to do in our own persons ; in the second, Christ is appointed and allowed to do it for us. He fulfilled all the obligations of the law ; the duties thereof by active obedience in his life, and the curses thereof by passive obedience in his death. Now then we, by faith, becoming one with Christ, the grace of God doth number us up in the same mass and sum with him, and so imputeth and accounteth that ours which was done by him. There is no righteousness but doth originally refer and bear proportion to the law of God ; and yet we are not justified by the law, but by grace; because it is the favour of God, contrary to the rigour and exaction of the law, which alloweth the righteousness of the law, by one fulfilled, to be unto another accounted. A man is denominated righteous, as a wall may be esteemed red or green. Now that comes to pass two manners of ways ; either by the colour inherent and belonging unto the wall itself, or by the same colour in some diaphanous transparent body; as glass, which, by the beam of the sun shining on the wall, doth externally affect the same, as if it were its own, and covers that true inherent colour which it hath of itself. In like manner, by the strict covenant of the law, we ought to be righteous from a righteousness inherent in, and performed by, ourselves: but in the new covenant of grace, we are righteous by the righteousness of Christ, which shineth upon us, and presenteth us in his colour unto the sight of his Father. Here, in both covenants, the righteousness from whence the denomination groweth, is the same; namely the satisfying of the demands of the whole law; but the manner of our right and propriety thereunto is much varied. In the one, we have right unto it by law, because we have done it ourselves: in the other, we have right unto it only by grace and favour, because another man's doing of it is bestowed upon us, and accounted ours. And this is that gracious covenant, of which the Lord here saith, " *I have sworn and will not repent.*"

For resolving of the second question, upon what reasons the immutability of the covenant of grace standeth, we must note, That as things are of several sorts, so accordingly they may be mutable or immutable several ways. Some things are absolutely immutable, out of the nature of the thing itself; and that is, when the abrogation or alteration of the thing would unavoidably infer some prodigious consequences and notorious pravity with it, as certain dishonour to God, and confusion upon other things. As if we should conceive a man free from worshipping, reverencing, acknowledging, loving, or trusting in God; herein the creature would be unsubordinated to the Creator, which would infer desperate pravity and disorder, and God should be robbed of his essential honour, which he can no more part from than cease to be God. But now it is repugnant to the nature of an entire covenant, to be in this manner immutable. For, in a covenant, there is a mutual stipulation and consent between God and man; and after performance of man's duty, God maketh promise of bestowing a reward. Now there can be no binding necessity in God to confer, nor absolute power in man to challenge any good from God, who doth, freely and by no necessity, good unto his creatures.

Secondly, Some things are merely ' juris positivi,' not of any intrinsecal necessity, resulting out of the condition of their nature, such as are free either to be or not to be of themselves, or, when they are, free to continue or to cease; not in themselves determined unto any condition of being invariably belonging unto their nature. And such are all covenants: for God might have dealt with men, as with lapsed angels, never have entered anew into covenant with them: he might have reserved unto himself a power of revocation and calling in his patent, shutting up his office of mercy again. How then comes it, that this covenant is immutable, and Christ's priesthood of everlasting and unchangeable vigour to all ages and generations of men? That there shall never be erected, in the church, any other form of God's worship, or any other instruments of man's salvation, than those which we now enjoy? The apostle groundeth it upon two reasons [z]: The promise and the oath of God. First, The promise putteth a right in the creature, which he had not before, and that promise determineth the will of God to the being; and leaveth not it indifferent to the being or not being of the covenant. For it is the foundation of a just claim, which we, by faith, may make upon the fidelity, justice, and power of God, to make it good. "He is faithful and just to forgive us our sins [a];" "The righteous God shall give unto me a crown of righteousness [b]:" righteousness and justice, as well as mercy, is the ground of forgiveness of sin, and salvation, not in relation or respect to merit in us, but to promise in God. Only mercy it was which moved him to promise; and having promised, only truth, and fidelity, and righteousness, bindeth him to perform. As impossible it is for God to break any promise, and to lie unto David, as it is to be an unholy God, or to deny himself [c]. Secondly, The oath of God; for that pawns his own being, life, power, truth, holiness, to make good that which he hath so ratified; and upon these two, doth the immutability of the second covenant, and of Christ's priesthood depend.

Here then we see, upon what ground all our comfort and assurance subsisteth; not upon any strength, power, liberty, or inherent grace already received, which we of ourselves are every day apt to waste, and be cheated of by Satan and the world; but upon God's unchangeable mercy and covenant. This was all David's salvation and desire, all that his heart rested upon,—that though his house were not so with God, that is, did fail much of that beauty and purity, which therein God required, and therefore did deserve to be cast off,—yet God had made with him an everlasting covenant, "ordered in all things and sure [d]." When the conscience is afflicted with the sense of sin, with the fear of its own slip-

---

z Heb. vi. 17, 18.   a 1 John i. 9.   b 2 Tim. iv. 8.   c Psal.
lxxxix. 35. 2 Tim. ii. 13. 1 Thes. v. 24.   d 2 Sam. xxiii. 5.

periness and unsteadfastness in God's covenant, this is all it
hath to support it, "That God is one[e];" that Christ is
"the same yesterday, and to-day, and for ever[f];" that he is
where he ever was, "ready to meet those that return[g]." If
I should do to men, as I have done to God, they would
despise, forsake, revenge themselves on me; I should never
receive grace nor favour again.   But God is not as man[h]:
the whole cause of his compassion is in and from himself;
and therefore he doth not take the advantage of our failings
and exasperations, to alter the course of his dealing towards
us[i]. Though we fail every day, yet his compassions fail not;
and therefore from his immutable mercy it is, that we are not
consumed.[k] His blessing of an adopted people is an irreversible thing, because he is God and not-man; and therefore cannot repent, nor call in the promise which he hath
made; for which purpose "He doth not behold iniquity in
Jacob, nor perverseness in Israel[l]."   If the sun should be
always immovably fixed in one place, as it was a little while
in Joshua's time, at the destruction of the kings[m]; though I
might shut out the light of the sun from me, yet as soon as
I remove the curtain, the sun is still where it was, ready to
be found, and to shine upon me.   The case were lamentable
with us, if, so often as man provokes God's justice, he should
presently revoke his mercy; if the issue of our salvation
should depend upon the frailty and mutability of our own nature, and our life should be in our own keeping.   If the pure
angels of Heaven fell from their created condition, to be
most black and hideous adversaries of the God that made
them; if Adam stood not firm with all that stock of strength
and integrity of will, which he had in Paradise; how can I,
who have so many lusts within, so many enemies without,
such armies of fears and temptations round about me, be
able to resist and stand?   Grace inherent is as mutable in
me, as it was in Adam; Satan as malicious and impetuous
against me, as against Adam; propensions to sin, and falling
away, strong in me, which were none in Adam; snares as
many, weaknesses more; enemies as many, temptations
more.   From the grace which is deposited in mine own

e Gal. iii. 19.   f Heb. xiii. 8.   g Isai. lxiv. 5. Luke xv. 20.
h Hos. xi. 9.   i Psal. ciii. 8, 14.   k Lam. iii. 22. Mal. iii. 6.   l Numb.
xxiii. 19, 20, 21.   m Josh. x. 12, 13.

keeping, I cannot but depart daily, if the Lord should leave me in the hand of mine own counsel : even as water, though it could be made as hot as fire, yet being left unto itself, will quickly reduce and work itself to its own original coldness again. We have grace abiding in our hearts, as we have light in our houses, always by emanation, effusion, and supportance from the Sun of Righteousness which shines upon us. Therefore this is all the comfort which a man hath remaining, that though I am wanting to myself, and do often turn from God, yet he is not wanting to me, nor returns from me ; for " the gifts and calling of God are without repentance [n]." The heart of the best man is like the wheels in Ezekiel's vision [o]; as mutable, and movable several ways as wheels ; as perplexed, hindered, and distracted in itself, as cross wheels in one another ; grace swaying one way, and flesh another ;—who can expect stability in such a thing ? Surely, of itself, it hath none : but the constancy and uniformity of motion in the wheels was this, that they were joined to the living creatures, who in their motion returned not when they went.[p] Such is the stability of the faithful in the covenant ; they have it not from themselves, for they are all like wheels,—but from him unto whom by the same Spirit of life they are united ; who cannot repent, nor return from the covenant of mercy which he hath made.

" *Thou art a priest for ever, after the order of Melchizedek.*" We now come to speak of the priesthood of Christ itself, which is thus sealed and made immutable by the oath of God. " Every high priest," saith the apostle, " is ordained for men in things pertaining to God, that he may offer both gifts and sacrifices for sin [q]." These sacrifices are of two sorts, some eucharistical, as testifications of homage, subjection, duty, and service, as the dedication of the firstfruits, the offerings of Abel and Cain, the meat and drinkofferings, &c. ; some ilastical or expiatory, for the washing away of sins, for making compensation to the justice of God, which had been in sin violated, and to propitiate him again. So that, in this regard, a priest was to be a middle person, by God appointed to stand and to minister between him and men in their behalf ; to be impartial and faithful towards

[n] Rom. xi. 29.   [o] Ezek. i. 16.   [p] Ezek. i. 17, 21   [q] Heb. v. 1.

the justice and truth of God, and not to be overruled by his love to men to injure him; and to be compassionate and merciful towards the errors of men, and not to be overruled by his zeal to God's justice, to give over the care or service of them. And such a High-priest was Christ, zealous of his Father's righteousness and glory, for he was "set forth to declare the righteousness of God [r];" and he did glorify him on earth, by finishing the things which he had given him to do [s]; compassionate towards the errors and miseries of his church,—for he was appointed to expiate and to remove them out of the way [t].

Touching this priesthood, we will thus proceed: First, To enquire into the necessity we have of such a priest. Secondly, What kind of qualifications are requisite in him, who must be unto us such a priest. Thirdly, Wherein the acts or offices of such a priesthood do principally consist. Fourthly, What is the virtue, fruits, ends, events, of such a priesthood. Fifthly, What are the duties which the execution of that office doth enforce upon us, or what uses we should make of it. In these five particulars, I conceive, will the substance of most things which pertain unto the priesthood of Christ, be absolved.

For the first of these we must premise this general rule, There can be no necessity of a priest (in that sense which is most proper and here intended) but between a guilty creature, and a righteous God: for if man were innocent in his relations towards God, he would stand in no need of an expiation; and if God were unrighteous in the passages of man's sin, there would not be due unto him any just debt of satisfaction. This being premised, I shall, through many steps and gradations, bring you to this necessity of Christ's priesthood which we enquire into.

First, Every creature is unavoidably subject to the Creator; for he made all things for himself, and all is to return that glory to him, for which he made them [u]. And this subjection of the creature to the Creator, doth suppose a debt of service to the will of the Creator. Impossible it is, and utterly repugnant to the quality of a creature, not to be subject to some law, and indebted, in

r Rom. iii. 25. s John xvii. 4. t Col. ii. 14. u Prov. xvi. 4.
Rom. ix. 21.

some obedience or other, to him that made it. 'Omne esse' is 'propter operari;' it is a certain rule in creatures, that God giveth every creature a being to this end, that it might put forth that being in some such operations as he hath fitted it for, and prescribed it to observe. The most excellent of all creatures, that excel in strength, are "ministers to do his pleasure, and to hear his voice [x]:" and all the rest have their several laws, and rules of working by his wisdom set them, in the which they wait upon him, and according unto which they move, like Ezekiel's wheels, by the conduct of an invisible Spirit, and by the command of a voice that is above them, as if they understood the law of their Creator, and knew the precepts which they do obey [y]. No creature is for itself only, or its own end: for that which hath not its being of itself, cannot be an end unto itself; inasmuch as the end of every thing which is made, is antecedent to the being of it in the mind and intention of him that made it. The end of things is as a mark, fixed and unmovable in the purpose of the supreme cause; the creature as the arrow, ordered by a most wise and efficacious providence, some through natural and necessary, others voluntary and contingent motions, unto one and the same end, the glory and service of the Creator.

Secondly, No creature is, in its being, or in any of those operations and services which to God it owes, intrinsecally, and, of itself, immutable. It is God's own peculiar honour, to be without variableness or shadow of changing [z]. There was a time when the sun stood still, and moved backward, and was filled with darkness, as with an internal cloud; when the lions have forgotten to devour, and the fire to consume, and the whales to conduct. God can, as he will, alter the courses of nature, let go the reins, and dispense with the rules, which himself had secretly imposed upon the creatures to observe; which shows that they are not in themselves immutable. That constancy which in their motions they observe, is from the regular government of that most wise providence, which carries them to their end, " without any turning [a]:" but when his glory requires, and his will commands it, the mountains tremble, the seas cleave asunder, the rivers run

---

[x] Psalm ciii. 20, 21.   [y] Ezek. xxv. 26. Psalm civ. 19.   [z] James. i. 17.
Mal. iii. 6.   [a] Ezek. i. 17.

back, the earth opens, the laws of nature stand still for a while without any execution, as if they were suspended or repealed by him that made them : and therefore in that place, things are said to " move by a voice," which is above them, namely, by the command of the supreme cause [b].

Thirdly, Man, being, in his nature and formal constitution, a reasonable creature, was appointed by God to serve him after a reasonable manner, out of judgement, discretion, and election, to make choice of his way above all others, as being most excellent, and beautiful in itself, and most convenient and advantageous unto man. Therefore, our service is called " a reasonable service [c]," and David is said to have chosen the way of truth, and the precepts of the Lord [d]; and Moses, to have chosen the afflictions of God's people, and the reproaches of Christ, before the pleasures of sin, or the treasures of Egypt [e]. And hence it is, that holiness, in the phrase of Scripture, is called " judgement :"—" he shall convince the world of judgement [f]," and " he shall bring forth judgement unto victory [g] :" noting, that the Spirit of holiness ruleth and worketh in the spirit of obedience by the way of reason and conviction ;—therefore he is called " a Spirit of judgement [h]." And for this cause, God did not set any over-ruling law, or determinating virtue over the operations of man, as of other creatures, that so he might truly work out of the conduct of judgement, and election of will.

Fourthly, There is no deviation from a reasonable service, or true active obedience, properly so called (for the obedience of brutes and inanimate creatures is rather passive than active), which hath not some intrinsecal pravity in it, and, by consequence, some fundamental demerit, or obligation unto punishment : for guilt is the proper passion of sin, resultant out of it, and therefore inseparable from it. It cannot be, that a creature should, of itself, and out of the corruption of its own reason and judgement, choose to relinquish the service of him to whom it is naturally and unavoidably subject, and, by that means, become altogether unprofitable, abominable, and unfit for the Master's use, and for those holy ends to which it was originally ordered ;—but it must withal incur

b Ezek. i. 24, 25.   c Rom. xii. 1.   d Psalm cxix. 30.   e Heb. xi. 25, 26.
f John xvi. 11.   g Matth. xii. 20.   h Isai. iv. 4.

the displeasure, and thereupon provoke the revenge, of that righteous Creator, who, out of great reasons, had put it under such a service.

Fifthly, By all this which hath hitherto been spoken, it appears, that God is not unjust, but most holy and righteous, First, In making a law for man to observe, when he forbade the eating of the fruit of the tree of knowledge of good and evil, to show that man had nothing by personal, immediate, and underived right, but all by donation and indulgence. Any law God might justly make, the obedience whereof he gave the creature an original power to perform, by reason of the natural and necessary subjection of the creature unto him. Secondly, In annexing a curse and penalty to the violation of that law; which, for the declaration of his glorious justice, he might most righteously do, because of the inevitable demerit, or liableness unto censure, from the disobedience of that law, resulting. Thirdly, In making man in such a mutable condition, as in the which he might stand or fall by his own election, because he would be obeyed by judgement and free choice, not by fatal necessity, or absolute determination [i].

Sixthly, Here then comes in the fall of man, being a wilful or chosen transgression of a law, under the precepts whereof he was most justly created, and unto the malediction whereof he was as necessarily and righteously subject if he transgressed: for as, by being God's creature, he was subject to his will,—so, by being his prisoner, he was as justly subject unto his wrath; and that so much the more, by how much the precept was more just, the obedience more easy, the transgression more unreasonable, and the punishment more certain.

Now, by this fall of man, there came great mischief into the world, and intolerable injury was done by the creature to him that made him: First, His dominion and authority in his holy command was violated. Secondly, His justice, truth, and power in his most righteous threatenings were despised. Thirdly, His most pure and perfect image, wherein man was created in righteousness and true holiness, was utterly defaced. Fourthly, His glory, which, by an active service, the

---

[i] *Basil.* tom. 1. Homil. ' Quod Deus non est Auctor mali.'—*Justin. Mart.*Apol. 1. Τὸ αὐτεξούσιον, οὐ τὸ ἠναγκασμένον, Θεῷ φιλόν. Vid. *Tert.* advers. Marc. 1. 2. c. 6, 7, 9. Prov. i. 29. Eccles. vii. 29. Isai. lxvi. 3, 4.

creature should have brought unto him, was lost and despoiled. So that now things will not return to their primitive order and perfection again, till these two things be first effected: First, A satisfaction of God's justice; and secondly, A reparation of man's nature: which two must needs be effected by such a middle and common person, as hath both zeal towards God, that he may be satisfied,—and compassion towards man, that he may be repaired: such a person, as having man's guilt and punishment on him translated, may satisfy the justice of God; and, as having a fulness of God's Spirit and Holiness in him, may sanctify and repair the nature of man. And this person is the priest here spoken of by David.

Here the learned frame a kind of conflict in God's holy attributes, and by a liberty which the Holy Ghost from the language of holy Scripture alloweth them, they speak of God after the manner of men, as if he were reduced unto some straits and difficulties by the cross demands of his several attributes. Justice called upon him for the condemnation of a sinful, and therefore worthily accursed creature, which demand was seconded by his truth, to make good that threatening, " In the day that thou eatest thereof, thou shalt die the death." Mercy, on the other side, pleaded for favour and compassion towards man, wofully seduced and overthrown by Satan; and peace, for reconcilement and pacification between an offended judge and an undone creature. Hereupon the infinite wisdom and counsel of the blessed Trinity found out a way, which the angels of Heaven gaze on with admiration and astonishment, how to reconcile these different pleas of his attributes together. A priest then is resolved upon, one of the same blessed Trinity, who, by his Father's ordination, his own voluntary susception, and the Holy Spirit's sanctification, should be fitted for the business. He was to be both a surety, and a head over sinful men, to suffer their punishments, and to sanctify their natures; in the relation of a surety, to pay man's debt unto God; and in the relation of a head, to restore God's image unto man : and thus in him, " Mercy and truth have met together, righteousness and peace have kissed each other [k]."

k Psalm lxxxv. 10.

So then the necessity which man fallen hath of this priesthood here spoken of, is grounded upon the sweet harmony
and mutual kisses of God's mercy, truth, righteousness, and
peace, which will more distinctly appear, by considering
three things :—First, God did purpose not utterly to destroy
his creature, and that principally for these two reasons, as
we may observe out of the Scriptures: First, His own free
and everlasting love, and that infinite delight which he hath in
mercy, which disposeth him abundantly to pardon, and to exercise loving-kindness in the earth [1]. Secondly, His delight
to be actively glorified by his creatures' voluntary service and
subjection : "Herein is my Father glorified, that ye bear
much fruit [m];" "I have no pleasure in the death of the
wicked, but that he turn from his way and live [n]." He delighteth most in unbloody conquest, when, by his patience,
goodness, and forbearance, he subdueth the hearts, affections, and consciences of men unto himself, so leading them
unto repentance, and bringing down their thoughts unto the
obedience of Christ: he loveth to see things in their primitive rectitude and beauty, and therefore, esteemeth himself
more glorified in the services, than in the sufferings of men.
He loveth to have a church and generation of men, which
shall serve him in the midst of all his enemies : "The Lord
loveth the gates of Sion, more than all the dwellings of Jacob [o]:" namely, because he was there more solemnly worshipped and served. And therefore he resolved not to destroy
all men, lest there should be no religion upon the earth.
When the angels fell, they fell not all ; many were still left
to glorify him actively in their service of him; but when
Adam fell, all mankind fell in him ; so that there was no tree
of this paradise left to bring forth any fruit unto God. And
this is most certain, God had rather have his trees for fruit,
than for fuel : and for this reason, he was pleased to restore
mankind again. These are the causes, why the Lord would
not utterly destroy man ; but these alone show not the necessity of a priest to come between God and man.

Secondly, God did purpose not to suffer sin to pass
utterly unrevenged, and that for these two reasons : First,
Because of his great hatred thereunto. He is of purer eyes

[1] Mich. vii. 18. Exod. xxxiv. 6, 7. Psalm ciii. 8. Isai. lv. 7. Jer. ix. 24.
[m] John xv. 8. [n] Ezek. xxxiii. 11. [o] Psalm lxxxvii. 2.

than to behold evil, he cannot look on iniquity [p] ; it provoketh a nauseousness and abhorrency in him [q]. Secondly,
Because of his truth and the law, which he had established
against sin, which he will in no wise abolish ; " one jot or
tittle shall, in no ways, pass from the law, till all be fulfilled [r] ;" for it is altogether indecent, especially to the wisdom
and righteousness of God, that that which provoketh the
execution, should procure the abrogation of his law ; that
that should supplant and undermine the law, for the alone
preventing whereof the law was before established [s]. Thirdly, Because of his terror and fearful majesty ; for God will
have men always to tremble before him, and by his terror
to be persuaded from sinning [t]. God will, for this cause,
have men always to fear before him, because he referreth to
himself entire the punishment of sin ; " Fear him who is
able to destroy both body and soul in Hell ; I say unto you,
fear him," saith our Saviour [u]. For " it is a fearful thing
to fall into the hands of the living God ;" and therefore we
ought to serve him with reverence and godly fear, because
he is ' a consuming fire [x].'

Thirdly, Add unto all this, the everlasting impotency
which is in man, either to satisfy God, or to repair himself.
God's justice is infinite which is wronged ; and his glory infinite, of which man had attempted to spoil and rob him ;
and man is both finite in himself, and very impotent, by
reason of sin ; for to be a sinner, and without strength, are
terms equivalent in the apostle [y]. Now, then, between
finite and infinite there can be no proportion ; and therefore
from the one to the other, there can be no satisfaction :
man is utterly unable to do any of God's will, because he is
altogether carnal [z]. And he is utterly unable either to suffer,
or to break through the wrath of God, because he hath not
strength enough to endure it, nor obedience to submit unto
it. Now, then, join all these things together, and we shall
see the absolute necessity we had of a priest. God will not
execute the severity of his law ; for thereby the creature

---

[p] Hab. i. 13.   [q] Psal. v. 6. Zech. viii. 17. Rev. iii. 16. Amos. v. 21, 22.
Isai. i. 13, 14.   [r] Matt. v. 18.   [s] ῞Ινα μὴ διαφθαρῇ τὸ ἅπαξ κεκυρωμένον.
Ælian. de Zaleuc.—Vid. Grot. de satisfactione Christi, cap. 5.   [t] 2 Cor. v. 10, 11.
[u] Matt. x. 28. Luke xii. 4.   [x] Heb. x. 30. xii. 28, 29.   [y] Rom. v. 6, 8.
[z] Rom. viii. 7. 1 Cor. ii. 14.

should everlastingly lose the fruition of him, and he should likewise lose the service and voluntary subjection of his creature. And yet he will not abolish his law neither; lest thereby his justice should be more securely abused, his hatred against sin the less declared, his truth in all his threatenings questioned; and his dreadful majesty by men neglected, as the wooden king by the frogs in the fable. He will not punish those persons whom he loves, because he is pitiful to them; he will not pass over the sins which he hates, because he is jealous towards himself. Man and sin are as inseparably joined together since the fall, as fire and heat: yet God will have mercy on the man, and he will take vengeance of the sin. Some course then or other must there be found out to translate this man's sin on another's person, who may be able to bear them; and to interest this man's person in another's righteousness, which may be able to cover him. Some way must be found out, that things may be all one in regard of man, as if the law had been utterly abrogated, and that they may be all one in regard of God too, as if the creature had been utterly condemned. And all this is done in our High-priest. On him was executed the curse of the law; by him was fulfilled the righteousness of the law; for him was remitted the sin of man; and through him were all things made new again. The world was in Christ, as in its surety, making satisfaction to the justice of God; and God was in Christ, as in his ambassador, reconciling the world unto himself again. By all which we see the necessity which man, lapsed, had of a priest to restore him.

Hence then we may learn, First, How much we ought to hate sin, which arms the law, justice, and power of God against us. As hateful as it is unto God, so hateful it is in itself. For he judgeth uprightly; he seeth things just as they are, without passion, prejudice, or partiality: and as hateful as it is in itself, so hateful should it be unto us, as the only ground of our misery, of the creature's vanity, and of God's dishonour. We see it is so hateful unto God, that he will most certainly be avenged of it. If he spare me, yet he will not spare my sin, though his own beloved Son must be punished for it. O then, why should that be light to me, which was as heavy as a millstone to the soul of Christ?

Why should that be my pleasure, which was his passion? Why that be on a throne with me, which was upon a cross with him? Why should I allow that to be really in me, which the Lord so severely punished, when the guilt thereof was but imputed to his son?—Many sins there are which others, Papists in their practice, as well as in their doctrine and profession, esteem for light and venial sins. And venial indeed they are, ' per exoratorem Patris Christum,' as Tertullian states the question, By Christ who is a prevailing advocate with the Father. But, however, let not us dare esteem that a light thing, for which Christ died. And woe it had been for men, if Christ had not, in his body, on the tree, carried as well the guilt of our idle words, our vain thoughts, our loose and impertinent actions, as of our oaths, execrations, and blasphemies. If great sins were as the spear and nails, certainly small sins were as the thorns which pierced his head. And therefore we should learn with David to ' hate every evil way,' because God hates it, and suffers it not to pass unpunished ; to revenge the quarrel of Christ against those lusts of ours, which nailed him to his cross, and to crucify them for him again; for, for that end was Christ crucified, that " our old man might be crucified with him, that the body of sin might be destroyed, that henceforth we should not serve sin [a]."

Again, We see, by this necessity of a priest, how deeply we stand engaged to our merciful God, who hath vouchsafed to help us in our greatest necessity : how we ought to love him, who hath first of all loved us : how we ought, in our bodies and in our spirits, to glorify him, who hath so dearly bought us : how we should, like volunteers, fight for him who overcame for us : how thankful we should be to him, who was so compassionate unto us : how we should admire and adore the unsearchable riches of his wisdom and goodness, who, when we were desperately and incurably gone, had found out a way of escape and deliverance for us. God stood not in need of us, or any service of ours; he could have glorified himself in our just destruction. Who then can enough express either the mercy of God, or the duty of man, when he considers that God should call together

[a] Rom. vi. 6.

all the depths of his own wisdom and counsel, to save a company of desperate fugitives, who had joined in combination with his greatest enemies, to resist and dishonour him? It would have posed all the wisdom of the world (though misery be commonly very witty to shape and fashion to itself images of deliverance) to have found out a way to Heaven between the wrath of God and the sin of man. It would have posed all the heavenly intelligences, and the united consultations of the blessed angels, to have reconciled God's mercy in the salvation of man, and his justice in the condemnation of sin; to have poured out Hell upon the sin, and yet to have bestowed Heaven upon the sinner. If God should have instructed us thus far, "Ye are miserable creatures, but I am a merciful God: the demands of my justice I must not deny, neither will I deny the entreaties of my mercy: find me out a sacrifice answerable to my justice, and it shall be accepted for you all:"—O where could man have found a creature of capacity enough to hold, or of strength enough to bear, the sins of the world, or the wrath of God? Where could he have found out in Heaven or earth, amongst men or angels, a priest that durst accompany such a sacrifice into the presence of so consuming a fire? Or where could he have found out an altar whereon to offer, and whereby to sanctify so great a sacrifice? No, no! the misery of man was too deep and inextricable for all the created counsel in the world to invent a deliverance. Now, then, if God himself did study to save me, how great reason is there that I should study to serve him! How ought all my wisdom, and counsel, and thoughts, and desires, be directed to this one resolution, to live acceptably and thankfully unto him, who, when he might have produced glory to himself out of my confusion, chose rather to humble, and, as it were, for a while to unglorify himself for my salvation! Certainly that man did never rightly understand the horror of sin, the infinite hatred of God against it, the heaviness of his wrath, the malediction of the law, the mystery and vast dimensions of God's love in Christ, the preciousness of his sacrifice, the end, purpose, or merit of his death, any of those unsearchable riches of God, manifested in the flesh,—who will not crucify a vanity, a lust, a pleasure, an earthly member, unto him again; who finds more content and satisfaction in

his own ways of sin and death, more wisdom in the temptations and deceits of Satan, and his own fleshly mind, than
in those deep mysteries of grace, and contrivances of mercy,
which the angels desire to pry into.

Therefore, in the last place, we should labour to feel this
necessity we have of such a priest. This is the only reason
why so few make use of so precious a fountain, because they
trust in their own muddy and broken cisterns at home, and
are never sensibly and thoroughly touched with the sense of
their own wants. For it is not the saying and confessing,
' ore tenus,' that I have nothing,—nor the knowing in speculation only that I have nothing,—but the feeling and smart-
ing, by reason of my want, which will drive me to seek for
relief abroad. If a man did seriously consider and lay together such thoughts as these ; " I am very busy for the
affairs and passages of this present life, which will quickly
vanish and pass away like a weaver's shuttle, or a tale that is
told ; I have another, and an abiding life to live, after this is
over. All that I toil for here, is but for the back, the belly,
the bag, and posterity. And am I not nearer to myself, than
I am to my money ? Am I not nearer to my soul, than I
am to my carcase, or to my seed ? Must I not have a being
in that, when neither I nor my posterity have either back to
be clothed, or belly to be fed, or name to be supported ?
O why am I not as sadly employed ? why spend I not some,
at least as serious and inquisitive, thoughts about this as
about the other ? Do I not know that I must one day stand
before him who is a consuming fire, that I must one day be
weighed in the balance, and woe be unto me if I am found
too light ? Appear before him I dare not of myself alone,
without a priest to mediate for me, to cover and protect me
from his fury, and to reconcile me unto him again. My person wants a priest ; it is clogged with infinite guilt, which
without him cannot be covered. My nature wants a priest ;
it is overspread with a deep and universal corruption, which,
without him, cannot be cured. My sins want a priest ; they
are, in number and in quality, above measure sinful, which
without him cannot be pardoned. My services want a
priest ; they are blemished and poisoned with many failings
and corruptions, without him they cannot be accepted :"—I
say, if men did seriously lay together such thoughts as these,

it could not be, that rational and sad men, men of deep
thoughts in other matters, who love to bolt out things to the
bran, and to be very solicitous for evidence and certainty in
them,—should suffer such a business as this, their interest in
that priest, who must alone clothe their persons with his
righteousness, and cleanse their nature with his Spirit, and
wash away their sins with his blood, and sanctify their prayers and alms and all religious devotions with his incense and
intercession, or else all of them must pass through the trial
of such a fire as will consume them all,—to be slubbered
over with loose and slender thoughts, and to be rested in,
and resolved upon rather by the lying presumptions of a
deceitful heart, than by the evidences and testimony of God's
holy Spirit.—Consider what I say, and the Lord give you
understanding in all things.

The second thing, proposed to be considered in the priesthood of Christ, was the qualification of that person, who
was to be a fit High-priest for us. Legal sacrifices would not
serve the turn to purge away sin, because of their baseness.
They are not expiations of sin[b]; but were only remem-
brances and commemorations of sin[c]. Necessary it was,
that heavenly things themselves should be purified with
better sacrifices[d]; for they, of themselves, without that
typical relation which they had unto Christ[e], and that in-
strumental virtue which in that relation they had from him[f],
were utterly weak and unprofitable[g]: as the shadow hath
neither being in itself, nor can give refreshment unto another, but dependency on the body to which it belongeth.
And this appeareth, first, By their reiteration. Where the
conscience is once purged, and there is remission of sin,
there is no more offering[h]: for the repeating of the sacrifice, shows that the person, for whose sake it is repeated, is
' in statu quo prius,' in the same condition now, as he was
in at the time of the former oblation. Secondly, By their
variety: there were both gifts and sacrifices for sin[i]. Bulls,
and goats, and calves, and lambs[k]: and that shows that no
one thing was fit to typify the full expiation wrought by

[b] Heb. ix. 9, 12.   [c] Heb. x. 3.   [d] Heb. ix. 23.   [e] Gal. iii. 23.
[f] Heb. ix. 13.   [g] Heb. vii. 18.   [h] Heb. x. 2, 18.   [i] Heb. v. 1. viii. 3.
[k] Heb. ix. 9, xii. 13.

Christ; whereas he offered but one sacrifice, and, by that, perfected for ever them that are sanctified[l]. And if legal sacrifices would not serve the turn, then neither would legal priests be fit for so great a work : for all the good which the priest doth, is in the virtue of the sacrifice which he brings. And this likewise the apostle proves by many arguments. First, because of their sinfulness : for they themselves wanted an expiation, and therefore could not be mediators for the sins of others[m]. Secondly, because of the carnalness of their institution : they were made after the law of a carnal commandment; that is, of a temporary, perishable, and merely external ordinance[n], which prescribed only the examples and shadows of heavenly things. Thirdly, because of their mortality : they were not suffered to continue by reason of death, whereas our priest must live to make intercession. Fourthly, because of their ministry, and the revolution of their services, which never came to a period or perfection in which the priest might give over, and ' sit down:' they ' stood daily ministering,' and oftentimes offering (their service did daily return upon them again); whereas Christ, after he had offered " one sacrifice for sin," for ever " sat down on the right hand of God[o]."

To show you then the qualifications of this priest:—a priest, in general, is ordained for men in things pertaining to God, to offer sacrifice for the obtaining of righteousness and remission of sins.

First, then, Christ, being a priest, must of necessity be a mediator and a surety between parties, that he might have one unto whom, and others for whom and in whose behalf, to offer a sacrifice. Every priest must be a mediator, to stand between God and the people, and to intercept and bear the iniquity[p] even of their holy things. And unto this mediation there must concur the consent of the parties between whom it is negotiated ; for a mediator is not a mediator of one. Now God giveth his consent by laying on him our iniquities, and making his soul an offering for sin[q], and thereby declaring himself to be one with us[r]. And man gives his consent, when by faith he receiveth Christ ; and so becometh not only the friend, but the son of God[s].

[l] Heb. x. 12, 14.   [m] Heb. v. 3. vii. 27.   [n] Heb. vii. 16.   [o] Heb. x. 11, 12.   [p] Exod. xxviii. 38.   [q] Isai. liii. 6, 10.   [r] Gal. iii. 20.   [s] John i. 12.

Secondly, But every mediator is not presently a priest; for there is a mediation only by way of entreaty, prayer, and request, wherein men do obtain but not deserve or purchase remission for others: such mediators were Joab and the widow of Tekoah in the behalf of Absalom [t]. And there are mediators by way of satisfaction; as sureties are between the creditor and the debtor; and such a mediator was Christ, not only a mediator, but also a surety of a better covenant [u]. He was not to procure remission of our sins by way of favour and request; but he was set forth " to declare the righteousness of God [x]:" and such a mediator between God and us must needs be a priest too; for the debt which we owed unto God, was blood: " Without shedding of blood, there is no remission [y]."

Thirdly, Being such a priest, he must have a sacrifice answerable to the debt, which was owed to his Father. The debt we owed, was the forfeiture and subjection of our souls and bodies to the wrath of God, and curse of the law. God is able " to destroy both soul and body in Hell [z]." It is not to be understood only of his absolute power, but of that power which, as our judge, he hath power over us ' per modum judicii,' as we are his prisoners, and so obnoxious to the curses of his law. Therefore our priest was to have a soul and a body, to pay as a surety for our souls and bodies : —" Thou shalt make his soul an offering for sin [a]." " My soul is exceeding sorrowful, even unto death [b]." And again; " A body hast thou prepared me :" we are sanctified " through the offering of the body of Jesus Christ once for all [c]." " His ownself bare our sins in his own body on the tree [d]." So he was to be man, that he might have a fit and answerable sacrifice to offer, σῶμα κατηρτίσω μοι, " Thou hast fitted," or prepared, " a body for me," that my sacrifice might be proportionable to that in the place whereof it stood.—And thereby as he is fit for passion, so also for compassion : he was to be our kinsman, and of our blood, that he might be a merciful and faithful High-priest [e]; and fit for derivation of his righteousness, and transfusion of his Spirit upon us ; for " he that sanctifieth and they that are sanctified, are both of

---

[t] 2 Sam. xiv.   [u] Heb. viii. 6. vii. 22.   [x] Rom. iii. 25.   [y] Heb. ix. 22.
[z] Matt. x. 28.   [a] Isai. liii. 10.   [b] Matt. xxvi. 38.   [c] Heb. x. 5, 10.
[d] 1 Pet. ii. 24.   [e] Heb. ii. 11, 14, 17. Deut. xviii. 15.

one." And as it must be thus fitted to the sinner, that it may be a proper and suitable sacrifice for his sin ; so must it be perfect likewise. First, without blemish or sin :— " Such an High-priest became us who is holy, harmless, undefiled, separate from sinners [f];" that so " he might offer himself without spot unto God," and have no need of a sacrifice for himself [g]. Secondly, without any manner of defect, which should stand in need of supplement and contribution from something else ; that, of itself alone, it might be sufficient and available to bring perfection and salvation unto men, and to leave no more conscience of sin behind it [h].

Fourthly, As there was to be such a sacrifice, perfect in itself, and fit for the use and occasion for which it was appointed, so there must be an altar upon which to offer it unto the Father ; for it is " the altar which sanctifieth the offering :" that is, which, in regard of God, giveth it acceptance ; and which, in regard of man, giveth it virtue, merit, and value, answerable to his occasions. This sacrifice was to be sufficient for the satisfaction of God, and for the justification and reparation of man ; and both these by means of the altar on which it was offered, which was the Divine nature :—Through the Eternal Spirit he offered himself without spot unto God, and so by his blood purgeth our consciences from dead works [i]." For Christ as God sanctified himself as man, that so we, through the virtue and merit of his sacrifice, might be sanctified likewise [k]. He was to be God as well as man, ' Medium participationis,' before he could be ' medium reconciliationis,'—so that he might be himself supported to undergo and break through the weight of sin and the law; and, having so done, might have compass enough in his sacrifice to satisfy the justice of God, and to swallow up the sins of the world.

Fifthly, Inasmuch as the virtue of the Deity was to be attributed truly to the sacrifice ;—else it could have no value nor virtue in it ;—and that sacrifice was to be his own life, soul and body, who is the priest to offer it, because he was not barely a priest, but a surety,—and so his person stood instead of ours, to pay our debt, which was a debt of blood, and therefore he was to offer himself [l]:—and inasmuch as

[f] Heb. vii. 26.   [g] Heb. ix. 14. 1 Pet. i. 19.   [h] Heb. vii. 19. x. 14.
[i] Heb. ix. 14.   [k] John xvii. 19.   [l] Heb. ix. 26. 1 Pet. ii. 24.

his person must needs be equivalent in dignity and representation to the persons of all those for whom he mediated, and
who were, for his sake only, delivered from suffering; for
these causes necessary it was, that God and man should
make but one Christ, in the unity of the same infinite person, whose natures they both were, that which suffered, and
that which sanctified. The human nature was not to be left
to subsist in and for itself, but was to have dependence and
supportance in the person of the Son, and a kind of inexist-
ence in him, as the graft of an apple may have in the stock
of a plumb. From whence ariseth ; First, The communication of properties between the natures ; when, by reason of
the unity of the person, we attribute that to one nature
which is common to the other, not by confusion or transfusion, but by communion in one end, and in one person : as
when the Scriptures attribute human properties to the Divine nature ; " The Lord of life was slain [m] ;" " God purchased the church with his own blood [n] ;" " They crucified
the Lord of glory [o]." Or Divine to the human nature : as,
" The Son of man came down from Heaven [p] ;"—and " The
Son of man shall ascend where he was before [q]." Or when
both natures work with their several concurrence unto the
same work, as to ' walk on the waters,' to ' rise out of the
grave,' &c. By which communication of properties, virtue
is derived from the altar to the sacrifice, inasmuch as it was
the Lord of glory which was crucified. So that his passions
were, in regard of the person which bore them, Θεανδρικαὶ,
both human and Divine, because the person was Θεάνθρωπος,
God and man. Secondly, From the unity of the person supporting the human nature with the Divine, ariseth the appliableness of one sacrifice unto all men. Because the person of the Son is infinitely more than equivalent to the persons of all men, as one diamond to many thousand pebbles :
and because the obedience of this sacrifice was the obedience
of God, and therefore cannot but have more virtue and well-
pleasingness in it, than there can be demerit or malignity in
the sin of man.

Now this person, in whose unity the two natures are con-
joined, is the second person in the holy Trinity. He was

[m] Acts iii 15.   [n] Acts xx. 28.   [o] 1 Cor. ii. 8.   [p] John iii. 13.
[q] John vi. 62

the person, against whom the first sin was principally committed; for it was an affectation of wisdom and to be like unto God (as the falling sin is now the sin against the third person); and therefore the mercy is the more glorious, that he did undertake the expiation. " By him the world was made[r];" and therefore, being spoiled, he was pleased to new make it again, and " to bring many sons unto glory[s]." He was " the express image of his Father[t];" and therefore by him are we " renewed after God's image[u]" again. He was the Son of God by nature; and therefore the mercy was again the more glorified in his making us sons by adoption, and so 'joint-heirs' with himself, who was the heir of all things.

So then such a High-priest it became us to have, as should be first an equal middle person between God and man: in regard of God towards man, an officer appointed to declare his righteousness; and in regard of man towards God, a surety ready to purchase their pardon and deliverance. Secondly, Such a one as should be 'one with us' in the fellowship of our nature, passions, infirmities, and temptations; that so he might the more readily suffer for us, who, in so many things, suffered with us: and 'one with God' the Father in his Divine nature; that so, by the virtue of his sufferings and resurrection, he might be able both to satisfy his justice, and to justify our persons, to sanctify our nature, to perfume and purify our services, to raise up our dead bodies, and to present us to his Father a glorious church, without spot or wrinkle. And both these in the unity of one person; that so, by that means, the Divine nature might communicate virtue, merit, and acceptableness to the sufferings of the human; and that the dignity of that person might countervail the persons of all other men.—And this person, that person of the Three, by whom the glory of the mercy should be the more wonderfully magnified. In one word, two things are requisite to our High-priest:—a grace of union, to make the person God and man in one Christ; and a grace of unction, to fit him with such fulness of the Spirit, as may enable him to the performance of so great a work[w].

By all which we should learn; First, To adore this " great

[r] Col. i. 16, 17. John i. 3.   [s] Heb. ii. 10.   [t] Heb. i. 3. Col. i. 15.
[u] Col. iii. 10.   [w] Isai. xi. 2.

mystery of God manifested in the flesh, and justified in the
Spirit;" the unsearchableness of that love, which appointed
God to be man, the Creator of the world to be despised as a
worm, for the salvation of such rebels as might justly have
been left under chains of darkness, and reserved to the same
inevitable destruction with the devils which fell before them.
Secondly, To have always before our eyes the great hateful-
ness of sin, which no sacrifice could have expiated but the
blood of God himself; and the great severity and inexorableness of God's justice against it, which no satisfaction could
pacify, no obedience compensate, but the suffering and ex-
inanition of himself. O what a condition shall that man be in,
who must stand, or rather everlastingly sink and be crushed,
unto the weight of that wrath against sin, which amazed and
made heavy unto death the soul of Christ himself! which
made him who had the strength of the Deity to support him,
the fulness of the Spirit to sanctify and prepare him, the
message of an angel to comfort him, the relation of a beloved Son to refresh him, the voice of his Father from Heaven testifying unto him that he was heard in that he feared,
the assurance of an ensuing glory, and victory to encourage
him (none of which shall be allowed the wicked in Hell,
who shall not only be the vessels of his vengeance, but,
which will be as grievous as that, the everlasting objects of
his hatred and destestation), which made, I say, even the Son
of God himself, notwithstanding all these abatements, to
pray with strong cries, and bloody drops, and woful conflicts of the soul against the cup of his Father's wrath, and
to shrink and decline that very work, for which only he came
into the world! Thirdly, To praise God for that great honour, which he hath conferred upon our nature in the flesh
of his Son, which, in him, is anointed with more grace and
glory, and filled with more vast and unmatchable perfection,
than all the angels in Heaven are together capable of. For
though, for a little while, he was made lower than the angels
for the purpose of his suffering, yet he is " now sat down on
the right hand of Majesty on high ; angels, and authorities,
and powers being made subject unto him [x]." And for the
infinite mercy which he hath showed to our souls, bodies,

---

[x] Heb. ii. 6, 9.   1 Pet. iii. 22.   Heb. i. 4, 13.

and persons in the sacrifice of his Son; in our reconciliation
and favour with him; in the justification of our persons from
the guilt of sin; in the sanctification of our nature from the
corruption of sin; in the inheritance reserved in Heaven for
us; in the communion and fellowship we have with Christ in
his merits, power, privileges, and heavenly likeness. "Now,"
saith the apostle, "we are sons; and it doth not yet appear
what we shall be: but we know, that when he shall appear,
we shall be like him; for we shall see him as he is [y]."

From these things which have been spoken of the personal
qualifications of our High-priest, it will be easy to find out
the third particular enquired into, touching the acts or offices
of Christ's priesthood; or rather touching the parts of the
same action; for it is all but one [z]. Two acts there are,
wherein the execution of this office doth consist. The first,
An act of oblation of himself once for all, as an adequate
sacrifice, and full compensation for the sins of the whole
world [a]. Our debt unto God was twofold: as we were his
creatures, so we owed unto him a debt of active obedience,
in doing the duties of the whole law; and as we are his prisoners, so we owed unto him a debt of passive obedience, in
suffering, willingly and thoroughly, the curses of the law.
And under this law Christ was made to redeem us by his
fulfilling all that righteousness, who were under the precepts
and penalties of the law ourselves. Therefore the apostle
saith, "He was sin for us;" that is, a sacrifice for sin, to
meet and intercept that wrath, which was breaking out upon
us [b]. Herein was the great mercy of God seen to us, that
he would not punish sinners, though he would not spare sin.
If he should have resolved to have judged sinners, we must
have perished in our own persons; but being pleased to deal
with sin only 'in abstracto,' and to spare the sinner, he was
contented to accept of a sacrifice, which (under the relation
and title of a sacrifice) stood in his sight like the body of
sin alone by itself: in which respect he is likewise said to
be made 'a curse for us [c].' Now that which together with
these things giveth the complete and ultimate formality of a

[y] 1 John iii. 2.   [z] *Aug.* Enchirid. c. 41. et *Danæi* Comment. de Mendacio,
c. 15. et Ep. 120.—*Greg. Nazian.* Orat. 2. de filio.—*Chrysost.* in 2. Cor. 5.
[a] Heb. ix. 14, 26.   [b] 2 Cor. v. 21.   [c] Gal. iii. 13.

sacrifice unto the death of Christ, was his own willingness thereunto in that he offered himself [b]. And therefore he is called "the Lamb of God, that taketh away the sins of the world," because "he was dumb, and opened not his mouth, —but was obedient unto death, even the death of the cross [c]." Christ's death, in regard of God the Father, was a necessary death; for he had 'before determined' that it should be done [d]. "Thus it is written, and thus it behoved Christ to suffer [e]:"—"The Son of man must be lifted up [f]," and therefore he is said to be "a Lamb, slain from the beginning of the world," in regard of God's decree and pre-ordination. But this gave it not the formality of a sacrifice : for God the Father was not the priest; and it is the action of the priest, which giveth the being of a sacrifice to that which is offered. Again ; Christ's death in regard of men was violent ; they slew him with wicked hands, and "killed the Prince of life [g]." And, in this sense, it was no sacrifice neither; for they were not priests, but butchers of Christ. Thirdly, His death in regard of himself was voluntary [h]. "I lay down my life; no man taketh it from me, but I lay it down of myself. I have power to lay it down, and I have power to take it again [i]." And this oblation, and willing obedience, or rendering himself to God, is that which gives being to a sacrifice. He was delivered by God [j]; he was delivered by Judas [k] and the Jews [l]; and he was yielded and given up by himself [m]: in regard of God, it was justice and mercy [n]; in regard of man, it was murder and cruelty [o]; in regard of Christ, it was obedience and humility , and that voluntary act of his that which made it a sacrifice. "He gave *himself for us*, an offering and a sacrifice to God for a sweet smelling savour [q]." His death [r] did not grow out of

[b] Hostia si ad aras reluctata fuisset, invito Deo offerri putabant. *Macrob.* Saturn. lib. 3. cap. 5.—Imò non nisi volentem et velut annuentem mactabant. *Plut.* Sympos. lib. 8. cap. 8. Παραφυλάτlουσιν ἰσχυρῶς τὸ μὴ σφάτlειν πρὶν ἐπινεῦσαι κατασπενδόμενον. [c] Phil. ii. 8. [d] Acts iv. 28. [e] Luke xxiv. 46. [f] John iii. 14. [g] Acts ii. 23, ii. 15. [h] Quia voluit quando voluit. *Aug.* de Trin. 1. 4. cap. 13.—Passiones animi et corporis dispensationis voluntate sine ulla necessitate suscepit. lib. 83. Quæst. cap. 80.—Spiritum cum verbo sponte dimisit, prævento carnificis officio. *Tert.* Apol. cap. 21. [i] John x. 17, 18. [j] Acts ii. 23. [k] De traditione Christi facta à Patre et à Filio, à Juda et Judæis, vide (ex Augustino) *Lumb.* 3. Sent. Dist. 20. C. D. [l] Matt. xxvii. 2. Acts iii. 13. [m] Gal. ii. 20. Eph. v. 25. [n] John iii. 16, 17. Rom. iii. 25. [o] Acts vii. 52. [p] Phil. ii. 8. [q] Eph. v. 2. [r] Non conditionis ne-

the condition of his nature, neither was it inflicted on him
by reason of an excess of strength in those that executed it
(for he was the Lord of glory) ; but only out of mercy towards men, out of obedience towards God, and out of power
in himself. For ' omnis Christi infirmitas fuit ex potestate :'
by his power he assumed those infirmities, which the economy
and dispensation of his priesthood on the earth required;
and by the same power, he laid them aside again, when the
service was ended. And this, I say, was that which made
it a sacrifice. As martyrdom, when men lay down their
lives for the profession of the truth and the service of the
church, is called a sacrifice [6].

If it be here objected, that Christ's death was against
his own will, for he exceedingly feared it [t], and prayed earnestly against it, as a thing contrary to his will,[u]—To this I
answer, That all this doth not hinder but commend his willingness and obedience. Consider him in private as a man,
of the same natural affections, desires, and abhorrences with
other men ; and consider the cup as it was ' calix amaritu-
dinis,' a very bitter cup ; and so he most justly feared and
declined it, as knowing that it would be a most woful and
a heavy combat which he was entering upon. But consider
him in his public relation, as a mediator, a surety, a merciful and faithful High-priest; and so he most willingly and
obediently submitted unto it. And this willingness, ' ratione
officii,' was much the greater, because 'ratione naturæ,' his
will could not but shrink from it. It is easy to be willing
in such a service, as is suitable to our natural condition and
affections ; but when nature shall necessarily shrink, sweat,
startle, and stand amazed at a service, then not to repent, nor
decline, nor fling off the burden, but, with submission of heart,
to lie down under it,—this is, of all other, the greatest obedience [x]. It was the voice of nature, and the presentation of
the just and implanted desires of the flesh, to say " Tran-
seat," Let it pass from me. It was the retractation of mercy

cessitate, sed miserationis voluntate. *Aug.* in Psal. 78.—Vid. *Parker* de Descensu,
lib. 3. num. 116.   • Phil. ii. 17.   t Heb. v. 7.   u Matt. xxvi. 39.
x See *Hooker*, lib. 5, num. 48. *Field*, of the Church, lib. 5. cap. 18. Between
these divers desires, no Repugnancy, but a Subordination.—Filius Dei, qui dixit
et facta sunt ; mandavit et creata sunt omnia : secundum hoc quod Filius hominis temperat sententiam, &c. *Hier.* Ep. 702. lib. 2. advers. Pelagium.

and duty to say, " Glorify thyself:" whatever my nature
desires, whatever my will declines, whatever becomes of me,
yet still glorify thyself and save thy church. If it cannot
otherwise be, than by my drinking this bitter cup, " Thy
will be done."

The second act in the work of Christ's priesthood, is the
act of application or virtual continuation of this sacrifice to
the end of the world ; and that is in the intercession of
Christ ; unto which there is pre-required a power and prevalency over all his enemies, to break through the guilt of sin,
the curse of the law, and the chains of death, with which it
was impossible that he should be held. The vision which
Moses had of the burning bush, was an excellent resemblance of the sacrifice of Christ. The bush noted the sacrifice ; the fire, the suffering ; the continuance and prevailing
of the bush against the fire, the victory of Christ, and breaking through all those sufferings which would utterly have
devoured any other man. And this power of Christ was
showed in his resurrection, wherein " he was declared to be
the Son of God with power [y] ;" and in his ascension, when
" he led all his enemies captive [z];" and " in his sitting at the
right hand of God," far above all principalities and powers [a].
All which did make way to the presenting of his sacrifice
before the mercy-seat, which is the consummation thereof ;
and without which he had not been a priest. " We have
such a High-priest," saith the apostle, " as is set down
on the right hand of the Majesty in the heavens : for if he
were on earth, he should not be a priest, seeing that there
are priests which offer gifts according to the law [b]." It was
the same continued action, whereby the priest did offer
without the Holy place, and did then bring the blood into
the Holiest of all [c]. For the reason why it was shed, was, to
present it to the mercy-seat, and to show it unto the Lord
there. So Christ's act or office was not ended, nor fit to
denominate him a complete priest, till he did enter with
blood, and present his offering, in the Holiest of all, not
made with hands [d]. And therefore he had not been a priest,
if he should have continued on the earth : for there was

[y] Rom. i. 4.   [z] Eph. iv. 8.   [a] Eph. i. 19, 20.   [b] Heb. viii. 14.
[c] Heb. xiii. 11.   [d] Heb. ix. 24.

another priesthood there, which was not to give place but
upon the accomplishment of his ; for the whole figure was
to pass away, when the whole truth was come. Now Christ's
oblation was the τὸ ἀληθινὸν, 'the Truth,' prefigured in the
priest's sacrificing of the beast; and his entrance into Heaven, was the truth, prefigured in the priest's carrying of the
blood into the Holiest of all : and therefore both these were
to be accomplished, before the Levitical priesthood did give
place.

Here then it will be needful, for the more full unfolding
of the priesthood of Christ, to open the doctrine of his intercession at the right hand of his Father. The apostle calleth
it " the *appearing* of Christ for us [e]," which is ' verbum
forense,' an expression borrowed from the custom of human
courts ; for as in them, when the plaintiff or defendant is
called, their attorney appeareth in their name and behalf ;
so when we are summoned by the justice of God to defend
ourselves against those exceptions and complaints, which it
preferreth against us, we have " an advocate with the Father,
Jesus Christ the righteous," who standeth out and appeareth
for us.[f] As the High-priest went into the sanctuary with the
names of the twelve tribes upon his breast ; so Christ entered into the Holiest of all, with our persons, and in our
behalf ; in which respect the apostle saith, that " he was
apprehended of Christ [g]," and that " we do sit together in
heavenly places with him [h]." Merit and efficacy are the
two things, which set forth the virtue of Christ's sacrifice, by
which he hath reconciled us to his Father. The merit of
Christ, being a redundant merit, and having in it a plentiful
redemption, and a sufficient salvation, hath in it two things :
First, there is ἀπολύτρωσις, an expiation, or satisfaction, by
way of price :—Secondly, there is περιποίησις, an inheritance
by way of purchase and acquisition.[i] " He was made of a
woman, made under the law," for two ends, ἵνα ἐξαγοράσῃ, and
ἵνα ἀπολάβωμεν υἱοθεσίαν, that he might redeem us from the
curse under which we lay, and that he might purchase for
us the *inheritance* which we had forfeited before ; for so by
adoption, in that place, I understand in a complexed and

---

[e] Heb. ix. 24.   [f] 1 John ii. 2.   [g] Phil. iii. 12.   [h] Eph. ii. 6.
[i] Eph. i. 14.

general sense ; every good thing, which belongs unto us in the right of our sonship with Christ, and that is the inheritance of glory.[k]

Now all this is effected by the obedience of Christ's death ; for in that, was the act of impetration or procurement, consisting in the treaty between God and Christ. But there is yet farther required an execution, a real effectualness, and actual application of these to us. As it must be, in regard of God, a satisfaction and a purchase,—so it must be likewise, in regard of us, an actual redemption and inheritance. And this is done by the intercession of Christ, which is the commemoration, or rather continuation of his sacrifice. He offered it but once, and yet he is a priest for ever ; because the sacrifice, once offered, doth for ever remain before the mercy-seat. Thus as, in many of the legal oblations, there was first ' mactatio,' and then ' ostensio :';—first, the beast was slain on the altar, and then the blood was, together with the incense, brought before the mercy-seat[l] ;—so Christ was first slain, and then by his own blood he entered into the Holy place[m]. *That* was done on the earth without the gate ; *this,* in Heaven [n] ; *That* the sacrifice or obtaining of redemption ; *this* the application, or conferring of redemption. The sacrifice consisted in the death of Christ alone : the application thereof is grounded upon Christ's death as its merit, but effected by the life of Christ as its immediate cause. His death did obtain, his life did confer, redemption upon us. And therefore, in the Scriptures, our justification and salvation are attributed to the Life of Christ. " He was delivered for our offences, and rose again for our justification[o] ;"—" If Christ be not raised, your faith is vain, ye are yet in your sins[p] ;"—" He shall convince the world of righteousness, because I go to my Father[q] ;"—" Because I live, ye shall live also[r]." " If we be dead with Christ, we believe that we shall also live with him[s] ;"—" Being made perfect," or consecrated for ever, " he became the author of eternal salvation unto all them that obey him[t] ;"—" He is able perfectly to save, because he ever liveth[u]." We were

---

k Rom. viii. 17. 10.   l Levit. xvi. 11, 15.   m Heb. ix. 12. x. 12.
n Heb. xiii. 11, 12.   o Rom. iv. 25.   p 1 Cor. xv. 17.   q John xvi. 10.
r John xiv. 19.   s Rom. vi. 8.   t Heb. v. 8. vii. 28.   u Heb. vii. 25.

reconciled in his death : but had he there rested, we could
never have been acquitted nor entered in, for he was to be
our forerunner. And therefore the apostle addeth a ϖολλῷ
μᾶλλαν, " a *much more*" to the life of Christ ;—" *Much more*,
being reconciled, shall we be saved by his life ˣ." Not in
point of merit, but only of efficacy for us. As, in buying
land, the laying down of the price giveth a man a merito-
rious interest,—but the delivering up of the deeds, the re-
signing up of the property, the yielding up of the possession,
giveth a man an actual interest in that which he hath purchased; so the death of Christ *deserveth,* but the intercession
and life of Christ *applieth,* salvation unto us. It was not
barely Christ's dying, but his dying victoriously, so that it
was impossible for death to hold him ʸ, which was the
ground of our salvation. He could not justify us, till he
was declared to be justified himself: therefore the apostle
saith " that he was justified by the Spirit ᶻ ;' namely, by that
Spirit which quickened him ᵃ. When Christ offered himself a
sacrifice for sin, he was numbered amongst transgressors ᵇ.
He bore our sins along with him on the tree ; and so died
under the wrongs of men, and under the wrath of God, in
both respects, as a guilty person. But when he was quickened by the Spirit of Holiness, he then threw off the sins of
the world from his shoulder, and made it appear, that he
was a righteous person, and that his righteousness was the
righteousness of the world. So then, our faith and hope
was begun in Christ's death, but was finished in his life : he
was the author of it, by enduring the cross ; and he was
the finisher of it, by sitting down on the right hand of the
throne of God ᶜ. The apostle sums up all together; " It
is God that justifieth; who is he that condemneth ? It is
Christ that died, yea rather that is risen again, who is even
at the right hand of God, who also maketh intercession
for us ᵈ."

Now then to show, more distinctly, the nature and excellency of Christ's intercesssion. It consisteth in these particulars :—First, His appearance, or the presenting of his per-

ˣ Rom. v. 10.   ʸ Acts ii. 24.   ᶻ 1 Tim. iii. 16.   ᵃ Rom. i. 4.
viii. 11. 1 Peter iii. 18.   ᵇ Mark xv. 28.   ᶜ Heb. xii. 2.   ᵈ Rom.
viii. 33. 34.

son in our nature, and in his own, as a public person, a
mediator, a sponsor, and a pledge for us; as Judah was
both a mediator to request, and a surety to engage himself
to bear the blame for ever with his Father, for his brother
Benjamin [e]. And Paul for Onesimus, a mediator; "1 beseech thee for my son Onesimus [f]:" and a sponsor; "If he
hath wronged thee, or oweth thee ought, put that on mine
account, I will repay it [g]." So Christ is both a mediator and
surety for us [h].

Secondly, The presenting of his merits as a public satisfaction for the debt of sin, and as a public price for the purchase of glory. For the justice of God was not to be entreated or pacified without a satisfaction; and therefore
where Christ is called an 'advocate,' he is called a 'propitiation' too [i]; because he doth not intercede for us, but in
the right and virtue of the price which he paid. For "the
Lord spared not his Son, but delivered him up for us all [k]:"
he dealt in the full rigour of his justice with him.

Thirdly, In the name of his person, and for the vigour
and virtue of his merits, there is a presenting of his desires,
his will, his request, and interpellation for us, and so applying both unto us. " Father, I will that they also whom thou
hast given me, be with me where I am [l]," &c.

Fourthly, To all this doth answer the consent of the Father, in whose bosom he is, " who heareth him always [m];"
and " in whom he is well pleased [n];" who called him to
this office of being, as it were, Master of Requests in the behalf of his church, and promised to hear him in his petitions—" Ask of me, and I will give thee [o]," &c. Thus as
once when Æschylus [p] the tragedian was accused 'in Areopa-
go' for impiety, his brother Amyntas stood out as his advocate, using no other plea but this ;—he opened his garments
and showed them ' cubitum sine manu,' how he had lost his
hand in the service of the state, and so vindicated his brother. Or as Zaleucus [q], when he put out one of his own
eyes for his son, who had been deprehended in adultery,
delivered him from half the punishment which himself had

---

[e] Gen. xliii. 8, 9.   [f] Phil. ver. 9, 10.   [g] Phil. ver. 18, 19.   [h] Heb.
vii. 22, 8, 6.   [i] 1 John ii. 2.   [k] Rom. viii. 32.   [l] John xvii. 24.   [m] John
xi. 42.   [n] Matth. xvii. 5.   [o] Psal. ii. 8.   [p] Ælian. Var. Hist. l. 5. c. 19.
[q] Ælian. lib. 13, cap. 24.

decreed against that sin. Or to come nearer, as when the
hand steals, if the back be scourged [r], the tongue may, in
matters that are not capital, intercede for a dismission: so
Christ when he suffered for us (which he might more justly
do, than any one man can for another, because he was, by
divine pre-ordination and command, and by his own power,
more lord of his own life, than any other man is of his [s]),
may justly, in the virtue of those his sufferings, intercede in
our behalf for all that which those his sufferings did deserve,
either for the expiation of sin, or for the purchase of salvation. In which sense the apostle saith, that " The blood of
Christ is a speaking or interceding blood [t]."

By all which we may observe the impiety of the popish
doctrine, which distinguisheth between mediators of redemption, and mediators of intercession ; affirming that, though
the saints are not redeemers of the world, yet they are (as
the courtiers of Heaven) mediators of intercession for us,
and so may be sought unto by us. To which I answer, That
we must distinguish of interceding or praying for another.
There is one private and another public (which some learned men [u] have observed in Christ's own prayers) ; or praying
out of charity, and out of justice or office: or Thirdly,
praying out of humility with fear and trembling, or out of
authority, which is not properly prayer,—for prayer, in its
strictest sense, is a proposing of requests for things unmerit-
ed, which we expect ' ex vi promissi,' out of God's gracious
promise, and not ' ex vi pretii,' out of any price or purchase;—
but the presenting of the will and good pleasure of Christ to
his Father, that he may thereunto put his seal and consent,
the desiring of a thing so, as that he hath withal a right
jointly of bestowing it, who doth desire it. That the saints
in Heaven and the blessed angels, do pray for the state of
the church militant, as well as rejoice at their conversion,
inasmuch as charity remaineth after this life, seemeth to be
granted by Cyprian [w] and Jerome[x] ; neither know I any danger in so affirming. But if so, they do it only ' ex caritate,
ut fratres,' not ' ex officio, ut mediatores ;' out of a habit of

---

[r] Ὥσπερ ἁμαρτήσας ὁ ἄνθρωπος ἁμάρτημα διὰ χειρὸς κἂν τυφθῇ εἰς τὸν
νῶτον, οὐκ ἀδικεῖ ὁ τυπτήσας αὐτό. *Just. Mart.* Quæst. et Resp. ad Orthodox.
[s] John x. 18. 1 Cor. vi. 19.   [t] Heb. xii. 24.   [u] *Cameron.* de Eccles. p. 122.
[w] *Cyprian.* Ep. i.   [x] *Hieron.* lib. adversus vigilant.

charity to the general condition of the church (for it reacheth not to particular men); not out of an office of mediation, as if they were set up for public persons, appointed not only to pray for the Church in general, but to present the prayers of particular men to God in their behalf. To be such a mediator belongs only to Christ; because true intercession (as it is a public, and authoritative act) is founded upon the satisfactory merits of the person interceding. He cannot be a right advocate, who is not a propitiation too. And therefore the papists are fain to venture so far as to affirm, That the intercession of the saints with God for us, is grounded upon the virtue of their own merits : " We pray the saints to intercede for us [y], that is, that we may enjoy the suffrage of their merits."—But this is a very wicked doctrine [z]: First, Because it shareth the glory of Christ, and communicateth it to others. Secondly, Because it communicateth God's worship to others. Thirdly, Because, under pretence of modesty and humility, it bringeth in a cursed boldness " to deny the faith," and driveth children from their Father unto servants ; expressly therein gainsaying the apostle, who biddeth us " make our requests known to God [a];" and assured us, that, " by Christ, we have boldness so to do [b]," and " free access" allowed us by the Spirit [c]: whereas one chief reason of turning to the saints and angels, is, because sinful men must not dare to present themselves or their services unto God in their own persons, but by the help of those saints that are in more favour with God, and with whom they may be bolder.

Now from this doctrine of Christ's intercession, many and great are the benefits, which come unto the church of God. As first, Our fellowship with the Father and his Son : " I pray for these, that as thou, Father, art in me, and I in thee, they also may be one in us [d]." Secondly, The gift of the Holy Ghost; " I will pray the Father, and he shall give you another Comforter, that he may abide with you for ever, even the Spirit of truth [e]." All the comforts and workings

[y] Oramus Sanctos ut intercedant pro nobis; id est, ut merita eorum nobis suffragentur. *P. Lumb.* l. 4. dist. 45.   [z] See Dr. *Usher's* Answer to the Jesuit's Challenge, chap. of prayer to saints, p. 411. and the quotations out of *Hales* and *Biel* there.   [a] Phil. iv. 6.   [b] Heb. x. 9.   [c] Eph. ii. 18.   [d] John xvii. 21.   [e] John xiv. 16, 17.

of the Spirit in our hearts which we enjoy, are fruits of the
intercession of Christ. Thirdly, Protection against all our
spiritual enemies: " Who is he that condemneth ? It is
Christ that died, yea, rather that is risen again, who is even
at the right hand of God, who also maketh intercession for
us [f]." " I pray, that thou wouldst keep them from the evil [g]."
But are not the faithful subject to evils, corruptions, and
temptations, still ? How then is that part of the intercession of Christ made good unto us ? For understanding
hereof, we must know that the intercession of Christ is
available to a faithful man presently; but yet in a manner
suitable and convenient to the present estate and condition
of the church, so that there may be left room for another
life ; and therefore we must not conceive all presently done.
As the sun shineth on the moon by leisurely degrees, till she
come to her full light; or as if the king grant a pardon to
be drawn ; though the grant be of the whole thing at once,
yet it cannot be written and sealed, but word after word,
and line after line, and action after action ; so the grant of
our holiness is made unto Christ at first,—but in the execution thereof, there is line upon line, precept upon precept,
here a little and there a little ; such an order by Christ observed in the distribution of his Spirit and grace, as is most
suitable to a life of faith, and to the hope we have of a better
kingdom. " I have prayed for thee, that thy faith fail not,"
saith Christ unto Peter: yet we see it did shake and totter ;
" non rogavit ut ne deficeret, sed ut ne prorsus deficeret ;"
the prayer was not, that there might be no failing at all, but
that it might not utterly and totally fail.

Fourthly, The assurance of our sitting in heavenly places.
His sitting in heavenly places " hath raised us up together,
and made us sit with him [h]." First, Because he sitteth there
in our flesh. Secondly, Because he sitteth there in our behalf. Thirdly, Because he sitteth there as our centre [i], and
so is near unto us, ' natura officii et spiritu ;' by the unity of
the same nature with us ; by the quality of his office or
sponsorship for us ; and by the communion and fellowship of
his Spirit.

Fifthly, Strength against our sins : for from his priesthood

[f] Rom. viii. 34.   [g] John xvii. 15.   [h] Ephes. ii. 6.   [i] Col. iii. 1, 2.

in Heaven, which is his intercession, the apostle infers " the writing of the law in our hearts [k]."

Sixthly, The sanctification of our services: of which the Levitical priests were a type, who were to " bear the iniquity of the holy things of the children of Israel," that they might be accepted [l]. He is the angel of the covenant, who hath a golden censer, to offer up the prayers of saints [m]. There is a threefold evil in man : First, An evil of state or condition under the guilt of sin. Secondly, An evil of nature, under the corruption of sin, and under the indisposition and ineptitude of all our faculties unto good. Thirdly, An evil in all our services, by the adherency of sin : for that which toucheth an unclean thing, is made unclean ; and the best wine, mixed with water, will lose much of its strength and native spirits. Now Christ, by his righteousness and merits, justifieth our persons from the guilt of sin ; and, by the grace and Spirit, doth in measure purify our faculties, and cure them of that corruption of sin which cleaves unto them. And lastly, By his incense and intercession, doth cleanse our services from the noisomeness and adherency of sin ; so that in them the Lord smelleth a sweet savour : and so the apostle calleth the contributions of the saints towards his necessities, " an odour of a sweet smell, a sacrifice acceptable, and well-pleasing unto God [n]." And this is a benefit which runneth through the whole life of a Christian : all the ordinary works of our calling (being parts of our services unto God, for in them we work as servants to the same Master) are unto us sanctified, and to the Father made acceptable by the intercession of his Son, " who hath made us priests, to offer all our sacrifices with acceptance unto this altar [o]."

Seventhly, The inward interpellation of the soul itself for itself, which is, as it were, the echo of Christ's intercession in our hearts : " The Spirit maketh intercession for us with groans which cannot be uttered [p]." The same Spirit groaneth in us, and more fully and distinctly by Christ, prayeth for us.—" These things I speak in the world," saith our Saviour, " that they might have my joy fulfilled in themselves [q] ;" that is, as I conceive,—" I have made this prayer in the

- [k] Heb. viii. 4, 6, 9, 10.   [l] Exod. xxviii. 38.   [m] Revel. viii. 3.   [n] Phil. iv. 18. Gen. viii. 21.   [o] Rev. i. 6. 1 Pet. ii. 5. Isai. lxv. 7.   [p] Rom. viii. 26. [q] John xvii. 13.

world, and left a record and pattern of it in the church, that
they, feeling the same heavenly desires kindled in their hearts,
may be comforted in the workings of that Spirit of prayer in
them, which testifieth to their souls the quality of that intercession, which I will make for them in Heaven."

Eighthly, Patience and unweariedness in God's service :
" Let us run with patience that race that is set before us,
looking unto Jesus the author and finisher of our faith, who
for the joy that was set before him, endured the cross, despising the shame, and is set down at the right hand of the
throne of God [r]."

Lastly, Confidence in our approaches to the throne of
Grace. " Seeing then that we have a great High-priest that
is passed into the heavens, Jesus the Son of God, let us hold
fast our profession, and come boldly unto the throne of
grace [s]."   And again, " This man after he had offered one
sacrifice for sins, for ever sat down on the right hand of
God, from henceforth expecting till his enemies be made his
footstool :" from whence the apostle inferreth, " Having
therefore the boldness to enter into the Holiest by the blood
of Jesus ; and having a High-priest over the house of God,
let us draw near with a true heart, in full assurance of
faith[t]," &c.

And all these things are certain to us, in the virtue of this
intercession of Christ : First, Because the Father " heareth
him, and answereth him [u];" and appointed him to this office [x].
Secondly, Because the Father loveth us ;—" I say not unto
you, that I will pray the Father for you, for the Father himself loveth you, because ye have loved me [y]," &c.   Thirdly,
Because as Christ hath a prayer to intercede for us, so hath
he also a power to confer that upon us for which he inter-
cedeth.   " I will pray the Father, and he will give you
another Comforter [z];" " If I go not away, the Comforter will
not come unto you : but if I depart, I will send him unto
you [a]." That which Christ, by his prayer, obtained for us,—
by his power he conferreth upon us.   And therefore in the
Psalm, he is said to " Receive gifts for men," noting the fruit
of his intercession [b] ; and in the apostle, " to give gifts unto

[r] Heb. xii. 1, 2, 3.   [s] Heb. iv. 14, 16.   [t] Heb. x. 12, 32.   [u] John
xi. 42, xii. 28.   [x] Heb. v. 4, 5.   [y] John xvi. 26, 27.   [z] John xiv. 16.
[a] John xvi. 7.   [b] Psalm lxviii. 18.

men," noting the power and fulness of his person [b]. " Having
received of the Father the promise of the Holy Ghost, he
hath shed forth this, which you now see and hear [c]." Thus
great, and thus certain are the benefits, which come unto the
church, from the intercession of Christ.

The fourth thing enquired into, about the priesthood of
Christ, was, What is the virtue and fruits thereof: and they
may be all comprised in two general words : there is ' solutio
debiti,' the payment of our debt,—and ' redundantia meriti,'
an overplus and redundancy of merit. Satisfaction, whereby we are redeemed from under the law; and an acquisition,
or purchase of an inheritance and privileges for us. The
obedience of Christ hath a double relation in it ; First, There
is ' ratio legalis justitiæ,' the relation of a legal righteousness ; as it bears exact and complete conformity to the law,
will, and decree of his Father. Secondly, There is ' ratio
superlegalis meriti,' relation of a merit over and beyond the
law. For though it were ' nostrum debitum,' that which we
did necessarily owe ; yet it was ' suum indebitum,' that which
of himself he was not bound unto, but by voluntary susception, and covenant with his Father : for it was the blood and
obedience of God himself.

Here then, first, it is to be considered his payment of that
debt, which we did owe unto God; in which respect he is
said to " bear our sins." To *bear sin,* is to have the burden
of the guilt of sin and malediction of the law to lie upon a
man. So it is said, " He that troubleth you, shall bear his
judgement [d]."—" The son shall not bear the iniquity of the
father, neither shall the father bear the iniquity of the son ;
the wickedness of the wicked shall be upon him [e]." So
wrath is said to " abide on a man [f]," and sin is said " to be
retained," or held in its place [g]. So Christ is said " to bear
our sins in his body on the tree [h];" and, by so bearing them,
he took them off from us, cancelled the obligations of the
law against us, and did all whatsoever was requisite to satisfy
an offended justice; for " he fulfilled the law," which was our
debt of service. It becometh us to ' fulfil all righteousness [i],' and he 'endured the cross,' and curse, the bloody agony

[b] Ephes. iv. 8.   [c] Acts ii. 33.   [d] Gal. v. 10.   [e] Ezek. xviii. 20.
[f] John iii. 36.   [g] John xx. 23.   [h] 1 Pet. ii. 24. Isai. liii. 4, 6.   [i] Matth. iii. 15.

and ignominy of that death which was the ' debt of suffering [k].' And the covenant between him and his Father, was,
That all that should be done by him, as our head and surety ;
and so he was "to taste death for every man [l]." So there is
a commutation [m] allowed, that he should be in our stead, as
it were, Ἀντίψυχος, his soul a sacrifice, and his life a price, and
his death a conquest of ours, and therefore is called Ἀντίλυ-
τρον ὑπὲρ πάντων [n]; " a price or ransom" for all those, in whose
place he was made sin and a curse [o]. Though he had not
any demerit or proper guilt of sin upon him, which is a deserving of punishment (for that ever grows out of sin, either
personally inherent, or at least naturally imputed, by reason
that he to whom it is accounted, was seminally and naturally
contained in the loins of him, from whom it is on him derived); yet he had the guilt of sin, so far as it notes an obligation and subjection unto punishment, as he was our surety,
and so ' in sensu forensi,' in the sight of God's court of justice, one with us, who had deserved punishment, imputed
unto him.

The fruit which redounds to us hereby, is the expiation or
remission of our sins, by the imputing of our righteousness
unto us. " This is my blood of the New Testament which is
shed for many, for the remission of sins [p]." " In whom we
have redemption through his blood, the forgiveness of sins,
according to the riches of his glory [q]." And this must needs
be a wonderful mercy, to have so many thousand talents forgiven us, such an infinite weight taken off from our consciences, the penalty and curse of so many sins removed from
us. Our natural condition is to be an heir of everlasting
vengeance, the object of God's hatred and fiery indignation,
exiles from the presence of his glory, vessels fit and full of
misery, written within and without with curses, to be miserable, to be all over miserable, to be without strength in ourselves, to be without pity from other, to be without hope
from God, to be without end of cursedness :—this is the condition of a sinner ; and from all this doth the mercy of God
deliver us.

[k] Heb. xii. 2.   [l] Heb. ii. 9. Rom. v. 8.   [m] Notant qui de legum relax-
atione scripserunt, eas esse optimas relaxationes, quibus annexa est commutatio
sive compensatio. *Grot.* de Satisfact. Christi, cap. 5.   [n] 1 Tim. ii. 6.   [o] 2 Cor.
v. 21. Gal. iii. 13.   [p] Matth. xxvi. 28.   [q] Ephes. i. 7. Heb. xii.

The manner whereby the satisfaction of Christ becomes profitable unto us, unto the remission of sin and righteousness, is by 'imputation [r].' No man is able to stand before God's justice, for he is 'a consuming fire [s].' No flesh can be righteous, if he enter into judgement. He is of purer eyes than to behold iniquity [t]; for his eyes are not eyes of flesh [u]. Now all the world is guilty before God, and cometh short of his glory: ἐν πονηρῷ κεῖται, "it lieth in mischief [x];" and therefore must be justified by a foreign righteousness, and that equal to the justice offended, which is the righteousness of God unto us graciously imputed. "We are justified freely by his grace, through the redemption that is in Jesus Christ [y]."

To open this point of justification by imputed righteousness, we must note, That two things are pre-required to denominate a man, a righteous man. First, There must be extant a righteousness, which is apt and able to justify. Secondly, There must be a right and propriety to it, whereby it cometh to pass, that it doth actually justify. We must then, first, enquire what the righteousness is, whereby a man may be justified. Righteousness consisteth in a relation of rectitude and conformity. " God made man upright, but they have sought out many inventions," and turned into many crooked diverticles of their own [z]. A wicked man loveth " crooked ways," to wander up and down in his own course [a]; whereas a righteous man loveth " straight ways [b]," because righteousness consisteth in rectitude ; and this presupposeth some rule, unto which this conformity must refer. The primitive and original prototype, or rule of Holiness, is the righteousness of God himself, so far forth as his image is communicable to the creature, or at least so far forth as it was at the first implanted in man : " Be ye perfect, as your Father which is Heaven, is perfect [c]." It is not meant of his infinite perfection (for it was the sin of Adam, to aim at being as God, in absoluteness and independent excellency); but of that perfection of his, which is in the Word set forth unto us for an image and pattern, whereunto to conform our-

---

[r] Rom. iv. 3, 5, 8. v. 19. [s] Heb. xii. 29. [t] Hab. i. 13. [u] Job x. 4.
[x] 1 John v. 19. [y] Rom. iii. 12, 24. [z] Eccles. vii. 29. Deut. xxxii. 5.
[a] Jer. xxxi. 22. Hos. iv. 16. [b] Heb. xii. 13. Psal. v. 8. [c] Matth. v. 48.

selves. Therefore the secondary rule of righteousness, or rather the same rule unto us revealed, is the law of God written in his Word; in the which, God's holiness, so far as it is our example, exhibiteth itself to the soul, as the sun doth communicate its light through the beam which conveys it. Now in the law there are two things; one principal, obedience; the other secondary, malediction, upon supposition of disobedience: " Cursed is every one, that continueth not in all things which are written in the book of the law, to do them [d]." So then, upon supposition of the sin of man, two things are required unto justification; The expiation of sin, by suffering the curse; and the fulfilling of righteousness 'de novo,' again. Man, created, might have been justified by obedience only; but man, lapsed, cannot otherwise appear righteous in God's sight, but by a double obedience: the one passive, for the satisfaction of his vindicative justice, as we are his prisoners; the other active, in proportion to his remunerative justice, as we are his creatures.

But besides this, that there must be a righteousness extant, there is required, in the person to be justified or denominated thereby, a propriety thereunto, that it may be "his righteousness [e]." Now there may be a twofold propriety to righteousness, according to a twofold manner of unity: " Unitas enim præstantis est fundamentum proprietatis ad officium præstitum." First, There is a personal and individual unity, whereby a man is 'unus in se,' one in and by himself; and so hath propriety to a duty performed, because it is performed in his own person, and by himself alone. Secondly, There is a common unity, whereby a man is 'unus cum alio,' one with another; or whereby many are 'unum in aliquo primo,' one in and with some other thing, which is the fountain and original of them all. And this is the ground of righteousness imputed: for, in the law, a man is justified by performing entire obedience in his own person. For the law requireth righteousness to be performed by a created and implanted strength, and doth not put, suppose, or indulge, any common principle thereof, out of a man's self. Therefore legal righteousness is most properly called ' Our own

---

[d] Gal. iii. 10.   [e] Jer. xxxiii. 16.

righteousness,' and is set in opposition to the righteousness of God, or that which is by grace imputed [f]. We see then, that, in this matter of imputation, either of sin or righteousness, for the clearing of God from any injustice or partiality in his proceedings, there must ever be some unity or other between the parties; he, whose fact is imputed,—and the other, to whom it is imputed. It would be prodigious, and against reason, to conceive, that the fall of angels should be imputed unto men, because men had no unity in condition, either of nature or covenant with the angels, as we have in both with Adam.

This common unity is twofold; either natural, as between us and Adam, in whom we were seminally contained, and originally represented ; for otherwise than in and with Adam, there could, at the beginning, be no covenant made with mankind, which should, ' ex æquo,' reach unto all particular persons in all ages and places of the world :—or voluntary, as between a man and his surety, who, ' in conspectu fori,' are but as one person. And this must be mutual, the one party undertaking to do for the other, and the other yielding and consenting thereunto ; as between us and Christ: for Christ voluntarily undertook for us; and we, by the Spirit of Christ, are persuaded and made willing to consent, and, by faith, to cast our sins upon Christ, and to lay hold on him. And besides the will of the parties, who are, the one by default, the other by compassion and suretyship, engaged in the debt,—there is required the will and consent of the judge, to whom the debt is due, and to whom it belongeth in the right of his jurisdiction, to appoint such a form of proceeding for the recovery of his right, as may stand best with the honour of his person, and the satisfaction of his justice; who if he would, might, in rigour, have refused any surety, and have exacted the whole debt of those very persons, by whose only default it grew. And thus it comes to pass, that, by grace, we have fellowship with the second Adam, as, by nature, with the first [g]. So then, between Christ and us, there must be a unity, or else there can be no imputation. And therefore it is, that we are said to be ' justified by faith," and that " faith is imputed for righteous-

[f] Rom. x. 3. Phil. iii. 8, 9.   [g] 1 Cor. xv. 45, 48.

ness ᵇ;" not the τὸ 'credere,' the act of believing, as if that were, 'in se,' accounted righteousness as it is a work, proceeding from us by grace; because it is ' vinculum' and ' instrumentum unionis,' the bond of union between us and Christ; and, by that means, makes way to the imputation of Christ's righteousness unto us. Therefore we are said to be "buried," and "crucified" in and with Christ, by the virtue of faith, concorporating Christ and a Christian together, and communicating the fellowship of his sufferings and resurrection ⁱ. "If I be lifted up," saith our Saviour, "I will draw all men after me." 'Crucem conscendit, et me illuc adduxit;' when Christ hanged on the cross, we, in a sort, were there too. As, in Adam, we were all in Paradise, by a natural and seminal virtue; so, in Christ, by a spiritual virtue, whereby, in due time, faith was to be begotten in us, and so we to have an actual being of grace from him, as after our real existence we have an actual being of nature from Adam. Thus we see, that Christ did for us fulfil all righteousness, by his passive meriting and making satisfaction unto the remission of sins: by his active, covering our inabilities, and doing that in perfection for us, which we could not do for ourselves. First, he suffered our punishment: "he was wounded for our transgressions, he was bruised for our iniquities; the chastisement of our peace was upon him; and with his stripes we are healed ᵏ." If it be here objected, that an innocent person ought not to suffer for a nocent, for guilt is inseparable from sin; "The son shall not bear the iniquity of the father, neither shall the father bear the iniquity of the son; the soul that sinneth, the same shall die ¹;"—for the clearing of this objection, we must note, that there is a twofold manner of guilt (as I have before touched); either such as grows out of sin inherent, which is the deserving of punishment, as it is in us; or such as grows out of sin imputed, and that not by reason of union natural, as the guilt of Adam's sin is imputed unto us (which manner of imputation is likewise ' fundamentum demeriti,' and cause thus to deserve punishment), but voluntary, by way of vadimony and susception. And so guilt is only a

---

ʰ Rom. iv. 5.　　ⁱ Rom. vi. 6. Gal. vi. 14. Ephes. iii. 17. Phil. iii. 10.
ᵏ Isai. liii. 5.　　ˡ Ezek. xviii. 20.

free and willing obnoxiousness unto that punishment, which another hath deserved. Amongst sinful men it is true, that the son shall not bear the punishment of the father's sin : First, Because he is altogether personally distinct. Secondly, Because he is not appointed so to do, as Christ was [m]. Thirdly, Because he is not able to bear them, so as to take them off from his father, as Christ did ours : he was himself able to stand under our punishment without sinking ; and was able, by suffering them, to take them off from us, because his person was answerable in dignity, and therefore (by the grace of God, and the act of his divine jurisdiction, in ordering the way to his own satisfaction) equivalent in justice unto all ours. Fourthly, Because he hath already too many of his own to bear. But yet, if the will of the son go along with the father in sinning,—it is not strange, nor unusual for him to suffer for his father's and his own sin together, as for the continuation of the same offence ; because though he do not will the punishment (as Christ did ours), yet imitating and continuing the sin, there is 'volitum in causa,' for the punishment too.

Now for an answer and resolution of the question, Whether an innocent person may suffer for a nocent,—we must note, First, That God, out of his dominion over all things, may cast pains upon an innocent person, as it is manifest he did upon Christ. And what ground of complaint could any creature have against God [n], if he should have created it in fire, and made the place of its habitation the instrument of its pain ? Do not we ourselves, without cruelty upon many occasions, put creatures that have not offended us, unto pain ?

Secondly, It is not universally against equity for one to suffer the punishment of another's sin. We see the infants of Sodom, Babylon, Egypt, of Corah, Dathan, and Abiram, were involved in the punishment of those sins, of which themselves were not guilty : the Lord reserveth [o] to himself the punishment of the fathers on the children [p]; he punished the sins of three hundred and ninety years altogether [q].

---

[m] John x. 18. [n] Vid. *Grot.* de Satisfactione Christi, c. 4, 5. [o] *Tertul.* contr. Marcion. lib. 2. cap. 15. [p] *Lumbard.* lib. 2. distinct. 33.—*Aquin.* 22. quæst. 108. art. 4.—*Coquius* in Aug. Civ. Dei, l. 16. cap. 1. num. 1.—*Danæus* in Aug. Enchirid. cap. 46. [q] Ezck. iv. 2, 5.

Cham committed the sin; and yet Canaan was cursed for it [r]. The sin was Gehazi's alone; and yet the leprosy cleaved not to him only, but to his posterity [s]. The sin of crucifying Christ was the Jews' in that age alone; and yet wrath is come upon them to the uttermost even unto this day [t]. Achan trespassed alone; but he perished not alone, but his sons and daughters, and all that he had with him [u].

Thirdly, The equity hereof in the case of Christ doth here plainly appear: when all parties are glorified, and all parties are willing and well pleased, there is no injury done unto any: and in this the case is so; First, All parties are glorified, the Father is glorified in the obedience of his Son. " I have both glorified my name, and I will glorify it again [w]." " I have glorified thee on earth, I have finished the work, which thou gavest me to do [x]."—The Son is glorified: " thou madest him a little lower than the angels, and crownedst him with glory and honour [y]." And the sinner is glorified: " I will that where I am, they may be also, that they may behold my glory [z]." &c. Secondly, All parties are willing. First, The Father is willing; for, by his ordination, he appointed Christ to it [a]; by his love and tender compassion, he bestowed Christ upon us [b]; by his divine acceptation, he rested well pleased in it [c]: in one word, by his wonderful wisdom he fitteth it to the manifestation of his glory and mercy, to the reconciliation of him and his creature, and to the exaltation of his Son. Secondly, The Son is willing: he cheerfully submitteth unto it [d], and freely loved us, and gave himself unto us [e]. Thirdly, the sinner is willing, and accepteth and relieth upon it, as we have seen at large before in the third verse; so that there can be no injury done to any party, where all are willing, and where all are glorified.

Fourthly, That an innocent person may thus, in justice and equity, suffer for a nocent, there is required (besides these acts of ordination in the supreme, of submission in the

[r] Gen. ix. 22, 25.   [s] 2 Kings v. 27.   [t] Matth. xxvii. 25. 1 Thes. ii. 16. [u] Josh. vii. 24.   1 Kings xxi. 21.   Judg. ix. 56.   1 Kings ii. 33.   Jer. xxii. 30. [w] John xii. 27, 28.   [x] John xvii. 4.   [y] Heb. ii. 7. John xvii. 5.   [z] John xvii. 24.   [a] Acts iv. 27, 28.   [b] John iii. 16.   [c] Matth. xvii. 5.   [d] Heb. x. 9.   [e] Gal. ii. 20.

surety, and of consent in the delinquent) First, An intimate
and near conjunction in him that suffereth, with those that
should have suffered. Several unions and conjunctions there
are ; as politic, between the members and subjects in a
state; and thus in a commonwealth universally sinful[f], a
few righteous men may, as parts of that sinful society,
be justly subject to those temporary evils, which the sins
of the society have contracted : and the people may
justly suffer for the sins of the prince[g] and he for theirs[h].
Secondly, Natural, as between parents and children : so
the Lord visited the sins of Dathan upon his little ones[i].
Thirdly, Mystical, as between man and wife: so the Lord
punished the sins of Amaziah the priest of Bethel, by giving
over his wife unto whoredom[j]. And we see, in many cases,
the husband is liable to be charged and censured for the ex-
orbitances of his wife. Fourthly, Stipulatory, and by consent : as in the case of ' fide jussores' or ' obsides,' who are
punished for the sins of others whom they represent, and in
whose place they stand as a caution and muniment against
injuries which might be feared ; as we see in the parable of
the prisoner, committed to the custody of another person.[k]
Fifthly, Possessory, as between a man and his goods : and
so we find that a man was to offer no beast for a sin-offering
but that which was his own[l]. Now, in all these respects,
there was, in some manner, a conjunction between us and
Christ. He conversed amongst men, and was a member of
that tribe and society amongst whom he lived ; and therefore was altogether with them under that Roman yoke,
which was then upon the people, and in that relation paid
tribute unto Cæsar : he had the nature and seed of man, and
so was subject to all human and natural infirmities without
sin. He was mystically married unto his church; and therefore was answerable for the debts and misdemeanors of the
church. He entered into covenant and became surety for
man ; and therefore was liable to man's engagements.
Lastly, He became the possession, in some sort, of his

---

[f] Navicula, in qua erat Judas, turbabatur ; unde et Petrus, qui erat firmus me-
ritis suis, turbabatur alienis. *Ambros.* in Luc. 5. ʺΟφρ' ἀποτίσῃ Δῆμος ἀτασθαλίας
Βασιλήων, *Hesiod.*—Delirant reges, plectuntur Achivi. [g] 2 Sam. xxiv. 17.
[h] 1 Sam. xii. 25. [i] Num. xvi. 27, 33. [j] Amos vii. 17. [k] 1 Kings
xx. 39, 42. [l] Levit. v. 6, 7.

church : whence it is that we are said to ' receive' him, and to ' have' him [m] : not by way of dominion (for so we are his[n]), but by way of communion and propriety : and therefore, though we cannot offer him up unto God in sacrifice for our sins, yet we may, in our faith and prayers, show him unto his Father, and hold him up as our own armour and fence against the wrath of God.[o]

Secondly, There is required in the innocent person suffering, that he have a free and full dominion over that, from which he parteth in his suffering for another. As in suretyship, a man hath free dominion over his money ; and therefore, in that respect, he may engage himself to pay another man's debt: but he hath a free dominion over himself or his own life ; and therefore he may not part with a member of his own in commutation for another's, as Zaleucus did for his son ; nor be 'Αντίψυχος, to lay down his own life for the delivering of another from death, except in such cases as the Word of God limiteth and alloweth. But Christ was Lord of his own life ; and had therefore power to lay it down and to take it up. And this power he had (though he were in all points subject to the law, as we are) not solely by virtue of the hypostatical union, which did not, for the time, exempt him from any of the obligations of the law,—but by virtue of a particular command, constitution, and designation to that service of laying down his life. " This commandment have I received of my Father [p]."

Lastly, It is required, that this power be ample enough to break through the suffering he undertaketh, and to re-assume his life, and former condition again. " I have power to lay it down, and I have power to take it up." So then the sum of all is this ; by the most just, wise, and merciful will of God, by his own most obedient and voluntary susception, Christ Jesus,—being one with us in a manifold and most secret union, and having full power to lay down, and to take up his life again by special command and allowance of his Father given him,—did, most justly, without injury to himself, or dishonour to or injustice in his Father, suffer the punishment of their sins, with whom he had so near an

---

[m] 1 John v. 12.   [n] 1 Cor. vi. 19.   [o] Rom. xiii. 14.   [p] John xviii. 10.

union; and who could not themselves have suffered them with obedience in their own persons, or with so much glory to God's justice, mercy, and wisdom.

If it be here again objected, That sin in the Scripture is said to be " pardoned," which seems contrary to this payment and satisfaction; to answer this, we must note, first That, in the rigour of the law, ' Noxa sequitur caput,' the delinquent himself is in person to suffer the penalty denounced : for the law is, " In the day that thou eatest, thou shalt die : and the soul that sinneth, it shall die.—Every man shall bear his own burden q." So that the law, as it stands in its own rigour, doth not admit of any commutation, of substitution of one for another. Secondly, therefore, That another person, suffering, may procure a discharge to the person guilty, and be valid to free him,—the will, consent, and mercy of him to whom the infliction of the punishment belongeth, must concur ; and his overruling power must dispense, though not with the substance of the law's demands, yet with the manner of execution, and with that rigour which binds wrath peremptorily upon the head only of him, that hath deserved it. So then we see both these things do sweetly concur: first, a precedent satisfaction by paying the debt; and yet, secondly, a true pardon and remission thereof to that party which should have paid it,—and, out of mercy towards him, a dispensing with the rigour of that law, which, in strictness, would not admit any other to pay it for him.

Thus we see how Christ hath suffered our punishment. Secondly, he did all obedience, and fulfilled all actions of righteousness for us ; " For such a High-priest became us, who is holy, harmless, undefiled, separate from sinners r." He came not into the world but for us ; and therefore he neither suffered, nor did any thing, but for us. As the colour of the glass is, by the favour of the sun-beam shining through it, made the colour of the wall, not inherent in it, but relucent upon it, by an extrinsecal affection ; so the righteousness of Christ, by the favour of God, is so " imputed unto us," as that we are, ' quoad gratiosum Dei con-

q Gal. vi. 5.   r Heb. vii. 26.

spectum,' righteous too. In which sense I understand those
words, " He hath not beheld iniquity in Jacob, neither hath
he seen perverseness in Israel[s]." Though it is indeed in
him, yet the Lord looketh on him as clothed with the righteousness of Christ; and so is said not to see it, as the eye
seeth the colour of the glass in the wall ; and therefore cannot behold that other inherent colour of its own, which yet
it knoweth to be in it.

Now of this doctrine of justification, by Christ's righteousness imputed, we may make a double use. First, It may
teach us that great duty of self-denial : we see no righteousness will justify us but Christ's ; and his will not consist but
with the denial of our own. And surely, whatever the professions of men in word may be, there is not any one duty
in all Christian religion of more difficulty than this,—to
trust Christ only with our salvation ; to do holy duties of
hearing, reading, praying, meditating, almsgiving, or any
other actions of charity or devotion, and yet still to abhor
ourselves and our works ; to esteem ourselves, after we have
done all, unprofitable servants, and worthy of many stripes ;
to do good things, and not to rest in them ; to own the
shame and dung of our solemn services ; when we have done
all the good works we can, to say, with Nehemiah, " Remember me, O my God, concerning this, and spare me according to the greatness of thy mercy[t];" and with David, " To
thee, O Lord, belongeth mercy, for thou renderest to every
man according to his work[u];" it is thy mercy to reward us
according to the uprightness of our works, who mightest, in
judgement, confound us for the imperfection of our works ;
to give God the praise of our working, and to take to ourselves the shame of polluting his works in us. There is no
doctrine so diametrically contrary to the merits of Christ,
and the redemption of the world thereby, as justification by
works. No papist in the world is or can be more contentious for good works than we, both in our doctrine and our
prayers, and in our exhortations to the people. We say, no
faith justifieth us before God, but a working faith ; no man
is righteous in the sight of men, nor to be so esteemed, but
by works of holiness ; without holiness no man shall see

---

[s] Numb. xviii. 21.   [t] Neh. xiii. 22.   [u] Psal. lxii. 12

God ; he that is Christ's, is " zealous of good works," purifieth himself even as he is pure, and walketh as he did in this world.   Here only is the difference : We do them because they are our duty, and testifications of our love and thankfulness to Christ, and of the workings of his Spirit in our hearts ;—but we dare not trust in them, as that by which we hope to stand or fall before the tribunal of God's justice, because they are, at best, mingled with our corruptions, and therefore do themselves stand in need of a High-priest to take off their iniquity.   We know enough in Christ to depend on ; we never can find enough in ourselves.   And this confidence we have, if God would ever have had us justified by works, he would have given us grace enough to fulfil the whole law, and not to have left a prayer upon public record for us every day to repeat, and to regulate all our own prayers by, *Forgive us our trespasses.*   For how dares that man say, ' I shall be justified by my works,' who must every day say, ' Lord forgive my sin, and be merciful unto me a sinner !' Nay, though we could fulfil the whole law perfectly, yet from the guilt of sins, formerly contracted, we could no other way be justified, than by laying hold, by faith, on the satisfaction and sufferings of Christ.

Secondly, It may teach us confidence against all sins, corruptions, and temptations. " Who shall lay any thing to the charge of God's elect ?   It is God that justifieth ; who is he that condemneth ?   It is Christ that died," &c.   Satan is the blackest enemy, and sin is the worst thing he can allege against me, or my soul is or can be subject unto : for Hell is not so evil as sin ; inasmuch as Hell is of God's making, but sin only of mine.   Hell is made against me, but sin is committed against God.   Now I know Christ came to destroy the works, and to answer the arguments and reasonings, of the Devil.   ' Thou canst not stand before God,' saith Satan, ' for thou art a grievous sinner, and he is a devouring fire.'— But Faith can answer, ' Christ is able both to cover and to cure my sin, to make it vanish as a mist, and to put it as far out of mine own sight as the East is from the West.'— But thou hast nothing to do with Christ, thy sins are so many and so foul.'—' Surely the blood of Christ is more acceptable to my soul, and much more honourable and precious in itself, when it covereth a multitude of sins.   Paul was a persecutor, a blasphemer, and injurious, the greatest of all sinners; and yet he obtained mercy, that he might be for a pattern of all long-suffering to those that should after believe in Christ. If I had as much sin upon my soul as thou hast, yet faith could unload them all upon Christ, and Christ could swallow them all up in his mercy.'—' But thou hast still nothing to do with him, because thou continuest in thy sin.'—' But doth he not call me, invite me, beseech me, command me to come unto him? If then I have a heart to answer his call, he hath a hand to draw me to himself, though all the gates of Hell and powers of darkness, or sins of the world, stood between.'—' But thou obeyest not this call.'—' True indeed, and pitiful it is, that I am dull of hearing, and slow of following, the voice of Christ; I want much faith: but yet, Lord, thou dost not use to quench the smoking flax, or to break the bruised reed; I believe, and thou art able to help mine unbelief. I am resolved to venture my soul upon thy mercy, to throw away all my own loading, and to cleave only to this plank of salvation.'—' But faith purifieth the heart; whereas thou art unclean still.'—' True indeed; and miserable man I am therefore, that the motions of sin do work in my members. But yet, Lord, I hate every false way; I delight in thy law with my inner man; I do that which I would not, but I consent to thy law that it is good; I desire to know thy will, to fear thy name, and to follow thee whithersoever thou leadest me.'—' But these are but empty velleities, the wishings and wouldings of an evil heart.'—' Lord, to me belongeth the shame of my failings, but to thee belongeth the glory of thy mercy and forgiveness. Too true it is that I do not all I should: but do I allow myself in any thing that I should not? Do I make use of mine infirmities to justify myself by them, or shelter myself under them, or dispense with myself in them? Though I do not the things I should, yet I love them, and delight in them; my heart and spirit, and all the desires of my soul are towards them: I hate, abhor, and fight with myself for not doing them; I am ashamed of mine infirmities, as the blemishes of my profession; I am weary of them, and groan under them as the burdens of my soul: I have no lust, but I am willing to know it, and when I know, to crucify it. I hear of no farther measure of grace, but I admire it, and hunger after it, and press on to it. I can take Christ and affliction, Christ and persecution together. I can take Christ without the world, I can take Christ without myself. I have no unjust gain, but I am ready to restore it. No time have I lost by earthly business from God's service, but I am ready to redeem it. I have followed no sinful pleasure, but I am ready to abandon it; no evil company, but I mightily abhor it. I never swore an oath, but I can remember it with a bleeding conscience. I never neglected a duty, but I can recount it with revenge and indignation. I do not in any man see the image of Christ, but I love him the more dearly for it, and abhor myself for being so much unlike it. I know, Satan, I shall speed never the worse with God, because I have thee for mine enemy. I know I shall speed much the better, because I have myself for mine enemy.'— Certainly, he that can take Christ offered, that can in all points admit him, as well to purify as to justify, as well to rule as save, as well his grace as his mercy,—need not fear all the powers of darkness, nor all the armies of the foulest sins, which Satan can charge his conscience withal.

The second great virtue and fruit of the priesthood of Christ was, ' ex redundantia meriti,' from the redundancy and overflowing of his merit. First, He doth merit to have a church; for the very being of the Church is the effect of that great price which he paid : therefore the church is called a " purchased people [x]." " Ask of me, and I will give thee the heathen for thine inheritance [y]." " When he made his soul an offering for sin, he did by that means see his seed, and divide a portion with the great [z]." The delivering and selecting of the saints out of the present evil world, was the end of Christ's sacrifice [a]. Secondly, He did merit all such good things for the church, as the great love of himself and his Father towards the Church did resolve to confer upon it. They may, I conceive, be reduced to two heads : First, Immunity from evil, whatsoever is left to be removed after the payment of our debt; or taking off from us the guilt and obligation unto punishment. Such are the dominion of sin : " Sin shall not have dominion over you [b]:—The law

[x] 1 Pet. ii. 9. [y] Psal. ii. 8. [z] Isai. liii. 10, 11, 12. [a] Gal. i. 4
[b] Rom. vi. 14.

of the spirit of life in Christ Jesus, hath made me free from
the law of sin and death : [c] He that committeth sin, is the servant of sin ; but if the Son shall make you free, you shall be
free indeed':[d]. He that is born of God, doth not commit
sin [e] :" That is, he is not an artificer of sin, one that maketh
it his trade and profession, and therefore bringeth it to any
perfection. He hath received " a spirit of judgement," that
chaineth up his lusts, and a " spirit of burning," which
worketh out his dross [f].—Such is the vanity of our mind,
whereby we are naturally unable to think, or to cherish a
good thought [g] : The ignorance and hardness of our hearts,
unable to perceive or delight in any spiritual thing [h]: The
spirit of disobedience and habitual strangeness and averseness from God [i].—Such are also all those slavish, affrightful,
and contumacious effects of the law in terrifying the conscience, irritating the concupiscence, and compelling the
froward heart to an unwilling and unwelcome conformity.
The law is now made our counsellor, a delight to the inner
man : that which was a lion before, hath now food and
sweetness in it.

Secondly, Many privileges and dignities in the virtue of
that principal and general one, which is our unity unto
Christ : from whence, by the fellowship of his holy and
quickening spirit, we have an unction which teacheth us his
ways, and his voice which sanctifieth our nature, by the participation of the divine nature ; that is, by the renewing of
God's most holy and righteous image in us, which sanctifieth
our persons, that they may be spiritual kings and priests :—
Kings, to order our own thoughts, affections, desires, studies
towards him ; to fight with principalities, powers, corruptions and spiritual enemies :—*Priests,* to offer up our bodies,
souls, prayers, thanksgivings, alms, spiritual services upon
that altar, which is before his mercy-seat, and to slay and
mortify our lusts and earthly members ; which sanctifieth all
our actions, that they may be services to him and his church,
acceptable to him, and profitable to others.

Secondly, From this unity with him grows our adoption,
which is another fruit of his sacrifice. " He was made of a

---

　　c Rom. viii. 2.　　d John viii. 34, 36.　　e John iii. 9.　　f Isai. iv. 4.
Mal. iii. 2, 3. Matth. ii. 3.　　g 2 Cor. iii. 5. Ephes. iv. 17.　　h Ephes. iv. 18.
John i. 5. Luke xxiv 25. 45.　　i Ephes. iv. 18. Job xx. 14.

woman, made under the law, that we might receive the *adoption* of Sons [k]." By which we have free access to call upon God in the virtue of his sacrifice, sure supplies in all our wants, because our heavenly Father knoweth all our needs ; a most certain inheritance and salvation in hope ; for we are already "saved by hope [l]." And Christ is to us " the hope of glory [m]." Lastly, There is from hence our exaltation, in our final victory and resurrection, by the fellowship and virtue of his victory over death, as the fruits of ours [n]:" and in our complete salvation, being carried in our souls and bodies to be presented to himself without spot and blameless [o], and to be brought unto God [p]. Now to take all in one view, what a sum of mercy is here together! Remission of all sins, discharge of all debts, deliverance from all curses ; joy, peace, triumph, security, exaltation above all evils, enemies, or fears ; a peculiar, purchased, royal seed (the gift of God the Father to his Son); deliverance from the dominion and service of all sin, vanity, ignorance, hardness, disobedience, bondage, coaction, terror ; sanctification of our persons, natures, lives, actions ; adoption, hope, victory, resurrection, salvation, glory. O what a price was that which procured it ! O what manner of persons ought we to be for whom it was procured !

The fifth thing to be spoken of about the priesthood of Christ, I shall despatch in one word, which is the duty we owe upon all this. First, Then, we should not receive so great a grace in vain, but, by faith, lay hold upon it, and make use of it. " Let us fear," saith the apostle, " lest, a promise being left us of entering into his rest, any of you should seem to come short of it ; for unto us was the gospel preached, as well as unto them : but the Word preached did not profit them, not being mixed with faith in them that heard it [q]." God in Christ is but reconcilable unto us, one with us in his good will, and in his proclamation of peace. When two parties are at a variance, there is no actual peace without the mutual consent of both again. Till we by faith give our consent, and actually turn unto God, and seek his favour, and lay hold on the mercy which is set before us ; though

[k] Gal. iv. 5.   [l] Rom. viii. 24.   [m] Col. i. 27.   [n] 1 Cor. xv. 20, 49.
Phil. iii. 21.   [o] Ephes. v. 26, 27.   [p] 1 Pet. iii. 18.   [q] Heb. iv. 1, 2.

God be one, in that he sendeth a mediator, and maketh tender of reconcilement with us,—yet this grace of his is to us in vain, because we continue his enemies still. The sun is set in the heavens for a public light, yet it benefiteth none but those who open their eyes, to admit and make use of its light. A court of justice or equity, is a public sanctuary; yet it actually relieveth none but those that seek unto it. Christ is a public and universal salvation, set up for all comers, and appliable to all particulars [r]. " He is not willing that any should perish, but that all should come to repentance [s];"— " He tasted death for every man [t];" but all this is not beneficial unto life, but only to those that receive him. Only those that receive him, are, by these mercies of his, made the sons of God [u]; without faith, they abide his enemies still. God in Christ publisheth himself a God of peace and unity towards us [x],—and setteth forth Christ, as an all-sufficient treasure of mercy to all, that, in the sense of their misery, will fly unto him [y]. But till men believe, and are thus willing to yield their own consents, and to meet his reconciliation towards them, with theirs towards him, his wrath abideth upon them still; for by believing only, he will have his Son's death actually effectual, though it were sufficient before. O, therefore, let us not venture to bear the wrath of God, the curse of sin, the weight of the law, upon our own shoulders, when we have so present a remedy, and so willing a friend at hand to ease us.

Secondly, We should labour to feel the virtue of the priesthood and sacrifice of Christ working in us, purging our consciences from dead works, renewing our nature, cleansing us from the power and pollution of sin: for when, by the hand of faith, and the sweet operations of the Spirit, we are therewithal sprinkled, we shall then make it all our study to hate and to forbear sin, which squeezed out so precious blood, and wrung such bitter cries from so merciful a High-priest; to live no longer to ourselves (that is, ' secundum hominem,' as men [z]; after our own lusts and ways), but (as men that are not their own, but his that bought them,) to live in his service, and to his glory [a]. All that we can do, is too little to

[r] John iii. 16. [s] 2 Pet. iii. 9. [t] Heb. ii. 9. [u] John i. 12. [x] Gal. iii. 20. [y] Revel. xxii. 17. [z] 1 Cor. iii. 3. Hos. vi. 7. [a] 1 Cor. vi. 19, 20. 2 Cor. v. 14. 1 Pet. iv. 2.

answer so great love ;—love to empty himself, to humble himself ; to be God in the flesh, to be God on a cross ; to take off from us the hatred, fury, and vengeance of his Father ; to restore us to our primitive purity and condition again. Why should it be esteemed a needless thing, to be most rigorously conscionable, and exactly circumspect, in such a service, as unto which we are engaged with so infinite and unsearchable bounty ? He paid our debt to the uttermost farthing, drunk every drop of our bitter cup, and saved us *εἰς παντελὲς,* ' thoroughly :' why should not we labour to perform his service, and to fulfil every one of his most sweet commands to the uttermost too ?

Thirdly, We should learn to walk before him with all reverence and fear, as men that have received a kingdom which cannot be moved [b]. And with frequent consideration of the High-priest of our profession, that we may not, in presumption of his mercy, harden our hearts, or depart from God [c] ; but in due remembrance of the end of his sacrifice, which was to purchase to himself a peculiar people, zealous of all good works [d].

Fourthly, We should learn confidence and boldness towards him, who is a great, a faithful, and a merciful High-priest. This use the apostle makes of it : " Seeing we have a great High-priest, let us hold fast our profession, and come with boldness unto the throne of grace [e]." And again ; " Having therefore boldness to enter into the Holiest, by the blood of Jesus ; and having a High-priest over the house of God ; let us draw near, with a true heart, in full assurance of faith [f]," &c.

Fifthly, We learn perseverance and steadfastness in our profession, because he is able to carry us through, and save us to the uttermost. This is that which indeed makes us partakers of Christ. " We are made partakers of him, if we hold the beginning of our confidence steadfast to the end [g]." The considering of him, of his perseverance in finishing of his own work, and our faith, and his power and ability to save us to the uttermost, will keep us from fainting in our service and the profession we have taken [h].

Sixthly, We have hereby access to present our prayers,

[b] Heb. xii. 28.   [c] Heb. iii. 1, 8.   [d] Tit. ii. 14.   [e] Heb. iv. 14, 15, 16.
[f] Heb. x. 19, 22.   [g] Heb. iii. 14,   [h] Heb. xii. 2, 3. x. 23.

and all our spiritual sacrifices upon this altar, sprinkled with
the blood of that great sacrifice, and liberty to come unto
God by him, who liveth to make intercession for us[i]. " In
him we have access with confidence by faith [k]." Therefore
the Lord is said to have his " eyes open to our prayers, to
hearken unto them[l];" because he first looketh upon our persons in Christ, before he receiveth or admitteth any of our
services.

Lastly, We ought frequently to celebrate the memory, and
to commemorate the benefits of this sacrifice, wherein God
hath been so much glorified, and we so wonderfully saved.
Therefore the Lord hath of purpose instituted a sacred ordinance in his church, in the room of the paschal lamb ; that
as that was a prefiguration of Christ's death expected, so
this should, to all ages of the church, be a resemblance and
commemoration of the same exhibited. " So often as ye eat
this bread, and drink this cup, ye show forth the Lord's
death till he come[m]." For in the ordinances he is " crucified
before our eyes[n]." Therefore the apostle more than once
infers, from the consideration of this sacrifice and office of
Christ, our duty of not forsaking the assemblies of the saints,
and of exhorting and provoking one another[o].

Now I proceed to the last thing mentioned in the words,
concerning the priesthood of Christ ; and that is about the
order of it. *Thou art a priest for ever after the order of
Melchizedek.* ' Secundum verbum,' or ' secundum morem et
rationem :' the apostle readeth it κατὰ τάξιν, according to the
order of Melchizedek's priesthood. Of this Melchizedek,
we find mention made but in two places only of the Old Testament, and in both very briefly : the first, in the history of
Abraham returning from the slaughter of the kings, when
Melchizedek, being the priest of the Most High God,
brought forth bread and wine, and blessed him[p] ; and the
other, in this place. And for this cause the things, concerning him and his order, are δυσερμήνευτα, " hard to be understood[q]." It was so then, and so it would be still, if St. Paul
had not cleared the difficulties, and showed wherein the type
and the antitype did fully answer ; which he hath largely
done in Heb. vii.

i Heb. vii. 25.   k Ephes. iii. 12.   l 1 Kings viii. 52.   m 1 Cor. xi. 26.
n Gal. iii. 1.   o Heb. iii. 13. x. 24, 24.   p Gen. xiv. 18, 19, 20.
q Heb. v. 11.

For understanding and clearing the particulars which are herein considerable [s], here are some questions which offer themselves. First, Who Melchizedek was? Secondly, What is meant by τάξις, his order? Thirdly, Why Christ was to be a priest after his order, and not after Aaron's? Fourthly, Why he brought forth bread and wine? Fifthly, What kind of blessing it was, with which he blessed Abraham? Sixthly, In what manner he received tithes? Lastly, In what sense he was without father, and without mother, without beginning of days, or end of life?

First, For Melchizedek, who he was, much hath been said by many men, and with much confidence. Some heretics of old affirmed [t], that he was the Holy Ghost. Others [u], that he was an angel. Others [x], that he was Shem the son of Noah. Others [y], that he was a Canaanite, extraordinarily raised up by God to be a priest of the Gentiles. Others [z], that he was Christ himself, manifested by a special dispensation and privilege unto Abraham in the flesh, who is said "to have seen his day, and rejoiced [a]." Difference also there is about Salem, the place of which he was king. Some take it for Jerusalem, as Josephus [b], and most of the ancients. Others for a city in the half tribe of Manasseh, within the river Jordan, where Jerome reports, that some ruins of the palace of Melchizedek, were, in his days, conceived to remain. Tedious I might be in insisting on this point, who Melchizedek was. But when I find the Holy Ghost purposely concealing his name, genealogy, beginning, ending, and descent, and that to special purpose; I cannot but wonder, that men should toil themselves in the dark, to find out that of which they have not the least ground of solid conjecture; and the inevidence whereof is expressly recorded, to make Melchizedek thereby the fitter type of Christ's everlasting priesthood.

Secondly, What is meant by τάξις. It is as much as the state, condition, or prescribed rule of Melchizedek; and that was κατὰ δύναμιν ζωῆς ἀκαταλύτου, "after the power

[s] Vid. *Cameron.* Quæst. in Heb.   [t] Apud *Hieron.* Epist. To. 3. Epist. 136. et Epiphan. lib. 2. Heræs. 55.   [u] *Origen.* apud Hieronym.   [x] Hebræi apud *Epiphan.* et *Hieron.*   [y] *Tertull.* cont. Judæos.   *Just. Epiphan. Pareus* in Gen. [z] Quidam apud *Epiphan.* et nuper *Petrus Cunæus,* de Repub. Hebræor. cap. iii. vid. *Coqu.* in *Aug.* de Civ. Dei lib. 16. cap. 22.   [a] John viii. 56.   [b] Antiq. Jud. lib. i. cap. 11.

of an endless life. [c] Not by a corporeal unction, legal ceremony, or the intervening act of a human ordination ; but by
a heavenly institution, and immediate unction of the Spirit
of life, by that extraordinary manner, whereby he was to be
both king and priest unto God, as Melchizedek was.

Thirdly, Why was he not a priest after the order of Aaron?
The apostle giveth us this answer, " Because the law made
nothing perfect," but was " weak and unprofitable ;" and
therefore was to be abolished, and to give place to another
priesthood. Men were not to rest in it ; but by it to be led
to him, who was to abolish it [d], as the morning-star leadeth to
the sun, and, at the rising thereof, vanisheth. The ministry
and promises of Christ were better than those of the law :
and therefore his priesthood, which was the office of dispensing them, was to be " more excellent" likewise [e]. For when
the law and covenant were to be abolished, the priesthood
in which they were established, was to die likewise.

Fourthly, Why Melchizedek brought forth bread and
wine ? The papists, that they may have something to build
the idolatry of their mass upon, make Melchizedek to sacrifice bread and wine, as a type of the Eucharist. I will
not fall into so tedious a controversy, as no way tending to
edification ; and infinite litigations there have been between
the parties already about it. In one word ; we grant that
the ancients [f] do frequently make it a type of the Eucharist;
but only by way of allusion, not of literal prediction, or
strict prefiguration : as that, " Out of Egypt have I called
my Son," and, " In Rama was there a voice heard ;" which
were literally and historically true in another sense, but are
yet, by way of allusion, applied by the evangelist unto the history of Christ [g]. But we may note, First, It is not ' Sacri-
ficavit,' but ' Protulit,' ' he brought it forth,' he did not
offer it up. Secondly, He brought it forth to Abraham as a
prince, to entertain him after his conquest, as Josephus [h],
and from him, Cajetan understand it ; not as a priest, to
God. Thirdly, If he did offer, he offered bread and wine
truly ; these men, only the lying shapes thereof, and not
bread and wine itself ; which, they say, are transubstan-

---

[c] Heb. vii. 16.   [d] Heb. vii. 11, 12.   [e] Heb. viii. 6.   [f] *Glass.* Philol.
Sacra. p. 423.   [g] Matth. ii. 15, 18.   [h] Loco suprà citato.

tiated into another thing. Fourthly, The priesthood of Melchizedek, as type, and of Christ, as the substance, was
ἀκαταβατὸς, a priesthood, which could not pass unto any
other, either as successor or vicar, to one or the other; and
it was only by divine aud immediate unction: but the Papists make themselves priests, by human and ecclesiastical
ordination, to offer that which (they say) Melchizedek offered; and by that means most insolently make themselves
either successors, or vicars, or sharers, and co-partners, and
workers together with him and his antitype, Christ Jesus,
in the offices of such a priesthood as was totally uncommunicable, and intransient[i]; and so most sacrilegiously rob
him of that honour, which he hath assumed to himself as
his peculiar office.

Fifthly, What kind of blessing it was, wherewith Melchizedek blessed Abraham? To this I answer, that there is
a twofold benediction: the one ' Caritativa,' out of love;
and so any man may bless another by way of euprecation
or well-wishing: " The blessing of the Lord be upon you;
we bless you in the name of the Lord[k]:—the other ' Aucto-
ritativa,' as a king, a priest, an extraordinary superior and
public person, by way of office, and to the purpose of effecting and real conveying the blessing itself desired: " Without all contradiction," saith the apostle, " the less is blessed
of the greater[l]:" and such was this of Melchizedek, ' Bene-
dictio obsignans,' a seal, assurance, and effectual confirmation, of the promise before made[m].

Sixthly, In what manner he received tithes? I answer
with Calvin[n], that he had ' Jus decimarum,' and received
them as testifications of homage, duty, and obedience from
Abraham: for the apostle useth it as an argument to prove
his greatness above Abraham; which could be no argument
in the case of pure gift; since gifts, ' quatenus' gifts, though
they prove not a general inferiority in him that receives
them, yet they prove, that, in that case, there is something
which may be imputed, and which deserves acknowledgment. But, in this particular, all the acknowledgments are

---

i Heb. vii. 24.   k Psal. cxxvi. 8.   l Heb. vii. 7.   m Gen. xii. 2, 3.
n Quod debebat Abraham Deo, solvit in manum Melchizedec. Decimarum
ergo solutione, se minorem professus est. *Calv.* in Heb. vii. 5, 8, 9.

from Abraham to Melchizedek. Besides, nothing was
here, by Abraham or Melchizedek, done after an arbitrary
manner, but ' extraordinario spiritus afflatu et ex officio,'
on both sides, as learned Cameron hath observed.

Lastly, In what sense he was ἀπάτωρ and ἀμήτωρ, &c. without father, mother, or genealogy? I answer with Chrysostom[o], that it is not meant literally and strictly; but only
the Scripture takes notice of him, as an extraordinary man,
without signifying his line, beginning, end, or race (as
Tiberius said of Rufus, that he was ' Homo ex se natus');
that so he might be the fitter to typify Christ's person and
excellency, in whom those things were really true, which
are only, ' quoad nos,' spoken of the type, of whose beginning, end, or parentage, we neither have nor can have
any knowledge. These things thus premised, it will be easy
for you to preoccupate those observations which grow between the type and the antitype, which therefore I will but
cursorily propose. Note, First, That Christ's priesthood is
such as did induce a kingdom with it; for Melchizedek
was King of Salem, and priest of the Most High God. This
St. Jerome, and from him Ambrose, report to have been
meant by the order of Melchizedek, namely, ' Regale
Sacerdotium,' that Christ was to be a royal priest; by way
of merit, purchasing a kingdom of his Father,—and by way
of conquest, recovering it to himself out of the hands of his
enemies.

Note, Secondly, That Christ, by offering up himself a
sacrifice unto God, is become unto his people " a king of
righteousness," or, " the Lord our righteousness;" in which
sense he is called "The Prince of life[p];" that is, he hath all
power given him as a prince, to quicken and to justify whom
he will[q]. And this comes from his sacrifice, and perfect obedience to us imputed, and by faith employed and apprehended: for having fulfilled the righteousness of the law,
and justified himself by rising from the dead, he became,
being thus made perfect, the author of righteousness and
salvation to us[r]. We had in us a whole kingdom of sin;
and therefore requisite there was in him what should justify

---

[o] Διὰ τὸ μὴ μνημονευθῆναι τοὺς γεγενηκότας αὐτόν.   [p] Acts iii. 15.
[q] John v. 20, 21.   [r] Heb. v. 9.

us, a kingdom of grace and righteousness : that " as sin
reigned unto death, even so might grace through righteousness reign unto eternal life, by Jesus Christ our Lord ˢ.
And therefore we are said to be justified by " the righteousness of God ᵗ," that is, such a righteousness as is ours by
gift and grace, not by nature ᵘ; and such a righteousness
as God himself did perform, though in the human nature, in
our behalf ˣ.

And this is the ground of all our comfort, the best direction in all our miseries and extremities whither to fly. A
king is the greatest officer amongst men, and his honour
and state is for the support, defence, and honour of his people : he is ' Custos Tabularum,' the father and the keeper of
the laws. If I want any of that justice and equity, of which
his sacred bosom is the public treasure, I may freely beg it
of him, because he is an officer to dispense righteousness
unto his subjects ; so also is Christ unto his church. I
find myself in a miserable condition, condemned by the
conscience of sin, by the testimony of the Word, by
the accusations of Satan, full of discomforts: God is a
God of justice, and all fire ; myself a creature of sin, and
all stubble ; Satan the accuser of the brethren, who labours
to blow up the wrath of God against me. In this case
what shall I do ? Surely God " hath set his king on
Sion ;" and he is a king that hath life and righteousness to
give to me; that hath grace enough to quench all sin, and
the envenomed darts of Satan ; in whom there is erected a
court of peace and mercy, whereunto to appeal from the
severity of God, from the importunity of the Devil, and from
the accusations and testimonies of our own hearts. And indeed he had need be a king of righteousness that shall justify men; for our justification is in the remission of our sins;
and to pardon sins, and dispense with laws, is a regal dignity ; and God taketh it as his own high and peculiar prerogative, " I, even I, am he that blotteth out thine iniquity
for mine own sake, and will not remember thy sins ʸ." No
man, or angel, or created power, no merit, no obedience,
no rivers of oil, nor mountains of cattle, no prayers, tears,
or torments, can wipe out the stains, or remove the guilt

ˢ Rom. v. 21.   ᵗ Rom. iii. 21, 22.   ᵘ Rom. x. 4.   ˣ Acts xx. 28.
Phil. ii. 6, 7, 8.   ʸ Isai. xliii. 25.

of any sin; " I only, even I," and none else can do it; none but a divine and royal power can subdue sin ˢ.

And this is a ground of a second comfort, that, being a king of righteousness, he is rich in it, and hath treasures to bestow; that as we have a kingdom, a treasure, and abundance of sin; so we have a king, that hath always a residue of spirit and grace, that hath a most redundant righteousness " from faith to faith ᵃ." A man's faith can never overgrow the righteousness of our king. If we had all the faith that ever was in the world, put into one man, all that could not overclasp the righteousness of Christ, or be too big for it. As if a man had a thousand eyes, and they should, one after another, look on the sun, yet still the light would be revealed from eye to eye; or as if a man should go up by ten thousand steps to the top of the highest mountain, yet he could never overlook all the earth, or fix his eye beyond all visible objects, but should still have more earth and Heaven discovered unto him from step to step : so there is an immensity in the righteousness and mercy of God, which cannot be exhausted by any sins, or overlooked and comprehended by any faith of men. As God doth more and more reveal himself, and the righteousness of Christ unto the soul, so man maketh further progresses from " faith to faith." And therefore we should learn everlasting thankfulness unto this our king, that is pleased to be unto us a Melchizedek, a priest to satisfy his Father's justice, and a prince to bestow his own.

Note, Thirdly, Melchizedek was " king of Salem," that is, *of peace.* Here are two things to be noted; the place, a city of the Canaanites, and the signification thereof, which is *peace.* First, Then, we must observe, that Christ is a king of Canaanites, of Gentiles, of those that lived in abominable lusts : " Such were some of you; but ye are washed, but ye are sanctified, but ye are justified in the name of the Lord Jesus ᵇ." Be a man never so sinful or unclean, he hath not enough to pose or nonplus the mercy and righteousness of Christ; he can bring reconciliation and peace amongst Jebusites themselves. Though our father were an Amorite, our mother a Hittite; though we were Gentiles, estranged

ˢ Micah vii. 18.   ᵃ Rom. i. 17.   ᵇ 1 Cor. vi. 11.

from God in our thoughts, lives, hopes, ends; though we had justified Sodom and Samaria by our abominations;— yet he can make us "nigh by his blood," he can make our "crimson sins as white as snow," he can, for all that, estab- lish "an everlasting covenant" unto us [c]. I was a blas- phemer, a persecutor, very injurious to the Spirit of grace in his saints; I wasted, I worried, I haled into prison; I breathed out threatenings, I was mad, I made havock of the church, I was within one step of the unpardonable sin, nothing but ignorance between that and my soul: "How- beit for this cause I obtained mercy, that, in me first, Jesus Christ might show forth all long-suffering, for a pattern to them who should hereafter believe on him to life everlast- ing," saith St. Paul [d].

Let us make St. Paul's use of it: First, To love, and to believe in Christ, to accept as a most faithful and worthy saying, "That Christ came to save sinners;" indefinitely, without restriction, without limitation; and me, "though the chiefest of all others." Though I had more sins than earth or hell can lay upon me, yet if I feel them as heavy weights, and if I am willing to forsake them all,—let me not dishonour the power and unsearchable riches of Christ's blood,—even for such a sinner there is mercy. Secondly, To break forth into St. Paul's acknowledgment, "Now unto the King eternal, immortal, invisible, and only wise God;" to him that is a king of righteousness, and therefore hath abundance for me; that is eternal, and yet was born in time for me; immortal, yet died for me; invisible, yet was mani- fested in the flesh for me; the only wise God, and who made use of that wisdom to reconcile himself to me, and by the foolishness of preaching doth save the world, "be ho- nour and glory for ever and ever, Amen."

Secondly, From the signification of the Word, we may note, Where Christ is a king of righteousness, he is a king of peace too. So the prophet calleth him, "the Prince of Peace [e];" a creator and dispenser of peace. It is his own by propriety and purchase, and he leaves it unto us: "Peace I leave with you, my peace I give unto you; not as the world

---

[c] Ephes. ii. 11, 14. Isai. i. 18. Ezek. xvi. 60, 63.   [d] 1 Tim. i. 13, 1C.
[e] Isai. vi. 9.

giveth, give I unto you [f]." The world is either 'fallax' or
'inops;' either it deceives, or it is deficient: but peace is
mine, and I can give it. Therefore as the prophet Jeremiah
calleth him by the name of " Righteousness [g] ;" so the prophet
Micah calleth him by the name of " Peace:" " This man
shall be the peace, when the Assyrian shall come into our
land [h]." To which St. Paul alluding, calleth him εἰρήνη ἡμῶν,
" our peace [i] " By him, we have peace with God, being reconciled and ' recti in curia' again; " being justified by
faith, we have peace with God, through our Lord Jesus
Christ [j]." So that the heart can challenge all the world to
lay any thing to its charge. By him, we have peace with our
own consciences; for being sprinkled with his blood, they
are cleansed from dead works, and so we have " the witness
in ourselves," as the apostle speaketh [k]. By him, we have
peace with men. No more malice, envy, or hatred of one
another, after once " the kindness and love of God our Saviour towards men appeared [l]." All partition-walls are taken
down; and they which were two before, are both made
" one in him [m]:" and then there is towards the brethren a
love of communion,—towards the weak, a love of pity,—towards the poor, a love of bounty, either φιλαδελφία or ἀγάπη [n],
either brotherly love, or general love,—towards those without,
mercy, charity, compassion, forgiveness,—towards all, good
works. By him, we have peace with the creatures; we use
them with comfort, with liberty, with delight, with piety,
with charity, with mercy,—as glasses in the which we see,
and as steps by the which we draw nearer to, God. No rust
in our gold or silver; no moth nor pride in our garment; no
lewdness in our liberty; no hand against the wall; no flying
roll against the stone or beam of the house; no gravel in our
bread; no gall in our drink; no snare on our table; no
fears in our bed; no destruction in our prosperity: in all
estates we can rejoice; we can do and suffer all through
Christ that strengtheneth us. We are under the custody of
peace; it keeps our hearts and minds from fear of enemies,
and maketh us serve the Lord with confidence, boldness and
security [o]. " The works of righteousness are in peace, and

---

[f] John xiv. 27.   [g] Jer. xxxiii. 16.   [h] Micah v. 5.   [i] Ephes. ii. 14.
[j] Rom. v. 1.   [k] Heb. ix. 14. 1 John v. 10. Rom. viii. 16.   [l] Tit. iii. 3, 4.
[m] Ephes. ii. 14.   [n] 2 Pet. i. 7.   [o] Phil. iv. 7.

the effect of righteousness is quietness and assurance for
ever[o]."

Note, Fourthly, From both these, that is, from a peace
grounded in righteousness, needs must blessedness result:
for it is the blessedness of a creature to be re-united and one
with his Maker; to have all controversies ended, all dis-
tances swallowed up, all partitions taken down, and therefore the apostle useth[p] "righteousness" and "blessedness"
as terms promiscuous. All men seek for blessedness; it is
the sum and collection of all desires; a man loveth nothing
but in order and subordination unto that. And by nature
we are all children of wrath, and held under by the curse.
So many sins as we have committed, so many deaths and
curses have we heaped upon our souls, so many walls of separation have we set up between us and God, who is the
fountain of blessedness. Till all they be covered, removed,
forgiven, and forgotten, the creature cannot be blessed.
"Blessed are they whose iniquities are forgiven, and whose
sins are covered[q]." All the benedictions which we have
from the most high God, come unto us from the intercession
and mediation of Christ. His sacrifice and prayers give us
interest in the all-sufficiency of him that is above all, and so
are a security unto us against all adverse power or fear; for
what, or whom need that man fear, that is one with the most
high God? "If God be for us, who can be against us[r]?"
When God blesseth, his blessing is ever with effect and success; it cannot be reversed, it cannot be disappointed:
"Hath he said, and shall he not do it? or hath he spoken,
and shall he not make it good? Behold," saith Balaam, "I
have received commandment to bless; and he hath blessed,
and I cannot reverse it[s]."

Note, Fifthly, From Melchizedek's meeting Abraham returning from the slaughter of the kings, we may observe the
great forwardness that is in Christ, to meet and to bless his
people, when they have been in his service. "Thou meetest
him that rejoiceth and worketh righteousness[t].—I said I will
confess my sins, and thou forgavest the iniquity of my
sin[u]." No sooner did David resolve in his heart to return

---

[o] Isai. xxxii. 17.   [p] Rom. iv. 5, 9.   [q] Rom. iv. 7.   [r] Rom. viii. 31.
[s] Numb. xxiii. 19, 20.   [t] Isai. lxiv. 5.   [u] Psalm xxxii. 5.

to God, but presently the Lord prevented him with his
mercy, and anticipated his servant's confession with pardon
and forgiveness ;—"Thou preventest him with the blessings
of goodness ˣ." As the father of the prodigal, when he was
yet a great way off, far from that perfection which might in
strictness be required,—yet because he had set his face
homeward, and was now resolved to sue for pardon and re-
admittance, when he saw him, he had compassion, and *ran*
(the father's mercy was swifter than the son's repentance)
and fell on his neck and kissed him ʸ. We do not find the
Lord so hasty in his punishments, " He is slow to anger, and
doth not stir up all his wrath " together. He is patient and
long-suffering, " not willing that any should perish, but that
all should come to repentance." He comes, and he comes
again, and the third year he forbears, before he cuts down a
barren tree : but when he comes with a blessing, he doth not
delay, but prevents his people with goodness and mercy. O
how forward ought we to be to serve him, who is so ready to
meet us in his way, and to bless us!

Note, Sixthly, From the refection and preparations which
Melchizedek made for Abraham and for his men, we may
observe, That Christ, as king and priest, is a comforter and
refresher of his people in all their spiritual weariness, and
after all their services. This was the end of his unction, to
heal and to comfort his people : " The Spirit of the Lord is
upon me, because he hath anointed me to preach the gospel
to the poor ; he hath sent me to heal the broken-hearted, to
preach deliverance to the captives, and recovering of sight to
the blind, to set at liberty them that are bruised, and to
preach the acceptable year of the Lord ᶻ." To provide a
feast of fatted things, of wines on the lees, of fat things full
of marrow, of wine on the lees well refined ᵃ; to milk out
unto his people consolations and abundance of glory ᵇ; to
speak words in season to those that are weary, and to make
broken and dry bones to rejoice, and to flourish like a
herb ᶜ.

And this is a strong argument to hold up the patience,
faith, and hope of men in his service, and in all spiritual

ˣ Psal. xxi. 3.   ʸ Luke xv. 20.   ᶻ Luke iv. 18, 19.   ᵃ Isai. xxv. 6.
ᵇ Isai. lxvi. 11.   ᶜ Isai. l. 4. Psal. li. 8. Isai. lxvi. 14.

assaults ; we have a Melchizedek, which, after our combat
is ended, and our victory obtained, will give us refreshments at the last, and will meet us with his mercies. If we
faint not, but wait a while, " we shall see the salvation of
the Lord," that in the end " he is very pitiful and of tender
mercy [d]." " He is near at hand, his coming draweth nigh :
He is near that justifieth me ; who will contend with me?
Let us stand together. Who is mine adversary ? Let him
come near to me." The readiness of the Lord to help, is a
ground of challenge and defiance to enemies [e]. Job went
forth mourning, and had a great war to fight ; but the Lord
blessed his latter end more than his beginning ; and after his
battle was ended, met him, like Melchizedek, with re-
doubled mercies. David, Hezekiah, Heman the Ezrahite,
and many of the saints after their example, have had sore
and dismal conflicts, but at length their comforts have been
proportionable to their wrestlings ; they never wanted a
Melchizedek after their combats, to refresh them. " Rejoice
not against me, O mine enemy ; when I fall, I shall rise ;
when I sit in darkness, the Lord shall be a light unto me : I
will bear the indignation of the Lord, because I have sinned
against him, until he plead my cause, and execute judgement for me ; he will bring me forth to the light, and I shall
behold his righteousness [f]." He hath strength, courage, refection, spirit, to put into those that fight his battles ;
though they be but as Abraham, a family of three hundred
men, against four kings, yet he can cut Rahab, and wound
the dragon, and make a way in the sea for the ransomed to
pass over, and cause his redeemed to return with singing,
and with joy and gladness upon their heads : " I, even I, am
he that comforteth you ; who art thou that thou shouldst be
afraid of a man that shall die, and of the son of man that
shall be as grass [g]."

Note, Seventhly, From Melchizedek's receiving of tithes
from Abraham (which the apostle taketh special notice of,
four or five times together, in one chapter [h]), we may observe, that Christ is a receiver of homage and tribute from
his people. There was never any type of Christ as a priest,

---

[d] Exod. xiv. 13. James v. 11.   [e] Phil. iv. 5. James v. 8. Isai. l. 8, 9.
[f] Micah vii. 8, 9.   [g] Isai. li. 12.   [h] Heb. vii. 2, 4, 6, 8, 9.

but he received tithes; and that not in the right of any thing
in himself, but merely in the virtue of his typical office,—so
that originally they did manifestly pertain to that principal
priest, whom these represented, whose personal priesthood [i]
is standing, unalterable, and eternal, and therefore the rights
thereunto belonging are such too.

If it be objected, Why then did not Christ in his life receive tithes? I answer, First, Because though he were
the substance, yet the standing typical priesthood was not
abolished, till after his ministry on earth was finished : for
his priesthood was not consummate till his sitting at the
right hand of God. Secondly, Because he took upon him a
voluntary poverty for especial reasons belonging to the state
of his humiliation, and to the dispensation of man's redemption [k]. You will say, Now Christ's priesthood is consummate, and he himself is in Heaven, whither no tithes can be
sent, therefere none are due, because he hath no typical
priests on earth to represent him.—I answer, Though he be
in Heaven in his body, yet he is on earth in his ministry,
and in the dispensation of the virtue of his sacrifice ; and
the ministers of the gospel are " in his stead [l]" and ought to
be received as " Christ himself[m]." So then men are not by
this excused from rendering God's dues unto him ; First,
Because there is, in respect of him, whose sacrifice we commemorate and show forth to the people, due a testification
of homage unto him : Secondly, Because in respect of us,
there is due a reward of our labour; for " the labourer is
worthy of his hire." To lay all together in one view, inasmuch as all the types of Christ as a priest, have received
tithes as due ; and inasmuch as that right was not grounded
upon any thing in or from themselves, but upon their typical
office, and so did originally pertain to the principal priest
whom they typified ; and inasmuch as his person and office
is eternal, and therefore such are all the ' annexa' and dues
thereof; and inasmuch as he hath no where dispensed with,
or denied, or refused, or revoked this right which from him,
as the principal, all his types ever enjoyed ; and lastly, inas-

i Dicit Apostolus, ad tempus decimas Levitis solutas fuisse, quia non semper
viverent ; Melchizedek vero, quia immortalis fit, retinere usque in finem quod à
Deo semel illi datum est.   Calv. in Heb. vii. 8.   k 2 Cor. viii. 9.   l 2 Cor.
v. 20.   m Gal. iii. 14.

much as he hath left to the ministers of his Word, the dispensation of his sacrifice, and made them his " ambassadors," and in " his stead" to the church, to set forth him crucified in his ordinances ; for my part I do not see why unto them, in the name and right of their master, those rights should not be due, which were manifestly his in his types, and of which himself hath no where in his Word declared any revocation.

But not to enter upon any disputes or unwelcome controversies, thus much I cannot by the way but observe, That these,—who labour in the Word and doctrine, and therein are ambassadors for Christ, and stand in his stead to reveal the mysteries, and dispense the treasures of his blood in the church,—ought to have, by way of homage to Christ, and by way of recompense and retribution to themselves, a liberal maintenance, befitting the honour and dignity of that person whom they represent, and of that service wherein they minister : The apostle saith, That they are worthy of double honour [n], an honour of reverence, and an honour of maintenance ;—and doubtless the very heathen shall rise up in judgement against many, who profess the truth in both these respects; for the heathen themselves did show so much honour to their devilish priests, that I remember one of the Roman consuls [o] seeing a priest and some vestal virgins going on foot, and he riding on his chariot, descended, and would not go into it again, till those diabolical votaries were first placed ; nay, the very kings and emperors in Greece, Egypt, Rome, &c. thought it one of the greatest honours to be withal the priests of the people. Amongst the Christians, when the Synod of Nice was assembled by Constantine's command, and some accusations, or (as the historian [p] calleth them) calumniations were presented to the emperor against some bishops and ministers, he looked not on the particulars, but sealed them up with his own signet; and having first reconciled the parties, commanded the libels to be burnt, adding withal, that if he should himself see a bishop in adultery, he would cover his nakedness with his own royal robe ; " Because," saith he, " the sins of such

[n] 1 Tim. v. 17, 18.   Lam. iv. 16.   Phil. ii. 29.   2 Cor. i. 41.   Hosea iv. 4.
[o] Liv.—Alex. ab Alex. lib 2. cap. 8. Clem. Alex. Stro. lib. 7.—Diodor, Sicul. lib. 2.—Theodoret. Hist. lib. 1. cap. 11.—Socrat. lib. 1. cap. 8.

men ought not to be divulged, lest their example do as much
hurt to the souls of others, as their fact to their own : for as
a good life is necessary for themselves, so is their good fame
necessary for others [r]." The meaning of that noble prince,
was not that such men's sins should go unexamined, or ex-
empted from punishment, but to show both in how high
honour they who are worthy in that function, ought to be
had for their work's sake [s]; and how wary men should be in
giving liberty to their tongues or distempered passions to
censure, mis-report, or scandalize the persons and parts of
such men, against whom Timothy was not to receive an ac-
cusation without two or three witnesses [t]; and to give notice
of those ill consequences, which would ensue upon the public observation of the sins of those men, who in their doctrine preach the truth, and build up the church.   For doubtless of other men who preach lies in hypocrisy, there cannot
too much of their secret villanies and personal uncleanness
be detected, that so the lewdness of their lives may stop the
progress and growth of their evil doctrine.

But to return to the point that I am upon : liberal maintenance is due to those that labour in the Word and doctrine,
out of justice, and not out mercy, for their work's sake.   I
will not press the examples of heathens themselves in this
duty, for the shame of Christians.   We find that the priests
of Egypt [u] had portions out of the king's own treasuries, and
that their lands were still reserved unto them [x].   And we find
besides these lands, that they had the third part of all yearly
tributes and levies, as Diodorus Siculus [y] tells us.   But we
will first look upon the example of God's own priests and
Levites under the law : Secondly, Upon the precepts and
commands of the gospel.   God is not less mindful of ministers under the gospel, than of those under the law.   Now
then, if you will not believe that a liberal maintenance is
now by God allotted unto us, look what he did allot unto
them [z]: first, look upon the proportion of their persons, and
then upon the proportion of their maintenance : for their
persons, it would not be hard to prove that the tribe of Levi,
though the thirteenth part of the people in regard of their
civil division, were not yet the fortieth part of the people.

---

[r] Vita Episcoporum sibi, fama aliis necessaria. *Aug.*   [s] 1 Thes. v. 12, 13.
[t] 1 Tim. v. 19.   [u] *Plin.* lib. 12. cap. 14.—*Alex. ab Alex.* lib. 3. cap. 22.
[x] Gen. xlvii. 22.   [y] Lib. 2.   [z] Vid. *Selden's* Review of his History, cap. 2.

Look into the numbering of them, and compare Number i. 46. with iii. 39. The other tribes were numbered from twenty years old and upward, all that were able to bear arms, which was to the age of fifty years, as Josephus reports; for, at that age, they were supposed to be unserviceable for war;—and yet thus their number amounted to six hundred and three thousand five hundred and fifty men, able to go to war. The Levites, on the other side, were numbered from one month old and upward ; and yet the whole sum amounted but to twenty and two thousand. Now conjecture the number of those in the other tribes, who were under twenty years of age, and who were too old for warlike service, to be but half as many as the rest ; yet the whole number of the tribes, reckoned from their infancy upward, will amount, at the least, to nine hundred and two thousand men. Of which number, the number of the Levites is just the one and fortieth part. After, we find, that they increased to a mighty number more [b]; but the whole people increased accordingly : for the tribe of Judah, which was before but seventy-four thousand, was then five hundred thousand, and, in Jehoshaphat's time, eleven hundred thousand at least [c]. Well then, the Levites were but the fortieth part of the people (not so much), so that that tribe was but almost a quarter as numerous as the rest. Now look in the next place to the proportion of their mainteance. One would think, that the fortieth part of the people could require but the fortieth part of the maintenance in proportion. But, First, They had the tenth of all the increase of seed, and fruit, and great and small cattle [d]. Secondly, They had forty-eight cities with suburbs for gardens, and for cattle [e] :—which cities were next to the best, and, in many tribes, the best of all ; in Judah, Hebron,—in Benjamin, Gibeon, both royal cities: so that those, with about a mile suburb to every one of them, can come to little less than the wealth of one tribe alone, in that little country, which from Dan to Beersheba was about a hundred and sixty miles long. Thirdly, They had all the first-fruits of clean and unclean beasts [f]; of the fruits of the earth, and the fleece of the sheep [g] ; of men to be redeemed [h]. Fourthly, The meat-

---

[b] 1 Chron. xxxiii. 3   [c] 2 Sam. xxiv. 2. Chron. vii.   [d] Levit. xxvii. 30.
[e] Numb. xxxv. 2.   [f] Numb. xviii. 13.   [g] Deut. xviii. 4. Neh. x. 35.
[h] Numb. xviii. 15.

offerings, the sin-offerings, the trespass-offerings, the heave-offerings, and the wave-offerings, were all theirs [i]. Fifthly, They had all vows and voluntary oblations, and consecrations, and every hallowed thing [k]. Sixthly, Excepting the Holocaust, they had either the shoulder, or the breast, or the skin, or something of every sacrifice which was offered [l]. Seventhly, The males were to appear three times a-year before the Lord, and they were not to come empty handed [m]. Lastly, Unto them did belong many recompenses of injury, which was the restitution of the principal, and a fifth part [n]. Now put the tithes, the cities, and these other constant revenues together; and the priests and Levites, who were but about a quarter as many as one tribe, had yet about three times the revenues of one tribe.

But to leave this argument. Let us consider what the apostle saith ; " Let him that is taught in the Word, communicate to him that teacheth, ἐν πᾶσιν ἀγαθοῖς, in all *his goods,*" as Beza well expounds it [o].—" The elders that labour in the Word and doctrine, are worthy of double honour: for the Scripture saith, Thou shalt not muzzle the ox that treadeth out the corn, and the labourer is worthy of his reward [p]."— "Who goeth a warfare, at any time, at his own charges? Who planteth a vineyard, and eateth not of the fruit thereof? or who feedeth a flock, and eateth not of the milk of the flock ? Say I these things as a man" (that is, am I partial ? do I speak merely out of affection, and human favour to mine own cause, or calling ?) " or saith not the law the same also ? For it is written in the law of Moses, Thou shalt not muzzle the mouth of the ox that treadeth out the corn. Doth God take care for oxen ? or saith he it altogether for our sakes ?" That is, Doth God provide laws for rewarding and encouraging the labour of brute beasts, and doth he leave the maintenance and honour of his own immediate officers to the arbitrary and pinching allowances of covetous and cruel men ? "For our sakes, no doubt, this is written, That he that plougheth, should plough in hope; and he that thresheth in hope, should be partaker of his hope: " That is, that the encouragement of the ministers, in their service, might

i Numb. xviii. 9, 10, 11.　k Numb. xviii. 8, 9.　l Numb. xviii. 18. Lev. vii. Deut. xviii. 3.　m Exod. xxiii. 15, 17.　n Numb. v. 7, 8.　o Gal. vi. 6 p 1 Tim. v. 17, 18.

depend upon such a hope, as is grounded on God's law and provision ; and that they might not be left to the wills and allowances of those men, against whose sins they were sent. And this the apostle proveth by an argument, drawn from a most answerable equity : — " If we have sown unto you spiritual things, is it a great thing if we shall reap your carnal things ?" If ye do rightly judge of those heavenly treasures which we bring in abundance unto you, impossible it is that ye should judge our pains and service towards your immortal and precious souls, sufficiently rewarded with a narrow and hungry proportion of earthly and perishable things. " Do ye not know, that they which minister about holy things, live of the things of the temple ? And they which wait at the altar, are partakers with the altar ?" To note that they receive their maintenance from the hand of God himself, whose only the things of the altar are, and not from men. " Even so hath the Lord ordained, that they which preach the gospel, should live by the gospel ꟼ." And what is it *to live?* First, They must live as men : they must have for necessity and for delight. Secondly, They must live as believers : " He that provideth not for his own, is worse than an infidel ʳ." They must therefore have, by the gospel, sufficient to lay up for those, whom the law of common humanity, much more of faith, commands them to provide for. Thirdly, They must live as ministers. They must have wherewith to maintain the duties of their calling, a good example of piety and charity and hospitality, that they may confirm by practice, what in doctrine they teach ˢ. And the instruments of their calling, which is a profession of so vast and unlimited a compass of learning (for there is no part of learning in the whole circle thereof which is not helpful, and may not contribute to the understanding of holy Scriptures, and to some part or other of a divine employment), cannot but be very chargeable. And alas, how many men preach the gospel, and yet scarce find the first and meanest of all these supplies! This is the great ingratitude of the world, and withal the malice and policy of Satan,—by the poverty and contempt of the ministers, to bring the gospel itself into contempt, and to deter able men from adventuring on so

ꟼ 1 Cor. ix. 7, 13.   ʳ 1 Tim. v. 8.   ˢ 1 Tim. iii. 2.

unrewarded a calling, as Calvin [t] justly complains. All that
can, with colour or countenance, be pretended by those who
are guilty of this neglect, is poverty and disability to maintain the gospel. And it were well, if there were not places
to be found, wherein dogs and horses, hawks and hounds,
grow fat with God's portion; and the mercenary preacher,
when he grows lean with want, is accused of too much study.
But suppose that poverty be truly alleged : do we think poverty a just pretext for the neglect of a moral duty? May a
man spend the Lord's day on his shopboard, because he is
poor, and wants means? And if I may not rob God of his
time, upon pretence of poverty, neither then is the same any
argument to rob him of his portion. " Be not deceived, God
is not mocked ;" namely, with pretence of poverty and necessity, as Calvin expounds that place [u]. St. Paul bears witness unto some men, that " they did good beyond their
power," that they were richly liberal, though they were
deeply poor [x] : And yet those were but contributions out of
mercy; whereas, double honour is due to the ministers of the
gospel by a law of justice. It is a wrong and foolish apology,
to pretend the punishment for the continuance of the fault.
The poverty of many men is, doubtless, a just recompense
for their neglect of the honour of the gospel :—for God hath
ever severely punished the contempt and dishonour done to
his messengers [y]. Whereas, on the other side, do thou deal
faithfully with God ; fulfil to thy power his appointment and
decree, that they which preach the gospel, may live by the
gospel, and then hearken unto God : " Honour the Lord
with thy substance and the first-fruits of all thine increase;
so shall thy barns be filled with plenty, and thy presses burst
out with new wine [z]." — " Consider now from this day and
upward, from the day that the foundation of the Lord's tem-

---

t Hic est actus Satanæ, alimentis fraudare pios Ministros, ut Ecclesia talibus de-
stituatur, &c. *Calvin.* in Gal. vi. 6. Satan hac arte tentat doctrinâ privare Ecclesiam,
dum, inopiæ et famis metu, plurimos absterret, ne id oneris suscipiant. *Idem* in
1 Tim. v. 17.—Vid. *Muscul.* in Gal. vi. 6. et in 1 Tim. iii. 2.—Bishop *Jewel's*
Sermons on Hag. i, 2, 3, 4, page 181, 182, on Psalm xcix. 9, page 191, 194.—
Perkins in his Sermon of ' The Duties and Dignities of the Ministry.'—*Hooker's*
Eccl. policy, lib. 5. Num. 79.—*Hildersham* on John iv. page 300, 301, 319, 323.—
Bolton in his epistle dedicatory to his discourse of True Happiness.—*Greg. Tholos.*
de Repub. lib. 13, cap. 17.   u Gal. vi. 7.   x 2 Cor. viii. 2, 3.   y 2 Chron.
xvi. 10, 12. xxiv. 11, 25. xxvi. 19, 20. xxxvi. 16, 17.   z Prov. iii. 9. 10.

ple was laid, consider it. Is the seed yet in the barn? From this day I will bless you [a]." — " Ye are cursed with a curse; for ye have robbed me, even this whole nation. Bring ye all the tithes into the storehouse, that there may be meat in mine house, and prove me herewith, saith the Lord of Hosts" (if ye will not do it out of duty, yet do it out of experiment), " if I will not open you the windows of Heaven, and pour you out a blessing, that there shall not be room enough to receive it [b]." There was never any man lost by paying God his dues; there was never any man thrived by grudging, or pittancing the Almighty. I will conclude this point with the apostle. It is his doctrine; " Faithful ministers are worthy of double honour." And it is his exhortation; " Render to all their dues, tribute to whom tribute, custom to whom custom, fear to whom fear, honour to whom honour [c]."

Note, Lastly [d], The priesthood of Christ is an everlasting priesthood. He also was without father, and without mother, without beginning of days, or end of life. As man, without a father; as God, without a mother; " The same, yesterday and to-day, and for ever [e]." His name was " Everlasting Father [f]." His gospel an " Everlasting gospel [g]." He was " a Lamb, slain from the beginning of the world [h]." The virtue of his blood goes backward, as high as Adam. He was fore-ordained before the foundation of the world [i]. The redemption of those, that transgressed under the first testament, the remission of sins that were past, were procured by this sacrifice [k]. It goeth downward to the end of the world; he must reign, till all be put under his feet, and he must raise up all by the power and virtue of his victory over death [l]; and lastly, It goeth onward to all immortality: for though the acts and administration of his priesthood shall cease, when he shall have delivered the kingdom to his Father, and have brought the whole church into God's presence; yet the virtue and fruits of those acts shall be absolutely eternal: for so long as the saints shall be in Heaven, so long they shall enjoy the benefit of that sacrifice, which did purchase not a lease, or expiring term; but ζωὴν ἀκατάλυτον, " an endless life," an everlasting glory, an inheritance incorruptible, and that fadeth not away, reserved in the Heaven for them.

[a] Hag. ii. 18, 19.   [b] Mal. iii. 9, 12.   [c] Rom. xiii. 3.   [d] *Greg. Naz.* Orat. 36. de Folio.   [e] Heb. xiii. 8.   [f] Isai. ix. 6.   [g] Rev. xiv. 6.   [h] 1 Pet. i. 19.   [i] 2 Tim. i. 9.   [k] Heb. ix. 15. Rom. iii. 25.   [l] John v. 26, 29.

VERSES V. AND VI.

The Lord, at thy right hand, shall strike through kings in the day of his wrath. He shall judge amongst the heathen; he shall fill the places with dead bodies; he shall wound the heads over many countries.

In the former part of the Psalm, we have had the description of Christ's offices, of *king* and *priest*, together with the effects thereof in gathering a *willing people* unto himself. Now here the prophet showeth another effect of the powerful administration of these offices, containing his victories over all his enemies, allegorically expressed in an hypotyposis, or lively allusion unto the manner of human victories: wherein, First, I shall, in a few words, labour to clear the sense; and then the observations which are natural, will the more evidently arise.

" *The Lord at thy right hand*." To lay aside their exposition who understand these words of God the Father,—the words are an apostrophe of the prophet to those, at whose right hand the Lord Jesus is. Some make it an apostrophe to God the Father, a triumphal and thankful prediction of that power and judgement, which he hath given to this his Benjamin, the Son at his right hand; because that thereby the phrase retaineth the same signification and sense, which it had in the first verse. As if David had said, ' O God, the Father of all power and majesty, worthy art thou of all praise, thanksgiving, and honour, who hast given such power to thy son in the behalf of thy church, as to smite through kings, and judge heathen, and pull down the chief of his enemies, and to subdue all things to himself:' and these read it thus, " O *Lord. he that is at thy right hand, shall strike through kings*," &c. Others make it to be an apostrophe to the church, and so to be a phrase not expressing Christ's exaltation, as verse 1. but his care and protection over his church, his readiness to assist and defend his own people against all the injuries and assaults of

adverse power. Solomon saith, "A wise man's heart is
at his right hand, but a fool's heart is at his left ᵃ:" That is,
his heart is ready and prepared to execute any wise counsels
or godly resolutions; as the prophet David saith, "My
heart is prepared, O God, my heart is prepared ; I will sing
and give thanks." But a fool's heart, when he should do any
thing, is like his left hand, to seek of skill, inactive, and
unprepared ; when he walketh by the way, "his heart faileth him ᵇ." And this readiness and present help of God, to
defend and guide his church, is expressed frequently by his
being at the right hand thereof;—" Because the Lord is at
my right hand, I shall not be moved ᶜ."—" He shall stand at
the right hand of the poor to save him ᵈ."—" I the Lord thy
God will hold thy right hand, saying unto thee, Fear not, I
will help thee ᵉ." As if David had said, ' Be not dismayed
nor cast down, O ye subjects of this king ; as if, being exalted to God's right hand, he had given over the care and
protection of his people : for as he is at the right hand of
his Father in glory and majesty ; so is he at your right hand
too, standing to execute judgement on your enemies, and to
reveal the power of his arm towards you in your protection.'

Now the reasons of this phrase and expression, as I conceive, are these two:—First, To note that Christ's power,
providence, and protection, do not exclude, but only
strengthen, assist, and prosper the ordinary and just endeavours of the church for themselves. The Lord is not at our
left hand to succour us in our idleness and negligence, but at
our *working* hand, to give success to our honest endeavours.
The sword of the Lord doth not fight without the sword of
Gideon ᶠ. In the miracles of Christ, when he fed and feasted
men, he never created wine or bread of nothing ; but
blessed, and so changed, or multiplied that which was, by
human industry, prepared before. Our Saviour had fish and
bread of his own; and yet he would have his disciples put
in their net and catch, and bring of their own ;—to note
unto us, that God's power and providence must not exclude
but encourage man's industry ᵍ. He protecteth us ' in viis
nostris, non in præcipitiis,' in our own ways, not in our

ᵃ Eccles. x. 2.　　ᵇ Eccles. x. 3.　　ᶜ Psalm xvi. 8.　　ᵈ Psalm cix. 31.
ᵉ Isai. xxxi. 13.　　ᶠ Judg. vii. 18.　　John xxi. 9, 10.

precipices or presumptions [h]. So long then as the church
is valiant and constant in withstanding the enemies of
her peace and prosperity, God is undoubtedly with her
to bless that courage, and to strengthen that right hand.
So long as Moses held up his hand, God fought for
Israel. There was Joshua's sword, and Moses' hand or
prayer, and, upon those, God's blessing [i]. And they
were all to concur: if the sword should cease, the prayer
would do no good; for God will not be tempted: if the
prayer faint, the sword is in vain; for God will not be
neglected:—as, in a curious clock, stop any wheel, and
you hinder the whole motion. If God promise to be
present, Joshua must promise to be courageous [k]. Secondly, To note unto us the care and military wisdom of
Christ our captain, to meet with and to prevent our enemies,
and to intercept their blows against us; for we may observe
in the Scripture, that Satan plieth the right hand of the
church, laboureth to weaken and assault us, where there is
most danger towards him. " Let Satan stand at his right
hand [l]; " that is, Give him over to the rage of Satan, that he
may be hurried to execute his will.—Thus "Satan stood at
the right hand of Joshua, the High-priest, to resist him [m]; "
noting the assiduous and indefatigable endeavours of Satan
to resist, disappoint, and overthrow the works of the
worthies in God's church, ("I would have come unto you,
even I Paul, once again, but Satan hindered us [n]; ") and to
divert the strength of men upon his service. And therefore
to rebuke him, and to show to the church that our strength
is from him, and due unto him, he also stands there to out-
vie the temptations and impulsions of Satan.

These are the two expositions, which are given of these
words, " *The Lord at thy right hand.*" Now though, of all
places of Scripture, there is indeed but one literal sense; yet
when two are given, which both tend unto the same general
scope, and are suitable not only to the analogy of faith, but
to the meaning mainly aimed at by the Holy Ghost in the
place, and when there is no apparent evidence in the face
of the text, for preferring one before the other; I think it is

h Psalm xci. 11.   i Exod. xvii. 12, 13.   k Josh. i. 5, 6, 9.   l Psalm cix. 6.
m Zech. iii. 1.   n 1 Thes. ii. 18.

not unfit to embrace both ; and so something I shall touch
upon both senses.

"*Shall strike through,*" or wound, or make gore-bloody,
"*kings in the day of his wrath.*" The word is, "*Hath
stricken* through kings." It is a prophecy of things future,
spoken as of things to be done : *To strike through,* notes a
complete victory and full confusion of the enemy,—an incu-
rable wound, that they may stagger, and fall, and rise up no
more, and that affliction may not arise a second time [o]. The
only difficulty is, what is meant by "*kings :*" for which we
must note, That the kingdom of Christ is spiritual, and his
war spiritual, and therefore his enemies, for the most part,
spiritual. Therefore I take it, we are hereby to understand the most potent enemies of Christ ; whether spiritual,
" We wrestle not against flesh and blood, but against principalities and powers, and spiritual wickedness in high
places [p] :" or carnal, as heathen and wicked men [q] ; the
fat and the strong enemies of the church [r]. Our spiritual
enemies in Scripture are called "kings :" " Satan the *prince*
of this world [s], the god of this world [t], the *prince* of the
power of the air [u], the *king* of the locusts [x]," &c. Sin and
original concupiscence is a king : " Let not sin *reign* in your
mortal bodies." And the earthly enemies of Christ are
called kings : " The ten horns [y], that is, *ten kings,* make war"
with the Lamb ;—" The *kings* of the earth stood up, and the
rulers were gathered together against the Lord, and his
Christ [z]." And death, which is the last enemy, is a king :
" The king of terrors," that reigneth over men. And over
all these kings do the victories of Christ reach.—Some, by
kings, understand the Roman emperors, who are called
" kings [a]," and their overthrow, for persecuting the church.
But since all sorts of Christ's enemies are called kings in
Scripture, and all of them do push at his kingdom in the
church,—I see no ground why we may not, by *kings,* understand them all, with their subjects, armies, and associates.
As in great victories the lords and principal men are said to

o Nahum i. 9. 1 Sam. xxvi 8.   p Ephes. vi. 12. 2 Cor. x. 4.   q Psal.
ii. 8, 9.   r Ezek. xxxiv. 16.   s John xvi. 11.   t 2 Cor. iv. 4.
u Ephes. ii. 2.   x Rev. ix. 11.   y Rev. xvii. 12, 14.   z Psal. ii. 9.
Acts iv. 27. 1 Cor. ii. 8.   a 1 Pet. ii. 13, 17.

be overcome, when the servants and soldiers are routed and slain.

" *In the day of his wrath:*" That is, when time hath ripened the insolency and malice of the enemy, when his fury is fully stirred up and provoked, when the just and full time of his glory is come; that it may appear that they are overcome not by time, or chance, or human power, or secular concurrence, but only by the power of his wrath he will do it. Christ is never destitute of power; but in wisdom he hath ordered the times of his church, when to have his church suffer and bear witness to him, and when to triumph in his deliverances. So the meaning of this clause is this, When the day of recompense is come, when the sins and provocation of his enemy is ripe, when the utmost period of his patience is expired, ἐν προθεσμίᾳ, in the fixed and immovable day which he hath set, be the probabilities never so poor, and preparations never so small, the expectations never so low, the means in human view never so impossible,—yet then, by his wrath, he will utterly and incurably wound his enemies, both spiritual and temporal, that they shall not rise a second time.

" *He shall judge amongst the Heathen.*" The word "judgement" noteth both government and punishment. "The Lord shall judge his people, and repent himself for his servants, when he seeth that their power is gone [b]:" there, "to judge" noteth government.—"The Lord standeth up to plead, and to judge his people [c]:" "That nation whom they serve, will I judge [d]:" there, "to judge" noteth punishment. Here it is taken for executing condemnation upon the contumacious adversaries of the gospel of Christ amongst the Gentiles, as in the great victory of Gog and Magog [e]: some, by Gentiles [f], understand all enemies, both spiritual and earthly.

" *He shall fill the places with dead bodies.*" That notes both the swiftness of the victory, and the greatness of the victory. That it shall be so general and so speedy, that the enemy shall have either none left; or they that are

---

[b] Deut. xxxii. 36.   [c] Isai. iii. 13.   [d] Gen. xv. 14.   [e] Ezek. 39.
[f] *Glass.* in Isai. lxiii. 6.

left, shall not be able nor have leisure to bury their dead bodies [g].

" *He shall wound the head over divers countries* [h]." That is, either the principal of his enemies every where ; or Satan, who is the god of the world, that ruleth as head over the children of disobedience in all places ; or antichrist, the head of nations, the chief of God's enemies [i].

" *The Lord at thy right hand.*" According to the twofold apostrophe before mentioned, here are two observations which I will but touch.   First, That God the Father is worthy to have all the power, majesty, and judgement, which he hath given to his Son our Mediator, for our protection, salvation, and defence, most thankfully and triumphantly acknowledged to him.   We find our Saviour himself praising God in this behalf, that he had delivered all things into his hand, even power to make babes believe on him [k].   And this St. Paul is frequent in, namely, in praising and glorifying God for Christ : " O wretched man that I am, who shall deliver me ? &c.   I thank God through Jesus Christ our Lord. [l]"   All the promises of God are in him Yea, and in him Amen, " to the glory of God " by us. [m] He gave himself for our sins, that he might deliver us from this present evil world, according to the will of God and our Father, " To whom be glory " for ever and ever, Amen [n].—Every tongue must confess that Jesus Christ is Lord " to the glory" of God the Father [o].

And reason there is, that it should thus be acknowledged to the Father ; because he hath all his kingdom and power in the church from the Father : " All power is given unto me."—" He hath given him a name above every name:" and this the Son hath revealed to us, that so he might " manifest the name ;" that is, get glory to his Father thereby [p].   For, in Christ, it was God that reconciled the world to himself.   Secondly, He hath it all given unto him in our nature, in our behalf, and as our head ; so that we, in the gifts of God to him, were only respected ;

---

[g] Ezck. xxxix. 11.   [h] Hab. iii. 13. Psal. lxviii. 21.   [i] Rev. xiii. 7, 8.
xiv. 8, 17. xv. 18.   [k] Matth. xi. 25, 27.   [l] Rom. vii. 25. 1 Tim. i. 16, 17.
[m] 2 Cor. i. 19, 20.   [n] Gal. i. 4, 5.   [o] Phil. ii. 11.   [p] John xvii. 6, 7.

and therefore we have reason to praise God for them. It
was not indeed given to him strictly (for it was not to him
' Beneficium,' but ' Onus,' an office, but not a benefit), but
to him for us, or to us in and by him. In all the victories,
deliverances, refreshments, experiences of God's power and
goodness, we must ever remember to praise God in and
through his Son ; to acknowledge the power of his right
hand, which is not now against his church, but against the
enemies of his church. For therefore the deliverance of his
church is ascribed to God's *right hand ;* because he hath
there one to plead, to entreat, to move his right hand in
our behalf. Therefore in all our distresses, in all conflicts and
temptations, we must, by faith, look up unto God's right
hand ; put him in remembrance of that faithfulness, righteousness, atonement, and intercession, which is there made
in our behalf. There we have matter enough to fill our
mouths and hearts with praises and triumph and rejoicing
in him : " It is Christ who is at the right hand of God ; who
shall separate us from the love of Christ q ?" Here are two arguments of the church's safety and triumph. The ' love ' of
Christ, and the ' honour' of Christ. He loveth all his to
the end. But what good can love do without power ?
Therefore he that loveth us, is exalted by God, and hath
all power given him for this purpose, that his love may do
us good. In the conflicts of my corruptions (which are an
adversary too wise, too subtile, too numberless for me to
vanquish) I may yet, when I am driven to Paul's extremity,
rest in his thanksgiving ; and looking up to Jesus, who will
be the finisher of every good work which he begins, and
seeing him at God's right hand, may triumph in the power
and office which God hath given to his Son there,—which
is, to subdue our iniquities, and to sanctify us by his truth,
and by that residue of Spirit which he keepeth for the
church r ; for that prayer is a model, as it were, and coun-
terpart of Christ's intercession : for, saith he, " I come to
thee, and speak these things in the world, that they may
have my joy fulfilled in them s ;" that is, That they, having
a specimen and form of that intercession which with thee
I shall make for them, left upon public record for them to

q Rom. viii. 34, 35.   r John xvii. 17, 19.   s John verse 13.

look on,—and there finding that their sanctification is the
business of my sitting at thy right hand, may, in the midst
of the discomforts and conflicts of their corruptions, have a
full joy and triumph in the honour which thou hast given
me.'—I am beset with the temptations of mine enemies, and
persecutions for the name of Christ: –in this case I may
give God praise for the power, which he hath given to his
Son : I may, from mine enemies, appeal unto God's right
hand : I may, like Stephen, when the stones and buffets
are about my soul, look up by faith, and see there my captain standing up in my defence [t] : I may acknowledge unto
God the power given unto his Son ; that though nothing of
all this fall upon me without his provision and permission,
yet sure I am, that he hath power and mercy in his right
hand, that though mine enemies were as strong as a combination and army of kings, yet the Lord at his right hand
hath, from him in my behalf, received power enough to
strike through kings, when the day of his wrath is come.

Note, Secondly, Christ is at the right hand of his people,
present with them, and prepared to defend them from all
their enemies : present by his Spirit to strengthen, comfort,
and uphold them, enabling them to glory and rejoice in all
their sufferings, as knowing that they are but for a moment,
and that which is needful to purge their faith, and to make
them bear their shame[u], and to glorify the consequent power
of Christ, which shall be revealed to their joy[x], when he will
recompense double to us in mercy, and to our enemies in
severity[y]: present by his mighty power, and by his angels, to
rescue, deliver, and protect them ; to be as a wall of fire, as
a shield, a buckler, a rock, a captain to his people [z].

And this is the ground of all the church's comfort, That
more is with them than against them. The enemies have
combinations and confederacies of men; but the church
hath Emmanuel, God with them[a] : none can pull Christ
from the hand of God, or from the right hand of his people;
that is, none can take away either his power or his love
from his people. The church and truth can never be crushed
and overthrown, no more than a rock with the raging of

---

[t] Acts vii. 55.   [u] 1 Peter i. 6, 7. Jam. i. 2, 3. Isai. xxvii. 8, 9.   [x] 1 Pet.
iv. 13.   [y] Isai. liv. 7, 8. lxi. 7.   [z] Zech. ii. 5.   [a] Isai. viii. 9, 10.

the waves : they are heavenly things; and therefore nothing
of earth or hell can reach to corrupt them. It was but a
vain attempt of the giants to build a tower to heaven. The
world was made, that there might be therein a church to
worship and contemplate that God which made it: therefore
in the creation, God never rested till he came to a church,
to note, that that was the end thereof: and therefore it is
easier to pull down the world, and to shake in pieces the
frame of nature, than to ruin the church. The church hath
Christ for her husband, he to whom all knees must bend,
he whom every tongue must confess, he who will subdue all
things to himself: so she hath love, power, and jealousy, all
three very strong things, on her side. And therefore the only
way to be safe, is to keep Christ at our right hand, to hold
fast his truth, worship, and obedience : for so long as we
have Emmanuel, all adverse power is but flesh, and all flesh
is but grass, withered in a moment when God will blow
upon it.

Note, Thirdly, Christ, in his appointed time, will utterly
overthrow the greatest enemies of his kingdom, and deliver
his church from under the sorest oppressions. There
is not any one argument in the holy Scriptures more
frequently repeated, than this of Christ's victories: prefigured they were in the deliverance of Israel out of Egypt [b];
in the deliverances of the ark out of the waters [c]; in the deliverance of the Jews from Babylon [d];—to note, that, in the
sorest extremities and greatest improbabilities, God will
show himself jealous for his people. This victory is expressed by " treading of a wine-press [e]:" when there are none
to help, when the church is brought to sorest extremities,
though multitudes meet against her, as many as the grapes
in a vintage, they shall all be but as clusters of grapes ; he
shall squeeze out their blood like wine, and make his Church
to thresh them [f].—By the dissipation of smoke out of a
chimney: they shall be " as the smoke out of the chimney [g]." As Athanasius used to say of Julian the apostate,
that he was but ' Nubecula quæ citò transiret,' a little cloud

[b] 1 Cor. x. 2, 4.   [c] 1 Pet. iii. 21, 22.   [d] Rev. xiv. 8. Isai. xi. 10, 12, 15.
[e] Isai. lxiii. 1, 6.   [f] Lam. i. 15. Rev. xiv. 20. Joel iii. 12. Micah iv. 13.
[g] Hos. xiii. 3.

which would quickly be blown away. Smoke when it breaks out of a chimney with a horrible blackness, threateneth to blot out the sun, and to invade and choke up all the air; but a little blast of wind scattereth it, and anon nothing thereof appears.—By 'fire consuming thorns and briers[h]:' "while they be folded together as thorns, and while they are drunken as drunkards," that is, while they have plotted their counsels and confederacies so curiously that no man dares so much as touch them, and while they are drunken with the pride and confidence of their own strength, "they shall then be devoured as stubble that is full dry[i]."

Therefore the Scripture calleth Christ 'a man of war[k];' because he is furnished with all arts of victory: power invincible; as a lion amongst shepherds, so is he amongst his enemies[l]: wisdom unsearchable, which must stand[m] if he purpose, none can disappoint him[n]: authority—by the least intimation, to gather together all the forces of the world against the enemies of his church. If he but hiss unto them, they presently come in troops[o]. He can command help for his people[p]; and if that should fail, he can create help for his people, as he did for Israel, when he wrought miracles to deliver them[q].

We may, more profitably, consider the truth and comfort of this point, by discovering it in the several enemies of Christ and his people. First, The great enemy of the seed of the woman, is the serpent, that great red dragon, whose names are all names of enmity: the Accuser, the Tempter, the Destroyer, the Devourer, the Envious man, furnished with much strength and mighty succour, legions of principalities and powers attending on him; and with much wisdom, which the Scripture calleth νοήματα, the wiles and trains and craftiness of Satan. And his arts of destroying men are two: To tempt and to accuse. His temptations are twofold: either unto sin, or unto discomfort; either to make us offend God, or to make us disquiet ourselves; either to wound us, or to vex us. And in all these his arts, Christ our captain will tread him under

h Isai. x. 17.   i Nahum i. 10. Isai. xxvii. 4. xxxi. 9.   k Exod. xv. 3.
l Isai. xxxi. 4.   m Isai. i. 2.   n Isai. xiv. 27.   o Isai. v. 26. vii. 18.
p Psal. xliv. 4. lxxi. 3. Jer. xlvii. 7.   q Psal. cvi. 22.

our feet, and will give his church the victory at the last,
either by arming us with sufficiency of grace and faith in his
victories; putting us, by his Spirit, in mind of his temptations, which taught him compassion towards us, who are so
much weaker, and encouraging our hearts to cry out unto
him, who is our merciful and compassionate High-priest,
like a ravished woman, in our extremities, as Paul did [r]; stirring up our faith to lay hold on him, when we are in darkness; and our spirit of adoption to cry unto him, when we
are in danger; and our spirit of wisdom to solve the objections, to discern the devices of Satan, and to prepare and
arm our hearts accordingly to wrestle with him. Or else by
rebuking of him, pulling in his chain, and chasing him away;
and, as our second, undertaking the combat in person for us,
when he is ready to prevail [s]. Thus he overcometh him as a
tempter, and ever giveth some comfortable or profitable issue
out of them.

He likewise overcometh him as an accuser. Satan accuseth the saints, either by way of complaint and narration
of the things which they have done [t]; which the apostle
calleth ἐγκαλέσῃ, his laying of crimes to the charge of men [u];
and thus Christ overcometh him by his intercession, and, in
the hearts of his saints, by making them judge and accuse
themselves, that they may be able to clear themselves too [x].
Or he accuseth by way of suspicion or pre-conjecture, as he
did Job [y]; and herein likewise Christ overcometh him in his
servants, by permitting him to tempt and vex them, that they
may come the purer out of the fire,—and by putting a holy
suspicion and jealousy into them, over their own hearts,
which may still be a means to prevent them against evils,
that are likely to assault them,—to teach them in every condition, 'as well possible as present, how to walk acceptably
before God [z].

Another great enemy of the kingdom of Christ is, the
lust of our own evil nature. " The carnal mind is enmity
against God, for it is not subject to the law of God, neither
indeed can be [a]." Enmity in grieving, vexing, and quench-

    [r] 2 Cor. xii. 8, 9.   [s] Zech. iii. 1, 2.   [t] Rev. xi. 10.   [u] Rom. viii. 33.
[x] 1 Cor. xi. 31. 2 Cor. vii. 11.   [y] Job i. 9, 10, 11.   [z] Phil. iv. 11, 13.
[a] Rom. viii. 7. Phil. iii. 8.

ing the holy Spirit in us, and lusting enviously against his
grace [b]. And here also Christ overcometh by the prevailing
power of his Spirit, giving us more grace, demolishing the
kingdom of sin, and judging the prince of this world, which
before did rule in the children of disobedience. And this
he doth by the judgement-seat and sceptre of his Spirit in
the heart: for the judgement of the Spirit is too hard for the
principality of Satan [c]. The Spirit of Christ is a victorious
Spirit: "He bringeth forth his judgement unto victory [d]."
He worketh out by degrees the dross and impurity of our
nature and services. First, By faith, fixing upon better promises and hopes than lust can make [e]. Secondly, By watchfulness eyeing corruptions, and so stirring up those arguments and principles, which are strongest against them [f].
Thirdly, By leading us to more acquaintance with God in
knowledge, love, and communion [g]; and so fetching more
wisdom and strength from him : for this is the way that we
get all our strength, even by learning of him [h]. Fourthly,
By inclining the heart to hate and to complain of corruptions, to bemoan itself, as Paul and Ephraim did [i]. Fifthly,
By bringing the heart into the light, there to approve and
judge his actions [k]; by setting it always in God's eye, that it
may not sin against him [l]. Sixthly, By convincing the heart
of the beauty and excellency of Grace, of the unlikeness of
sin to God, and so making the soul more full of desires for
the one and against the other [m]; and thus kindling lust
against lust [n]. Seventhly, By being always a present moni-
tor and watchman in the soul, to supply it with spiritual
weapons and reasoning against the temptation of lust [o].
Lastly, In one word, by daily supplies from the residue of
Spirit which is in our head, whereby, according to the proportion and exigence of the members, he floweth into them [p].
This is that seed, that leaven. that vital instinct, which is
ever in the heart, setting itself against the workings and life

---

[b] Jam. iv. 4, 5.   [c] John xvi. 11.   [d] Matth. xii. 20. Isai. iv. 4.
[e] 1 John v. 4. Heb. xi. 24, 26.   [f] Job xxxi. 1. Psal. xxxix. 1.   [g] Job
xxii. 21. 1 John i. 3.   [h] Phil. iv. 12.   [i] Rom. vii. 23. Mark ix. 24.
Jer. xxxi. 18, 19.   [k] John iii. 20.   [l] Psal. xvi. 8.   [m] Isai. xxvi. 8.
Ezek. xxxvi. 31.   [n] Gal. v. 17.   [o] Isai. xxx. 31. John xiv. 26.
[p] Mal. ii. 15. Phil. i. 19.

of lust, and by little and little wasting it away, as fire doth water.

The grand instrument of Satan and lust (who are the two leaders in this war against Christ) is the wicked world: the power, malice, wisdom, learning, or any other, either natural or acquired abilities of evil men: for even, in an earthly respect, by the word 'kings,' we are not only to understand those monarchs and princes of the earth, who set themselves against Christ; but all such as excel in any such worldly abilities, as may further that opposition. It notes the strength, policy, pride, and greatness of mind, or scorn of subjection, which is in the heart against Christ. So that *king* here stands in opposition to *subject:* they who reject Christ's yoke, and break his bonds asunder, and will not have him to reign over them, those are the *kings* in the text. And these also will he smite through, and confound by the power of his Word and the strength of his arm. " The Lord gave the Word: great was the company of those that published it. Kings of armies did flee apace, and she that tarried at home, divided the spoil q." " Tophet is prepared of old, for the king it is prepared r." " Come and gather yourselves together to the supper of the great God, that ye may eat the flesh of kings, and the flesh of captains, and the flesh of mighty men, and the flesh of horses, and of them that sit on them, and the flesh of all men, both free and bond, both small and great s," &c. " As for mine enemies, which would not that I should reign over them, bring them hither and slay them before me t." " Be wise now, ye kings; be instructed, ye judges of the earth. Serve the Lord with fear, and rejoice with trembling; kiss the Son lest he be angry, and ye perish from the way, when his wrath is kindled but a little u." Thus the Lord overthroweth his church's enemies, and protecteth it against all their greatest preparations, and most formidable power.

And this he doth several ways: sometimes by diverting their forces from his church into some other necessary channel, or ambitious design of their own. Thus Rabshakeh and his host were called from Judah x. So the Lord promised

q Psal. lxviii. 11, 12.　　r Isai. xxx. 33.　　s Rev. xix. 17, 18.　　t Luke xix. 27.　　u Psal. ii. 10, 11, 12.　　x 2 Kings xix. 7, 8.

his people, that when they went up to appear before him
thrice a year, he would divert the desires of their enemies
from their land [y]. Thus Julian the apostate, having but two
main plots to honour (as he supposed) his government and
his idols withal—the subduing of the Persian, and the rooting out of the Galileans, as he called them,—was prevented
from this, by being first overthrown in the other: for the
prosperous success of which expedition he vowed unto his
idol-gods a sacrifice of all the Christians in the empire, as
Gregory Nazianzen [z] relateth.—Sometimes by infatuating and
implanting a spirit of giddiness and distraction in the enemies of his church, making them destitute both of counsel
and courage. When God would punish Babylon (which is
a type of the enemies of Christ's kingdom) he made their
hearts melt, that they should be amazed at one another, and
" their faces should be like flames [a]:" that is, not only pale,
like a flame, but rather, as I conceive, full of variety of fearful impressions and distracted passions: nothing so tremu-
lous, so various, so easily bended every way with the smallest blast, as a flame : so their fear should make their blood
and spirits in their faces to tremble, quiver, and vary, to
come and go like a thin flame in them ; so God threateneth
" to mingle a perverse spirit," to make the spirit of Egypt
fail in them, and their wisdom to perish [b]. And thus likewise
the Lord dealt with Julian [c] in that Persian expedition : he
put a spirit of folly in him to burn his ships, and so to put a
necessity of courage in his people, as the old Gauls did
against Cæsar [d], and then to leave them all destitute of necessary relief.—Sometimes by ordering casualties, and particular emergences for the deliverance of his church ; a
thing wonderfully seen in the histories of Joseph and Esther.
Thus as a man, by a chain made up of several links, some
of gold, others of silver, others of brass, iron, or tin, may
be drawn out of a pit ; so the Lord, by the concurrence of
several unsubordinate things, which have no manner of dependence or natural coincidency amongst themselves, hath
oftentimes wrought the deliverance of his church, that it
might appear to be the work of his own hand.—Sometimes

---

[y] Exod. xxxiv. 24.   [z] *Greg. Naz. Orat.* 4. in Julian. 2.   [a] Isai. xiii. 7, 8.
[b] Isai. xix. 1, 2, 3, 14, 17.   [c] *Theodoret.* Hist. lib. 3. cap. 20.   [d] *Naz.*
Orat. 4. *Cæsar*, Comm. lib. 1.

by ordering and arming natural causes to defend his church, and to amaze the enemy. Thus the stars in their courses, are said to fight against Sisera [e]. A mighty wind from Heaven, beating on their faces, discomfited them, as Josephus [f] reports. So the Christian armies under Theodosius [g] against Eugenius the tyrant, were defended by winds from Heaven, which snatched away their weapons out of their hands; to make good that promise, " No weapon that is formed against thee, shall prosper." So the Lord slew the enemies of Joshua with hail [h]. And thus the Moabites were overthrown, by occasion of the sun shining upon the water [i].—Sometimes by implanting fantasies and frightful apprehensions into the minds of the enemy, as into the Midianites [k], and the Assyrians [l]. Thus the Lord caused a voice to be heard in the temple, before the destruction of Jerusalem, warning the faithful to go out of the city [m].—Sometimes by stirring up and prospering weak and contemptible means, to show his glory thereby. The Medes [n] and Persians were an effeminate and luxurious people ; Cyrus a mean prince, for he was not at this time emperor of the Medes or Persians, but only son-in-law to Darius or Cyaxares; and yet these are made instruments to overthrow that most valiant people, the Babylonians [o]. As Jeremiah [p] was drawn out of the dungeon by old rotten rags, which were thrown aside as good for nothing; so the Lord can deliver his church by such instruments as the enemies thereof, before, would have looked upon with scorn, as upon cast and despicable creatures. For God, as he useth to infatuate those whom he will destroy ; so he doth guide with a spirit of wonderful wisdom, those whom he raiseth to defend his kingdom. The Babylonians [q] were feasting, and counted their city impregnable, being fortified with walls and the great river ; and God gave wisdom beyond the very conjectures of men, to attempt a business which might seem unfeasible in nature, to dry up Euphrates, and divide it into several small branches : and so he made a way to bring his army into the city while they were feasting, the

[e] Judges v. 20.   [f] *Joseph.* Antiq. Jud. l. 5. c. 6.   [g] *Aug.* de Civ. Dei. l. 5. c. 26.   [h] Josh. xi. 11.   [i] 2 Kings ii. 22, 23.   [k] Judges vii. 13, 14. [l] 2 Kings vii. 6.   [m] *Euseb.* l. 3. c. 8.   [n] *Brisson.* de Reg. Pers. lib. 2. [o] Isai. xlv. 1, 13. iii. 17.   [p] Jer. xxxviii. 11.   [q] *Herodot.* lib. 1.—*Xenoph.* de expedit. Cyri, lib. 7.

gates thereof being in great confidence and security left open [r].
—Sometimes by turning the hearts of others to compassionate
the church, to hate the enemies, and not to help them, but
to rejoice when he is sinking [s].—Sometimes by the immediate stroke of God upon their bodies or consciences. Thus
God gave the church rest by smiting Herod [t]. Thus Maxi-
minus [u], being smitten with a horrible and stinking disease
in his bowels, confessed that it was Christ which overcame
him; and Julian, being smitten with an unknown blow from
Heaven, as is supposed, confessed that Christ was too hard
for him; and another Julian, uncle to the apostate, for
pissing on the Lord's table, had his bowels rotted, and his
excrements issued out, ' non per secessum, sed per vulnera,'
as the same historian reports.—Sometimes by tiring them
quite out, and making them, for very vexation and successless-
ness, give over their vain attempts; or else disheartening
them, that they may not begin them. So Dioclesian retired
to a private life, because he could not root out the Christians;
and Julian was afraid to persecute the Christians, as his
predecessors had done, lest they should thereby increase:
he forbore it out of envy, and not out of mercy, as Nazianzen [x]
observes.—Sometimes by turning their own devices upon
their heads, ruining them with their own counsels, and, it
may be, despatching them with their own hands. Thus the
Lord set every man's sword against his fellow, in the huge
host of the Midianites [y]. So Pilate and Nero, the one the
murderer of Christ, the other the dedicator of all the consequent great persecutions,—both [z] died by their own hands,
as being most wicked and most cruel, and therefore fittest to
revenge the cause of Christ and his people upon themselves.
Thus God did not only curse the counsel, but revenge the
treason, of Ahithophel, by an act of the most desperate folly
and inhumanity which could be committed.—Sometimes by
hardening them unto a most desperate prosecution of their
own ruin, as in the case of Pharaoh; suffering them to lift
at the stone so long, till it loosen, and fall upon them [a].—

[r] Isai. xliv. 27, 28. xlv. 1. Jer. li. 36.   [s] Isai. xiv. 6, 10, 16. Nahum iii. 7.
[t] Acts xii. 23, 24.   [u] *Fuseb.* de vita Constant. lib. 1. cap. 50.—*Theodor.* lib. 3.
cap. 20. vid. *Tertul.* contr. Scapulam cap. 3. et *Laurent. de la Barr.*—*Euseb.* Hist.
lib. 8. cap. 26. et *Zonaras.*   [x] *Naz.* Orat. 3. in Julian. 1.   [y] Judges vii. 22.
[z] *Tertul.* Apolog cap. 5.—*Euseb.* lib. 2. cap. 7.   [a] Zech. xii 3. Matth. xxi. 44.

Sometimes by ingratiating the church with them to their own destruction, as he did Israel with the Egyptians [b]. By these, and a world the like means, doth the Lord overthrow the enemies of his kingdom.

Now all this is "*in the day of his wrath*," or in his own due time: where we may note by the way, That Christ hath wrath in him as well as mercy. Though he be, by wicked and secure men, misconceived, as if he were only compassionate; yet 'læsa patientia fit furor,' he will more sorely judge them hereafter, whom he doth not by persuasions and allurements prevail with here. So merciful he is, that he is called 'a Lamb' for meekness; and yet so terrible, that he is called 'a Lion' for fury. It is true, " fury is not in him," namely, to those that apprehend his strength, and make their peace with him [c] : but yet to those that will not kiss, that is, not love, worship, nor obey him, he can with a little wrath show himself very terrible [d]. He cometh first with peace [e]; but it is 'pax concessa,' not 'pax emendicata,' a peace mercifully offered, not a peace growing out of any necessity or exigences on his part, and so wrought by way of composition for his own advantages. The peace of a conqueror [f]: A peace which putteth conditions to those to whom it is granted, that they shall be tributaries and servants unto him [g]. Therefore the apostle saith, that he came " to preach" or to proclaim " peace [h];" but if we reject it, he then follows the directions of Joshua, " These mine enemies which would not have me to reign over them, bring them hither, and slay them before me [i]."

But the main thing here to be noted is, That Christ hath a day, a προθεσμία, a prefixed and constituted time, wherein he will be avenged on the greatest of his enemies. When he forbears, and suffers them to prevail, yet still he holdeth the line in his own hand; the hook of his decree is in their nostrils, and he can take them short, when he will. It is never want of power, wisdom, or love to his church, that their quarrel is not presently revenged ; but all these are fitted to his greater glory. The Lord seemeth to neglect, to break up the hedge, to sleep while his church is sinking, as Christ

[b] Exod. xii. 35, 36.   [c] Isai. xxvii. 4, 6.   [d] Psalm ii. 12.   [e] Luke x. 5.
[f] Zech. ix. 10.   [g] Deut. xx. 10, 11, 12.   [h] Ephes. ii. 17.   [i] Luke xix. 27.

to his disciples seemed careless [k] : so frequently in Scripture, the saints expostulate with God in an humble and mourning debate, " Why sleepest thou, O Lord? Arise, cast us not off for ever [l]." But God hath his ' quare' against us too, for this infirmity and haste of ours ; " Why sayest thou, O Jacob, and speakest, O Israel, my way is hid from the Lord, and my judgement is passed over from my God ?" That is, he hath not taken notice of my calamity. " Hast thou not known, hast thou not heard, that the everlasting God, the Lord, the Creator of the ends of the earth fainteth not, neither is weary ? There is no searching of his understanding [m]." He is wonderful in counsel, and excellent in working; and therefore he doth not slumber nor sleep : but only in wisdom ordereth times and seasons, that there may, in the end, be the greater glory unto him,—and in the things done, the more beauty. " Every thing," saith Solomon, " is beautiful in its time :" if you gather it before, it looseth both its beauty and virtue. It would be madness for a man to mow down his corn, when it is in the green blade. " He waiteth," saith the apostle, " for the precious fruit of the earth, and hath long patience." James v. 7. Now the prophet assureth us, that *light*, that is, comfort, refreshment, peace, deliverance, " is sown for the righteous [n]." It was sown for the people of God, when they were in captivity ; though to themselves they seemed as dead men in their graves ; yet indeed they were dead, but as seed in the furrows, which revived again [o]. And therefore the Lord likewise (like St. James's husbandman) is said to wait, that he may be gracious to his people [p], Though a man suffer never so much injury, and be most violently kept out of his own right, yet he must wait till time and mature proceedings have brought on his matters to a trial : therefore the Lord calleth it " the year of recompenses for the controversies of Sion [q]." It is not for private men to order the periods, or stints, or revolutions of times, wherein businesses are to be tried ; but public authority constitutes that, and every man must wait for the appointed time : so the church must not set God the times when it would be heard or eased ; but must trust his

---

[k] Mark iv. 38, 39.   [l] Psalm xliv. 23. Jer. xiv. 8, 9.   [m] Isai. xl. 27, 28.
[n] Psalm xcvii. 11.   [o] Psalm cxxvi. 5, 6.   [p] Isai. xxx. 18.   [q] Isai. xxxiv. 8.

wisdom and power[s], for there is a set time, wherein he will have mercy upon Sion[t].

Now this time is ruled and bounded by these considerations : First, When the sin of the enemy is grown ripe, and his heart proud and insolent against God and his people; when he trampleth upon the poor; when he sacrificeth to his own net; when he adoreth his own counsels; when he defieth his own condition, and thinketh that none can pull him down ;—then it is a time for God to show himself, and to stir up his glory. " It is time," saith David, " for thee, O Lord, to work, for they have made void thy law[u]." So outrageous they are, that their fury runneth over from thy servants to thine ordinances, to blot out the very records of Heaven, the name and fear of God out of the earth. And this reason and period of time, we find frequently in the Scriptures given: " In the fourth generation they shall come hither again, for the iniquity of the Amorites is not yet full[x];" it is not grown to that ripeness and compass, as I, in my wise, secret, and patient providence, will permit. " O thou that dwellest upon many waters, abundant in treasures," saith the Lord to Babylon, " thine end is come, and the measure of thy covetousness[y]" When men have filled up the measure of their sins, then is their end come ; be their wealth, or safety, or their natural or acquired munition never so great. " Put ye in the sickle," saith the prophet, " for the harvest is ripe ; come, get you down ; for the press is full, the fats overflow, for the wickedness is great[z]." When wickedness is so great, that it filleth all vessels, then is the Lord ready to put in his sickle, and to cut it down.

It is further demanded, When sin is full? To this I answer, That there are three things principally, which set forth the sinfulness of sin, Universality, Impudence, and Obstinacy. First, When a whole land is filled with it, that there are none to intercede, or to stand in the gap; when, from streets to palaces, from houses to courts, from schools to churches, from every corner sin breaketh forth, so that blood toucheth blood. " The land is full of adulterers," saith the prophet; " because of swearers, the land mourneth;

[s] Jer. xlix. 19.   [t] Psalm cii. 13.   [u] Psalm cxix. 126.   [x] Gen. xv. 16.
[y] Jer. li. 13.   [z] Joel iii. 13.

for both priest and prophet are profane; yea, in my
house have I found their wickedness, saith the Lord [a] :"
when, in every place, and at every view, there are new and
more abominations [b]. Secondly, When sin is impudent [c],
whorish [d], and outrageous; when there is no fear, modesty,
or restraint, but it breaketh all bonds, and, like a raging
sea, overrunneth the banks: " They declare their sin as
Sodom," saith the prophet, " and hide it not; woe unto
their souls [e] :" it is so full that it breaks out into their countenance [f]; hypocrisy itself is too narrow to cover it. This
is that which the apostle calleth " an excess of riot [g];" and
the prophet, " a rushing like a horse into the battle [h]." Now
when God thus gives a man over, sin will not be long filling up : when lusts break forth and throng together; when,
from concupiscence [i], sin goes on to conception and delight,
to formation and contrivance, to birth and execution, to
education and custom, to maintenance and defence, to glory
and boasting, to insensibility, hardness, and a reprobate
sense,—then there is such a fulness in sin, as is near unto
cursing ; the very next step is hell. Lastly, When sin holds
out in stubbornness, and is incorrigible; when the remedy is
refused, the pardon rejected, peace not accepted,—then is
sin come to its fulness. The sins of the Amorites were
never quite full, but when they rejected that peace, mercy,
and subjection to God's people, which was offered them
first. But when men sin against those means of grace which
are sent unto them, and leave no remedy to themselves; no
marvel if the Lord give them over, and let in the enemy
upon them [k]. Therefore we must take heed of finishing sin,
for it is not sin alone, but the consummation and finishing
of sin which condemns a man.

Now when thus the sin of the enemy is grown so ripe,
that it breaketh forth into pride and insultation against God's
people, then is the Lord's time to show himself. " I will
restore health unto thee," saith the Lord to his church;

---

[a] Jer. xxiii. 10, 11.   [b] Ezek. viii. 17. Jer. v. 1, 6.   [c] Isai. xlviii. 4.
[d] Jer. iii. 3.   [e] Isai. iii. 9.   [f] Delicti durior frons est, ab ipso et in ipso
delicto, impudentiam docta. *Tertul.* de Vel. Virg. cap. i.   [g] Rom. i. 24, 26.
[h] Isai. lxix. 27.   [i] Dum servitur libidini, facta est consuetudo ; dum con-
suetudini, necessitas. *Aug.* Confess. lib. 8. cap. 5.—Vid. *Bernard.* de Gradibus
Superbiae.   [k] 2 Chron. xxxvi. 16.

" and I will heal thee of thy wounds, because they called thee
an outcast, saying, This is Sion whom no man seeketh after[1]."
When the highways were waste, and the wayfaring man
ceased, and the enemy regarded no man, " Now, saith the
Lord, will I arise, now will I be exalted[m]," &c. When the
enemies help forward the affliction of God's people, and, by
their pride and insultation, do double the misery which is
upon them,—then will the Lord return them in mercies, and
be sore displeased with his enemies[n].

Secondly, When God's people are thoroughly humbled
and purged : for God useth wicked men, as his staff or weapon, as his fire or fan, to correct and purge them[o]. He intended not in his punishments such severity against them, as
against their enemies : if the rod be for the child, the fire is
for the rod[p]. When men are so smitten, that they can return
to him that smiteth them, and not revolt more and more: for
God will not throw any more darts at those who are sunk
and dead already, —when they are stirred in their hearts
jointly to seek the Lord, and to meet him in the way of his
judgements, and to compassionate and favour the dust of
Sion : for when God's time to deliver a people is come, he
will more abundantly stir up the hearts of his people to
pray for it than in the day of his wrath[q] : whereas, when he
will destroy a people, he will not suffer his saints to pray[r].

Thirdly, When all human hopes and expectations are
gone, when a people is so pilled and broken, that they have
no courage, means, succours, or probabilities left; then
is God's time to deliver his church, and to punish his enemies. " The Lord shall judge his people, and repent
himself for his servants, when he seeth that their power is
gone[s]." In one word, when the preparation and premises,
as it were, unto God's glory are best ordered and put together, then is the day of his wrath come.

The church then need not to be cast down[t] with the insultation of her enemies, since Christ is the same yesterday,
and to-day, and for ever; such as he was ever to his church,

l Jer. xxx. 7. Jer. l. 11. Ezek. xxv. 3, 28. vi. 9. Obad. verse 3, 4.   m Isai.
xxxiii. 8, 11.   n Zech. i. 15, 16.   Isai. xl. 2. xlvii. 5, 6.   o Isai. x. 12.
p Isai. xxvii. 7, 8, 9.   q Psalm cii. 16, 17. Dan. ix. 2, 3.   r Jer. xiv. 11.
s Deut. xxxii. 36. Psalm lxviii. 20. cix. 31.   t Deut xx. 3, 4. Isai. li. 12, 13.
Deut. xxxi. 6, 7, 8.

such he is still. If he have delivered his church from the
pride of her enemies heretofore, his power, truth, watchfulness, compassion, is the same still: and by faith in them,
we may rebuke Satan; we may chide away the weakness
and fear of our own hearts; we may rejoice against those
that insult over us; when they rage most, we may hope
their time is short, and that it is but the biting of a wounded
beast. Therefore we find the saints, in Scripture, arm themselves against present dangers, with the consideration of
what God hath done for his church in times past[u]; and in
the confidence of the same truth and power[x], break forth
into a holy scorn of their enemies[y]. In the sorest extremities, we may fix our faith on God; and he delighteth to be
depended upon alone, when all outward helps and probabilities fail[z]. A million of men came against Asa, one of
the hugest hosts of men that we ever read of; yet, by relying on God, they were all delivered into his hand: and
the reason is added, because God hath eyes and strength,
or, as he is described, Rev. v. 6, seven horns and seven
eyes, much wisdom and much power to show himself valiant in the behalf of those that walk uprightly[a].

We should learn likewise to rejoice and triumph with all
thankfulness of heart, when Christ subdueth the enemies of
his kingdom, and giveth deliverance and refreshment to his
people. When he maketh his hand known to his servants,
and his fury to his enemies, then should all they that love
Jerusalem, rejoice[b]. Thus the church, after they were delivered from the malice of Haman, instituted days of joy and
feasting[c]. It is a sign of an evil heart against the peace and
prosperity of the church of Christ, to envy, or slight, or
think basely of the instruments and ways, whereby Christ
delivereth it; as we see in Tobiah and Sanballat[d].

Lastly, We should learn wisdom to lay hold on the times
and seasons of God's peace, because he hath a day of wrath
too; to apprehend the offers and opportunities of grace.
Christ had been at the church's door, and had knocked for
admittance; but neglecting that season, he was gone, and

<hr/>

u Psalm lxviii. 7, 8. lxxiv. 13, 18. Isai. li. 9,10, 11. Habak. iii.   x Jer. xxx. 8.
y Micah vii. 8, 9, 10. Isai. 1. 8, 9.   z Isai. xli. 17, 18. Habak. iii. 17, 18.
a 2 Chron. xvi. 8, 9.   b Isai. lxvi. 10.   c Esther ix. 22.   d Neh. iv. 2. 3.

much she suffered, before she could find him again [f]. When the Lord speaketh unto us in his ordinances, and by the secret motions and persuasions of his holy Spirit, we should not defer, nor put him off, as Felix did Paul, to some other time; but pursue the occasion, and set ourselves to do every duty in God's time. There is a time for every work, and it is beautiful only in its time: and therefore fit it is, that we should observe wisely the signs and nature of the times [g], and accordingly proportion our devotions for the church and ourselves. It is the worst loss of time to let slip the seasons of grace and spiritual wisdom, till, it may be, God's time of mercy is passed over. If thou hadst known, in this thy day, the things that concern thy peace! But now thy day is over, and my day of wrath is come; they are now hidden from thine eyes.

" *He shall judge amongst the heathen.*"—By *heathen* we are to understand the same with *enemies*, verse 1, and *people* [h]; meaning all the armies and swarms of Christ's enemies, either spiritual or secular. The word " Gentiles" was a word of great contempt and detestation amongst God's people [i], as the word " Jew" is now amongst us: a proverbial word to cast reproach and shame upon men. Therefore the apostle saith of the Ephesians, that, in times past, " they had been Gentiles in the flesh [k]." As if, by being Christians, they had ceased to be Gentiles; or rather that word had ceased to be a term of reproach. So that " Gentile" was a word of scorn, as " Samaritan [l]," or " Canaanite [m]," or " Publican [n]." And therefore we find those two joined together, " Publicans and Sinners;" and so the apostle joineth these two words, " Gentiles and Sinners [o]." So then the word " *heathen*" is added by David to the enemies of Christ, to render them the more odious, and to express their more abject and hateful condition: and therefore, when God would cast notable reproach upon his people, he calleth them " Sodomites and Gentiles [p]." So then the meaning is, His most abject and hateful enemies, that are unto him as Canaanites

---

[f] Cant. v. 2, 7.   [g] Matth. xvi. 2.   [h] Isai. lxiii. 6.   [i] *Cameron.* de Ecclesia, page 33, 34.   *Weem's* Christian Synag. page 137.   [k] Ephes. ii. 11.   [l] John viii. 48.   [m] Ezek. xvi. 3.   [n] Matth. xviii. 17. Luke xviii. 11.   [o] Gal. ii. 15.   [p] Isai. i. 10. Ezek. ii. 3.

and Samaritans, *he shall judge;* that is, he shall condemn and punish them.

Whence we may note, That Christ's victories over his enemies shall be by way of pleading and disceptation. His military is likewise a judiciary proceeding, grounded upon righteous and established laws. Therefore the day of God's wrath is called a time of vengeance, and recompense for the " controversies of Sion q;"—to show that the Lord doth not take vengeance but by way of debate: and therefore when he punisheth, he is said to " plead" with men. The priest said not, Where is the Lord? and they that handle the law, knew me not, &c. "Wherefore I will yet plead with you, saith the Lord, and with your children's children will I plead r." So to ' plead' and to ' take vengeance' go together s: and the Lord is said to ' reprove with equity,' and to smite the earth with the rod of his mouth ; that is, to convince and argue before he doth punish t; as we see in the case of Sodom u. Herein the Lord showeth, that all our misery begins at ourselves ; that if we perish, it is because we would not take his counsel, nor be guided by his will. That he did not sell us to any of his creditors ; but that for our iniquities, we " sold ourselves x." In human wars, though never so regularly and righteously ordered, yet many particular men may perish without any personal guilt of their own. ' Delirant reges, plectuntur Achivi.' But, in these wars of Christ, there shall not a man perish, till he be first convinced, by a judiciary proceeding, of his own demerit. " Every mouth must be stopped, and all the world," by the evidence and acknowledgment of their own conscience, "become guilty before God," before his wrath shall seizo upon them. The Lord sent Noah to preach, before he sent a flood to destroy the world. He argued with Adam, before he thrust him out of Paradise. The ' voice' goeth ever before the ' rod y.' This course our Saviour observed towards him, who had not the wedding-garment: first, convinced him till he was speechless, and then cast him into outer darkness z. And this course the Lord took with his people, when he punished them a. For he will have the consciences of

q Isai. xxxiv. 8.   r Jer. ii. 8, 9.   s Jer. li. 36.   t Isai. xi. 4.   u Gen. xviii. 21, 23.   x Isai. l. 1.   y Micah vi. 9.   z Matth. xxii. 12, 13. a Isai. v. 3, 4. Amos ii. 11. iii. 7.

men to subscribe and acknowledge the justness of his proceedings, and to condemn themselves by their own witness.
When he entereth into judgement, he doth it by line and
plummet [b], in proportion to the means of grace neglected, to
the patience and forbearance abused, to the times of grace
overslipped, to the purity of the law violated and profaned.
We must take heed, therefore, of continuing Gentiles, of
being aliens from that commonwealth of Israel, and strangers
from that covenant of promise, of living without God in the
world. No man can, with hope or comfort, say, " Enter not
into judgement," but he who is the " Lord's servant" and of
his household. We must be all ingrafted into the natural
olive, and become the seed of Abraham, and Jews by covenant, before Christ will be our peace, or reconcile us unto
his Father [c].

" *He shall fill the places with dead bodies.*"—This notes the
greatness of the victory, That none should be left to bury
their dead. There shall be a universal destruction of wicked
men together in the day of God's wrath ; they shall be bound
up in bundles and heaped for damnation [d]. And it notes
the shame and dishonour of the enemy: They shall lie like
dung upon the face of the earth, and shall be beholden to
their victors for a base and dishonourable burial; as we see
in the great battle with Gog and Magog [e].

" *He shall wound the head over many countries.*"—Either
literally, Antichrist [f]; who taketh upon him to be œcumeni-
cal bishop and monarch, and to dispose of crowns and dispense kingdoms at his pleasure. Or spiritually, Satan, who
is the prince of this world, whose head Christ was to crush
and tread under our feet [g]. Or figuratively, the Head, that
is, the counsel and power of many nations, which shall at
last appear to have been but a vain thing [h]. What sense soever we follow, the main thing to be observed is, that which
we handled before; that Christ will, in due time, utterly
destroy the greatest, the highest, the wisest of his enemies.—
And therefore this may suffice upon this verse.

[b] Isai. xxviii. 17.   [c] Rom. ii. 29. xi. 17, 24. Gal. vi. 16. Ephes. ii. 11, 14.
[d] Matth. xiii. 30. Psalm xxxvii. 38. Isai. i. 28. lxvi. 17.   [e] Ezekiel
xxxix. 11, 16.   [f] Revel. xvii. 2, 18.   [g] Gen. iii. 15. Rom. xvi. 20.
[h] Psalm ii. 2. 1 Cor. i. 19.

VERSE VII.

*He shall drink of the Brook in the Way: therefore shall he
lift up the Head.*

SOME understand these words in the sense of the two
former, for a figurative expression of the victories of Christ,
and they in a twofold manner. Some, by *brook*, understand
the blood of the adversary, with which the way should be
filled as with a stream : and, by *drinking* hereof, the satiating,
refreshing, and delighting himself in the confusion of his
enemies ; for the Lord is eased, when his enemies are subdued [a]. Others, that he should pursue his victory with such
heat and importunity, that he should not allow any time
of usual repast, but should content himself with such obvious
refreshment, as should offer itself in the way : and should immediately lift up his head again, to pursue the enemy at the
heel;—and in this sense, there is no more new matter here
intimated, than that which hath been before handled.

Others understand the means, whereby Christ should thus
lift up his head, and exalt himself above all the enemies of
his kingdom, namely, by his passion and sufferings ; by death
destroying death, and him that had the power of death, which
is the devil. I will not undertake to define which sense is
most agreeable to the place ; it being so difficult. But upon
occasion of this latter (which, I think, is more generally embraced) I shall speak something of the means and grounds
of Christ's victories over his enemies, and of his government
in his church, namely, his sufferings and resurrection.

" *He shall drink of the brook in the way.*"—By *brook* then,
or *torrent*, we may understand the wrath of God, and the
rage of men ; the afflictions and sufferings which befel Christ.
And this is a very frequent metaphor in holy Scriptures, to
understand ' afflictions' by ' water [b].' So the wrath of the
Lord is called a stream, and a lake, Isai. xxx. 33. Revel.

[a] Isai. i. 24.   [b] Psalm xviii. 4, 5. xlii. 7. lxix. 1. cxxiv. 4, 5.

xix. 20.—in regard of the rage and irresistibleness thereof,—
'Sternit agros, sternit sata læta, boumque labores ;'—and in
regard of the turbidness and thickness thereof : for God's
wrath is full of dregs [c]. It is said in the history of Christ's
passion, when he was going to wrestle with that woful
Agony in the garden, that "He passed over the brook
Cedron [d]." And we may observe in the History of the Kings,
that when the good kings Hezekiah, and Asa, and Josiah,
purged the city and the temple of idolatry, " They burnt the
cursed things at the brook Kidron, and cast them therein-
to [e];"—to note unto us, that that brook was the sink, as it were,
of the temple, that into which all the 'purgamenta' and uncleanness of God's house, all the cursed things were to be
cast. With relation whereunto it is not improbable, that the
prophet David, by a prophetical spirit, might notify the sufferings of Christ, by drinking of that cursed brook over
which he was to pass,—to signify, that on him all the faithful
might lay and pour out their sins, who is therefore said to be
' made sin and a curse for us [f] ;' — as the people, when they
laid their hands on the head of the sacrifice, did thereby, as
it were, unload all their sins upon it.

Now as waters signify afflictions, so there are two words
with relation thereunto, which signify suffering of afflictions ;
and they are both applied unto Christ [g] : " Are ye able to
drink of the cup that I shall drink of, or be baptized
with that baptism that I am baptized with ?" He that
drinketh, hath the water in him ; he that is dipped or
plunged, hath the water about him. So it notes the universality of the wrath which Christ suffered : it was within
him ; " my soul is heavy unto death :"—and it was all about
him ; betrayed by Judas, accused by Jews, forsaken by disciples, mocked by Herod, condemned by Pilate, buffed by
the servants, nailed by the soldiers, reviled by the thieves
and standers by, and, which was all in all, forsaken by his
Father. So then *drinking of the brook* is meant suffering of
the curses ; and it is frequently so used [h].

By "*the way*" we must understand either the life of
Christ on earth, his passage between his assumed voluntary

---

[c] Isai. li. 17. Psalm lxxv. 8.   [d] John xviii. 1.   [e] 2 Chron. xv. 16. 2 Chron.
xxix. 16. xxx. 14. 2 Kings xxiii. 6.   [f] 2 Cor. v. 21. Gal. iii. 13.   [g] Matth.
xx. 22.   [h] Jerem. xxv. 27. xlix. 12. Ezck. xxiii. 32, 34. Habak. ii. 16. Revel.
xiv. 9, 10.

humility and his exaltation again ; or the way between mankind and Heaven, which, by that flood of wrath and torrent
of curses, which were ἐν μέσῳ [i], was made utterly impassable,—
till Christ, by his sufferings, made a path through it for the
ransomed of the Lord to pass over.

" *Therefore shall he lift up the head.*"—It noteth in the
Scripture-phrase victory, eluctation, and breaking through
those evils, which did urge and press a man before [k] ; and also
boldness, confidence, and security to the whole body [l]. And
farther, it is not, he *shall be lifted up*, but he *shall do it himself* [m]. He hath the power of life, and the fountain of life in
himself [n]. So that following this sense of the words, the
meaning is,—" He shall suffer and remove all those curses
which were in the way between mankind and Heaven ; and
then he shall lift up his head in the resurrection, and break
through all those sufferings into glory again ;"—which sense
is most punctually and expressly unfolded in those parallel
places, Luke xxiv. 26, 46. Philip ii. 8, 9. 1 Pet. i. 11.

" *He shall drink of the brook in the way :*"—From hence we
may note, First, That between mankind and Heaven there
is a torrent of wrath and curses, which doth everlastingly separate between us and glory ; μέγα χάσμα ἐστήρικται, a great and
fixed gulf, which all the world can neither wade through nor
remove. The law at first was an easy and smooth way to
righteousness, and from thence to salvation ; but now every
step thereof sinks as low as Hell. It is written within and
without, with curses ; which way soever a man stirs, he finds
nothing but death before him :—one man's way, by the
civility of his education, the ingenuity of his disposition,
the engagement of other ends or relations, may seem more
smooth, plausible, than another's ; but, by nature, they all
run into Hell ; as all rivers, though never so different in other
circumstances, run into the sea. It is as impossible for a natural man of himself to escape damnation, as it is to make
himself no child of the old Adam, or not to have been begotten by fleshly parents. The gulf of sin in our nature
cannot be cleansed, and therefore the guilt thereof cannot be
removed. The image we have lost is, by us, irreparable ;

---

[i] Col. ii. 14.   [k] Psalm xxvii. 6.   [l] Luke xxi. 28.   [m] Qui se humiliaverat,
ipse exaltabit. *Hieron.*   [n] John v. 26. x. 18.

the law we have violated, inexorable; the justice we have injured, unsatisfiable; the concupiscence of our nature, insati-
able; sin, an aversion from an infinite good, and a conversion
to the creature, infinite: and therefore the guilt thereof infinite and unremovable too.

We should learn often to meditate on this point, to find
ourselves reduced unto these straits and impossibilities, that
we cannot see which way to turn, or to help ourselves, for
that is the only way to draw us unto Christ. Every man
naturally loves to be, in the first place, beholding to himself;
in any extremity, if his own wits, purse, projects, or endeavours will help him out, he looks no farther; but when all
his own succours have forsaken them, then he seeks abroad.
It is much more true in the matter of salvation: No man
never did begin at Christ, but went unto him upon mere necessity, when he had experience of the emptiness of all his
other succours and dependences. We all, by nature, are
offended at him, and will not have him to reign over us, till
thereunto we be forced by the evidence of that infinite and
unpreventable misery, under which, without him, we must
sink for ever. This is, of all other, the most urging argument unto men at first to consider, That there is a torrent of
curses, a sea of death, a reign of condemnation, a hell of
sin within, and a hell of torments without, between them and
their salvation;—and there is no drop of that sea, no scruple of that curse, no tittle of that law, which must not all be
either fulfilled or endured. Suppose that God should sum-
mon thy guilty soul to a sudden appearance before his tribunal of justice; and should there begin to deal with thee
even at thy mother's womb: alas, thou wouldst be utterly
gone there; even there, a seed of evil doers, the spawn of
viperous and serpentine parents, a cursed child, a child of
wrath, an exact image of the old Adam, and of the blood of
Satan. But then here is, after this, produced a catalogue
and history of sins of forty, fifty, or threescore years long;
and in them every inordinate motion of the will, every sudden
stirring and secret working of inward lust, every idle word,
every unclean aspect, every impertinency and irregularity of
life, scored up against thy poor soul; and each of them to
be produced at the last, and either answered or revenged.
O where shall the ungodly and sinners appear, if they have

not right in Christ! And how should men labour to be se-
cured in that right! Who would suffer so many millions of
obligations and indictments to lie between him and God un-
cancelled, and not labour to have them taken out of the
way? Now the only way to be brought hereunto is, to deny
ourselves, and all we do; to do no good thing for this end,
that we may rest in it, or rely upon it when we have done,
but after all to judge ourselves unprofitable servants : when
we have prayed, to see Hell between Heaven and our prayers;
when we have preached, to see Hell between Heaven and our
sermons ;—when we have done any work of devotion, to see
Hell between Heaven and all our services, if God should
mark what is amiss in them, and should enter into judgement
with us :—in one word, to see Hell between Heaven and any
thing in the world else, save only between Christ and Heaven. Till, in this manner, men be qualified for mercy, they
will have no heart to desire it, and God hath no purpose to
confer it. Christ must be esteemed worthy of all acceptation, before God bestows him ; and the way so to esteem of
him is, to feel ourselves the greatest of sinners. And when
the soul is thus once humbled with the taste and remembrance
of that wormwood and gall which is in sin, there is then an
immediate passage unto hope and mercy [o], and that hope is
this :—

"That Christ hath drunken up and dried that torrent of
curses," which was between us and Heaven, and hath made a
passage through them all by himself unto his Father's kingdom.
He was made sin, and a curse for us; that so he might
swallow up sin and death, and might be the destruction of
Hell [p]. I will here but touch upon two things. First, What
Christ suffered. Secondly, Why he suffered. For understanding of the first, we must note, First, That Christ's human
nature was, by the hypostatical union, exalted unto many
dignities, which, to all the creatures in the world besides,
are utterly incommunicable ; as the communication of properties, the adoration of angels, the primogeniture of the
creatures, the co-operation with the Deity in many mighty
works, the satisfaction of an infinite justice by a finite
passion, &c. Exalted likewise it was by his spiritual unction

---

[o] Lament. iii. 19, 22.   [p] Hosea xiii. 14.

above all his fellows, with that unmeasurable fulness of grace, as wonderfully surpasseth the united and cumulated perfections of all the angels in Heaven. Secondly, We must note likewise, That all these things Christ received for the work of man's redemption; and therefore he had them in such a manner, as was most suitable and convenient for the execution of that work. Now Christ was to fulfil that work by a way of suffering and obedience; by death to destroy him that had the power of death, as David, by Goliah's sword, slew him that was master of the sword. As there fell a mighty tempestuous wind upon the Red Sea, whereby the passage was opened for Israel to go out of Egypt into Canaan; so Christ was to be torn and divided by his sufferings, that so there might be a passage for us to God, through that sea of wrath which was between our Egypt and our Canaan, our sin and our salvation. Here, then, are two general rules to be observed concerning the sufferings of Christ: First, That the economy or dispensation of his mediatorship, is the measure of all that he suffered. So much as that required, he did suffer, and more he did not: for though he suffered as man, yet he suffered not because he was a man, but because he was a mediator. Secondly, Inasmuch as a mediator between God and sinners was to be holy and separate from sinners (for if he should have been a sinner, he had been one of the parties, and not a mediator), therefore none of those sufferings which are repugnant to his holiness, and by consequence unserviceable to the administration of his office, could belong unto him. Such things then as did no way prejudice the plenitude of his grace, the union of his natures, the quality of his mediation, such things as were suitable to his person, and requisite for our pardon, such as were possible for him, and such as were necessary for us,— those things he suffered as the punishment of our sins.

Now punishments are of several sorts: some, are sins; some, only from sins. Some things, in several respects, are both sins and punishments. In relation to the law q, as deviations, so they are sins: in relation to the order and dispo-

---

q Deus naturarum bonarum Creator optimus, malarum voluntatum justissimus ordinator. *Aug.* de Civit. Dei, lib. 11. cap. 17. lib. 14. cap. 26. et Tom. 7. cont. Julian. Pelag. lib. 5. cap. 3. De Grat. et Lib. Arbitr. cap. 23. de Prædest. cap. 10.

sition of God's providence, so they are punishments: as hardness of heart, and a reprobate sense. Other punishments are from sin ; and, in this regard, sin is two ways considerable, either as inherent, or as imputed: from sin as inherent, or from the consciousness of sin in a man's self, doth arise remorse, or torment, and the worm of conscience. Again; Sin, as imputed, may be considered two ways: Either it is imputed upon a ground in nature ; because the persons to whom it is imputed, are naturally one with him that originally committed it, and so it doth seminally descend, and is derived upon them ;—thus Adam's sin of eating the forbidden fruit is imputed unto us, and the punishment thereof on us derived, namely, the privation of God's image, and the corruption of our nature. Or else it is imputed upon a ground of voluntary contract, vadimony, or susception ; so that the guilt thereupon growing, is not a derived, but an assumed guilt, which did not bring with it any desert or worthiness to suffer, but only an obligation and obnoxiousness thereunto. As if a sober and honest person be surety for a prodigal and luxurious man, who, spending his estate upon courses of intemperance and excess, hath disabled himself to pay any of his debts ; the one doth for his vicious disability deserve imprisonment, unto which the other is as liable as he, though without any such personal desert. Now then the punishments which Christ suffered, are only such as agree unto sin thus imputed [r], as all our sins were unto Christ. Again; In punishments, we are to distinguish between punishments inflicted from without, and punishments ingenerated, and immediately resulting from the condition of the person that suffereth. Or between the passions and actions of the men that are punished. Punishments, inflicted, are those pains and dolorous impressions, which God, either by his own immediate hand, or by the ministry of such instruments as he is pleased to use, doth lay upon the soul or body of a man. Punishments, ingenerated, are those which grow out of the weakness and wickedness of the person, lying under the sore and invincible pressure of those

---

[r] Τὸ ἐμὸν ἀνυπότακτον ἑαυτοῦ ποιεῖται, ὡς κεφαλὴ τοῦ παντὸς σώματος· ἕως μὲν οὖν ἀνυπότακτος ἐγὼ καὶ στασιώδης, 'Ανυπότακτος τὸ κατ' ἐμὲ καὶ ὁ Χριστὸς λέγεται. Greg. Nazian. Orat. 36.

pains which are thus inflicted ; as blasphemy, despair, and the worm of conscience. In one word, some evils of punishment are vicious [s], either formally in themselves, or fundamentally and by way of connotation in regard of the originals thereof, in the person suffering them. Others are only dolorous and miserable, which press nature, but do no way defile it ; nor refer to any either pollution or impotency, in the person suffering them ; and of this sort only were the punishments of Christ.

Now these punishments which Christ thus suffered, are either inchoate or consummate : inchoate, as all those defects of our nature, which neither were sins, nor grounded upon the inherence of sins (for he took not our personal, but only our natural defects), so far as they have pain and anguish in them. And these were either corporeal, as hunger, thirst, weariness, and the like ; or spiritual, as fear, grief, sorrow, temptations, &c. Consummate were those, which he suffered at last. And these likewise were either corporeal, as shame, mockings, buffets, trials, scourgings, condemnation, an ignominious and a cursed death. Or spiritual ; and those were principally two. First, A punishment of dereliction : " My God, my God, why hast thou forsaken me [t] ? " There was some kind of separation between God and Christ, during the time of his sufferings for sin in that cursed manner. For understanding whereof we must note, That he had a fourfold union unto God. First, In his human nature, which was so fast united in his person to the divine, that death itself did not separate it, either from the person, or from the deity. It was the Lord that lay in the grave.—Secondly, In love, and so there was never any separation neither ; but when he hung on the cross, he was still the beloved Son of his Father, in whom he was well pleased.—Thirdly, In the communion of his Spirit and holiness ; and in that regard likewise there was no disunion, for he was offered up as a Lamb without spot or blemish.—Lastly, In the fruition of the light of his countenance, and of his glory and favour ; and, in this respect, there was, for the time of his sufferings, a dereliction, ' subtractione visionis, non dissolutione unionis,' by the withdrawing of his countenance, not by the dissolving of his

---

[s] Infirmitates quædam vitiosæ, quædam miseræ. *Aug.*   [t] Matth. xxvii. 46.

union. He looked upon Christ as a God armed against the
sins of the world, which were then upon him. Secondly,
There was a punishment of malediction. He did undergo
the curse of the law ; he did grapple with the wrath of God,
and with the powers of darkness ; he felt the scourges due
unto our sins in his human nature, which squeezed and
wrung from him those strong cries, those deep and woful
complaints, that bloody and bitter sweat, which drew compassion from the very rocks. And surely it is no derogation
to the dignity of Christ's person, but, on the other side, a
great magnifying of the justice of God against sin, of the
power of Christ against the law, and of the mercy of them
both towards sinners,—to affirm, that the sufferings of Christ,
whatever they were in ' specie,' in the kind of them, were
yet ' in pondere,' in their weight and pressure, equally grievous with those which we should have suffered : for being in
all things, save sin, like unto us, and most of all in his liableness to the curse of the law (so far as it did not necessarily denote either sin inherent, or weakness to break
through in the person suffering), why he should not be obnoxious to as great extremities of pain, I see no reason ; for
no degree of mere anguish and dolor can be unbefitting the
person of him who was to be known by that title, " A man
of sorrows." And surely, far more indignity it was to him
to suffer a violent death of body from the hands of base
men, than to suffer with patience, obedience, and victory,
far sorer stripes from the hand of God his Father, who was
pleased upon him to lay the iniquity of us all.

For the second thing proposed, Why Christ suffered these
things ; the Scripture giveth principally these five reasons :
First, To execute the decree of his Father [u]. Secondly, To
fulfil the prophecies, prefigurations, and predictions of holy
Scriptures [x]. Thirdly, To magnify his mercy and free love
to sinners, and most impotent enemies [y]. Fourthly, To declare the righteousness and truth of God against sin, who
would not be reconciled with sinners [z], but upon a legal expiation [a]. For although we may not limit the unsearchable
wisdom and ways of God, as if he could no other way have

[u] Acts iv. 27, 28.   [x] Luke xxiv. 46.   [y] Rom. v. 8.   [z] *Aug.* de Trin.
lib. 13. cap. 10. et de Agone Christiano, Tom. 3. cap. 11.   [a] Rom. iii. 25.

saved man ; yet we are bound to adore this means, as being by him selected out of that infinite treasure of his own counsel, as most convenient to set forth his wonderful hate of sin, his inexorable justice and severity against it, his unsearchable riches of love and mercy towards sinners, and, in all things, to make way to the manifestation of his glory.— Lastly, To show forth his own power, which had strength to stand under all this punishment of sin, and at last to shake it off, and to declare himself to be the Son of God, by the resurrection from the dead [b]. For though Christ did exceedingly fear, and for that seems to decline and pray against these his passions ; yet none of that was out of jealousy, or suspicion that he should not break through them. But he feared them, as being pains unavoidable, which he was most certain to suffer ; and as pains very heavy and grievous, which he should not overcome without much bitterness, and very woful conflict. Now for a word of the last clause.

" *Therefore shall he lift up the head.*"—We may hence observe, that Christ hath conquered all his sufferings by his own power. As in his passion, when he suffered, he bowed down his head beforehand, and gave up the ghost with a loud voice, to note, that his sufferings were voluntary [c] ; so, in his resurrection, he is said to *lift up his head himself*, to note, that he had life in himself ; that he was the prince of life ; that it was impossible for him to be held under by death (as we were by the law [d]) ; and that his exaltation was voluntary likewise, and from his own power,—for he was not to have any assistant in the work of our redemption, but to do all alone [e].

If it be objected, That Christ was raised from the dead " by the glory of his Father," and that he raised him up [f] ;— to this I answer, That this was not by way of supplement and succour, to make up any defect of power in Christ ; but only by way of consent to Christ's own power and action, that so men might jointly honour the Son and the Father [g]. Or, by " the glory of the Father," we may understand that glorious power which the Father gave unto his Son in the flesh, to have life in himself [h], annexing thereunto a com-

---

[b] Rom. i. 4.   [c] John xix. 30.   [d] Rom. vii. 6.   [e] John ii. 19. v. 26.
x. 17. Acts iii. 15.   [f] Rom. vi. 4. Acts xiii. 33.   [g] John v. 19. 26.
[h] John v. 26.

mand to exercise the same power[i]. Or he is said to be
raised by himself and his Father both, because that Holy Spirit which immediately quickened him [k], was both his and his
Father's. It was not any personal thing wherein the Son differed from the Father, which raised Jesus from the dead,
but that Spirit which was common to them both.

To conclude, then, with the consideration of those great
benefits, and that excellent use which this resurrection of
Christ doth serve for unto us. First, It assureth us of the
accomplishment of his works of mediation on earth, and that
he is now in the execution of those other offices, which remain
to be fulfilled by him in Heaven for the application of his sacrifice unto us : for having in the resurrection justified himself, he thereby rose for our justification likewise[l]. For if
the debt had not been taken quite off by the surety, it would
have lain upon the principal still. And therefore the apostle
proveth the resurrection by this, That God's mercies are
" sure[m]." Whereas, if Christ were not risen from the dead,
we should be yet in our sins ; and so, by consequence, the
mercies of David should have failed us[n]. And for this reason it is (as I conceive) that the Lord sent an angel to remove the stone from the mouth of the sepulchre; not to
supply any want of power in him, who could himself have
rolled away the stone with one of his fingers; but as a
judge, when the law is satisfied, sendeth an officer to open
the prison-doors to him, who hath made that satisfaction ;
so the Father, to testify that his justice was fully satisfied
with the price which his Son had paid, sent an officer of
Heaven to open the doors of the grave, and, as it were, to
hold away the hanging, while his Lord came forth of his bed-
chamber.

Secondly, It assureth us of our resurrection; for as the
head must rise before the members, so the members are sure
to follow the head. The wicked shall rise by his judiciary
power, but not by the virtue and fellowship of his resurrection, as the faithful, who are therefore called " children of
the resurrection[o]." Thirdly, It doth, by a secret and spiritual virtue, renew and " sanctify our nature[p];" for the acts

---

i John x. 18.　k Rom. i. 4.　1 Tim. iii. 16.　1 Pet. iii. 18.　l Rom. iv. 25.
m Acts xiii. 34.　n 1 Cor. xv. 17, 18.　o Luke xx. 36. 1 Cor. xv. 20, 23.
p Rom. vi. 4.

of Christ's mediation in his sufferings and victories, are s͟ͅ-
ritually appliable and effectual in us unto answerable effects:
his death, to the mortification of sin [q]; and his resurrection,
to the quickening of us in holiness [r]: Fourthly, It comforteth
us in all other calamities of life which may befall us; he
that raised up himself from the dead, hath compassion and
power to deliver us from all evil, and to keep us from falling.
This is the sum of Job's argument,—" God will raise me up
at the last day; therefore undoubtedly he is able (if it stand
with my good and his own glory) to lift me up from this
dunghill again [s]." And this is God's argument to comfort
his people in patient waiting upon him in their afflictions;—
because their dead bodies shall live, and they that dwell in
the dust, shall awake and sing [t]. Lastly, It serveth to draw
our thoughts and affections from earth unto Heaven; because things of a nature should move unto one another.
Now saith the apostle, "Our conversation is in Heaven,
from whence we look for a Saviour, even the Lord Jesus
Christ; who shall change our vile body, and make it like
unto his glorious body, according to the working whereby
he is able to subdue all things unto himself." To him with
the Father and the Holy Ghost, three persons and one God,
be all honour, glory, majesty, and thanksgiving, for ever.
Amen.

q Heb. ix. 14.   1 John i. 7.   r Ephes. ii. 5.   Col. ii. 12.   s Job xix. 27.
t Isai. xxvi. 19.

END OF VOL. II.

LONDON:
PRINTED BY S. AND R. BENTLEY, DORSET STREET.